MUSIC LAW

CHANGING LANDSCAPES IN THE MUSIC INDUSTRY AND THE LAW THAT GOVERNS IT

■ ■ ■

Julie L. Ross

Professor of Law, Legal Practice
Georgetown University Law Center

Michael J. Huppe

President and CEO, SoundExchange, Inc.
Adjunct Professor of Law
Georgetown University Law Center

AMERICAN CASEBOOK SERIES®

American Casebook Series is a trademark registered in the U.S. Patent and Trademark Office.

© 2021 LEG, Inc. d/b/a West Academic
    444 Cedar Street, Suite 700
    St. Paul, MN 55101
    1-877-888-1330

West, West Academic Publishing, and West Academic are trademarks of West Publishing Corporation, used under license.

Printed in the United States of America

ISBN: 978-1-68467-612-5

ACKNOWLEDGMENTS FROM THE AUTHORS

This textbook has been an ongoing work in progress since we first started talking about teaching a music law course in 2005. Our work together began when Mike was a guest lecturer for several years in the music law unit of Julie's Entertainment Law Seminar. Both of us have extensive experience in music issues and music copyright litigation, and it has always been one of our favorite areas of practice. We quickly coalesced around the concept of teaching a dedicated music law class. As we began to design this course, we soon discovered that there was no existing textbook that covered the topic, at least not in the way that we wanted to address it—with a mix of cases & statutes, policy issues, history of the industry, artistic concerns, and a healthy dose of industry business concepts.

So, we began the laborious task of creating our own materials, building them out over the years based on student feedback, the development of the law, and the lightning-fast evolution of the industry. In that process, many of our students and research assistants provided invaluable assistance. Most recently, as the textbook became a reality, David Kolokolo and Julia Weber worked incredibly hard to help us with editing and refining the text and to create graphics to illustrate key points; we deeply appreciate their help with this project.

Other students who were key contributors in providing both constructive feedback on our course materials and researching additional materials that ultimately made their way into the textbook include Robert Strong, Samantha Kosarzycki; Barr Benyamin; Xiaoxiang Sean Deng; Eric Vissichelli; Tom King; Josh Landau; Samantha Walls; Bill Broome; John Lichtefeld; and Joseph Anderson. Other students—too many to name here—provided helpful feedback in their course evaluations and in their seminar participation over the more than ten years that we have taught the course and worked on refining the materials. Our students brought a range of insightful and diverging perspectives to the issues in this book, which helped us expand our own thinking as much as we hope that the course expanded theirs. We also appreciate the enthusiasm and support exhibited by everyone at West Academic, with a special shout-out to Jon Harkness.

Julie wants to acknowledge and express gratitude for the support provided by Georgetown, particularly in the form of research assistant compensation and summer research grants over the many years that it took to compile and finalize this textbook, and for the ongoing and tireless assistance of Noelle Adgerson. She is also grateful for all of the musicians in her life who have shown her how difficult it is to quit their day jobs and make a living in the music business, but who still find ways to use their talents to brighten the world around them. A special thank you goes to Julie's mentors, Judge Lee Sarokin, Ken Sidle, and Vince Chieffo, who trusted her with important, interesting work and who were the best teachers and role models one could ask for. Finally, but most importantly, she wants to thank her support network: her husband, Bill; her son, Jake; her Mom, Jane; the Fab Five; her Hamily; her Legal Practice colleagues at Georgetown; the wind-down team; and, of course, her favorite co-teacher, Mike. Without all of your support, help, patience, wisdom, and encouragement, this book would still be on her bucket list rather than a reality.

Mike wishes to thank the many people he has worked with in and around the music industry, from whom he has learned so much. The multiple constituents, clients, customers, board members and organizations that he has had the pleasure of engaging these past 20+ years have allowed him to glimpse the industry through many lenses. He extends a special thanks to the team at SoundExchange, including the best executives and staff he's ever had the pleasure of working with, and to John Simson (who helped build the foundation of what has become such an amazing company). He is grateful to Judge Leonie Brinkema (who helped fuel the fire of his interest in intellectual property), and to the team at the Recording Industry Association of America (especially Cary Sherman, who was there for so many iterations of his career). Thanks also to his colleagues who contributed to this book, including Kyle Funn, Brad Prendergast, Tim Dadson, Katie Beiter and Marni Rochkind. He especially wants to acknowledge the tireless dedication and judgment of Emily Fulp, an invaluable partner in so many ways related to this book and beyond. He is forever indebted to Julie Ross; it was her fateful call over a decade ago that brought him into the rewarding world of teaching, and an even more rewarding friendship. And finally, Mike wishes to express the greatest thanks and appreciation to his family (wife Maria, and kids Ellie & Ryan), who endured countless absences and the long hours that this book—and the job—have required. Their love, patience and understanding have been more helpful than they realize.

SUMMARY OF CONTENTS

TABLE OF CONTENTS

TABLE OF CASES

The principal cases are in bold type.

MUSIC LAW

CHANGING LANDSCAPES IN THE MUSIC INDUSTRY AND THE LAW THAT GOVERNS IT

CHAPTER I

INTRODUCTION: *ROLL OVER BEETHOVEN*[1]

■ ■ ■

What is music law? Unlike tax law, or election law, tort law, or securities law, there is no easily-defined set of legal principles that one can point to as making up the relevant body of law in the subject area. It is perhaps more like "the law of the horse," criticized by Judge Frank Easterbrook as an ineffective way to organize and analyze what might otherwise be unrelated legal principles,[2] in that many of the legal principles affecting participants in the music industry find their sources in multiple disciplines and often are general principles that are not limited in their application to the world of music. However, within general bodies of law such as copyright, contract, antitrust, and the right of publicity, legislatures and courts have carved out an identifiable set of rules that apply particularly to musical compositions, sound recordings, musicians, songwriters, publishers, labels, studio producers and other participants in the music industry. This textbook presumes a basic background in copyright[3] and contract, which is essential to understanding the more complex rules that apply in the context of the music industry, but takes on a broad array of legal issues and examines their application in the creation, distribution, and consumption of music. The law and the industry are both evolving rapidly, and it is thus an exciting and dynamic area of law to follow and analyze; we hope that you find it as fascinating as we do.

We begin this chapter with some introductory materials: the Copyright Clause of the U.S. Constitution and the basic provisions of the 1976

---

[1] Chuck Berry (1956); released by the Beatles on WITH THE BEATLES (1963).

[2] Frank H. Easterbrook, Cyberspace and the Law of the Horse, 1996 U. CHI. LEGAL F. 207 (1996). As Judge Easterbrook put it, "Lots of cases deal with sales of horses; others deal with people kicked by horses; still more deal with the licensing and racing of horses, or with the care veterinarians give to horses, or with prizes at horse shows. Any effort to collect these strands into a course on 'The Law of the Horse' is doomed to be shallow and to miss unifying principles. Teaching 100 percent of the cases on people kicked by horses will not convey the law of torts very well. Far better for most students—better, even, for those who plan to go into the horse trade—to take courses in property, torts, commercial transactions, and the like, adding to the diet of horse cases a smattering of transactions in cucumbers, cats, coal, and cribs. Only by putting the law of the horse in the context of broader rules about commercial endeavors could one really understand the law about horses." Id. at 207–08. Unlike the hypothetical "law of the horse" course criticized by Judge Easterbrook, which lacks a unifying principle, a music law course provides an opportunity to focus on how the law has shaped the music industry in the U.S. and how the music industry has shaped U.S. law over the course of the past century.

[3] For those students who have not previously taken a course in copyright, we suggest a review of COPYRIGHT IN A NUTSHELL as a complement to this textbook, which provides a basic understanding of general copyright principles.

Copyright Act with which one must be familiar to gain an understanding of the more complex copyright provisions relevant to the music industry. We then move to an overview of the many different components and participants within today's music industry, and a historical overview of the development of the conception of music as property.

Chapters 2 and 3 introduce the state of legal protection for music and those involved in creating and distributing it at the turn of the 20th century, immediately before and after the enactment of the Copyright Act of 1909. These early cases and statutory provisions are essential to an understanding of why and how the music industry developed into its current state, and they illustrate some common themes in music law that are repeated in current case law and in the debate over the future of the industry. Chapter 2 focuses on legal issues regarding duplication and performance of sound recordings, and Chapter 3 focuses on the performance right in compositions and the legal issues that arose from the formation of performing rights organizations to collectively enforce and administer the performance right.

In Chapter 4, the textbook covers the grant of limited federal copyright protection to sound recordings and the continuing debate over performance rights in sound recordings, as well as some of the legal issues arising out of the provisions of the 1976 Copyright Act. Chapter 5 addresses the multitude of legal and business issues that arose as music entered the digital era, and the next two chapters turn to music licensing issues, with Chapter 6 introducing statutory licensing in the context of the digital public performance right in sound recordings and Chapter 7 covering the mechanical right in compositions and the implications of the recently-enacted Music Modernization Act.

Chapter 8 provides an overview of what we refer to as "garden variety" music copyright cases, where the owner of a composition or sound recording claims that a new work is substantially similar to the original work. In Chapter 9, the textbook introduces the state law right of publicity and federal Lanham Act and their roles in the music industry, including protections against misappropriation of a recording artist's voice, band name disputes, and use of songs in political campaigns. Chapter 10 introduces recording and songwriting agreements and addresses provisions relating to ownership of copyright, duration of the contractual relationship, and compensation that are often at issue in recording and songwriting agreements. Chapter 11 continues the discussion of contract issues within the recording and publishing branches of the music industry, focusing on provisions ranging from the obligation to exploit (or lack thereof) to choice of law. Finally, Chapter 12 provides a brief introduction to additional legal issues in the music industry that have arisen over the years and that are likely to be relevant in the coming years as the industry continues to change, including copyright termination rights, state statutes governing artist representatives, consolidation in the industry, and payola statutes.

The materials within this textbook were designed to illustrate some of the most important legal issues faced by today's musicians and other participants in the music industry and how those issues parallel and/or differ from those that have arisen throughout the history of the industry. It is our hope that they will also spark discussion of how the law and the industry might or should evolve in the future in the face of new technologies and conceptions of music, new demands and uses by consumers, and new models for providing access to musical works.

CONSIDER AS YOU READ . . .

- As applied to music, how does the U.S. Constitution's Copyright Clause support the creation of new works and the ability of the public to access those works?

- Why and how are recordings of musical performances (sound recordings) and compositions treated in distinct manners under U.S. law?

- Is a more simplified model for the music industry either desirable or possible? Does it matter from whose perspective the question is considered?

- What lessons or models can we take from history (even ancient history) to better understand how the industry developed into its current state in the U.S. and inform our vision of what the music industry might look like in the future?

A. UNITED STATES CONSTITUTION: COPYRIGHT CLAUSE

The Congress shall have Power . . . To promote the Progress of Science and useful Arts, by securing for limited Times to Authors and Inventors the exclusive Right to their respective Writings and Discoveries. . .

U.S. CONSTITUTION, Article I, Section 8, clause 8.

B. UNITED STATES COPYRIGHT ACT:
DEFINITIONS OF RELEVANT TERMS (§ 101) AND
SCOPE OF COPYRIGHT PROTECTION (§ 106)

Even though we will not get to the current interpretation of U.S. copyright law until a few chapters down the road, we note two components of modern copyright law that are relevant in considering the historical materials that follow. First, Section 101 provides definitions of terms. Some of these definitions will seem obvious to you, but the nature of what is protected by copyright is heavily influenced by statutes that have changed over time, and thus the meanings of terms and phrases used in copyright law are important—as is the manner in which those meanings have changed and adapted to technological innovations (or failed to change and adapt, as we will see in some of the most difficult legal cases). Keep the current definitions of terms in mind as you read the sections and chapters below that illustrate how music copyright developed over the past century and how technological innovation continuously tested the boundaries of existing definitions and understandings of what copyright law did, and did not, protect.

Second, Section 106 defines the scope of the rights granted to owners of various types of copyrightable works. Pay particular attention to the current scope of rights granted to sound recordings as compared to other types of copyrightable works, including musical compositions. The historical summary in Section D and the materials in Chapters 2 and 3 will provide some perspective as to why and how the scope of copyright protection for compositions and sound recordings ended up differing in important respects. Many of the disputes involving music copyright, under the 1909 Copyright Act and under current law, are fundamentally grounded both in the key definitions and the limitations of scope contained in Sections 101 and 106 and their predecessors within U.S. copyright law. Note, too, that music is often treated differently from other types of copyrighted works; it is important to recognize those differences and to pay particular attention to whether a provision applies to a composition or a sound recording (or both).

17 U.S.C. § 101. DEFINITIONS

Except as otherwise provided in this title, as used in this title, the following terms and their variant forms mean the following:

. . . **"Copies"** are material objects, other than phonorecords, in which a work is fixed by any method now known or later developed, and from which the work can be perceived, reproduced, or otherwise communicated, either directly or with the aid of a machine or device. The term "copies" includes the material object, other than a phonorecord, in which the work is first fixed.

. . . A work is **"created"** when it is fixed in a copy or phonorecord for the first time; where a work is prepared over a period of time, the portion of it that has been fixed at any particular time constitutes the work as of that time, and where the work has been prepared in different versions, each version constitutes a separate work.

. . . A work is **"fixed"** in a tangible medium of expression when its embodiment in a copy or phonorecord, by or under the authority of the author, is sufficiently permanent or stable to permit it to be perceived, reproduced, or otherwise communicated for a period of more than transitory duration. A work consisting of sounds, images, or both, that are being transmitted, is "fixed" for purposes of this title if a fixation of the work is being made simultaneously with its transmission.

. . . To **"perform"** a work means to recite, render, play, dance, or act it, either directly or by means of any device or process or, in the case of a motion picture or other audiovisual work, to show its images in any sequence or to make the sounds accompanying it audible.

A **"performing rights society"** is an association, corporation, or other entity that licenses the public performance of nondramatic musical works on behalf of copyright owners of such works, such as the American Society of Composers, Authors and Publishers (ASCAP), Broadcast Music, Inc. (BMI), and SESAC, Inc.

"Phonorecords" are material objects in which sounds, other than those accompanying a motion picture or other audiovisual work, are fixed by any method now known or later developed, and from which the sounds can be perceived, reproduced, or otherwise communicated, either directly or with the aid of a machine or device. The term "phonorecords" includes the material object in which the sounds are first fixed.

. . . **"Publication"** is the distribution of copies or phonorecords of a work to the public by sale or other transfer of ownership, or by rental, lease, or lending. The offering to distribute copies or phonorecords to a group of persons for purposes of further distribution, public performance, or public display, constitutes publication. A public performance or display of a work does not of itself constitute publication.

To perform or display a work "publicly" means—

    (1)   to perform or display it at a place open to the public or at any place where a substantial number of persons outside of a normal circle of a family and its social acquaintances is gathered; or

    (2)   to transmit or otherwise communicate a performance or display of the work to a place specified by clause (1) or to the public, by means of any device or process, whether the members of the public capable of receiving the performance or display receive it in the same place or in separate places and at the same time or at different times.

. . . **"Sound recordings"** are works that result from the fixation of a series of musical, spoken, or other sounds, but not including the sounds accompanying a motion picture or other audiovisual work, regardless of the nature of the material objects, such as disks, tapes, or other phonorecords, in which they are embodied.

17 U.S.C. § 106. EXCLUSIVE RIGHTS
IN COPYRIGHTED WORKS

Subject to sections 107 through 122, the owner of copyright under this title has the exclusive rights to do and to authorize any of the following:

(1) to **reproduce** the copyrighted work in copies or phonorecords;

(2) to prepare **derivative works** based upon the copyrighted work;

(3) to **distribute** copies or phonorecords of the copyrighted work to the public by sale or other transfer of ownership, or by rental, lease, or lending;

(4) in the case of literary, musical, dramatic, and choreographic works, pantomimes, and motion pictures and other audiovisual works, to **perform** the copyrighted work **publicly**;

(5) in the case of literary, musical, dramatic, and choreographic works, pantomimes, and pictorial, graphic, or sculptural works, including the individual images of a motion picture or other audiovisual work, to **display** the copyrighted work **publicly**; and

(6) in the case of sound recordings, to **perform** the copyrighted work **publicly by means of a digital audio transmission**.

NOTES AND QUESTIONS

1. Is the model adopted by the U.S. Constitution—copyright protection via a "property model" as a means for promoting creation—the best (or only) way to support the creation of new works and make them available to the public? What other models might be effective in promoting the creation of musical works and making them accessible to the public?

2. Note the differing definitions for "copy," "phonorecord," and "sound recording" in Section 101 and keep them in mind throughout this textbook. Do the distinctions make sense to you? What questions do they raise?

3. Pay particular attention to the nature of the rights granted to owners of different types of copyrighted works in Section 106, specifically with respect to musical compositions and sound recordings. The materials below will provide some historical context for the different scope of rights for these works. As you read them, think about how you might expand or amend the definitions and nature of rights granted in compositions and sound recordings in the modern era.

C. OVERVIEW OF THE MUSIC INDUSTRY

The above provisions of U.S. copyright law hint at the nature and structure of the music industry, as most of the key participants in the industry grew up around the rights protected by law—and the law developed to create or protect new rights as technology changed the industry. The key "players" in the music industry[4] are currently expanding and changing at a rapid pace: only several years ago, Spotify was just a European startup that was having trouble making inroads in the U.S. because of licensing issues. As of 2019, it had become the primary source of music for most of the students in our seminar—although only two years before that, YouTube was the most popular source of music for our seminar students. Similarly, while just ten years earlier physical sales constituted about 60% of the revenue in the U.S. recorded music sector, in 2019 that dominance had been replaced by streaming, which constituted 75% of recorded music revenue.

Physical/ Digital Sales

Total U.S. Revenue (Recorded Music)

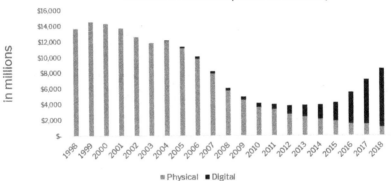

© 2008–18 SoundExchange, used with permission

---

⁴ Most references in this textbook are to the popular music industry in the U.S. Other aspects of U.S. music, such as musical theater, opera, jazz, and classical music, involve additional "players" and some unique industry practices due to the nature of those musical forms that are outside the scope of this text. However, the basic distinctions between types of work (composition versus sound recording) and protected rights (reproduction and distribution versus performance) apply broadly to all aspects of music.

U.S. Music Industry Revenues 1H 2018
Source: RIAA

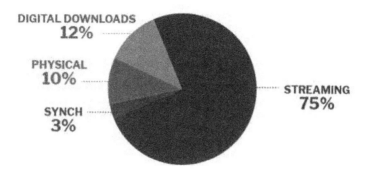

Streaming Music Revenues
Source: RIAA

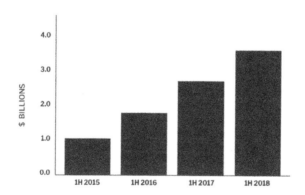

© 2019 SoundExchange, charts used with permission

With that caveat about rapid transitions within the industry in recent years that continue today, this section will introduce some of the primary participants in the industry and the roles that they play, in the hope of giving you an overview of the breadth and depth of the music industry. We will also explore what positions some of the key constituencies have taken in the debates over music law and policy that have dominated the industry in the twenty-first century.

So, where does your music come from? If your answer is Spotify, or some new service or source launched recently, that is only the tip of the iceberg—it identifies how you access music, but it does not identify the source or the path by which a particular song makes it to your playlist and your ears. You likely know the names of your favorite artists, although you might also listen to genres of music and hear songs by artists that you cannot identify simply by hearing their performance of a song. But do you know who wrote the songs you love? Do you know who produced them, and what label financed the recording of the song and likely owns the copyright to it? Do you know what music publisher owns or administers the rights to the composition? In fact, for a song to make it from an idea in a composer's head to your ears, a host of different "players" are involved, and the law and/or lawyers play a part at many steps in the process.

Even though a composer/songwriter[5] and performing artist might be the same person—think of famous singer-songwriters like Bob Dylan and Paul McCartney—both the law and the music business treat them as separate entities, with distinct roles, governing laws, and business structures that apply to their rights and revenues. The product of their work is also viewed as distinct under the law, with different rights applying to "musical works"—i.e., the composition or song, including the notes, chord progressions and lyrics—and to "sound recordings"—i.e., the fixed (recorded) performance of the composition by a performing artist that emanates from your speaker or earbuds. Note that the term "copy" refers to musical works, but "phonorecord" is the term of art used by the Copyright Act to refer to the physical object in which a sound recording is fixed. In the recording business, the term "master recording" is used to refer to the original work that is owned by the copyright owner of the sound recording.

A further distinction involves the nature of the rights at issue, with separate players and separate legal rules governing reproduction and distribution rights, on the one hand, and performance rights, on the other hand. Flip back to the provisions of Section 106 of the Copyright Act and

---

[5] Throughout this textbook, we will use the terms "composer" and "songwriter," as well as the terms "composition" and "song," interchangeably. Within the popular music genre, the terms "songwriter" and "song" are more common, whereas "composer" and "composition" are used more often in the context of classical music. The Copyright Act uses the term "musical work" to refer exclusively to compositions/songs; within the statute, the term "musical work" does not encompass sound recordings.

you will note that musical works and sound recordings are singled out (among other types of copyrightable works) with distinct rights. For example, not all copyrightable works are granted public performance rights, and the scope of the public performance right granted to sound recordings is narrower than that of musical works.

In addition to focusing on who owns or controls the particular right at issue—and note that different rights in the same work may be licensed to and administered by different entities—it is helpful to "follow the money"[6] by understanding who gets paid and who is obligated to pay for each type of use of the musical work or sound recording. As you do so, consider the distinct "products" created under copyright law (such as the sound recording and the musical work) and how copyright law handles each of the "activities" that those products may encounter in commerce.

The following graphic provides a high-level (and oversimplified) approach to some of the more important commercial activities that occur in the industry: reproduction, distribution & performance. For each of these activities, we have set forth examples of the types of organizations that oversee those activities for both sound recordings and musical works. Think of this as a visual representation of the distinct quadrants of the music industry that have developed in tandem with the legal rights granted to owners of compositions and owners of sound recordings under federal law, with some examples of different entities that own, or are responsible for, administering and enforcing the distinct rights for distinct types of works:

---

[6]   Catchphrase made famous in the 1976 film *All the President's Men.*

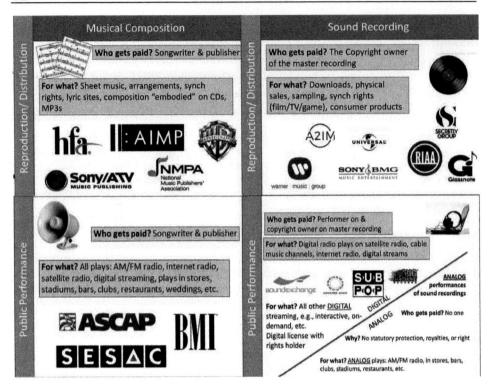

© 2008–2020 MH Presentations, used with permission

The Composition: Music Publishers and Songwriters

Of course, as the City of Nashville touts on its web page, "It All Begins with a Song."[7] Once a composer has fixed her idea in some form—whether humming it into a voice recorder, writing notes and lyrics on a page, working with cowriters in a recording studio, or even inking it on the back of a napkin—the musical work is presumptively protected by U.S. copyright. Some composers retain the copyright interest in their musical works; many others assign the copyright to music publishers. Regardless of who owns the copyright, however, music publishers play a primary role in promoting the compositions in their catalog to performing and recording artists and in administering the rights associated with those compositions.

Although music publishers started out as entities that focused on publishing printed songbooks and sheet music, their role in today's music economy stretches far beyond print. In addition, today's music publishers may own or administer the mechanical rights, synchronization rights, and public performance rights stemming from live, digital, and analog performances of the compositions in their catalog. Revenue is earned

---

7   *See* Nashville: Music City home page at https://www.visitmusiccity.com/itallbeginswitha song.

whenever a copy of sheet music is sold (reproduction royalties); whenever a recording of a composition is made and distributed, as in a LP or CD or download (mechanical royalties); whenever a composition is integrated into an audiovisual work, electronic game, or other non-audio usage (synchronization, or "synch," revenues); and whenever a composition is publicly performed in any manner (performance royalties), among other revenue sources from uses of the composition.[8] Sheet music now makes up only a small percentage of music publishing revenues, with revenue from the performance right in musical works—particularly from broadcast radio, but increasingly from digital streaming—making up the greatest share.

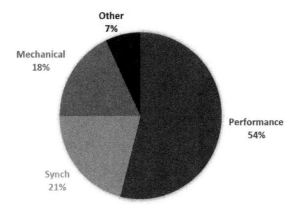

U.S. Publishing Industry Revenues (1st Half 2018)
(Source: NMPA)

As will be discussed in more detail in Chapter 10, even when the music publisher is assigned the copyright to a composition, it is typical for the publisher and composer to share revenue from most sources 50–50, although shared ownership (co-publishing) arrangements or those in which the composer retains the copyright and the publisher merely administers it can increase the composer's share.

The mechanical right is governed by 17 U.S.C. § 115 and is subject to a statutory license; once the owner of a composition authorizes it to be mechanically reproduced (i.e., recorded), the statute permits anyone else to record it as long as the statutory rate or a separately negotiated rate is paid. In recent years, the Harry Fox Agency has often been the primary entity that administers negotiated mechanical royalties, although the passage of the Music Modernization Act in 2018 created a new "Mechanical Licensing Collective" to provide a central resource for administering a new

---

8   For example, "grand rights" in a musical work include incorporation of the work in a dramatic presentation, such as in musical theater or opera.

blanket license for certain digital mechanical reproductions in the U.S.[9] Digital distribution of recorded compositions is included in what "counts" as a mechanical reproduction, and thus, for example, digital downloads of songs and the use of music in cell phone ringtones both implicate the mechanical right.

The public performance right in musical works is administered through entities referred to as "performing rights societies" in Section 101 of the Copyright Act, but also known as performing rights organizations, or PROs. The best-known PROs with respect to compositions are ASCAP and BMI, although there are other competing PROs that have developed (e.g. SESAC and GMR). PROs negotiate and enter into agreements with music publishers and composers to license public performances of compositions, and they provide what are often blanket licenses to organizations and venues that permit these licensees to publicly perform all works in the PRO's catalog. The PROs collect license fees from the variety of entities that publicly perform compositions—ranging from corner bars to the biggest sports arenas to broadcast radio and digital streaming companies, and including live performances and performances of pre-recorded music in the analog and digital realms. They then distribute those revenues to their publisher and composer members, generally on a 50/50 split between publisher and composer for a given work. The history of PROs in the U.S. is discussed in some detail in Chapter 3, including the decades of antitrust regulation of PROs and the complicated rate-setting process that has developed as a result of antitrust oversight.

Music publishers and composers also seek out opportunities to license their musical works for use in audiovisual works such as motion pictures, television or cable productions, commercials, and Internet videos. These "synchronization licenses" are typically individually negotiated, with the price varying widely depending upon the manner in which the composition is used, how prominent it will be in the audiovisual work, and how successful the composition has been.

The Sound Recording: Performing Artists and Record Labels

While what we call music starts with a song, that is typically just the first step towards commercial success. There is also significant value in today's music industry that results from performances of the song, whether recorded or live, by a performing artist. Revenue earned by songwriters and music publishers is partly reliant upon performing artists (whether the songwriter herself or another person/group) to bring their musical works to life and upon audiences for those performances to make them profitable.

Music and the theater have in common one element that distinguishes them from the other arts. . . . [B]oth require the

---

[9] See Chapter 7 for a more detailed introduction to the Section 115 mechanical license and the changes adopted by the 2018 Music Modernization Act.

intervention of outsiders to set before us the patterned ideas of the composer or playwright. Masterpieces may be created by a painter or poet for his own delight, unseen or unsung by any besides himself. But a symphony, like a drama, does not fulful [sic] its meaning unless it is projected by performers before an audience. The printed score of the Brahms First Symphony, or the pregnant pages of Shakespeare's *Macbeth*, are merely blueprints of the creators' intentions, of full value only to exceptionally skilled and imaginative readers. They do not come to life without performers and without audience.[10]

Just as the fixation of a composition in some medium creates a copyrightable "musical work," the fixation of a recording of a musical performance creates a copyrightable "sound recording." Creating a sound recording is often a collective work, involving lead performers, backup singers, studio musicians, sound engineers, and producers—typically making the endeavor both more costly than writing a composition and potentially complicating the ability of any one person to claim "authorship" of the finished recording. Traditionally, most sound recordings have been created pursuant to a recording agreement between the performers and a recording company, commonly referred to as a record label. A "typical" recording agreement gives copyright ownership of the master sound recording to the record label, usually in exchange for an advance guaranty and payment of royalties resulting from sales and licenses of the recording.

Income from exploitation of sound recordings, like that from exploitation of compositions, comes from several different sources that involve many different types of entities within the music industry. Importantly, the "bundle of rights" granted by U.S. copyright law in sound recordings is more limited than that granted in compositions. As a result of this difference in the scope of rights granted, the U.S. recording industry was historically structured around a "sales model." In other words, the industry was designed primarily to promote the sales of recordings, which drove the vast majority of revenue. This contrasted with the publishing industry, which historically benefitted from more diverse sources of significant revenue.

Until the creation of a digital performance right in sound recordings and the advent of Internet streaming services, the primary source of revenue for record labels was sales of records (which includes vinyl, cassette and 8-track tape, and CD) and then digital downloads. Record labels distributed the records to third party distributors—record stores, department stores, iTunes—which then sold those records to consumers. Performing artists were contractually entitled to royalties from these sales

---

10 FREDERICK DORIAN, THE HISTORY OF MUSIC IN PERFORMANCE: THE ART OF MUSICAL INTERPRETATION FROM THE RENAISSANCE TO OUR DAY, *Foreword by Eugene Ormandy* 7 (W. W. Norton & Company 1966).

through their agreements with the labels, but labels deducted their costs (including advances paid to the artists) before paying any royalty to the artists. Recording agreements are discussed in more detail in Chapter 10, including how the traditional structures are changing in the digital era.

Another significant difference between the recording and publishing sides of the industry relates to the fact that terrestrial radio stations (i.e., traditional "AM/FM" broadcasters) still pay only composers and music publishers for broadcasts of music. There is no royalty owed under U.S. copyright law to recording artists or labels for the broadcast of their recordings. An important exception to that rule was created in 1995 when a limited digital public performance right was created for sound recordings. With the incredible growth of digital streaming services in recent years, the revenue stream from the digital public performance right now surpasses that from physical sales of records, making up almost seventy-five percent of revenue for U.S. sound recordings by 2018. Digital streaming royalties are administered either by master owners or by SoundExchange, which makes payments directly to record labels, featured artists, and backup musicians. Chapter 6 details the manner in which the digital public performance right in sound recordings is administered.

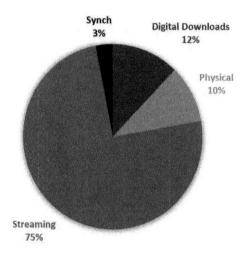

U.S. Recording Industry Revenues (1st Half 2018)
(Source: RIAA)

Licensing of sound recordings for synchronization in motion pictures, television and cable productions, and commercials is also a source of revenue that is typically administered by record labels, with a contractual share of revenues going to the recording artists. These licenses are individually negotiated with licensees, with fees dependent upon similar factors as those relevant to synchronization licenses for compositions.

Other primary sources of revenues for performing artists, and increasingly for record labels, are ancillary to the sale, distribution, or digital public performance rights created by copyright. Significant revenues can be earned from touring—live performances by artists—and merchandising—sales of branded T-shirts, hats, water bottles, etc., that feature the performer's name, trademark, and image. A nationwide tour often involves the participation of multiple entities, including promoters; venues; ticket vendors; road crews; technical crews; touring musicians; backup singers and dancers; transportation companies; insurers; and advertisers. Merchandising often involves the participation of artistic designers, third-party manufacturers, and both online and physical sales outlets.

In addition to those who directly participate in the revenue-generating aspects of the modern music industry, there are a host of additional important roles played by individuals and entities. For example, key policies affecting the music industry are developed through the work of trade organizations and unions, lawyers and lobbyists, Congress, International Treaties, courts, and government agencies like the Copyright Office, Copyright Royalty Board, and Antitrust Division of the Department of Justice. Lawyers, in particular, are involved in almost all aspects of the music industry, from developing legal policy to enforcing property rights to negotiating the contracts that make it possible for the idea of a song to become a product available to the public. The figure below summarizes some of the key players involved in all aspects of the modern music industry, from the creation of the composition through the consumer's experience of the performance:

Music Industry Participants from Idea to Consumer

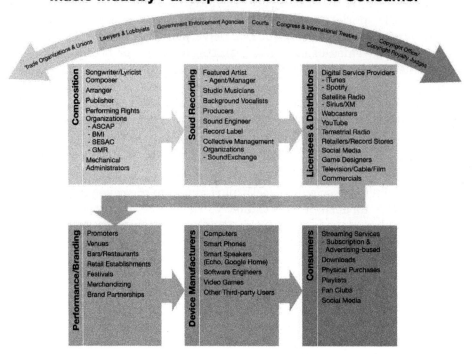

For many users (i.e., licensees) of music, it is necessary to obtain a license from *both* the owner of the musical work and the owner of the sound recording. However, the necessity of licenses from the owners of both works will vary depending upon the nature of the right implicated by the use. If, for example, the owner of a baseball stadium wanted to play John Fogerty's *Centerfield* at a game, it could rely solely on a blanket license from the PRO that included that particular composition in its catalog. The stadium would not need any license at all from the owner of the sound recording, as there is no public performance right in sound recordings that applies to performances in physical spaces like stadiums; the public performance right in sound recordings applies only to digital transmissions.[11] By contrast, if the producer of a motion picture wished to include Fogerty's recording of *Centerfield* in the opening sequence of its film, it would need a synchronization license from the copyright owner of the composition (Fogerty or his music publisher or another assignee of the rights) as well as a license from the copyright owner of the sound recording (Fogerty or his record label or another assignee of the rights). It is easy to see how complicated and fraught with potential error the music licensing process can be, given the variety of rights, owners, assignees, licensees, and administrators that are potentially involved in gaining authority to use a

---

[11] *See* 17 U.S.C. §§ 106, 114.

single song. In later chapters, we will explore music licensing in more detail, with a focus on the growing use of statutory licensing as an effort to simplify the process for certain types of uses.

We have often heard (and said) that if the music industry were to be created from a clean slate today, it would look quite different from what it does now. The modern music industry has many vibrant components that make up the overall marketplace, including the sound recording industry. But sound recordings were not always a significant driver of music law and policy, especially considering that commercial recordings and record labels are a comparatively new addition to our history of musical enjoyment (which dates back centuries). Indeed, the modern record label as we know it did not evolve until the early 20th century, which may be one reason the law has been slower to protect sound recordings. So it is understandable that compositions and those who published them were the first to receive legal protections, and it is the logical starting point for our study of music law from the American perspective. To give you a better understanding of how and why the music industry developed as it has in the U.S., the section below gives you a broad overview of the history of music pertinent to the development of the music industry in America.

D. AMERICAN MUSIC LAW IN HISTORICAL CONTEXT[12]

The concept of music as a commodity—something that can be owned and controlled, bought and sold, and protected by law from "theft"—is a relatively new one. Music is found in every culture in the world. "Indeed, poets, philosophers, and scientists have contended that music is part of what makes us distinctly human."[13] The first musical instrument was most likely the human voice, but anthropologists have discovered musical instruments that are believed to be as much as 44,000 years old.[14] The word "music" itself, derived from the Greek word mousikè, meaning (the art) of the Muse,[15] reflects a long-standing and deeply ingrained belief in music as a gift from God rather than the creation of any individual human being as an author.[16]

Music as an Oral Tradition and Divine Inspiration

For most of human history, musical works were oral traditions, passed down from generation to generation. As Harvard musicologist Thomas Forrest Kelly notes, "The oldest recording device, and the newest, is the memory; without it, nothing would be possible."[17] The earliest form of musical notation dates back to 1400 BCE in Mesopotamia—or perhaps 1200 BCE in ancient Babylonia, given some dispute over whether representations on the ancient tablet discovered in Mesopotamia were intended as musical notation[18]—and the ancient Greeks used musical

---

[12] Note that this is only a cursory overview, with some broad generalizations made solely for purposes of conciseness. The cited sources in this section provide a much more detailed and nuanced review of music history and are recommended for those of you who are interested in how music developed as a human art and, ultimately, as a commodity and industry. Of course, as is expected, some of these sources are framed from a particular point of view about what influences directed the development of musical innovation and protection and how and whether music should be protected in the present day; by citing them, we do not mean to take a stand in that debate for purposes of this text. We trust our readers to make their own evaluation of the arguments offered in those sources.

[13] DAVID SUISMAN, SELLING SOUNDS: THE COMMERCIAL REVOLUTION IN AMERICAN MUSIC 6–7 (Harvard University Press 2009).

[14] See, e.g., NILS LENNART WALLIN, STEVEN BROWN, & BJÖRN MERKER, THE ORIGINS OF MUSIC 4, 10 (Cambridge: MIT Press 2001) ("It is probably safe to assume that musical instruments are at least as old as anatomically modern humans if not much older.").

[15] Music, Dictionary.com, at http://www.dictionary.com/browse/music (last visited 9/9/19).

[16] Michael W. Carroll, Whose Music Is It Anyway?: How We Came to View Musical Expression as a Form of Property, 72 U. CIN. L. REV. 1405, 1426–27 (2004). We highly recommend reading this article in its entirety for a detailed exploration of the development of the concept of music as property. As Carroll explains, the focus here is on the development of music in Western Europe because U.S. copyright law and policy stems from those roots, tracing back through the formation of the publishing industry in England, which was influenced by European conventions adopted in the late Middle Ages and early Renaissance, which in turn was influenced by conventions adopted in ancient Greece and Rome. See id. at 1408 n. 9.

[17] THOMAS FORREST KELLY, CAPTURING MUSIC: THE STORY OF NOTATION 3 (W.W. Norton & Co. 2015).

[18] See JAMES BOYLE, JENNIFER JENKINS, & KEITH AOKI, TALES FROM THE PUBLIC DOMAIN: THEFT, THE HISTORY OF MUSIC 12 (CreateSpace Independent Publishing Platform February 14,

notation, albeit infrequently, as a historical record of songs. In practice, most music in ancient Greece was likely made up of the repetition of common themes, improvised by individual musicians.[19]

Close-up of a portion of the original stone at Delphi, Greece, with the second of the two hymns to Apollo. (The music notation is represented by the symbols above the main, uninterrupted line of Greek lettering.)[20]

Transcription of a portion of the Delphi Hymn of Apollo inscription in modern musical notation from David Binning Monro, The Modes of Ancient Greek Music 134 (Oxford: Clarendon Press 1894), Urbana, Illinois: Project Gutenberg (scanned public domain material from the Google Print Project).[21]

2017), *available at* https://law.duke.edu/musiccomic/download/; RICHARD TARUSKIN & CHRISTOPHER H. GIBBS, THE OXFORD HISTORY OF WESTERN MUSIC, COLLEGE EDITION 4 (2d ed. Oxford Univ. Press NY/Oxford 2019).

[19] JAMES BOYLE, JENNIFER JENKINS, & KEITH AOKI, TALES FROM THE PUBLIC DOMAIN: THEFT, THE HISTORY OF MUSIC 12–15 (CreateSpace Independent Publishing Platform February 14, 2017), *available at* https://law.duke.edu/musiccomic/download/.

[20] http://en.wikipedia.org/wiki/Image:Delphichymn.jpg photo by Ziggur.

[21] Retrieved July 11, 2020, from www.gutenberg.org/files/40288/40288-h/40288-h.htm.

However, the ancient Greeks still sought to impose control over music. Some musical forms were considered too emotional or dangerous; Plato even advanced an argument against musical innovation, asserting that "changes in styles of music are always politically revolutionary."[22] Aristotle agreed with Plato that the state needed to regulate music, urging that the state control the musical curriculum by banning certain instruments (flutes were deemed to be "too exciting") and teaching only the "ethical" melodies. Although music was viewed as potentially dangerous if it veered too far from cultural norms, the idea of a musician or his patron "owning" a particular melody was absent in ancient times. "The system for generating music was in their view part of a larger, beautiful system created by divine power and which ordered the cosmos. The specific conventions governing musical expression reflected the norms and collective culture of the Greeks and could not be individually appropriated."[23]

Statue of Plato in front of the Academy of Athens. Original Work of Leonidas Drosis (d. 1880), photograph by C. Messier 7 February 2016

Similarly, after the Roman Empire rose to power, it embraced music as a part of its everyday culture, but it did not treat music as something that could be "owned." As in Greek culture, much of both musical performance and instruction was the work of slaves in the Roman Empire; it was in that sense that the Roman elite could own and control the means for creating music (as opposed to owning the musical product itself). The

---

[22]   PLATO, THE REPUBLIC, Book 4, 424c at 117 (Cambridge University Press, ed. G.R.F. Ferrari) (dialog of Socrates and Adeimantus). Plato's dialogue continued by arguing that the guardians of the state should "build their watchtower" in music, because breaking rules in music can easily "become a habit" without people realizing it, and "once the idea of breaking rules has gradually established itself, it seeps imperceptibly into people's characters and habits. From there it brims over, increasing as it goes, into their contracts with one another. And from contracts, Socrates, it extends its course of wanton disruption to laws and political institutions, until finally it destroys everything in private and public life." *Id.* at 424d–e, 117. Socrates' response was that a disciplined musical education would prevent this parade of horribles, noting that it would be absurd to pass laws about many matters of discipline but that a disciplined education would instill a disciplined approach to all things in adulthood. *Id.* at 425a–b, 117–18.

[23]   Michael W. Carroll, *Whose Music Is It Anyway?: How We Came to View Musical Expression as a Form of Property*, 72 U. CIN. L. REV. 1405, 1424–25, 1427 (2004).

elite in Roman society were patrons of music, funding the development of performers with "star" qualities, but music itself was "viewed as evanescent" rather than being commodified. Thus, unlike the authors of literary texts in ancient Greece and Rome, the identities of composers of music are largely lost to history and no trade in compositions existed, even though the tools were available for preserving compositions with musical notation systems.[24]

Development of Written Musical Notation and the Role of the Church

During the Middle Ages, new emphasis was placed on the creation of musical notation systems, because the ancient Greek notation systems were largely lost to history by the sixth century A.D. This new effort was largely driven by the Church as a means of controlling the forms of music to be performed during services for the purpose of achieving uniformity, although the early Christian Church is also thought to have made a practice of adopting popular melodies for Christian hymns that could be sung at home instead of pagan hymns.[25] The Church's effort to create a system of notation unfolded over several centuries, from about the ninth to the fourteenth centuries, moving from being merely descriptive, with no means of indicating pitch or tempo, to being more and more detailed and prescriptive, using staff notation to convey relative pitch by identifying specific notes to be played and, later, to convey the duration of notes.[26]

> Musicians of the Middle Ages figured out how to make marks on parchment to capture sound in space, an achievement that required extraordinary conceptual leaps and technological advances. What began as a method to represent the general shape of a song evolved over several centuries to become not only a recording but a playback device, allowing musicians to transport music and learn songs they had never heard before.[27]

---

[24] *Id.* at 1432–33; JAMES BOYLE, JENNIFER JENKINS, & KEITH AOKI, TALES FROM THE PUBLIC DOMAIN: THEFT, THE HISTORY OF MUSIC 14–15 (CreateSpace Independent Publishing Platform February 14, 2017), *available at* https://law.duke.edu/musiccomic/download/.

[25] Michael W. Carroll, *Whose Music Is It Anyway?: How We Came to View Musical Expression as a Form of Property*, 72 U. CIN. L. REV. 1405, 1436–43 (2004); JAMES BOYLE, JENNIFER JENKINS, & KEITH AOKI, TALES FROM THE PUBLIC DOMAIN: THEFT, THE HISTORY OF MUSIC 26–29 (CreateSpace Independent Publishing Platform February 14, 2017), *available at* https://law.duke.edu/musiccomic/download/; C.F. ABDY WILLIAMS, THE STORY OF NOTATION 42–43 (Haskell House Publishers 1969).

[26] Michael W. Carroll, *Whose Music Is It Anyway?: How We Came to View Musical Expression as a Form of Property*, 72 U. CIN. L. REV. 1405, 1440–43 (2004). The early forms of notation that were incapable of conveying pitch, tempo, or duration of notes relied on the longstanding oral tradition, wherein music was learned through listening, repetition, and memorization; these compositions could not be performed based upon the notation alone. *See* RICHARD TARUSKIN & CHRISTOPHER H. GIBBS, THE OXFORD HISTORY OF WESTERN MUSIC, COLLEGE EDITION 14–33 (2d ed. Oxford Univ. Press NY/Oxford 2019).

[27] THOMAS FORREST KELLY, CAPTURING MUSIC: THE STORY OF NOTATION, *Preface* at xiii (W.W. Norton & Co. 2015); *see also* RICHARD TARUSKIN & CHRISTOPHER H. GIBBS, THE OXFORD

By the fourteenth century, "a combination of scientific, logical, philosophical, and poetic advances" had coalesced to produce "a standard and universal form of musical notation" that still largely applies in the West today.[28] That is not to say that the system of notation developed in the Middle Ages could perfectly transmit the composer's intended sound of the performance even with increasingly complex indications of pitch, tempo, duration, and emotion.

> Musical notation, however perfect, can never entirely represent the composer's meaning. Much must be left to the imagination of the performer . . . . The more emotion and artistic power felt by the composer, the less satisfactory is a mechanical and unintellectual performance . . . . [F]or, as in the drama, so in music, every highly skilled and intellectual performer has his own idea of what the composer intends to convey.[29]

One telling illustration of the difficulty in creating a system of notation that could fully convey the intended nature of the performance comes from the reign of Emperor Leopold I, a Habsburg who ruled the Holy Roman Empire and was King of Hungary, Croatia, and Bohemia from 1658 until his death in 1705. As the story goes, Leopold had successfully urged his ambassador to Rome to convince the Pope to send him a copy of the famed *Miserere* of Allegri, which had never been heard outside of the Sistine Chapel. Apparently, Leopold was so disappointed with the performance of the piece that he wrote in anger to the Pope, accusing the chapel master of sending him a different composition in order to keep the true composition a "mystery." The Pope fired the chapel master on receipt of the letter, but he later allowed a cardinal to plead in the master's defense that the "style of singing in the Sistine Chapel, and especially in performing the *Miserere*, was such as could not be expressed by notes, nor taught, nor transmitted to any other place, except by example. . . ." Although the Pope could not understand how the same notes could sound so different when performed in different places, he sent the master's defense to Vienna, and Leopold ultimately arranged for the Pope to send musicians to Vienna to teach his musicians the proper way of performing the piece.[30] Even though musical notation had come far in the centuries since the Church had begun its efforts to standardize liturgical performances, it still did not fully achieve the goal of uniformity across time and distance.

HISTORY OF WESTERN MUSIC, COLLEGE EDITION 3–4 (2d ed. Oxford Univ. Press NY/Oxford 2019) ("What had previously been transmitted from generation to generation through singing and playing came to be partially written down, preserved, and disseminated. This was an enormously important change.").

[28] THOMAS FORREST KELLY, CAPTURING MUSIC: THE STORY OF NOTATION 174, 208 (W.W. Norton & Co. 2015).

[29] C.F. ABDY WILLIAMS, THE STORY OF NOTATION 218–19 (Haskell House Publishers 1969).

[30] *Id.* at 219–20.

As noted above, the Church viewed musical notation as a means of regulating the form of performances rather than a means of spurring the creation of new compositions. In this regard, the Church actively sought to suppress forms of musical expression that were not officially sanctioned.[31] In spite of its original purpose—limiting music to specific, accepted compositions—the system of notation developed by the Church ended up allowing composers to experiment with new, more complex compositions, and the Church was ultimately not able to suppress the creation of new musical expression, particularly among secular musicians.[32] Once a system of musical notation existed, the idea of authorship in music could more readily take root, and it grew as secular musicians gained independence and stature in society over the course of the tenth through fourteenth centuries.[33]

Development of Musical Performance and Composition as a Profession

During the latter part of the Middle Ages, traveling musicians—referred to as minstrels or "jongleurs"—traveled the countryside, providing musical entertainment for audiences ranging from peasants at festivals to nobles at annual banquets.

> They sang all sorts of ditties, played on various instruments for money, especially for dancers, accompanied the bands of warriors, amused the ladies and nobles in their castles, recounted deeds of valour in rude verse, carried news from town to town, were often the secret messengers of Cupid and always the welcome merry-makers of the people. But they were vagrant, homeless, and, on the whole, despised, even though gladly greeted on all festive occasions for the entertainment they unfailingly provided.[34]

Joining the minstrels in the late eleventh and twelfth centuries were French nobles—called troubadours—who chose to become traveling musicians, serving as poet-composers who brought along instrumentalists most likely hired from the community of traveling minstrels. Their music focused mainly on expounding upon either courtly love or heroic deeds.

---

[31] Michael W. Carroll, Whose Music Is It Anyway?: How We Came to View Musical Expression as a Form of Property, 72 U. CIN. L. REV. 1405, 1436–37 (2004).

[32] JAMES BOYLE, JENNIFER JENKINS, & KEITH AOKI, TALES FROM THE PUBLIC DOMAIN: THEFT, THE HISTORY OF MUSIC 30 (CreateSpace Independent Publishing Platform February 14, 2017), available at https://law.duke.edu/musiccomic/download/; Michael W. Carroll, Whose Music Is It Anyway?: How We Came to View Musical Expression as a Form of Property, 72 U. CIN. L. REV. 1405, 1443 (2004).

[33] See, e.g., THOMAS TAPPER & PERCY GOETSCHIUS, ESSENTIALS IN MUSIC HISTORY 79–82 (New York: Charles Scribner's Sons 1914).

[34] Id. at 79–80; see also Michael W. Carroll, Whose Music Is It Anyway?: How We Came to View Musical Expression as a Form of Property, 72 U. CIN. L. REV. 1405, 1444–45 (2004).

Portrait of one of the few female troubadours,
Comtessa Beatriz de Dia,
a French poet and composer born in 1175[35]

Unlike minstrels and jongleurs, troubadours had more resources to support themselves and greater respect in society. However, the nomadic life of all of these traveling musicians made them more independent from political/religious authorities. As a result, they were considered to be potentially troublesome influences by those in power in the places to which they traveled.[36]

Troubadour offrant un poème à sa bien-aimée
(Troubadour offering a poem to his beloved).
Illustration by Master of the Codex Manesse
(Foundation Painter), circa 1305–1340.

During the twelfth through fourteenth centuries, with the growth of European cities and formation of universities, many traveling musicians ended up finding employment as town watchmen and timekeepers, using their instruments to announce the arrival of visitors or to warn of danger. They also provided music for both public and private celebrations, and with the emergence of a middle class, musicians gained increased stature and

---

[35]   From Bibliothèque Nationale, MS cod. fr. 12473.

[36]   THOMAS TAPPER & PERCY GOETSCHIUS, ESSENTIALS IN MUSIC HISTORY 79–80 (New York: Charles Scribner's Sons 1914); Michael W. Carroll, *Whose Music Is It Anyway?: How We Came to View Musical Expression as a Form of Property*, 72 U. CIN. L. REV. 1405, 1445–46 (2004); RICHARD TARUSKIN & CHRISTOPHER H. GIBBS, THE OXFORD HISTORY OF WESTERN MUSIC, COLLEGE EDITION 36–41 (2d ed. Oxford Univ. Press NY/Oxford 2019).

the demand for their services increased. Starting in Vienna and ultimately spreading throughout Germany, England, and France, these town musicians formed guilds as a means of limiting competition from traveling musicians:[37] "The guild was granted an official, regulated monopoly on public performance by the town council, and the exclusive privileges of guild membership, marked by gowns and insignia, made a career as a musician an attractive choice to pursue."[38] Thus, the guilds were able to regulate music within the town walls by limiting who was authorized to perform.

One of the enduring legacies of the early "professional" musicians—traveling minstrels and troubadours and more rooted members of musical guilds—was their interest in and advancement of the use of musical instruments. During much of the Middle Ages, when vocal music dominated the Church and folk-song within the home, the traveling musicians and guilds were the only group of musicians who kept alive the tradition of the fiddle and pipe, both alone and in group performances. Their embrace of instrumental music helped to pave the way for the Renaissance period in which instrumental composition flourished.[39]

The coalescence of growth in stature and independence of secular musicians and development of more complex musical notation systems by the Church began to lead to a more general acceptance of the idea of musical composition as a human art, rather than an activity involving repetition of common themes handed down by the divine. During the late twelfth century, the Notre Dame cathedral in Paris became a center of musical activity, particularly for the development of the notation of polyphonic music, and individual composers began to gain recognition.[40] "A significant feature illustrating the importance of this period is the fact that here, for the first time, musical activity steps out of the obscurity of anonymous and collective creation, and enters the stage of individual achievement and personal contribution."[41] By the fourteenth century,

---

[37] *See* THOMAS TAPPER & PERCY GOETSCHIUS, ESSENTIALS IN MUSIC HISTORY 80 (New York: Charles Scribner's Sons 1914); Michael W. Carroll, *Whose Music Is It Anyway?: How We Came to View Musical Expression as a Form of Property*, 72 U. CIN. L. REV. 1405, 1446–47 (2004).

[38] Michael W. Carroll, *Whose Music Is It Anyway?: How We Came to View Musical Expression as a Form of Property*, 72 U. CIN. L. REV. 1405, 1447 (2004).

[39] THOMAS TAPPER & PERCY GOETSCHIUS, ESSENTIALS IN MUSIC HISTORY 81–82 (New York: Charles Scribner's Sons 1914).

[40] WILLI APEL, THE NOTATION OF POLYPHONIC MUSIC 900–1600 at 215 (rev. 5th ed., Mediaeval Academy of America, Cambridge MA 1953). For example, Magister Leoninus is credited as being one of the earliest composers of organum—a form of plainchant with harmony—and Magister Perotinus Magnus, a composer of discant, is recognized as one of the earliest composers whose name is attached to individual compositions. *Id.* Polyphonic music is that which has more than a single line of melody; monophonic music (think of the classic Gregorian chant as an example) consists of only a single line of melody. *See, e.g.*, WILLI APEL, THE NOTATION OF POLYPHONIC MUSIC 900–1600, *Introduction* at xix–xxiv (rev. 5th ed., Mediaeval Academy of America, Cambridge MA 1953).

[41] *Id.*

composition had developed into a recognized art in which individual composers could frequently claim attribution, and the more wealthy composers—often the troubadours, with their aristocratic backgrounds— began to pay to have their compositions transcribed.[42] Guild endowments, funded by members, also provided funding for the composition of new musical works, and the guilds began to expand their monopoly to cover the music itself rather than merely the musical performers, complaining when traveling jongleurs borrowed from and reworked popular melodies created by guild members. However, well into the fourteenth century, the general practice was still for composers to freely borrow from one another without permission or attribution.[43]

Commodification of Printed Music and Legal Protections for Publishers

Johannes Gutenberg's invention of a movable type printing press in about 1440 was another watershed moment in the history of Western music.[44] Although more difficult (and less profitable) than book printing, musical printing began by the 1470s.[45] The nascent music publishing industry first began to thrive in Italy, buoyed by a combination of the role of the Church as a primary sponsor of composers and musicians during the early Renaissance, the resources invested in artistic creation and innovation within the nobility in Italy, and the central role that Italy played in the trade networks of the time. By about 1530, with improvements in print technology that allowed for a single-impression technique in lieu of the original triple-, and then double-, impression techniques, printed music became "increasingly accessible to middle-class buyers" and music publishing as a commercial enterprise spread to other parts of Europe.[46]

> With the advent of commercial music printing almost five hundred years ago (and thus some five hundred years after the introduction of music writing), reproduction became easier and

---

[42]　Michael W. Carroll, *Whose Music Is It Anyway?: How We Came to View Musical Expression as a Form of Property*, 72 U. CIN. L. REV. 1405, 1449 (2004).

[43]　*Id.* at 1450–51.

[44]　*See* RICHARD TARUSKIN & CHRISTOPHER H. GIBBS, THE OXFORD HISTORY OF WESTERN MUSIC, COLLEGE EDITION 174–75 (2d ed. Oxford Univ. Press NY/Oxford 2019); Michael W. Carroll, *Whose Music Is It Anyway?: How We Came to View Musical Expression as a Form of Property*, 72 U. CIN. L. REV. 1405, 1456–57 (2004); JAMES BOYLE, JENNIFER JENKINS, & KEITH AOKI, TALES FROM THE PUBLIC DOMAIN: THEFT, THE HISTORY OF MUSIC 38–39 (CreateSpace Independent Publishing Platform February 14, 2017), *available at* https://law.duke.edu/musiccomic/download/.

[45]　*See, e.g.*, JAMES BOYLE, JENNIFER JENKINS, & KEITH AOKI, TALES FROM THE PUBLIC DOMAIN: THEFT, THE HISTORY OF MUSIC 41–42 (CreateSpace Independent Publishing Platform February 14, 2017), *available at* https://law.duke.edu/musiccomic/download/; Michael W. Carroll, *Whose Music Is It Anyway?: How We Came to View Musical Expression as a Form of Property*, 72 U. CIN. L. REV. 1405, 1456 (2004).

[46]　See Michael W. Carroll, *Whose Music Is It Anyway?: How We Came to View Musical Expression as a Form of Property*, 72 U. CIN. L. REV. 1405, 1454–56, 1457 (2004).

cheaper. . . . Music could now spread much more widely than ever before and much more impersonally.[47]

As publishers began to embrace printed music, they sought protection from competitors in the form of royal privileges that granted a monopoly on publishing certain types of works within the royal territories.[48] At the time, books containing multiple compositions were printed and published, not individual compositions. The main expense in early music publishing was not the cost of creating the composition—patrons or the composer himself bore those costs. Although making printed copies required the same amount of work and expense in those days as type-setting the original printed work, competitors could gain an advantage by waiting to see which compositions within a book of many compositions gained popularity and then supplant sales of the original work by compiling what was essentially a book of "greatest hits." Because the original publisher had incurred the expense of investing in the publishing of many works, only some of which became popular, it was at a competitive disadvantage if other publishers were allowed to profit from publishing the same works once their popularity was established.[49]

The royal privilege, or "letter patent," system created property-like rights for music publishers, but it was not available to all publishers of original works; it was often limited to narrow geographical areas; it typically focused on "exclusive rights to print music using a specific technique or specific type of font"; and privileges could be revoked or expanded to competitors at the whim of the monarch.[50] In many parts of Europe and England, licensing requirements—used as a form of censorship—merged with music printing privileges, serving dual purposes of protecting publishers against competition and limiting published works to those approved by the monarch.

This system of limited monopolies on publishing also protected publishers, not composers—with the prominent exception of Orlando di Lasso, an Italian composer who in the 1570s was able to obtain the

---

[47]   RICHARD TARUSKIN & CHRISTOPHER H. GIBBS, THE OXFORD HISTORY OF WESTERN MUSIC, COLLEGE EDITION 30 (2d ed. Oxford Univ. Press NY/Oxford 2019).

[48]   One of the first publishers to do so was Petrucci, who created a unique way to print musical scores and, after arguing that his method allowed convenient printing of plainchant ("a thing very important to the Christian religion"), was granted a twenty-year "monopoly over all musical printing in Venice as a reward." JAMES BOYLE, JENNIFER JENKINS, & KEITH AOKI, TALES FROM THE PUBLIC DOMAIN: THEFT, THE HISTORY OF MUSIC 41–42 (CreateSpace Independent Publishing Platform February 14, 2017), available at https://law.duke.edu/musiccomic/download/.

[49]   See Michael W. Carroll, Whose Music Is It Anyway?: How We Came to View Musical Expression as a Form of Property, 72 U. CIN. L. REV. 1405, 1468–71, 1486 (2004). We note the similarity of this business model of the early music publishers to the business model that has predominated within the American recording industry, both in terms of the album format (where one "hit" single on an album could drive sales) and in terms of the labels' practice of signing many new acts with advance monetary guarantees, only a fraction of which are repaid by successful sales.

[50]   Id. at 1458–60.

exclusive right to determine who printed his work, based largely on his close ties to both the French and German courts and an argument for control over the quality of work attributed to him after inaccurate versions of his compositions had been printed. "Lasso set a noteworthy precedent in two respects: (1) he was the first composer to obtain a legal monopoly over publication of his entire body of work and (2) he successfully pursued international publication and legal control over his music across political domains."[51]

One of the problems with the system of privileges was that it covered entire books, not individual works, and thus it was often difficult for individual publishers to know what material was subject to privilege and what was free to print. In addition, some privileges came with express limitations on price as a condition of the privilege, so that the monopoly could not be abused. Because privileges were often limited to small geographic areas, publishers would often obtain privileges from multiple authorities to extend the reach of their monopoly. The privilege was also not easy for publishers to enforce. Even where the courts were an available avenue of recourse, like in England, publishers would often go directly to their political patrons for help. In Venice, music publishers often opted for a form of private dispute resolution, where the parties would each name another printer, who would together name a third, and the three would reach a binding decision in the dispute.

In spite of the benefits of the royal privileges granted to music publishers, it was not a profitable branch of the early publishing business; it only began to become profitable in the mid-1500s after single-impression printing began to spread throughout Europe and cheaper costs led to increased demand, particularly by the professionals in the emerging middle class.[52] This, in turn, led to an increased demand by publishers for new compositions to print. Most composers earned their livelihood through patronage rather than from publication of their works; some composers sought to have their patrons finance the publication of their works in exchange for a dedication, but composers rarely received any share in the profits from publication. In Italy, "[m]any Venetian composers paid for the privilege of having their works printed, and by doing so became partners in the printing venture. These early commissioned works signaled to composers that the middle classes were a supplement for, or even an alternative to, the aristocracy as a source of financial support."[53] Thus, by

---

[51]   Michael W. Carroll, *Whose Music Is It Anyway?: How We Came to View Musical Expression as a Form of Property*, 72 U. CIN. L. REV. 1405, 1461, 1482–83 (2004); *see also* JAMES BOYLE, JENNIFER JENKINS, & KEITH AOKI, TALES FROM THE PUBLIC DOMAIN: THEFT, THE HISTORY OF MUSIC 44–46 (CreateSpace Independent Publishing Platform February 14, 2017), *available at* https://law.duke.edu/musiccomic/download/.

[52]   Carroll, *supra* n. 47 at 1466–67, 1469, 1472. Notably, for early music publishers, "[p]aper alone represented up to seventy-five percent of the direct costs of production." *Id.* at 1471.

[53]   *Id.* at 1470–71, 1475–76.

the start of the seventeenth century, the music marketplace—represented by sales of books compiling many compositions—had expanded to reflect the increasing music literacy and expendable income of the growing middle class in England and Europe.

Rights Granted to Composers

Growing side-by-side with the expanding marketplace for printed compositions was composers' knowledge that their works could travel to distant places and last beyond their lifetimes, which naturally led to their awareness that they could gain attribution for their authorship of musical works. Some composers sought out publication of their works in the hope of gaining accolades; others sought to prevent publication of their works to maintain some control over their performance. Publishers began to advertise their music books by highlighting individual composers, and the music-buying public began to seek out works by specific composers based on those composers' reputations.[54]

Although composers began to gain recognition as authors of compositions during the Renaissance period, they did not (with the important exception of Lasso mentioned above, who gained royal privileges giving him control over his body of work in the late sixteenth century) have any legal basis for exercising control over their creative works. "The formation of a bourgeois listening and performing public (that is, a body of people with the surplus income, leisure time and interest to devote to musical activities) created sufficient demand for musical publications and thus enabled unauthorized editions to become feasible and then commonplace."[55] The prevalence of unauthorized publications, referred to at the time as "piracy," were of concern to composers who sought to protect the integrity of their original work and to control its dissemination, and even when composers did sell their works to authorized publishers, it was for a one-time fee, leaving publishers to profit from successful works while the authors gained only notoriety.[56]

Other than a handful of composers who obtained royal privileges in England in the 1700s, composers had no legal recourse for unauthorized printing of their works until passage of the Statute of Anne ("A Bill for Encouragement of Learning") in England in 1710.[57] Even then, it was not until 1777 that an English court determined that musical compositions were "writings," and thus protected. In *Bach v. Longman*, the son of

---

[54] *Id.* at 1476–81.

[55] David Hunter, *Music Copyright in Britain to 1800*, 67 MUSIC & LETTERS 269, 271 (July 1986).

[56] *Id.* at 272–76.

[57] *See, e.g., id.* at 277 ("[b]etween 1710 and 1770 at least sixteen privileges were granted to composers"); JAMES BOYLE, JENNIFER JENKINS, & KEITH AOKI, TALES FROM THE PUBLIC DOMAIN: THEFT, THE HISTORY OF MUSIC 47 (CreateSpace Independent Publishing Platform February 14, 2017), *available at* https://law.duke.edu/musiccomic/download/.

Johannes Sebastian Bach succeeded in an infringement claim against an unauthorized publisher, with Lord Mansfield ruling, "[W]e are of opinion, that a musical composition is a writing within the Statute of the 8th of Queen Anne."[58] However, the Statute of Anne covered only printing rights for the entire work; it did not give authors any right to control or profit from performances of the work, and it did not apply to "borrowing" of parts of the work.[59]

In America, due to the influence of author and lawyer Noah Webster (who is perhaps best known for his 1828 dictionary), in 1783 Connecticut was the first state to enact copyright protection for authors, modeling its statute after the Statute of Anne. The first federal Copyright Act of 1790, signed into law by President George Washington, only protected maps, charts, and books.[60] At the urging of Congressman William Wolcott Ellsworth, son-in-law of Noah Webster, musical compositions were added to the list of works covered by statutory copyright protection in the U.S. in 1831, and the first musical work was registered for copyright protection under that law by Philadelphia music publisher George Willig only ten days after the law was enacted.[61]

---

[58]   *Bach v. Longman*, 2 Cowper 623, 624 (1777).

[59]   *See* JAMES BOYLE, JENNIFER JENKINS, & KEITH AOKI, TALES FROM THE PUBLIC DOMAIN: THEFT, THE HISTORY OF MUSIC 62 (CreateSpace Independent Publishing Platform February 14, 2017), *available at* https://law.duke.edu/musiccomic/download/.

[60]   Copyright Act of 1790, *available at* https://www.copyright.gov/about/1790-copyright-act. html.

[61]   *See* U.S. Copyright Office, Copyright Timeline, 19th Century, at https://www.copyright. gov/timeline/timeline_19th_century.html. Originally, claims to copyright were recorded by the clerks of the U.S. District Courts; it was not until the 1870 that the Library of Congress was charged with registering and recording copyrights.

Maid of My Love, with lyrics by David Richardson and music by I.T. Norton:
First Musical Composition Registered under U.S. Copyright Law, E.D. Pa. 1831[62]

The scope of protected rights under the 1831 general copyright revision only included protection against unauthorized printing and vending; a public performance right for musical compositions was not granted until 1897.[63]

Music Industry in America at the Turn of the Twentieth Century

A rapid commodification of music took place over the course of the twentieth century, influenced by a combination of technological advances, innovative business enterprises, and the creation of laws and enforcement mechanisms for protecting musical creations as property. The first foundation for the modern music industry in America was the growth of music publishing at the turn of the century, grounded more in a desire to sell sheet music rather than a desire to create lasting art.[64] Close on the

---

[62] U.S. Copyright Office Timeline, 19th Century, https://www.copyright.gov/timeline/timeline_19th_century.html.

[63] Copyright Office Circular 1a, available at https://www.copyright.gov/circs/circ1a.html. The 1897 statute's provisions regarding the performance right are discussed in more detail in Chapter 3.

[64] *See* DAVID SUISMAN, SELLING SOUNDS: THE COMMERCIAL REVOLUTION IN AMERICAN MUSIC 18 (Harvard University Press, 2009) (describing the advent of the popular song after the Civil War as marking "the beginning of a new era in the political economy of music, by refashioning

heels of the commercialization of the popular song was the invention and commercial exploitation of the "talking machine"—revolutionary technology that allowed sounds to be recorded and replayed and thereby furthered the acceptance of music as a thing that one could own rather than as something one did or one experienced in the moment.[65]

America's music publishing industry did not really begin to take off until the advent of the "Tin Pan Alley"[66] era at the end of the nineteenth century, in which aggressive marketing of "popular" songs led to huge increases in sales of sheet music and the development of a consumer economy in music. A precondition to the growth of the music publishing industry was the broad acceptance in the U.S. of the nineteenth century ideal of "music as a means to elevate the mind, body, and character of individuals and the spirit of the nation as a whole,"[67] which made it commonplace across the country for keyboard instruments—pianos and organs of all levels of price and quality—to be found in the home. Although this ideal contemplated the benefits of bringing "serious" music into the home, it created a condition precedent for a new brand of music publishers to establish a market for popular songs.[68]

Centered in New York City, the new music publishing empire in the U.S. had its roots in vaudeville in the 1880s. Recognizing the popular appeal of vaudeville, music publishers began to advertise their songs in theater trade journals, and young publishing firms enlisted vaudeville performers in performing and promoting their new songs onstage. The Witmark brothers—Isidore, Julius (who had previously had an act as a minstrel performer), and Jay—founded M. Witmark and Sons, which became a pioneer in promoting its arsenal of songs. Charles K. Harris, a songwriter and publisher who wrote and promoted the first, truly national "hit song" in 1892–93 with *After the Ball*, moved to New York City just after the start of the twentieth century and inspired other young music publishing firms to try their luck on Tin Pan Alley.[69] By 1900, most hit songs (based on sheet music sales) originated in New York, and by 1910, Tin Pan Alley was described as a collection of "popular song factories." In

---

one of the most basic and universal forms of cultural expression—the song—according to the inexorable logic of business"). Suisman goes on to note, "What distinguished Tin Pan Alley from other modes of making music was that the *primary* motivation for writing a song was to sell it, not to express some inherently human feeling or musical impulse." *Id.* at 22.

[65] *E.g.*, THOMAS FORREST KELLY, CAPTURING MUSIC: THE STORY OF NOTATION 207–08 (W.W. Norton & Co. 2015); DAVID SUISMAN, SELLING SOUNDS: THE COMMERCIAL REVOLUTION IN AMERICAN MUSIC 10–12 (Harvard University Press, 2009). The early years of the recording industry will be discussed in more detail in Chapter 2.

[66] The origination of this term is not clear, although one author asserts that it likely "involved Harry Von Tilzer and the songwriter and journalist Monroe Rosenfeld and referred to the cacophony created in the music publishers' studios." DAVID SUISMAN, SELLING SOUNDS: THE COMMERCIAL REVOLUTION IN AMERICAN MUSIC 21 (Harvard University Press, 2009).

[67] *Id.* at 19.

[68] *Id.* at 18–32.

[69] *See id.* at 25–30.

fact, these music publishers had turned music into a commodity just like soap or pencils, with systems in place for production, distribution, promotion, and sales of their products. To maintain a steady stream of "product," the publishers hired staff songwriters—on the one hand making it possible for more composers to earn a living creating music, but on the other hand giving publishers more control over the nature and form of the musical works that they sold, with an emphasis on catchy titles and a strong chorus.[70] With the success of the marketing and promotion campaigns driven by the Tin Pan Alley publishers, a demand for a constant stream of new music was created and the foundation for a new industry was built.

Although musical notation allowed compositions to be preserved in written form and thus eventually protected as property and commodified, giving music publishers both profit and power, musical performances were not capable of being recorded until after recording technologies were invented in the late 1800s and did not receive legal protection until much later. In Chapter 2, we will discuss the early days of this branch of the music industry in more depth.

NOTES AND QUESTIONS

1.   Does anything surprise you about the historical development of music as a commodity? What? Why?

2.   As illustrated in the brief history above, efforts by authorities to exercise control over both the form and performance of music predate efforts by individuals to claim authorship over musical works. Given the rich array of musical works that existed before the law began to recognize and protect authors (e.g., classical works, folk music, religious hymns), do you think that copyright protection is necessary for promoting the creation of musical works? Why or why not?

---

[70]   *Id.* at 32, 41, 43, 49–50.

CHAPTER II

THE DAWN OF THE RECORDING INDUSTRY AND THE 1909 COPYRIGHT ACT: *GOOD MORNING GOOD MORNING*[1]

■ ■ ■

"Maybe sometimes,
we've got it wrong but it's alright,
the more things seem to change,
the more they stay the same.
Don't you hesitate.
Girl put your records on. . ."

Put Your Records On, by Corinne Bailey Rae, John Beck, & Steve Chrisanthou (2006).

One of the themes that we expect you to see throughout these materials is that expressed by Corinne Bailey Rae in the above lyrics to her 2006 hit song—"the more things seem to change, the more they stay the same." This chapter deals with amazing new technology that revolutionized the way that people communicated and the way that they interacted with music. In recent years, we have seen the impact of the different technological innovations that have similarly revolutionized the way that we communicate and the way that we interact with music. We doubt that these will be the last such revolutions in these areas, and each presents similar challenges to both the law and to the existing methods of communicating and accessing musical works.

---

[1]   John Lennon & Paul McCartney (1967); released by the Beatles on SGT. PEPPER'S LONELY HEARTS CLUB BAND (1967).

CONSIDER AS YOU READ . . .

- What analytical themes and arguments do you see repeated in the case law excerpted below?

- How did technology disrupt existing law and business models in the early years of the music industry, and how did the courts deal with efforts to establish property rights in sound recordings?

- Do you see any analogs in the modern music industry for the issues faced by the parties to the cases discussed below?

A. THE BATTLE OVER FORMAT AT THE BIRTH OF THE RECORD INDUSTRY

Close to the turn of the twentieth century, just as New York was becoming the center for what would become the modern music publishing industry, across the Hudson River, New Jersey was becoming the center for innovations that would become the foundation for the modern recording industry. When Alexander Graham Bell patented his invention of the telephone in Boston in 1876, Thomas Edison had already been engaged in similar work to improve upon the telegraph by transferring sounds over a wire. Bell's original device only worked over short distances and produced only faint sound, and Edison devoted resources in his Menlo Park, New Jersey laboratory to creating a better transmitter. Emile Berliner, a German immigrant who began studying physics and electricity in his own workshop in Washington D.C., was simultaneously engaged in efforts to create a marketable device for transmitting sound across long distances.[2] The efforts of these innovators, among many others who devoted years of trial and error experimentation to developing devices for transmitting and recording sound, would end up being instrumental to the creation of devices that would ultimately be used to play recorded music in homes all over the world and objects—records—that could successfully store these musical sounds for repeated playback.

The first recording technology used a wax cylinder, invented in the 1870s, and Thomas Edison recorded the first human voice on a phonograph in 1877, receiving a patent for his recording technique that year.[3] Edison's cylinder was capable of both playing pre-recorded sound and recording original sounds; he initially focused on its use as a dictation device rather

---

[2]   ANDRE MILLARD, AMERICA ON RECORD: A HISTORY OF RECORDED SOUND 18, 22 (Cambridge Univ. Press 2d ed. 2005).

[3]   ALAN BARGFREDE, MUSIC LAW IN THE DIGITAL AGE: COPYRIGHT ESSENTIALS FOR TODAY'S MUSIC BUSINESS 1–2 (Berklee Press 2017, 2d ed.).

than as a vehicle for bringing music into people's homes, but it was difficult to operate as a business tool and his dictation machine ultimately failed in the marketplace. However, the popularity of the coin-operated "amusement phonograph," where people would pay a nickel a turn to listen to prerecorded material on exhibition phonographs, led to renewed focus by Edison and others in development of the device for entertainment, rather than business, use. Their initial idea was that members of the public would purchase the devices and use them to record and replay their own violin and piano performances, complementing the existing musical instruments in the home rather than supplanting them.[4]

Edison soon realized, though, "that the record business could be the most profitable part of the industry of recorded sound."[5] After a decade of experimenting for an inexpensive but consistent process to copy recorded sound, Edison's team came up with a formula and process for wax cylinders that could be mass-produced to play prerecorded music on his phonograph devices. Emile Berliner, who in 1888 had first demonstrated a different design for his own talking machine—the gramophone—and who had headquartered his Gramophone Company in Camden, New Jersey, was also searching for a method for duplicating the flat discs that the gramophone used for playback of sounds. He contracted with Eldridge Johnson, a machinist in Camden, who focused his research on the recording and duplication process in an effort to improve sound quality in mass-produced duplicates of recordings. Using techniques developed by Edison for the phonograph cylinder, Johnson was able to create a system for duplicating thousands of discs a day, with a record plant opening in Camden in 1902. Edison's cylinder duplicating facility opened in West Orange, New Jersey, in 1903.[6]

---

[4]   ANDRE MILLARD, AMERICA ON RECORD: A HISTORY OF RECORDED SOUND 41–44 (Cambridge Univ. Press 2d ed. 2005).

[5]   *Id.* at 44.

[6]   ANDRE MILLARD, AMERICA ON RECORD: A HISTORY OF RECORDED SOUND 44–48 (Cambridge Univ. Press 2d ed. 2005).

Thomas Edison listening to a wax cylinder
phonograph at the Edison laboratory,
Orange, N.J. 6/16/1888
From the Museum of Innovation and
Science, Schenectady, N.Y.

The ability to mass produce recordings on both cylinders for the phonograph and discs for the gramophone, along with the development of more inexpensive and easier to operate players powered by spring-operated motors, led to a huge surge in sales of both talking machines and records. Three companies emerged at the top of the budding record industry: (1) Edison's National Phonograph Company, with its cylinder recordings; (2) Victor Talking Machine Company, founded by Johnson in 1901 after purchasing Berliner's patents when Berliner withdrew from the gramophone business at the turn of the twentieth century,[7] with its flat disc recordings; and (3) Columbia of Washington, D.C., which took the pragmatic approach of manufacturing machines and records in both the cylinder and disc formats. Together, the Edison, Victor, and Columbia companies were known as the "Big Three," offering both inexpensive and deluxe models of their record players, building manufacturing plants to mass produce both players and records, and developing nationwide marketing and distribution networks for their products.[8]

During the first two decades of the young recording industry, there was no standardization, with a confusing array of options available to the consumer: cylinder versus disc; discs with a lateral versus a vertical cut; different sized cylinders with different numbers of grooves per inch; different recording speeds, ranging from fifty to 120 rpm. Records (whether cylinders or discs) made by one company might not work on a player made by a different company. Consumers needed to know how to adjust their player's speed to match the recording speed of individual records, or the

---

[7]   DAVID SUISMAN, SELLING SOUNDS: THE COMMERCIAL REVOLUTION IN AMERICAN MUSIC 101–02, 104 (Harvard University press 2009).

[8]   ANDRE MILLARD, AMERICA ON RECORD: A HISTORY OF RECORDED SOUND 49–53 (Cambridge Univ. Press 2d ed. 2005).

sound would be distorted. Moreover, the early technology was limited in both the possible duration of recordings—just 2–3 minutes—and the types of sounds that could be best captured. For example, drums and strings were difficult to record, as were soprano and bass voices, but the range of the early recording technology was ideal for tenors and brass instruments. Not surprisingly, some of the earliest "hits" were recordings of performers whose voices or instruments were best suited to the limitations of the technology, with compositions that could be performed (or adapted to be performed) within the short duration allowed by the recording device.[9]

A number of factors ultimately led to the triumph of the gramophone over the phonograph (although disc record players were called phonographs for many decades after the demise of Edison's invention), having nothing to do with the quality of the sound produced by the device or its cylinder recordings.[10] First, consumers found it easier to store a collection of disc records rather than a collection of cylinder records. Second, the gramophone was easier to operate than the phonograph; changing discs was simpler than changing cylinders. Third, in 1906, Johnson's Victor Talking Machine Co. released the Victrola, a reinvention of the appearance of the talking machine that hid its functioning parts and made it look like an expensive piece of furniture, making it a substitute for the more expensive piano in many wealthy homes and appealing to middle-class buyers. Although Edison introduced a disc player in 1913 with high-quality sound, it did not sell—the discs that could be played on an Edison Diamond Disc were not compatible with those that could be played on a Victrola, and vice versa, and Victor had a far more extensive catalog of recordings available for purchase than did Edison. By the start of World War I, "the cylinder record was considered old-fashioned."[11]

---

[9] DAVID SUISMAN, SELLING SOUNDS: THE COMMERCIAL REVOLUTION IN AMERICAN MUSIC 108–09 (Harvard University press 2009); ANDRE MILLARD, AMERICA ON RECORD: A HISTORY OF RECORDED SOUND 80–84, 125 (Cambridge Univ. Press 2d ed. 2005). Millard notes that some of the earliest records, from the 1880s and 1890s, were recordings of "artistic whistling," and that the roots of the phonograph as a business machine, intended for dictation, help to explain why the phonograph initially was better at recording the male voice than musical instruments or female voices. *Id.* at 81.

[10] *See* ANDRE MILLARD, AMERICA ON RECORD: A HISTORY OF RECORDED SOUND 129 (Cambridge Univ. Press 2d ed. 2005); ALAN BARGFREDE, MUSIC LAW IN THE DIGITAL AGE: COPYRIGHT ESSENTIALS FOR TODAY'S MUSIC BUSINESS 2 (Berklee Press 2017, 2d ed.).

[11] ANDRE MILLARD, AMERICA ON RECORD: A HISTORY OF RECORDED SOUND 129–33 (Cambridge Univ. Press 2d ed. 2005).

An early Victrola, designed to look like
an expensive piece of furniture rather
than a mechanical device.
Photo by Julie Ross

Another important reason for Victor's success in the battle between cylinder and disc record formats was Victor's aggressive advertising of its exclusive recording arrangements with elite opera stars—tenor Enrico Caruso was Victor's most famous featured artist, and their relationship was mutually beneficial, gaining them both fame and fortune. Caruso was a relative unknown in the U.S. when one of Victor's agents, Frederick Gaisberg, encountered Caruso on a visit to Italy in 1902 and agreed to pay him what was then a huge sum for Victor to exclusively record him on its newly-adopted "Red Seal" series of expensive, "high culture" recordings. His powerful tenor voice was ideally suited to the existing recording technology, and Caruso became the first true recording star of the record industry. With Caruso and a stable of other virtuoso performers exclusively signed to record for it, Victor succeeded by marketing the quality of music and performers it offered, whereas Edison ultimately failed by marketing based upon his reputation as an inventor and the quality of the sound of his talking machines and records.[12]

---

[12] DAVID SUISMAN, SELLING SOUNDS: THE COMMERCIAL REVOLUTION IN AMERICAN MUSIC 106–14, 125–26, 145–48 (Harvard University Press, 2009); ANDRE MILLARD, AMERICA ON RECORD: A HISTORY OF RECORDED SOUND 59–60, 78, 132–34 (Cambridge Univ. Press 2d ed. 2005).

Enrico Caruso, signing an autograph
in Italy (circa 1919)

As a result of these new technologies that made it possible for consumers to listen to music at a different time and place from when it was first performed, the modern music industry began to emerge. Music became embedded in everyday life in ways that had previously not been possible, becoming a presence in both private and commercial spaces and also integrated within other aspects of the entertainment business. The use of gramophones and player pianos made it possible to play music within the home without being trained in a musical instrument. As they had begun to do for the Tin Pan Alley sheet music marketplace that took off at the turn of the twentieth century, composers continued to write "light, catchy songs" for the new music market, while opera and classical music were now readily available to the masses. As David Suisman has described it, "Music, which had once been produced in the home, by hand, was now something to be purchased, like a newspaper or ready-to-wear dress."[13]

With this new technology came disputes regarding both the nature and scope of legal protection for the manufacturers of records and the amount of control, if any, composers and publishers had over uses of their compositions in these new devices. We start below with litigation between music publishers and piano roll makers and the impact those disputes had on the 1909 Copyright Act. Ultimately, the recording industry's "talking machine" technology surpassed player pianos and piano rolls as the preferred method of bringing music into consumers' homes. The makers of player pianos, like Edison's phonograph record company, focused more on popular compositions to fuel sales, as opposed to the gramophone industry, which highlighted the new generation of celebrity performers.[14] The consuming public was drawn more to the latter, and player pianos steadily

---

[13] DAVID SUISMAN, SELLING SOUNDS: THE COMMERCIAL REVOLUTION IN AMERICAN MUSIC 10–11 (Harvard University Press, 2009).

[14] An expensive brand of player pianos played rolls that essentially reproduced the actual performance of virtuoso pianists, playing the notes exactly as the pianist did rather than being mechanically cut from preset notes of the composition itself, but this was the exception to the rule.

lost favor as recordings by celebrity performers were available for as little as twenty-five cents apiece and more compact record players were widely marketed for anywhere from $10 to $400.[15]

Thus, after enactment of the 1909 Copyright Act, it was the creators of sound recordings—the companies that produced them and the performers that made them possible—that ultimately were the primary litigants in efforts to obtain legal protection for the recordings. Initially, patents protected the sound recordings, and in 1909, the U.S. Supreme Court affirmed an injunction against the sale of records that could be played on the Victor gramophone, finding that the patent covered both the gramophone device and the pre-recorded records that were designed to play on it.[16] As a result, absent a license from the major device manufacturers, it was unlawful to make records that could be played on those devices until expiration of the patents. Of course, piracy existed, and some of the cases below illustrate how the law dealt with claims by record companies against competitors who made and sold "counterfeit" records that were copied from the originals sold by the plaintiff record companies.

After 1917, by which time most of the relevant patents for the gramophone, phonograph, and their recording devices had expired, serious competitors for the Big Three (Edison, Victor, and Columbia) began to enter the market. Several of the leading competitors around this time were player piano and piano roll manufacturers who recognized the impact of recorded music on their profits; Aeolian Piano Company was among them, releasing a high-end line of talking machines and creating the Vocalion record label. However, because the Big Three had exclusive agreements with well-known classical artists and vaudeville performers, new recording companies began to record a wider range of musical genres and performers, bringing recordings of blues, jazz, folk, and other previously-unrecorded styles of music to a wider range of audiences.[17]

By 1921, the Big Three had seen their sales decline dramatically. Further disrupting the still-developing music industry, radio started distributing music to the masses in the 1920s. At the outset, radio provided an additional vehicle for performers to earn income as they performed for various live broadcasts. Professional musicians would gather around a studio microphone, often at regular times, to broadcast live music to the new radio listeners. However, this symbiotic relationship between performers and radio began to alter as recording technology advanced.[18]

---

[15] *See* DAVID SUISMAN, SELLING SOUNDS: THE COMMERCIAL REVOLUTION IN AMERICAN MUSIC 148 (Harvard University Press, 2009); ANDRE MILLARD, AMERICA ON RECORD: A HISTORY OF RECORDED SOUND (Cambridge Univ. Press 2d ed. 2005).

[16] *Leeds & Catlin Co. v. Victor Talking Mach. Co.*, 213 U.S. 301 (1909).

[17] *See* ANDRE MILLARD, AMERICA ON RECORD: A HISTORY OF RECORDED SOUND 72–75 (Cambridge Univ. Press 2d ed. 2005).

[18] ALAN BARGFREDE, MUSIC LAW IN THE DIGITAL AGE: COPYRIGHT ESSENTIALS FOR TODAY'S MUSIC BUSINESS 3 (Berklee Press 2017, 2d ed.).

When technology developed to the point that radio stations could simply play a record purchased for seventy-five cents rather than paying artists to perform live on the radio, the courts struggled to deal with claims by recording artists and labels that radio broadcasts of records were unauthorized and thus impermissible, as is illustrated below by the *Waring* and *Whiteman* cases. The modern relationship between broadcast radio, musicians, record labels, composers, and music publishers remains complex and will be addressed in later chapters, but understanding the issues and dynamics of these early years of the industry informs our understanding of the current issues and dynamics.

In the next section, we provide excerpts from a case that predated the 1909 copyright revision but that set the stage for the manner in which the law would treat sound recordings for many decades and, relatedly, the manner in which the American music industry would develop.

B. MECHANICAL REPRODUCTIONS OF COMPOSITIONS UNDER PRE-1909 ACT CASELAW

To provide a sense of why the 1909 Copyright Act dealt with use of musical compositions by the budding record industry in the way that it did, we first include an excerpt from a case that laid the foundation for Congress' evaluation of how to deal with innovations in technology that made it possible to reproduce musical compositions by mechanical means. Much of the law and policy surrounding the modern American music industry deals with the impact that technology can have on new ways of experiencing music. But as the below case will show, "technological disruption" is not a new phenomenon, and music creators (as well as the entire industry) have been grappling with adjusting to new technologies since the turn of the century. Moreover, this modern experience is simply a continuation of the challenges that advances in technology have presented to creators of music since the time of the printing press, and before.

In the case below, owners of compositions were not asserting violations of a performance right. Instead, they were challenging the right of manufacturers of machines that could play compositions—in the case below, player pianos—to reproduce the compositions in machine-readable form. The creation and marketing of "piano rolls" was just as revolutionary at the time as other digital inventions are to the modern industry, not only in terms of the impact on the public's manner of interacting with music, but also in terms of the impact on existing participants within the industry and the law's ability to keep up with those changes.

Player piano with perforated roll.
Photograph taken by Daderot 18 May 2013 of Exhibit in the Bayernhof Museum,
Pittsburgh, Pennsylvania, and dedicated to the public domain.

WHITE-SMITH MUSIC PUBLISHING CO. V. APOLLO CO.

209 U.S. 1 (1908)

MR. JUSTICE DAY delivered the opinion of the court:

[¶]... The actions were brought to restrain infringement of the copyrights of two certain musical compositions, published in the form of sheet music, entitled respectively, 'Little Cotton Dolly' and 'Kentucky Babe.' The appellee, defendant below, is engaged in the sale of player pianos known as the 'Apollo,' and of perforated rolls of music used in connection therewith. The appellant, as assignee of Adam Geibel, the composer, alleged compliance with the copyright act, and that a copyright was duly obtained by it on or about March 17, 1897. The answer was general in its nature, and upon the testimony adduced a decree was rendered, as stated, in favor of the Apollo Company, defendant below, appellee here.

The action was brought under the provisions of the copyright act, § 4952 (U. S. Comp. Stat. Supp. 1907, p. 1021), giving to the author, inventor, designer, or proprietor of any book, map, chart, dramatic or musical composition the sole liberty of printing, reprinting, publishing, completing, copying, executing, finishing and vending the same.... The appellee is the manufacturer of certain musical instruments adapted to be used with perforated rolls. The testimony discloses that certain of these rolls, used in connection with such instruments, and being connected with the mechanism to which they apply, reproduce in sound the melody recorded in the two pieces of music copyrighted by the appellant.

The manufacture of such instruments and the use of such musical rolls has developed rapidly in recent years in this country and abroad. The record discloses that in the year 1902 from seventy to seventy-five thousand of such instruments were in use in the United States and that from one million to one million and a half of such perforated musical rolls, to be more fully described hereafter, were made in this country in that year.

It is evident that the question involved in the use of such rolls is one of very considerable importance, involving large property interests and closely touching the rights of composers and music publishers. . . .

Without entering into a detailed discussion of the mechanical construction of such instruments and rolls, it is enough to say that they are what has become familiar to the public in the form of mechanical attachments to pianos, such as the pianola, and the musical rolls consist of perforated sheets, which are passed over ducts connected with the operating parts of the mechanism in such manner that the same are kept sealed until, by means of perforations in the rolls, air pressure is admitted to the ducts which operate the pneumatic devices to sound the notes. This is done with the aid of an operator, upon whose skill and experience the success of the rendition largely depends. As the roll is drawn over the tracker board the notes are sounded as the perforations admit the atmospheric pressure, the perforations having been so arranged that the effect is to produce the melody or tune for which the roll has been cut.

Speaking in a general way, it may be said that these rolls are made in three ways. First. With the score or staff notation before him the arranger, with the aid of a rule or guide and a graduated schedule, marks the position and size of the perforations on a sheet of paper to correspond to the order of notes in the composition. The marked sheet is then passed into the hands of an operator who cuts the apertures, by hand, in the paper. This perforated sheet is inspected and corrected, and when corrected is called 'the original.' This original is used as a stencil and bypassing ink rollers over it a pattern is prepared. The stenciled perforations are then cut, producing the master or templet. The master is placed in the perforating machine and reproductions thereof obtained, which are the perforated rolls in question. . . . Second. A perforated music roll made by another manufacturer may be used from which to make a new record. Third. By playing upon a piano to which is attached an automatic recording device producing a perforated matrix from which a perforated music roll may be produced.

It is evident, therefore, that persons skilled in the art can take such pieces of sheet music in staff notation, and, by means of the proper instruments, make drawings indicating the perforations, which are afterwards outlined and cut upon the rolls in such wise as to reproduce, with the aid of the other mechanism, the music which is recorded in the copyrighted sheets.

The learned counsel for the parties to this action advance opposing theories as to the nature and extent of the copyright given by statutory laws enacted by Congress for the protection of copyright, and a determination of which is the true one will go far to decide the rights of the parties in this case. On behalf of the appellant it is insisted that it is the intention of the copyright act to protect the intellectual conception which has resulted in the compilation of notes which, when properly played, produce the melody which is the real invention of the composer. It is insisted that this is the thing which Congress intended to protect, and that the protection covers all means of expression of the order of notes which produce the air or melody which the composer has invented.

Music, it is argued, is intended for the ear as writing is for the eye, and that it is the intention of the copyright act to prevent the multiplication of every means of reproducing the music of the composer to the ear.

On the other hand, it is contended that while it is true that copyright statutes are intended to reward mental creations or conceptions, that the extent of this protection is a matter of statutory law, and that it has been extended only to the tangible results of mental conception, and that only the tangible thing is dealt with by the law, and its multiplication or reproduction is all that is protected by the statute.

. . . . [T]he decisions so far as brought to our attention in the full discussion had at the bar and upon the briefs have been uniformly to the effect that these perforated rolls operated in connection with mechanical devices for the production of music are not within the copyright act. It was so held in Kennedy v. McTammany, 33 Fed. 584. The decision was written by Judge Colt in the first circuit; the case was subsequently brought to this court, where it was dismissed for failure to print the record. 145 U.S. 643, 36 L. ed. 853, 12 Sup. Ct. Rep. 983. In that case the learned judge said:

'I cannot convince myself that these perforated strips of paper are copies of sheet music within the meaning of the copyright law. They are not made to be addressed to the eye as sheet music, but they form part of a machine. They are not designed to be used for such purposes as sheet music, nor do they in any sense occupy the same field as sheet music. They are a mechanical invention made for the sole purpose of performing tunes mechanically upon a musical instrument.'

[¶]. . . . Since these cases were decided Congress has repeatedly had occasion to amend the copyright law. The English cases, the decision of the District of Columbia court of appeals, and Judge Colt's decision must have been well known to the members of Congress; and although the manufacture of mechanical musical instruments had not grown to the proportions which they have since attained, they were well known, and the omission of Congress to specifically legislate concerning them might well be taken to be an acquiescence in the judicial construction given to the copyright laws.

This country was not a party to the Berne convention of 1886, concerning international copyright, in which it was specifically provided:

> 'It is understood that the manufacture and sale of instruments serving to reproduce mechanically the airs of music borrowed from the private domain are not considered as constituting musical infringement.'

But the proceedings of this convention were doubtless well known to Congress. . . .

[¶] In the last analysis this case turns upon the construction of a statute, for it is perfectly well settled that the protection given to copyrights in this country is wholly statutory. . . .

Musical compositions have been the subject of copyright protection since the statute of February 3, 1831 (4 Stat. at L. 436, chap. 16), and laws have been passed including them since that time. When we turn to the consideration of the act it seems evident that Congress has dealt with the tangible thing, a copy of which is required to be filed with the Librarian of Congress, and wherever the words are used (copy or copies) they seem to refer to the term in its ordinary sense of indicating reproduction or duplication of the original. Section 4956 (U. S. Comp. Stat. 1901, p. 3407) provides that two copies of a book, map, chart, or musical composition, etc., shall be delivered at the office of the Librarian of Congress. Notice of copyright must be inserted in the several copies of every edition published, if a book, or, if a musical composition, etc., upon some visible portion thereof. Section 4962, copyright act ([18 Stat. at L. 78, chap. 301] U. S. Comp. Stat. 1901, p. 3411). Section 4965 (U. S. Comp. Stat. 1901, p. 3414) provides in part that the infringer 'shall forfeit . . . every sheet thereof, and . . . one dollar for every sheet of the same found in his possession,' etc., evidently referring to musical compositions in sheets. Throughout the act it is apparent that Congress has dealt with the concrete, and not with an abstract, right of property in ideas or mental conceptions. . . .

[¶] What is meant by a copy? We have already referred to the common understanding of it as a reproduction or duplication of a thing. A definition was given by Bailey, J., in West v. Francis, 5 Barn. & Ald. 743, quoted with approval in Boosey v. Whight, supra. He said: 'A copy is that which comes so near to the original as to give to every person seeing it the idea created by the original.'

Various definitions have been given by the experts called in the case. The one which most commends itself to our judgment is perhaps as clear as can be made, and defines a copy of a musical composition to be 'a written or printed record of it in intelligible notation.' It may be true that in a broad sense a mechanical instrument which reproduces a tune copies it; but this is a strained and artificial meaning. When the combination of musical sounds is reproduced to the ear it is the original tune as conceived by the author which is heard. These musical tones are not a copy which appeals to the eye. In no sense can musical sounds which reach us through the sense of hearing be said to be copies, as that term is generally understood, and as we believe it was intended to be understood in the statutes under consideration. A musical composition is an intellectual creation which first exists in the mind of the composer; he may play it for the first time upon an instrument. It is not susceptible of being copied until it has been put in a form which others can see and read. The statute has not provided for the protection of the intellectual conception apart from the thing produced, however meritorious such conception may be, but has provided for the making and filing of a tangible thing, against the publication and duplication of which it is the purpose of the statute to protect the composer.

Also it may be noted in this connection that if the broad construction of publishing and copying contended for by the appellants is to be given to this statute it would seem equally applicable to the cylinder of a music box, with its mechanical arrangement for the reproduction of melodious sounds, or the record of the graphophone, or to the pipe organ operated by devices similar to those in use in the pianola. All these instruments were well known when these various copyright acts were passed. Can it be that it was the intention of Congress to permit them to be held as infringements and suppressed by injunctions?

After all, what is the perforated roll? The fact is clearly established in the testimony in this case that even those skilled in the making of these rolls are unable to read them as musical compositions, as those in staff notations are read by the performer. It is true that there is some testimony to the effect that great skill and patience might enable the operator to read this record as he could a piece of music written in staff notation. But the weight of the testimony is emphatically the other way, and they are not intended to be read as an ordinary piece of sheet music, which, to those skilled in the art, conveys, by reading, in playing or singing, definite impressions of the melody.

These perforated rolls are parts of a machine which, when duly applied and properly operated in connection with the mechanism to which they are adapted, produce musical tones in harmonious combination. But we cannot think that they are copies within the meaning of the copyright act.

It may be true that the use of these perforated rolls, in the absence of statutory protection, enables the manufacturers thereof to enjoy the use of musical compositions for which they pay no value. But such considerations properly address themselves to the legislative, and not to the judicial, branch of the government. As the act of Congress now stands we believe it does not include these records as copies or publications of the copyrighted music involved in these cases.

The decrees of the Circuit Court of Appeals are affirmed.

MR. JUSTICE HOLMES, concurring specially:

In view of the facts and opinions in this country and abroad to which my brother Day has called attention, I do not feel justified in dissenting from the judgment of the court, but the result is to give to copyright less scope than its rational significance and the ground on which it is granted seem to me to demand. Therefore I desire to add a few words to what he has said.

The notion of property starts, I suppose, from confirmed possession of a tangible object, and consists in the right to exclude others from interference with the more or less free doing with it as one wills. But in copyright property has reached a more abstract expression. The right to exclude is not directed to an object in possession or owned, but is *in vacuo*, so to speak. It restrains the spontaneity of men where, but for it, there would be nothing of any kind to hinder their doing as they saw fit. It is a prohibition of conduct remote from the persons or tangibles of the party having the right. It may be infringed a thousand miles from the owner and without his ever becoming aware of the wrong. It is a right which could not be recognized or endured for more than a limited time and therefore, I may remark, in passing, it is one which hardly can be conceived except as a product of statute, as the authorities now agree.

The ground of this extraordinary right is that the person to whom it is given has invented some new collocation of visible or audible points,—of lines, colors, sounds, or words. The restraint is directed against reproducing this collocation, although, but for the invention and the statute, anyone would be free to combine the contents of the dictionary, the elements of the spectrum, or the notes of the gamut in any way that he had the wit to devise. The restriction is confined to the specific form, to the collocation devised, of course, but one would expect that, if it was to be protected at all, that collocation would be protected according to what was its essence. One would expect the protection to be coextensive not only with the invention, which, though free to all, only one had the ability to achieve, but with the possibility of reproducing the result which gives to the invention its meaning and worth. A musical composition is a rational collocation of sounds apart from concepts, reduced to a tangible expression from which the collocation can be reproduced either with or without continuous human intervention. On principle anything that mechanically reproduces that collocation of sounds ought to be held a copy, or, if the statute is too narrow, ought to be made so by a further act, except so far as some extraneous consideration of policy may oppose. What license may be implied from a sale of the copyrighted article is a different and harder question, but I leave it untouched, as license is not relied upon as a ground for the judgment of the court.

NOTES AND QUESTIONS

1. The foregoing case provides an introduction to several themes that you will see repeating themselves throughout the development of music copyright law and other legal issues affecting the music industry through the current time, as well as an introduction to the manner in which the structure of the law (i.e., the bundles of rights protected by the law) has affected the structure of the music industry.

2. Try to identify some of these themes in the *White-Smith Music* case. For example, what issues do you see the court struggling with in this case? Do you see any issues that might have analogs to modern disputes among the various participants in the music industry? What was the basis for the Court's decision in this case? Do you think that the Court's view of the issues raised by this 1908 case is consistent with a property-rights model of music, or does the Court's approach reflect a different model?

3. One interesting note about the *White-Smith Music* case is the fact that, before the Supreme Court decided the case, the Aeolian Company, a leading player piano and piano roll manufacturer, had entered into contracts with almost all of the country's major music publishers that granted Aeolian the exclusive right to make piano rolls of these publishers' compositions for thirty-five years if the ultimate ruling in the litigation was that the making of piano rolls without consent of the copyright owners was infringement and that exempted Aeolian from liability for any royalties for uses prior to the date of any such ruling.[19] Of course, as you saw above, the Supreme Court ruled that piano rolls were not infringing copies of compositions. When you look at the language of the 1909 Act in the next subsection, note the provisions governing the mechanical license and how they operated to prevent the type of monopoly over mechanical reproduction of compositions that Aeolian would have exercised under its contracts if the *White-Smith Music* case had been decided differently.

---

[19] DAVID SUISMAN, SELLING SOUNDS: THE COMMERCIAL REVOLUTION IN AMERICAN MUSIC 165 (Harvard University Press, 2009).

C. RELEVANT PORTIONS OF THE 1909 COPYRIGHT ACT: SECTIONS 1, 4, 5, 25

AN ACT TO AMEND AND CONSOLIDATE
THE ACTS RESPECTING COPYRIGHT.

Be it enacted by the Senate and House of Representatives of the United States of America in Congress assembled,

[SEC. 1] That any person entitled thereto, upon complying with the provisions of this Act, shall have the exclusive right:

(a) to print, reprint, publish, copy, and vend the copyrighted work;

(b) To translate the copyrighted work into other languages or dialects or make any other version thereof if it be a literary work; to dramatize it if it be a nondramatic work; to convert it into a novel or other nondramatic work if it be a drama; to arrange or adapt it if it be a musical work; to complete, execute, and finish it if it be a model or design for a work of art;

(c) To deliver or authorize the delivery of the copyrighted work in public for profit if it be a lecture, sermon, address, or similar production;

(d) To perform or represent the copyrighted work publicly if it be a drama or if it be a dramatic work and not reproduced in copies for sale, to vend any manuscript form, *etc.* or any record whatsoever thereof; to make or to procure the making of any transcription or record thereof by or from which, in whole or in part, it may in any manner or by any method be exhibited, performed, represented, produced, or reproduced; and to exhibit, perform, represent, produce, or reproduce it in any manner or by any method whatsoever;

(e) To perform the copyrighted work publicly for profit if it be a musical composition and for the purpose of public performance for profit; and for the purposes set forth in subsection (a) hereof, to make any arrangement or setting of it or of the melody of it in any system of notation or any form of record in which the thought of an author may be recorded and from which it may be read or reproduced: *provided,* That the provisions of this Act, so far as they secure copyright controlling the parts of instruments serving to reproduce mechanically the musical work, shall include only compositions published and copyrighted after this Act goes into effect, and shall not include the works of a foreign author or composer unless the foreign state or nation of which such author or composer is a citizen or subject grants, either by treaty, convention, agreement, or law, to citizens of the United States similar rights:

And provided further, and as a condition of extending the copyright control to such mechanical reproductions, That whenever the owner of a musical copyright has used or permitted or knowingly acquiesced in the use of the copyrighted work upon the parts of instruments serving to reproduce mechanically the musical work, any other person may make similar use of the copyrighted work upon the payment to the copyright proprietor of a royalty of two cents on each such part manufactured, to be paid by the manufacturer thereof; and the copyright proprietor may require, and if the manufacturer shall furnish, a report under oath on the twentieth day of each month on the number of parts of instruments manufactured during the previous month serving to reproduce mechanically said musical work, and royalties shall be due on the parts manufactured during any month upon the twentieth of the next succeeding month. The payment of the royalty provided for by this section shall free the articles or devices for which such royalty has been paid from further contribution to the copyright except in case of public performance for profit:

And provided further, That it shall be the duty of the copyright owner, if he uses the musical composition himself for the manufacture of parts of instruments serving to reproduce mechanically the musical work, or licenses others to do so, to file notice thereof, accompanied by a recording fee, in the copyright office, and any failure to file such notice shall be a complete defense to any suit, action, or proceeding for any infringement of such copyright.

In case of the failure of such manufacturer to pay to the copyright proprietor within thirty days after demand in writing the full sum of royalties due at said rate at the date of such demand the court may award taxable costs to the plaintiff and a reasonable counsel fee, and the court may, in its discretion, enter judgment therein for any sum in addition over the amount found to be due as royalty in accordance with the terms of this Act, not exceeding three times such amount.

The reproduction or rendition of a musical composition by or upon coin-operated machines shall not be deemed a public performance for profit unless a fee is charged for admission to the place where such reproduction or rendition occurs.

. . . .

SEC. 4. That the works for which copyright may be secured under this Act shall include all the writings of an author.

. . . .

SEC. 25. That if any person shall infringe the copyright in any work protected under the copyright laws of the United States such person shall be liable:

. . . .

(e) Whenever the owner of a musical copyright has used or permitted the use of the copyrighted work upon the parts of musical instruments serving to reproduce mechanically the musical work, then in case of infringement of such copyright by the unauthorized manufacture, use, or sale of interchangeable parts, such as disks, rolls, bands, or cylinders for use in mechanical music-producing machines adapted to reproduce the copyrighted music, no criminal action shall be brought, but in a civil action an injunction may be granted upon such terms as the court may impose, and the plaintiff shall be entitled to recover in lieu of profits and damages a royalty as provided in section one, subsection (e), of this Act:

Provided also, That whenever any person, in the absence of a license agreement, intends to use a copyrighted musical composition upon the parts of instruments serving to reproduce mechanically the musical work, relying upon the compulsory license provision of this Act, he shall serve notice of such intention, by registered mail, upon the copyright proprietor at his last address disclosed by the records of the copyright office, sending to the copyright office a duplicate of such notice; and in case of his failure so to do the court may, in its discretion, in addition to sums hereinabove mentioned, award the complainant a further sum, not to exceed three times the amount provided by section one, subsection (e), by way of damages, and not as a penalty, and also a temporary injunction until the full award is paid.

Rules and regulations for practice and procedure under this section shall be prescribed by the Supreme Court of the United States.

NOTES AND QUESTIONS

1. At the time that the 1909 Act was passed, sound recordings were still viewed as inventions and protected by patent law. How does this background affect your understanding of the new mechanical licensing provisions of the 1909 Act?

2. What provisions of the 1909 Act excerpted above deal with the concerns about potential monopolies over the mechanical rights to compositions that were mentioned in Note 3 at the end of the last section? How do the provisions address those concerns?

3. Of particular import is Section 1(e) of the 1909 Act, as it created the first statutory copyright license for use of a work that does not require permission from the owner so long as the statutory requirements are met. Try to list out these requirements and consider how easy or difficult each requirement might be for a potential licensee to meet.

4. Can you think of alternative ways that Congress might have dealt with the issue of "mechanical" reproduction of compositions in forms that could not be "read" like a printed score but that made it possible for the composition to be "played" by a mechanical device?

5. At the time of its enactment, composers argued that the two-cent per record fixed royalty was both "arbitrary and inadequate compensation," noting the perceived unfairness in charging the same royalty for recordings of songs by successful composers like Irving Berlin and Oscar Hammerstein as for songs by unknown composers. See HARRY P. WARNER, RADIO & TELEVISION RIGHTS: THE LAW OF COPYRIGHT, TRADE-MARKS AND UNFAIR COMPETITION AND THE BROADCASTING INDUSTRY at 333 (Matthew Bender & Co. 1953). What do you think about these arguments? Is it either desirable or possible to have a statutory license that requires different rates based upon the popularity of the work or author in question? Currently, the mechanical rate for use of a composition in a physical recording under five minutes in length is 9.1¢, but a host of other rates exist for various other media in which compositions are mechanically reproduced (e.g., streaming services, ring tones, toys, greeting cards). Note that Chapters 6 and 7 will deal more in depth with statutory licenses in the current music industry. In the next section, we will consider the more immediate impact of the 1909 Copyright Act and how it helped to shape the evolution of the music industry.

D. CASES DISCUSSING AND APPLYING THE 1909 ACT: DUPLICATION AND PERFORMANCE RIGHT ISSUES IN SOUND RECORDINGS

One of the earliest cases to interpret the scope and meaning of the mechanical reproduction rights set forth in Sections 1(e) and 25 of the 1909 Act was *Aeolian Co. v. Royal Music Roll Co.*,[20] in which the licensee of the right to manufacture perforated music rolls sued a competitor who simply copied the perforated rolls created by the licensee rather than creating its own perforated rolls from the musical composition at issue. There, the court recognized that, "[w]hile, under the provisions of the copyright law, such music rolls or records are not strictly matters of copyright, Congress in passing the enactment evidently intended to protect copyright proprietors in their right to their productions, and to give them an exclusive right to print, publish, and vend the same."[21]

In finding that the licensee had the right to pursue the action in its capacity as licensee, the court stated:

> The provision of the statute (section 1e) that 'any other person may make similar use of the copyrighted work' becomes automatically operative by the grant of the license; but the subsequent user does not thereby secure the right to copy the perforated rolls or records. He cannot avail himself of the skill and labor of the original manufacturer of the perforated roll or record by copying or duplicating the same, but must resort to the copyrighted composition or sheet music, and not pirate the work of a competitor who has made an original perforated roll.[22]

In *Standard Music Roll Co. v. F. A. Mills, Inc.*,[23] the compulsory license was construed to apply only to the extent of the original license granted by the copyright owner. Thus, where the initial license agreement authorized only the mechanical reproduction of a composition and did not authorize the separate reproduction of printed lyrics to the composition, the compulsory license only applied to the reproduction of perforated music rolls and did not authorize the defendant to include printed lyric sheets with the music rolls. In interpreting the scope of the compulsory license provisions of Section 1(e) of the 1909 Act, the court stated:

> The object of these provisos seems to be the prevention of monopoly or favoritism in granting the right to reproduce a musical work mechanically. If the owner authorizes one person to reproduce the work mechanically, other persons also may

---

[20] 196 F. 926 (W.D.N.Y. 1912).

[21] *Id.* at 926.

[22] *Id.* at 926–27.

[23] 241 F. 360 (3d Cir. 1917).

reproduce it in a similar mechanical manner, subject to the payment of the statutory royalty. And, in order to compel the owner to make the license public by filing a notice in the office at Washington, the statute provides as a penalty that failure to file shall be a 'complete defense to any suit, action, or proceeding for any infringement of such copyright.' What does 'such copyright' refer to? Manifestly, as we think, some particular right to reproduce the musical work mechanically. Just how the reproduction is to be made, and whether it is to be confined to the music or shall extend to the words also, is in the first instance left for the owner to determine. But after he has determined it, and has granted a license to one person, he thereby opens the field to all others to do the same, or a similar, thing. If he license one person to reproduce both words and music by the phonograph method, other persons may reproduce them both by using the phonograph. If he license one person to reproduce the music by the automatic roll, others also may use the roll, but they do not thereby acquire the right to print the words. In brief, 'such copyright' means the particular right covering mechanical reproduction that happens to be in controversy—in the present case, the right to reproduce, not the words but the music, mechanically.[24]

As you will see in the cases below, the inclusion of a compulsory mechanical license in the 1909 Act may have addressed the problem recognized by the Court in *White-Smith Publishing*, but there were still a host of issues that the emerging recording and broadcasting technologies created that led to litigation, the outcome of which helped to shape the way in which the music industry developed. The materials below raise thorny issues in the context of musical recordings that courts and policy-makers still wrestle with today in many other contexts.

As you read the cases, try to identify where you see any of the following themes discussed:

(1) the impact of technology on the law and business of music and the inability of the law to keep pace with future uses of technology (let alone current uses);

(2) the tensions and competing claims of right between creators of devices, creators of content, and consumers;

(3) rights of composers versus rights of the owners of sound recordings;

(4) conflict (or complement) between federal and state law;

---

[24] *Id.*

(5) a "Lockean Theory" approach that provides one the benefit of the fruits of his or her labor;

(6) the balance between promotion (conduct that increases the demand for a product) and substitution (conduct that decreases sales of a product by providing a substitute);

(7) the tension between the efficiency of collective action in enforcing rights and a free market approach to property.

What other themes/issues do you see raised in the materials? Do you see any potential corollaries to current issues in the music industry?

In addition, as you read the cases below, pay particular attention to the following questions:

- Who is suing? Is it the owner of the musical composition? The owner of a recording of a performance of a musical composition? A licensee of one of the above? What differences can you see in the scope of protection provided to each of these categories of potential plaintiffs and the claims and defenses asserted?

- What is the nature of the claims asserted? What intellectual property rights are implicated in the case—copyright, trademark, patent, or some combination? What state law and equitable claims are asserted and recognized?

- Who is the defendant and how did his/her/its actions implicate the rights asserted in the action?

- What policy concerns are addressed in each of the cases, either expressly or implicitly?

Berliner patented gramophone disc,
photo by Julie Ross

FONOTIPIA LTD. V. BRADLEY

171 F. 951 (E.D.N.Y. Cir. 1909)

CHATFIELD, DISTRICT JUDGE.

[¶] The complainants at the present time are producing and putting upon the market records of vocal and instrumental music, for use upon machines for the reproduction of sound, and constructed in a form suitable for operation with these records in the flat and circular or disc form described in the patent to Berliner, No. 534,543, February 19, 1895 (Victor v. Amer. Grapho. Co., 145 Fed. 350, 76 C.C.A. 180), and Jones, No. 688,739, December 10, 1901 (Amer. Grapho. Co. v. Universal Co., 151 Fed. 595, 81 C.C.A. 13 9).

It is unnecessary to consider in detail the machines made by either company, further than to say that those manufactured by the complainant the Victor Talking Machine Company are known generally as the 'Victor talking machines,' and those put upon the market by the Columbia Company are called 'graphophones,' and the discs described can be interchangeably used upon either type of instrument.

The discs themselves, as at present made, are of some such substance as hard rubber, and are said to be made by causing the music to be sung or played into a receiving instrument, which records the waves of sound upon a disc properly prepared, which, in turn, by an electroplating process, is used to yield a matrix of metal. From this matrix numberless reproductions, substantially duplicates even in minute details of the original record, are produced by processes perfected by each company, and these reproduced discs, when used upon the talking machine or graphophone, turn back, by means of the diaphragm of the instrument, the lines of the record into sound waves, which are the equivalent of those originally sung or played.

In the case of the Victor Company, the discs sold by it within the United States are plainly marked with notice of the patent, and also with notice that the disc is sold for use only upon a talking machine, for the reproduction of sound. The price at which the discs are to be sold is also printed upon each disc, and the maintenance of this price is made a condition of the sale under license. Thus actual notice is given to each purchaser or user of the Victor Company's discs, of the conditions under which they have been sold, and that the article has to do with a patented product. . . .

[¶] Particular attention has been called to the trade-mark of the Victor Company, which, both as a trade-mark and as an advertisement, in the shape of a dog listening to the sounds from a talking machine horn, and labeled 'His master's voice,' has become familiar to the public. The methods employed by all of the complainant companies, the uniform care and excellent reproducing qualities of their products (both machines and records), has educated the public to expect the successful reproduction of music of a high standard of quality in the reproduction, and, as shown by the record, the grade of goods produced by the complainant companies upholds the standards which they have established. The public is protected in its purchases by the evenness and excellence of the output.

Victor Company Logos

In addition to the expense and the rights represented by the business indicated, all three of the complainant companies have entered into separate contracts with individual singers and musicians, and particularly in the case of singers under contracts with the so-called 'Grand Opera

Companies' of New York, Paris, London, Berlin, Milan, etc. Under these contracts with artists able to command large prices, the initial cost of producing the record is great, and the companies are under an agreement to pay a royalty for each record produced from the original matrix, thus furnishing a continuing contract and expense, of which the benefit is going to the singer.

. . . . The court must also take into account, in any such matter as the present, not only questions of public policy, but questions of public benefit, and it is evident, from the common use of various forms of talking machines or phonographs and graphophones, that the better class of music is brought within the observation and study of many persons who would have neither time nor opportunity to become familiar with it in other ways. The reproduction of songs by famous singers and artists is both educational and beneficial to the people as a whole, and the court cannot but take notice of the fact that such music has an educational side, and appeals to substantially everyone, even though they be unconscious of this result.

[¶] . . . . The defendant has been for some months advertising by circular letter and in other ways his ability to sell records of the Continental Record Company, stating in these advertisements that the records are sold at prices not more than half those now charged for the original records. The advertisements claim that the records themselves are pressed upon the very highest class of material finished equal to the original, that the character of the record itself is identical with the original record, and that experts who have listened to samples are unable to determine between the original and the copy. The catalogue contains a statement that the records offered by Bradley are 'all duplicates from the original records made by the artists whose names are used herein.'

It is apparent from the explanation which has been already made that the commercial records sold by the complainants are copies or duplicates, in the sense that they are made from a matrix or metallic plate, but are in no sense duplicate originals; that is, actually made by the sound waves of the singer at the time of the original song. . . . The testimony shows that the defendant the Continental Record Company makes its records from commercial discs of the complainants and must produce a second matrix before the copies can be pressed or stamped.

[¶] . . . . If the defendant is selling to customers records reproduced by processes of the Continental Record Company, by means of discs purchased in the market by that company for the purpose, and if he advertises and guarantees to his customers that the Continental records are duplicates equal in all respects, including composition and finish, and that it is impossible to distinguish between the Continental records and those produced by the complainants, we have a question of fact presented in which the public is interested, namely, do the records submitted as evidence in the case lead to any determination upon the question of deception or imitation of the product, and the resultant benefit to the imitator, with corresponding injury to the imitated, by the results of the sales, and by the effect upon future sales if the product of the imitation be unsatisfactory?

It may be argued that the imitation would go out of the market and be removed from interference with the original if the product proved unsatisfactory; but it would seem that business reputation and excellence of product are entitled to some protection from imitations which discourage further use and prove unsatisfactory as a whole, because the result of the sale of such a product must necessarily affect adversely the opinion of the very class of customers which is sought to be enlarged by the sale of a satisfactory product.

A comparison, in order to observe points of similarity between the records put in evidence by the complainants, and made by themselves, with the records produced by the defendant and introduced as purchases from him, leads irresistibly to the conclusion that the material used in the Continental Record Company's discs is greatly inferior, contains imperfections which cause scratchings and irritating sounds, is subject to warp, and is so much softer or destructible in character that the commercial value of the defendant's records is much less than that of the complainant companies' records. Actual comparison of the discs warrants the finding that the Continental records are not in every way the equal, even when played upon the same machine, of the complainants' records, and it is impossible to hold that they are duplicates in the sense that they cannot, in most cases, be distinguished from the genuine, or that the imitation product is the duplicate in the sense of being the equal of the original. The defendant's records do not show the use of as good material in the discs, nor as much durability and freedom from warping as those of the complainants, and a comparison shows in many instances a dulling or far away effect in the defendant's discs.

[¶] . . . . [W]e must therefore consider the broad question presented by the issue, namely, whether the taking of property in the shape of valuable ideas and products, by mechanical imitation or reproduction, is susceptible of notice by a court of equity, and whether any remedy therefor can exist apart from the questions of patent, trade-mark, and intentional deception or imitation and deceitful substitution of the product.

[¶] . . . . We therefore reach the broad question of the power of a court of equity to secure to an individual by injunction the full enjoyment of both corporeal and incorporeal rights in property created by him or at his expense, and capable of a taking by another, where such taking either diminishes or destroys the enjoyment of those rights by the owner and diverts a part of the enjoyment or profits from the rights to the one complained of.

[¶] . . . . No case cited and decided strictly upon the question of unfair competition, so far as called to the attention of the court, has ever granted relief in instances outside of imitation or deception, and where the public would be likely to be misled by the points of similarity involved; but equity has granted relief in certain typical lines of cases where the doctrine of unfair competition seems to have been the guide to the decision, but where the basis upon which the relief was granted was the unfair taking of the complainant's property, rather than the deception of the purchaser, or the imitation of a patented or copyrighted article, or a registered trade-mark or trade-name. . . . [¶]

The present case is extremely like these just considered in principle. It is almost as if the court should be asked to enjoin individuals from theft, upon the ground that the criminal statutes did not make the taking of the particular kind of property in question larceny, and in cases where equitable relief was therefore appealed to because of the absence of any adequate remedy at law.

The principle involved is far-reaching, especially in that it carries the scope of equitable jurisdiction into matters frequently considered to be purely the result of business competition, and which, even if in themselves morally or financially wrong, are supposed to be without remedy where no contractual relations have existed from which suits for damages could arise. Various statutes have been passed in an attempt by legislation to protect certain classes of rights, such as the recording acts of the various states, and the lien laws of different jurisdictions. The patent, trade-mark, and copyright laws of different governments and the history of legislation as well as law, prove that where an act is admittedly wrong in the eyes of the public, and where the interests of individuals are being interfered with by commissions of the acts in question, legislation in the appropriate jurisdiction usually follows, and a legal remedy is created; but such legal remedies must be with relation to a specific class of acts. The jurisdiction of a court of equity has always been invoked to prevent the continuance of acts of injury to property and to personal rights generally, where the law had not provided a specific legal remedy, and it would seem that the appropriation of what has come to be recognized as property rights or incorporeal interests in material objects, out of which pecuniary profits can fairly be secured, may properly, in certain kinds of cases, be protected by legislation; but such intangible or abstract property rights would seem to have claims upon the protection of equity, where the ground for legislation is uncertain or difficult of determination, and where the principles of equity plainly apply. The so-called 'common-law right' in literary property before its publication has long been recognized in the law. After the passage of legislation, literary property was secured, even in the published article, by the various copyright statutes of the different nations.

When such a copyright statute has been passed, all property rights in the published article must be secured and controlled by strict compliance with the statute.

It has been held that under the copyright law in effect prior to the 1st day of July, 1909, musical compositions, unless transcribed in print or musical characters, upon paper, were incapable of copyright (White-Smith Music Pub. Co. v. Apollo Co., 209 U.S. 1, 28 Sup.Ct. 319, 52 L.Ed. 655). Since the beginning of the present action, the copyright law has been amended, and since the 1st day of July, 1909, any form of recording or transcribing a musical composition, or rendition of such composition, has been capable of registration, and the property rights therein secured under the copyright statute (Act March 4, 1909, c. 320, 35 Stat. 1075).

It would seem therefore that the questions raised in the present case may be avoided as to future compositions by copyrighting the original rendition of the song, provided the singer has the right to use it for that purpose, and the disc record by which the rendition is preserved; but question will still remain as to the records produced prior to the present copyright law, and serious discussion may arise over the right obtained, for instance, by a grand opera singer who files a copyright for the resinging of a song already recorded by him or her, and sold to the public upon a disc record. With that we have nothing to do here, and the relief asked in this case would protect those who have already sung or played compositions having a pecuniary value, because of their musical excellence, and also the persons who have invested capital and labor in putting a valuable product upon the market. The education of the public by the dissemination of good music is an object worthy of protection, and it is apparent that such results could not be attained if the production of the original records was stopped by the wrongful taking of both product and profit by any one who could produce sound discs free from the expense of obtaining the original record.

It has been said in the case of American Washboard Co. v. Saginaw Mfg. Co., 103 Fed. 281, 43 C.C.A. 233, 50 L.R.A. 609, that the basis of recovery is the damage to property rights of the complainant, rather than the deception of the public. It is from this contended: The better the imitation, the greater reason there is for issuing an injunction. And, in the sense that the marketable qualities of an article can be appropriated by a good substitute, this statement is true; but it necessarily follows that the injury to reputation and to the demand for the article would be greater if the imitations do not prove satisfactory, and there be no way of informing the public that the genuine is preferable or superior. In the case of sound discs such as those involved in the present action, a careful comparison of the records is necessary to emphasize the superiority of the discs made with better material, more careful and experienced workmanship, and improved methods; and it is also evident that to the untrained ear such differences cannot be carried in mind and appreciated, unless the opportunity for direct comparison be immediately present. An actual playing of the discs introduced as evidence in this case illustrates the point involved, for the testimony and also experiments show that in some cases the records sold by the defendant are with difficulty distinguished from those sold by the complainant, unless one is played immediately following the other and under the same circumstances, so that comparison would be fair.

Reference has been made to the rights of a photographer who should make a film for moving pictures, of some historical or unique occasion, and should sell the film to parties who should reproduce it in a moving-picture machine. Other parties might make pictures from the film, or from the exposures, and a question, in some respects, similar to the present, might be involved. . . . Sculptors might carve statues of great commercial value, and stone carvers might copy these sculptures.

It cannot now be determined how far such appropriation of ideas could be prevented; but it would seem that where a product is placed upon the market, under advertisement and statement that the substitute or imitating product is a duplicate of the original, and where the commercial value of the imitation lies in the fact that it takes advantage of and appropriates to itself the commercial qualities, reputation, and salable properties of the original, equity should grant relief.

That is the particular proposition presented in the present case, and to that extent it seems to the court that the principles applied in the stock-ticker and similar cases above recited should be followed, and relief by injunction granted.

Fred Waring's Pennsylvanians
Victor Recording with "Not Licensed for Radio Broadcast" Notice

WARING V. WDAS BROADCASTING STATION

327 Pa. 433, 194 A. 631 (1937)

STERN, JUSTICE.

The problems involved in this case have never before been presented to an American or an English court. They challenge the vaunted genius of the law to adapt itself to new social and industrial conditions and to the progress of science and invention. For the first time in history human action can be photographed and visually reportrayed by the motion picture. Sound can now be mechanically captured and reproduced, not only by means of the phonographs for an audience physically present, but, through broadcasting, for practically all the world as simultaneous auditors. Just as the birth of the printing press made it necessary for equity to inaugurate a protection for literary and intellectual property, so these latter-day inventions make demands upon the creative and ever-evolving energy of equity to extend that protection so as adequately to do justice under current conditions of life.

Plaintiff, since 1917, has been the conductor of an orchestra which is incorporated under the laws of the state of New York as 'Fred Waring's Pennsylvanians, Inc.' Plaintiff owns 98 shares of the corporation out of a total of 100, the other 2 being issued merely for the purpose of qualifying the necessary directors. The orchestra consists of about 25 musicians; it has achieved an outstanding reputation in the musical world for artistic rendition of popular music. Originally it confined its performances to dance halls and the vaudeville stage; later it began to play over the radio, and entered into a contract with the Ford Motor Company to broadcast on one night of each week for the sum of $13,500 for each performance.

Some years ago the orchestra started to make phonograph records for the Victor Talking Machine Company. The two which are the subject of the present controversy were manufactured in 1932; they consisted of two songs, the publishers of the songs, who owned the copyright, licensing the Talking Machine Company to use them for making records, but not for public performance for profit. The Talking Machine Company paid the orchestra $250 for each recording. Plaintiff, foreseeing the likelihood of the records being used by broadcasting companies for reproduction over the radio, discussed the matter with the Talking Machine Company, and, as a result, it was agreed between them that a label should be placed upon the records reading: 'Not licensed for radio broadcast.'[1] They were then sold in the ordinary course of business to the Talking Machine Company's dealers, and by the latter to individual purchasers, the retail price being 75 cents apiece.

Defendant, a Delaware corporation, is the owner of a radio station and engaged in operating it for profit. Some of its programs over the air are accompanied by advertising for which it receives a direct remuneration; others are part of its general service of entertainment for the public and for the commercial benefit of its advertisers as a whole. Having purchased one of the records made by plaintiff's orchestra, and having obtained a license to broadcast the songs from the American Society of Composers, Authors and Publishers, to which both the publishers and the composers had assigned the exclusive right of public performance under the copyright, defendant broadcast the records as a part of its sustaining programs. The playing of the records was accompanied by the customary announcement over the radio that they were mechanical reproductions of the orchestra's renditions. Plaintiff filed a bill in equity to enjoin defendant from broadcasting the records. The court below granted the injunction prayed for, from which decree defendant has taken the present appeal.

There are three major questions involved: (1) Have performers-in this case an orchestra-any enforceable property rights in their artistic interpretation of the work of a composer? (2) If so, to what extent can such rights be reserved at the time of what the law designates as 'publication?' (3) As ancillary to such rights, under what circumstances can performers be afforded equitable relief on the ground of unfair competition?

1.   The property rights claimed by plaintiff are admittedly not the subject of protection under existing copyright laws. The Act of March 4, 1909, c. 320, section 5, 35 Stat. 1076, as amended by the Act of August 24, 1912, c. 356, 37 Stat. 488, 17 U.S.C.A. § 5, enumerates the various literary

---

[1]   The license given to the Victor Talking Machine Company by the publishers also expressly required that the company place such a legend upon the records.

and artistic productions which may be copyrighted, including books, lectures, dramatic and musical compositions, works of art, photographs, and motion pictures. The creator of such a work may protect his property rights therein, but the statute does not recognize any right of a performing artist in his interpretative rendition of a musical composition, or in the acting of a play, composed by another.[2] It is to the common law, therefore, that the performer must turn, and the question arises whether an actor or a musician has any property rights at common law in his performance. This problem is presented now for the first time because, until the invention of the motion picture and the sound films, an actor's interpretation of a play was necessarily evanescent and ephemeral. It might be made the subject of mimicry,[3] but the actual performance itself, the postures, gestures, voices, and motions, could not be identically reproduced. So also in the case of music, an instrumental or vocal performance by a soloist or an orchestra, once rendered, was lost forever except as repeated by the artist himself, until the advent of sound-recording devices permitted the fixation of the performance upon a disc or record which could be played and replayed, and even broadcast, at will, with the result that a single performance by the artist is now sufficient, generally speaking, to allow the rendition to be heard over and over again through an indefinite course of years. Under such circumstances it naturally has become important for the artist—in the present case we are concerned more particularly with the musician—to guard against his field of lucrative return being thus drastically narrowed, and to protect his artistic product against its indiscriminate

---

[2] Prior to 1909 mechanical devices, such as music rolls, discs, and records, for the reproduction of sound, were held to be beyond the scope of the copyright laws and not to infringe protected works which they were the means for audibly reproducing. Stern v. Rosey, 17 App.D.C. 562; White-Smith Music Publishing Co. v. Apollo Company, 209 U.S. 1, 28 S.Ct. 319, 52 L.Ed. 655, 14 Ann.Cas. 628. By the statute of that year, however, the composer or copyright proprietor was given control, in accordance with the provisions of the act, of the manufacture and use of such devices, although the right of copyright was not extended to the mechanical reproductions themselves. (See the report of the Patent Committee to the House of Representatives which accompanied the presentation of the act and purported to explain its scope.) By the provisions of the act, if the owner of the musical copyright uses or permits the use of records for mechanical reproduction of the work, any other person may make similar records upon the payment to the copyright proprietor of a royalty of 2 cents on each record, although this does not permit their use for public performances for profit. See Irving Berlin, Inc., v. Daigle (C.C.A.) 31 F.(2d) 832. The measure of protection thus given in the case of pianola records and phonograph discs is to the composer, not the performer. Plaintiff, in 1935, made application to the Register for a copyright on the 'personal interpretation by Fred Waring' of the musical composition 'Lullaby of Broadway.' The application was rejected, the Register of Copyrights saying, inter alia: 'There is not and never has been any provision in the Act for the protection of an artist's personal interpretation or rendition of a musical work not expressible by musical notation in the form of 'legible' copies although the subject has been extensively discussed both here and abroad.'

[3] It has been said that the owner of the production rights of a play cannot enjoin an imitation of the actors and stage business. See Savage v. Hoffmann (C.C.) 159 F. 584; Chappell & Co., Ltd. v. Fields (C.C.A.) 210 F. 864; Shafter's 'Musical Copyright,' pp. 66, 67. Such imitations, while they may resemble the original, are not identical with it. In the present case, however, it is not a copy or imitation but the exact reproduction of the performance itself, transfixed by a mechanical process, for which protection is sought.

reproduction, especially by those who, in a commercial sense, are in the nature of competitors.

At common law, rights in a literary or artistic work were recognized on substantially the same basis as title to other property. Such rights antedated the original copyright act of 8 Anne c. 19, and, while it has been uniformly held that the rights given by the act supersede those of the common law so far as the act applies,[FN4 omitted] the common-law rights in regard to any field of literary or artistic production which does not fall within the purview of the copyright statute are not affected thereby.[FN5 omitted]

Does the performer's interpretation of a musical composition constitute a product of such novel and artistic creation as to invest him with a property right therein?[6] It may be said that the ordinary musician does nothing more than render articulate the silent composition of the author. But it must be clear that such actors, for example, as David Garrick, Mrs. Siddons, Rachel, Booth, Coquelin, Sarah Bernhardt, and Sir Henry Irving, or such vocal and instrumental artists as Jenny Lind, Melba, Caruso, Paderewski, Kreisler, and Toscanini, by their interpretations, definitely added something to the work of authors and composers which not only gained for themselves enduring fame but enabled them to enjoy financial rewards from the public in recognition of their unique genius; indeed, the large compensation frequently paid to such artists is testimony in itself of the distinctive and creative nature of their performances. The law has never considered it necessary for the establishment of property rights in intellectual or artistic productions that the entire ultimate product should be the work of a single creator; such rights may be acquired by one who perfects the original work or substantially adds to it in some manner. Thus, in Wood v. Boosey, 2 L.R.Q.B. 340, it was held that a person who arranged the score of an opera for the pianoforte thereby created an independent musical composition in which he had a right of property apart from that of the composer of the opera itself. . . . A musical composition in itself is an incomplete work; the written page evidences only one of the creative acts which are necessary for its enjoyment; it is the performer who must consummate the work by transforming it into sound. If, in so doing, he contributes by his interpretation something of novel intellectual or artistic value, he has undoubtedly participated in the creation of a product in which he is entitled to a right of property, which in no way overlaps or duplicates that of the author in the musical composition. All that need now

---

[6]   The case of Musical Performers' Protection Association, Ltd., v. British International Pictures, Ltd., 46 T.L.R. 485, was concerned with the construction of an English statute, passed in 1925, known as the Dramatic and Musical Performers' Protection Act, which imposed a fine upon any one making, selling, or using a record of a performance of any dramatic or musical work without the written consent of the performers. It held that this act was not intended to confer upon musicians any property rights in their rendition which they could enforce by enjoining the use of a sound record of their performance, but merely provided a fine as the penalty for violation of its provisions.

be decided is that such a property right inheres in the case of those artists who elevate interpretations to the realm of independent works of art.

In the present case the evidence is uncontradicted that plaintiff's orchestra measured up to this standard. A number of witnesses, themselves of fame in the musical world, testified, and the learned chancellor found, that 'Waring's Pennsylvanians' were nationally and even internationally acclaimed as unique in their artistry. Indeed, as already stated, the fact that they receive from the Ford Motor Company $13,500 for a radio performance is striking testimony to that effect. That their performances lie in the field of popular rather than classical music has no bearing upon the question of the existence of a property right in their productions. [¶] . . .

2.   It being established that plaintiff has common-law property rights which are the subject of protection in equity, we come to a consideration of the question whether they were lost by such a 'publication' as would, according to the general American doctrine, completely terminate them. When plaintiff and his orchestra performed for the Talking Machine Company they knew that, although intended for use in phonographs, the records could be played before a microphone and broadcast over the radio. Indeed, it was to prevent such use that the arrangement was made to stamp them with the legend, 'Not licensed for radio broadcast.' Was this attempted restriction, of which notice was thus given to all who came into possession of the records, legally effective to accomplish the purpose for which it was designed? Could the publication effected by the making and sale of the records be limited in its generality so as to enable plaintiff to prevent their use for broadcasting?

The law has consistently distinguished between performance and publication—between what is sometimes referred to as a 'limited' or 'qualified' and a 'general' publication.

> 'When the communication is to a select number upon condition, express or implied, that it is not intended to be thereafter common property, the publication is then said to be limited. . . . 'It is a fundamental rule that to constitute publication there must be such a dissemination of the work of art itself among the public as to justify the belief that it took place with the intention of rendering such work common property.' * * * 'The test is whether there is or is not such a surrender as permits the absolute and unqualified enjoyment of the subject-matter by the public or the members thereof to whom it may be committed.' Werckmeister v. Amer. Lith. Co. (C.C.A.) 134 F. 321, 68 L.R.A. 591, 596.'

Berry v. Hoffman, 125 Pa.Super. 261, 267, 268, 189 A. 516, 519. Thus the production of a play, . . . the delivery of a lecture, . . . the playing of a musical composition, . . . the exhibition of a painting, . . . a performance over the radio, . . . does not constitute a publication which operates as an abandonment to public use. In determining whether or not there has been such a publication, the courts look partly to the objective character of the dissemination and partly to the proprietor's intent in regard to the relinquishment of his property rights. . . .

Where public policy or some other determinative consideration is not involved, why should the law adopt an immutable principle that no restrictions, reservations, or limitations can ever be allowed to accompany the sale of an article of personal property? As a matter of fact, there have been many cases, notably in England, in which restrictive covenants and conditions accompanying the alienation of chattels have been enforced.[8] . . . Familiar examples in this country are the 'ticket-scalper' cases, . . . and the 'trading stamp' cases . . . . It is true that in addition to the question of public policy other factors may weigh against the imposition of such restrictions in many, perhaps most, instances.

Thus an attempted restriction, instead of being aimed at the accomplishment of a useful commercial, industrial, or social purpose, may be merely capricious and serve only to clog the free and untrammeled circulation of personal property. Again, in the case of some restrictive covenants limiting the use of chattels, it might be difficult, if not impossible, to detect breaches so as to make legal enforcement practical. There is no reason, however, why an ancient generalization of law should be held invariably to apply to cases in which modern conditions of commerce and industry and the nature of new scientific inventions make restrictions highly desirable. Mere aphorisms should not be permitted to fetter the law in furthering proper social and economic purposes.[9]

Since a rule of law ceases when its reason ceases, latitude should be allowed for intelligent discrimination in the enforcement of equitable servitudes on chattels similar to those upheld by the courts in the case of building restrictions and other limitations upon the use of land.[10]

---

[8] 'The tendency in the United States has been to apply the doctrine of restrictive agreements to personal property when not regarded as an unlawful restraint of trade or in violation of public policy.' Harlan F. Stone, 'The Equitable Rights and Liabilities of Strangers to a Contract,' 18 Columbia Law Review 291, 310.

[9] 'I think that at least it is safe to say that the most enlightened judicial policy is to let people manage their own business in their own way, unless the ground for interference is very clear.' Dissenting opinion of Mr. Justice Holmes in Dr. Miles Medical Co. v. Park & Sons Co., 220 U.S. 373, 411, 31 S.Ct. 376, 386, 55 L.Ed. 502. See, also, dissenting opinion of Mr. Justice Holmes in Motion Picture Patents Co. v. Universal Film Mfg. Co., 243 U.S. 502, 519, 37 S.Ct. 416, 61 L.Ed. 871, L.R.A.1917E, 1187, Ann.Cas.1918A, 959, and concurring opinion of Mr. Justice Brandeis in Boston Store of Chicago v. American Graphophone Co., 246 U.S. 8, 27, 38 S.Ct. 257, 62 L.Ed. 551, Ann.Cas.1918C, 447. See, also, Prof. E. C. S. Wade, 'Restrictions on User,' 44 Law Quarterly Review 51, 64.

[10] 'Just as modern needs have brought equitable restrictions on land, of which the old common law knew nothing, into existence, they may also call for a limited departure from the free transfer of chattels for the sake of promoting desirable business practices wholly strange to Coke's day.' Chafee, 'Equitable Servitudes on Chattels,' 41 Harvard Law Review 945, 983.

In the present case it is clear that the restriction affixed to the records, 'Not licensed for Radio Broadcast,' was not unreasonable, nor did it operate in restraint of trade. It was intended to effect a legitimate purpose; indeed, unless such a restriction can be imposed and enforced, it will be impossible for distinguished musicians to commit their renditions to phonograph records—except possibly for a prohibitive financial compensation—without subjecting themselves to the disadvantages and losses which they would inevitably suffer from the use of the records for broadcasting. Such a restriction, therefore, works for the encouragement of art and artists. Moreover, it does not limit the use of the records in private homes or even public halls where a breach could not readily be detected or enjoined; the employment of the records for radio broadcasting would immediately become a matter of general knowledge. Uses of the records on phonographs and for broadcasting purposes are so radically distinct as to belong practically to two totally different fields of operation.

It thus appears that no valid reason exists why the restriction attached to the manufacture and sale of the records in this case should not be enforced in equity. It may, indeed, be said, in conclusion upon this point, that in a sense plaintiff was not imposing a restriction in connection with a sale by him of a chattel. The chattel here consisted of the phonograph record. This the plaintiff never owned. What he granted was merely the incorporeal privilege of reproducing the rendition of the song indented upon the chattel sold by the Talking Machine Company. The reservation or restriction imposed by him was to limit the extent of this privilege. The title to the physical substance and the right to the use of literary or artistic property which may be printed upon or embodied in it are entirely distinct and independent of each other. Werckmeister v. American Lithographic Co. (C.C.) 142 F. 827, 830; Stephens v. Cady, 14 How. (55 U.S.) 528, 14 L.Ed. 528; Stevens v. Gladding, 17 How. (58 U.S.) 447, 15 L.Ed. 155. . . .

The notice used was fairly and reasonably sufficient to make purchasers realize the existence and extent of the restriction imposed upon their use of the records.

3.   It having been demonstrated, first, the plaintiff had common-law rights of property in his orchestra's renditions of the songs, and, second, that there is no logical or practical reason why the restriction placed upon the use of the records should not be enforced in equity, it remains to point out an additional ground upon which plaintiff may rely for the protection of such rights against invasion and abuse by defendant, namely, that of 'unfair competition.' A leading authority on this aspect of the case is International News Service v. Associated Press, 248 U.S. 215, 39 S.Ct. 68, 63 L.Ed. 211, 2 A.L.R. 293. The Associated Press, at a great expenditure of labor and capital, gathered and distributed the news among its members. The International News Service, a rival organization, 'pirated' the news thus accumulated. The Associated claimed that this was accomplished

partly by . . . copying the news from bulletin boards and the early editions of the newspapers of Associated members and embodying it in the newspapers of its own members in competition with those of the Associated. . . . [I]t was ruled in the Associated Press Case that . . . the Associated could enjoin the International from publishing in its own newspapers the news which had been gathered by the Associated and which appeared on the bulletin boards and in the Associated newspapers, until a sufficient time had elapsed to destroy its commercial value as news. The court held that, while there was probably no absolute property in the news as such, an injunction should be granted on the ground of unfair competition, saying (248 U.S. 215, at page 236, 39 S.Ct. 68, 71, 63 L.Ed. 211, 2 A.L.R. 293):

'Obviously, the question of what is unfair competition in business must be determined with particular reference to the character and circumstances of the business. The question here is not so much the rights of either party as against the public but their rights as between themselves. . . . * * * Regarding the news, therefore, as but the material out of which both parties are seeking to make profits at the same time and in the same field, we hardly can fail to recognize that for this purpose, and as between them, it must be regarded as quasi property, irrespective of the rights of either as against the public.'

Extending this thought, the court further said (248 U.S. 215, at pages 239–242, 39 S.Ct. 68, 63 L.Ed. 211, 2 A.L.R. 293):

'Defendant insists that when, with the sanction and approval of complainant, and as the result of the use of its news for the very purpose for which it is distributed, a portion of complainant's members communicate it to the general public by posting it upon bulletin boards so that all may read, or by issuing it to newspapers and distributing it indiscriminately, complainant no longer has the right to control the use to be made of it; that when it thus reaches the light of day it becomes the common possession of all to whom it is accessible; and that any purchaser of a newspaper has the right to communicate the intelligence which it contains to anybody and for any purpose, even for the purpose of selling it for profit to newspapers published for profit in competition with complainant's members.

'The fault in the reasoning lies in applying as a test the right of the complainant as against the public, instead of considering the rights of complainant and defendant, competitors in business, as between themselves. The right of the purchaser of a single newspaper to spread knowledge of its contents gratuitously, for any legitimate purpose not unreasonably interfering with complainant's right to make merchandise of it, may be admitted; but to transmit that news for commercial use, in competition with complainant—which is what defendant has done and seeks to justify—is a very different matter. In doing this defendant, by its very act, admits that it is taking material that has been acquired by complainant as the result of organization and the expenditure of labor, skill, and money, and which is salable by complainant for money, and that defendant in appropriating it and selling it as its own is endeavoring to reap where it has not sown, and by disposing of it to newspapers that are competitors of complainant's members is appropriating to itself the harvest of those who have sown. Stripped of all disguises, the process amounts to an unauthorized interference with the normal operation of complainant's legitimate business precisely at the point where the profit is to be reaped, in order to divert a material portion of the profit from those who have earned it to those who have not; with special advantage to defendant in the competition because of the fact that it is not burdened with any part of the expense of gathering the news. The transaction speaks for itself and a court of equity ought not to hesitate long in characterizing it as unfair competition in business.'

It appears from the Associated Press Case that while, generally speaking the doctrine of unfair competition rests upon the practice of fraud or deception, the presence of such elements is not an indispensable condition for equitable relief, but, under certain circumstances, equity will protect an unfair appropriation of the product of another's labor or talent.[FN13 omitted] In the present case, while defendant did not obtain the property of plaintiff in a fraudulent or surreptitious manner, it did appropriate and utilize for its own profit the musical genius and artistry of plaintiff's orchestra in commercial competition with the orchestra itself. In line with the theory of the Associated Press Case, the 'publication' of the orchestra's renditions was a dedication of them only to purchasers for use of the records on phonographs, and not to competitive interests to profit therefrom at plaintiff's expense. Indeed, in the Associated Press Case the intent against an unqualified abandonment had to be inferred from the circumstances, whereas here it was expressed on the records themselves, and defendant's use of them was a violation of the explicit notice to that effect.

In Fonotipia, Ltd., v. Bradley (C.C.) 171 F. 951, an injunction was granted to manufacturers of musical records against the manufacture and sale of duplicates made by taking a matrix from one of plaintiff's records and making copies therefrom. As the duplicates were made prior to the present Copyright Law of 1909, relief could not be obtained under the Copyright Act (17 U.S.C.A. § 1 et seq.). It was held, aside from any question of deception or fraud, that plaintiffs were entitled to restrain the sale of such copies as a wrongful appropriation of their property rights, although the original records had been sold indiscriminately to the public for years and the copies were clearly marked as such. The court cited the 'ticket-scalper' and 'trading stamp' cases, and said (171 F. 951, at pages 961, 962): 'Equity has granted relief in certain typical lines of cases where the doctrine of unfair competition seems to have been the guide to the decision, but where the basis upon which the relief was granted was the unfair taking of the complainant's property, rather than the deception of the purchaser, or the imitation of a patented or copyrighted article, or a registered trademark or trade-name.' . . .

That plaintiff's orchestra and defendant are in competition admits of but little doubt. They both furnish entertainment to the public over the radio. The orchestra obtains its remuneration from contracts with advertisers who pay it for the music rendered as supplementary to their advertising. Defendant's revenue also is derived from advertisers, and presumably it can exact a greater compensation from them by being able to furnish mechanized music of an attractive quality at nominal cost— partly because this makes it unnecessary for the advertisers to pay for 'live talent,' and partly because by thus entertaining the radio public a more receptive field is created for the advertising. Thus defendant can in effect 'sell' to its advertising customers and to the public, at practically no expense to itself, the identical musical renditions of plaintiff's orchestra. That such competition is extremely harmful to plaintiff and his orchestra is obvious. It probably must become increasingly difficult for them to demand and obtain $13,500 for a single performance over the radio if innumerable reiterations of their renditions can be furnished at a cost of 75 cents. There was testimony to the effect, and the learned chancellor found, that the constant broadcasting of the records[14] diminished the commercial value of the orchestra's performances. Moreover, the records being, as it happened in this case, old ones, the public were led to judge the ability of the orchestra by work rendered at a time when it probably had not attained its present high degree of excellence. In Associated Press v. KVOS, Inc. (C.C.A.) 80 F. (2d) 575,[FN15 omitted] an injunction was granted to a news agency to restrain a radio station from broadcasting news reports taken from the newspapers published by plaintiff's members, it being held that the radio station and the newspapers alike disseminated advertising together with news which helped to make it attractive, and therefore they were just as much in commercial competition in the field of publishing news as in that of the sale of advertising. Even though no direct charge is made by a broadcasting station for the entertainment which it furnishes, its broadcast performances are nevertheless for profit in the eyes of the law,

---

[14] It was testified that between 350 and 450 broadcasting stations in the United States use records almost exclusively instead of 'live talent,' both for their commercial and their sustaining programs.

as they are designed to aid in the obtaining of advertising business. Witmark v. Bamberger (D.C.) 291 F. 776 . . . .

On the facts in the present case, therefore, and having in mind the many unique factors which enter into its consideration, we are of opinion that on the ground of unfair competition, apart from any other theory of equitable relief, plaintiff is entitled to the injunction which the court below awarded. . . .

Finally, defendant maintains that, by becoming a member of the National Association of Performing Artists, plaintiff automatically assigned to that association whatever rights he may have had in the records made by his orchestra. Even if that were so, however, it would be of no available concern to defendant. Purdy v. Massey, 306 Pa. 288, 159 A. 545.

The decree of the court below is affirmed; costs to be paid by defendant.

Paul Whiteman and his orchestra in 1921
Photo from sheet music cover in the
collection of Fredrik Tersmeden
(Lund, Sweden)

RCA MFG. CO. V. WHITEMAN
114 F.2d 86 (2d Cir. 1940)

L. HAND, CIRCUIT JUDGE.

This case comes up upon appeals by the plaintiff, RCA Manufacturing Company, Inc., and the defendants, Paul Whiteman and W.B.O. Broadcasting Corporation. Before the action was brought Whiteman had filed a complaint against W.B.O. Broadcasting Corporation and Elin, Inc., to restrain the broadcasting of phonograph records of musical performances by Whiteman's orchestra. By leave of court RCA Manufacturing Company, Inc., then filed the complaint at bar, as ancillary to Whiteman's action, asking the same relief against W.B.O. Broadcasting Corporation and Elin, Inc., as Whiteman had asked in his action, and in addition asking that Whiteman be adjudged to have no interest in the records of his performances, because of contracts between him and itself. Whiteman thereupon discontinued his action, leaving only the ancillary action in which the judgment on appeal was entered. The dispute is as to whether W.B.O. Broadcasting Corporation, as the purchaser of phonographic records prepared by RCA Manufacturing Company, Inc., of Whiteman's orchestral performances, may broadcast them by radio. Whiteman's performances took place in studios of RCA Manufacturing Company, Inc., which arranged for their reproduction upon ordinary phonographic disc records, and which, with the consent of Whiteman, sold the records to the public at large. Of the nine records here in question five were sold between November, 1932, and August 15, 1937, during which period every record bore the legend: 'Not Licensed for Radio Broadcast'. (Apparently the four earlier records did not advise the purchaser of any such limitation.) After August 15, 1937, this notice was changed to read as follows: 'Licensed by Mfr. under U.S. Pats. 1625705, 1637544, RE. 16588 (& other Pats. Pending) Only For Non-Commercial Use on Phonographs in Homes. Mfr. & Original Purchaser Have Agreed This Record Shall Not Be Resold Or Used For Any Other Purpose. See Detailed Notice on Envelope.' These later records were enclosed in envelopes which even more clearly gave notice of the same limitations. W.B.O. Broadcasting Corporation every week bought from a New York company, Bruno-New York, Inc., such records as it needed; it used them thereafter to broadcast over its radio system. Bruno-New York, Inc., had bought the records in question under a contract with RCA Manufacturing Company, Inc. in which they agreed after its date (August 9, 1937) to resell 'only for non-commercial use on phonographs in homes as per the notice appearing on the record labels and envelopes.' It may be assumed that W.B.O. Broadcasting Corporation is charged with notice of the legends on the records, and with the contract of Bruno-New York, Inc., and that it broadcasts them on its radio system in disregard of both.

Paul Whiteman Orchestra Record with notice
limiting resale and use for commercial purposes

The questions raised below were whether Whiteman and/or RCA Manufacturing Company, Inc., had any musical property at common-law in the records which radio broadcasting invaded; whether Whiteman had passed any rights which he may have had to RCA Manufacturing Company, Inc., under certain agreements, not necessary to be set out; and whether, if either Whiteman or RCA Manufacturing Company, Inc., had any such common-law property, the legends and notice enabled them, or either of them, to limit the uses which the buyer might make of the records. The judge held that all of Whiteman's rights had passed to RCA Manufacturing Company, Inc., which for that reason was entitled to enjoin the broadcasting of these records; and that Whiteman was also entitled to an injunction against W.B.O. Broadcasting Corporation because it was unfair competition to broadcast his performances without his consent. All parties appealed except Elin, Inc. The RCA Manufacturing Company, Inc., appealed because the judge did not recognize its common-law artistic property, arising out of the skill and art necessary to obtain good recording, and also because of the affirmative relief granted to Whiteman. Whiteman appealed because of the holding that he had lost all his rights to RCA Manufacturing Company, Inc., under its contracts with him. W.B.O. Broadcasting Corporation appealed because any relief was granted against it.

It is only in comparatively recent times that a virtuoso, conductor, actor, lecturer, or preacher could have any interest in the reproduction of his performance. Until the phonographic record made possible the preservation and reproduction of sound, all audible renditions were of necessity fugitive and transitory; once uttered they died; the nearest approach to their reproduction was mimicry. Of late, however, the power to reproduce the exact quality and sequence of sounds has become possible, and the right to do so, exceedingly valuable; people easily distinguish, or think they distinguish, the rendition of the same score or the same text by their favorites, and they will pay large sums to hear them. Hence this action. It was settled at least a century ago that the monopoly of the right to reproduce the compositions of any author—his 'common-law property' in them—was not limited to words; pictures were included. Turner v. Robinson, 10 Ir.Ch. 121; S.C. 10 Ir.Ch. 522; Prince Albert v. Strange, 1 McN. & G. 25. This right has at times been stated as though it extended to all productions demanding 'intellectual' effort; and for the purposes of this case we shall assume that it covers the performances of an orchestra conductor, and—what is far more doubtful—the skill and art by which a phonographic record maker makes possible the proper recording of those performances upon a disc. It would follow from this that, if a conductor played over the radio, and if his performance was not an abandonment of his rights, it would be unlawful without his consent to record it as it was received from a receiving set and to use the record. Arguendo, we shall also assume that such a performance would not be an abandonment, just as performance of a play, or the delivery of a lecture is not; that is, that it does not 'publish' the work and dedicate it to the public. Ferris v. Frohman, 223 U.S. 424, 435, 32 S.Ct. 263, 56 L.Ed. 492; Nutt v. National Institute, 2 Cir.,

31 F.2d 236; McCarty & Fischer v. White, D.C., 259 F. 364; Uproar Co. v. National Broadcasting Co., D.C., 8 F.Supp. 358. Nevertheless, even if Whiteman's 'common-law property' in his performances survived the sale of the records on which they were inscribed, it would be very difficult to see how he, or a fortiori the maker of the records, could impose valid restrictions upon their resale. Concededly that could not be done (regardless of the present statutory prohibition) if the restriction went to the resale price. Bobbs-Merrill Co. v. Straus, 210 U.S. 339, 28 S.Ct. 722, 52 L.Ed. 1086. . . . We do not, however, have that question to decide, for we think that the 'common-law property' in these performances ended with the sale of the records and that the restriction did not save it; and that if it did, the records themselves could not be clogged with a servitude.

Copyright in any form, whether statutory or at common-law, is a monopoly; it consists only in the power to prevent others from reproducing the copyrighted work. W.B.O. Broadcasting Corporation has never invaded any such right of Whiteman; they have never copied his performances at all; they have merely used those copies which he and the RCA Manufacturing Company, Inc. made and distributed. The putatively protected performances were themselves intended for that purpose and for that alone; the situation was precisely the same as though Whiteman and RCA Manufacturing Company, Inc., had combined to produce an original musical score and inscribe it upon records. The records at bar embodied Whiteman's 'common-law property'—his contribution as a conductor—in precisely the same way that the record of such a score would embody his composition. Hence the question is no different from whether he might disseminate a musical score to the public at large, but impose a limitation upon it that buyers should not use it to broadcast for profit. Whatever might be said of that—if the sale were not a 'publication'—it will hardly be argued that if it was a 'publication' in the sense that that destroys the 'common-law property', the restriction upon the use of the record would be valid notwithstanding. Restrictions upon the uses of chattels once absolutely sold are at least prima facie invalid; they must be justified for some exceptional reason, normally they are 'repugnant' to the transfer of title. If 'the common-law property' in the rendition be gone, then anyone may copy it who chances to hear it, and may use it as he pleases. It would be the height of 'unreasonableness' to forbid any uses to the owner of the record which were open to anyone who might choose to copy the rendition from the record. To revert to the illustration of a musical score, it would be absurd to forbid the broadcast for profit of its record, if any hearer might copy it and broadcast the copy. Thus, even if Whiteman and RCA Manufacturing Company, Inc., have a 'common-law property' which performance does not end, it is immaterial, unless the right to copy the rendition from the records was preserved through the notice of the restriction.

As applied to books, where the problem is precisely the same, there is not very much law as to whether such restrictions prevent complete dedication, but the judges who have passed upon the question have declared, at times with much certainty, that they are nugatory. In 1898 the Court of Appeals of New York flatly so decided in Jewelers Mercantile Agency v. Jewelers Publishing Co., 155 N.Y. 241, 49 N.E. 872, 41 L.R.A. 846, 63 Am.St.Rep. 666, and that is the leading case. . . . In his dissenting opinion in International News Service v. Associated Press, 248 U.S. 215, 256, 39 S.Ct. 68, 63 L.Ed. 211, 2 A.L.R. 293, Mr. Justice Brandeis spoke of the law as 'well-settled' to that effect. . . . It is quite true that if 'publication' were merely a question of intent, these decisions are wrong, for the intent is obvious not to dedicate the whole right. The problem is not so simple; in dealing with a monopoly the law imposes its own limits. Certainly when the 'common-law property' is in a work which the Copyright Act, 17 U.S.C.A. 1 et seq., covers, there can be no doubt; Congress has created the monopoly in exchange for a dedication, and when the monopoly expires the dedication must be complete. If the records were registrable under the act, the restriction would therefore certainly not limit the dedication. The fact that they are not within the act should make no difference. It is indeed argued that by virtue of Donaldson v. Becket, 4 Burr. 2408, there is a perpetual common-law copyright in works not copyrightable under the act; we have answered that argument in Fashion Originators Guild v. Federal Trade Commission, 2 Cir., 114 F.2d 80, and need not repeat what we said. That being true, we see no reason why the same acts that unconditionally dedicate the common-law copyright in works copyrightable under the act, should not do the same in the case of works not copyrightable. Otherwise it would be possible, at least pro tanto, to have the advantage of dissemination of the work at large, and to retain a perpetual though partial, monopoly in it. That is contrary to the whole policy of the Copyright Act and of the Constitution. Any relief which justice demands must be found in extending statutory copyright to such works, not in recognizing perpetual monopolies, however limited their scope.

It is true that the law is otherwise in Pennsylvania, whose Supreme Court in 1937 decided that such a legend as the records at bar bore, fixed a servitude upon the discs in the hands of any buyer. Waring v. WDAS Broadcasting Company, 327 Pa. 433, 194 A. 631. We have of course given the most respectful consideration to the conclusions of that great court, but with much regret we find ourselves unconvinced for the reasons we have tried to state. However, since that is the law of Pennsylvania and since the broadcasting will reach receiving sets in that state, it will constitute a tort committed there; and if an injunction could be confined to those sets alone, it would be proper. It cannot; for even if it be mechanically possible to prevent any broadcasting through the angle which the state of Pennsylvania subtends at the transmission station, that would shut out points both in front of, and beyond, Pennsylvania. We must therefore choose between denying any injunction whatever—since in our judgment the act is unlawful only in Pennsylvania—or enjoining W.B.O. Broadcasting Corporation from broadcasting throughout the Union and in Canada in order to prevent a tort in Pennsylvania alone. This would be an obvious misuse of the writ which goes only in aid of justice.

Whiteman and the plaintiff also rest their case upon the theory of unfair competition, depending for that upon International News Service v. Associated Press, supra, 248 U.S. 215, 39 S.Ct. 68, 63 L.Ed. 211, 2 A.L.R. 293. That much discussed decision really held no more than that a western newspaper might not take advantage of the fact that it was published some hours later than papers in the east, to copy the news which the plaintiff had collected at its own expense. In spite of some general language it must be confined to that situation (Cheney Bros. v. Doris Silk Corp., 2 Cir., 35 F.2d 279, 281), certainly it cannot be used as a cover to prevent competitors from ever appropriating the results of the industry, skill, and expense of others. 'Property' is a historical concept; one may bestow much labor and ingenuity which inures only to the public benefit; 'ideas', for instance, though upon them all civilization is built, may never be 'owned'. The law does not protect them at all, but only their expression; and how far that protection shall go is a question of more or less; an author has no 'natural right' even so far, and is not free to make his own terms with the public.

In the case at bar if Whiteman and RCA Manufacturing Company, Inc., cannot bring themselves within the law of common-law copyright, there is nothing to justify a priori any continuance of their control over the activities of the public to which they have seen fit to dedicate the larger part of their contribution. We are adjured that courts must adjust themselves to new conditions, and that in the case at bar justice clearly points the way to some relief. We cannot agree; no doubt we should be jealous to execute all reasonable implications of established doctrines; but we should be equally jealous not to undertake the composition of substantial conflicts of interests, between which neither the common-law, nor the statute, has given any clue to its preference. We cannot know how Congress would solve this issue; we can guess—and our guess is that it would refuse relief as we are refusing it—but if our guess were the opposite, we should have no right to enforce it. If the talents of conductors of orchestras are denied that compensation which is necessary to evoke their efforts because they get too little for phonographic records, we have no means of knowing it, or any right to assume it; and it is idle to invoke the deus ex machina of a 'progress' which is probably spurious, and would not be for us to realize, if it were genuine. . . . [¶]

It follows that the complaint must be dismissed, and for reasons which make it unnecessary to determine how far Whiteman's contracts with RCA Manufacturing Company, Inc., preserved any common-law copyrights he might have had, if they had survived the sale of the records.

Judgment   reversed;   complaint   dismissed;   costs   to   W.B.O.
Broadcasting Corporation.

Ed. Note: In December, 1940, the U.S. Supreme Court denied a
petition for a writ of certiorari in the above case, 61 S.Ct. 393,
effectively upholding the Second Circuit's conclusion that property
rights in a sound recording ended with the sale of the record.

NOTES AND QUESTIONS

1.   In *Capitol Records, Inc. v. Mercury Records Corp.*, 221 F.2d 657 (2d
Cir. 1955), the Second Circuit considered an appeal from an injunction against
the   manufacture   and   distribution   of   phonograph   records   containing
"recordings of performances by highly gifted artists." The case raised several
issues regarding the right to protect phonograph records against unauthorized
copying and distribution, but it is often cited for its analysis of the question of
whether phonograph records were copyrightable under federal law. In that
regard, the Second Circuit stated:

> There can be no doubt that, under the Constitution, Congress could
> give to one who performs a public domain musical composition the
> exclusive right to make and vend phonograph records of that
> rendition. The question is whether Congress has done so.

> It is plain that, prior to the 1909 amendment of the Copyright Act,
> Congress had not accorded to one who performed such a composition
> that exclusive right. The Supreme Court held in White-Smith Music
> Publishing Company v. Apollo Company, 209 U.S. 1, 28 S.Ct. 319, 52
> L.Ed. 655, that the holder of the copyright of a musical composition
> did not have the exclusive right to make and vend music rolls for
> mechanical pianos. It was determined that the music rolls were not
> 'copies' of the musical composition within the copyright owner's
> exclusive right to make 'copies' of the composition. . . .

> To meet the holding that the owner of the copyright of a musical
> composition could not enjoin the making and vending of music rolls
> and records, Congress amended the Act in 1909, Act March 4, 1909,
> c. 320, 35 Stat. 1075. To change that result it could have declared that
> a mechanical reproduction of a musical composition should constitute
> a 'copy' thereof within the meaning of the Act. Under such an
> amendment a virtuoso might copyright his rendition by depositing
> two records with the Librarian of Congress under section 4956 above
> quoted and thereafter be entitled to enjoin the reproduction of copies
> of those records. Congress, however, did not adopt that plan. Instead
> it enacted in section 1(e), 17 U.S.C. § 1(e), that any person complying

with the provisions of the Act should have the exclusive right 'to perform the copyrighted work publicly for profit if it be a musical composition; and * * * to make * * * any form of record (of it) in which the thought of an author may be recorded and from which it may be read or reproduced'.

Thus Congress met the narrow problem presented by the Apollo case. . . . No attempt was made to meet a case like that at bar where, in the nature of things, the performance of the artist could be copyrighted only in the form of a record. . . .

That the actual intent of Congress coincided with the intent as expressed in these words of the statute as amended in 1909 appears from the Report of the Committee on Patents which accompanied the House of Representatives bill that embodied the amendment. That Report, H.R.Rep., No. 2222, 60th Cong., 2d Sess. 10, stated, immediately following the discussion of section 1(e):

> 'It is not the intention of the committee to extend the right of copyright to the mechanical reproductions themselves, but only to give the composer or copyright proprietor the control, in accordance with the provisions of the bill, of the manufacture and use of such devices.'

The Second Circuit went on, however, to affirm the grant of injunctive relief, finding that the distribution of the recordings was not a "publication" under federal law and thus that New York common law copyright applied to provide a remedy to the plaintiff for protection against unauthorized copying of the recordings. **Judge Learned Hand dissented** from this result, agreeing in large part with the court's analysis of the federal question:

> I also believe that the performance or rendition of a 'musical composition' is a 'Writing' under Article I, § 8, Cl. 8 of the Constitution separate from, and additional to, the 'composition' itself. It follows that Congress could grant the performer a copyright upon it, provided it was embodied in a physical form capable of being copied. The propriety of this appears, when we reflect that a musical score in ordinary notation does not determine the entire performance, certainly not when it is sung or played on a stringed or wind instrument. Musical notes are composed of a 'fundamental note' with harmonics and overtones which do not appear on the score. There may indeed be instruments—e.g. percussive—which do not allow any latitude, though I doubt even that; but in the vast number of renditions, the performer has a wide choice, depending upon his gifts, and this makes his rendition pro tanto quite as original a 'composition' as an 'arrangement' or 'adaptation' of the score itself, which § 1(b) makes copyrightable. Now that it has become possible to capture these contributions of the individual performer upon a physical object that can be made to reproduce them, there should be no doubt that this is within the Copyright Clause of the Constitution.

That, however, does not answer the question whether Congress has protected this 'common-law property' by copyright; and I am also disposed to believe that it has not done so. . . .

2.   The *Fonotipia* case was decided shortly after the 1909 Act went into effect. Take another look at the court's *dicta* discussing the possible impact of the 1909 Act above. Was the court's characterization of the impact of the 1909 Act's provisions regarding recordings of musical compositions accurate? Why or why not? Based upon the language of Section 1(e) of the 1909 Act and the court's reasoning in *Mercury Records* quoted in Note 1, above, consider the possible arguments about whether the Act provided a copyright or some other interest in sound recordings of a musical composition. How could the *Fonotipia* court have arrived at its understanding of the possible reach of the 1909 Act?

3.   Why was the focus of the court's discussion and analysis in *Fonotipia*, *Waring*, and *Whiteman* on the equitable claim of unfair competition?

4.   In *Waring*, the court limited the property right that it recognized for performers to "those artists who elevate interpretations to the realm of independent works of art." Later, in Chapter 9, you will see a similar standard in the context of state law misappropriation of voice claims. What do you think about this legal standard? What evidence might a court need to consider to decide whether this standard is met? Should judges and juries be charged with making these kinds of evaluations? If not, can you think of other ways to distinguish between performances (or voices) that deserve protection and those that do not, or should all performances be treated equally? Why or why not?

5.   As between *Waring* and *Whiteman*, which case do you think reaches the most appropriate resolution? Why?

6.   Which of the themes introduced at the start of subsection D did you see recurring most often in the case analyses above, and which do you think were the most compelling?

Note that some of these issues and themes will be particularly pertinent to the current state of the music industry. For example, performance rights in sound recordings like those addressed in *Waring* re-emerged as a hot topic in music law in the context of the digital performance right and state law protections afforded to pre-1972 sound recordings—a topic expressly addressed in the 2018 Music Modernization Act.

CHAPTER III

EARLY CHALLENGES IN ENFORCING THE PERFORMANCE RIGHT IN COMPOSITIONS: *CAN'T BUY ME LOVE*[1]

■ ■ ■

Although a performance right in musical compositions had been created by federal statute in 1897, composers and publishers did not make any real effort to enforce that right until several years after the Copyright Revision of 1909. The House Report for the 1897 amendment stated that the first purpose of the proposed law was:

> [T]o secure to musical compositions the same measure of protection under the copyright law as is now afforded to productions of a strictly dramatic character. There can be no reason why the same protection should not be extended to one species of literary property of this general character as to the other, and the omission to include protective provisions for musical compositions in the law sought to be amended was doubtless the result of oversight.[2]

The 1897 statute grant of a performance right provided that:

> Any person publicly performing or representing any dramatic or musical composition for which a copyright has been obtained, without the consent of the proprietor of said dramatic or musical composition, . . . shall be liable for damages therefor, such damages in all cases to be assessed at such sum, not less than one hundred dollars for the first and fifty dollars for every subsequent performance, as to the court shall appear just. If the unlawful performance and representation be willful and for profit, such person or persons shall be guilty of a misdemeanor and upon conviction be imprisoned for a period not exceeding one year.[3]

As noted in Chapter 2, the 1909 Act adopted different governing language for the performance right in musical compositions than that in the 1897 Act. Section 1(e) granted the right to "perform the copyrighted

---

[1] John Lennon & Paul McCartney (1964); released by the Beatles on A HARD DAY'S NIGHT (1964).

[2] H. Rep. No. 54–2290 (Dec. 7, 1896).

[3] 29 Stat. 481, 481–82 (Jan. 6, 1897).

work publicly for profit if it be a musical composition and for the purpose of public performance for profit."[4] Note the difference in language between the 1897 Act, which only included proof that a performance be "for profit" in criminal prosecutions, and the general "for profit" requirement in the 1909 Act. The 1909 Act also makes no mention of lack of consent as a precondition for liability, although of course a license by the owner of the composition would serve as a defense to any claimed liability for publicly performing a composition for profit.

In fact, there was some debate in Congress about the nature of the right that was granted in 1897 and whether mere publication of a composition was sufficient to prove consent to perform. Some representatives felt the criminal penalties (which were a new addition to U.S. copyright law) were too draconian; others complained about the nationwide form of injunctions that was adopted for enforcement of the right (primarily against traveling shows).[5] But there was also an important debate about what the performance right should encompass, and a proposed amendment would have added the following statement: "The printing, publication, and sale of such dramatic or musical composition by the proprietor thereof shall be deemed a sufficient consent to the public performance or representation thereof."[6] Even the congressmen sponsoring the bill seemed to agree with the following characterization:

> Mr. COOPER of Wisconsin. But there is no necessity for [the proposed amendment], because the bill as it stands [and as it was ultimately enacted] is absolutely correct on that point. There can be no unlawful performance unless it be without the consent of the owner, and if I copyright a song and sell it to dealers to be sold by them over the counter, anybody who purchases it from them buys with it my consent that he use it in any way he may choose, and for profit or otherwise, in his discretion. It is the property of the music dealer, and not my property, as soon as I have sold it to him to put on his shelves. . . . [If the owner of a copyright] places the articles with storekeepers generally to be sold by them absolutely and without condition, then the people who buy do so with his consent that they use the article for profit if they desire.[7]

---

4   Copyright Act of 1909, Pub. L. 60–349 (March 4, 1909).

5   *E.g.*, CONG. REC., CR-1896-1210, 89–90 (Dec. 10, 1896), *available at* http://www.copyright history.org/cam/tools/request/showRepresentation?id=representation_us_1896e&pagenumber=1_ 1&show=transcription. In a passionate argument for the need for greater punishment for violation of intellectual property rights than physical property rights that was repeated in support of modern expansions to penalties for copyright infringement, Representative Lemuel Quigg from New York stated, "I say that unless you draw the law so strictly that you can stop this piracy by everybody everywhere, you have not drawn it strictly enough to protect anybody anywhere." *Id.* at 90.

6   *Id.* at 89.

7   *Id.* at 90.

This argument—that publication for sale of the sheet music for a song is deemed consent for its public performance for profit—may be one reason why there was no effort by music publishers to enforce the performance right granted in 1897 until after enactment of the 1909 Copyright Act. You will also see in some of the cases that follow that it was an argument made against liability on the part of the defendants in lawsuits brought to enforce the 1909 Act's performance right. Other reasons for the initial lack of enforcement of the performance right by composers and publishers likely include both a failure to appreciate the commercial value of the right, as well as the publishing industry's increasing need to look for alternative revenue sources after the growth of the phonograph industry began to impact sales of sheet music.[8]

Yet another likely factor in a lack of effort to enforce the performance right prior to enactment of the 1909 Act was that the growth in music publishing income in the Tin Pan Alley era relied heavily on song "plugging" by music publishers, where performers (often the composers themselves) were paid by the publishing houses to take their songs to the public as a means of increasing sales of sheet music. Professional performers were also given incentives by music publishers to incorporate their newest songs into minstrel shows and concerts as a method of advertising their collections and increasing demand. The idea that the performance of compositions enhanced their sales and was a necessary part of promoting them was a powerful one, grounded in the realities of the business, and was likely an initial reason for restraint in seeking recompense for performances of compositions. However, as more and more public venues began incorporating background music—first via live performances, and later via phonographs and radio—music publishers recognized that these venues were making commercial use of their property without permission or compensation and sought to capitalize on the performance right.[9]

Finally, the right itself is inherently difficult to enforce, particularly by an individual copyright owner. Performances were by their nature ephemeral and disparate in time and place, making proof of infringement of the performance right more circumstantial than direct. For this relatively new right to be effectively enforced, its scope needed to be tested and mechanisms needed to be established for copyright owners to be able

---

[8]   See Harry P. Warner, Radio & Television Rights: The Law of Copyright, Trade-marks and Unfair Competition and the Broadcasting Industry 336 (Matthew Bender & Co. 1953).

[9]   See DAVID SUISMAN, SELLING SOUNDS: THE COMMERCIAL REVOLUTION IN AMERICAN MUSIC 59–89, 159–60 (Harvard University Press, 2009). In fact, music publishers were heavily involved in the drafting of the 1909 Copyright Act, not only with respect to the crafting of the mechanical right, but also with respect to performances for profit. "As far as the publishers were concerned, . . . the difference was between unregulated and regulated distribution and between someone else's profits and their own. Even if the revenues of publishers as a group were increasing, they objected to their musical products' being systematically used as raw material in other increasingly profitable businesses." *Id.* at 160.

to police the multitude of venues where music might be performed publicly for profit within the meaning of the statute. Because the Copyright Act itself did not provide these answers, copyright owners developed their own collective enforcement mechanisms by establishing performing rights organizations.

The first performing rights organization (PRO)—the Société des Auteurs, Compositeurs, et Editeurs de Musique (SACEM)—was formed in France in 1851; other European countries followed suit in the years from 1882–1903. After SACEM opened a New York branch in 1911, in 1913 a group of music publishers and composers, including Victor Herbert, Irving Berlin, Ernest R. Ball, and Gene Buck, gathered together to form the American Society of Composers, Authors, and Publishers (ASCAP) for the purpose of protecting the performance rights of U.S. composers and publishers. As described by the court in *Broadcast Music v. Taylor*, 55 N.Y.S.2d 94, 100 (Sup. Ct. 1945), before ASCAP's founding, songwriters went largely uncompensated for public performances of their songs in the first years after the performance right was granted, "largely . . . due to the inherent difficulties which confronted them individually in enforcing their rights to such compensation. Individually they lacked the means and the ability to detect infringers throughout the country, and to call them to account."

Although ASCAP was inspired by its European predecessors, it took a different approach to collective enforcement of the performance right.

> Unlike SACEM, which sought to collect a fee based on each performance of a member's work, the aim of ASCAP was to license its members' works en masse to subscriber organizations (hotels, restaurants, and so on) and at the end of year, after covering its operating costs, to divide its revenues among its members (split equally between composers and publishers), prorated according to class.[10]

The "class structure" was controversial from the start but persisted for decades—it was based upon factors including "seniority, catalogue size, sheet music sales, and number of hits"[11] and tended to weigh more heavily in favor of the powerhouse Tin Pan Alley publishers and their star composers.

ASCAP's initial attempts to collect payments in exchange for blanket licenses to perform compositions in its repertoire were largely rebuffed, with owners of venues asserting that they did not charge the public for the music that was played and thus that it was not a public performance "for profit" covered by the 1909 Act. In response, ASCAP brought several carefully planned lawsuits, with well-known composers and publishing

---

[10]　*Id.* at 170–71.

[11]　*Id.* at 171.

houses as plaintiffs.[12] Their success in these test cases, first in the context of live performances of compositions in hotel restaurants and later in the context of radio broadcasts, helped to create the blueprint for the structure of the modern music industry.

CONSIDER AS YOU READ . . .

- Keep the themes introduced in Chapter 2 in mind as you read the materials below. Do any reappear? Do you see any new analytical themes or arguments arising? What are they?

- Can you think of alternative methods of enforcing the performance right in compositions than those that arose with the formation of PROs? Does it appear that PROs are focused more on control over how and when a work is performed, or are they focused primarily on revenue?

- Is antitrust regulation necessary when, as now, competing PROs exist? Is music different from other types of commodities? How, and why might those differences matter for purposes of antitrust oversight? And how are the antitrust arguments impacted today when licensees on the "other side of the table" from the PROs are some of the largest companies in the world?

- What are the most important factors that should be considered in determining a fair rate for a performance license? Should all compositions be treated the same? Should all types of performances be treated the same?

- Given the 2015 recommendations of the Copyright Office and 2016 conclusions from the DOJ's review of the ASCAP and BMI consent decrees, what do you think Congress should do, if anything, to modernize the licensing process for performance rights in compositions?

---

[12] DAVID SUISMAN, SELLING SOUNDS: THE COMMERCIAL REVOLUTION IN AMERICAN MUSIC 172 (Harvard University Press, 2009).

A. EARLY CASES ADDRESSING THE PERFORMANCE RIGHT IN MUSICAL COMPOSITIONS

As you read the materials that follow, first in connection with the meaning and scope of the performance right and then in connection with antitrust and other issues that arose out of the formation of performance rights organizations to enforce composers' performance rights, consider what the music industry might look like today if the results in these cases had been different.

1. PUBLIC PERFORMANCE FOR PROFIT

Two weeks' vacation in New York, the nation's best summer resort (circa 1918),
by the Vanderbilt Hotel (New York, N.Y.)
From the Library of Congress

HERBERT V. SHANLEY CO.
242 U.S. 591 (1917)

MR. JUSTICE HOLMES delivered the opinion of the court:

These two cases present the same question: whether the performance of a copyrighted musical composition in a restaurant or hotel without charge for admission to hear it infringes the exclusive right of the owner of the copyright to perform the work publicly for profit. Act of March 4, 1909, chap. 320, § 1(e), 35 Stat. at L. 1075, Comp. Stat. 1913, § 9517. The last-numbered case was decided before the other and may be stated first. The plaintiff owns the copyright of a lyric comedy in which is a march called 'From Maine to Oregon.' It took out a separate copyright for the march and published it separately. The defendant hotel company caused this march to be performed in the dining room of the Vanderbilt Hotel for the entertainment of guests during meal times, in the way now common, by an orchestra employed and paid by the company. It was held by the circuit court of appeals, reversing the decision of the district court, that this was not a performance for profit within the meaning of the act. 136 C. C. A. 639, 221 Fed. 229.

The other case is similar so far as the present discussion is concerned. The plaintiffs were the composers and owners of a comic opera entitled 'Sweethearts,' containing a song of the same title as a leading feature in the performance. There is a copyright for the opera and also one for the song, which is published and sold separately. This the Shanley Company caused to be sung by professional singers, upon a stage in its restaurant on Broadway, accompanied by an orchestra. The district court . . . followed the decision in 136 C. C. A. 639, 221 Fed. 229, as to public performance for profit. 222 Fed. 344. The decree was affirmed by the circuit court of appeals. 143 C. C. A. 460, 229 Fed. 340.

If the rights under the copyright are infringed only by a performance where money is taken at the door, they are very imperfectly protected. Performances not different in kind from those of the defendants could be given that might compete with and even destroy the success of the monopoly that the law intends the plaintiffs to have. It is enough to say that there is no need to construe the statute so narrowly. The defendants' performances are not eleemosynary. They are part of a total for which the public pays, and the fact that the price of the whole is attributed to a particular item which those present are expected to order is not important. It is true that the music is not the sole object, but neither is the food, which probably could be got cheaper elsewhere. The object is a repast in surroundings that to people having limited powers of conversation, or disliking the rival noise, give a luxurious pleasure not to be had from eating a silent meal. If music did not pay, it would be given up. If it pays, it pays out of the public's pocket. Whether it pays or not, the purpose of employing it is profit, and that is enough.

Decree reversed.

2. PERFORMING MUSIC IN MOVIE THEATERS

Advertisement for Movie Theater Organ, Exhibitor's Trade Review (Sep–Nov 1922)
Lib. Cong. Packard Campus, available at
https://archive.org/download/exhibitorstr00newy/exhibitorstr00newy.pdf
(at 765)(9/2/22 vol. 12, no. 14)

HARMS V. COHEN
279 F. 276 (E.D. Pa. 1922)

THOMPSON, DISTRICT JUDGE.

The plaintiff, a corporation engaged in the business of publishing and selling musical compositions, has brought this suit as owner of the copyright in a musical composition entitled 'Tulip Time,' from 'Ziegfield Follies, 1919.' The defendant is alleged to be the owner and manager and operator of the Model Theater, where moving pictures and photo plays are exhibited and musical compositions are played, and to which the general public is admitted upon the payment of an admission fee. It is charged that the defendant, in infringement of the copyright, has given public performances for profit of the musical composition in question, by causing it to be played and performed in his theater for the entertainment and amusement of his patrons.

The answer, after denying ownership and control of the theater on the part of the defendant, and denying knowledge of many of the averments of the bill, avers, inter alia, in paragraph 12 of the answer:

'Defendant avers that no musical composition is performed or has been performed in said theater for profit.'

And in paragraph 16:

'That there is employed an organist, who has contracted to play while the motion picture and photoplays are being exhibited, such short excerpts of musical selections as may appear to her fitting and appropriate to the action of that portion of the motion picture at that precise instant being shown upon the screen. The said organist is an independent contractor, over whose actions while playing the defendant has no control. The defendant further avers that entire musical compositions are not played, but that merely short excerpts, continuously changing with the theme of the motion picture, are given. Defendant avers that no charge is made for the privilege of listening to the playing of music, which music is purely incidental, and not a part of the motion picture exhibited by the defendant in the conduct of his motion picture business; that the songs played in said theater were not performed by the defendant, or caused to be performed by him, publicly for profit.'

While the defendant denies that he owns or operated the Model Theater, the answer admits that at the theater daily exhibitions of motion pictures and photo plays are given, to which the general public is admitted, on payment of an admission fee. I fail to see any distinction in law in favor of the performance of copyright musical compositions in moving picture theaters to which a charge for admission is made, as opposed to their performance in public restaurants, as an additional attraction to the customers of such restaurants, which latter were held to be performances for profit within the meaning of the Copyright Act in the case of Herbert v. Shanley Co., 242 U.S. 591, 37 Sup.Ct. 232, 61 L.Ed. 511. It may be assumed that music selected because it is 'fitting and appropriate to the action of that portion of the motion picture at that precise instant being shown upon the screen,' and 'continuously changing with the theme of the motion picture,' is played for the additional attraction to the audience and for its enjoyment and amusement. As Mr. Justice Holmes says in the case above cited:

'If music did not pay, it would be given up. If it pays, it pays out of the public's pocket. Whether it pays or not, the purpose of employing it is profit, and that is enough.'

As to the averments that the organist is an independent contractor, over whose actions, while playing, the defendant has no control, and that she plays only such short excerpts as may to her appear fitting and appropriate, they do not constitute a defense against the charge in the bill. He who employs a musician to perform in an exhibition for profit, under a contract by which the musician has authority to play whatever compositions are in accordance with her judgment appropriate and fitting, must be held responsible for all that is done by the musician. By giving her that authority the employer acquiesces in and ratifies whatever she does. If under his contract he has parted with the right to exercise this control over her actions, without making inquiry as to what she intends to play, he yet must be deemed to have taken part, and to have given her general authority to perform copyright compositions. . . .

That the playing consisted of short excerpts is no defense. . . .

[¶]. . . . Paragraph 17 of the answer is as follows:

"Defendant is informed, believes, and therefore charges, that it has become a universal custom of musical composers and publishers to issue, and to send out to musicians in every part of the United States, what are known as 'professional copies' of their musical compositions, with a request that these musicians publicly perform said compositions and thereby 'plug' or popularize and advertise said compositions to the ultimate benefit of the authors and publishers. Defendant is informed, believes, and therefore charges, that professional copies of this selection, to wit, 'Tulip Time,' as well as others published by the plaintiff, were furnished by it, or through its agents, to the organist employed by the owner; that the issuance of such professional copies constituted a license to the recipient thereof to publicly perform such musical composition; that the plaintiff acquiesced in such public performance of the musical selection wherever and in what manner it was so played, and that the plaintiff was greatly benefited, and not damaged, by any such performance."

If the custom is as stated, the issuing and sending out of professional copies is, as part of the custom, accompanied by the request for public performance by the musicians to whom the copies are sent. The charge that the professional copies of 'Tulip Time' were furnished to the organist is insufficient to bring the plaintiff within the custom, because there is no averment that the sending out was accompanied with the request constituting a part of the custom. The mere giving of professional copies does not constitute a license. The averment of acquiescence in public performance clearly is intended to imply that the acquiescence was through the sending out of the professional copies, for there are no other facts averred upon which the conclusion of acquiescence is based. The averment that the plaintiff was greatly benefited, and not damaged, by any such performance, is clearly immaterial, and the seventeenth paragraph as a whole must be stricken out.

Paragraph 18 of the answer avers in substance that the plaintiff is a member of the American Association of Composers, Authors, and Publishers, which includes a majority, if not all, of the composers, authors, and publishers in the United States; that the members thereof, for the purpose of securing to themselves 'an unreasonable and extortionate profit, and for the purpose of establishing and maintaining an unreasonable and extortionate license fee for the performance of their musical numbers,' have combined and assigned to the society the privilege to issue licenses for the performance of the music of the members, and to charge such sums as the society might fix; that the society appointed an agent to issue licenses for the performance of the musical compositions in Philadelphia; that the agent demanded extortionate fees for such licenses, which the defendant refused to pay.

It is averred that the plaintiff is therefore engaged with others in a combination or conspiracy in restraint of interstate trade or commerce, in violation of section 1 of the Sherman Act; that the present bill is one of eight simultaneously brought by members of the alleged combination; and that the present suit is not a bona fide action to protect the plaintiff's rights, but is part of a combination or conspiracy to create a monopoly in the musical composing and publishing business, in restraint of trade, and to demand unreasonable and extortionate profit from moving picture theater owners and lessees.

Under the Copyright Act (section 1 (Comp. St. Sec. 9517)) the copyright owner has the exclusive right to print, reprint, publish, copy, and vend the copyrighted work, and under section 41 (Comp. St. Sec. 9562) the copyright is distinct from the property in the material object copyrighted, and the sale or conveyance by gift or otherwise of the material object does not, of itself, constitute a transfer of the copyright, nor does the assignment of the copyright constitute a transfer of the title to the material object.

Does a combination of composers, authors, and publishers, under which extortionate license fees are demanded for public performances for profit of the musical numbers copyrighted by the various members, constitute a violation of the Sherman Act (Comp. St. Secs. 8820–8823, 8827–8830)? The agreement under which the alleged unlawful combination was formed is not before the court, and the question must be decided upon the averments in the answer. In order to constitute a defense, it must be established that one charged with infringement may be relieved from liability if the plaintiff is engaged in an alleged unlawful combination. Congress has declared in the Sherman Act that all such contracts and combinations in the form of trust or otherwise are illegal, but, on the other hand, has granted to musical composers a monopoly in their works, and has provided methods for enforcing their rights in the courts. If an infringer, when those remedies are invoked, may set up as a defense that the copyright is the object of an unlawful combination, and is being used to carry into effect the purposes of an unlawful combination, may he thus escape the results of his own wrongful act? If he can set up an unlawful combination as a defense against his infringement of the copyright, then any one who wrongfully trespasses upon or takes the property of another may set up as a defense that the property was being held and used by a member of an unlawful combination in carrying out the purposes of that combination. It would follow, if one took possession of cattle or beef belonging to a corporation or individual, a member of a combination for fixing the price of cattle or beef in restraint of trade, he would be relieved from liability to pay for the property so taken, or from returning it to its owner, upon producing proof that the owner was engaged in such unlawful combination. In the same manner one might with impunity take possession of oil, gasoline, sugar, or other commodities belonging to members of an alleged trust or combination in restraint of trade. But there is no provision in the Sherman Act divesting members of combinations in restraint of trade of their property. The remedies under that act are clearly defined and are exclusive. . . .

But a copyright is an intangible thing, and it is separate and distinct from the material object copyrighted, and the right under a copyright to perform musical compositions is not trade or commerce, any more than producing plays is trade or commerce, People v. Klaw, 55 Misc.Rep. 72, 106 N.Y.Supp. 341; or producing grand opera, Metropolitan Opera Co. v. Hammerstein, 162 App.Div. 691, 147 N.Y.Supp. 532; or the giving of exhibitions of baseball games, National League et al. v. Federal Baseball Club et al., 269 Fed. 681, 50 App.D.C. 165.

The answer does not set up that the defendant is affected in any other way by the alleged unlawful combination, except by his being prevented from producing the plaintiff's copyrighted music. The material object, the sheets of music, are not involved. If, therefore, the material object is not involved, so far as the defendant is concerned, the answer does not show that interstate commerce is directly affected by the combination, and it is therefore no defense. . . . Paragraph 18 of the answer must therefore be stricken out.

It is ordered that the motion to strike out be granted, in so far as is consistent with this opinion, and otherwise be denied.

3. RADIO BROADCASTS OF LIVE MUSICAL PERFORMANCES

Bamberger's Department Store at
131 Market Street in Newark, NJ,
with WOR radio towers on top.

M. WITMARK & SONS V. L. BAMBERGER & CO.
291 F. 776 (D.N.J. 1923)

LYNCH, DISTRICT JUDGE.

The defendant conducts a gigantic department store in the city of Newark, N.J., and sells its wares at retail throughout the state of New Jersey, if not in adjacent states. Since February, 1922, it has conducted a radio department wherein radio equipment of all sorts is sold. It has also established and conducts a licensed radio broadcasting station known as Station WOR, from which vocal and instrumental concerts and other entertainment and information are broadcasted on a wave length of 405 meters. The plaintiff owns the musical composition entitled 'Mother Machree,' and under the Copyright Act of 1909 (Comp. St. Sec. 9517 et seq.) possesses the exclusive right to perform that composition publicly for profit.

The plaintiff, alleging that the defendant performed, or caused to be performed, its composition 'Mother Machree' by means of singing from the broadcasting station WOR and that this performance by the defendant was publicly for profit, prays that a preliminary injunction issue restraining the defendant from the further performance of its copyrighted song. The defendant denies that this broadcasting of the copyrighted 'Mother Machree' was or is for profit, its contention being that because everything it broadcasts is broadcasted without charge or cost to radio listeners, there is no performance publicly for profit within the meaning of the Copyright Act.

It being extremely unlikely that any facts developed upon final hearing will alter the undisputed situation now presented, and both parties desiring a speedy final determination of the issue, the court is disposed, at this time, to register its conclusions as to the law.

The question simmered down is: What is meant by the words 'publicly for profit'? Fortunately, those words have been construed by the United States Supreme Court in the case of Herbert v. Shanley Co., 242 U.S. 591, 37 Sup.Ct. 232, 61 L.Ed. 511, a case frequently referred to by counsel on both sides of this cause. . . . Justice Holmes, in speaking for the court of last resort, had this to say:

> "If the rights under the copyright are infringed only by a performance where money is taken at the door they are very imperfectly protected. . . . The defendants' performances are not eleemosynary. They are part of a total for which the public pays, and the fact that the price of the whole is attributed to a particular item which those present are expected to order, is not important. . . . If music did not pay it would be given up. If it pays it pays out of the public's pocket. Whether it pays or not the purpose of employing it is profit and that is enough. Decrees reversed."

It is strenuously argued in behalf of the defendant in the instant cause that it was the view of the court of last resort that the facts, as developed in the Shanley situation, showed that there was a direct charge to those who patronized the restaurant—a direct charge for and on account of music which was collected from persons dining there. So far as appears, there was only one 'item' charged for, to wit, food. In fixing the charge for food the restaurant proprietor undoubtedly took into consideration many items in addition to the cost of the food and the preparation and service of it. There was 'attributed to' the 'item' food the musical entertainment and other attractions afforded the patrons. The diner at no time had the subject of entertainment charge called to his attention except in the high price of the food which he was permitted to procure. This, in our opinion, was an indirect way of collecting the charge for musical entertainment from those who were there to pay. To constitute a direct charge, it seems to us that there would have to be an admission fee charged at the entrance to the dining hall or a specific fee for entertainment would have to be charged the listener either while in or about to leave the premises.

There is another case which strikes us as being quite helpful. In the case of Harms et al. v. Cohen, 279 Fed. 276, District Judge Thompson held that the playing of copyrighted music by a pianist in a motion picture theater was an infringement of the copyright and relief was accorded the owner thereof. In that case an admission charge was collected from all who entered the theater for the purpose of viewing motion pictures. Incidental to the exhibition was the playing by a pianist of music which, to the pianist, seemed appropriate to the development of the play or events which were being portrayed on the screen. . . . [¶] It was held by Judge Thompson that the furnishing of music was an attraction which added to the enjoyment of persons viewing the motion pictures, and that although the proprietor had nothing whatever to do with the selection of the musical compositions rendered, the fact that the pianist was paid by the proprietor to supply the music moved the court to hold that the proprietor was furnishing music publicly for profit. There being no direct charge on account of musical entertainment furnished, there was what we term an indirect charge or fee therefor.

If our construction of the opinion of the Supreme Court in the Shanley Case, supra, be sound, that is to say, if there was found to be an indirect charge for the use of copyrighted musical compositions because of which the court held that the owner of the copyright was entitled to relief, the problem now presented for solution is not so difficult.

We have already stated that the Bamberger Co. makes no direct charge to those who avail themselves of the opportunity to listen to its daily broadcasting programmes. The question then is: Is the broadcasting done for an indirect profit? In determining this we think it is proper to look to the reason for broadcasting at all. Why was it done? What was it done for? What was the object, or to use the term of Justice Holmes: What was the 'purpose'? We know the purpose of the restaurant proprietor, and we know the purpose of the proprietor of the moving picture theater. What was the purpose of the defendant in expending thousands of dollars in establishing and operating this broadcasting station?

Adopting the language of Justice Holmes, the defendant is not an 'eleemosynary institution.' A department store is conducted for profit, which leads us to the very significant fact that the cost of the broadcasting was charged against the general expenses of the business. It was made a part of the business system.

Next we have the fact, already referred to, that the defendant sells radio receiving instruments and accessories. Whether a profit has resulted from such sales is not material in determining the object. It is within the realms of probability that many departments of a large store at times show losses rather than profits. Paraphrasing the comments of Justice Holmes, 'Whether it pays or not the purpose is profit, and that is enough.' While the defendant does not broadcast the sale prices of its wares, or refer specifically thereto, it does broadcast a slogan which appears in all of the defendant's printed advertisements. . . . 'L. Bamberger & Co., One of America's Great Stores, Newark, N.J.,' is broadcasted at the beginning of every periodical programme and also at the conclusion thereof. . . .

WOR's first studio - 1922
J. R. Poppele, chief engineer on phone at right
Photo from WOR RADIO 1922 - 1982
The First Sixty Years

If the development or enlargement of the business of the department store was completely out of the minds of the promoters of this broadcasting enterprise, is it reasonable to believe that the slogan, 'L. Bamberger & Co., One of America's Great Stores, Newark, N.J.,' would be announced to all listeners one, two, three, four, five, or six times a day? If the defendant desired to broadcast for purely eleemosynary reasons, as is urged, is it not likely that it would have adopted some anonymous name or initial? Undoubtedly the proprietors in their individual capacities have done and do many things of a public spirited and charitable nature on account of which they are entitled to the highest commendation. But it does not appear, and the court cannot believe, that those charitable acts are all labeled or stamped, 'L. Bamberger & Co., One of America's Great Stores, Newark, N.J.'

There is another point which, although striking us as immaterial, deserves some comment. The defendant argues that the plaintiff should not complain of the broadcasting of its song because of the great advertising service thereby accorded the copyrighted number. Our own opinion of the possibilities of advertising by radio leads us to the belief that the broadcasting of a newly copyrighted musical composition would greatly enhance the sales of the printed sheet. But the copyright owners and the music publishers themselves are perhaps the best judges of the method of popularizing musical selections. . . . [T]he method, we think, is the privilege of the owner. He has the exclusive right to publish and vend, as well as to perform.

Considering all of the facts and circumstances, it is the conclusion of the court that the broadcasting of the defendant was publicly for profit within the meaning of the Copyright Act as that meaning has been construed by the United States Supreme Court.

A decree will be entered in favor of the plaintiff, but restraint will be withheld pending a review of this opinion.

The *M. Witmark & Sons* case, above, challenged the right of radio stations to broadcast performances of compositions without a license from or compensation to the composer. The performance right was extended even further in 1931, when the U.S. Supreme Court decided ***Buck v. Jewell-La Salle Realty Co.***, 283 U.S. 191 (1931). In *Buck*, the defendant hotel had a master radio receiver and installed loudspeakers in the hotel's rooms and common spaces, making headsets available to guests of the hotel who wished to listen to whatever program the hotel tuned its receiver to at that particular time.

ASCAP and one of its member composers sued the hotel after it tuned its receiver in to a radio show that did not have permission to broadcast a performance of the composer's music. The trial court denied relief, finding that the hotel's actions were not a public performance for profit. The Supreme Court disagreed in an opinion authored by Justice Brandeis, relevant portions of which are excerpted below.

---

4. RADIO BROADCASTS OF MUSIC OVER HOTEL LOUDSPEAKERS

BUCK V. JEWELL-LASALLE REALTY CO.
283 U.S. 191 (1931)[13]

MR. JUSTICE BRANDEIS delivered the opinion of the Court. . . . [¶]

The parties agree that the owner of a private radio receiving set who in his own home invites friends to hear a musical composition which is being broadcast would not be liable for infringement. For, even if this be deemed a performance, it is neither public nor for profit. Compare Herbert v. Shanley Co., 242 U.S. 591, 37 S.Ct. 232, 61 L. Ed. 511. The contention that what the hotel company does is not a performance within the meaning of the Copyright Act is urged on three grounds.

First. The defendant contends that the Copyright Act may not reasonably be construed as applicable to one who merely receives a composition which is being broadcast. Although the art of radio broadcasting was unknown at the time the Copyright Act of 1909 was passed, and the means of transmission and reception now employed is wholly unlike any then in use, it is not denied that such broadcasting may

---

[13] Footnotes are omitted from this excerpt.

be within the scope of the act [citations omitted]. The argument here urged, however, is that, since the transmitting of a musical composition by a commercial broadcasting station is a public performance for profit, control of the initial radio rendition exhausts the monopolies conferred, both that of making copies (including records) and that of giving public performances for profit (including mechanical performances from a record); and that a monopoly of the reception, for commercial purposes, of this same rendition, is not warranted by the act. The analogy is invoked of the rule under which an author who permits copies of his writings to be made cannot, by virtue of his copyright, prevent or restrict the transfer of such copies. Compare Bobbs-Merrill Co. v. Straus, 210 U.S. 339, 28 S.Ct. 722, 52 L. Ed. 1086. This analogy is inapplicable. It is true that control of the sale of copies is not permitted by the act, but a monopoly is expressly granted of all public performances for profit.

The defendant next urges that it did not perform because there can be but one actual performance each time a copyrighted selection is rendered, and that, if the broadcaster is held to be a performer, one who, without connivance, receives and distributes the transmitted selection, cannot also be held to have performed it. But nothing in the act circumscribes the meaning to be attributed to the term 'performance,' or prevents a single rendition of a copyrighted selection from resulting in more than one public performance for profit. While this may not have been possible before the development of radio broadcasting, the novelty of the means used does not lessen the duty of the courts to give full protection to the monopoly of public performance for profit which Congress has secured to the composer. Compare Kalem Co. v. Harper Bros., 222 U.S. 55, 63, 32 S.Ct. 20, 56 L. Ed. 92, Ann. Cas. 1913A, 1285. No reason is suggested why there may not be more than one liability. And, since the public reception for profit in itself constitutes an infringement, we have no occasion to determine under what circumstances a broadcaster will be held to be a performer, or the effect upon others of his paying a license fee.

The defendant contends further that the acts of the hotel company were not a performance because no detailed choice of selections was given to it. In support of this contention it is pointed out that the operator of a radio receiving set cannot render at will a performance of any composition, but must accept whatever program is transmitted during the broadcasting period. Intention to infringe is not essential under the act. Compare Hein v. Harris (C. C.) 175 F. 875, affirmed (C. C. A.) 183 F. 107; Stern v. Jerome H. Remick & Co. (C. C.) 175 F. 282; Haas v. Leo Feist, Inc. (D. C.) 234 F. 105; M. Witmark & Sons v. Calloway (D. C.) 22 F.2d 412, 414. And knowledge of the particular selection to be played or received is immaterial. One who hires an orchestra for a public performance for profit is not relieved from a charge of infringement merely because he does not select the particular program to be played. Similarly, when he tunes in on a broadcasting station, for his own commercial purposes, he necessarily assumes the risk that in so doing he may infringe the performing rights of another. Compare Harms v. Cohen (D. C.) 279 F. 276, 278; M. Witmark & Sons v. Pastime Amusement Co. (D. C.) 298 F. 470, 475, affirmed (C. C. A.) 2 F.(2d) 1020; M. Witmark & Sons v. Calloway (D. C.) 22 F.(2d) 412, 413. It may be that proper control over broadcasting programs would automatically secure to the copyright owner sufficient protection from unauthorized public performances by use of a radio receiving set, and that this might justify legislation denying relief against those who in using the receiving set innocently invade the copyright, but the existing statute makes no such exception.

Second. The defendant contends that there was no performance because the reception of a radio broadcast is no different from listening to a distant rendition of the same program. We are satisfied that the reception of a radio broadcast and its translation into audible sound is not a mere audition of the original program. It is essentially a reproduction. As to the general theory of radio transmission, there is no disagreement. All sounds consist of waves of relatively low frequencies which ordinarily pass through the air and are locally audible. Thus music played at a distant broadcasting studio is not directly heard at the receiving set. In the microphone of the radio transmitter the sound waves are used to modulate electrical currents of relatively high frequencies which are broadcast through an entirely different medium, conventionally known as the 'either.' These radio waves are not audible. In the receiving set they are rectified; that is, converted into direct currents which actuate the loud-speaker to produce again in the air sound waves of audible frequencies. The modulation of the radio waves in the transmitting apparatus, by the audible sound waves, is comparable to the manner in which the wax phonograph record is impressed by these same waves through the medium of a recording stylus. The transmitted radio waves require a receiving set for their detection and translation into audible sound waves, just as the record requires another mechanism for the reproduction of the recorded composition. In neither case is the original program heard; and, in the former, complicated electrical instrumentalities are necessary for its adequate reception and distribution. Reproduction in both cases amounts to a performance. Compare Buck v. Heretis (D. C.) 24 F.(2d) 876; Irving Berlin, Inc., v. Daigle (C. C. A.) 31 F.(2d) 832, 833. In addition, the ordinary receiving set, and the distributing apparatus here employed by the hotel company are equipped to amplify the broadcast program after it has been received. Such acts clearly are more than the use of mere mechanical acoustic devices for the better hearing of the original program. The guests of the hotel hear a reproduction brought about by the acts of the hotel in (1) installing, (2) supplying electric current to, and (3) operating the radio receiving set and loud-speakers. There is no difference in substance between the case where a hotel engages an orchestra to furnish the music and that where, by means of the radio set and loudspeakers here employed, it furnishes the same music for the same purpose. In each the music is produced by instrumentalities under its control.

Third. The defendant contends that there was no performance within the meaning of the act because it is not shown that the hotel operated the receiving set and loud-speakers for profit. Unless such acts were carried on for profit, there can, of course, be no liability. But whether there was a performance does not depend upon the existence of the profit motive. The question submitted does not call for a determination whether the acts of the hotel company recited in the certificate constitute operation for profit.

NOTES AND QUESTIONS

1.   Go back to the themes outlined near the beginning of section D in Chapter 2, as well as any additional recurring themes that you have identified in these early music law cases. Do you see similar or new themes emerging from the above cases involving the performance right in musical compositions as in the cases dealing with duplication and performance rights in sound recordings? In which of the cases do you see disputes over promotion and substitution? Where and how does the Lockean theory appear? Consider the bundle of rights in music as defined by copyright law and the manner in which various parties in the industry have sought to carve out and enforce those rights; how do those issues come into play in the cases above? Do you see any differences between the ways in which these issues have played out in the context of protection of compositions versus protection of sound recordings? To what do you attribute any such differences? Does it make sense to treat these rights differently? Why or why not?

2.   The notion of "profit" has been handled differently over the course of the law's treatment of the performance right. What exactly does it mean to "profit" from a performance of a work? What are some other ways that a licensee might benefit from performing these works?

3.   Once the Court resolved the question of the scope of the performance right in musical compositions, the difficult issue of enforcement of that right moved to the fore. As you saw in the excerpts above, efforts by composers and publishers who had joined ASCAP to enforce the performance right were often met by defenses based on antitrust law. Angered by the license fees charged by ASCAP and the string of court rulings that required radio stations to obtain a license from the copyright owner of a musical work before broadcasting a performance of that work, in 1939 the broadcast industry formed its own competing organization, Broadcast Music, Inc. ("BMI"), seeking to acquire a catalog of musical works that could be broadcast by radio stations at a lower cost than ASCAP works. The next section provides you with a cross-section of materials to give you some perspective on the legal and policy arguments that arose in connection with the formation and ultimate antitrust regulation of ASCAP and BMI, competing organizations that were authorized by their

members to license and collect license fees for public performances of musical compositions.

B. ANTITRUST AND STATUTORY CHALLENGES TO PERFORMANCE RIGHTS ORGANIZATIONS

Victor Herbert, Irving Berlin, John Phillip Sousa—three of
the founding members of ASCAP, pictured in 1924
From Library of Congress National Photo Company Collection [Public domain]

1. BACKGROUND OF GOVERNMENT ANTITRUST OVERSIGHT OF PROs

It is impossible to fully understand why and how the licensing of musical works in the U.S. takes its present shape without some background on the long history of antitrust challenges to performing rights organizations—first, the American Society of Composers, Authors, and Publishers (ASCAP); then Broadcast Music Inc. (BMI), and, more recently, to a smaller, specialized PRO (SESAC). Of course, U.S. copyright law is designed to create a monopoly of sorts, albeit a "limited" one. Collective efforts to enforce that monopoly against entities and individuals believed to be infringing on copyright, however, were almost immediately met with claimed violations of federal and state antitrust laws, ultimately leading to decades-long oversight of PROs by the Antitrust Division of the United States Department of Justice. As aptly noted by Bernard Korman, who once served as ASCAP's General Counsel:

> [T]he government agency with which authors acting collectively through ASCAP or BMI must deal is not a cultural agency, as it is in some European countries. It is the Antitrust Division of the

Department of Justice. And that does make a difference. Cultural agencies are, naturally, supportive of authors and their societies: antitrust agencies are, equally naturally, hostile to large organizations that are dominant in any market.[14]

As mentioned above, ASCAP, like most performing rights societies around the world, is owned by its composer and music publisher members. By contrast, BMI was founded and owned by broadcast radio networks (i.e. the licensees of composers and publishers), and its mission was "to create a repertory large enough so that the radio industry would have access to music other than the ASCAP repertory."[15] At its inception, BMI's catalog of music available to license to broadcast radio was mostly arrangements of public domain works that BMI itself published. BMI advertised its organization as having the purpose of lowering the license fees paid by broadcasters for performances of compositions. Although it ultimately served an important role in representing composers and publishers of musical works that had been excluded from or overlooked by ASCAP—most notably African American, Latin American, and "hillbilly" music—BMI did not exist to enhance the earnings of composers and publishers. It was created as an alternative to ASCAP that would benefit broadcasters.[16]

In addition to forming BMI, the broadcasting industry also asserted antitrust claims relating to ASCAP's efforts to collectively enforce the performance right in compositions. Some of those claims were asserted in defense to lawsuits brought by ASCAP to enforce its members' performance rights; broadcasters also lobbied, successfully in some cases, for state legislatures to enact "anti-ASCAP" statutes that expressly barred collective enforcement of copyright interests. Radio broadcasters also complained to the Department of Justice Antitrust Division, asserting that ASCAP's collective licensing activities, which attempted to set a fee for access to all works within their repertoire and which gave broadcasters no option for obtaining licenses directly from the copyright owners of compositions, were anti-competitive and violated federal antitrust laws. Bernard Korman has described these efforts as follows:

> From the time it was created in 1914, ASCAP's licensing efforts met with opposition from each new industry or group it sought to license. Indeed, the powerful trade organization of the radio and

---

[14] Bernard Korman, *U.S. Position on Collective Administration of Copyright and Anti-Trust Law*, 43 J. COPYRIGHT SOC'Y U.S.A. 158, 160 (Winter 1995).

[15] Bernard Korman, *U.S. Position on Collective Administration of Copyright and Anti-Trust Law*, 43 J. COPYRIGHT SOC'Y U.S.A. 158, 162 (Winter 1995).

[16] *See generally* RUSSELL SANJEK, PENNIES FROM HEAVEN: THE AMERICAN POPULAR MUSIC BUSINESS IN THE TWENTIETH CENTURY, chapters 12, 13, 19 (Da Capo Press 1996) (describing in detail the many years of negotiations and battles between ASCAP, the National Association of Broadcasters, and BMI); HARRY P. WARNER, RADIO & TELEVISION RIGHTS: THE LAW OF COPYRIGHT, TRADE-MARKS AND UNFAIR COMPETITION AND THE BROADCASTING INDUSTRY, ch. 13 (Matthew Bender & Co. 1953).

television broadcasting industry, the National Association of Broadcasters (NAB), was created in the early 1920's for the express purpose of resisting ASCAP's licensing efforts among broadcasters. The growth of the society was greatly stimulated by the development of the radio broadcasting industry. Virtually from its inception, broadcasters recognized that music was an effective and cheap means of attracting audiences for advertising messages. By the 1930's, license fees were paid on the basis of a percentage of each station's advertising revenues. As those revenues grew, so too did ASCAP's fees and the resentment of the broadcasters. Many believed that ASCAP's members should pay them—after all, they argued unsuccessfully in court, it was radio broadcasting that popularized music and led to enhanced sheet music and record sales. . . .

In 1939, differences between ASCAP and the radio industry over the fees to be charged in the next license term to begin on 1 January, 1941 came to a head. . . . [M]ost broadcasters boycotted ASCAP music for a year beginning in November 1940.

Early in 1941, the government . . . filed new civil and criminal complaints against ASCAP. It is a sign of the hostile view the Government then had of ASCAP that, although ASCAP's main office was in New York and the Attorney General's office was in Washington, these complaints were not filed in either city. Instead, they were filed more than a thousand miles from both cities, in Milwaukee, Wisconsin, before Federal Judge Duffy who, as United States Senator Duffy, had unsuccessfully sponsored bills to abolish the minimum damage provisions of the copyright law on which the success of ASCAP's enforcement activities depended. In March, ASCAP signed a consent decree resolving the civil action. *Nolo contendere* pleas led to fines disposing of the criminal charges. . . .

The decree was entered in March, but final new radio license terms were not agreed upon until the fall, and the boycott by substantially all of the stations in the United States continued until November 1941. ASCAP's belief that the radio industry could not survive without performing the popular works of the world's greatest songwriters, American and foreign, proved wrong. The power was in the radio industry.[17]

The broadcasters, not surprisingly in retrospect, were also argued to be engaging in anticompetitive conduct by their continued boycott of ASCAP

---

[17]   Bernard Korman, *U.S. Position on Collective Administration of Copyright and Anti-Trust Law*, 43 J. COPYRIGHT SOC'Y U.S.A. 158, 161–63 (Winter 1995).

music.[18] In its new civil and criminal complaints filed at the beginning of 1941, the DOJ Antitrust Division named not only ASCAP, but also BMI, CBS, NBC, and others. Shortly thereafter, BMI also agreed to a consent decree to resolve the civil action. The resolution of those antitrust complaints through consent decrees led to what is now almost eighty years of antitrust oversight of U.S. PROs that governs their structure, licensing arrangements, and rate-setting process.

2. BACKGROUND OF PRIVATE ANTITRUST LITIGATION REGARDING PERFORMING RIGHTS ORGANIZATIONS

Private antitrust litigation has also served to constrain U.S. performing rights organizations (PROs) over the years, although as a practical matter the continuing oversight by the DOJ through the consent decrees has often made it difficult for private suits by licensees not happy with their rate negotiations with ASCAP and BMI to succeed. For example, in *Broadcast Music, Inc. v. Columbia Broadcasting System, Inc.*, 441 U.S. 1 (1979), the Supreme Court noted that even though consent judgments entered into with the Antitrust Division of the DOJ do not immunize PROs from private antitrust liability,

> it cannot be ignored that the Federal Executive and Judiciary have carefully scrutinized ASCAP and the challenged conduct, have imposed restrictions on various of ASCAP's practices, and, by the terms of the decree, stand ready to provide further consideration, supervision, and perhaps invalidation of asserted anticompetitive practices. In these circumstances, we have a unique indicator that the challenged practice may have redeeming competitive virtues and that the search for those values is not almost sure to be in vain.[19]

The Supreme Court went on to reject CBS's argument that ASCAP and BMI's blanket licensing practices were per se violations of the Sherman Act, reversing the contrary ruling of the Circuit Court below:

> Here, the blanket-license fee is not set by competition among individual copyright owners, and it is a fee for the use of any of the compositions covered by the license. But the blanket license cannot be wholly equated with a simple horizontal arrangement among competitors. ASCAP does set the price for its blanket license, but that license is quite different from anything any individual owner could issue. The individual composers and authors have neither agreed not to sell individually in any other

---

[18]   RUSSELL SANJEK, PENNIES FROM HEAVEN: THE AMERICAN POPULAR MUSIC BUSINESS IN THE TWENTIETH CENTURY, 207–11 (Da Capo Press 1996).

[19]   441 U.S. at 13 (footnotes omitted).

market nor use the blanket license to mask price fixing in such other markets. Moreover, the substantial restraints placed on ASCAP and its members by the consent decree must not be ignored. The District Court found that there was no legal, practical, or conspiratorial impediment to CBS's obtaining individual licenses; CBS, in short, had a real choice.

With this background in mind, which plainly enough indicates that over the years, and in the face of available alternatives, the blanket license has provided an acceptable mechanism for at least a large part of the market for the performing rights to copyrighted musical compositions, we cannot agree that it should automatically be declared illegal in all of its many manifestations.[20]

On remand, the Second Circuit concluded that the blanket license satisfied the rule of reason because CBS could feasibly obtain direct licenses from copyright owners and thus the blanket license did not unreasonably restrain competition.[21]

In addition to private antitrust litigation brought by potential licensees of PROs to challenge the collective licensing of copyrighted works, in the early years of BMI's existence, members of ASCAP sued BMI, alleging violations of the Clayton Act. In *Schwartz v. Broadcast Music Inc.*, excerpted below, the main issue addressed in the opinion is the question of whether individual members of ASCAP had standing to bring antitrust claims against BMI under the Clayton Act. However, resolving the standing issue required the court to explore in some depth both the nature of the substantive arguments asserted by the various parties and the inner workings of both ASCAP and BMI. As you read the *Schwartz* case, take note of the complexity in both the different rights implicated by the lawsuit and the various entities who owned or controlled those rights and consider what those complexities mean for the ability of authors of copyrighted works to protect their interests.

---

[20]   *Id.* at 23–24 (footnotes omitted).
[21]   *CBS v. ASCAP*, 620 F.2d 930, 938–39 (2d Cir. 1980).

Portrait of Composer Arthur Schwartz,
Library of Congress,
Prints & Photographs Division,
Carl Van Vechten Collection

SCHWARTZ V. BROADCAST MUSIC INC.

180 F. Supp. 322 (S.D.N.Y. 1959)[22]

WEINFELD, DISTRICT JUDGE.

This is a motion by the defendants for summary judgment in a private antitrust suit brought under sections 4, 12 and 16 of the Clayton Act. The motion is based solely on plaintiffs' alleged lack of standing to sue and hence the merits of the action are not involved.

[¶]. . . The issue here falls within a very narrow compass—whether the alleged antitrust conduct of the defendants has injured the plaintiffs in their business or property within the meaning of the antitrust statutes so as to give them standing to maintain this action for treble damages. [¶] . . . . The plaintiffs, thirty-three in number, professional composers and authors, are engaged in the writing of musical compositions. They bring this action, in their individual capacities, and, also, as a spurious class action pursuant to Rule 23(a)(3) of the Federal Rules of Civil Procedure on behalf of approximately 3,000 professional authors and composers of music who allegedly have suffered and will continue to 'suffer loss and damage in their business and property' by reason of defendants' conduct in violation of the antitrust laws, as set forth in the complaint. Plaintiffs are members of ASCAP.

The defendants include Broadcast Music, Inc., (hereafter referred to as BMI), which is wholly owned by radio and television broadcasting companies. BMI is engaged primarily in the acquisition and licensing of performance rights in musical compositions. The other defendants include

---

[22] Footnotes omitted except where indicated.

the leading radio and television networks, each of which owns and operates radio and television stations. These defendants, together with other broadcasters, organized BMI. Each broadcasting company defendant is a stockholder of BMI. . . .

The gist of the plaintiffs' charges is that the defendants conspired to dominate and control the market for the use and exploitation of musical compositions, particularly the rights to public performance for profit, to establish and maintain a monopoly thereof and to restrain trade and commerce therein. The ultimate goal, say the plaintiffs, was to control the music industry and thereby to fix and reduce the price to be paid by the defendant networks and their co-conspirators in the broadcasting industry for the use of music on their programs.

Plaintiffs charge that to achieve their conspiratorial objective, the defendants organized BMI in 1939, as the vehicle to maintain a music pool for their joint use and benefit, and have dominated it ever since. In general they allege that to effectuate the conspiracy, the defendants have given preference to the performance of BMI controlled music, have discriminated against the musical compositions written by the plaintiffs and other writers similarly situated, have boycotted, restricted and limited their musical compositions both in broadcasting and recording and have induced other broadcasters and record companies to do the same.

Specific acts and conduct of the defendants in furtherance of the conspiracy are enumerated in the complaint. Plaintiffs charge that such conspiratorial acts and conduct have . . . limited, restricted and prevented (1) the publication of musical compositions written by plaintiffs and others similarly situated; (2) the marketing and sale of published versions thereof; (3) the use and utilization thereof by radio and television broadcasting stations and networks; (4) the use and utilization thereof in the manufacture and sale of phonograph records; (5) the public performance for profit thereof in places of public gathering and entertainment, and (6) the stimulation which use and popularization in each of said segments of the market provides for exploitation in other segments thereof.

In consequence, the plaintiffs claim that they and other writers similarly situated have been injured by an annual loss of income from their musical compositions, depreciation of the price of performance fees and loss of prestige and recognition as authors and composers. Plaintiffs seek treble damages in the sum of $150,000,000 and injunctive relief. . . .

[¶] . . . . The burden of the defendants' challenge to the plaintiffs' standing to sue centers about the separate dispositions by plaintiffs of (1) printing, publishing and mechanical reproduction rights, sometimes referred to hereafter as the publishing and recording rights, and (2) the nondramatic public performance rights for profit, hereafter referred to as the public performance rights. The claims which center about these rights may be considered separately.

To support their position, the defendants note that the complaint alleges, and the pre-trial record establishes, that plaintiffs' and other writers' compositions are marketed through (1) the printing and sale of sheet music, (2) the licensing of recordings on phonograph records and other mechanical reproductions, and (3) the licensing of public performance rights. Accordingly, the defendants argue that since the plaintiffs have granted, for commercial exploitation, their public performance rights to ASCAP and their recording and publishing rights to the publishers, from whom they receive payments therefor, any injury to plaintiffs is indirect and secondary; that the conspiracy, if it injures anyone directly, injures ASCAP and the music publishers; that the right to sue for damages for such direct injuries is with them and not with the plaintiffs.

In all, 7,000 songs have been composed by the plaintiffs herein. As to all, the public performance rights are the subject of agreements with ASCAP by virtue of plaintiffs' membership therein.

As to 5,800 of the total number, the publishing and recording rights are the subject of agreements entered into by plaintiffs with publishers.

As to the remaining 1,200, no publishing or recording contracts are in effect. The plaintiffs are the common law or statutory copyright owners.

The Nondramatic Public Performance Rights and ASCAP

The complaint emphasizes that a principal objective of the conspiracy was control of the public performance rights in musical compositions. Hence, we turn first to this aspect of the defendants' attack upon plaintiffs' standing to sue. This involves a consideration of ASCAP and the agreement under which it licenses the nondramatic public performance for profit of plaintiffs' compositions.

ASCAP is a nonprofit unincorporated association which was formed in 1914 to protect its members against piracies of their works and generally to promote their interests. It grants licenses and collects royalties for the nondramatic public performance for profit of the works of its members. Its duration is 99 years. Its membership includes two groups, authors and composers of music, referred to as 'writer members', and music publishers. . . . Under the Articles of Association, all members, writers and publishers alike, execute agreements vesting in ASCAP the right to license, upon a nonexclusive basis, the nondramatic public performance of works written or published by the members. Pursuant thereto, these plaintiffs, writer members, entered into uniform agreements with ASCAP. The agreements provide in part that: 'The Owner (the publisher or writer member) sells, assigns, transfers and sets over unto (ASCAP) for the term hereof, the entire exclusive[22] right of public performance * * * in each musical work,' of which he is the copyright owner either alone or jointly with others, or in which he has any right, title or interest, or which during the term of the agreement may be written, composed, acquired, owned, published or copyrighted by the owner, alone, jointly, or in collaboration with others." . . .

ASCAP, through its licensing department, grants performance licenses . . . of two kinds: (1) a blanket license, and (2) a program license. The blanket license is the type generally issued. It grants to the music user for its term the right to perform all the music in ASCAP's catalogue upon payment of a flat fee which does not vary according to the number of ASCAP compositions used by the licensee or the number of programs in which they are played. Under the program license the broadcaster pays ASCAP a fee only for each program in which ASCAP's music is used. The terms of the licenses and the rates to be charged are decided by ASCAP's Board of Directors. Individual members do not pass upon, approve, ratify or reject license terms agreed to by the Board.

. . . . [¶] With respect to the 7,000 songs, public performance licenses have been granted only by ASCAP. Plaintiff members since 1941 have not granted a single license although they assert an equal right to grant nonexclusive licenses, a point hereafter considered.

. . . . [¶] The thrust of the alleged conspiracy insofar as the public performance rights are concerned is directed against ASCAP as the licensor of the totality of all its members' compositions and not as against particular members or particular compositions. The licensing activities of ASCAP are extensive and represent a vast business enterprise. . . . No matter what name may be applied to ASCAP, no matter what its jural character, as a consequence of the grant of rights by its members to it, the competition in the field of nondramatic public performances for profit is between ASCAP and BMI and not between plaintiffs or other composers and BMI. . . . No matter how phrased, it cannot obscure the fact that ASCAP, and not the individual composers, is the direct target of the alleged conspiracy. Any other conclusion flies in the face of reality.

[¶]. . . . The conclusion is compelled that in practice and in fact it is ASCAP which was and is engaged in the business of licensing plaintiffs' compositions for public performance; that for that purpose plaintiffs have so divested themselves of their public performance rights to ASCAP that any injury resulting from the conspiracy was primarily and directly upon

---

[22] Despite this provision, ASCAP only has a nonexclusive right to license such performances. A provision in a consent decree entered in 1941 (United States v. ASCAP, Civ. No. 13–95, S.D.N.Y., Mar. 4, 1941) enjoined ASCAP from acquiring or asserting exclusive performance rights in the compositions. Thereafter, a clause was added at the end of the agreements stating that the grant made by the owner was modified by the consent decree. Following the entry of an amended decree in 1950 the word 'exclusive' was omitted from the agreements.

ASCAP; that injury if any, sustained by the plaintiffs is secondary and remote.

. . . . [¶] No substantial reason has been advanced why ASCAP has not brought the action or why it has not been vouched into the action. The fact that ASCAP is a nonprofit organization does not mean that direct injury cannot be inflicted upon it by illegal antitrust conduct of others, just as that fact does not mean that ASCAP cannot itself indulge in antitrust conduct. The fact is that ASCAP has sued and has been sued. Indeed, were ASCAP to bring an action based upon the alleged illegal conduct of the defendants by reason of claimed injury and recover a judgment, the proceeds in the first instance would be the property of the association, and subject to the payment of its debts. A recovery would permit distribution to be made to the individual plaintiffs and other members of ASCAP as determined by the Writers' Classification Committee in accordance with the by-laws.

Upon all the foregoing, the Court holds that with respect to the nondramatic public performance rights, the plaintiffs are without standing to sue.

We now consider whether the plaintiffs have standing to sue with respect to publishing and recording rights.

The Publishing and Recording Rights and the Publishers

The plaintiffs have entered into agreements with 300 music publishers, who are also members of ASCAP. Under these they have transferred to the publishers their unpublished original compositions with the right to secure copyright therein and all rights thereunder, subject to the performance rights granted to ASCAP. The agreements cover approximately 5,800 of the 7,000 compositions written by the plaintiffs. They are substantially similar and provide:

> 'The Writer hereby sells, assigns, transfers and delivers to the Publisher a certain heretofore unpublished original musical composition written and/or composed by the above-named Writer now entitled * * * including the title, words and music thereof, and the right to secure copyright therein throughout the entire world, to have and to hold the said copyright and all rights of whatsoever nature thereunder existing * * *.'

[¶] . . . . [The plaintiffs] charge that music publishers with whom they had contracts were induced by subsidies, restrictive covenants, incentive payments and other devices including payments of salaries of publishers' employees, to refrain from publishing and exploiting plaintiffs' songs; that recording companies were induced by various methods not to record plaintiffs' songs; that these activities were all for the purpose of suppressing plaintiffs' musical compositions altogether or to discriminate in favor of BMI songs. Plaintiffs further allege that some publishers, who were ASCAP houses, organized BMI companies and although in theory functioning separately, in fact, because of special concessions granted by BMI to the publishers, refrained from promoting non-BMI music or curtailed its exploitation. Plaintiffs name firms who engaged in this practice.

Publishers to whom plaintiffs transferred their compositions with the right to secure the copyrights were obligated to exploit them in good faith for the benefit of the composers, as well as for themselves.

The essence of these charges is that the defendants, in furtherance of the alleged conspiratorial objective to control the music market, induced publishers, including some under contract to plaintiffs, by various means, to withhold exploitation and marketing of plaintiffs' compositions in printed and recorded form; that in order to induce the publishers to do so, the defendants made payments to the publishers to cover their loss in income by reason of nonexploitation of plaintiffs' songs, thus making them whole to the detriment of the plaintiffs; that by such payments, defendants removed the incentive for, and interfered with the duty upon, the publishers to promote the marketing of plaintiffs' songs.

The Court's function on this motion is not to weigh and pass upon the merits of the charges. Should the proof sustain the charges, it would be difficult to challenge plaintiffs' claim of direct injury. This branch of the conspiracy appears, upon the facts alleged, to be directed not against the publishers but rather against the songwriters. A conspiracy may have more than one objective and its force directed against one or more intended victims. The target area of the conspiracy was broad enough to include plaintiffs insofar as the publication and recording rights are concerned. Upon the facts alleged, the publishers were not damaged since they received compensating payments from the defendants; the only persons damaged were the songwriters. The wrongful acts had a direct impact upon the composers who were injured thereby and not upon the publishers who were made whole. The bounties granted to the publishers removed them from the target area of the defendants' attack and placed plaintiffs directly in the line of fire. . . .

The fact that the plaintiffs divested themselves of the publishing and recording rights does not deprive them of standing to sue. They could receive royalties only if the publishers, in good faith, worked their compositions. Here the charge is that the very function which the publishers undertook to perform had been interfered with and rendered sterile by the acts of the defendants.

The significant distinction in the ASCAP situation is that no claim is made that ASCAP participated in or lent itself to any conduct in violation of its duty to market plaintiffs' compositions, which resulted in diminution of income to the plaintiffs. On the contrary, as already noted, the force of the conspiracy was directed against ASCAP as the licensor of its entire catalogue of songs.

[¶] .... Under all the circumstances presented, plaintiffs have set forth enough to support their claim of direct injury due to the acts and conduct charged against the defendants so as to entitle them to maintain this claim. Accordingly, this aspect of the defendants' motion is denied.

Plaintiffs' 1200 Songs as to Which No Publisher Contracts Are in Effect

There remains for final consideration the defendants' contention with respect to the 1,200 songs as to which no publisher contracts are in effect. These constitute works of which the respective plaintiffs were either a registered proprietor of statutory copyright, a holder of legal title to common law copyright, or are compositions in which a publisher's right has terminated because of cancellation of the contract. The interest of plaintiffs therein was susceptible to damage by the charged conspiracy. Here the plaintiffs claim the publishing and recording market was entirely foreclosed to them by reason of defendants' action. While defendants acknowledge that plaintiffs are the common law or statutory copyright owners of these compositions, they minimize their value and contend that any injury was only collateral and any damage inconsequential. This contention is without substance. Whether the damage is great or slight is a question of fact to be decided by the trier of the fact. Accordingly, the defendants' motion likewise is denied with respect to the 1,200 songs.

NOTES AND QUESTIONS

1.   Do you agree with the court's reasoning and conclusion in *Schwartz* regarding the lack of standing on the part of individual composers to sue BMI and its member broadcasters for their alleged anticompetitive conduct in preferencing performances of non-ASCAP affiliated compositions? Why or why not? Does the distinction that the court makes between standing to sue with respect to the performance rights and recording/publishing rights make sense to you? Why or why not?

2.   Given that standing was the primary issue in the *Schwartz* case, you might wonder why ASCAP did not join in the action. Although the reasons were many and complex, both some history and context can provide insights. First, at the time, there was growing disagreement within the membership of ASCAP as to the best course for the organization to take in administering the performance right. Not only were the composer and publisher members at odds, but the more well-established composers were given more favorable treatment (i.e., higher distributions from the performance license fees collected by ASCAP) than composers who were newer members of the organization or whose music was viewed as being of lesser artistic value—and the *Schwartz*

plaintiffs were a group of newer members who had been at odds with the ASCAP board for many years. The consent decree entered into in 1941 expressly permitted the ASCAP board to allocate royalty distributions to members based upon the "number, nature, character and prestige of a member's works, the seniority of a member's works, and popularity and vogue of such works."[23] Under this system, established composers received the lion's share of distributions from ASCAP; younger, up-and-coming composers, including screen composers, were relegated to much smaller, fixed distributions rather than participating in a percentage of revenues collected. Votes among the membership were also weighted according to the share of past royalties the members had been allocated, giving control over most membership decisions to those who benefited most from the existing allocation system.

Second, the growth of music licensing for film and emergence of television enhanced the tensions between publishers and composers and among groups of composers. In negotiations over the renewal of the contract between screen composers and the Hollywood publishing houses that dragged out through the mid-to-late 1940s, screen composers sought to retain the copyrights to their compositions. They wanted ASCAP to separate film performance royalties from other performance royalties; instead of those royalties going into the larger pool of all collected performance royalties and being allocated under a system that paid a higher proportion of royalties to composers whose works were broadcast on radio, they argued that film performance royalties should be allocated solely among film composers. There was also a movement by publishers to withhold television performance licensing from ASCAP so that they could individually license their catalogs to television networks for potentially greater fees than ASCAP could obtain under the consent decree.

Third, as discussed in the summary above, ASCAP had been subject to antitrust oversight by the Department of Justice since entry of the consent decree in 1941 and had suffered from the 1941 broadcast industry boycott of the ASCAP catalog. The society focused its attention on renewing its licensing arrangements among radio networks and smaller stations and on solidifying its role in licensing music for film and television, which were both expanding markets. It also was concerned about the potential impact of decisions in civil antitrust cases relating to music licensing in the film industry that raised the question of whether any reversion of rights granted in the antitrust proceedings would go to composers or to their publishers[24]—pitting the publisher and composer members of ASCAP and its board against one another.

---

[23] *See* Russell Sanjek, Pennies from Heaven: The American Popular Music Business in the Twentieth Century 256 (De Capo Press 1996); David Suisman, Selling Sounds: The Commercial Revolution in American Music 171 (Harvard University Press, 2009). This provision was modified in 1950, when the court administering the consent decree permitted an amendment to require allocations of performance royalties by ASCAP to be based primarily on objective surveys of performances rather than on the subjective determinations of ASCAP's Board.

[24] See *Alden-Rochelle, Inc. v. Am. Soc. of Composers, Authors & Publishers*, 80 F. Supp. 900, 903 (S.D.N.Y. 1948), amending 80 F. Supp. 888 (S.D.N.Y. 1948).

Ultimately, many of the concerns about BMI's practices that were raised in the *Schwartz* case were addressed in the 1966 consent decree between BMI and the Department of Justice after ASCAP complained. The 1966 consent decree prohibited BMI from preventing publishers under contract with it from publishing or promoting compositions licensed through ASCAP. The 1966 consent decree also prohibited BMI from requiring its publisher members that were affiliated with recording companies to favor BMI-licensed compositions and from providing guarantees to publishers who withdrew from ASCAP to join BMI.[25]

The sections that follow provide an overview of antitrust proceedings in the decades since the original 1941 consent decree. The summaries below take you up to the modern copyright era, including changes made to the existing consent decree rate-setting process for collective licensing of performance rights in compositions implemented as part of the 2018 Music Modernization Act. We will pick up on a discussion of collective licensing of other protected rights—the digital performance right in sound recordings and the mechanical right in compositions—in later chapters.

The following excerpt is from a 2015 report by the U.S. Copyright Office, the result of a several-year review process as Congress considered changes to the copyright provisions governing aspects of the music industry that ultimately led to enactment of the Music Modernization Act of 2018. It provides you with a broad overview of how antitrust oversight of PROs has evolved over time to influence licensing and the rate-setting process in the modern music industry.

---

3. COPYRIGHT OFFICE AND DEPARTMENT OF JUSTICE SUMMARIES REGARDING MODERN OVERSIGHT OF PROs AND RATE SETTING

COPYRIGHT AND THE MUSIC MARKETPLACE REPORT
U.S. Copyright Office, Feb. 2015[26]

[¶] . . . . Today, the PROs provide various different types of licenses depending upon the nature of the use. Anyone who publicly performs a musical work may obtain a license from a PRO, including terrestrial, satellite and internet radio stations, broadcast and cable television

---

[25] For a detailed discussion of the "music wars" that had a profound effect on the music industry's development and spawned both civil and criminal antitrust proceedings from the mid-1930s through the mid-1950s, see Russell Sanjek, Pennies from Heaven: The American Popular Music Business in the Twentieth Century (De Capo Press 1996), Parts 3, 4 & 5.

[26] U.S. Copyright Office, COPYRIGHT AND THE MUSIC MARKETPLACE §II(B)(3) at 32–42 & §IV(C)(1)–(2) at 145–62 (Feb. 2015), *available at* https://www.copyright.gov/policy/musiclicensing study/copyright-and-the-music-marketplace.pdf (second printing, May 2016).

stations, online services, bars, restaurants, live performance venues, and commercial establishments that play background music.

Most commonly, licensees obtain a blanket license, which allows the licensee to publicly perform any of the musical works in a PRO's repertoire for a flat fee or a percentage of total revenues.[111] Some users opt for a blanket license due to its broad coverage of musical works and relative simplicity as compared to other types of licenses. Large commercial establishments such as bars, restaurants, concert venues, stores, and hotels often enter into blanket licenses to cover their uses, paying either a percentage of gross revenues or an annual flat fee, depending on the establishment and the type and amount of use.[112] Terrestrial radio stations obtain blanket licenses from PROs as well, usually by means of the RMLC [Radio Music License Committee].[113] Many television stations, through the TMLC [Television Music License Committee], also obtain blanket licenses.[114]

Less commonly used licenses include the per-program or per-segment license, which allows the licensee to publicly perform any of the musical works in the PRO's repertoire for specified programs or parts of their programming, in exchange for a flat fee or a percentage of that program's advertising revenue.[115] Unlike a blanket license, the per-program or per-segment license requires more detailed reporting information, including program titles, the specific music selections used, and usage dates, making the license more burdensome for the licensee to administer.[116]

Users can also license music directly from music publishers through a direct license or a source license. A direct license is simply a license agreement directly negotiated between the copyright owner and the user who intends to publicly perform the musical work. Source licenses are commonly used in the motion picture industry, because the PROs are prohibited from licensing public performance rights directly to movie theater owners.[117] . . . In the context of motion pictures, source licenses do

---

[111] *Meredith Corp.*, 1 F. Supp. 3d at 190; *BMI v. CBS*, 441 U.S. at 5.

[112] *See* KOHN at 1263, 1275–80. The Copyright Act exempts many small commercial establishments from the need to obtain a public performance license. *See* 17 U.S.C. § 110(5).

[113] David Oxenford, *What is the RMLC, And Why Should a Radio Station Pay Their Bill?*, BROAD. L. BLOG (Aug. 24, 2012), http://www.broadcastlawblog.com/2012/08/articles/what-is-the-rmlc-and-why-should-a-radio-station-pay-their-bill.

[114] *Meredith Corp.*, 1 F. Supp. 3d at 189–90.

[115] *See generally* Lauren M. Bilasz, *Note: Copyrights, Campaigns, and the Collective Administration of Performance Rights: A Call to End Blanket Licensing of Political Events*, 32 CARDOZO L.REV. 305, 323 & nn.111–112 (2010) (descriptions of each license).

[116] *See, e.g.*, KOHN at 1266 (discussing per-program licenses).

[117] This prohibition was a result of antitrust litigation brought by movie theater owners in the 1940s. *Alden-Rochelle*, 80 F. Supp. 888; *see also* Christian Seyfert, *Copyright and Anti-Trust Law: Public Performance Rights Licensing of Musical Works into Audiovisual Media* 19 (Sept. 1, 2005) (unpublished LL.M. thesis, Golden Gate University School of Law) ("Seyfert"), *available at* http://digitalcommons.law.ggu.edu/theses/13.

not typically encompass non-theatrical performances, such as on television. Thus, television stations, cable companies, and online services such as Netflix and Hulu must obtain public performance licenses from the PROs to cover the public performance of musical works in the shows and movies they transmit to end users.[119]

b. Antitrust Oversight

Basic Antitrust Principles

Unlike the mechanical right, the public performance of musical works is not subject to compulsory licensing under the Copyright Act. But, as described below, ASCAP and BMI are subject to government antitrust regulation through longstanding consent decrees. And while neither SESAC nor GMR is subject to such direct antitrust regulation, each, of course, must abide by generally applicable antitrust law, which is enforceable by the government or through private causes of action. SESAC, for example, has recently been the subject of private antitrust suits. . . . A detailed explanation of the antitrust rationale that underlies the PRO consent decrees is beyond the scope of this study. But a brief discussion of some basic antitrust principles may be helpful in understanding the motivation behind the decrees.

Section 1 of the Sherman Antitrust Act prohibits "[e]very contract, combination in the form of trust or otherwise, or conspiracy, in restraint of trade or commerce among the several [s]tates."[120] As the Supreme Court has opined, however, "Congress could not have intended a literal interpretation of the word 'every,' " and as a result, courts "analyze[ ] most restraints under the so-called 'rule of reason.' "[121] The rule of reason test requires a court to not only find a restraint of trade, but also determine whether that restraint is unreasonable.[122]

. . . [¶] *Department of Justice Consent Decrees*

Since 1941, ASCAP and BMI's licensing practices have been subject to antitrust consent decrees overseen by the Antitrust Division of the DOJ and enforced by federal district courts in New York City.[129] Those consent decrees were implemented in reaction to alleged anticompetitive practices of ASCAP and BMI. Specifically, when originally formed, both PROs

---

[119] *Id.*; *see also* Netflix First Notice Comments at 1–2; *ASCAP Reports Increased Revenues in 2011*, ASCAP (Mar. 8, 2012), http://www.ascap.com/press/2012/0308_ascap-reports.aspx (reflecting blanket licenses with Netflix and Hulu). Licensing of performance rights from SESAC and GMR occurs without direct antitrust oversight, and those smaller PROs may refuse to license their repertoires to potential licensees.

[120] 15 U.S.C. § 1.

[121] *Arizona v. Maricopa Cnty. Med. Soc'y*, 457 U.S. 332, 342–43 (1982).

[122] *Associated Press v. United States*, 326 U.S. 1, 27 (1945).

[129] *See generally United States v. BMI*, 275 F.3d 168, 171–72 (2d Cir. 2001) (describing the history); *see also Antitrust Consent Decree Review*, U.S. DOJ, http://www.justice.gov/atr/cases/ascap-bmi-decree-review.html (last visited Jan. 26, 2015).

acquired the exclusive right to negotiate members' public performance rights, and forbade their members from entering into direct licensing arrangements. Additionally, both offered only blanket licenses covering all of the music in their respective repertoires.[130]

In the 1930s, the DOJ's Antitrust Division investigated ASCAP for anticompetitive conduct—specifically that ASCAP's licensing arrangements constituted price-fixing and/or unlawful tying.[131] The government subsequently filed federal court actions in 1934 and 1941, arguing that the exclusive blanket license—as the only license offered at the time—was an unlawful restraint of trade and that ASCAP was charging arbitrary prices as a result of an illegal copyright pool.[132] While the first case was never fully litigated after the government was granted a mid-trial continuance, the latter action was settled with the imposition of a consent decree in 1941.[133] That consent decree has been modified twice, first in 1950 and most recently in 2001.[134] The United States also pursued antitrust claims against BMI, resulting in a similar consent decree in 1941.[135] The 1941 BMI consent decree was superseded by a new decree in 1966, which was last amended in 1994.[136]

Although the ASCAP and BMI consent decrees are not identical, they share many of the same features. As most relevant here, the PROs may only acquire nonexclusive rights to license members' public performance rights; must grant a license to any user that applies, on terms that do not discriminate against similarly situated licensees; and must accept any songwriter or music publisher that applies to be a member, as long as the writer or publisher meets certain minimum standards.[137]

ASCAP and BMI are also required to offer alternative licenses to the blanket license. One option is the adjustable fee blanket license, a blanket license with a carve-out that reduces the flat fee to account for music directly licensed from PRO members. Under the consent decrees, ASCAP and BMI must also provide, when requested, "through-to-the-audience" licenses to broadcast networks that cover performances not only by the networks themselves, but also by affiliated stations that further transmit

---

[130] Seyfert at 6, 20; see also Wilf at 177.

[131] Seyfert at 20–21.

[132] *BMI v. CBS*, 441 U.S. at 10.

[133] Seyfert at 20–21.

[134] *BMI v. CBS*, 441 U.S. at 11.

[135] *Id.* at 12 n.20.

[136] Seyfert at 22; see also BMI Consent Decree.

[137] ASCAP Consent Decree §§ IV.B–C, VI, VIII, XI; BMI Consent Decree §§ IV.A, V, VIII.

those performances downstream.[138] ASCAP and BMI are also required to provide per-program and per-segment licenses, as are described above.[139]

ASCAP is expressly barred from licensing any rights other than its members' public performance rights (*i.e.*, ASCAP may not license mechanical or synchronization rights).[140] Although BMI's consent decree lacks a similar prohibition, in practice BMI does not license any rights other than public performance rights.[141]

Finally, and perhaps most significantly, prospective licensees that are unable to agree to a royalty rate with ASCAP or BMI may seek a determination of a reasonable license fee from one of two federal district court judges in the Southern District of New York.[142] The rate court procedures are discussed in greater detail below.

In response to requests by ASCAP and BMI to modify certain provisions of their decrees, the DOJ's Antitrust Division announced in June 2014 that it would be evaluating the consent decrees, and has solicited and received extensive public comments on whether and how the decrees might be amended. . . . [143] The DOJ has expressed its intent to "examine the operation and effectiveness of the Consent Decrees," particularly in light of the changes in the way music has been delivered and consumed since the most recent amendments to those decrees.[145] At the same time, the DOJ is conducting a related investigation to determine whether there has been a coordinated effort among music publishers and PROs to raise royalty rates.[146] [¶] . . . .

c. Consent Decree Procedures

As noted, ASCAP and BMI are required by their consent decrees to grant a nonexclusive license to publicly perform all of the works in their repertoires to any potential licensee who makes a written application.[164] An entity that seeks a public performance license begins the process by

---

[138] ASCAP Consent Decree § V; BMI Consent Decree § IX.

[139] ASCAP Consent Decree §§ II.J–K, VII; BMI Consent Decree § VIII.B. Note that under the ASCAP consent decree, the per-segment license has a number of conditions that must be met before it can be used. ASCAP Consent Decree § VII.

[140] ASCAP Consent Decree § IV.A.

[141] *See* BMI, Comments on Department of Commerce Green Paper at 4–5 (Nov. 13, 2013), *available at* http://www.ntia.doc.gov/files/ntia/bmi_comments.pdf.

[142] ASCAP Consent Decree § IX; BMI Consent Decree § XIV.

[143] *Antitrust Consent Decree Review*, U.S. DOJ, http://www.justice.gov/atr/cases/ascap-bmi-decree-review.html (last visited Jan. 26, 2015).

[145] *Antitrust Consent Decree Review*, U.S. DOJ, http://www.justice.gov/atr/cases/ascap-bmi-decree-review.html (last visited Jan. 26, 2015).

[146] Ed Christman, *Dept. of Justice Sends Doc Requests, Investigating UMPG, Sony/ATV, BMI and ASCAP Over Possible "Coordination,"* BILLBOARD (July 13, 2014), http://www.billboard.com/biz/articles/news/publishing/6157513/dept-of-justice-sends-doc-requests-investigating-umpg-sony atv. Members of the DOJ Antitrust Division attended and observed the Office's roundtables for this study in Nashville and New York.

[164] ASCAP Consent Decree § VI; BMI Consent Decree § IV.A.

submitting such a request to the PRO. In the absence of an established rate for the applicant's use, the PRO and the applicant may then engage in negotiations regarding the appropriate rate.[165] Significantly, however, under both consent decrees, the mere submission of the application gives the applicant the right immediately to begin using the musical works in the PRO's repertoire without payment of any fee or compensation during the pendency of negotiations or a ratesetting proceeding.[166]

If the PRO and licensee are unable to agree on a fee, either party may apply for a determination of a reasonable fee by the applicable rate court.[167] The term "rate court" is a bit of a misnomer, however; as noted above, rate disputes are handled by the federal district judge in the Southern District of New York who has been assigned ongoing responsibility for administration of the relevant consent decree.[168] Currently, the ASCAP decree and ratesetting cases are overseen by Judge Denise Cote, and Judge Louis L. Stanton oversees these matters with respect to BMI.

Ed. Update: The 2018 Music Modernization Act changed this practice of having only two judges assigned to the ratesetting process (one for ASCAP and one for BMI). Now, judges will be assigned on a rotating basis.

In a rate court proceeding, the PRO has the burden of proving that the royalty rate it seeks is "reasonable," and if the court determines that the proposed rate is not reasonable, it will determine a reasonable rate itself.[169] In determining a reasonable fee, the rate court is tasked with assessing the fair market value of the license, *i.e.*, "what a license applicant would pay in an arm's length transaction."[170] But antitrust concerns also play a direct role: according to the Second Circuit, the rate courts are also obligated to "tak[e] into account the fact that the PRO, as a monopolist, exercises disproportionate power over the market for music rights."[171]

Since negotiations between PROs and potential licensees—as well as rate court proceedings—can be lengthy, an applicant or a PRO may apply to the rate court to fix an interim rate, pending final determination of the applicable rate. Under the two decrees, such interim fees are supposed to

---

[165] ASCAP Consent Decree § IX.F; BMI Consent Decree § XIV.A.

[166] ASCAP Consent Decree § IX.E; BMI Consent Decree § XIV.A.

[167] ASCAP Consent Decree § IX.A; BMI Consent Decree § XIV.A.

[168] Paul Fakler, *Music Copyright Royalty Rate-Setting Litigation: Practice Before the Copyright Royalty Board and How It Differs from ASCAP and BMI Rate Court Litigation*, 33 LICENSING J. 1, 5 (2013), *available* at http://www.arentfox.com/sites/default/files/Fakler LicensingJournalArticle.pdf.

[169] ASCAP Consent Decree § IX.B–D; BMI Consent Decree § XIV.A.

[170] *Pandora Ratesetting*, 6 F. Supp. 3d at 353 (citation omitted).

[171] *BMI v. DMX*, 683 F.3d at 45 (internal quotation marks, citations, and alterations omitted).

be set by the court within three to four months.[172] Once the rate court fixes the interim rate, the licensee must pay the interim fee retroactively to the date of its license application.[173] Final royalty rates are also applied retroactively.[174] [¶] . . . .

IV. ANALYSIS AND RECOMMENDATIONS

C. Role of Government in Music Licensing

[¶]. . . . Government regulation of music has focused on the interrelated concerns of access, pricing and competition. As noted above, section 115—the first compulsory license in our copyright law—was enacted to prevent a single piano roll company from exercising exclusive control over song copyrights. The PRO consent decrees are the result of the government's attempt to balance the efficiencies of collective licensing with concerns about anticompetitive conduct. More recently, Congress chose to extend the public performance right for digital uses of sound recordings on the condition that certain of those uses would be subject to compulsory licensing under sections 112 and 114 of the Copyright Act, thus further extending the practice of regulatory oversight.

As a result of these policy determinations, an administrative tribunal, the CRB, sets the fees paid for the reproduction and distribution of musical works, as well as the royalties due for radio-style digital performance of sound recordings. Two federal judges in New York City are responsible for establishing the fees for the public performance of musical works across traditional and digital platforms. For better or worse, these decades-old regimes are deeply embedded in our licensing infrastructure.[782]

Viewed in the abstract, it is almost hard to believe that the U.S. government sets prices for music. In today's world, there is virtually no equivalent for this type of federal intervention—at least outside of the copyright arena.[783] The closest example is the retransmission by cable and satellite providers of copyrighted television programming (including the

---

[172] The interim fee proceedings are to be completed within 90 days in ASCAP's case and 120 days in BMI's case. *See* ASCAP Consent Decree § IX(F); BMI Consent Decree § XIV.B.

[173] *See id.*

[174] *See id.*

[782] Notably, in the deliberations leading to the adoption of the 1976 Act, then Register of Copyrights Abraham L. Kaminstein recommended elimination of the section 115 compulsory license, concluding that the underlying concerns about a publisher monopoly were no longer relevant. *See* GENERAL REVISION OF COPYRIGHT REPORT at 36. Publishers did not ultimately pursue that opportunity, however, instead agreeing to maintain the compulsory license in exchange for a statutory rate hike from 2 to 2.75 cents per use. *See Music Licensing Reform Hearing* (statement of Marybeth Peters, Register of Copyrights); S. REP. NO. 94–473, at 88–92.

[783] Outside of the copyright context, rare instances of government price-fixing involve commodities, not differentiated goods. The Federal Energy Regulatory Commission conducts a ratesetting process for interstate transmission of electricity and natural gas, *see* 16 U.S.C. § 824d-e; 15 U.S.C. § 717c-d, and the United States Department of Agriculture issues federal milk marketing orders that set minimum (not maximum) prices for the sale of milk in most regions of the United States, *see* 7 U.S.C. § 608c(5).

music embodied in that programming), which is also subject to compulsory licensing under the Copyright Act and government-set rates.[784] But retransmission rights represent a much more limited segment of the overall revenues for the television industry than do the core music markets subject to government ratesetting, and even there, broadcasters are permitted separately to negotiate non-government-controlled fees for access to the signals that carry the copyrighted works.[785]

1. Antitrust Considerations

[¶] . . . . Concerns about potential monopoly effects are heightened when would-be competitors decide on the prices to be charged for products that are or are required to be purchased together, as is the case when musical works are licensed by multiple owners on a blanket basis through ASCAP or BMI. The government, however, including the Supreme Court, has acknowledged the social benefits of this type of collective blanket licensing, and has endorsed it under a "rule of reason" approach rather than finding it *per se* unlawful.[786] But the government has also, since the World War II era, subjected ASCAP and BMI to extensive regulation under their respective consent decrees.

It is worth noting that the longevity of these two decrees represents a rather extreme exception to the modern DOJ guidelines which, since 1979, have required that such decrees terminate, generally after a period of no longer than ten years.[787] More recently, in March 2014, the DOJ announced a policy to facilitate the "fast track" review and termination of most perpetual or "legacy" decrees.[788] Under that policy, the DOJ will "advise courts that pre-1980 'legacy' decrees, except in limited circumstances, are presumptively no longer in the public interest."[789] The DOJ has suggested,

---

[784] 17 U.S.C. §§ 111, 119, 122; *see also* U.S. COPYRIGHT OFFICE, SATELLITE TELEVISION EXTENSION AND LOCALISM ACT: § 302 REPORT 129–40 (2011), *available at* http://www.copyright.gov/reports/section302-report.pdf ("STELA REPORT") (recommending ways in which the cable and satellite compulsory retransmission licenses might be phased out).

[785] *See* 47 U.S.C. § 325 (defining retransmission consent rights).

[786] *BMI v. CBS*, 441 U.S. at 23–25 (holding that the blanket license should be subject to rule of reason analysis and remanding to lower courts to apply that analysis); *CBS v. ASCAP*, 620 F.2d at 932 (on remand from Supreme Court, sustaining blanket license under rule of reason analysis because CBS had failed to prove the non-availability of alternatives to the blanket license); *Buffalo Broad. v. ASCAP*, 744 F.2d at 926–32 (sustaining blanket license under rule of reason analysis in context of local television stations).

[787] U.S. DOJ, ANTITRUST DIV., ANTITRUST DIV. MANUAL III 146–47 (5th ed. 2014), *available at* http://www.justice.gov/atr/public/divisionmanual/atrdivman.pdf.

[788] *Id.* (explaining that the DOJ's adoption of a policy that favors sunset provisions was "based on a judgment that perpetual decrees were not in the public interest"). In addition to policy concerns, there may be some interesting due process questions concerning the length of the consent decrees.

[789] Press Release, U.S. DOJ, Antitrust Div., Antitrust Division Announces New Streamlined Procedure for Parties Seeking to Modify or Terminate Old Settlements and Litigated Judgments (Mar. 28, 2014), *available at* http://www.justice.gov/atr/public/press_releases/2014/304744.pdf (noting that "[s]ince 1980, there have been significant changes in markets and technology and substantial changes in antitrust law").

however, that among those "limited circumstances" is "when there is a long-standing reliance by industry participants on the decree."[790] The revised DOJ policy would thus appear to exclude the PRO decrees.

The word "monopoly" came up many times in the written and oral presentations of participants in this study in discussing the continuing significance of the decrees and antitrust oversight. But it is important to understand that there are two distinct types of "monopoly" being referenced, and each requires separate analysis.

The first type of "monopoly" refers to alleged anticompetitive practices on the part of the PROs, and also sometimes of the major publishers and record labels with significant market share. Here the concern is that licensees—for example, a television network or online service—have insufficient leverage to negotiate appropriate licensing fees with the licensor.[791] Excessive market power is the linchpin of antitrust analysis, whether in a government-initiated enforcement action or private litigation;[792] typically, however—and as discussed below in connection with the *Pandora* litigation—the remedies for civil antitrust violations do not involve long-term government price controls. Such remedies instead tend to focus on injunctive relief to address the particular anticompetitive behavior in question and/or the payment of one-time fines.[793]

The second type of monopoly referenced by participants is a wholly different one, namely, the limited "monopoly" in an individual work that is conferred by virtue of the exclusive rights granted under the Copyright Act. Even though it is not a product of collective activity, these exclusive rights

---

[790] *Id.*

[791] Interestingly, the Office heard considerably less about the market power of large technology companies or other dominant distributors of music and whether that poses similar concerns. *But see, e.g.*, MMF & FAC Second Notice Comments at 21–22 (noting the "market power of a few tech giants").

[792] *See* U.S. DOJ & FTC, Antitrust Enforcement and Intellectual Property Rights: Promoting Innovation and Competition 110 (2007), *available at* http://www.justice.gov/atr/public/hearings/ip/ 222655.pdf ("ANTITRUST ENFORCEMENT AND IP RIGHTS REPORT") ("Whether the legal analysis applied to intellectual property bundling is some form of the per se rule or the more searching rule of reason, a plaintiff will have to establish that a defendant has market power in the tying product."); *cf. Illinois Tool Works Inc. v. Indep. Ink, Inc.*, 547 U.S. 28, 42–43 (2006) (explaining the following about tying arrangement involving patented products: "While some such arrangements are still unlawful, such as those that are the product of a true monopoly or a market wide conspiracy, . . . that conclusion must be supported by proof of power in the relevant market rather than by a mere presumption thereof."); *see also* Herbert Hovenkamp, Federal Antitrust Policy: The Law of Competition and Its Practice 2 (4th ed. 2011) ("An important goal of antitrust law—arguably its only goal—is to ensure that markets are competitive.").

[793] *See, e.g.*, Farrell Malone & J. Gregory Sidak, *Should Antitrust Consent Decrees Regulate Post-Merger Pricing?*, 3 J. Competition L. & Econ. 471, 477 (2007) (explaining that, in expressing its preference for structural remedies over conduct remedies in situations involving anticompetitive merger, the DOJ "explicitly criticizes price agreements as a component of consent decrees" and that the "[DOJ] disfavors using consent decrees to fix a price or an allowable range of prices for the post-merger firm"); *see also* Herbert Hovenkamp, Mark D. Janis, Mark A. Lemley & Christopher R. Leslie, IP and Antitrust: An Analysis of Antitrust Principles Applied to Intellectual Property Law 22–62 (2d ed. Supp. 2013) ("As a general matter, antitrust should not favor solutions that turn the federal courts into price control agencies.").

probably play no less of a significant role in debates about music licensing. Many licensees—for example, large online providers—believe they must have access to complete, or virtually complete, catalogs of sound recordings and musical works in order to compete in the marketplace. A compulsory license—at least in theory—can make that possible.

But compulsory licensing removes choice and control from copyright owners who seek to protect and maximize the value of their assets. An increasingly vocal number of copyright owners believe they should be able to withhold their works from low-paying or otherwise objectionable digital services, in part because such services may cannibalize sales or higher-paying subscription models. Taylor Swift's widely publicized decision to pull her catalog from the leading streaming provider Spotify because she did not want her songs available on Spotify's free tier of service has been widely reported, and other artists appear to be following suit.[794] Similarly, artist manager Irving Azoff of GMR has reportedly threatened YouTube with a billion-dollar lawsuit if it does not remove his clients' repertoire from their site.[795] In order to take such action—and demand higher compensation—the use cannot be subject to mandatory licensing.[796] But for those under a compulsory license or a consent decree, it is not possible to say no.

In this regard, it is interesting to compare music to other types of copyrighted works, for example, television shows and movies. Like music, a particular television show or movie may not be a fully satisfying substitute for another—or a substitute at all. But consumers do not expect to be able to access every television show through Hulu, or every movie through Netflix. It is understood that different services can and will offer different content. . . . [¶]

The Office believes that the question of whether music copyright owners should be able to choose whether to agree to a license is an especially critical one. Understandably, those seeking permission to use music appreciate the security of compulsory licensing processes and certainty of government-set rates—as buyers of content likely would in any

---

[794] Dickey, *Taylor Swift on 1989, Spotify, Her Next Tour and Female Role Model* (quoting Taylor Swift: "I think that people should feel that there is a value to what musicians have created, and that's that."); *see also* Mitchell Peters, *Big Machine's Scott Borchetta Explains Why Taylor Swift Was Removed From Spotify*, BILLBOARD (Nov. 8, 2014), http://www.billboard.com/articles/news/6312143/big-machine-scott-borchetta-explains-taylor-swift-1989-removal-from-spotify-nikki-sixx (quoting Big Machine Label Group CEO Scott Borchetta: "We determined that her fan base is so in on her, let's pull everything off of Spotify, and any other service that doesn't offer a premium service . . . Now if you are a premium subscriber to Beats or Rdio or any of the other services that don't offer just a free-only, then you will find her catalogue."); Bogursky, *Taylor Swift, Garth Brooks and other artists lead the fight against Spotify*.

[795] Gardner, *Pharrell Williams' Lawyer to YouTube: Remove Our Songs or Face $1 Billion Lawsuit*.

[796] Notably, Swift's sound recordings are not subject to compulsory licensing when used for interactive services, and GMR's clients—who are not represented by ACSCAP or BMI—have asserted rights not covered by the consent decrees.

context.[798] But modern competition law does not view the rights enjoyed by copyright owners as intrinsically anathema to efficient markets. As the DOJ itself has explained, "antitrust doctrine does not presume the existence of market power from the mere presence of an intellectual property right."[799]

As a general matter, the Office believes that certain aspects of our compulsory licensing processes can and should be relaxed. But this does not mean that antitrust concerns should be overlooked. Many pertinent considerations have been raised in the DOJ's parallel consideration of the ASCAP and BMI consent decrees. The Office strongly endorses that review, and—in light of the significant impact of the decrees in today's performance-driven music market—hopes it will result in a productive reconsideration of the 75-year-old decrees. At the same time, the Office observes that it is Congress, not the DOJ, that has the ability to address the full range of issues that encumber our music licensing system, which go far beyond the consent decrees.

2.   The PROs and the Consent Decrees

Since the first part of the twentieth century, ASCAP and BMI have provided critical services to songwriters and music publishers on the one hand, and myriad licensees on the other, in facilitating the licensing of public performance rights in musical works. SESAC, though smaller, has also played an important role in this area, administering performance rights for a select group of clients. More recently, GMR has come onto the scene as a fourth contender in the performance rights arena, with an impressive client roster. Each of these organizations offers repertoire-wide—or "blanket"—licenses for the musical works they represent, with the four together essentially representing the entire spectrum of musical works available for licensing in the U.S., including many foreign works. . . .

As detailed above, both ASCAP and BMI, unlike their smaller competitors SESAC and GMR, are subject to continuing consent decrees. The decrees, overseen by federal district courts in New York City (typically referred to as the "rate courts"), were last updated before the rise of licensed digital music services—in the case of BMI, in 1994, and in the case of ASCAP, in 2001. The consent decrees impose significant government-mandated constraints on the manner in which ASCAP and BMI may operate. . . . Except to the extent a licensee seeks a narrower license—such as a "per-program" license or a blanket license with "carveouts" for directly licensed works—ASCAP and BMI are required to license all works in their repertoire.

---

[798] For example, in a 2011 study conducted by the Copyright Office, cable and satellite operators operating under the section 111, 119 and 122 compulsory licenses expressed strong opposition to the possibility of phasing them out. STELA REPORT at 8.

[799] Antitrust Enforcement and IP Rights Report at 2.

a. *Pandora* Analysis

Publisher Withdrawals

In 2013, as part of pending ratesetting litigation with the internet radio service Pandora, both the ASCAP and BMI rate courts—applying slightly different logic—interpreted the consent decrees as prohibiting music publishers from withdrawing authorization to license their songs for particular types of uses.[800] Major music publishers had sought to withdraw their "new media" (*i.e.*, online and mobile usage)[801] rights from the PROs in an effort to negotiate with Pandora directly to achieve higher rates than what they believed they would otherwise be awarded in court.[802]

Following their decisions to withdraw, EMI agreed to a rate equivalent to the existing ASCAP rate of 1.85% for services like Pandora (but without deductions for ASCAP's fees); Sony/ATV negotiated for a prorated share of an industrywide rate of 5% (which translated to a 2.28% implied rate for ASCAP); and UMG obtained a prorated share of 7.5% (or a 3.42% ASCAP rate).[803] Subsequently, however, the two rate courts held that these publishers could not selectively withdraw specific rights from ASCAP or BMI to be negotiated independently. Instead, the publishers had to be "all in" or "all out."[804]

In the wake of these decisions, the three publishers who had sought to withdraw (now two, as Sony/ATV has since become affiliated with EMI) are, for the moment, back "in," and ASCAP and BMI have petitioned the DOJ to modify their decrees to allow these sorts of partial withdrawals by their publisher members. With the petitions pending, however, both Sony/ATV and UMPG—which together represent some 50% of the music publishing market[805]—have made it clear that they may well choose to withdraw *all* rights from the PROs in the future.

The specter of across-the-board withdrawal by the major publishers from ASCAP and BMI is concerning to many in the music sector. The three major publishers—Sony/ATV, UMPG, and Warner/Chappell—together

---

[800] *In re Pandora*, 2013 WL 5211927, at *11; *BMI v. Pandora*, 2013 WL 6697788, at *5.

[801] "New media" services are those available by means of the internet, a wireless mobile telecommunications network, and/or a computer network. *In re Pandora*, 2013 WL 5211927, at *2; *BMI v. Pandora*, 2013 WL 6697788, at *2.

[802] To some degree, the move to withdraw was also likely spurred by technological evolution. Unlike traditional media such as broadcast radio stations, digital providers are equipped to track and report each use of a musical work (for example, each time a song is streamed to an individual subscriber) and thus provide full census reporting to a copyright owner. When such census reporting is available, there is no need for an intermediary organization such as a PRO to survey or sample the service to allocate royalty payments among songwriters; a publisher has the means to allocate the royalties itself. Thus, it is more feasible for the publisher to self-administer a directly negotiated license.

[803] *Pandora Ratesetting*, 6 F. Supp. 3d at 330, 339–40, 355.

[804] *In re Pandora*, 2013 WL 5211927, at *11; *BMI v. Pandora*, 2013 WL 6697788, at *5.

[805] Christman, *First-Quarter Music Publishing Rankings: SONGS Surges Again.*

represent approximately 63% of the U.S. music publishing market,[806] and the songwriters they in turn represent (as well as the publishers themselves) currently license the vast majority of their performance rights through the PROs.[807] The Office agrees that the full withdrawal of leading publishers from ASCAP and BMI would likely significantly disrupt the music market by fundamentally altering the licensing and payment process for the public performance of musical works without an established framework to replace it, at least in the short run.

On the user side, as might be predicted, many strongly prefer the government-supervised PRO system over the unregulated negotiation of rights, and oppose the movement toward withdrawal. While many licensees—such as commercial radio and television stations represented by RMLC and TMLC—are successful in negotiating (rather than litigating) rates with ASCAP and BMI under the current regime, it is reassuring to them to know that they can turn to a federal court if they view it as a better option. Like the radio and television sectors, digital services, including Pandora (whose recent rate court litigation is discussed below), also strongly favor government oversight of music publishers' licensing practices.

[¶] . . . . Concerns about the impact of large publisher withdrawals are not limited to the user side. Songwriters, too, are apprehensive. According to longstanding industry practice, songwriters are paid their "writer's share" of performance royalties directly by the PROs; these monies do not flow through the publishers. In a world of direct licensing, publishers would not be required to adhere to established standards for the reporting and payment of royalties, such as those employed by ASCAP and BMI. Songwriters worry that direct licensing could thus result in a system with much less accountability and transparency than they currently enjoy under the PROs.

There is a particular concern about publishers' treatment of advance payments and licensing fees by music services, as such monies may not be accounted for by the publisher in a transparent fashion. This, in turn, raises a question in songwriters' minds as to whether withdrawal would exacerbate this problem. . . .[810] On top of all this, a precipitous decline in overall royalty throughput would almost certainly result in markedly increased—and perhaps prohibitive—administrative costs for those who remained affiliated with ASCAP and BMI.

An interesting question is whether significantly decreased market shares on the part of ASCAP and BMI due to major publisher withdrawals would, paradoxically, obviate the need for ongoing government control of

---

[806] *See id.*

[807] *See* Sisario, *Pandora Suit May Upend Century-Old Royalty Plan.*

[810] *See, e.g.,* SGA First Notice Comments at 8–9.

those organizations. From a practical perspective, one might question why ASCAP and BMI would remain subject to significant government controls if larger market competitors (*i.e.*, the major publishers) were not subject to such supervision. We assume that the DOJ may address this issue in its forthcoming analysis. [¶] . . . .

b. PRO Ratesetting Process

This above section reviews the *Pandora* decision in some detail because it illuminates an important policy concern: namely, whether we should continue to blend antitrust oversight with industry rate proceedings as envisioned under the consent decrees. In the *Pandora* litigation, this approach appears to have yielded a mixture of competition and ratesetting considerations, without a satisfying analysis of either. The Office is of the view that allegations of anticompetitive conduct are worthy of evaluation (and, if appropriate, remedial action) separate and apart from the question of a fair rate—and vice versa. Each of these two critical policy objectives merits government attention in its own right.[821]

The Office therefore proposes that the ratesetting aspects of PRO oversight be separated from whatever government supervision is determined still to be necessary to address antitrust concerns.

Migrate to Copyright Royalty Board

Assuming PRO ratesetting is separated from any ongoing antitrust oversight, the Office proposes that the function of establishing rates be migrated to the CRB.[822] Industry ratesetting is, of course, a primary function of the CRB, and the CRB has the benefit of experience assessing a broader spectrum of rate-related questions than the federal rate courts. Significantly, the CRB sets rates on the sound recording side as well as for musical works. It also has in-house economic expertise. . . .

[¶] . . . .

c. Partial Withdrawal of Rights

A primary focus of the commentary to the Copyright Office—and to the DOJ in its review of the consent decrees—is music publishers' ability (or

---

[821] *See* EPSTEIN at 36 (concluding that "there is no comparative advantage in using a judicial body as opposed to some administrative agency" for ratesetting).

[822] ASCAP and BMI also seek to have rate disputes decided outside of federal court. Both have recommended some sort of system of (apparently private) arbitration without providing much detail. ASCAP First Notice Comments at 4, 23–24 (recommending "expedited private arbitration"); *Music Licensing Hearings* at 52 (statement of Michael O'Neill, CEO, BMI) ("We believe that replacing the current rate court with arbitration in New York under the American Arbitration Association rules would be a faster, less expensive, and a more market-responsive mechanism for all parties to obtain fair, market-value rate decisions."). For the reasons discussed above, the Office believes the CRB is the logical venue to determine public performance rates. As an added benefit, the CRB does not depend upon the payment of private arbitration fees (a significant factor in the demise of the CARPs that preceded the CRB). *See* H.R. REP. NO. 108–408, at 21, 99–100. At the same time, based on stakeholders' input, the Office is recommending certain changes to the CRB system, which are outlined below.

inability) to withdraw specific categories of licensing rights from their authorizations to the PROs. The purpose of such withdrawals would be to allow music owners to negotiate in the marketplace for the exploitation of their songs—or, if not satisfied with the price offered, to withhold their songs from particular services. This has an analog in much of the discussion surrounding section 115, another area where publishers and songwriters seek the ability to escape from mandatory licensing. . . .

. . . . The Office is therefore sympathetic to the publishers' position that they should be permitted to withdraw certain rights from the PROs to permit market negotiations. The Office believes that partial withdrawal—in the form of a limited right to "opt out"—should be made available to those who want it. This view is reinforced by the possibility of wholesale defections by major (and perhaps other) publishers from ASCAP and BMI if government controls are not relaxed, and the potential chaos that would likely follow.

Any such opt-out process would need to be carefully managed to ensure licensees did not face undue burdens in the licensing process as a result. At least for now, the Office believes that withdrawal of performance rights should be limited to digital rights equivalent to those that the record labels are free to negotiate outside of sections 112 and 114—essentially, interactive streaming rights for new media services. In the case of such a partial withdrawal, the publisher would be free to pursue a direct deal for the rights in question (or, if not satisfied with a licensee's offer, withhold songs from the service in question).

Publishers who chose to opt out would need publicly to identify the particular uses subject to withdrawal, the licensing organization from which they were being withdrawn, each of the affected works, where a direct license might be sought, and other pertinent information.[831] As discussed below, it is the Office's recommendation that a non-profit general music rights organization ("GMRO") be designated by the Copyright Office to receive, maintain and offer access to this information. . . .

---

[831] The proposed opt-out right would be by publisher, not by individual work.

The following excerpt is from the DOJ's Closing Statement at the completion of its 2016 antitrust consent decree review of the ASCAP and BMI consent decrees. It provides more context and details about the concerns raised in those proceedings and the ongoing work of the Antitrust Division in overseeing compliance with the consent decrees, with a particular focus on the recent debates about whether the consent decrees do, or should, require ASCAP and BMI to offer "full-work" licenses or allow partial withdrawal of rights (e.g. new media rights) from blanket licensing. The latter issue—partial withdrawal of rights—was introduced in the Copyright Office Report excerpted above. The issue of "full work" licensing involves situations in which there are multiple authors/owners of a composition who are not all members of the same PRO, creating uncertainty as to whether licenses from multiple PROs or individuals are needed for a licensee to be fully authorized to perform the work.

CLOSING STATEMENT OF DEPARTMENT OF JUSTICE, ANTITRUST DIVISION, ANTITRUST CONSENT DECREE REVIEW

ASCAP and BMI 2016[27]

At the request of ASCAP and BMI, in 2014 the Antitrust Division of the U.S. Department of Justice opened an inquiry into the operation and effectiveness of the consent decrees.... During the discussions surrounding these requested modifications, it became apparent that industry participants had differing understandings of whether the PROs' licenses provide licensees the ability to publicly perform, without risk of copyright infringement, all of the works in each of the PROs' repertories. The requests for modifications therefore required the Division to examine the question of whether the consent decrees obligate ASCAP and BMI to offer "full-work" licenses.

The Division has now concluded its investigation and has decided not to seek to modify the consent decrees. As discussed in detail below, the consent decrees, which describe the PROs' licenses as providing the ability to perform "works" or "compositions," require ASCAP and BMI to offer full-work licenses. The Division reaches this determination based not only on the language of the consent decrees and its assessment of historical practices, but also because only full-work licensing can yield the substantial procompetitive benefits associated with blanket licenses that

---

[27] U.S. Dept. of Justice, Antitrust Division, Antitrust Consent Decree Review—ASCAP and BMI 2016, Statement of the Department of Justice on the Closing of the Antitrust Division's Review of the ASCAP and BMI Consent Decree (August 4, 2016), *at* https://www.justice.gov/atr/file/882101/download (last visited Sept. 23, 2019).

distinguish ASCAP's and BMI's activities from other agreements among competitors that present serious issues under the antitrust laws. Moreover, the Division has determined not to support modifying the consent decrees to allow ASCAP and BMI to offer "fractional" licenses that convey only rights to fractional shares and require additional licenses to perform works. Although stakeholders on all sides have raised some concerns with the status quo, the Division's investigation confirmed that the current system has well served music creators and music users for decades and should remain intact. The Division's confirmation that the consent decrees require full-work licensing is fully consistent with preserving the significant licensing and payment benefits that the PROs have provided music creators and music users for decades.

.... This statement seeks to explain the bases for the Division's determination and describe why an express recognition that ASCAP and BMI do currently and must continue to offer full-work licenses should not meaningfully disrupt the status quo in the licensing of public performance rights. . . .

The Division has also decided that it will not at this time support other proposed decree modifications. The most significant of the proposed modifications was a proposal supported by ASCAP, BMI, and music publishers to allow music publishers to "partially withdraw" from ASCAP and BMI, thereby prohibiting the PROs from licensing the withdrawing publishers' music to digital services such as Pandora or Spotify. The lack of industry consensus as to whether the PROs offer full-work licenses creates too much uncertainty to properly evaluate the competitive impact of allowing partial withdrawal, a necessary predicate to a determination that a decree modification to allow partial withdrawal would be in the public interest. [¶] . . .

I. Background

Purpose and Operations of ASCAP and BMI. In order to publicly perform musical works, businesses must obtain permission from copyright holders. Every day, hundreds of thousands of restaurants, radio stations, online services, television stations, performance venues, and countless other establishments publicly perform musical works. These music users have historically relied in large part on PROs to provide licenses to perform these works. PROs pool the copyrights held by their composer, songwriter, and publisher members or affiliates and collectively license those rights to music users. . . .

Individual songwriters, composers, and publishers that participate in a PRO execute an agreement with that PRO to do so. Today, a songwriter joins ASCAP by executing a membership agreement in which it grants to ASCAP the right to license any work that "may be written, composed, acquired, owned, published, or copyrighted by the owner, alone, jointly or in collaboration with others . . . ." ASCAP Writer Agreement, *available at* http://www.ascap.com/~/media/files/pdf/join/ascap-writer-agreement.pdf. The ASACP writer further warrants "that there are no existing assignments or licenses, direct or indirect, of non-dramatic performing rights in my musical works, except to or with the publisher(s)" that would restrict ASCAP's ability to license under the terms of the grant of rights. *Id.* Similarly, a songwriter affiliating with BMI grants to BMI the right to license non-dramatic public performances of "all musical compositions . . . composed by [the member] alone or with one or more co-writers" and promises that "no performing rights in [these compositions] have been granted to or reserved by others except as specifically set forth therein in connection with Works heretofore written or co-written by [the author]." BMI Writer Agreement, *available at* http://www.bmi.com/forms/affiliation/bmi_writer_kit.pdf.

The ASCAP and BMI Consent Decrees. [¶] . . . .

Consistent with the Supreme Court's guidance, the consent decrees seek to preserve the transformative benefits of blanket licensing, including the "immediate use" of the works within the PROs' repertories. To this end, the ASCAP consent decree requires ASCAP to offer users a "license to perform *all the works in the ASCAP repertory*." ASCAP Consent Decree § VI (emphasis added). The BMI consent decree similarly requires BMI's licenses to provide music users with access to its "repertory," which includes "those compositions, the right of public performance of which [BMI] has or hereafter shall have the right to license or sublicense." BMI Consent Decree § II(C). The decrees also provide for the creation of two separate "rate courts," to which either music users or the PROs may resort if the two sides are unable to reach a mutually agreeable price for a license. *See* ASCAP Consent Decree § IX; BMI Consent Decree § XIV.

Existence of Multi-Owner Works. Many musical works have multiple authors. Under the copyright law, joint authors of a single work are treated as tenants-in-common, so "[e]ach co-owner may thus grant a nonexclusive license to use the entire work without the consent of other co-owners, provided that the licensor accounts for and pays over to his or her co-owners their pro-rata shares of the proceeds." United States Copyright Office, VIEWS OF THE UNITED STATES COPYRIGHT OFFICE CONCERNING PRO LICENSING OF JOINTLY OWNED WORKS (2016), at 6, *available at* http://www.copyright.gov/policy/pro-licensing.pdf. Copyright holders may, however, depart from the default rules under the Copyright Act. *See generally id.* ("[T]he default rules are only a 'starting point,' with collaborators . . . free to alter this statutory allocation of rights and liabilities by contract.") (citations and quotations omitted). There are therefore at least two possible frameworks under which PROs may license works with multiple owners belonging to multiple PROs. Under a "full-work" license, each PRO would offer non-exclusive licenses to the work entitling the user to perform the work without risk of infringement liability. Under a "fractional" license, each PRO would offer a license only to the interests it holds in a work, and require that the licensee obtain additional licenses from the PROs representing other co-owners before performing the work.

Division Review of the Consent Decrees. In 2014, the Antitrust Division opened an investigation into potential modifications of the consent decrees requested by various stakeholders. The Division issued a public request for comments and received more than 200 responses, primarily from industry stakeholders such as composers, publishers, and music licensees, as well as from advocacy groups. (The solicitation and responses are available here: https://www.justice.gov/atr/ascap-bmi-decree-review.) The PROs proposed three significant modifications: first, to allow publishers to partially withdraw works from the PROs, thereby preventing the PROs from licensing such works to digital music users; second, to streamline the process by which fee disputes are resolved; and, third, to permit the PROs to offer licenses to rights other than the public performance right, particularly for users who also need a performance license. . . .

As the Division considered the implications of these proposed changes, particularly partial withdrawal, stakeholders on all sides raised questions about the treatment of multi-owner works. Music users claimed that the PROs had always offered licenses to perform all works in their repertories, whether partially or fully owned, and urged modifications to confirm their view. Rightsholders, by contrast, claimed that the PROs had never offered full licenses to perform fractionally owned works, and also urged modifications to confirm their view. ASCAP and BMI did not concede that the existing consent decrees prohibited fractional licensing, but proposed that their consent decrees be modified to explicitly allow them to offer fractional licenses. *Historically, the industry has largely avoided a definitive determination of whether ASCAP and BMI offered full-work or fractional licenses because the vast majority of music users obtain a license from ASCAP, BMI, and SESAC and pay those PROs based on fractional market shares. These practices made it unnecessary, from both the user and rightsholders' perspective, to sort out whether the ASCAP and BMI licenses are full-work or fractional; users have held licenses that collectively cover all works and rightsholders have been paid for their works by their own PROs without having to worry about accounting* (emphasis added). However, recent events, including the Division's review, have made it necessary to confront the question.

The question of whether ASCAP and BMI licenses are or should be fractional or full-work has significant implications for the PROs, their members, and their licensees. If PROs offer fractional licenses, a music user, before performing any multi-owner work in a PRO's repertory, would need a license to the fractional interests held by each of the work's co-owners. A full-work license from a PRO, on the other hand, would provide infringement protection to a music user seeking to perform any work in the repertory of the PRO. . . .

II. There is broad consensus that ASCAP and BMI as currently constituted fill important and procompetitive roles in the music licensing industry.

Despite strong areas of disagreement among industry stakeholders as to issues raised in the Division's solicitations of public comments, there is broad consensus that ASCAP and BMI provide a valuable service to both music users and PRO members. The PROs allow music users to obtain immediate access through licenses that protect them from copyright infringement risk to millions of works controlled by the hundreds of thousands of songwriters, composers, and publishers that have contributed songs to the PROs.

Music creators also benefit from the PROs' licensing practices. For many songwriters and composers, affiliating with a PRO and contributing their works to the PRO's repertory provides the only practical way of licensing their works. While direct licensing to individual music users always remains available as an alternative for music creators, individual music creators would often find it infeasible to themselves enter into licenses with all of the bars, restaurants, radio stations, television stations, and other music users to which ASCAP and BMI license. Even where direct negotiations are possible, users and creators may find PRO licenses more efficient. Moreover, the PROs have developed valuable expertise in distributing revenues among the hundreds of thousands of copyright holders, and creators generally trust that ASCAP and BMI will fairly distribute licensing proceeds.

[¶] . . . .

III. The consent decrees require full-work licensing.

The Division's review has made clear that the consent decrees require ASCAP's and BMI's licenses to provide users with the ability to publicly perform, without risk of infringement liability, any of the songs in the respective PRO's repertory. This determination is compelled by the language and intent of the decrees and years of interpretations by federal courts. First, the plain text of the decrees cannot be squared with an interpretation that allows fractional licensing: the consent decrees require ASCAP to offer users the ability to perform all "works" in its repertory and BMI's licenses to offer users the ability to perform all "compositions" in its repertory. ASCAP's and BMI's licenses have for decades purported to do exactly that. *See, e.g.*, BMI Music License for Eating & Drinking Establishments, *available at* http://www.bmi.com/forms/licensing/gl/ede. pdf ("BMI grants you a non-exclusive license to publicly perform at the Licensed Premises *all of the musical works* of which BMI controls the rights to grant public performances during the terms.") (emphasis added).

Moreover, only full-work licensing achieves the benefits that underlie the courts' descriptions and understandings of ASCAP's and BMI's licenses. For example, the Supreme Court explained that the ASCAP and BMI blanket license "allows the licensee *immediate use* of covered compositions, *without the delay of prior individual negotiations*, and great flexibility in the choice of musical material." *BMI*, 441 U.S. at 21–22 (emphasis added). In so doing, they provide "unplanned, rapid, and indemnified access" to the works in ASCAP's and BMI's repertories. *Id.* at 20. If the licenses were fractional, they would not provide *immediate* use of covered compositions; users would need to obtain additional licenses before using many of the covered compositions. And such fractional licenses would *not* avoid the delay of additional negotiations, because users would need to clear rights from additional owners of fractional interests in songs before performing the works in the ASCAP and BMI repertories. Similarly, the Second Circuit has held that ASCAP is "required to license its entire repertory to all eligible users," and that the repertory includes "all works contained in the ASCAP repertory." *Pandora Media, Inc. v. ASCAP*, 785 F.3d 73, 77–78 (2d Cir. 2015) (emphasis removed). The Second Circuit rejected arguments that this decree requirement conflicted with copyright law, noting that "[i]ndividual copyright holders remain free to choose whether to license their works through ASCAP." *Id.* at 78. The logic of the Second Circuit's decision applies to BMI as well.

Accordingly, the consent decrees must be read as requiring full-work licensing. ASCAP and BMI can include in their repertories only those songs they can license on such a basis. These songs include works written by a single songwriter who is a member of the PRO; works written by multiple writers, all of whom are members of the PRO; and works written by multiple writers, one or more of whom are members of the PRO and possess the right under the default tenancy in common or pursuant to other arrangements among the songwriters to grant a full-work license. Moreover, nothing in this interpretation contradicts copyright law. To the extent allowed by copyright law, co-owners of a song remain free to impose limitations on one another's ability to license the song. Such an action may, however, make it impossible for ASCAP or BMI—consistent with the full-work licensing requirement of the antitrust consent decrees—to include that song in their blanket licenses.

IV. The Division has determined that modification of the consent decrees to permit fractional licensing by ASCAP and BMI would not be in the public interest.

The Division also considered ASCAP's and BMI's requests to modify the decrees to permit fractional licensing. Based on the public comments and meetings and communications with stakeholders, the Division has concluded that it would not be in the public interest to modify the ASCAP and BMI consent decrees to permit ASCAP and BMI to offer fractional licenses.

Modifying the consent decrees to permit fractional licensing would undermine the traditional role of the ASCAP and BMI licenses in providing protection from unintended copyright infringement liability and immediate access to the works in the organizations' repertories, which the Division and the courts have viewed as key procompetitive benefits of the PROs preserved by the consent decrees.

Allowing fractional licensing would also impair the functioning of the market for public performance licensing and potentially reduce the playing of music. If ASCAP and BMI were permitted to offer fractional licenses, music users seeking to avoid potential infringement liability would need to meticulously track song ownership before playing music. As the experience of ASCAP and BMI themselves shows, this would be no easy task. Today, in the context of compensating song owners, ASCAP, BMI, and other PROs must track and rely on song ownership information they possess to determine to whom to distribute funds collected from music users. But even with their years of experience in finding and compensating song owners and their established relationships with music creators, the PROs often do not make distributions until weeks or months *after* a song is played, and even then do so imperfectly. The difficulties, delays, and imperfections that are tolerated in the context of PRO payments would prove fatal to the businesses of music users, who need to resolve ownership questions *before* playing music to avoid infringement exposure.

A comparison between the licensing of public performance rights and the licensing of synchronization rights further illustrates the problem faced by music users who rely on PRO licenses. Producers of movies or television programming have traditionally entered separate synchronization licenses with each owner of a fractional interest in a song the producer seeks to include in his or her television show or movie, generally on a song-by-song basis. Unlike many ASCAP and BMI licensees, the producer can identify a song before it is used and has the ability to substitute to a different song if the producer cannot reach agreements for the synchronization rights with each of the song's fractional owners. Indeed, it is not uncommon for a producer to fail to obtain synchronization licenses from all of a song's fractional owners and to turn instead to a different song. In contrast, music users publicly performing music are often using music selected by others— for example, by the producer who placed a song in a television show or the disk jockey selecting songs for the radio (which may be played in a bar or restaurant that cannot control the music chosen). These users rely on blanket licenses to allow them to perform music without first determining whether they have cleared the rights in a work. Unlike a movie or television producer, these music users cannot switch to a different song if they lack the rights to publicly perform a song. Their only recourse under a fractional licensing regime, under which their PRO blanket licenses leave them exposed to infringement liability, might be to simply turn off the music.

[¶] . . . . Finally, allowing fractional licensing might also impede the licensed performance of many songs by incentivizing owners of fractional interests in songs to withhold their partial interests from the PROs. A user with a license from ASCAP or BMI would then be unable to play that song unless it acceded to the hold-out owner's demands, providing the hold-out owner substantial bargaining leverage to extract significant returns. The result would be a further reduction in the benefits of the ASCAP and BMI licenses and the creation of additional impediments to the public performance of music.

For all of these reasons, the Division believes that modifying the consent decrees to permit fractional licensing would not be in the public interest. Although PROs, songwriters, and publishers suggested there are problems associated with full-work licensing, especially the creation of works that would be unlicensable by the PROs, the Division believes that the potential costs associated with these concerns are far outweighed by the benefits of full-work licensing. In particular, the Division believes . . . that songwriters possess several options that would allow PROs to continue to license their works as well as allow those songwriters to continue to be paid by the PRO of their choice.

V.   The Division has also determined that other modifications to the consent decrees would not be appropriate at this time.

Industry stakeholders also proposed to the Division that the consent decrees be modified in other ways. The most significant of the proposed modifications, and the one that received the greatest attention among industry stakeholders, was that the consent decrees be modified to allow PRO members to "partially withdraw" rights and thereby prevent the PROs from granting licenses that include those rights to certain users (in particular, digital music services) but not to other music users. [¶] . . . .

VIII. The consent decrees remain vital to an industry that has grown up in reliance on them. But the consent decrees are inherently limited in scope, and a more comprehensive legislative solution may be possible and preferable.

During the course of its review, the Division considered whether the ASCAP and BMI consent decrees continue to serve the purposes for which they were put in place in 1941. After carefully considering the information obtained during its investigation, the Division has concluded that the industry has developed in the context of, and in reliance on, these consent decrees and that they therefore should remain in place. However, the Division recognizes the incongruity in the oversight over the licensing of performance rights and other copyrights in compositions and sound recordings and believes that the protections provided by the consent decrees could be addressed through a legislative solution that brings performance rights licensing under a similar regulatory umbrella as other rights. The Division encourages the development of a comprehensive legislative solution that ensures a competitive marketplace and obviates the need for continued Division oversight of the PROs.

DOJ ANTITRUST DIVISION ANTITRUST CONSENT DECREE REVIEW

ASCAP and BMI 2019[28]

The DOJ has since opened up a new Consent Decree Review for both United States v. ASCAP, 41 Civ. 1395 (S.D.N.Y.) and United States v. BMI, 64 Civ. 3787 (S.D.N.Y.), "to address competitive concerns arising from the market power each organization acquired through the aggregation of public performance rights held by their member songwriters and music publishers."[29] It accepted comments from the public, "including songwriters, publishers, licensees, and other industry stakeholders"[30] through early August of 2019 on the following questions:

- Do the Consent Decrees continue to serve important competitive purposes today? Why or why not? Are there provisions that are no longer necessary to protect competition? Which ones and why? Are there provisions that are ineffective in protecting competition? Which ones and why?

- What, if any, modifications to the Consent Decrees would enhance competition and efficiency?

- Would termination of the Consent Decrees serve the public interest? If so, should termination be immediate or should there instead be a sunset period? What, if any, modifications to the Consent Decrees would provide an efficient transitionary period before any decree termination?

- Do differences between the two Consent Decrees adversely affect competition? How?

- Are there differences between ASCAP/BMI and PROs that are not subject to the Consent Decrees that adversely affect competition?

---

[28] U.S. Dept. of Justice, Antitrust Division, Antitrust Consent Decree Review—ASCAP and BMI 2019, at https://www.justice.gov/atr/antitrust-consent-decree-review-ascap-and-bmi-2019 (last visited Sept. 23, 2019).

[29] *Id.*

[30] *Id.*

- Are existing antitrust statutes and applicable caselaw sufficient to protect competition in the absence of the Consent Decrees?[31]

NOTES AND QUESTIONS

1. By the time you read this chapter, the DOJ will most likely have published the results of its 2019 review, providing a summary of the answers it received to the above questions from the various interested parties in the industry and giving its own evaluation based upon those responses. What do you think some of the arguments are? Can you make a case for greater antitrust oversight? Can you make a case for reduced oversight or termination of the consent decrees?

2. The summaries above provide a comparative framework for viewing United States performance rights collectives and the tension between efficient mechanisms for licensing rights and monopolistic control of pricing. In the musical composition context, competing organizations arose and yet were still ultimately subject to antitrust oversight, with judges in the Southern District of New York resolving fee disputes. Do you think antitrust oversight is still necessary for licensing performance rights in compositions?

3. Both the Copyright Office and the DOJ discuss concerns about partial or wholesale withdrawal of rights by publishers (particularly large publishers) from blanket licensing, both in terms of fragmentation of the market and difficulty for users who perform large catalogs of compositions, such as non-interactive streaming services like Pandora. Compare the DOJ's stated position on partial withdrawal of new media rights in its discussion of the *Pandora* litigation with the Copyright Office's stated position in the 2015 Report. Which view do you think is better reasoned? Why?

4. The efforts by publishers to withhold "new media rights" from blanket licensing, mentioned in the 2015 Copyright Office Report and 2016 DOJ Consent Decree Review Conclusion excerpted above, find a parallel in the efforts by music publishers to withhold television performance licensing from ASCAP in the late 1940s and early 1950s—both instances reflect a desire to potentially negotiate greater licensing fees through individual licensing of the publisher's catalog of works than ASCAP could obtain under the consent decree rate setting process. How can the copyright owner's interest in negotiating what she views as fair license fees be balanced with the increasing demand by licensees for efficient licensing systems?

5. The 2105 Copyright Office Report includes a strong recommendation that the rate setting process be separated from antitrust oversight, with the Copyright Royalty Board (an entity within the Copyright Office already responsible for setting rates for licensing other types of music rights) taking

---

[31] *Id.*

over the rate setting process. However, the 2018 Music Modernization Act did not take any action on this recommendation; as noted in the Update above, it only made relatively minor adjustments to the current rate setting procedure for licensing performance rights in compositions that requires disputes to be submitted to the Southern District of New York. Why do you suppose Congress took no action on this proposal? What parties might be opposed to it, and why? Who might it favor? Do you think that antitrust oversight and rate-setting inform one another and should remain intertwined, or do you think that the two issues can be effectively separated?

6. In a 1995 article, Bernard Korman, former General Counsel to ASCAP, noted some important differences between the U.S. approach to collective administration of copyrights and that of other countries, particularly those in Europe: (1) with multiple PROs, the U.S. is the only country where it is not possible to obtain "a single public performance license granting access to virtually all of the world's copyrighted music"; (2) U.S. antitrust law places limits on collective action by copyright owners not found in other countries; (3) not only do collectives need to be concerned about federal antitrust law in the U.S., but they are also subject to state laws (from 50 states and the District of Columbia) prohibiting anti-competitive conduct; and (4) collectives in the U.S. are not governed by a cultural agency, as in most European countries, but are instead under the oversight of the Antitrust Division.[32] Do you think it would be better or worse to have a single collective? Why? Is the Antitrust Division of the DOJ the best entity to exercise oversight over PROs?

7. In any licensing system, the licensors will argue that rates are too low and licensees will argue that rates are too high. What factors should be most important in determining a fair license fee? If the music publishing industry were given a clean slate to reinvent its licensing system, what would you recommend?

8. Note that Chapters 6 and 7 will return to licensing, rate setting, and the pros and cons of statutory licenses, discussing related issues that have arisen since the creation of a federal digital performance right in sound recordings and the growth of digital streaming as the preferred music-delivery method for many consumers, as well as the likely impact of changes adopted in the 2018 Music Modernization Act regarding the compulsory license for the mechanical right (among other changes). Next, though, we turn to developments in the 1970s relating to federal protections for sound recordings and the efforts of record companies and recording artists to obtain a performance right in the sound recordings that are the product of their work.

---

[32] Bernard Korman, *U.S. Position on Collective Administration of Copyright and Anti-Trust Law*, 43 J. Copyright Soc'y U.S.A. 158, 162–64 (Winter 1995).

CHAPTER IV

FEDERAL PROTECTION FOR SOUND RECORDINGS AND STATE LAW PREEMPTION: *THE LONG AND WINDING ROAD*[1]

■ ■ ■

The last chapter took you from the first efforts to enforce the statutory performance right in *compositions* in the early part of the twentieth century to modern oversight of the licensing process for those performance rights. This chapter takes a step back again, looking at the first federal recognition of copyright protection for *sound recordings* and the ensuing battle over performance rights in sound recordings that continues today. Although Chapter 2 introduced you to some of the efforts to seek legal protection for sound recordings by both performers and record labels in the early years of the record industry, the Copyright Act did not recognize sound recordings as federally protected works until the Sound Recording Act ("SRA") of 1971 was passed. And even then, the protection that the SRA granted was limited and prospective only. A patchwork of state law protections had developed over the prior decades, many of which criminalized unauthorized duplication of records, but no nationwide remedy had existed against large-scale record piracy. This chapter thus begins with the text of the Sound Recording Act, which granted only limited rights to owners of sound recordings, followed by excerpts from a report by Barbara Ringer, then the Register of Copyrights, who summed up recommendations to Congress regarding a performance right in sound recordings.

It was not until 1995, when the Digital Performance Right in Sound Recordings Act was passed, that federal law granted any performance right to sound recordings, and that right was limited to certain digital transmissions. This chapter will address the debate over performance rights in sound recordings that continues to this day even as the existing, limited digital performance right has become a primary source of revenue for the recording industry.

In addition, this chapter discusses one of the most impactful changes to U.S. copyright law for the music industry in the 1976 Copyright Act—

---

[1]   John Lennon & Paul McCartney (1969); released by the Beatles on LET IT BE (1970).

section 301's preemption of state laws that had previously protected sound recordings and its carve-out that allowed state law protections to continue for pre-1972 sound recordings. Owners of pre-1972 sound recordings lobbied for years to obtain federal protection for their works, and beginning in 2014 there was a flurry of litigation in which pre-1972 sound recording owners asserted state law performance rights in lawsuits against digital streaming services. As you will see, the 2018 Music Modernization Act finally addressed at least some of the arguments made by advocates for these "legacy" recordings.

CONSIDER AS YOU READ . . .

- What are the strongest arguments for expanding the performance right in sound recordings beyond digital transmissions? What are the strongest arguments against doing so? Has the music marketplace changed enough since the 1978 Ringer Report to render any of the arguments (pro or con) either stronger or weaker than they were at the time?

- Should the 1971 Sound Recording Act have applied retroactively to sound recordings made prior to its effective date? Why or why not?

- What do you think of the merits of arguments regarding a state law performance right in sound recordings for pre-1972 sound recordings?

- What types of state law protections for musical works and sound recordings, if any, should survive preemption analysis?

A. THE LIMITED FEDERAL PROTECTION OF SOUND RECORDINGS

SOUND RECORDING ACT OF 1971
Excerpt from Public Law 92–140, 85 Stat. 391–92, October 15, 1971

AN ACT

To amend title 17 of the United States Code to provide for the creation of a limited copyright in sound recordings for the purpose of protecting against unauthorized duplication and piracy of sound recording, and for other purposes.

Be it enacted by the Senate and House of Representatives of the United States of America in Congress assembled, That title 17 of the United States Code is amended in the following respects:

(a) In section 1, title 17, of the United States Code, add a subsection (f) to read:

"To reproduce and distribute to the public by sale or other transfer of ownership, or by rental, lease, or lending, reproductions of the copyrighted work if it be a sound recording: *Provided*, That the exclusive right of the owner of a copyright in a sound recording to reproduce it is limited to the right to duplicate the sound recording in a tangible form that directly or indirectly recaptures the actual sounds fixed in the recording: *Provided further*, That this right does not extend to the making or duplication of another sound recording that is an independent fixation of other sounds, even though such sounds imitate or simulate those in the copyrighted sound recording; or to reproductions made by transmitting organizations exclusively for their own use."

[¶¶]. . . . Sec. 3. This Act shall take effect four months after its enactment except that section 2 of this Act shall take effect immediately upon its enactment. The provisions of title 17, United States Code, as amended by section 1 of this Act, shall apply only to sound recordings fixed, published, and copyrighted on and after the effective date of this Act and before January 1, 1975, and nothing in title 17, United States Code, as amended by section 1 of this Act, shall be applied retroactively or be construed as affecting in any way any rights with respect to sound recordings fixed before the effective date of this Act.

Approved October 15, 1971.

Barbara Ringer, Register of Copyrights 1973–1980
From U.S. Copyright Office, https://www.copyright.
gov/about/registers/ringer/ringer.html

RINGER REPORT ON PERFORMANCE RIGHTS IN SOUND RECORDINGS, ADDENDUM TO REPORT
42 Fed. Reg. 12,763–8 (March 27, 1978)

Barbara Ringer, the first woman to serve as Register of Copyrights, is viewed as one of the architects of the 1976 copyright revision. In that role, she was tasked with overseeing the production by the Copyright Office of a Report on Performance Rights in Sound Recordings—an almost 1,000-page document provided to Congress in January of 1978 to inform its consideration of the merits of providing a performance right in sound recordings. Below are excerpts from her separately-submitted Statement to Congress that summarizes her conclusions and recommendations based upon the Report.

[1410–03]
LIBRARY OF CONGRESS
Copyright Office
[Docket NO. S77–6D]

PERFORMANCE RIGHTS IN SOUND RECORDINGS

Addenda to Report

On Tuesday. March 21, 1978, the Federal Register published a notice that addenda to the January 3, 1978 Report of the Register of Copyrights were transmitted to Congress and are available for public inspection (43 FR 11773). The following is the Register's Statement referred to in the previous notice at 43 FR 11774, preceded by that Statement's letter of transmittal. . . .

ADDENDUM TO THE REPORT OF THE REGISTER OF COPYRIGHTS
ON PERFORMANCE RIGHTS IN SOUND RECORDINGS

Statement of the Register of Copyrights containing a Summary of Conclusions and Specific Legislative Recommendations.

INTRODUCTION

The Congressional mandate to the Register of Copyrights contained in section 114(d) of the new copyright statute reads as follows:

> "On January 3, 1978, the Register of Copyrights, after consulting with representatives of owners of copyrighted materials, representatives of the broadcasting, recording, motion picture, entertainment industries, and arts organizations, representatives of organized labor and performers of copyrighted materials, shall submit to the Congress a report setting forth recommendations as to whether this section should be amended to provide for performers and copyright owners of copyrighted material any performance rights in such material. The report should describe the status of such rights in foreign countries, the views of major interested parties, and specific legislative or other recommendations, if any."

On January 3, 1978, I submitted to Congress our basic documentary report, consisting of some 2,600 pages, including appendices. The basic report includes analyses of the constitutional and legal issues presented by proposals for performance rights in sound recordings, the legislative history of previous proposals to create these rights under Federal Copyright law, and testimony and written comments representing current views on the subject in this country. The basic report seeks to review and analyze foreign systems for the protection of performance rights in sound recordings, and the existing structure for international protection in this field, including the Rome Convention for the Protection of Performers, Producers of Phonograms, and Broadcasting Organizations. The basic report also includes an "economic impact analysis" of the proposals for performance royalty legislation, prepared by an independent economic consultant under contract with the Copyright Office.

After reviewing all of the material in the basic report, together with additional supplementary material,[FN1 omitted] I have prepared this statement in an effort to summarize the conclusions I have drawn from our research and analysis and to present specific recommendations for legislation. With the presentation of this statement, the Copyright Office believes that it has discharged all of its responsibilities under section 114(d).

It was understandable that enactment of section 114(d) was greeted with raised eyebrows and cynical smiles. Some of those who favored performance rights in sound recordings viewed it as a temporizing move, aimed at ducking the issue and delaying Congress' obligation to come to grips with the problem. Others, opponents of the principle of royalties for performance of sound recordings, expressed derision at the idea of entrusting a full-scale study of the problem to an official who had, in testimony before both Houses of Congress, expressed a personal commitment to that principle. The Register's Report could either be looked on as a time-consuming nuisance that had to be gotten out of the way before Congress could be induced to look at the problem again, or as something that could be dismissed as worthless because the views of the official responsible for it were already fixed and her conclusions were predictable.

Neither the idea nor the drafting of section 114(d) originated with anyone in the Copyright Office. When approached with the proposed compromise that subsection (d) reflects, we accepted the responsibility and the short deadline imposed by the new subsection with two thoughts in mind:

First, we agreed with those who felt that any full-scale effort to tie enactment of performance royalty legislation directly to the bill for general revision of the copyright law would seriously impair the chances for enactment of omnibus revision. Keeping the subject of performance royalty alive but splitting it off for later Congressional consideration reduced the twin dangers of lack of time to complete work on the bill for general revision, and concerted opposition to the bill as a whole.

Second, we also agreed that, with a problem as important and hotly contested as this one, Congress should have a fuller record and more thorough research and analysis on which to base its consideration of proposed legislation. Although the deadline for the report (January 3, 1978) coincided with the date on which the Copyright Office was required to implement the whole new copyright statute, we felt that it would be possible for us to complete both jobs on time.

As I viewed the mandate in section 114(d), the important thing was to provide Congress with a body of reliable information that would help it to legislate intelligently and effectively on the subject of performance rights in sound recordings. Regarded in this way, the basic documentary report, together with the other three addenda, are far more important than this statement of conclusions and recommendations.

[¶ . . .] As Register of Copyrights since 1973 I have taken a consistent and rather strong public position in favor of the principle of performance royalties for sound recordings. This was no secret to anyone when section 114(d) was added to the revision bill and, in enacting that provision, Congress could hardly have expected me to abandon beliefs and convictions based on many years of personal research and experience in the field. What it could expect were two separate things: first, as full and objective a study by the Copyright Office of the problem as possible; and, second, an honest and unbiased statement of my conclusions and recommendations, as Register of Copyright, based on a fresh review of the Copyright Office study.

This statement is intended to fulfill the second of these two obligations. My hope is that it will be of some help to Congress in considering this difficult problem, but that no one attach undue weight to any of its conclusions or recommendations. In particular, I hope that it will be considered as entirely separate from the Copyright Office's basic documentary report, so that the attacks on my conclusions and recommendations will not undermine the usefulness of the body of information brought together in the basic report.

BASIC ISSUES AND CONCLUSIONS

The following is an effort to present, in outline form, the basic issues of public policy, constitutional law, economics, and Federal statutory law raised by proposals for performing rights in sound recordings, together with a bare statement of the conclusion I have reached on each of them, and a highly condensed discussion of the reasons behind each conclusion.

1. The Fundamental Public Policy Issue

Issue: Should performers, or record producers, or both, enjoy any rights under Federal law with respect to public performances of sound recordings to which they have contributed?

Conclusion: Yes.

Discussion: The Copyright Office supports the principle of copyright protection for the public performance of sound recordings. The lack of copyright protection for performers since the commercial development of phonograph records has had a drastic and destructive effect on both the performing and the recording arts. Professor Gorman's fascinating study shows that in seeking to combat the vast technological unemployment resulting from the use of recorded rather than live performances, the labor union movement in the United States may in some ways have made the problem worse. It is too late to repair past wrongs, but this does not mean they should be allowed to continue. Congress should now do whatever it can to protect and encourage a vital artistic profession under the statute constitutionally intended for this purpose: the copyright law.

Broadcasters and other commercial users of recordings have performed them without permission or payment for generations. Users today look upon any requirement that they pay royalties as an unfair imposition in the nature of a "tax." However, any economic burden on the users of recordings for public performance is heavily outweighed not only by the commercial benefits accruing directly from the use of copyrighted sound recordings, but also by the direct and indirect damage done to performers whenever recordings are used as a substitute for live performances. In all other areas the unauthorized use of a creative work is considered a copyright infringement if it results either in damage to the creator or in profits to the user. Sound recordings are creative works, and their unauthorized performance results in both damage and profits. To leave the creators of sound recordings without any protection or compensation for their widespread commercial use can no longer be justified.

2. *Constitutional Issues*

a. *Issue*: Are sound recordings "the writings of an author" within the meaning of the Constitution?

Conclusion: Yes.

Discussion: Arguments that sound recordings are not "writings" and that performers and record producers are not "authors" have become untenable. The courts have consistently upheld the constitutional eligibility of sound recordings for protection under the copyright law. Passage of the 1971 Sound Recording Amendment was a legislative declaration of this principle, which was reaffirmed in the Copyright Act of 1976.

b. *Issue*: Can sound recordings be "the writings of an author" for purposes of protection against unauthorized duplication (piracy or counterfeiting), but not for purposes of protection against unauthorized public performance?

Conclusion: No.

Discussion: Either a work is the "writing of an author" or it is not. If it is, the Constitution empowers Congress to grant it any protection that is considered justified. There is no basis, in logic or precedent, for suggesting that a work is a "writing" for some purposes and not for others.

c. *Issue*: Would Federal legislation to protect sound recordings against unauthorized public performance be unconstitutional: (i) if there has been no affirmative showing of a "need" on the part of the intended beneficiaries and hence no basis for asserting Congressional authority to "promote the progress of science and useful arts"; or (ii) if there has been an affirmative showing that compensation to the intended beneficiaries is "adequate" without protection of performing rights?

Conclusion: No.

Discussion: These are actually disguised economic arguments, not constitutional objections. Congressional authority to grant copyright protection has never been conditioned on any findings of need, or of the likelihood that productivity or creativity will increase. The established standard is that Congress has complete discretion to grant or withhold protection for the writings of authors, and that the courts will not look behind a Congressional enactment to determine whether or not it will actually provide incentives for creation and dissemination. It is perfectly appropriate to argue that a particular group of creators is adequately compensated through the exercise of certain rights under copyright law, and therefore Congress should not grant them additional rights. It is not appropriate to argue that a Federal statute granting these rights could be attacked on the constitutional ground that it did not "promote the progress of science and useful arts."

d.   *Issue*: Would the establishment of performance rights interfere with the First Amendment rights of broadcasters and other users of sound recordings?

Conclusion: No.

Discussion: The courts have been generally unreceptive to arguments that the news media have a right to use copyrighted material, beyond the limits of fair use in particular cases, under theories of freedom of the press or freedom of speech. These arguments seem much weaker where the copyrighted material is being used for entertainment purposes, where the user is benefiting commercially from the use, or where the use is subject to compulsory licensing.

3.   *Economic Issues*

a.   *Issue*: Do the benefits accruing to performers and record producers from the "free airplay" of sound recordings represent adequate compensation in the form of increased record sales, increased attendance at live performances, and increased popularity of individual artists?

Conclusion: No, on balance and on consideration of all performers and record producers affected.

Discussion: This is the strongest argument put forward by broadcasters and other users. There is no question that broadcasting and jukebox performances give some recordings the kind of exposure that benefits their producers and individual performers through increased sales and popularity. The benefits are hit-or-miss and, if realized, are the result of acts that are outside the legal control of the creators of the works being exploited, that are of direct commercial advantage to the user, and that may damage other creators. The opportunity for benefit through increased sales, no matter how significant it may be temporarily for some "hit records," can hardly justify the outright denial of any performing rights to any sound recordings. That denial is inconsistent with the underlying philosophy of the copyright law: that of securing the benefits of creativity to the public by the encouragement of individual effort through private gain (*Mazer v. Stein*, 347 U.S. 201 (1954)).

b.   *Issue*: Would the imposition of performance royalties represent a financial burden on broadcasters so severe that stations would be forced to curtail or abandon certain kinds of programming (public service, classical, etc.) in favor of high-income producing programming in order to survive?

Conclusion: There is no hard economic evidence in the record to support arguments that a performance royalty would disrupt the broadcasting industry, adversely affect programming, and drive marginal stations out of business.

Discussion: This has been the single most difficult issue to assess accurately, because the arguments have consisted of polemics rather than facts. An independent economic analysis of potential financial effects on broadcasters was commissioned by the Copyright Office in an effort to provide an objective basis for evaluating the arguments and assertions on both sides of this issue. This study concludes on the basis of statistical analysis that the payment of royalties is unlikely to cause serious disruption within the broadcasting industry. There are arguments aplenty to the contrary, but there is no hard evidence to support them.

c.   *Issue*: Would the imposition of a performance royalty be an unwarranted windfall for performers and record producers?

Conclusion: No.

Discussion: As for performers, the independent economic survey commissioned by the Copyright Office indicates that only a small proportion of performers participating in the production of recordings receive royalties from the sale of records and that, even if they do, royalties represent a very small proportion of their annual earnings. While the statistics collected with respect to record producers is less conclusive, the economic analysis concludes that the amount generated by the Danielson bill for record companies would be less than one-half of one percent of their estimated net sales.

4.   *Legal Issues*

a.   *Issue*: Assuming that some legal protection should be given to sound recordings against unauthorized public performance, should it be given under the Federal copyright statute?

Conclusion: Yes.

Discussion: Considerations of national uniformity, equal treatment, and practical effectiveness all point to the importance of Federal protection for sound recordings, and under the Constitution the copyright law provides the appropriate legal framework. Preemption of state law under the new copyright statute leaves sound recordings worse off than they were before 1978, since previously an argument could be made for common law performance rights in sound recordings.

b. *Issue*: What form should protection take?

Conclusion: The best approach appears to be a form of compulsory licensing, as procedurally simple as possible.

Discussion: No one is arguing for exclusive rights, and it would be unrealistic to do so. The Danielson bill represents a good starting point for the development of definitive legislation.

c. *Issue*: Who should be the beneficiaries of protection?

Conclusion: There are several possibilities; since performers and record producers both contribute copyrightable authorship to sound recordings, they should both benefit.

Discussion: Special considerations that must be taken into account include the fact that many performers on records are "employees for hire," the unequal bargaining positions in some cases, and the status of arrangers.

d. *Issue*: How should the rates be set?

Conclusion: Congress should establish an initial schedule, which the Copyright Royalty Tribunal would be mandated to reexamine at stated intervals.

Discussion: It would seem necessary to establish minimum statutory rates at the outset, rather than leaving the initial task to the Tribunal. Review of the statutory rates by the Copyright Royalty Tribunal should be mandatory after a period of time sufficient to permit the development of a functioning collection and distribution system.

LEGISLATIVE RECOMMENDATIONS

Section 114(d) asks the Register of Copyrights, among other things, to set forth "recommendations as to whether this section should be amended to provide for performers and copyright owners of copyrighted material by performance rights in such material," and to describe "specific legislative or other recommendations, if any."

Based on the conclusions outlined above, my general recommendation is that section 114 be amended to provide performance rights, subject to compulsory licensing, in copyrighted sound recordings, and that the benefits of this right be extended both to performers (including employees for hire) and to record producers as joint authors of sound recordings.

Specific legislative recommendations are embodied in the following draft bill, which is essentially a revision of the Danielson Bill (H.R. 6063, 95th cong., 1st Sess. 1977).

[¶ . . .]

Among the many detailed questions raised by the Danielson Bill, the draft bill set out above, or both, the following deserve special considerations:

1. *Definitions.* The draft bill revises the definition of "perform" in section 101 to embrace sound recordings. Another possible amendment in that section might expand the definition of "fixed" to include cases where a work is being fixed simultaneously with its performance. An important question involves the rights of performers who are employees for hire; the draft bill does not change the definition of "work made for hire" in section 101, but defines "performers" in section 114 in a way that is intended to insure their right to share in performance royalties despite their employee status.

. . . .

3. *Exemption for Public Broadcasting.* The draft bill retains the exemptions for public broadcasting now in section 114.

4. *Act that Triggers the Compulsory License.* The draft bill follows the Danielson Bill in making compulsory licenses available when phonorecords of a sound recording have been publicly distributed anywhere. It does not limit the place of distribution to the United States (as in section 115), and it does not adopt proposals to allow a period of free use (30 days was suggested) before any liability would accrue.

5. *Administration.* The draft bill follows the pattern established in sections 111 and 116 of the Copyright Act of 1976, providing for filing in the Copyright Office and payment of fees there, but entrusting to the Copyright Royalty Tribunal the tasks of distributing royalties and adjusting rates.

. . . .

7. *Royalty Rates.* The draft bill recasts the rate provisions of the Danielson Bill in an effort to make them a little simpler, but it leaves the basic system and amounts largely untouched. The compulsory licensing rates for jukebox and cable performances are not increased in sections 116 and 111, so the beneficiaries of those sections would be required to share their pot with performers and record producers.

8. *Substitution of Negotiated Licenses.* The Danielson Bill allowed for the substitution of negotiated licenses and urged the formation of collecting agencies to make this possible. This raised a number of practical problems and inconsistencies, and the existence of the Copyright Royalty Tribunal adds a new factor. The draft bill is based on the premise that all licensing in this area will be compulsory.

9. *Distribution of Royalties.* The Danielson Bill provided for a mandatory fifty-fifty split between performers and "copyright owners". It

did not come to grips with the status of performers who are employees for hire. The draft bill gives at least fifty percent of the royalties to performers on a per capita basis, regardless of their employment status, but allows performers to negotiate for more (not less) than a fifty percent share.

10. *Exemptions.* Both the Danielson Bill and the draft provide outright exemptions to smaller radio and television stations and music services.

11. *Definition of Performers.* Neither draft mentions arrangers, although in practice they are often assimilated to performers. Arguments can be made that employed arrangers should be entitled to share in the royalties under section 114.

12. *Soundtracks.* The draft bill seeks to clarify a difficult question: are "soundtrack recordings" subject to compulsory licensing when they are publicly performed?

. . . .

[FR Doc. 78–7878 Filed 3–24–78; 8:45 am]

NOTES AND QUESTIONS

1.   The Ringer Report's recommendations have not yet been adopted by Congress. A limited performance right in sound recordings was granted to artists and copyright owners in 1995 for certain digital transmissions of sound recordings (see Chapter 6, *infra*), but all other performances of sound recordings remain unprotected by the Copyright Act, even after the October 2018 enactment of the Music Modernization Act.

Thus, for example, although the author of a musical composition is compensated when a recording of the composition is played on a terrestrial radio station or at a sporting event, neither the copyright owner of the sound recording itself nor the artists who performed the musical work are required to be compensated under current copyright law—and their permission is not needed for such uses.

2.   Below, you will read about the ongoing debate about performance rights in sound recordings. As you read the materials below, keep in mind the issues raised in the Ringer Report. What do you think the best, current answers to those questions might be in light of how the music industry has evolved over time since the Ringer Report was released in 1978?

B. THE PERFORMANCE RIGHT IN SOUND RECORDINGS DEBATE IN RECENT YEARS

For many years after being granted a digital performance right, the recording industry lobbied—both in Congress and in the court of public opinion—for an expanded performance right in sound recordings that extended beyond the digital realm to terrestrial radio. The fact that broadcast radio compensated songwriters and music publishers for use of their works but did not compensate recording artists and labels has been a point of contention since the advent of radio, as illustrated by the *Waring* and *Whiteman* cases excerpted in Chapter 2. In fact, many bills have been introduced over the years to attempt to expand the performance right in sound recordings to include terrestrial radio broadcasts, but none have been passed.

The ongoing campaign to obtain a performance right in sound recordings that treated recording artists similarly to composers with respect to broadcast radio plays of recordings is aptly illustrated in a December, 1988 letter from Frank Sinatra, who saw no royalties from radio plays of his recordings even though the composers of the songs he sang were compensated. The letter was sent to recording artists that included the Beach Boys, Paul McCartney, George Harrison, Neil Diamond, Bob Dylan, Ella Fitzgerald, Michael Jackson, Waylon Jennings, Liza Minelli, Willie Nelson, Bruce Springsteen, Barbara Streisand, and Stevie Wonder. Below is an image of the first page:

FRANK SINATRA

December 12, 1988

Bruce Springsteen

New York, NY 10022

Dear Bruce:

As you may or may not be aware, whenever one of your performances is played on the radio or on a jukebox, the writer of the song is compensated for the performance, but the performer is not.

I am of course the songwriter's biggest fan, but there is no logical reason to distinguish why the writer and publisher should be compensated for the performance of a song on the radio or a jukebox but the performer should not. Neither the United States Copyright Act nor any state statutes, however, have affirmatively recognized such a performance right for recording artists. Over 60 foreign countries presently recognize a performance royalty right for artists, but American artists cannot participate in any income received for a performance of their music in a foreign country because the United States does not offer a reciprocal right.

The Copyright Revision Act of 1976 flagged the inconsistency, and a bill was introduced to amend the Copyright Act and provide for payment of royalties to artists and record companies for the use of their copyrighted performances. Unfortunately, the legislation was never enacted.

We are of the opinion that legislation has not been enacted in part because recording artists have not been aware of the problem, while others with vested interests have lobbied heavily for the defeat of such legislation. We believe that with a unified effort from fellow recording artists, we may be able to pass such legislation.

Sinatra's letter read in pertinent part:

> *As you may or may not be aware, whenever one of your performances is played on the radio or on a jukebox, the writer of the song is compensated for the performance, but the performer is not.*
>
> *I am of course the songwriter's biggest fan, but there is no logical reason to distinguish why the writer and publisher should be compensated for the performance of a song on the radio or a jukebox but the performer should not. Neither the United States Copyright Act nor any state statutes, however, have affirmatively recognized such a performance right for recording artists. Over 60 foreign countries presently recognize a performance right for artists, but American artists cannot participate in any income received for a performance of their music in a foreign country because the United States does not offer a reciprocal right.*
>
> *The Copyright Revision Act of 1976 flagged the inconsistency, and a bill was introduced to amend the Copyright Act and provide for payment of royalties to artists and record companies for the use of their copyrighted performances. Unfortunately, the legislation was never enacted.*
>
> *I am willing to be part of an initial small group of performers who would establish a non-profit society tentatively entitled the Performance Society of America, for the purpose of implementing legislation to procure performance royalties for artists, and to subsequently collect and distribute such royalties. To give you an idea of some of the numbers involved, ASCAP and BMI, which administer such performance rights for composers, last year collected over $500,000,000 in the United States alone. I should point out that a performance royalty for recording artists would in no way reduce the royalties payable to the composer—rather, it would create an additional royalty payable to those whose performances appear on a sound recording. . . .*
>
> *Very truly yours,*
> *Frank Sinatra*

While recording artists and record labels characterized broadcast radio's use of sound recordings without compensation as an unfair "free ride," broadcast radio characterized the efforts to create a terrestrial performance right in sound recordings as a "tax" on their use of the music in their broadcasts. Certainly, for decades, radio performances of sound recordings served as a form of promotion for those recordings, enhancing sales in a measurable way and leading to efforts by record labels to get airplay for their recordings. However, with the marked decrease in record sales after the digital revolution and the rise of online streaming services as the "go-to" source for consumers' music expenditures, the arguments about promotion have carried less weight.

In 2015, the Fair Play, Fair Pay Act was introduced in Congress with much fanfare.[2] It did not make it out of committee in that Congress, and it was reintroduced in 2017 as H.R. 1836.[3] One of the main focuses of that proposed legislation was to require terrestrial radio to pay royalties for broadcasts of sound recordings, and it would have required payments for pre-1972 sound recordings in the same manner as for recordings made after that date. However, this bill also never made it out of committee.

Music First promotion of the Fair Play Fair Pay Act
Used with permission

---

[2]   *See, e.g.*, Roger N. Behle, Jr., *Fair Play, Fair Pay—Not a Fair Fight*, INSIDE COUNSEL (Dec. 15, 2015), *available at* http://foleybezek.com/news/fair-play-fair-pay-not-a-fair-fight.html.

[3]   *See* https://www.congress.gov/bill/115th-congress/house-bill/1836.

The 2018 Music Modernization Act did address longstanding issues about protections (or lack thereof) for pre-1972 sound recordings, as will be discussed below, but it did not expand the performance right in sound recordings beyond digital transmissions. Thus, as of the date of this writing, federal law still permits broadcast radio to perform sound recordings without compensation to recording artists or record labels.

NOTES AND QUESTIONS

1.   As noted in the Ringer Report and the discussion immediately above, over the decades since the grant of federal copyright protection to sound recordings, several bills have been introduced in Congress that would have provided expanded performance rights to sound recordings. The Fair Play, Fair Pay Act was one of the most recent examples. None of these proposed bills went so far as to propose a full performance right in sound recordings—the rights created by these legislative proposals would have been limited to a performance right for sound recordings on terrestrial radio, but not for bars, restaurants, arenas, and other venues in which music is played. Do you think that an expanded performance right for sound recordings should be created by Congress? Why or why not? If so, how far should the right extend?

2.   In the absence of a statutory solution, some in the industry have sought out private, contractual arrangements for compensation for use of their sound recordings in terrestrial radio broadcasts, although little information is publicly available regarding the nature of those arrangements or their ultimate fate. For example, in 2012, Big Machine Label Group announced that it had entered into an agreement with Clear Channel Media & Entertainment (now iHeartMedia) in which Clear Channel would pay performance royalties to Big Machine for terrestrial radio broadcasts of sound recordings by Big Machine's recording artists.[4] The details of the deal were not made publicly available, but press reports indicated that, in exchange for the payment of royalties for terrestrial radio broadcasts of Big Machine's recording acts, iHeartMedia would receive a cap on royalties for online streaming of its radio broadcasts, presumably leading to a lower rate paid to Big Machine (and ultimately its artists) for online streaming of sound recordings than that paid to other record labels and recording artists.[5] This deal was announced at the start of the Future of Audio congressional hearings before the House Subcommittee on Communications and Technology,[6] part of a series of

---

[4]   Big Machine Label Group is a Nashville company famous for breaking Taylor Swift's career, which signed artists such as Florida Georgia Line, Thomas Rhett, Reba McEntire, Rascal Flatts, Brantley Gilbert, Lady Antebellum, Cheap Trick, and Jennifer Nettles. Its business encompasses several record labels, a publishing branch, and a country music radio station.

[5]   *See, e.g.*, Richard Busch, *Look Before You Leap: Is Big Machine's New Deal with Clear Channel a Good Long Term Strategy?*, FORBES (June 28, 2012), *available at*: http://www.forbes.com/sites/richardbusch/2012/06/28/look-before-you-leap-is-big-machines-new-deal-with-clear-channel-a-good-long-term-strategy/.

[6]   *See, e.g.*, https://republicans-energycommerce.house.gov/hearings/future-audio/.

hearings and reports that ultimately led up to the Music Modernization Act of 2018. At the time, it was viewed by some as an effort to avoid a statutory resolution of the dispute regarding expansion of performance rights in sound recordings, in favor of private negotiations between interested parties.[7] The Clear Channel/iHeartMedia deal with Big Machine was followed in 2013 and 2014 by announcements of deals between the radio conglomerate and other record labels and artists, some of which were reported to include promises of promotional support by iHeartMedia for acts covered by these agreements, including special interviews and segments on the radio network and participation by those acts in iHeartRadio music festivals.[8]

3.   Do you think that private negotiations can adequately address the concerns raised in the Ringer Report and the Sinatra Letter regarding compensating record labels and recording artists for public performances of their works that benefit commercial entities? Put another way, should a performance right in terrestrial broadcasts of sound recordings only be available to those who have the power to negotiate such a right? Why or why not?

4.   What are the strongest justifications for treating sound recordings and musical compositions differently for purposes of the bundles of rights that attach to each? What are the strongest arguments for treating them the same?

---

[7]   *See, e.g.,* Richard Busch, *Look Before You Leap: Is Big Machine's New Deal with Clear Channel a Good Long Term Strategy?*, FORBES (June 28, 2012), *available at:* http://www.forbes.com/sites/richardbusch/2012/06/28/look-before-you-leap-is-big-machines-new-deal-with-clear-channel-a-good-long-term-strategy/.

[8]   *See* Clear Channel's iHeartMedia web page, with links to related press releases on other deals, *at* https://www.iheartmedia.com/press/clear-channel-and-bbr-music-group-imprints-broken-bow-and-stoney-creek-records-announce; Ben Sisario, *Clear Channel-Warner Music Deal Rewrites the Rules on Royalties*, NEW YORK TIMES (Sept. 12, 2013), *available at* http://www.nytimes.com/2013/09/13/business/media/clear-channel-warner-music-deal-rewrites-the-rules-on-royalties.html?emc=eta1.

C. PREEMPTION AND THE 1976 COPYRIGHT ACT

Because the 1976 omnibus revisions to the Copyright Act deferred any congressional action regarding performance rights in sound recordings, arguably the most impactful aspect of the 1976 Copyright Act for the music industry was the preemption of state laws that had previously provided additional protection to owners of sound recordings. Prior to the enactment of the 1976 Copyright Act, the only available form of preemption of state laws relating to unauthorized uses of sound recordings was under the United States Constitution; Section 301 of the 1976 Act created an additional federal statutory basis for preemption.

This section introduces preemption analysis in the context of state laws seeking to provide protection against unauthorized duplication and performances of sound recordings. Chapter 9 returns to statutory preemption in the context of state law claims for misappropriation of an artist's voice for commercial purposes.

1. PRE-1976 ACT PREEMPTION ARGUMENTS

GOLDSTEIN V. CALIFORNIA
412 U.S. 546 (1973)

MR. CHIEF JUSTICE BURGER delivered the opinion of the Court.

We granted certiorari to review petitioners' conviction under a California statute making it a criminal offense to 'pirate' recordings produced by others.

In 1971, an information was filed by the State of California, charging petitioners in 140 counts with violating § 653h of the California Penal Code. The information charged that, between April 1970 and March 1971, petitioners had copied several musical performances from commercially sold recordings without the permission of the owner of the master record or tape.[1] Petitioners moved to dismiss the complaint on the grounds that § 653h was in conflict with Art. I, § 8, cl. 8, of the Constitution,[FN2 omitted] the 'Copyright Clause,' and the federal statutes enacted thereunder. . . . On

---

[1] In pertinent part, the California statute provides: '(a) Every person is guilty of a misdemeanor who: '(1) Knowingly and willfully transfers or causes to be transferred any sounds recorded on a phonograph record, . . . tape, . . . or other article on which sounds are recorded, with intent to sell or cause to be sold, . . . such article on which such sounds are so transferred, without the consent of the owner. '(2) . . . '(b) As used in this section, 'person' means any individual, partnership, corporation or association; and 'owner' means the person who owns the master phonograph record, . . . master tape, . . . or other device used for reproducing recorded sounds on phonograph records, . . . tapes, . . . or other articles on which sound is recorded, and from which the transferred recorded sounds are directly or indirectly derived.' Specifically, each count of the information alleged that, in regard to a particular recording, petitioners had, 'at and in the City of Los Angeles, in the County of Los Angeles, State of California . . . willfully, unlawfully and knowingly transferred and caused to be transferred sounds recorded on a tape with the intent to sell and cause to be sold, such tape on which such sounds (were) so transferred . . . .'

appeal, the Appellate Department of the California Superior Court sustained the validity of the statute. After exhausting other state appellate remedies, petitioners sought review in this Court.

I

Petitioners were engaged in what has commonly been called 'record piracy' or 'tape piracy'—the unauthorized duplication of recordings of performances by major musical artists.[FN3 omitted] Petitioners would purchase from a retail distributor a single tape or phonograph recording of the popular performances they wished to duplicate. The original recordings were produced and marketed by recording companies with which petitioners had no contractual relationship. At petitioners' plant, the recording was reproduced on blank tapes, which could in turn be used to replay the music on a tape player. The tape was then wound on a cartridge. A label was attached, stating the title of the recorded performance-the same title as had appeared on the original recording, and the name of the performing artists.[4] After final packaging, the tapes were distributed to retail outlets for sale to the public, in competition with those petitioners had copied.

Petitioners made no payments to the artists whose performances they reproduced and sold [or] . . . . to the producer, technicians, or other staff personnel responsible for producing the original recording and paying the large expenses incurred in production. . . . [or] for the use of the artists' names or the album title.

The challenged California statute forbids petitioners to transfer any performance fixed on a tape or record onto other records or tapes with the intention of selling the duplicates, unless they have first received permission from those who, under state law, are the owners of the master recording. Although the protection afforded to each master recording is substantial, lasting for an unlimited time, the scope of the proscribed activities is narrow. No limitation is placed on the use of the music, lyrics, or arrangement employed in making the master recording. Petitioners are not precluded from hiring their own musicians and artists and recording an exact imitation of the performance embodied on the master recording. Petitioners are even free to hire the same artists who made the initial recording in order to duplicate the performance. In essence, the statute thus provides copyright protection solely for the specific expressions which compose the master record or tape.

Petitioners' attack on the constitutionality of § 653h has many facets. First, they contend that the statute establishes a state copyright of

---

[4] An additional label was attached to each cartridge by petitioners, stating that no relationship existed between petitioners and the producer of the original recording or the individuals whose performances had been recorded. Consequently, no claim is made that petitioners misrepresented the source of the original recordings or the manufacturer of the tapes.

unlimited duration, and thus conflicts with Art. I, § 8, cl. 8, of the Constitution. Second, petitioners claim that the state statute interferes with the implementation of federal policies inherent in the federal copyright statutes. 17 U.S.C. § 1 et seq. According to petitioners, it was the intention of Congress, as interpreted by this Court in Sears, Roebuck & Co. v. Stiffel Co., 376 U.S. 225, 84 S.Ct. 784, 11 L.Ed.2d 661 (1964), and Compco Corp. v. Day-Brite Lighting, 376 U.S. 234, 84 S.Ct. 779, 11 L.Ed.2d 669 (1964), to establish a uniform law throughout the United States to protect original writings. As part of the federal scheme, it is urged that Congress intended to allow individuals to copy any work which was not protected by a federal copyright. Since § 653h effectively prohibits the copying of works which are not entitled to federal protection, petitioners contend that it conflicts directly with congressional policy and must fall under the Supremacy Clause of the Constitution. . . .

We note at the outset that the federal copyright statutes to which petitioners refer were amended by Congress while their case was pending in the state courts. . . . The recordings which petitioners copied were all 'fixed' prior to February 15, 1972. Since, according to the language of the amendment, Congress did not intend to alter the legal relationships which govern these recordings, the amendments have no application in petitioners' case.[7]

II

Petitioners' first argument rests on the premise that the state statute under which they were convicted lies beyond the powers which the States reserved in our federal system. If this is correct, petitioners must prevail, since the States cannot exercise a sovereign power which, under the Constitution, they have relinquished to the Federal Government for its exclusive exercise.

The principles which the Court has followed in construing state power were stated by Alexander Hamilton in Number 32 of The Federalist:

'. . . [A]s the plan of the (Constitutional) convention aims only at a partial union or consolidation, the State governments would clearly retain all the rights of sovereignty which they before had, and which were not, by that act, exclusively delegated to the United States. This exclusive delegation, or rather this alienation, of State sovereignty, would only exist in three cases: where the Constitution in express terms granted an exclusive authority to the Union; where it granted in one instance an authority to the Union, and in another prohibited the States from exercising the like authority; and where it granted an authority to the Union, to

---

[7]   No question is raised in the present case as to the power of the States to protect recordings fixed after February 15, 1972.

which a similar authority in the States would be absolutely and totally contradictory and repugnant.'[8]

The first two instances mentioned present no barrier to a State's enactment of copyright statutes. . . .

In applying the third phase of the test, we must examine the manner in which the power to grant copyrights may operate in our federal system. The objectives of our inquiry were recognized in Cooley v. Board of Wardens, 12 How. 299, 13 L.Ed. 996 (1852), when, in determining whether the power granted to Congress to regulate commerce[9] was 'compatible with the existence of a similar power in the States,' the Court noted: 'Whatever subjects of this power are in their nature national, or admit only of one uniform system, or plan of regulation, may justly be said to be of such a nature as to require exclusive legislation by Congress.' 12 How., Id., at 319.

The Court's determination that Congress alone may legislate over matters which are necessarily national in import reflects the basic principle of federalism. . . . [¶]

We must also be careful to distinguish those situations in which the concurrent exercise of a power by the Federal Government and the States or by the States alone may possibly lead to conflicts and those situations where conflicts will necessarily arise. 'It is not . . . a mere possibility of inconvenience in the exercise of powers, but an immediate constitutional repugnancy that can by implication alienate and extinguish a pre-existing right of (state) sovereignty.' The Federalist No. 32, p. 243 (B. Wright ed. 1961).

Article I, § 8, cl. 8, of the Constitution gives to Congress the power—

'To promote the Progress of Science and useful Arts, by securing for limited Times to Authors and Inventors the exclusive Rights to their respective Writings and Discoveries . . . .' [¶] . . .

The objective of the Copyright Clause was clearly to facilitate the granting of rights national in scope. While the debates on the clause at the Constitutional Convention were extremely limited, its purpose was described by James Madison in the Federalist:

'The utility of this power will scarcely be questioned. . . . The right to useful inventions seems with equal reason to belong to the inventors. The public good fully coincides in both cases with the claims of individuals. The States cannot separately make effectual provision for either of the cases, and most of them have

---

8   The Federalist No. 32, p. 241 (B. Wright ed. 1961); see Cooley v. Board of Wardens, 12 How. 299, 318–319, 13 L.Ed. 996 (1851).

9   Art. I, § 8, cl. 3.

anticipated the decision of this point, by laws passed at the instance of Congress.'[11]

The difficulty noted by Madison relates to the burden placed on an author or inventor who wishes to achieve protection in all States when no federal system of protection is available. To do so, a separate application is required to each state government; the right which in turn may be granted has effect only within the granting State's borders.[12] The national system which Madison supported eliminates the need for multiple applications and the expense and difficulty involved. In effect, it allows Congress to provide a reward greater in scope than any particular State may grant to promote progress in those fields which Congress determines are worthy of national action.

Although the Copyright Clause thus recognizes the potential benefits of a national system, it does not indicate that all writings are of national interest or that state legislation is, in all cases, unnecessary or precluded. The patents granted by the States in the 18th century show, to the contrary, a willingness on the part of the States to promote those portions of science and the arts which were of local importance.[FN13 omitted] Whatever the diversity of people's backgrounds, origins, and interests, and whatever the variety of business and industry in the 13 Colonies, the range of diversity is obviously far greater today in a country of 210 million people in 50 States. In view of that enormous diversity, it is unlikely that all citizens in all parts of the country place the same importance on works relating to all subjects. Since the subject matter to which the Copyright Clause is addressed may thus be of purely local importance and not worthy of national attention or protection, we cannot discern such an unyielding national interest as to require an inference that state power to grant copyrights has been relinquished to exclusive federal control.

The question to which we next turn is whether, in actual operation, the exercise of the power to grant copyrights by some States will prejudice the interests of other States. As we have noted, a copyright granted by a particular State has effect only within its boundaries. If one State grants such protection, the interests of States which do not are not prejudiced since their citizens remain free to copy within their borders those works which may be protected elsewhere. The interests of a State which grants copyright protection may, however, be adversely affected by other States

---

[11]   The Federalist No. 43, p. 309 (B. Wright ed. 1961).

[12]   Numerous examples may be found in our early history of the difficulties which the creators of items of national import had in securing protection of their creations in all States. For example, Noah Webster, in his effort to obtain protection for his book, A Grammatical Institute of the English Language, brought his claim before the legislatures of at least six States, and perhaps as many as 12. See B. Bugbee, The Genesis of American Patent and Copyright Law 108–110, 120–124 (Wash., D.C., 1967); H.R.Rep.No.2222, 60th Cong., 2d Sess., 2 (1909). Similar difficulties were experienced by John Fitch and other inventors who desired to protect their efforts to perfect a steamboat. See Federico, State Patents, 13 J.Pat.Off.Soc. 166, 170–176 (1931).

that do not; individuals who wish to purchase a copy of a work protected in their own State will be able to buy unauthorized copies in other States where no protection exists. However, this conflict is neither so inevitable nor so severe as to compel the conclusion, that state power has been relinquished to the exclusive jurisdiction of the Congress. Obviously when some States do not grant copyright protection—and most do not—that circumstance reduces the economic value of a state copyright, but it will hardly render the copyright worthless. . . . [I]n the case of state copyrights, except as to individuals willing to travel across state lines in order to purchase records or other writings protected in their own State, each State's copyrights will still serve to induce new artistic creations within that State—the very objective of the grant of protection. . . .

Similarly, it is difficult to see how the concurrent exercise of the power to grant copyrights by Congress and the States will necessarily and inevitably lead to difficulty. At any time Congress determines that a particular category of "writing" is worthy of national protection and the incidental expenses of federal administration, federal copyright protection may be authorized. Where the need for free and unrestricted distribution of a writing is thought to be required by the national interest, the Copyright Clause and the Commerce Clause would allow Congress to eschew all protection. In such cases, a conflict would develop if a State attempted to protect that which Congress intended to be free from restraint or to free that which Congress had protected. However, where Congress determines that neither federal protection nor freedom from restraint is required by the national interest, it is at liberty to stay its hand entirely.[16] Since state protection would not then conflict with federal action, total relinquishment of the States' power to grant copyright protection cannot be inferred.

As we have seen, the language of the Constitution neither explicitly precludes the States from granting copyrights nor grants such authority exclusively to the Federal Government. The subject matter to which the Copyright Clause is addressed may at times be of purely local concern. No conflict will necessarily arise from a lack of uniform state regulation, nor will the interest of one State be significantly prejudiced by the actions of another. No reason exists why Congress must take affirmative action either to authorize protection of all categories of writings or to free them from all restraint. We therefor conclude that, under the Constitution, the States have not relinquished all power to grant to authors 'the exclusive Right to their respective Writings.' . . . [¶]

III

Our conclusion that California did not surrender its power to issue copyrights does not end the inquiry. We must proceed to determine

---

[16] For example, Congress has allowed writings which may eventually be the subject of a federal copyright, to be protected under state law prior to publication. 17 U.S.C. § 2.

whether the challenged state statute is void under the Supremacy Clause. No simple formula can capture the complexities of this determination; the conflicts which may develop between state and federal action are as varied as the fields to which congressional action may apply. 'Our primary function is to determine whether, under the circumstances of this particular case, (the state) law stands as an obstacle to the accomplishment and execution of the full purposes and objectives of Congress.' Hines v. Davidowitz, 312 U.S., 52, 67, 61 S.Ct. 399, 404, 85 L.Ed. 581 (1941). We turn, then, to federal copyright law to determine what objectives Congress intended to fulfill.

By Art. I, § 8, cl. 8, of the Constitution, the States granted to Congress the power to protect the 'Writings' of 'Authors.' . . . . While an 'author' may be viewed as an individual who writes an original composition, the term, in its constitutional sense, has been construed to mean an 'originator,' 'he to whom anything owes its origin.' Burrow-Giles Lithographic Co. v. Sarony, 111 U.S. 53, 58, 4 S.Ct. 279, 281, 28 L.Ed. 349 (1884). Similarly, although the word 'writings' might be limited to script or printed material, it may be interpreted to include any physical rendering of the fruits of creative intellectual or aesthetic labor. Ibid.; Trade-Mark Cases, 100 U.S. 82, 94, 25 L.Ed. 550 (1879). Thus, recordings of artistic performances may be within the reach of Clause 8.

While the area in which Congress may act is broad, the enabling provision of Clause 8 does not require that Congress act in regard to all categories of materials which meet the constitutional definitions. Rather, whether any specific category of 'Writings' is to be brought within the purview of the federal statutory scheme is left to the discretion of the Congress. . . . As our technology has expanded the means available for creative activity and has provided economical means for reproducing manifestations of such activity, new areas of federal protection have been initiated.[FN17 omitted]

Petitioners contend that the actions taken by Congress in establishing federal copyright protection preclude the States from granting similar protection to recordings of musical performances. According to petitioners, Congress addressed the question of whether recordings of performances should be granted protection in 1909; Congress determined that any individual who was entitled to a copyright on an original musical composition should have the right to control to a limited extent the use of that composition on recordings, but that the record itself, and the performance which it was capable of reproducing were not worthy of such protection.[18] In support of their claim, petitioners cite the House Report on the 1909 Act, which states:

---

[18]   17 U.S.C. § 1(e).

'It is not the intention of the committee to extend the right of copyright to the mechanical reproductions themselves, but only to give the composer or copyright proprietor the control, in accordance with the provisions of the bill, of the manufacture and use of such devices.' H.R.Rep.No. 2222, 60th Cong., 2d Sess., 9 (1909).

To interpret accurately Congress' intended purpose in passing the 1909 Act and the meaning of the House Report petitioners cite, we must remember that our modern technology differs greatly from that which existed in 1909. The Act and the report should not be read as if they were written today, for to do so would inevitably distort their intended meaning; rather, we must read them against the background of 1909, in which they were written.

In 1831, Congress first extended federal copyright protection to original musical compositions. An individual who possessed such a copyright had the exclusive authority to sell copies of the musical score; individuals who purchased such a copy did so for the most part to play the composition at home on a piano or other instrument. Between 1831 and 1909, numerous machines were invented which allowed the composition to be reproduced mechanically. For example, one had only to insert a piano roll or disc with perforations in appropriate places into a player piano to achieve almost the same results which previously required someone capable of playing the instrument. The mounting sales of such devices detracted from the value of the copyright granted for the musical composition. Individuals who had use of a piano roll and an appropriate instrument had little, if any, need for a copy of the sheet music.[19] The problems which arose eventually reached this Court in 1908 in the case of White-Smith Music Publishing Co. v. Apollo Co., 209 U.S. 1, 28 S.Ct. 319, 52 L.Ed. 655. . . . Despite the fact that the piano rolls employed the creative work of the composer, all protection was denied.

It is against this background that Congress passed the 1909 statute. . . . Congress determined that the copyright statutes should be amended to insure that composers of original musical works received adequate protection to encourage further artistic and creative effort. Henceforth, under § 1(e), records and piano rolls were to be considered as 'copies' of the original composition they were capable of reproducing, and could not be manufactured unless payment was made to the proprietor of the composition copyright. The section of the House Report cited by petitioners was intended only to establish the limits of the composer's right; composers were to have no control over the recordings themselves. Nowhere does the report indicate that Congress considered records as anything but a component part of a machine, capable of reproducing an

---

[19]   H.R.Rep.No.7083, 59th Cong., 2d Sess., pt. 2, p. 2 (1907) (Minority Report).

original composition[22] or that Congress intended records, as renderings of original artistic performance, to be free from state control.[FN23 omitted]

Petitioners' argument does not rest entirely on the belief that Congress intended specifically to exempt recordings of performances from state control. Assuming that no such intention may be found, they argue that Congress so occupied the field of copyright protection as to pre-empt all comparable state action. Rice v. Santa Fe Elevator Corp., 331 U.S. 218, 67 S.Ct. 1146, 91 L.Ed. 1447 (1947). This assertion is based on the language of 17 U.S.C. §§ 4 and 5, and on this Court's opinions in Sears, Roebuck & Co. v. Stiffel Co., 376 U.S. 225, 84 S.Ct. 784, 11 L.Ed.2d 661 (1964), and Compco Corp. v. Day-Brite Lighting, 376 U.S. 234, 84 S.Ct. 779, 11 L.Ed.2d 669 (1964).

Section 4 of the federal copyright laws provides:

'The works for which copyright may be secured under this title shall include all the writings of an author.' 17 U.S.C. § 4.

Section 5, which lists specific categories of protected works, adds:

'The above specifications shall not be held to limit the subject-matter of copyright as defined in section 4 of this title . . . .' 17 U.S.C. § 5.

Since section 4 employs the constitutional term 'writings,'[24] it may be argued that Congress intended to exercise its authority over all works to which the constitutional provision might apply. However, in the more than 60 years which have elapsed since enactment of this provision, neither the Copyright Office, the courts, nor the Congress has so interpreted it. The Register of Copyrights, who is charged with administration of the statute, has consistently ruled that 'claims to exclusive rights in mechanical recordings . . . or in the performances they reproduce' are not entitled to protection under § 4. 37 CFR § 202.8(b) (1972).[25] With one early

---

[22] This is especially clear from the comment made by the Committee on Patents in regard to a foreign statute which, to some extent, protected performances. The committee stated that the foreign statute 'in no way affects the reproduction of such music by photographs, graphophones, or the ordinary piano-playing instruments, for in these instruments the reproduction is purely mechanical.' H.R.Rep.No.2222, supra, n. 12, at 5.

[24] H.R.Rep.No.2222, supra, n. 12, at 10.

[25] The registration of records under the provisions of the 1909 Act would give rise to numerous administrative difficulties. It is difficult to discern how an individual who wished to copyright a record could comply with the notice and deposit provisions of the statute. 17 U.S.C. §§ 12, 13, 19, 20. Nor is it clear to whom the copyright could rightfully be issued or what constituted publication. Finally, the administrative and economic burden of classifying and maintaining copies of records would have been considerable. See Chafee, Reflections on the Laws of Copyright: II, 45 Col.L.Rev. 719, 735 (1945); Ringer, The Unauthorized Duplication of Sound Recordings, Studies Prepared for the Subcommittee on Patents, Trademarks, and Copyrights of the Senate Committee on the Judiciary, 86th Cong., 2d Sess., 2 (Comm.Print 1961); Hearings on S.646 and H.R.6927, supra, n. 5, at 11, 14.

exception,[26] American courts have agreed with this interpretation;[27] and in 1971, prior to passage of the statute which extended federal protection to recordings fixed on or after February 15, 1972, Congress acknowledged the validity of that interpretation. Both the House and Senate Reports on the proposed legislation recognized that recordings qualified as 'writings' within the meaning of the Constitution, but had not previously been protected under the federal copyright statute. H.R.Rep.No.92–487, pp. 2, 5 (1971); S.Rep.No.92–72, p. 4 (1971); U.S.Code Cong. & Admin.News p. 1566. In light of this consistent interpretation by the courts, the agency empowered to administer the copyright statutes, and Congress itself, we cannot agree that sections 4 and 5 have the broad scope petitioners claim. [¶]. . . .

V

. . . . [T]here is no fixed, immutable line to tell us which 'human productions' are private property and which are so general as to become 'free as the air.' In earlier times, a performing artist's work was largely restricted to the stage; once performed, it remained 'recorded' only in the memory of those who had seen or heard it. Today, we can record that performance in precise detail and reproduce it again and again with utmost fidelity. The California statutory scheme evidences a legislative policy to prohibit 'tape piracy' and 'record piracy,' conduct that may adversely affect the continued production of new recordings, a large industry in California. Accordingly, the State has, by statute, given to recordings the attributes of property. No restraint has been placed on the use of an idea or concept; rather, petitioners and other individuals remain free to record the same compositions in precisely the same manner and with the same personnel as appeared on the original recording.

In sum, we have shown that section 653h does not conflict with the federal copyright statute enacted by Congress in 1909. Similarly, no conflict exists between the federal copyright statute passed in 1971 and the present application of section 653h, since California charged petitioners only with copying recordings fixed prior to February 15, 1972.[29] Finally, we have concluded that our decisions in Sears and Compco, which we reaffirm today, have no application in the present case, since Congress has indicated neither that it wishes to protect, nor to free from protection, recordings of musical performances fixed prior to February 15, 1972.

We conclude that the State of California has exercised a power which it retained under the Constitution, and that the challenged statute, as

---

[26] Fonotipia, Ltd. v. Bradley, 171 F. 951, 963 (EDNY 1909).

[27] Aeolian Co. v. Royal Music Roll Co., 196 F. 926, 927 (WDNY 1912); Waring v. WDAS Broadcasting Station, 327 Pa. 433, 437–438, 194 A. 631, 633–634 (1937); Capitol Records v. Mercury Records Corp., 221 F.2d 657, 661–662 (CA2 1955); Jerome v. Twentieth Century Fox-Film Corp., 67 F.Supp. 736, 742 (SDNY 1946).

[29] Supra, at 2307.

applied in this case, does not intrude into an area which Congress has, up to now, preempted. Until and unless Congress takes further action with respect to recordings fixed prior to February 15, 1972, the California statute may be enforced against acts of piracy such as those which occurred in the present case.

Affirmed. [MR. JUSTICE DOUGLAS, MR. JUSTICE MARSHALL, MR. JUSTICE BRENNAN and MR. JUSTICE BLACKMUN dissented].

2. PREEMPTION AFTER THE 1976 ACT

17 U.S.C. § 301(a)–(c). PREEMPTION WITH RESPECT TO OTHER LAWS

(a) On and after January 1, 1978, all legal or equitable rights that are equivalent to any of the exclusive rights within the general scope of copyright as specified by section 106 in works of authorship that are fixed in a tangible medium of expression and come within the subject matter of copyright as specified by sections 102 and 103, whether created before or after that date and whether published or unpublished, are governed exclusively by this title. Thereafter, no person is entitled to any such right or equivalent right in any such work under the common law or statutes of any State.

(b) Nothing in this title annuls or limits any rights or remedies under the common law or statutes of any State with respect to—

(1) subject matter that does not come within the subject matter of copyright as specified by sections 102 and 103, including works of authorship not fixed in any tangible medium of expression; or

(2) any cause of action arising from undertakings commenced before January 1, 1978;

(3) activities violating legal or equitable rights that are not equivalent to any of the exclusive rights within the general scope of copyright as specified by section 106 . . . .

(c) Notwithstanding the provisions of section 303, and in accordance with chapter 14, no sound recording fixed before February 15, 1972, shall be subject to copyright under this title. With respect to sound recordings fixed before February 15, 1972, the preemptive provisions of subsection (a) shall apply to activities that are commenced on and after the date of enactment of the Classics Protection and Access Act. Nothing in this subsection may be construed to affirm or negate the preemption of rights and remedies pertaining to any cause of action arising from the nonsubscription broadcast transmission of sound recordings under the common law or statutes of any State for activities that do not qualify as covered activities under chapter 14 undertaken during the period between the date of enactment of the Classics Protection and Access Act and the date on which the term of prohibition on unauthorized acts under section 1401(a)(2) expires for such sound recordings. Any potential preemption of rights and remedies related to such activities undertaken during that period shall apply in all respects as it did the day before the date of enactment of the Classics Protection and Access Act.

Important Note: In October, 2018, the Music Modernization Act of 2018 ("MMA"), was signed into law and, among other things, amended section 301(c)'s "savings clause" against preemption of state law protection for pre-1972 sound recordings. The portion of the MMA dealing with pre-1972 sound recordings was titled the Classics Protection and Access Act, referred to in the new text of the section above. **Prior to October 11, 2018, the effective date of the MMA, section 301(c) of the Copyright Act read as follows:**

> **(c)** With respect to sound recordings fixed before February 15, 1972, any rights or remedies under the common law or statutes of any State shall not be annulled or limited by this title until February 15, 2067. The preemptive provisions of subsection (a) shall apply to any such rights and remedies pertaining to any cause of action arising from undertakings commenced on and after February 15, 2067. Notwithstanding the provisions of section 303, no sound recording fixed before February 15, 1972, shall be subject to copyright under this title before, on, or after February 15, 2067.

As you can see from the changed language above, the portion of the MMA referred to as the Classics Protection and Access Act carved out a much narrower category of state law claims that would be exempt from preemption for pre-1972 sound recordings than in the original version of section 301(c). In subsection 4, below, we discuss pre-1972 sound recordings and the impact of the MMA's changes to Section 301 and Chapter 14 of the Copyright Act with respect to state law

> copyright infringement claims for *digital public performances* of sound recordings made prior to February 15, 1972.
>
> First, in subsection 3, we illustrate efforts to preserve some state law claims regarding copyrighted works immediately following the enactment of the 1975 Act and its preemption of state laws equivalent to the federal copyright law.

3. STATE TRUE NAME AND ADDRESS STATUTES

One way that record labels sought to retain state law protections against unauthorized duplication of sound recordings even after enactment of the 1976 Copyright Act was through what became known as "true name and address" ("TN&A") statutes. Rather than criminalizing record piracy, these state statutes criminalized the failure to indicate the true identity of the manufacturer of the work. By fashioning these TN&A statutes in the nature of "consumer protection" laws, it avoided the potential preemption arguments that might have otherwise arisen had they been fashioned as straight piracy statutes. Below is an example of one such statute and a case illustrating how courts treated arguments that such statutes were preempted under section 301.

CAL. PENAL CODE § 653w. FAILURE TO DISCLOSE ORIGIN OF RECORDING OR AUDIOVISUAL WORK; VIOLATIONS; PUNISHMENT

(a)(1) A person is guilty of failure to disclose the origin of a recording or audiovisual work if, for commercial advantage or private financial gain, he or she knowingly advertises or offers for sale or resale, or sells or resells, or causes the rental, sale, or resale of, or rents, or manufactures, or possesses for these purposes, any recording or audiovisual work, the outside cover, box, jacket, or label of which does not clearly and conspicuously disclose the actual true name and address of the manufacturer thereof and the name of the actual author, artist, performer, producer, programmer, or group thereon. This section does not require the original manufacturer or authorized licensees of software producers to disclose the contributing authors or programmers. . . . [¶¶]

(b) Any person who has been convicted of a violation of subdivision (a) shall be punished as follows:

(1) If the offense involves the advertisement, offer for sale or resale, sale, rental, manufacture, or possession for these purposes, of at

least 100 articles of audio recordings or 100 articles of audiovisual works described in subdivision (a), or the commercial equivalent thereof, the person shall be punished by imprisonment in a county jail not to exceed one year, or by imprisonment pursuant to subdivision (h) of section 1170 for two, three, or five years, or by a fine not to exceed five hundred thousand dollars ($500,000), or by both that fine and imprisonment.

(2) Any other violation of subdivision (a) not described in paragraph (1), shall, upon a first offense, be punished by imprisonment in a county jail not to exceed one year, or by a fine not to exceed fifty thousand dollars ($50,000), or by both that fine and imprisonment.

(3) A second or subsequent conviction under subdivision (a) not described in paragraph (1), shall be punished by imprisonment in a county jail not to exceed one year or pursuant to subdivision (h) of section 1170, or by a fine of not less than one thousand dollars ($1,000), but not to exceed two hundred thousand dollars ($200,000), or by both that fine and imprisonment.

ANDERSON V. NIDORF
26 F.3d 100 (9th Cir. 1994)[9]

OVERVIEW

Cletus Robert Anderson appeals the district court's denial of his habeas corpus petition challenging his conviction under California Penal Code § 653w for failure to disclose the origin of a sound recording. Anderson claims that this California statute is preempted by federal copyright laws and violates the First Amendment. We have jurisdiction under 28 U.S.C. § 1291 and affirm.

BACKGROUND

At a flea market in May of 1990, a Los Angeles County Deputy Sheriff approached Cletus Anderson, who was selling almost 5,000 tapes which appeared to be pirated. When Anderson could not produce any documentation demonstrating the origin or manufacturer of the tapes, he was arrested for failure to disclose the origin of a sound recording, in violation of California Penal Code § 653w.

Anderson waived a jury trial and was convicted by the state court on November 20, 1990. He was sentenced to 180 days in county jail and five years' probation. A California Court of Appeals affirmed Anderson's conviction on appeal, rejecting his arguments that the California statute

---

[9] Footnotes are omitted from this excerpt.

was preempted by federal copyright laws and that his conviction violated the First Amendment. *People v. Anderson,* 235 Cal.App.3d 586, 286 Cal.Rptr. 734 (1991). The California Supreme Court denied review on January 22, 1992. Anderson then filed a petition for habeas corpus in federal district court, but accepted a dismissal without prejudice in order to petition the California courts for post-conviction relief. After the California Supreme Court denied Anderson's state petition for habeas corpus on May 27, 1992, Anderson filed a second petition in federal district court. The court adopted the magistrate judge's Report and Recommendation denying Anderson's petition for habeas corpus.

DISCUSSION

A district court's decision on a petition for writ of habeas corpus is reviewed *de novo. Lincoln v. Sunn,* 807 F.2d 805, 808 (9th Cir.1987).

I.   *Is California Penal Code § 653w preempted by federal copyright laws?*

The federal copyright laws preempt state-created "legal or equitable rights that are equivalent to any of the exclusive rights within the general scope of copyright." 17 U.S.C. § 301(a). We have held:

> Section 301(a) preempts a state-created right if that right "may be abridged by an act which, in and of itself, would infringe one of the exclusive rights [listed in § 106]." But if violation of the state right is "predicated upon an act incorporating elements beyond mere reproduction or the like," there is no preemption.

Oddo v. Ries, 743 F.2d 630, 635 (9th Cir.1984) (citations omitted). *See also G.S. Rasmussen & Assoc. v. Kalitta Flying Service, Inc.,* 958 F.2d 896, 904 (9th Cir.1992) (following *Oddo*), *cert. denied,* 508 U.S. 959, 113 S.Ct. 2927, 124 L.Ed.2d 678 (1993).

Anderson argues that § 653w is preempted by copyright laws because § 653w is intended to protect the rights of copyright owners through the prevention of pirating. It is clear that this is *one* of the purposes of the statute. The California Court of Appeals explained:

> Penal Code section 653w was enacted as part of a comprehensive statutory scheme designed to prevent and punish the misappropriation of recorded music for commercial advantage or private financial gain. (Pen.Code, § 653h.) .... The state's interest in enacting Penal Code section 653w is the desire to protect the public in general, and the many employees of the vast entertainment industry in particular, from the hundreds of millions of dollars in losses suffered as a result of the "piracy and bootlegging" of the industry's products.

Anderson, 286 Cal.Rptr. at 735, 737.

However, the statute also has the purpose of "protecting the public from being victimized by false and deceptive commercial practices." *Id.* at 737. This point was made by the district court:

> [Anderson's] argument ignores the other purpose the legislative materials ... show Section 653w was designed to serve: 'assist[ing] consumers in this state by mandating that manufacturers market product[s] for which consumers can go back to the source if there are any problems or complaints.' Preemption would frustrate the State's objective of consumer protection through disclosure.

[ER 18 n. 4. (emphasis in original; internal citations omitted).] Federal copyright laws do not serve this purpose of protecting consumers. They are designed to protect the property rights of copyright owners. *See, e.g., Wheaton v. Peters,* 33 U.S. (8 Pet.) 591, 603, 8 L.Ed. 1055 (1834).

Further, the California statute criminalizes selling recordings whose labels fail to disclose the manufacturer or author; it does not criminalize unauthorized duplication or "bootlegging" of copyrighted works. An act criminalized by § 653w thus does not "in and of itself . . . infringe one of the exclusive rights" listed in the copyright laws. *Oddo,* 743 F.2d at 635. The statute incorporates "elements beyond mere reproduction or the like," *id.,* i.e. failing to appropriately label recordings for sale.

Because § 653w does not prohibit the reproduction of copyrighted works, but rather prohibits selling recordings without disclosing the manufacturer and author of the recording (regardless of its copyright status), the federal copyright laws do not preempt the state statute. . . .

CONCLUSION

The district court's denial of Anderson's petition for writ of habeas corpus is AFFIRMED.

4. PRE-1972 SOUND RECORDINGS AND DIGITAL STREAMING: STATE LAW PERFORMANCE RIGHT LITIGATION

Starting in 2014, the battle for performance rights in sound recordings took an interesting turn in the context of pre-1972 sound recordings. You will recall that pre-1972 sound recordings received no federal copyright protection under the 1971 Sound Recording Act but retained existing state law protections—Section 301(c) expressly preserved those state law protections from the 1976 Act's preemption provisions that were in effect through 2018. Members of the band The Turtles, incorporated as Flo & Eddie Inc. and most famous for recording the song "Happy Together" in 1967, sued Sirius XM in federal court in California, New York, and Florida and Pandora Media Group in federal court in California, alleging that the defendants violated state law in streaming the band's recordings without a license or payment.

Trade ad by White Whale Records Licensing for The Turtles'
single *Happy Together*, BILLBOARD (March 4, 1967)

California Litigation: Sirius XM

Stunning many in the industry, in September of 2014, the district court in California issued an opinion in the case against Sirius XM, finding a state law performance right in pre-1972 sound recordings.[10] District Judge Philip Gutierrez granted plaintiff Flo & Eddie Inc.'s motion for partial summary judgment, holding as a matter of law that California law recognized performance rights in pre-1972 sound recordings.

It was undisputed that Flo & Eddie owned the copyrights in the pertinent Turtles' sound recordings; that Flo & Eddie had never granted licenses for the performance of its sound recordings during the more than four decades that those recordings had been broadcast on terrestrial radio;

---

[10] *Flo & Eddie Inc. v. Sirius XM Radio Inc.*, No. CV 13–5693 PSG RZX, 2014 WL 4725382, 2014 Copr. L. Dec. ¶ 30,665, 112 U.S.P.Q.2d 1307 (C.D. Cal. Sept. 22, 2014).

that Sirius XM had performed the Turtles' sound recordings over satellite and internet radio without obtaining a license or paying royalties to Flo & Eddie; and that, although Flo & Eddie had been aware of Sirius XM's performance of its sound recordings for more than seven years, it had not made any demands for Sirius XM to cease its performances or to pay royalties for those performances prior to commencing the litigation.

In opposition to Flo & Eddie's motion for summary judgment, Sirius XM argued that public performance rights are not included among the bundle of rights that attaches to state law copyright ownership of a pre-1972 sound recording. Once it purchased a copy of a Flo & Eddie recording, Sirius XM claimed that it had the lawful right to broadcast and stream that recording to its subscribers without obtaining a license from Flo & Eddie to do so. Flo & Eddie argued that California state law granted an exclusive public performance right to owners of pre-1972 recordings, and thus that permission must be obtained from those owners before the recordings may be publicly performed.

In ruling on the motion, Judge Guterriez interpreted section 980(a)(2) of the California Civil Code, which directly addresses pre-1972 sound recordings. Section 980(a)(2) provides:

> The author of an original work of authorship consisting of a sound recording initially fixed prior to February 15, 1972, has an exclusive ownership therein until February 15, 2047, as against all persons except one who independently makes or duplicates another sound recording that does not directly or indirectly recapture the actual sounds fixed in such prior recording, but consists entirely of an independent fixation of other sounds, even though such sounds imitate or simulate the sounds contained in the prior sound recording.[11]

The court found the plain meaning of the phrase "exclusive ownership" in the statute to convey that "the legislature intended ownership of a sound recording in California to include all rights that can attach to intellectual property, save the singular, expressly-stated exception for making 'covers' of a recording."[12] The court also noted the absence of California case law addressing performance rights in sound recordings to conclude that, prior to the legislature's enactment of section 980(a)(2), no common law performance right existed, and found that no subsequent case law interpreting section 980(a)(2) contradicts the statute's plain meaning.[13] Thus, Judge Guterriez concluded that "copyright ownership of a sound recording under § 980(a)(2) includes the exclusive right to publicly perform

---

[11]   Cal. Civ. Code § 980(a)(2).

[12]   2014 WL 4725382 at *5.

[13]   *Id.* at *7–8.

that recording."[14] Although the court found that Sirius XM had violated Flo & Eddie's performance rights in the Turtles' sound recordings, it found that material issues of disputed fact precluded summary judgment on the claims relating to reproduction of the recordings.[15]

In a footnote, the court briefly addressed Sirius XM's argument that recognition of a state law performance right in pre-1972 sound recordings would violate the Commerce Clause:

> Sirius XM's argument that state regulation of sound recording performances would violate the Commerce Clause is without merit. See Opp. 21:12–14. "Where state or local government action is specifically authorized by Congress, it is not subject to the Commerce Clause even if it interferes with interstate commerce." White v. Mass. Council of Constr. Emp'rs, Inc., 460 U.S. 204, 213, 103 S.Ct. 1042, 75 L.Ed.2d 1 (1983); see also S. Pac. Co. v. State of Ariz. ex rel. Sullivan, 325 U.S. 761, 769, 65 S.Ct. 1515, 89 L.Ed. 1915 (1945) ("Congress has undoubted power to redefine the distribution of power over interstate commerce. It may . . . permit the states to regulate the commerce in a manner which would otherwise not be permissible"). Because Congress specifically authorized protection of pre-1972 sound recording rights by the states in 17 U.S.C. § 301(c), the California statute protecting those rights is not subject to the Commerce Clause.[16]

The case proceeded, with the court granting class action certification, allowing other independent recording labels/artists to participate in the class action.

The case was settled on the eve of trial in the fall of 2016. That settlement included a minimum payment of $25 million to the class members, plus additional payments contingent upon the outcome of appeals in pending litigation in the Fifth, Ninth (in which Pandora was the defendant), and Eleventh Circuits that could make the figure rise to $40 million to resolve claims of past misappropriation. Additionally, the settlement included an estimated $45 to $59 million for a ten-year licensing deal moving forward—which, again, was contingent upon the outcome of the pending cases.

New York Litigation: Sirius XM

Shortly after the grant of partial summary judgment by the district court in California (which recognized a California state law public performance right in pre-1972 recordings), in November of 2014, the Southern District of New York also ruled that New York state law provided

---

[14]   *Id.* at *9.

[15]   *Id.* at *10, 12.

[16]   2014 WL 4725382 at *9 n. 1.

a performance right to owners of pre-1972 sound recordings.[17] Unlike the state statutory basis for the California federal court's decision, the judge in the S.D.N.Y. case based her ruling on her prediction of how the highest court in New York would interpret the scope of New York's common law copyright protection. Recognizing that the existence of exclusive rights to publicly perform sound recordings was a question of first impression under New York law, the judge acknowledged that the decision had "profound economic consequences for the recording industry and both the analog and digital broadcast industries."[18]

Judge McMahon rejected Sirius XM's defenses based upon laches, fair use, and the dormant Commerce Clause. She disagreed with the reasoning of Judge Guterriez relating to the Commerce Clause, quoted above, however, because she did not read 17 U.S.C. section 301(c) to expressly permit state regulation of interstate commerce relating to pre-1972 sound recordings. Instead, she found that "concluding that Sirius is liable under New York property law principles would not amount to a 'regulation' of interstate commerce by New York."[19] The opinion concluded by noting:

> Sirius is correct that this holding is unprecedented (aside from the companion California case, which reached the same result), and will have significant economic consequences. Radio broadcasters—terrestrial and satellite—have adapted to an environment in which they do not pay royalties for broadcasting pre-1972 sound recordings. Flo and Eddie's suit threatens to upset those settled expectations. Other broadcasters, including those who publicly perform media other than sound recordings, will undoubtedly be sued in follow-on actions, exposing them to significant liability. And if different states adopt varying regulatory schemes for pre-1972 sound recordings, or if holders of common law copyrights insist on licensing performance rights on a state-by-state basis (admittedly, an unlikely result, since such behavior could well cause broadcaster to lose interest in playing their recordings) it could upend the analog and digital broadcasting industries.
>
> But in the end, all this case presents me with is a suit between private parties seeking to vindicate private property rights—not a challenge to state regulation. That lawsuit can and will be resolved on its merits. The broader policy problems are not for me to consider. They are the province of Congress, the New York Legislature, and perhaps the New York Court of Appeals.[20]

---

[17]   *Flo & Eddie, Inc. v. Sirius XM Radio, Inc.*, 62 F. Supp. 3d 325, 338–39 (S.D.N.Y. 2014).

[18]   62 F. Supp. 3d at 338.

[19]   *Id.* at 351–52.

[20]   *Id.* at 352–53.

Judge McMahon certified the issue for immediate appeal, and Sirius XM appealed the ruling to the Second Circuit. The Second Circuit, in turn, found the question appropriate for certification to the New York Court of Appeals, the state's highest court. It declined to rule on the dormant Commerce Clause issue raised by Sirius XM, because "the question of whether such a right would violate the dormant Commerce Clause is not something we can adjudicate without knowing what, if any, limitations New York places on such rights, if they do exist."[21]

The New York Court of Appeals accepted the certified question,[22] and, in December, 2016 ruled that New York state law did *not* provide exclusive public performance rights to owners of pre-1972 sound recordings.[23] Because the existence of a public performance right in sound recordings was a question of first impression, the court found prior common law decisions addressing sound recording piracy—and thus the reproduction right of copyright owners under New York common law—to be non-dispositive. The court also analyzed societal expectations, which it found relevant to determining the scope of common law copyright protections, and cited lobbying efforts by recording industry representatives and various statements of the Register of Copyrights over several decades as evidence of wide-held belief that no performance right in sound recordings existed under either federal or state law. In declining to recognize the right as a matter of common law, the court noted that it was more appropriately a legislative question, stating:

> As Congress demonstrated when it enacted the DPRA—by including mandatory licensing and a rate-setting scheme, as well as exemptions—recognizing new rights in this complex area of law involves a delicate balancing of numerous competing interests, requiring an intricate regulatory scheme that can be crafted only by a legislative body. For instance, to make practical the exercise of the right of public performance, it would certainly be necessary to have a central agency or clearinghouse—as the DPRA has established—to maintain a record of ownership rights in sound recordings.[24]

As a result of the ruling by the New York Court of Appeals, the Second Circuit reversed the denial of summary judgment, remanding to the court below for entry of summary judgment in favor of Sirius XM and dismissal of the case with prejudice.[25]

---

[21] *Flo & Eddie, Inc. v. Sirius XM Radio, Inc.*, 821 F.3d 265, 272 (2d Cir. 2016).

[22] *Flo & Eddie, Inc. v. Sirius XM Radio, Inc.*, 27 N.Y.3d 1015, 52 N.E.3d 240 (2016).

[23] *Flo & Eddie, Inc. v. Sirius XM Radio, Inc.*, 28 N.Y.3d 583, 70 N.E.3d 936 (2016).

[24] *Id.*, 28 N.Y.3d at 606, 70 N.E.3d at 949.

[25] *Flo & Eddie, Inc. v. Sirius XM Radio, Inc.*, 849 F.3d 14, 17 (2d Cir. 2017).

Florida Litigation: Sirius XM

Although it followed a similar path as the New York litigation, the Florida litigation brought by Flo & Eddie against Sirius XM yielded a different result in the district court: Judge Gayles granted summary judgment in Sirius XM's favor, finding that Florida common law did not provide a public performance right in sound recordings, stating:

> If this Court adopts Flo & Eddie's position, it would be creating a new property right in Florida as opposed to interpreting the law. The Court declines to do so. . . . The Court finds that the issue of whether copyright protection for pre-1972 recordings should include the exclusive right to public performance is for the Florida legislature. Indeed, if this Court was to recognize and create this broad right in Florida, the music industry—including performers, copyright owners, and broadcasters—would be faced with many unanswered questions and difficult regulatory issues including: (1) who sets and administers the licensing rates; (2) who owns a sound recording when the owner or artist is dead or the record company is out of business; and (3) what, if any, are the exceptions to the public performance right. The Florida legislature is in the best position to address these issues, not the Court.[26]

Noting that the issue was moot in light of its ruling, the Florida district court also commented on Sirius XM's Commerce Clause defense, agreeing with the California district court's conclusion that Congress expressly authorized state regulation of pre-1972 sound recordings in section 301(c) of the Copyright Act.

Flo & Eddie appealed the ruling to the Eleventh Circuit, which, like the Second Circuit, certified the question to the Florida Supreme Court. In 2017, the Florida Supreme Court found no common law public performance right in sound recordings under Florida law, stating:

> Flo & Eddie essentially asks this Court to recognize an unworkable common law right in pre-1972 sound recordings that is broader than any right ever previously recognized in any sound recording. Doing so would require this Court to, among other things, ignore the lengthy and well-documented history of this topic—something we decline to do.[27]

The Florida Supreme Court relied heavily on the history of federal copyright protection for sound recordings in its reasoning:

> Unlike the carefully delineated and limited right of public performance for post-1972 sound recordings that Congress

---

[26] *Flo & Eddie, Inc. v. Sirius XM Radio, Inc.*, No. 13-23182-CIV, 2015 WL 3852692, at *5 (S.D. Fla. June 22, 2015), *aff'd*, 709 F. App'x 661 (11th Cir. 2018).

[27] *Flo & Eddie, Inc. v. Sirius XM Radio, Inc.*, 229 So. 3d 305, 316 (Fla. 2017).

eventually recognized in 1995 and circumscribed within the context of the various competing stakeholder interests, the Florida common law right sought by Flo & Eddie for pre-1972 sound recordings is unfettered. Thus, if this exclusive right of public performance has existed all along under the common law, then one would have to conclude that Congress actually took away that common law right for post-1972 recordings, on a going-forward basis, when enacting the Act of 1971—an act that recognized solely the right of reproduction in post-1972 sound recordings. See Act of 1971, § 1, 85 Stat. 391. And one would have to conclude that Congress then only partially restored that right when enacting the Act of 1995—an act that recognized the right of public performance in post-1972 recordings, but only in the context of digital transmissions. See Act of 1995, § 2, 109 Stat. 336. We decline to reach the conclusion that, despite decades of industry lobbying, Congress eventually granted a right in 1972 that was significantly less valuable than the right Flo & Eddie claims has existed all along under the common law in Florida and elsewhere. Accepting Flo & Eddie's position would require that we ignore the lengthy history of this issue on the federal level.[28]

As a result of the Florida Supreme Court's ruling, in January of 2018, the Eleventh Circuit entered an order affirming the judgment of the district court in favor of Sirius XM, ending the Florida litigation.[29]

California Litigation: Pandora Media

Flo & Eddie also filed suit against Pandora Media Group in October 2014 in federal court in California, with claims essentially identical to those asserted against Sirius XM. Relying on Judge Guterriez's prior ruling in the Sirius XM litigation, the district court ruled that section 980(a)(2) granted Flo & Eddie a property right in the public performance of its sound recordings.[30] Pandora appealed, and in March, 2017, the Ninth Circuit certified two questions of state law to the California Supreme Court: one addressing whether section 980(a)(2) provides a public performance right in published pre-1972 sound recordings, and one addressing whether a common law public performance right exists under California law for pre-1972 sound recordings.[31] After the Music Modernization Act ("MMA") was signed into law in October, 2018, the California Supreme Court dismissed consideration of the certified questions.

---

[28] *Id.* at 316–17.

[29] *Flo & Eddie, Inc. v. Sirius XM Radio, Inc.*, 709 F. App'x 661, 663 (11th Cir. 2018).

[30] *Flo & Eddie, Inc. v. Pandora Media, Inc.*, No. CV 14–7648 PSG (RZx), 2015 U.S. Dist. LEXIS 70551, at *27–29.

[31] *Flo & Eddie, Inc. v. Pandora Media, Inc.*, 851 F.3d 950 (9th Cir. 2017).

On October 17, 2019, the Ninth Circuit held that the passage of the MMA "warranted vacating the district court's order and remanding the claims in light of the new law."[32] As of this writing, the case was still pending and the district court had not yet ruled on the issue.

In addition to the revised language in section 301's preemption provisions provided above, a related change to federal copyright law made by the MMA that is of particular importance to the issues in the Flo & Eddie litigation was the addition of **Chapter 14**, governing pre-1972 sound recordings. Although the MMA did not grant federal copyright protection to pre-1972 works *per se*, it generally gives owners of pre-1972 sound recordings the benefit of the exclusive rights available to owners of post-1972 sound recordings, as well as the remedies available to copyright owners under sections 502 through 505 (addressing remedies for infringement) and 1203 (addressing remedies for circumvention of technological measures designed to protect against infringement) of the Copyright Act.[33]

For digital public performances of pre-1972 sound recordings made *after* the MMA's effective date, section 1401(b) also essentially subjects pre-1972 sound recordings to the compulsory license, treating such transmissions as "authorized and made with the consent of the rights owner" if they satisfy the requirements of the section 114 and section 112 statutory licenses and the statutory royalty is paid in the same manner as required for post-1972 sound recordings.

With respect to digital audio transmissions of pre-1972 sound recordings made *prior* to the effective date of the MMA, such as those that were the subject of the Flo & Eddie litigation, Section 1401(e) expressly preempts "any claim of common law copyright or equivalent right under the laws of any State arising from a digital audio transmission or reproduction that is made before the date of enactment of this section of a sound recording fixed before February 15, 1972" if certain conditions are met.[34] First, the transmission must have met the requirements for the statutory license or be exempt under section 114(d)(1)–(2), or, in the case of an ephemeral reproduction, meet the requirements of section 112(e). Second, unless the transmission would have been exempt under section 114(d)(1) or the rights owner had voluntarily negotiated an agreement that provides otherwise, the transmitting entity must provide notice of the past use and pay statutory royalties for that use for the 3 years preceding the

---

[32] *Flo & Eddie, Inc. v. Pandora Media, LLC*, 789 Fed. Appx. 569, 2019 Copr. L. Dec. ¶ 31,540 (9th Cir. 2019).

[33] Chapter 14, added by the MMA, also expressly applied the section 512 notice and takedown provisions, and related safe harbors for Internet Service Providers, to pre-1972 sound recordings. The application of section 512 in the context of sound recordings will be discussed in more detail in Chapter 5.

[34] 17 U.S.C. § 1401(e)(1).

MMA's enactment within 270 days of enactment of the MMA (i.e. July 13, 2020).[35]

NOTES AND QUESTIONS

1.   Why do you think that the preemption provision of the 1976 Act (section 301) has been described as one of the most important changes adopted in that Act? Do you think that the *Goldstein* and *Nidorf* cases above were rightly decided? Why or why not? What types of state law protections for musical works and sound recordings, if any, should survive preemption analysis?

2.   As suggested by the *Flo & Eddie* litigation, where the district court in California noted that Sirius XM included pre-1972 sound recordings in its webcasts without any payment to the owners of the sound recordings, a "hot topic" before the enactment of the MMA was the extent to which state laws protecting pre-1972 recordings might interfere with the ability of companies like Pandora and Sirius XM to rely solely on the Section 114 compulsory license of the performance right in operating their streaming/webcasting services. The 2018 MMA addresses these concerns in an interesting way—not by granting federal copyright protection to pre-1972 sound recordings, as some owners of those recordings have advocated for, but by giving owners of pre-1972 works many of the benefits of copyright ownership and expressly preempting state law claims based upon digital performances of pre-1972 sound recordings provided that certain royalties are paid at federally-prescribed rates. What do you think about this solution to the problem?

3.   One of the defenses raised by Sirius XM in these cases was laches—that the sound recording owners had never before asserted any performance right violation under the particular state law despite decades of radio broadcast of the recordings. With its roots in equity, the laches defense is grounded in the notion that an unreasonable and prejudicial delay in bringing suit may prevent recovery for infringement if granting relief would cause unjust hardship to the defendant or to third parties. In rejecting that defense, the S.D.N.Y. opinion noted: "[A]quiescence by participants in the recording industry in a status quo where recording artists and producers were not paid royalties while songwriters were does not show that they lacked an enforceable right under the common law—only that they failed to act on it." *Flo & Eddie, Inc. v. Sirius XM Radio, Inc.*, 62 F. Supp. 3d 325, 340 (S.D.N.Y. 2014). Ignoring the impact of the MMA on these claims for a moment, do you believe that owners of pre-1972 sound recordings should have been able to assert a state law-based performance right in their sound recordings even though they never sought to enforce such a right in the decades in which terrestrial radio broadcast their recordings without any payment?

---

[35]   17 U.S.C. § 1401(e)(1)(A)–(B).

4.   As noted in the excerpts from the *Flo & Eddie* litigation above, Sirius XM raised the Dormant Commerce Clause of the U.S. Constitution as a defense, arguing that individual state laws granting a performance right in digital streaming of pre-1972 sound recordings would interfere with interstate commerce. The Courts rejected the arguments without much discussion. Do you think that the Dormant Commerce Clause arguments were properly rejected, or do they merit more consideration?

5.   Prof. Ross argued in a 2015 article, as well as in amicus briefs filed jointly with Profs. Brandon Butler, Peter Jaszi, and Gary Pulsinelli in the Flo & Eddie litigation, that the Supremacy Clause of the U.S. Constitution preempts state laws in this area in light of the comprehensive digital statutory licensing scheme established by Congress in the 1995 amendments to the Copyright Act.[36] Given the Supreme Court's reasoning in *Goldstein v. California*, 412 U.S. 546 (1973) and the language of section 301(c) prior to its 2018 amendment by the MMA, what do you think about this constitutional argument? Does the MMA's new language in sections 301(c) and 1401 render the Supremacy Clause preemption argument moot?

6.   Take another look at the post-MMA language in section 301(c) in subsection 2, above. It is cumbersome to parse through, but, when read in conjunction with section 1401, it seems to set up essentially three categories of activities relating to pre-1972 sound recordings for purposes of preemption.

- First, activities commenced "on and after" enactment of the MMA are subject to the general preemption provisions of section 301(a), which preempt state law rights that are equivalent to copyright.

- Second, notwithstanding the forgoing language, Congress left unchanged any potential preemption of state law rights relating to activities involving "nonsubscription broadcast transmissions of sound recordings" that "do not qualify as covered activities under chapter 14" and that take place between enactment of the MMA and the date of termination of prohibition on unauthorized activities for those works specified in section 1401(a)(2)—in other words, preemption analysis is the same for these activities after October of 2018 as it would have been before the MMA.

- Third, by implication, there is *no statutory preemption* of state law rights in pre-1972 sound recordings relating to activities taking place *prior* to enactment of the MMA that are not covered by section 1401(e) (i.e., that do not involve digital audio transmissions/reproductions covered by the compulsory licenses in sections 114(d) and 112(e) or exempt transmissions under section 114(d)(1)). Thus, for example, making an unauthorized CD of a pre-1972 recording that took place in California in

---

[36]   Julie L. Ross, *[Un]Happy Together: Why the Supremacy Clause Preempts State Law Digital Public Performance Rights in Pre-1972 Sound Recordings*, 62 J. Copyright Soc'y U.S.A. 545 (Summer 2015).

September of 2018 might still be subject to state law remedies under California Civil Code section 980(a)(2), whereas the same conduct a month later would only be subject to federal copyright infringement remedies; the California law would be preempted.

Why do you think Congress adopted such a complicated approach to statutory preemption when it comes to pre-1972 sound recordings? What interests might it have been trying to reconcile—or what compromises by interested parties might have led to this approach?

The MMA and its impact beyond pre-1972 sound recordings are addressed in more detail in Chapters 6 and 7, *infra*.

CHAPTER V

THE RISE OF DIGITAL MUSIC DISTRIBUTION: *REVOLUTION*[1]

■ ■ ■

Although the 1976 copyright revision was the product of years of study, review, and comment by the Copyright Office, Congress, and interested parties, it did not adequately anticipate the problems that would arise as a result of digital technology—problems that had a particular impact on the music industry. Many of the cases that you will read in this section, like their historical predecessors, necessarily focus on the nature of the technology in determining whether its functioning violates any of the rights granted to copyright owners under the Copyright Act—e.g., the courts break down and analyze how the technology works to determine whether what it does meets the statutory definition of reproducing, distributing, performing, transmitting a work. We include those descriptions of the technology even though many of our readers might be familiar with how modern music technology works, because the analysis of the law often turns on the specifics of the technological process at issue.

Below, we provide a visual history of some of the key technological innovations relevant to the music industry since its inception. The early, "analog era" innovations and some of the legal issues they presented were introduced in Chapters 2 and 3. In this chapter, we will focus on the digital revolution and its impact on the music industry and laws that govern it, as well as on consumers and the way that they interact with music.

---

[1]   John Lennon & Paul McCartney (1968); released by the Beatles on THE BEATLES (WHITE ALBUM) (1968).

Innovations in Music Technology: The Analog Years (1880s–1990s)

Innovations in Music Technology: The Digital Years (1980s–?)

Graphics by Julia Weber

One of the earliest attempts by Congress to specifically deal with the impact of digital media on music copyright was the Audio Home Recording Act of 1992 ("AHRA"). As you will see in the first case below involving the Rio portable music player, the AHRA ended up providing little protection to copyright owners because its hyper-specific language limited protection to certain devices and media that were soon outdated. As we saw in the cases from the early 1900s, the strict interpretation of the language of the copyright statute once again came into conflict with the challenges created by new technology to leave both copyright owners and those who created (or made use of) that technology uncertain about the scope of the legal protection available under existing law.

The emergence of the Internet and peer-to-peer networks created a similar set of problems in the 1990s, illustrated in the *Grokster* case and subsequent cases addressing whether making copyrighted works available for download by others can constitute infringement, some of which are excerpted in Part B below. Part C of this chapter also addresses the effectiveness of the processes put into place by the Digital Millennium Copyright Act ("DMCA") in an effort to balance the competing interests of copyright owners, Internet service providers, and individual users of those Internet services. Finally, Part D of this chapter excerpts opinions in recent litigation involving the introduction of new platforms for distributing entertainment products to further illustrate some of the challenges facing entities who seek to enter the market for media works with innovative technology.

This series of case excerpts provides a snapshot of the response of both the industry and the law to new platforms for and methods of promoting/distributing music. It also highlights the continuing theme of how difficult it is for both the law and the players in the music industry to keep up with technology. You will also witness the difficulties experienced by new market entrants, who typically have invented new technology to exploit copyrighted works within a copyright system grounded in classic assumptions about who should control and profit from use of the music.

CONSIDER AS YOU READ . . .

- How does the *Diamond Multimedia* case illustrate the law's difficulty in keeping up with technology in the context of the music industry?

- Is civil litigation the best way to address unauthorized digital copying and distribution of sound recordings via the Internet, or should alternative processes be available? What might any alternatives look like? How can harm to copyright owners from widespread infringement be balanced with fairness to individuals who copy for private, rather than commercial, use?

- Do the notice and takedown provisions of the Digital Millennium Copyright Act and the current legal standards for secondary liability for copyright infringement make sense in the context of digital transfers of copyrighted works via the Internet? Why or why not? Can you think of effective alternatives?

- How can technological innovation be encouraged while still protecting authors (and their licensees) against unauthorized or uncompensated uses of their intellectual property?

A. MUSIC ENTERS THE DIGITAL AGE

Diamond Rio Portable Music Player,
Introduced in 1998

RECORDING INDUSTRY ASS'N OF AMERICA V. DIAMOND MULTIMEDIA SYSTEMS, INC.

180 F.3d 1072 (9th Cir. 1999)

O'SCANNLAIN, CIRCUIT JUDGE:

In this case involving the intersection of computer technology, the Internet, and music listening, we must decide whether the Rio portable music player is a digital audio recording device subject to the restrictions of the Audio Home Recording Act of 1992.

I

This appeal arises from the efforts of the Recording Industry Association of America and the Alliance of Artists and Recording Companies (collectively, "RIAA") to enjoin the manufacture and distribution by Diamond Multimedia Systems ("Diamond") of the Rio portable music player. The Rio is a small device (roughly the size of an audio cassette) with headphones that allows a user to download MP3 audio files from a computer and to listen to them elsewhere. The dispute over the Rio's design and function is difficult to comprehend without an understanding of the revolutionary new method of music distribution made possible by digital recording and the Internet; thus, we will explain in some detail the brave new world of Internet music distribution.

A

The introduction of digital audio recording to the consumer electronics market in the 1980's is at the root of this litigation. Before then, a person wishing to copy an original music recording—e.g., wishing to make a cassette tape of a record or compact disc-was limited to analog, rather than digital, recording technology. With analog recording, each successive generation of copies suffers from an increasingly pronounced degradation in sound quality. For example, when an analog cassette copy of a record or compact disc is itself copied by analog technology, the resulting "second-generation" copy of the original will most likely suffer from the hiss and lack of clarity characteristic of older recordings. With digital recording, by contrast, there is almost no degradation in sound quality, no matter how many generations of copies are made. Digital copying thus allows thousands of perfect or near perfect copies (and copies of copies) to be made from a single original recording. Music "pirates" use digital recording technology to make and to distribute near perfect copies of commercially prepared recordings for which they have not licensed the copyrights.

Until recently, the Internet was of little use for the distribution of music because the average music computer file was simply too big: the digital information on a single compact disc of music required hundreds of computer floppy discs to store, and downloading even a single song from the Internet took hours. However, various compression algorithms (which make an audio file "smaller" by limiting the audio bandwidth) now allow digital audio files to be transferred more quickly and stored more efficiently. MPEG-1 Audio Layer 3 (commonly known as "MP3") is the most popular digital audio compression algorithm in use on the Internet, and the compression it provides makes an audio file "smaller" by a factor of twelve to one without significantly reducing sound quality. MP3's popularity is due in large part to the fact that it is a standard, non-proprietary compression algorithm freely available for use by anyone, unlike various proprietary (and copyright-secure) competitor algorithms. Coupled with the use of cable modems, compression algorithms like MP3 may soon allow an hour of music to be downloaded from the Internet to a personal computer in just a few minutes.

These technological advances have occurred, at least in part, to the traditional music industry's disadvantage. By most accounts, the predominant use of MP3 is the trafficking in illicit audio recordings . . . . Various pirate websites offer free downloads of copyrighted material, and a single pirate site on the Internet may contain thousands of pirated audio computer files.

RIAA represents the roughly half-dozen major record companies (and the artists on their labels) that control approximately ninety percent of the distribution of recorded music in the United States. RIAA asserts that Internet distribution of serial digital copies of pirated copyrighted material will discourage the purchase of legitimate recordings, and predicts that losses to digital Internet piracy will soon surpass the $300 million that is allegedly lost annually to other more traditional forms of piracy.[1] RIAA fights a well-nigh constant battle against Internet piracy, monitoring the Internet daily, and routinely shutting down pirate websites by sending

---

[1]   Whether or not piracy causes such financial harm is a subject of dispute. Critics of the industry's piracy loss figures have noted that a willingness to download illicit files for free does not necessarily correlate to lost sales, for the simple reason that persons willing to accept an item for free often will not purchase the same item, even if no longer freely available. *See* Lewis Kurlantzick & Jacqueline E. Pennino, *The Audio Home Recording Act of 1992 and the Formation of Copyright Policy*, 45 J. Copyright Soc'y U.S.A. 497, 506 (1998). Critics further note that the price of commercially available recordings already reflects the existence of copying and the benefits and harms such copying causes; thus, they contend, the current price of recordings offsets, at least in part, the losses incurred by the industry from home taping and piracy. *See id.* at 509–10.

cease-and-desist letters and bringing lawsuits. There are conflicting views on RIAA's success-RIAA asserts that it can barely keep up with the pirate traffic, while others assert that few, if any, pirate sites remain in operation in the United States and illicit files are difficult to find and download from anywhere online.

In contrast to piracy, the Internet also supports a burgeoning traffic in legitimate audio computer files. Independent and wholly Internet record labels routinely sell and provide free samples of their artists' work online, while many unsigned artists distribute their own material from their own websites. . . . Diamond cites a 1998 "Music Industry and the Internet" report by Jupiter Communications which predicts that online sales for pre-recorded music will exceed $1.4 billion by 2002 in the United States alone.

Prior to the invention of devices like the Rio, MP3 users had little option other than to listen to their downloaded digital audio files through headphones or speakers at their computers, playing them from their hard drives. The Rio renders these files portable. More precisely, once an audio file has been downloaded onto a computer hard drive. . . , separate computer software provided with the Rio (called "Rio Manager") allows the user further to download the file to the Rio itself via a parallel port cable that plugs the Rio into the computer. The Rio device is incapable of effecting such a transfer, and is incapable of receiving audio files from anything other than a personal computer equipped with Rio Manager.

Generally, the Rio can store approximately one hour of music, or sixteen hours of spoken material (e.g., downloaded newscasts or books on tape). With the addition of flash memory cards, the Rio can store an additional half-hour or hour of music. The Rio's sole output is an analog audio signal sent to the user via headphones. The Rio cannot make duplicates of any digital audio file it stores, nor can it transfer or upload such a file to a computer, to another device, or to the Internet. However, a flash memory card to which a digital audio file has been downloaded can be removed from one Rio and played back in another.

B

RIAA brought suit to enjoin the manufacture and distribution of the Rio, alleging that the Rio does not meet the requirements for digital audio recording devices under the Audio Home Recording Act of 1992, 17 U.S.C. § 1001 *et seq.* (the "Act"), because it does not employ a Serial Copyright Management System ("SCMS") that sends, receives, and acts upon information about the generation and copyright status of the files that it plays. *See id.* § 1002(a)(2).[2] RIAA also sought payment of the royalties owed

---

[2]   At the time the preliminary injunction was sought and denied, the Rio did not incorporate SCMS; Diamond asserts that it has now incorporated such a system into the Rio Manager software, though not into the Rio itself.

by Diamond as the manufacturer and distributor of a digital audio recording device. *See id.* § 1003.

The district court denied RIAA's motion for a preliminary injunction, holding that RIAA's likelihood of success on the merits was mixed and the balance of hardships did not tip in RIAA's favor. *See generally Recording Indus. Ass'n of America, Inc. v. Diamond Multimedia Sys., Inc.,* 29 F.Supp.2d 624 (C.D.Cal.1998) (*"RIAA I"*). RIAA brought this appeal.

II

The initial question presented is whether the Rio falls within the ambit of the Act. The Act does not broadly prohibit digital serial copying of copyright protected audio recordings. Instead, the Act places restrictions only upon a specific type of recording device. Most relevant here, the Act provides that "[n]o person shall import, manufacture, or distribute any *digital audio recording device* . . . that does not conform to the Serial Copy Management System ["SCMS"] [or] a system that has the same functional characteristics." 17 U.S.C. § 1002(a)(1), (2) (emphasis added). The Act further provides that "[n]o person shall import into and distribute, or manufacture and distribute, any *digital audio recording device* . . . unless such person records the notice specified by this section and subsequently deposits the statements of account and applicable royalty payments." *Id.* § 1003(a) (emphasis added). Thus, to fall within the SCMS and royalty requirements in question, the Rio must be a "digital audio recording device," which the Act defines through a set of nested definitions.

The Act defines a "digital audio recording device" as:

> any machine or device of a type commonly distributed to individuals for use by individuals, whether or not included with or as part of some other machine or device, the digital recording function of which is designed or marketed for the primary purpose of, and that is capable of, making a *digital audio copied recording* for private use. . . .

Id. § 1001(3) (emphasis added).

A "digital audio copied recording" is defined as:

> a reproduction in a digital recording format of a *digital musical recording,* whether that reproduction is made directly from another digital musical recording or indirectly from a transmission.

Id. § 1001(1) (emphasis added).

A "digital musical recording" is defined as:

> *a material object—*
>
> (i)   in which are fixed, in a digital recording format, *only sounds, and material, statements, or instructions incidental to those fixed sounds*, if any, and
>
> (ii) from which the sounds and material can be perceived, reproduced, or otherwise communicated, either directly or with the aid of a machine or device.

Id. § 1001(5)(A) (emphasis added).

In sum, to be a digital audio recording device, the Rio must be able to reproduce, either "directly" or "from a transmission," a "digital music recording."

III

We first consider whether the Rio is able directly to reproduce a digital music recording-which is a specific type of material object in which only sounds are fixed (or material and instructions incidental to those sounds). *See id.*

A

The typical computer hard drive from which a Rio directly records is, of course, a material object. However, hard drives ordinarily contain much more than "only sounds, and material, statements, or instructions incidental to those fixed sounds." *Id.* Indeed, almost all hard drives contain numerous programs (e.g., for word processing, scheduling appointments, etc.) and databases that are not incidental to any sound files that may be stored on the hard drive. Thus, the Rio appears not to make copies from digital music recordings, and thus would not be a digital audio recording device under the Act's basic definition unless it makes copies from transmissions.

Moreover, the Act expressly provides that the term "digital musical recording" does not include:

> *a material object—*
>
> (i)   in which the fixed sounds consist entirely of spoken word recordings, or
>
> (ii) *in which one or more computer programs are fixed*, except that a digital recording may contain statements or instructions constituting the fixed sounds and incidental material, and statements or instructions to be used directly or indirectly in order to bring about the perception, reproduction, or communication of the fixed sounds and incidental material.

Id. § 1001(5)(B) (emphasis added). As noted previously, a hard drive is a material object in which one or more programs are fixed; thus, a hard drive is excluded from the definition of digital music recordings. This provides confirmation that the Rio does not record "directly" from "digital music recordings," and therefore could not be a digital audio recording device unless it makes copies "from transmissions." . . . [¶¶]

2

The district court concluded that the exemption of hard drives from the definition of digital music recording, and the exemption of computers generally from the Act's ambit, "would effectively eviscerate the [Act]" because "[a]ny recording device could evade [ ] regulation simply by passing the music through a computer and ensuring that the MP3 file resided momentarily on the hard drive." *RIAA I,* 29 F.Supp.2d at 630. While this may be true, the Act seems to have been expressly designed to create this loophole.

a

Under the plain meaning of the Act's definition of digital audio recording devices, computers (and their hard drives) are not digital audio recording devices because their "primary purpose" is not to make digital audio copied recordings. . . . The legislative history is consistent with this interpretation of the Act's provisions, stating that "the typical personal computer would not fall within the definition of 'digital audio recording device,'" S. Rep. 102–294, at *122, because a personal computer's "recording function is designed and marketed primarily for the recording of data and computer programs," *id.* at *121. Another portion of the Senate Report states that "[i]f the 'primary purpose' of the recording function is to make objects other than digital audio copied recordings, then the machine or device is not a 'digital audio recording device,' *even if the machine or device is technically capable of making such recordings." Id.* (emphasis added). The legislative history thus expressly recognizes that computers (and other devices) have recording functions capable of recording digital musical recordings, and thus implicate the home taping and piracy concerns to which the Act is responsive. Nonetheless, the legislative history is consistent with the Act's plain language-computers are *not* digital audio recording devices.[6]

. . . . [¶ ¶] c

In fact, the Rio's operation is entirely consistent with the Act's main purpose-the facilitation of personal use. As the Senate Report explains,

---

[6]   Indeed, Diamond asserted at oral argument (and supports the assertion with the affidavit of a direct participant in the negotiations and compromises that resulted in the final language of the Act) that the exclusion of computers from the Act's scope was part of a carefully negotiated compromise between the various industries with interests at stake, and without which, the computer industry would have vigorously opposed passage of the Act.

"[t]he purpose of [the Act] is to ensure the right of consumers to make analog or digital audio recordings of copyrighted music for their *private, noncommercial use.*" S. Rep. 102–294, at *86 (emphasis added). The Act does so through its home taping exemption, *see* 17 U.S.C. § 1008, which "protects all noncommercial copying by consumers of digital and analog musical recordings," H.R. Rep. 102–873(I), at *59. The Rio merely makes copies in order to render portable, or "space-shift," those files that already reside on a user's hard drive. *Cf. Sony Corp. of America v. Universal City Studios,* 464 U.S. 417, 455, 104 S.Ct. 774, 78 L.Ed.2d 574 (1984) (holding that "time-shifting" of copyrighted television shows with VCR's constitutes fair use under the Copyright Act, and thus is not an infringement). Such copying is paradigmatic noncommercial personal use entirely consistent with the purposes of the Act.

IV

Even though it cannot directly reproduce a digital music recording, the Rio would nevertheless be a digital audio recording device if it could reproduce a digital music recording "from a transmission." 17 U.S.C. § 1001(1).

A

The term "transmission" is not defined in Act, although the use of the term in the Act implies that a transmission is a communication to the public. *See id.* § 1002(e) (placing restrictions upon "[a]ny person who transmits or *otherwise communicates to the public* any sound recording in digital format") (emphasis added). In the context of copyright law (from which the term appears to have been taken), "[t]o 'transmit' a performance or display is to communicate it by any device or process whereby images or sounds are received beyond the place from which they are sent." 17 U.S.C. § 101. The legislative history confirms that the copyright definition of "transmission" is sufficient for our purposes here. The Act originally (and circularly) provided that "[a] 'transmission' is any audio or audiovisual transmission, now known or later developed, whether by a broadcast station, cable system, multipoint distribution service, subscription service, direct broadcast satellite, or other form of analog or digital communication." S. Rep. 102–294, at *10. The Senate Report provides a radio broadcast as an example of a transmission. *See id.,* at *119 (referring to "a transmission (e.g., a radio broadcast of a commercially released audio cassette)."). The parties do not really dispute the definition of transmission, but rather, whether *indirect* reproduction of a transmission of a digital music recording is covered by the Act.

B

RIAA asserts that indirect reproduction of a transmission is sufficient for the Rio to fall within the Act's ambit as a digital audio recording device. *See* 17 U.S.C. § 1001(1) (digital audio recording devices are those devices that are capable of making "a reproduction in a digital recording format of a digital musical recording, whether that reproduction is made directly from another digital musical recording or *indirectly* from a transmission") (emphasis added). Diamond asserts that the adverb "indirectly" modifies the recording of the underlying "digital music recording," rather than the recording "from the transmission." Diamond effectively asserts that the statute should be read as covering devices that are capable of making a reproduction of a digital musical recording, "whether that reproduction is made directly[,] from another digital musical recording[,] or indirectly[,] from a transmission."

While the Rio can only directly reproduce files from a computer hard drive via a cable linking the two devices (which is obviously not a transmission), the Rio can indirectly reproduce a transmission. For example, if a radio broadcast of a digital audio recording were recorded on a digital audio tape machine or compact disc recorder and then uploaded to a computer hard drive, the Rio could indirectly reproduce the transmission by downloading a copy from the hard drive. Thus, if indirect reproduction of a transmission falls within the statutory definition, the Rio would be a digital audio recording device.

1

RIAA's interpretation of the statutory language initially seems plausible, but closer analysis reveals that it is contrary to the statutory language and common sense. The focus of the statutory language seems to be on the two means of reproducing the underlying digital music recording-either directly from that recording, or indirectly, by reproducing the recording from a transmission. RIAA's interpretation of the Act's language (in which "indirectly" modifies copying "from a transmission," rather than the copying of the underlying digital music recording) would only cover the indirect recording of transmissions, and would omit restrictions on the direct recording of transmissions (e.g., recording songs from the radio) from the Act's ambit. This interpretation would significantly reduce the protection afforded by the Act to transmissions, and neither the statutory language nor structure provides any reason that the Act's protections should be so limited. Moreover, it makes little sense for the Act to restrict the indirect recording of transmissions, but to allow unrestricted direct recording of transmissions (e.g., to regulate second-hand recording of songs from the radio, but to allow unlimited direct recording of songs from the radio). Thus, the most logical reading of the Act extends protection to direct copying of digital music recordings, and to indirect copying of digital music recordings from transmissions of those recordings.

2

Because of the arguable ambiguity of this passage of the statute, recourse to the legislative history is necessary on this point. . . . The Senate

Report states that "a digital audio recording made from a commercially released compact disc or audio cassette, or *from a radio broadcast* of a commercially released compact disc or audio cassette, would be a 'digital audio copied recording.'" S. Rep. 102–294, at *119 (emphasis added). . . . Thus the legislative history confirms the most logical reading of the statute, which we adopt: "indirectly" modifies the verb "is made"—in other words, modifies the making of the reproduction of the underlying digital music recording. Thus, a device falls within the Act's provisions if it can indirectly copy a digital music recording by making a copy from a transmission of that recording. Because the Rio cannot make copies from transmissions, but instead, can only make copies from a computer hard drive, it is not a digital audio recording device.[7]

V

For the foregoing reasons, the Rio is not a digital audio recording device subject to the restrictions of the Audio Home Recording Act of 1992. The district court properly denied the motion for a preliminary injunction against the Rio's manufacture and distribution. Having so determined, we need not consider whether the balance of hardships or the possibility of irreparable harm supports injunctive relief.

AFFIRMED.

NOTES AND QUESTIONS

1.   The law has long struggled to keep up with technology, in part because of the difficulty in drafting statutory language that is neither so narrow that it fails to encompass new technologies nor so broad that it provides far greater protection than copyright policy would warrant. If you had to redraft the AHRA's language so that the Rio (or the iPod) fit within its provisions and thus change the result in the *Diamond Multimedia Systems* case, how would you do so?

2.   What do you think the impact on the development of devices like the Rio and the iPod might have been if the result in this case had been different and the court had broadly construed the application of the AHRA to newer technologies?

---

[7]   We further note that any transmission reproduced indirectly must pass through a computer, as an MP3 file, to reach the Rio. As we explained in part III.B.2, *supra,* computers are exempted from the requirement of reading and transmitting SCMS codes, and MP3 files do not incorporate such codes. Thus, requiring the Rio to implement SCMS because it can indirectly reproduce a transmission of a digital music recording would be, as the district court concluded, "an exercise in futility." *RIAA I,* 29 F.Supp.2d at 632. SCMS would not alter the Rio's ability to reproduce such transmissions, just as it would not alter the Rio's ability to reproduce digital music recordings uploaded to a computer hard drive.

B. P2P NETWORKS AND UNAUTHORIZED FILE SHARING

The advent of peer-to-peer networks was a technological revolution that upended the existing distribution chain for recorded music. Although, as some of the cases excerpted in earlier chapters illustrate, unauthorized copying and distribution of records had been common since the inception of the recording industry, unauthorized reproductions of vinyl records or cassette tapes were typically of poorer sound quality than the originals from which they were made and required physical distribution that was easier to discover and prosecute than Internet-based copying and distribution of sound recordings. Moreover, digital reproductions are perfect copies, capable of being replayed over and over without degrading in quality, and peer-to-peer networks allowed for recordings to be downloaded by millions of people throughout the world.

As you will see in some of the cases excerpted below, the recording industry responded to this threat to their distribution of sound recordings and resulting loss in sales revenues with litigation against peer-to-peer networks for contributory or vicarious infringement, seeking to hold the networks responsible for direct infringement by their users. In later efforts to stem the tide of unauthorized file sharing, the recording industry brought thousands of direct copyright infringement lawsuits against individuals who both uploaded and downloaded musical recordings through peer-to-peer file sharing services.

A Note on Secondary Liability for Infringement

Copyright law permits recovery under theories of both direct infringement—i.e., claims against those whose acts constitute infringement of an exclusive right of a copyright owner—and secondary infringement. Although the Copyright Act itself does not specifically address the means of proving secondary liability for infringement, it has long been recognized in the common law and was explicitly recognized by the Supreme Court in *Sony Corp. of America v. Universal City Studios, Inc.*, 464 U.S. 417 (1984). The two main types of secondary liability developed in the common law prior to Grokster were **contributory infringement** and **vicarious infringement**. To prove contributory infringement, the plaintiff must typically establish that the defendant (1) had actual or constructive knowledge of direct infringement by a third party and (2) materially contributed to the infringing activity. To prove vicarious infringement, the plaintiff must establish (1) the right and ability to supervise or control the infringing activity; and (2) a direct financial benefit from that activity.

METRO-GOLDWYN-MAYER STUDIOS, INC. V. GROKSTER, LTD.
545 U.S. 913 (2005)

JUSTICE SOUTER delivered the opinion of the Court.

The question is under what circumstances the distributor of a product capable of both lawful and unlawful use is liable for acts of copyright infringement by third parties using the product. We hold that one who distributes a device with the object of promoting its use to infringe copyright, as shown by clear expression or other affirmative steps taken to foster infringement, is liable for the resulting acts of infringement by third parties.

I. A.

Respondents, Grokster, Ltd., and StreamCast Networks, Inc., defendants in the trial court, distribute free software products that allow computer users to share electronic files through peer-to-peer networks, so called because users' computers communicate directly with each other, not through central servers. The advantage of peer-to-peer networks over information networks of other types shows up in their substantial and growing popularity. Because they need no central computer server to mediate the exchange of information or files among users, the high-bandwidth communications capacity for a server may be dispensed with, and the need for costly server storage space is eliminated. Since copies of a file (particularly a popular one) are available on many users' computers, file requests and retrievals may be faster than on other types of networks, and since file exchanges do not travel through a server, communications can take place between any computers that remain connected to the network without risk that a glitch in the server will disable the network in its entirety. Given these benefits in security, cost, and efficiency, peer-to-peer networks are employed to store and distribute electronic files by universities, government agencies, corporations, and libraries, among others.[FN1 omitted]

Other users of peer-to-peer networks include individual recipients of Grokster's and StreamCast's software, and although the networks that they enjoy through using the software can be used to share any type of digital file, they have prominently employed those networks in sharing copyrighted music and video files without authorization. A group of copyright holders (MGM for short, but including motion picture studios, recording companies, songwriters, and music publishers) sued Grokster and StreamCast for their users' copyright infringements, alleging that they knowingly and intentionally distributed their software to enable users to reproduce and distribute the copyrighted works in violation of the Copyright Act, 17 U.S.C. § 101 et seq. (2000 ed. and Supp. II).[FN2 omitted] MGM sought damages and an injunction.

Discovery during the litigation revealed the way the software worked, the business aims of each defendant company, and the predilections of the users. Grokster's eponymous software employs what is known as FastTrack technology, a protocol developed by others and licensed to Grokster. StreamCast distributes a very similar product except that its software, called Morpheus, relies on what is known as Gnutella technology.[3] A user who downloads and installs either software possesses the protocol to send requests for files directly to the computers of others using software compatible with FastTrack or Gnutella. On the FastTrack network opened by the Grokster software, the user's request goes to a computer given an indexing capacity by the software and designated a supernode, or to some other computer with comparable power and capacity to collect temporary indexes of the files available on the computers of users connected to it. The supernode (or indexing computer) searches its own index and may communicate the search request to other supernodes. If the file is found, the supernode discloses its location to the computer requesting it, and the requesting user can download the file directly from the computer located. The copied file is placed in a designated sharing folder on the requesting user's computer, where it is available for other users to download in turn, along with any other file in that folder.

In the Gnutella network made available by Morpheus, the process is mostly the same, except that in some versions of the Gnutella protocol there are no supernodes. In these versions, peer computers using the protocol communicate directly with each other. When a user enters a search request into the Morpheus software, it sends the request to computers connected with it, which in turn pass the request along to other connected peers. The search results are communicated to the requesting computer, and the user can download desired files directly from peers' computers. As this description indicates, Grokster and StreamCast use no servers to intercept the content of the search requests or to mediate the file transfers conducted by users of the software, there being no central point

---

[3] Subsequent versions of Morpheus, released after the record was made in this case, apparently rely not on Gnutella but on a technology called Neonet. These developments are not before us.

through which the substance of the communications passes in either direction.[FN4 omitted]

Although Grokster and StreamCast do not therefore know when particular files are copied, a few searches using their software would show what is available on the networks the software reaches.... [¶] As for quantification, the parties' anecdotal and statistical evidence entered thus far to show the content available on the FastTrack and Gnutella networks does not say much about which files are actually downloaded by users, and no one can say how often the software is used to obtain copies of unprotected material. But MGM's evidence gives reason to think that the vast majority of users' downloads are acts of infringement, and because well over 100 million copies of the software in question are known to have been downloaded, and billions of files are shared across the FastTrack and Gnutella networks each month, the probable scope of copyright infringement is staggering.

Grokster and StreamCast concede the infringement in most downloads, Brief for Respondents 10, n. 6, and it is uncontested that they are aware that users employ their software primarily to download copyrighted files, even if the decentralized FastTrack and Gnutella networks fail to reveal which files are being copied, and when. From time to time, moreover, the companies have learned about their users' infringement directly, as from users who have sent e-mail to each company with questions about playing copyrighted movies they had downloaded, to whom the companies have responded with guidance.[6] App. 559–563, 808–816, 939–954. And MGM notified the companies of 8 million copyrighted files that could be obtained using their software.

Grokster and StreamCast are not, however, merely passive recipients of information about infringing use. The record is replete with evidence that from the moment Grokster and StreamCast began to distribute their free software, each one clearly voiced the objective that recipients use it to download copyrighted works, and each took active steps to encourage infringement.... [¶] An internal e-mail from a [StreamCast] company executive stated: " 'We have put this network in place so that when Napster pulls the plug on their free service . . . or if the Court orders them shut down prior to that . . . we will be positioned to capture the flood of their 32 million users that will be actively looking for an alternative.' " *Id.*, at 588–589, 861.

Thus, StreamCast developed promotional materials to market its service as the best Napster alternative.... [¶]

The evidence that Grokster sought to capture the market of former Napster users is sparser but revealing, for Grokster launched its own

---

[6]   The Grokster founder contends that in answering these e-mails he often did not read them fully. App. 77, 769.

OpenNap system called Swaptor and inserted digital codes into its Web site so that computer users using Web search engines to look for "Napster" or "[f]ree file sharing" would be directed to the Grokster Web site, where they could download the Grokster software. *Id.,* at 992–993. . . . [A]n internal communication indicates they aimed to have a larger number of copyrighted songs available on their networks than other file-sharing networks. *Id.,* at 868. The point, of course, would be to attract users of a mind to infringe, just as it would be with their promotional materials developed showing copyrighted songs as examples of the kinds of files available through Morpheus. *Id.,* at 848. . . .

In addition to this evidence of express promotion, marketing, and intent to promote further, the business models employed by Grokster and StreamCast confirm that their principal object was use of their software to download copyrighted works. Grokster and StreamCast receive no revenue from users, who obtain the software itself for nothing. Instead, both companies generate income by selling advertising space, and they stream the advertising to Grokster and Morpheus users while they are employing the programs. As the number of users of each program increases, advertising opportunities become worth more. Cf. App. 539, 804. While there is doubtless some demand for free Shakespeare, the evidence shows that substantive volume is a function of free access to copyrighted work. Users seeking Top 40 songs, for example, or the latest release by Modest Mouse, are certain to be far more numerous than those seeking a free Decameron, and Grokster and StreamCast translated that demand into dollars.

Finally, there is no evidence that either company made an effort to filter copyrighted material from users' downloads or otherwise impede the sharing of copyrighted files. Although Grokster appears to have sent e-mails warning users about infringing content when it received threatening notice from the copyright holders, it never blocked anyone from continuing to use its software to share copyrighted files. Id., at 75–76. StreamCast not only rejected another company's offer of help to monitor infringement, id., at 928–929, but blocked the Internet Protocol addresses of entities it believed were trying to engage in such monitoring on its networks, id., at 917–922.

B.

. . . . The District Court held that those who used the Grokster and Morpheus software to download copyrighted media files directly infringed MGM's copyrights, a conclusion not contested on appeal, but the court nonetheless granted summary judgment in favor of Grokster and StreamCast as to any liability arising from distribution of the then-current versions of their software. Distributing that software gave rise to no liability in the court's view, because its use did not provide the distributors with actual knowledge of specific acts of infringement. Case No. CV 01 08541 SVW (PJWx) (CD Cal., June 18, 2003), App. 1213.

The Court of Appeals affirmed. 380 F.3d 1154 (C.A.9 2004). In the court's analysis, a defendant was liable as a contributory infringer when it had knowledge of direct infringement and materially contributed to the infringement. But the court read Sony Corp. of America v. Universal City Studios, Inc., 464 U.S. 417, 104 S.Ct. 774, 78 L.Ed.2d 574 (1984), as holding that distribution of a commercial product capable of substantial noninfringing uses could not give rise to contributory liability for infringement unless the distributor had actual knowledge of specific instances of infringement and failed to act on that knowledge. The fact that the software was capable of substantial noninfringing uses in the Ninth Circuit's view meant that Grokster and StreamCast were not liable, because they had no such actual knowledge, owing to the decentralized architecture of their software. The court also held that Grokster and StreamCast did not materially contribute to their users' infringement because it was the users themselves who searched for, retrieved, and stored the infringing files, with no involvement by the defendants beyond providing the software in the first place.

The Ninth Circuit also considered whether Grokster and StreamCast could be liable under a theory of vicarious infringement. The court held against liability because the defendants did not monitor or control the use of the software, had no agreed-upon right or current ability to supervise its use, and had no independent duty to police infringement. We granted certiorari. 543 U.S. 1032, 125 S.Ct. 686, 160 L.Ed.2d 518 (2004).

II. A.

MGM and many of the amici fault the Court of Appeals's holding for upsetting a sound balance between the respective values of supporting creative pursuits through copyright protection and promoting innovation in new communication technologies by limiting the incidence of liability for copyright infringement. The more artistic protection is favored, the more technological innovation may be discouraged; the administration of copyright law is an exercise in managing the tradeoff. . . .

The tension between the two values is the subject of this case, with its claim that digital distribution of copyrighted material threatens copyright holders as never before, because every copy is identical to the original, copying is easy, and many people (especially the young) use file-sharing software to download copyrighted works. This very breadth of the software's use may well draw the public directly into the debate over copyright policy, Peters, Brace Memorial Lecture: Copyright Enters the Public Domain, 51 J. Copyright Soc. 701, 705–717 (2004) (address by Register of Copyrights), and the indications are that the ease of copying songs or movies using software like Grokster's and Napster's is fostering disdain for copyright protection, Wu, When Code Isn't Law, 89 Va. L.Rev. 679, 724–726 (2003). As the case has been presented to us, these fears are said to be offset by the different concern that imposing liability, not only on infringers but on distributors of software based on its potential for unlawful use, could limit further development of beneficial technologies. See, e.g., Lemley & Reese, Reducing Digital Copyright Infringement Without Restricting Innovation, 56 Stan. L.Rev. 1345, 1386–1390 (2004); Brief for Innovation Scholars and Economists as Amici Curiae 15–20; Brief for Emerging Technology Companies as Amici Curiae 19–25; Brief for Intel Corporation as Amicus Curiae 20–22.[8]

The argument for imposing indirect liability in this case is, however, a powerful one, given the number of infringing downloads that occur every day using StreamCast's and Grokster's software. When a widely shared service or product is used to commit infringement, it may be impossible to enforce rights in the protected work effectively against all direct infringers, the only practical alternative being to go against the distributor of the copying device for secondary liability on a theory of contributory or vicarious infringement. See In re Aimster Copyright Litigation, 334 F.3d 643, 645–646 (C.A.7 2003).

One infringes contributorily by intentionally inducing or encouraging direct infringement, see Gershwin Pub. Corp. v. Columbia Artists Management, Inc., 443 F.2d 1159, 1162 (C.A.2 1971), and infringes vicariously by profiting from direct infringement while declining to exercise a right to stop or limit it, Shapiro, Bernstein & Co. v. H.L. Green Co., 316 F.2d 304, 307 (C.A.2 1963).[FN9 omitted] Although "[t]he Copyright Act does not expressly render anyone liable for infringement committed by another," Sony Corp. v. Universal City Studios, 464 U.S., at 434, 104 S.Ct. 774, these doctrines of secondary liability emerged from common law principles and are well established in the law, id., at 486, 104 S.Ct. 774 (Blackmun, J., dissenting); Kalem Co. v. Harper Brothers, 222 U.S. 55, 62–63, 32 S.Ct. 20, 56 L.Ed. 92 (1911); Gershwin Pub. Corp. v. Columbia Artists Management, supra, at 1162; 3 M. Nimmer & D. Nimmer, Copyright § 12.04[A] (2005).

B.

Despite the currency of these principles of secondary liability, this Court has dealt with secondary copyright infringement in only one recent

---

8 The mutual exclusivity of these values should not be overstated, however. On the one hand technological innovators, including those writing file-sharing computer programs, may wish for effective copyright protections for their work. See, e.g., Wu, When Code Isn't Law, 89 Va. L.Rev. 679, 750 (2003). (StreamCast itself was urged by an associate to "get [its] technology written down and [its intellectual property] protected." App. 866.) On the other hand the widespread distribution of creative works through improved technologies may enable the synthesis of new works or generate audiences for emerging artists. See Eldred v. Ashcroft, 537 U.S. 186, 223–226, 123 S.Ct. 769, 154 L.Ed.2d 683 (2003) (STEVENS, J., dissenting); Van Houweling, Distributive Values in Copyright, 83 Texas L.Rev. 1535, 1539–1540, 1562–1564 (2005); Brief for Sovereign Artists et al. as Amici Curiae 11.

case, and because MGM has tailored its principal claim to our opinion there, a look at our earlier holding is in order. In Sony Corp. v. Universal City Studios, supra, this Court addressed a claim that secondary liability for infringement can arise from the very distribution of a commercial product. There, the product, novel at the time, was what we know today as the videocassette recorder or VCR. Copyright holders sued Sony as the manufacturer, claiming it was contributorily liable for infringement that occurred when VCR owners taped copyrighted programs because it supplied the means used to infringe, and it had constructive knowledge that infringement would occur. At the trial on the merits, the evidence showed that the principal use of the VCR was for " 'time-shifting,' " or taping a program for later viewing at a more convenient time, which the Court found to be a fair, not an infringing, use. Id., at 423–424, 104 S.Ct. 774. There was no evidence that Sony had expressed an object of bringing about taping in violation of copyright or had taken active steps to increase its profits from unlawful taping. Id., at 438, 104 S.Ct. 774. Although Sony's advertisements urged consumers to buy the VCR to " 'record favorite shows' " or " 'build a library' " of recorded programs, id., at 459, 104 S.Ct. 774 (Blackmun, J., dissenting), neither of these uses was necessarily infringing, id., at 424, 454–455, 104 S.Ct. 774.

On those facts, with no evidence of stated or indicated intent to promote infringing uses, the only conceivable basis for imposing liability was on a theory of contributory infringement arising from its sale of VCRs to consumers with knowledge that some would use them to infringe. Id., at 439, 104 S.Ct. 774. But because the VCR was "capable of commercially significant noninfringing uses," we held the manufacturer could not be faulted solely on the basis of its distribution. Id., at 442, 104 S.Ct. 774. . . . [¶]

In sum, [under the patent law's traditional staple article of commerce doctrine], where an article is "good for nothing else" but infringement, Canda v. Michigan Malleable Iron Co., supra, at 489, there is no legitimate public interest in its unlicensed availability, and there is no injustice in presuming or imputing an intent to infringe, see Henry v. A.B. Dick Co., 224 U.S. 1, 48, 32 S.Ct. 364, 56 L.Ed. 645 (1912), overruled on other grounds, Motion Picture Patents Co. v. Universal Film Mfg. Co., 243 U.S. 502, 37 S.Ct. 416, 61 L.Ed. 871 (1917). Conversely, the doctrine absolves the equivocal conduct of selling an item with substantial lawful as well as unlawful uses, and limits liability to instances of more acute fault than the mere understanding that some of one's products will be misused. It leaves breathing room for innovation and a vigorous commerce. See Sony Corp. v. Universal City Studios, 464 U.S., at 442, 104 S.Ct. 774; Dawson Chemical Co. v. Rohm & Haas Co., 448 U.S. 176, 221, 100 S.Ct. 2601, 65 L.Ed.2d 696 (1980); Henry v. A.B. Dick Co., supra, at 48, 32 S.Ct. 364.

The parties and many of the amici in this case think the key to resolving it is the Sony rule and, in particular, what it means for a product to be "capable of commercially significant noninfringing uses." Sony Corp. v. Universal City Studios, supra, at 442, 104 S.Ct. 774. MGM advances the argument that granting summary judgment to Grokster and StreamCast as to their current activities gave too much weight to the value of innovative technology, and too little to the copyrights infringed by users of their software, given that 90% of works available on one of the networks was shown to be copyrighted. Assuming the remaining 10% to be its noninfringing use, MGM says this should not qualify as "substantial," and the Court should quantify Sony to the extent of holding that a product used "principally" for infringement does not qualify. See Brief for Motion Picture Studio and Recording Company Petitioners 31. As mentioned before, Grokster and StreamCast reply by citing evidence that their software can be used to reproduce public domain works, and they point to copyright holders who actually encourage copying. Even if infringement is the principal practice with their software today, they argue, the noninfringing uses are significant and will grow.

We agree with MGM that the Court of Appeals misapplied Sony, which it read as limiting secondary liability quite beyond the circumstances to which the case applied. Sony barred secondary liability based on presuming or imputing intent to cause infringement solely from the design or distribution of a product capable of substantial lawful use, which the distributor knows is in fact used for infringement. The Ninth Circuit has read Sony's limitation to mean that whenever a product is capable of substantial lawful use, the producer can never be held contributorily liable for third parties' infringing use of it; it read the rule as being this broad, even when an actual purpose to cause infringing use is shown by evidence independent of design and distribution of the product, unless the distributors had "specific knowledge of infringement at a time at which they contributed to the infringement, and failed to act upon that information." 380 F.3d, at 1162 (internal quotation marks and brackets omitted). Because the Circuit found the StreamCast and Grokster software capable of substantial lawful use, it concluded on the basis of its reading of Sony that neither company could be held liable, since there was no showing that their software, being without any central server, afforded them knowledge of specific unlawful uses.

This view of Sony, however, was error, converting the case from one about liability resting on imputed intent to one about liability on any theory. Because Sony did not displace other theories of secondary liability, and because we find below that it was error to grant summary judgment to the companies on MGM's inducement claim, we do not revisit Sony further, as MGM requests, to add a more quantified description of the point of balance between protection and commerce when liability rests solely on distribution with knowledge that unlawful use will occur. It is enough to note that the Ninth Circuit's judgment rested on an erroneous understanding of Sony and to leave further consideration of the Sony rule for a day when that may be required.

C

Sony's rule limits imputing culpable intent as a matter of law from the characteristics or uses of a distributed product. But nothing in Sony requires courts to ignore evidence of intent if there is such evidence, and the case was never meant to foreclose rules of fault-based liability derived from the common law.[FN10 omitted] Sony Corp. v. Universal City Studios, supra, at 439, 104 S.Ct. 774 ("If vicarious liability is to be imposed on Sony in this case, it must rest on the fact that it has sold equipment with constructive knowledge" of the potential for infringement). Thus, where evidence goes beyond a product's characteristics or the knowledge that it may be put to infringing uses, and shows statements or actions directed to promoting infringement, Sony's staple-article rule will not preclude liability.

The classic case of direct evidence of unlawful purpose occurs when one induces commission of infringement by another, or "entic[es] or persuad[es] another" to infringe, Black's Law Dictionary 790 (8th ed.2004), as by advertising. . . .

The rule on inducement of infringement as developed in the early cases is no different today.[FN11 omitted] Evidence of "active steps . . . taken to encourage direct infringement," Oak Industries, Inc. v. Zenith Electronics Corp., 697 F.Supp. 988, 992 (N.D.Ill.1988), such as advertising an infringing use or instructing how to engage in an infringing use, show an affirmative intent that the product be used to infringe, and a showing that infringement was encouraged overcomes the law's reluctance to find liability when a defendant merely sells a commercial product suitable for some lawful use, see, e.g., Water Technologies Corp. v. Calco, Ltd., 850 F.2d 660, 668 (C.A.Fed.1988) (liability for inducement where one "actively and knowingly aid [s] and abet[s] another's direct infringement" (emphasis deleted)) . . . .

For the same reasons that Sony took the staple-article doctrine of patent law as a model for its copyright safe-harbor rule, the inducement rule, too, is a sensible one for copyright. We adopt it here, holding that one who distributes a device with the object of promoting its use to infringe copyright, as shown by clear expression or other affirmative steps taken to foster infringement, is liable for the resulting acts of infringement by third parties. We are, of course, mindful of the need to keep from trenching on regular commerce or discouraging the development of technologies with lawful and unlawful potential. Accordingly, just as Sony did not find intentional inducement despite the knowledge of the VCR manufacturer that its device could be used to infringe, 464 U.S., at 439, n. 19, 104 S.Ct. 774, mere knowledge of infringing potential or of actual infringing uses would not be enough here to subject a distributor to liability. Nor would ordinary acts incident to product distribution, such as offering customers technical support or product updates, support liability in themselves. The inducement rule, instead, premises liability on purposeful, culpable expression and conduct, and thus does nothing to compromise legitimate commerce or discourage innovation having a lawful promise.

III. A.

The only apparent question about treating MGM's evidence as sufficient to withstand summary judgment under the theory of inducement goes to the need on MGM's part to adduce evidence that StreamCast and Grokster communicated an inducing message to their software users. The classic instance of inducement is by advertisement or solicitation that broadcasts a message designed to stimulate others to commit violations. MGM claims that such a message is shown here. . . .

. . . . The function of the message in the theory of inducement is to prove by a defendant's own statements that his unlawful purpose disqualifies him from claiming protection (and incidentally to point to actual violators likely to be found among those who hear or read the message). See supra, at 2779–2780. Proving that a message was sent out, then, is the preeminent but not exclusive way of showing that active steps were taken with the purpose of bringing about infringing acts, and of showing that infringing acts took place by using the device distributed. Here, the summary judgment record is replete with other evidence that Grokster and StreamCast, unlike the manufacturer and distributor in Sony, acted with a purpose to cause copyright violations by use of software suitable for illegal use. See supra, at 2772–2774.

Three features of this evidence of intent are particularly notable. First, each company showed itself to be aiming to satisfy a known source of demand for copyright infringement, the market comprising former Napster users. . . . Grokster and StreamCast's efforts to supply services to former Napster users, deprived of a mechanism to copy and distribute what were overwhelmingly infringing files, indicate a principal, if not exclusive, intent on the part of each to bring about infringement.

Second, this evidence of unlawful objective is given added significance by MGM's showing that neither company attempted to develop filtering tools or other mechanisms to diminish the infringing activity using their software. While the Ninth Circuit treated the defendants' failure to develop such tools as irrelevant because they lacked an independent duty to monitor their users' activity, we think this evidence underscores Grokster's and StreamCast's intentional facilitation of their users' infringement.[12]

Third, there is a further complement to the direct evidence of unlawful objective. It is useful to recall that StreamCast and Grokster make money by selling advertising space, by directing ads to the screens of computers employing their software. As the record shows, the more the software is used, the more ads are sent out and the greater the advertising revenue becomes. Since the extent of the software's use determines the gain to the distributors, the commercial sense of their enterprise turns on high-volume use, which the record shows is infringing.[FN13 omitted] This evidence alone would not justify an inference of unlawful intent, but viewed in the context of the entire record its import is clear.

The unlawful objective is unmistakable.

B.

In addition to intent to bring about infringement and distribution of a device suitable for infringing use, the inducement theory of course requires evidence of actual infringement by recipients of the device, the software in this case. As the account of the facts indicates, there is evidence of infringement on a gigantic scale, and there is no serious issue of the adequacy of MGM's showing on this point in order to survive the companies' summary judgment requests. Although an exact calculation of infringing use, as a basis for a claim of damages, is subject to dispute, there is no question that the summary judgment evidence is at least adequate to entitle MGM to go forward with claims for damages and equitable relief.

* * *

In sum, this case is significantly different from Sony and reliance on that case to rule in favor of StreamCast and Grokster was error. Sony dealt with a claim of liability based solely on distributing a product with alternative lawful and unlawful uses, with knowledge that some users would follow the unlawful course. The case struck a balance between the interests of protection and innovation by holding that the product's capability of substantial lawful employment should bar the imputation of fault and consequent secondary liability for the unlawful acts of others.

MGM's evidence in this case most obviously addresses a different basis of liability for distributing a product open to alternative uses. Here, evidence of the distributors' words and deeds going beyond distribution as such shows a purpose to cause and profit from third-party acts of copyright infringement. If liability for inducing infringement is ultimately found, it

---

[12] Of course, in the absence of other evidence of intent, a court would be unable to find contributory infringement liability merely based on a failure to take affirmative steps to prevent infringement, if the device otherwise was capable of substantial noninfringing uses. Such a holding would tread too close to the Sony safe harbor.

will not be on the basis of presuming or imputing fault, but from inferring a patently illegal objective from statements and actions showing what that objective was.

There is substantial evidence in MGM's favor on all elements of inducement, and summary judgment in favor of Grokster and StreamCast was error. On remand, reconsideration of MGM's motion for summary judgment will be in order.

The judgment of the Court of Appeals is vacated, and the case is remanded for further proceedings consistent with this opinion.

It is so ordered.

[Concurring opinions by JUSTICE GINSBURG, with whom THE CHIEF JUSTICE and JUSTICE KENNEDY join, and JUSTICE BREYER, with whom JUSTICE STEVENS and JUSTICE O'CONNOR join, are omitted.]

NOTES AND QUESTIONS

1.   As the Court made clear in its opinion, the evidence in *Grokster* of intentional marketing of the defendants' software to those seeking to obtain unauthorized copies of copyrighted sound recordings was important to the conclusion that the defendants could be liable under an "inducement" theory of secondary liability (even though they did not directly infringe any works themselves). Cases prior to the Supreme Court's *Grokster* ruling, however, had focused primarily on the architecture of the specific P2P file-sharing systems at issue and how the doctrines of contributory and vicarious infringement applied to that architecture, relying heavily on the Court's analysis in the *Sony* case. It is likely that the post-Napster file-sharing systems' architectural choices were also informed by the standards for proving contributory or vicarious infringement, with their decentralized systems deliberately designed to avoid supporting a case of actual knowledge of specific instances of infringement. Such systems were architected to prevent direct action by the system in retrieving or storing infringing files, and to ostensibly limit the system's ability to supervise or control individual users' conduct. Absent the type of strong evidence of intent to induce infringement by users that the Court emphasized in *Grokster*, do you think that technology developers should be permitted to design software or technology to avoid the centralized oversight and control that is needed for contributory or vicarious liability without fear of liability for infringement by third parties who use that technology? Why or why not?

2.   The *Diamond Multimedia* and *Grokster* cases arose in relation to new technology and/or devices that were capable of assisting in infringing conduct. These cases, as well as others, were focused on the manufacturers and distributors of devices (and software) in an attempt to address the problem at the source. However, as technology and consumer behavior developed, new

opportunities for infringement were constantly evolving. The content industry, and specifically the recording industry, eventually reached the point where they felt the need to confront individual users of some of these services in an effort to change behavior and address the increasing spread of online illicit file sharing. The cases below demonstrate some of these attempts and the issues the courts grappled with in evaluating both liability and damages.

A Note on the Fair Use Defense (17 U.S.C. § 107)

One recurring issue addressed in the cases that follow is the defense of **fair use**, codified in Section 107 of the Copyright Act. That section provides in pertinent part:

> [T]he fair use of a copyrighted work, including such use by reproduction in copies or phonorecords or by any other means specified by that section, for purposes such as criticism, comment, news reporting, teaching (including multiple copies for classroom use), scholarship, or research, is not an infringement of copyright. In determining whether the use made of a work in any particular case is a fair use the factors to be considered shall include—
>
> **(1)** the purpose and character of the use, including whether such use is of a commercial nature or is for nonprofit educational purposes;
>
> **(2)** the nature of the copyrighted work;
>
> **(3)** the amount and substantiality of the portion used in relation to the copyrighted work as a whole; and
>
> **(4)** the effect of the use upon the potential market for or value of the copyrighted work.

As you read the following case excerpts, pay particular attention to the courts' treatment of the fair use defense in the context of what were argued to be "private" uses of copyrighted works and how the four factors outlined in Section 107 are balanced in the context of online file sharing.

BMG MUSIC V. GONZALEZ
430 F.3d 888 (7th Cir. 2005)

Before EASTERBROOK, EVANS, and WILLIAMS, CIRCUIT JUDGES.

EASTERBROOK, CIRCUIT JUDGE.

Last June the Supreme Court held in MGM Studios, Inc. v. Grokster, Ltd., 545 U.S. 913, 125 S.Ct. 2764, 162 L.Ed.2d 781 (2005), that a distributed file-sharing system is engaged in contributory copyright infringement when its principal object is the dissemination of copyrighted material. The foundation of this holding is a belief that people who post or download music files are primary infringers. In re Aimster Copyright Litigation, 334 F.3d 643, 645 (7th Cir.2003), which anticipated Grokster, made the same assumption. In this appeal Cecilia Gonzalez, who downloaded copyrighted music through the KaZaA file-sharing network, denies the premise of Grokster and Aimster. She contends that her activities were fair use rather than infringement. The district court disagreed and granted summary judgment for the copyright proprietors (to which we refer collectively as BMG Music). 2005 WL 106592, 2005 U.S. Dist. LEXIS 910 (N.D.Ill. Jan. 7, 2005). The court enjoined Gonzalez from further infringement and awarded $22,500 in damages under 17 U.S.C. § 504(c).

A "fair use" of copyrighted material is not infringement. Gonzalez insists that she was engaged in fair use under the terms of 17 U.S.C. § 107—or at least that a material dispute entitles her to a trial. It is undisputed, however, that she downloaded more than 1,370 copyrighted songs during a few weeks and kept them on her computer until she was caught. Her position is that she was just sampling music to determine what she liked enough to buy at retail. Because this suit was resolved on summary judgment, we must assume that Gonzalez is telling the truth when she says that she owned compact discs containing some of the songs before she downloaded them and that she purchased others later. She concedes, however, that she has never owned legitimate copies of 30 songs that she downloaded. (How many of the remainder she owned is disputed.)

Instead of erasing songs that she decided not to buy, she retained them. It is these 30 songs about which there is no dispute concerning ownership that formed the basis of the damages award. This is not a form of time-shifting, along the lines of Sony Corp. of America v. Universal City Studios, Inc., 464 U.S. 417, 104 S.Ct. 774, 78 L.Ed.2d 574 (1984) (Betamax). A copy downloaded, played, and retained on one's hard drive for future use is a direct substitute for a purchased copy-and without the benefit of the license fee paid to the broadcaster. The premise of Betamax is that the broadcast was licensed for one transmission and thus one viewing. Betamax held that shifting the time of this single viewing is fair use. The files that Gonzalez obtained, by contrast, were posted in violation of copyright law; there was no license covering a single transmission or hearing-and, to repeat, Gonzalez kept the copies. Time-shifting by an authorized recipient this is not. See William M. Landes & Richard A. Posner, The Economic Structure of Intellectual Property Law 117–22 (2003).

. . . . Gonzalez was not engaged in a nonprofit use; she downloaded (and kept) whole copyrighted songs (for which, as with poetry, copying of more than a couplet or two is deemed excessive); and she did this despite the fact that these works often are sold per song as well as per album. . . .

As she tells the tale, downloading on a try-before-you-buy basis is good advertising for copyright proprietors, expanding the value of their inventory. The Supreme Court thought otherwise in Grokster, with considerable empirical support. As file sharing has increased over the last four years, the sales of recorded music have dropped by approximately 30%. Perhaps other economic factors contributed, but the events likely are related. Music downloaded for free from the Internet is a close substitute for purchased music; many people are bound to keep the downloaded files without buying originals. That is exactly what Gonzalez did for at least 30 songs. It is no surprise, therefore, that the only appellate decision on point has held that downloading copyrighted songs cannot be defended as fair use, whether or not the recipient plans to buy songs she likes well enough to spring for. See A & M Records, Inc. v. Napster, Inc., 239 F.3d 1004, 1014–19 (9th Cir.2001). See also UMG Recordings, Inc. v. MP3.com, Inc., 92 F.Supp.2d 349 (S.D.N.Y.2000) (holding that downloads are not fair use even if the downloader already owns one purchased copy).

Although BMG Music sought damages for only the 30 songs that Gonzalez concedes she has never purchased, all 1,000+ of her downloads violated the statute. All created copies of an entire work. All undermined the means by which authors seek to profit. Gonzalez proceeds as if the authors' only interest were in selling compact discs containing collections of works. Not so; there is also a market in ways to introduce potential consumers to music.

Think of radio. Authors and publishers collect royalties on the broadcast of recorded music, even though these broadcasts may boost sales. See Broadcast Music, Inc. v. Columbia Broadcasting System, Inc., 441 U.S. 1, 99 S.Ct. 1551, 60 L.Ed.2d 1 (1979) (discussing the licenses available from performing rights societies for radio and television broadcasts). Downloads from peer-to-peer networks such as KaZaA compete with licensed broadcasts and hence undermine the income available to authors. This is true even if a particular person never buys recorded media. Cf. United States v. Slater, 348 F.3d 666 (7th Cir.2003). Many radio stations stream their content over the Internet, paying a fee for the right to do so. Gonzalez could have listened to this streaming music to sample songs for purchase;

had she done so, the authors would have received royalties from the broadcasters (and reduced the risk that files saved to disk would diminish the urge to pay for the music in the end).

Licensed Internet sellers, such as the iTunes Music Store, offer samples-but again they pay authors a fee for the right to do so, and the teasers are just a portion of the original. Other intermediaries (not only Yahoo! Music Unlimited and Real Rhapsody but also the revived Napster, with a new business model) offer licensed access to large collections of music; customers may rent the whole library by the month or year, sample them all, and purchase any songs they want to keep. New technologies, such as SNOCAP, enable authorized trials over peer-to-peer systems. . . .

Authorized previews share the feature of evanescence: if a listener decides not to buy (or stops paying the rental fee), no copy remains behind. With all of these means available to consumers who want to choose where to spend their money, downloading full copies of copyrighted material without compensation to authors cannot be deemed "fair use." Copyright law lets authors make their own decisions about how best to promote their works; copiers such as Gonzalez cannot ask courts (and juries) to second-guess the market and call wholesale copying "fair use" if they think that authors err in understanding their own economic interests or that Congress erred in granting authors the rights in the copyright statute. . . .

BMG Music elected to seek statutory damages under 17 U.S.C. § 504(c)(1) instead of proving actual injury. . . . It is undisputed that BMG Music gave copyright notice as required—"on the surface of the phonorecord, or on the phonorecord label or container" (§ 402(c)). It is likewise undisputed that Gonzalez had "access" to records and compact disks bearing the proper notice. She downloaded data rather than discs, and the data lacked copyright notices, but the statutory question is whether "access" to legitimate works was available rather than whether infringers earlier in the chain attached copyright notices to the pirated works. Gonzalez readily could have learned, had she inquired, that the music was under copyright.

If BMG Music had requested more than $750 per work, then Gonzalez would have been entitled to a trial. See Feltner v. Columbia Pictures Television, Inc., 523 U.S. 340, 118 S.Ct. 1279, 140 L.Ed.2d 438 (1998). What number between $750 and $30,000 is "just" recompense is a question for the jury, unless both sides agree to decision by the court. But BMG Music was content with $750 per song, which the district judge awarded on summary judgment. . . . [¶¶]

As for the injunction: Gonzalez contends that this should be vacated because she has learned her lesson, has dropped her broadband access to the Internet, and is unlikely to download copyrighted material again. A private party's discontinuation of unlawful conduct does not make the dispute moot, however. An injunction remains appropriate to ensure that the misconduct does not recur as soon as the case ends. See United States v. W.T. Grant Co., 345 U.S. 629, 73 S.Ct. 894, 97 L.Ed. 1303 (1953). The district court did not abuse its discretion in awarding prospective relief.

Affirmed.

CAPITOL RECORDS INC. v. THOMAS
579 F. Supp. 2d 1210 (D. Minn. 2008)

MEMORANDUM OF LAW & ORDER

MICHAEL J. DAVIS, CHIEF JUDGE.

I. INTRODUCTION

This matter is before the Court on Defendant's Motion for New Trial, or in the Alternative, for Remittitur. [Docket No. 109] Defendant Jammie Thomas asserts that the amount of the statutory damages award is excessive and in violation of the due process clause of the United States Constitution. . . . The Court has sua sponte raised the issue of whether it erred in instructing the jury that making sound recordings available for distribution on a peer-to-peer network, regardless of whether actual distribution was shown, qualified as distribution under the Copyright Act. [Docket No. 139] . . . .

II. BACKGROUND

Plaintiffs are recording companies that owned or controlled exclusive rights to copyrights in sound recordings, including 24 at issue in this lawsuit. On April 19, 2006, Plaintiffs filed a Complaint against Defendant Jammie Thomas alleging that she infringed Plaintiffs' copyrighted sound recordings pursuant to the Copyright Act, 17 U.S.C. §§ 101, 106, 501–505, by illegally downloading and distributing the recordings via the online peer-to-peer file sharing application known as Kazaa. Plaintiffs sought injunctive relief, statutory damages, costs, and attorney fees. . . .

In Jury Instruction No. 15, the Court instructed: "The act of making copyrighted sound recordings available for electronic distribution on a peer-to-peer network, without license from the copyright owners, violates the copyright owners' exclusive right of distribution, regardless of whether actual distribution has been shown."

On October 4, 2007, the jury found that Thomas had willfully infringed on all 24 of Plaintiffs' sound recordings at issue, and awarded Plaintiffs statutory damages in the amount of $9,250 for each willful infringement. [Docket No. 100] . . .

[¶] .... On May 15, 2008, the Court issued an Order stating that it was contemplating granting a new trial on the grounds that it had committed a manifest error of law in giving Jury Instruction No. 15. [Docket No. 139] The Court ordered the parties to brief the issue ....

III. DISCUSSION [¶]...

C. Statutory Framework

The Copyright Act provides that "the owner of copyright under this title has the exclusive rights to do and to authorize any of the following: ... (3) to distribute copies or phonorecords of the copyrighted work to the public by sale or other transfer of ownership, or by rental, lease, or lending." 17 U.S.C. § 106(3). The Act does not define the term "distribute."

Courts have split regarding whether making copyrighted materials available for distribution constitutes distribution under § 106(3). The parties address four main arguments regarding the validity of the "making-available" interpretation: 1) whether the plain meaning of the term "distribution" requires actual dissemination of the copyrighted work; 2) whether the term "distribution" is synonymous with the term "publication," which, under the Copyright Act, does not require actual dissemination or transfer; 3) whether a defendant can be primarily liable for authorizing dissemination; and 4) whether U.S. treaty obligations and executive and legislative branch interpretations of the Copyright Act in relation to those obligations require a particular interpretation of the term "distribution."

D. Plain Meaning of the Term "Distribution"

There is a "strong presumption that the plain language of the statute expresses congressional intent [that] is rebutted only in rare and exceptional circumstances." United States v. Clintwood Elkhorn Mining Co., 128 S.Ct. 1511, 1518, 170 L.Ed.2d 392 (2008) (citations omitted). Each party asserts that the Court should adopt the plain meaning of the term "distribution;" however, they disagree on what that plain meaning is. Thomas and her supporters argue that the plain meaning of the statute compels the conclusion that merely making a work available to the public does not constitute a distribution. Instead, a distribution only occurs when a defendant actually transfers to the public the possession or ownership of copies or phonorecords of a work. Plaintiffs and their supporters assert that making a work available for distribution is sufficient.

1. Statutory Language

Starting with the language in § 106(3), the Court notes that Congress explains the manners in which distribution can be effected: sale, transfer of ownership, rental, lease, or lending. The provision does not state that an offer to do any of these acts constitutes distribution. Nor does § 106(3) provide that making a work available for any of these activities constitutes distribution. An initial reading of the provision at issue supports Thomas's interpretation.

2.   Secondary Sources

The ordinary dictionary meaning of the word "distribute" necessarily entails a transfer of ownership or possession from one person to another. See, e.g., Merriam-Webster's Collegiate Dictionary (10th ed.1999) (defining "distribute" as, among other things, "1: to divide among several or many: APPORTION . . . 2 . . . b: to give out or deliver esp. to members of a group").

Additionally, the leading copyright treatises conclude that making a work available is insufficient to establish distribution. See, e.g., 2–8 Nimmer on Copyright, § 8.11[A] (2008); 4 William F. Patry, Patry on Copyright, § 13.11.50 (2008).

3.   Opinion of the Register of Copyrights

Register of Copyrights, Marybeth Peters, has opined to Congress that making a copyrighted work available violates the distribution right. See, e.g., Letter from Marybeth Peters, Register of Copyrights, to Rep. Howard L. Berman, Rep. from the 28th Dist. of Cal. (Sept. 25, 2002) ("[M]aking [a work] available for other users of [a] peer to peer network to download . . . constitutes an infringement of the exclusive distribution right, as well as the production right."), quoted in Motown Record Co., LP v. DePietro, No. 04-CV-2246, 2007 WL 576284, at *3 n. 38 (E.D.Pa. Feb.16, 2007) (unpublished). However, opinion letters from the Copyright Office to Congress on matters of statutory interpretation are not binding and are "entitled to respect insofar as they are persuasive." Broadcast Music, Inc. v. Roger Miller Music, Inc., 396 F.3d 762, 778 (6th Cir.2005) (citation omitted).

4.   Use of the Term in Other Provisions of the U.S.Code

As Plaintiffs note, in other provisions of federal copyright law, Congress has explicitly defined "distribute" to include offers to distribute. See 17 U.S.C. § 901(a)(4) (stating, in context of copyright protection of semiconductor chip products, that "to 'distribute' means to sell, or to lease, bail, or otherwise transfer, or to offer to sell, lease, bail, or otherwise transfer"); 17 U.S.C. § 506(a)(1)(C) (imposing criminal penalties for "the distribution of a work being prepared for commercial distribution, by making it available on a computer network accessible to members of the public"). In other portions of the Copyright Act, Congress has explicitly confined the term "distribution" to a physical transfer of copyrighted material. For example, in the section of the Act providing compulsory licenses for nondramatic musical works, Congress provides: "For this purpose, and other than as provided [in Section 115(c)(3)], a phonorecord is considered 'distributed' if the person exercising the compulsory license has voluntarily and permanently parted with its possession." 17 U.S.C. § 115(c)(2).

The differing definitions of "distribute" within copyright law demonstrate that there is not one uniform definition of the term throughout copyright law. Cf. Firstar Bank, N.A. v. Faul, 253 F.3d 982, 990 (7th Cir.2001) (noting that "identical words used in different parts of the same act are intended to have the same meaning") (citation omitted). However, the Court notes that when Congress intends distribution to encompass making available or offering to transfer, it has demonstrated that it is quite capable of explicitly providing that definition within the statute. In this case, Congress provided the means by which a distribution occurs—"by sale or other transfer of ownership, or by rental, lease, or lending"—without also providing that a distribution occurs by an offer to do one of those actions, as it did in § 901(a)(4). While the Copyright Act does not offer a uniform definition of "distribution," the Court concludes that, in light of the examined provisions, Congress's choice to not include offers to do the enumerated acts or the making available of the work indicates its intent that an actual distribution or dissemination is required in § 106(3). [¶] . . .

The Court does not find the definitive interpretation of the term "distribute" in other titles of the U.S. Code. However, the Court does note that, while Congress has not added "offer to distribute" to § 106(3) of the Copyright Act, it has added "offers to sell" in the related field of patent law. 35 U.S.C. § 271(a). See also Eldred v. Ashcroft, 537 U.S. 186, 201–02, 123 S.Ct. 769, 154 L.Ed.2d 683 (2003) (citing patent practice as persuasive precedent in a copyright case). Before Congress amended the Patent Act to expressly include "offers to sell," courts strictly interpreted the statutory language, which expressly forbade sales but not offers to sell, as requiring proof of an actual sale. Rotec Indus. v. Mitsubishi Corp., 215 F.3d 1246, 1251 (Fed.Cir.2000). Court and congressional actions with regard to the Patent Act demonstrate two principles; 1) in the absence of a statutory definition that explicitly includes or excludes offers to sell or distribute, courts interpret liability narrowly to not include offers; and 2) Congress can and will amend a statute, when necessary, to explicitly include liability for an offer to do a prohibited act.

The Court's examination of the use of the term "distribution" in other provisions of the Copyright Act, as well as the evolution of liability for offers to sell in the analogous Patent Act, lead to the conclusion that the plain meaning of the term "distribution" does not including making available and, instead, requires actual dissemination. The Court now turns its attention to Plaintiffs' additional arguments regarding the existence of a making-available right.

E. Whether "Distribution" Is Synonymous with "Publication"

Plaintiffs advocate that, within the Copyright Act, the term "distribution" is synonymous with the term "publication."

> "Publication" is the distribution of copies or phonorecords of a work to the public by sale or other transfer of ownership, or by rental, lease, or lending. The offering to distribute copies or phonorecords to a group of persons for purposes of further distribution, public performance, or public display, constitutes publication. A public performance or display of a work does not of itself constitute publication.

17 U.S.C. § 101. Under this definition, making sound recordings available on Kazaa could be considered distribution.

The first sentence of the definition of "publication" and § 106(3) are substantially identical. However, there is additional language in the definition of "publication." Relying primarily on legislative history, Plaintiffs assert that the sentence defining publication as "[t]he offering to distribute copies or phonorecords to a group of persons for purposes of further distribution, public performance, or public display" should also apply to the definition of distribution.

[¶] . . . . A review of the Copyright Act as a whole also supports the conclusion that publication and distribution remain distinct concepts. Publication still triggers certain consequences such as a duty to deposit copies of the work with the Copyright Office, 17 U.S.C. § 407(a), and the calculation of the date of copyright termination for works made for hire, anonymous, and pseudonymous works, § 302(c).

The Court concludes that simply because all distributions within the meaning of § 106(3) are publications does not mean that all publications within the meaning of § 101 are distributions. The statutory definition of publication is broader than the term distribution as used in § 106(3). A publication can occur by means of the "distribution of copies or phonorecords of a work to the public by sale or other transfer of ownership, or by rental, lease or lending." § 101. This portion of the definition of publication defines a distribution as set forth in § 106(3). However, a publication may also occur by "offering to distribute copies or phonorecords to a group of persons for purposes of further distribution, public performance, or public display." § 101. While a publication effected by distributing copies or phonorecords of the work is a distribution, a publication effected by merely offering to distribute copies or phonorecords to the public is merely an offer of distribution, not an actual distribution.

Congress's choice to use both terms within the Copyright Act demonstrates an intent that the terms have different meanings. "It is untenable that the definition of a different word in a different section of the statute was meant to expand the meaning of 'distribution' and liability under § 106(3) to include offers to distribute." Atl. Recording Corp. v. Howell, 554 F.Supp.2d 976, 985 (D.Ariz.2008). The language of the Copyright Act definition of publication clearly includes distribution as part of its definition-so all distributions to the public are publications, but not all publications are distributions to the public.

F.   Existence of a Protected Right to Authorize Distribution

Plaintiffs and their supporters also take the position that authorizing distribution is an exclusive right protected by the Copyright Act. They base this argument on the fact that § 106 states "the owner of copyright under this title has the exclusive rights to do and to authorize any of the following . . . (3) to distribute . . . ." (emphasis added). Plaintiffs claim that the statute grants two separate rights-the right to "do" distribution and the right to "authorize" distribution. Therefore, making sound recordings available on Kazaa violates the copyright owner's exclusive right to authorize distribution.

The Court concludes that the authorization clause merely provides a statutory foundation for secondary liability, not a means of expanding the scope of direct infringement liability. See H.R. Rep. 94–1476, at 61 (1976), 1976 U.S.C.C.A.N. 5659, 5674 ("Use of the phrase 'to authorize' is intended to avoid any questions as to the liability of contributory infringers. For example, a person who lawfully acquires an authorized copy of a motion picture would be an infringer if he or she engages in the business of renting it to others for purposes of unauthorized public performance.") . . . . Without actual distribution, there can be no claim for authorization of distribution. See, e.g., Latin Amer. Music Co. v. Archdiocese of San Juan, 499 F.3d 32, 46 (1st Cir.2007) ("[T]o prove infringement, a claimant must show an infringing act after the authorization.") (citation omitted).

Equating making available with distribution would undermine settled case law holding that merely inducing or encouraging another to infringe does not, alone, constitute infringement unless the encouraged party actually infringes. See, e.g., Metro-Goldwyn-Mayer Studios Inc. v. Grokster, Ltd., 545 U.S. 913, 936–37, 125 S.Ct. 2764, 162 L.Ed.2d 781 (2005) ("[O]ne who distributes a device with the object of promoting its use to infringe copyright, as shown by clear expression or other affirmative steps taken to foster infringement, is liable for the resulting acts of infringement by third parties.") (emphasis added). If simply making a copyrighted work available to the public constituted a distribution, even if no member of the public ever accessed that work, copyright owners would be able to make an end run around the standards for assessing contributor copyright infringement.

. . . . [¶¶] The Court concludes that the text of § 106, case law, and legislative history clearly indicate that the authorization right is a means for secondary liability, which only applies if there is an actual dissemination.

.... [¶¶] The specter of impossible-to-meet evidentiary standards raised by amici is overstated. A person who makes an unauthorized copy or phonorecord of a copyrighted work for the purposes of uploading it onto a peer-to-peer network, absent a defense such as fair use, violates the reproduction right. 17 U.S.C. § 106(a). That person might also be liable for indirect infringement to the extent that her conduct caused others to engage in unauthorized reproduction, adaptation, public distribution, public performance, or public display of another's copyrighted work.

The end user who accesses or downloads the unauthorized copy or phonorecord may be liable for direct infringement, depending on the facts of the case and the applicability of defenses, such as the fair use defense. Under certain circumstances, a person who markets products or services that can enable others to infringe or to circumvent technological measures that control or restrict access to copyrighted works also may be liable for indirect infringement or for violation of the Digital Millennium Copyright Act, 17 U.S.C. §§ 1201(a)(2), (b).

Finally, while the Court does not adopt the deemed-disseminated theory based on Hotaling, it notes that direct proof of actual dissemination is not required by the Copyright Act. Plaintiffs are free to employ circumstantial evidence to attempt to prove actual dissemination. Overall, it is apparent that implementation of Congress's intent through a plain meaning interpretation of § 106(3) will not leave copyright holders without recourse when infringement occurs over a peer-to-peer network. [¶] ....

J.   Grant of a New Trial

Liability for violation of the exclusive distribution right found in § 106(3) requires actual dissemination. Jury Instruction No. 15 was erroneous and that error substantially prejudiced Thomas's rights. Based on the Court's error in instructing the jury, it grants Thomas a new trial.

... K. Need for Congressional Action

The Court would be remiss if it did not take this opportunity to implore Congress to amend the Copyright Act to address liability and damages in peer-to-peer network cases such as the one currently before this Court. The Court begins its analysis by recognizing the unique nature of this case. The defendant is an individual, a consumer. She is not a business. She sought no profit from her acts. The myriad of copyright cases cited by Plaintiffs and the Government, in which courts upheld large statutory damages awards far above the minimum, have limited relevance in this case. All of the cited cases involve corporate or business defendants and seek to deter future illegal commercial conduct. The parties point to no case in which large statutory damages were applied to a party who did not infringe in search of commercial gain.

The statutory damages awarded against Thomas are not a deterrent against those who pirate music in order to profit. Thomas's conduct was motivated by her desire to obtain the copyrighted music for her own use. The Court does not condone Thomas's actions, but it would be a farce to say that a single mother's acts of using Kazaa are the equivalent, for example, to the acts of global financial firms illegally infringing on copyrights in order to profit in the securities market. Cf. Lowry's Reports, Inc. v. Legg Mason, Inc., 271 F.Supp.2d 737, 741–42 (D.Md.2003) (describing defendants as a "global financial-services firm" and a corporation that brokers securities).

While the Court does not discount Plaintiffs' claim that, cumulatively, illegal downloading has far-reaching effects on their businesses, the damages awarded in this case are wholly disproportionate to the damages suffered by Plaintiffs. Thomas allegedly infringed on the copyrights of 24 songs-the equivalent of approximately three CDs, costing less than $54, and yet the total damages awarded is $222,000—more than five hundred times the cost of buying 24 separate CDs and more than four thousand times the cost of three CDs. While the Copyright Act was intended to permit statutory damages that are larger than the simple cost of the infringed works in order to make infringing a far less attractive alternative than legitimately purchasing the songs, surely damages that are more than one hundred times the cost of the works would serve as a sufficient deterrent.

Thomas not only gained no profits from her alleged illegal activities, she sought no profits. Part of the justification for large statutory damages awards in copyright cases is to deter actors by ensuring that the possible penalty for infringing substantially outweighs the potential gain from infringing. In the case of commercial actors, the potential gain in revenues is enormous and enticing to potential infringers. In the case of individuals who infringe by using peer-to-peer networks, the potential gain from infringement is access to free music, not the possibility of hundreds of thousands—or even millions—of dollars in profits. This fact means that statutory damages awards of hundreds of thousands of dollars is certainly far greater than necessary to accomplish Congress's goal of deterrence.

Unfortunately, by using Kazaa, Thomas acted like countless other Internet users. Her alleged acts were illegal, but common. Her status as a consumer who was not seeking to harm her competitors or make a profit does not excuse her behavior. But it does make the award of hundreds of thousands of dollars in damages unprecedented and oppressive.

Accordingly, based upon the files, records, and proceedings herein, IT IS HEREBY ORDERED:

1.   The Court hereby VACATES the verdict rendered in this case by the jury and grants Defendant a new trial to commence on a date to be set by the Court after consultation with the parties.

2.   The Judgment entered on October 5, 2007 [Docket No. 106] is VACATED.

3.   Defendant's Motion for New Trial, or in the Alternative, for Remittitur [Docket No. 109] is GRANTED on the grounds set forth in this Memorandum of Law & Order.

4.   Plaintiffs' unopposed Motion to Amend Judgment [Docket No. 116] is DENIED.

NOTES AND QUESTIONS

1.   The cases involving lawsuits against individual P2P users raise questions not only about interpretation of statutory terms such as "distribution" and "publication" in the Internet context, but also about the appropriate remedy in cases involving individual copying for personal use. In *Gonzalez*, the plaintiffs were awarded statutory damages of $750 each for 30 infringed works, for a total award of $22,500, which was upheld by the Seventh Circuit.

2.   In *Thomas*, after the case was remanded for a new trial, the jury found that Thomas had willfully infringed the 24 recordings at issue and awarded "statutory damages in the amount of $80,000 for each song, for a total verdict of $1,920,000." *Capitol Records Inc. v. Thomas-Rasset*, 680 F. Supp. 2d 1045, 1050 (D. Minn. 2010). After entry of judgment, both parties sought post-judgment relief, with mixed results:

> [T]he Court grants in part and denies in part Thomas-Rasset's motion and remits the damages award to $2,250 per song-three times the statutory minimum. The need for deterrence cannot justify a $2 million verdict for stealing and illegally distributing 24 songs for the sole purpose of obtaining free music. Moreover, although Plaintiffs were not required to prove their actual damages, statutory damages must still bear *some* relation to actual damages.
>
> The Court has labored to fashion a reasonable limit on statutory damages awards against noncommercial individuals who illegally download and upload music such that the award of statutory damages does not veer into the realm of gross injustice. Finding a precise dollar amount that delineates the border between the jury's wide discretion to calculate its own number to address Thomas-Rasset's willful violations, Plaintiffs' far-reaching, but nebulous damages, and the need to deter online piracy in general and the outrageousness of a $2 million verdict is a considerable task. The Court concludes that setting the limit at three times the minimum statutory damages amount in this case is the most reasoned solution.

This award constitutes the maximum amount a jury could reasonably award to both compensate Plaintiffs and address the deterrence aspect of the Copyright Act. **This reduced award is significant and harsh.** It is a higher award than the Court might have chosen to impose in its sole discretion, but the decision was not entrusted to this Court. It was the jury's province to determine the award of statutory damages and this Court has merely reduced that award to the maximum amount that is no longer monstrous and shocking.

Id. at *1. The plaintiff record companies appealed, seeking (for tactical reasons) recovery of $222,000 in damages, as well as a broader injunction that prohibited Thomas from making sound recordings available and a ruling that the district court had erred in finding that the copyright did not extend to prohibiting others from making a work available to others for copying. On September 11, 2012, the Eighth Circuit issued an opinion finding that the record companies were entitled to the damages and injunction they sought, but refused to rule on the "making available" issue, stating: "Important though the 'making available' legal issue may be to the recording companies, they are not entitled to an opinion on an issue of law that is unnecessary for the remedies sought or to a freestanding decision on whether Thomas-Rasset violated the law by making recordings available." *Capitol Records, Inc. v. Thomas-Rasset,* 692 F.3d 899, 902 (8th Cir. 2012).

3.   The decisions in the *Thomas* case illustrate the difficulty in answering the question of how to balance the harm to copyright owners from widespread infringement and Congress' intent to deter unauthorized copying through awards of statutory damages against concerns about fairness to individual defendants whose copying was for private, not commercial, use. How would you balance these competing interests? What do you think the best response is to the *Thomas* district court's plea for Congress to take action—what action would you recommend?

C. DMCA SAFE HARBORS AND NOTICE AND TAKEDOWN PROCEDURES: USE OF INTERNET SERVICES FOR UNAUTHORIZED COPYING AND DISTRIBUTION OF SOUND RECORDINGS

The cases below illustrate some of the difficulties faced by copyright owners in protecting their works from online infringement under existing law. Note that the burden is placed on copyright owners to identify infringing material; Internet service providers ("ISPs") have no affirmative duty under U.S. law to monitor their services to ensure that no infringing material or activity is taking place on their service. Out of concern that the development of the Internet as a communications medium would be hindered by any legal requirement for ISPs to "police" their services for violations of law, Congress adopted several "safe harbors" for ISPs in the Digital Millennium Copyright Act ("DMCA") (see the Note below for an overview of the requirements for these safe harbors). The provisions governing these safe harbors have been tested in recent cases, with the *Cox* and *Lenz* cases below as examples of how complex these provisions are in practice and of how the law often does not adequately address the realities of how current technology impacts the rights protected by copyright law.

A Note on the DMCA

The DMCA and its complex provisions, including those in Title II (the Online Copyright Infringement Liability Limitation Act) governing "safe harbors" for ISPs, is covered in most copyright courses. We do not provide its detailed provisions here, but three of its provisions are particularly relevant to the cases discussed in this part.

First, the DMCA creates safe harbors in Section 512 of Title 17. Four types of activities by ISPs are eligible for immunity from liability for third-party infringement:

1. **Transitory digital networking communications** (referred to in the Cox case when the court calls Cox a "conduit Internet services provider");

2. **System caching**;

3. **Information residing on systems or networks at the direction of users**; and

4. **Information location tools.** 17 U.S.C. §§ 512(a)–(d).

Second, an ISP may only take advantage of these safe harbors if it establishes a system for copyright owners to give notice to the ISP of what in good faith is believed to be infringing content on the ISP's service and adopts and reasonably implements a policy for "expeditiously" removing infringing information as to which notice is properly provided and terminating repeat infringers in "appropriate circumstances."

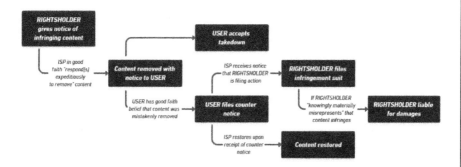

17 U.S.C. §§ 512(c), (g), & (f).

Third, anyone who "knowingly materially misrepresents" that material is infringing or was mistakenly removed will be liable for damages. 17 U.S.C. § 512(f).

BMG RIGHTS MANAGEMENT (US) LLC
v. COX COMMUNICATIONS, INC.
881 F.3d 293 (4th Cir. 2018)

DIANA GRIBBON MOTZ, CIRCUIT JUDGE:

BMG Rights Management (US) LLC ("BMG"), which owns copyrights in musical compositions, filed this suit alleging copyright infringement against Cox Communications, Inc. and CoxCom, LLC (collectively, "Cox"), providers of high-speed Internet access. BMG seeks to hold Cox contributorily liable for infringement of BMG's copyrights by subscribers to Cox's Internet service. Following extensive discovery, the district court held that Cox had not produced evidence that it had implemented a policy entitling it to a statutory safe harbor defense and so granted summary judgment on that issue to BMG. After a two-week trial, a jury found Cox liable for willful contributory infringement and awarded BMG $25 million in statutory damages. Cox appeals, asserting that the district court erred in denying it the safe harbor defense and incorrectly instructed the jury. We hold that Cox is not entitled to the safe harbor defense and affirm the district court's denial of it, but we reverse in part, vacate in part, and remand for a new trial because of certain errors in the jury instructions.

I. A.

Cox is a conduit Internet service provider ("ISP"), providing approximately 4.5 million subscribers with high-speed Internet access for a monthly fee. Some of Cox's subscribers shared and received copyrighted files, including music files, using a technology known as BitTorrent. BitTorrent is not a software program, but rather describes a protocol—a set of rules governing the communication between computers—that allows individual computers on the Internet to transfer files directly to other computers. This method of file sharing is commonly known as "peer-to-peer" file sharing, and contrasts with the traditional method of downloading a file from a central server using a Web browser.

Although peer-to-peer file sharing is not new, what makes BitTorrent unique is that it allows a user to download a file from multiple peers at the same time—even peers who only have a piece of the file, rather than the complete file. In other words, as soon as a user has downloaded a piece of the file, he or she can begin sharing that piece with others (while continuing to download the rest of the file). This innovation makes sharing via BitTorrent particularly fast and efficient. Although BitTorrent can be used to share any type of digital file, many use it to share copyrighted music and video files without authorization.

As a conduit ISP, Cox only provides Internet access to its subscribers. Cox does not create or sell software that operates using the BitTorrent protocol, store copyright-infringing material on its own computer servers, or control what its subscribers store on their personal computers.

Cox's agreement with its subscribers reserves the right to suspend or terminate subscribers who use Cox's service "to post, copy, transmit, or disseminate any content that infringes the patents, copyrights . . . or proprietary rights of any party." To enforce that agreement and protect itself from liability, however, Cox created only a very limited automated system to process notifications of alleged infringement received from copyright owners. Cox's automated system rests on a thirteen-strike policy that determines the action to be taken based on how many notices Cox has previously received regarding infringement by a particular subscriber. The first notice alleging a subscriber's infringement produces no action from Cox. The second through seventh notices result in warning emails from Cox to the subscriber. After the eighth and ninth notices, Cox limits the subscriber's Internet access to a single webpage that contains a warning, but the subscriber can reactivate complete service by clicking an acknowledgement. After the tenth and eleventh notices, Cox suspends services, requiring the subscriber to call a technician, who, after explaining the reason for suspension and advising removal of infringing content, reactivates service. After the twelfth notice, the subscriber is suspended and directed to a specialized technician, who, after another warning to cease infringing conduct, reactivates service. After the thirteenth notice, the subscriber is again suspended, and, for the first time, considered for termination. Cox never automatically terminates a subscriber.

The effectiveness of Cox's thirteen-strike policy as a deterrent to copyright infringement has several additional limitations. Cox restricts the number of notices it will process from any copyright holder or agent in one day; any notice received after this limit has been met does not count in Cox's graduated response escalation. Cox also counts only one notice per subscriber per day. And Cox resets a subscriber's thirteen-strike counter every six months.

BMG, a music publishing company, owns copyrights in musical compositions. To protect this copyrighted material, BMG hired Rightscorp, Inc., which monitors BitTorrent activity to determine when infringers share its clients' copyrighted works. When Rightscorp identifies such sharing, it emails an infringement notice to the alleged infringer's ISP (here, Cox). The notice contains the name of the copyright owner (here, BMG), the title of the copyrighted work, the alleged infringer's IP address, a time stamp, and a statement under penalty of perjury that Rightscorp is an authorized agent and the notice is accurate.

Rightscorp also asks the ISP to forward the notice to the allegedly infringing subscriber, since only the ISP can match the IP address to the subscriber's identity. For that purpose, the notice contains a settlement offer, allowing the alleged infringer to pay twenty or thirty dollars for a release from liability for the instance of infringement alleged in the notice. Cox has determined to refuse to forward or process notices that contain such settlement language. When Cox began receiving Rightscorp notices in the spring of 2011 (before Rightscorp had signed BMG as a client), Cox notified Rightscorp that it would process the notices only if Rightscorp removed the settlement language. Rightscorp did not do so. Cox never considered removing the settlement language itself or using other means to inform its subscribers of the allegedly infringing activity observed by Rightscorp.

Rightscorp continued to send Cox large numbers of settlement notices. In the fall of 2011, Cox decided to "blacklist" Rightscorp, meaning Cox would delete notices received from Rightscorp without acting on them or even viewing them. BMG hired Rightscorp in December 2011—after Cox blacklisted Rightscorp. Thus, Cox did not ever view a single one of the millions of notices that Rightscorp sent to Cox on BMG's behalf.

B.

On November 26, 2014, BMG initiated this action against Cox. BMG alleged that Cox was vicariously and contributorily liable for acts of copyright infringement by its subscribers.

At the conclusion of discovery, the parties filed multi-issue cross-motions for summary judgment, which the district court resolved in a careful written opinion. Among these issues, BMG asserted that Cox had not established a policy entitling it to the safe harbor defense contained in the Digital Millennium Copyright Act ("DMCA"), 17 U.S.C. § 512(a). To qualify for that safe harbor, an ISP, like Cox, must have "adopted and reasonably implemented . . . a policy that provides for the termination in appropriate circumstances of subscribers . . . who are repeat infringers." Id. § 512(i)(1)(A). The district court agreed with BMG and held that no reasonable jury could find that Cox implemented a policy that entitled it to that DMCA safe harbor. The court explained that BMG had offered evidence that "Cox knew accounts were being used repeatedly for infringing activity yet failed to terminate" those accounts and that Cox did "not come forward with any evidence" to the contrary. Accordingly, the court granted summary judgment to BMG on Cox's safe harbor defense.

The case proceeded to a jury trial that involved the testimony of more than a dozen witnesses and admission of numerous documents. . . .

The jury found Cox liable for willful contributory infringement and awarded BMG $25 million in statutory damages. The jury also found that Cox was not liable for vicarious infringement. The district court denied all post-trial motions and entered judgment in accordance with the verdict. Cox appeals, arguing that BMG should not have been granted summary judgment as to the DMCA safe harbor and that erroneous jury instructions entitle it to a new trial.[FN1 omitted]

II.

We first address Cox's contention that the district court erred in denying it the § 512(a) DMCA safe harbor defense. We review de novo the grant of summary judgment. Henry v. Purnell, 652 F.3d 524, 531 (4th Cir. 2011) (en banc).

A.

The DMCA provides a series of safe harbors that limit the copyright infringement liability of an ISP and related entities. As a conduit ISP, Cox seeks the benefit of the safe harbor contained in 17 U.S.C. § 512(a). To fall within that safe harbor, Cox must show that it meets the threshold requirement, common to all § 512 safe harbors, that it has "adopted and reasonably implemented . . . a policy that provides for the termination in appropriate circumstances of subscribers . . . who are repeat infringers." 17 U.S.C. § 512(i)(1)(A).

Cox's principal contention is that "repeat infringers" means adjudicated repeat infringers: people who have been held liable by a court for multiple instances of copyright infringement. Cox asserts that it complied with § 512(i)(1)(A)'s requirement and is therefore entitled to the § 512(a) DMCA safe harbor because BMG did not show that Cox failed to terminate any adjudicated infringers. BMG responds that Cox's interpretation of "repeat infringers" is contrary to "the DMCA's plain terms." Appellee Br. at 31. . . . [¶¶]

[O]ther provisions of the Copyright Act use the term "infringer" (and similar terms) to refer to all who engage in infringing activity, not just the narrow subset of those who have been so adjudicated by a court. For example, § 501(a), which creates a civil cause of action for copyright owners, states that "[a]nyone who violates any of the exclusive rights of the copyright owner" provided for in the statute "is an infringer of the copyright or right of the author." 17 U.S.C. § 501(a) (emphasis added).

Similarly, the DMCA itself provides that ISPs who store copyrighted material are generally not liable for removing "material or activity claimed to be infringing or based on facts or circumstances from which infringing activity is apparent, regardless of whether the material or activity is ultimately determined to be infringing." Id. § 512(g)(1) (emphases added). This provision expressly distinguishes among three categories of activity:

activity merely "claimed to be infringing," actual "infringing activity" (as is apparent from "facts or circumstances"), and activity "ultimately determined to be infringing." The distinction between "infringing activity" and activity "ultimately determined to be infringing" in § 512(g) shelters ISPs from being liable for taking down material that is "infringing," even if no court "ultimately determine[s]" that it is infringing—because, for example, the copyright holder simply does not file a lawsuit against the person who uploaded the infringing material. As this provision illustrates, Congress knew how to expressly refer to adjudicated infringement, but did not do so in the repeat infringer provision. See also id. § 512(b)(2)(E)(i) (addressing circumstance in which "a court has ordered that . . . material be removed"). That suggests the term "infringer" in § 512(i) is not limited to adjudicated infringers.

The legislative history of the repeat infringer provision supports this conclusion. Both the House Commerce and Senate Judiciary Committee Reports explained that "those who repeatedly or flagrantly abuse their access to the Internet through disrespect for the intellectual property rights of others should know that there is a realistic threat of losing that access." H.R. Rep. No. 105–551, pt. 2, at 61 (1998); S. Rep. No. 105–190, at 52 (1998). This passage makes clear that if persons "abuse their access to the Internet through disrespect for the intellectual property rights of others"—that is, if they infringe copyrights—they should face a "realistic threat of losing" their Internet access. The passage does not suggest that they should risk losing Internet access only once they have been sued in court and found liable for multiple instances of infringement. Indeed, the risk of losing one's Internet access would hardly constitute a "realistic threat" capable of deterring infringement if that punishment applied only to those already subject to civil penalties and legal fees as adjudicated infringers. . . .

Accordingly, we reject Cox's argument that the term "repeat infringers" in § 512(i) is limited to adjudicated infringers.[FN3 omitted]

B.

Section 512(i) thus requires that, to obtain the benefit of the DMCA safe harbor, Cox must have reasonably implemented "a policy that provides for the termination in appropriate circumstances" of its subscribers who repeatedly infringe copyrights. 17 U.S.C. § 512(i)(1)(A). We are mindful of the need to afford ISPs flexibility in crafting repeat infringer policies, and of the difficulty of determining when it is "appropriate" to terminate a person's access to the Internet. See id. At a minimum, however, an ISP has not "reasonably implemented" a repeat infringer policy if the ISP fails to enforce the terms of its policy in any meaningful fashion. See In re Aimster Copyright Litig., 252 F.Supp.2d 634, 659 (N.D. Ill. 2002), aff'd, 334 F.3d 643 (7th Cir. 2003) ("Adopting a repeat infringer policy and then purposely eviscerating any hope that such a policy could ever be carried out is not an 'implementation' as required by § 512(i)."). Here, Cox formally adopted a repeat infringer "policy," but, both before and after September 2012, made every effort to avoid reasonably implementing that policy. Indeed, in carrying out its thirteen-strike process, Cox very clearly determined not to terminate subscribers who in fact repeatedly violated the policy.

The words of Cox's own employees confirm this conclusion. In a 2009 email, Jason Zabek, the executive managing the Abuse Group, a team tasked with addressing subscribers' violations of Cox's policies, explained to his team that "if a customer is terminated for DMCA, you are able to reactivate them," and that "[a]fter you reactivate them the DMCA 'counter' restarts." The email continued, "This is to be an unwritten semi-policy." Zabek also advised a customer service representative asking whether she could reactivate a terminated subscriber that "[i]f it is for DMCA you can go ahead and reactivate." Zabek explained to another representative: "Once the customer has been terminated for DMCA, we have fulfilled the obligation of the DMCA safe harbor and can start over." He elaborated that this would allow Cox to "collect a few extra weeks of payments for their account. ;-)." Another email summarized Cox's practice more succinctly: "DMCA = reactivate." As a result of this practice, from the beginning of the litigated time period until September 2012, Cox never terminated a subscriber for infringement without reactivating them.

Cox nonetheless contends that it lacked "actual knowledge" of its subscribers' infringement and therefore did not have to terminate them. That argument misses the mark. The evidence shows that Cox always reactivated subscribers after termination, regardless of its knowledge of the subscriber's infringement. Cox did not, for example, advise employees not to reactivate a subscriber if the employees had reliable information regarding the subscriber's repeat infringement. An ISP cannot claim the protections of the DMCA safe harbor provisions merely by terminating customers as a symbolic gesture before indiscriminately reactivating them within a short timeframe.

In September 2012, Cox abandoned its practice of routine reactivation. An internal email advised a new customer service representative that "we now terminate, for real." BMG argues, however, that this was a change in form rather than substance, because instead of terminating and then reactivating subscribers, Cox simply stopped terminating them in the first place. The record evidence supports this view. Before September 2012, Cox was terminating (and reactivating) 15.5 subscribers per month on average; after September 2012, Cox abruptly began terminating less than one subscriber per month on average. From September 2012 until the end of October 2014, the month before BMG filed suit, Cox issued only 21 terminations in total. Moreover, at least 17 of those 21 terminations concerned subscribers who had either failed to pay their bills on time or used excessive bandwidth (something that Cox subjected to a strict three-strike termination policy). Cox did not provide evidence that the remaining four terminations were for repeat copyright infringement. But even assuming they were, they stand in stark contrast to the over 500,000 email warnings and temporary suspensions Cox issued to alleged infringers during the same time period.

Moreover, Cox dispensed with terminating subscribers who repeatedly infringed BMG's copyrights in particular when it decided to delete automatically all infringement notices received from BMG's agent, Rightscorp. As a result, Cox received none of the millions of infringement notices that Rightscorp sent to Cox on BMG's behalf during the relevant period. Although our inquiry concerns Cox's policy toward all of its repeatedly infringing subscribers, not just those who infringed BMG's copyrights, Cox's decision to categorically disregard all notices from Rightscorp provides further evidence that Cox did not reasonably implement a repeat infringer policy. See Ellison, 357 F.3d at 1080 (holding that "the district court erred in concluding on summary judgment that [the ISP] satisfied the requirements of § 512(i)" because the record showed that the ISP "allowed notices of potential copyright infringement to fall into a vacuum and to go unheeded," indicating it "had not reasonably implemented its policy against repeat infringers"); Aimster, 334 F.3d at 655 (holding that a defendant who "disabled itself from doing anything to prevent infringement" did not reasonably implement a repeat infringer policy).

BMG also provided evidence of particular instances in which Cox failed to terminate subscribers whom Cox employees regarded as repeat infringers. For example, one subscriber "was advised to stop sharing . . . and remove his PTP programs," and a Cox employee noted that the subscriber was "well aware of his actions" and was "upset that 'after years of doing this' he is now getting caught." Nonetheless, Cox did not terminate the subscriber. Another customer was advised that "further complaints would result in termination" and that it was the customer's "absolute last chance to . . . remove ALL" file-sharing software. But when Cox received another complaint, a manager directed the employee not to terminate, but rather to "suspend this Customer, one LAST time," noting that "[t]his customer pays us over $400/month" and that "[e]very terminated Customer becomes lost revenue."

Cox responds that these post-September 2012 emails do not necessarily "prove actual knowledge of repeat infringement." Appellants Br. at 59. Again, that argument is misplaced. Cox bears the burden of proof on the DMCA safe harbor defense; thus, Cox had to point to evidence showing that it reasonably implemented a repeat infringer policy. The emails show that Cox internally concluded that a subscriber should be terminated after the next strike, but then declined to do so because it did not want to lose revenue. In other words, Cox failed to follow through on its own policy. Cox argues that these emails only concerned "four cases," and that "occasional lapses" are forgivable. Id. at 58. But even four cases are significant when measured against Cox's equally small total number of relevant terminations in this period—also four. More importantly, Cox did not produce any evidence of instances in which it did follow through on its policy and terminate subscribers after giving them a final warning to stop infringing.

In addition, Cox suggests that because the DMCA merely requires termination of repeat infringers in "appropriate circumstances," Cox decided not to terminate certain subscribers only when "appropriate circumstances" were lacking. Appellants Br. at 56–57. But Cox failed to provide evidence that a determination of "appropriate circumstances" played any role in its decisions to terminate (or not to terminate). Cox did not, for example, point to any criteria that its employees used to determine whether "appropriate circumstances" for termination existed. Instead, the evidence shows that Cox's decisions not to terminate had nothing to do with "appropriate circumstances" but instead were based on one goal: not losing revenue from paying subscribers.

Cox failed to qualify for the DMCA safe harbor because it failed to implement its policy in any consistent or meaningful way—leaving it essentially with no policy. Accordingly, the district court did not err in holding that Cox failed to offer evidence supporting its entitlement to the § 512(a) safe harbor defense and therefore granting summary judgment on this issue to BMG.

III.

We turn to Cox's other principal challenge to the judgment: that the district court erred in instructing the jury as to contributory infringement.

* * * *

B.

. . . . Cox contends that the court erred in charging the jury as to the intent necessary to prove contributory infringement. Specifically, Cox challenges the district court's instructions that the jury could impose liability for contributory infringement if the jury found "Cox knew or should have known of such infringing activity." We agree that in so instructing the jury, the court erred.

i.

Grokster teaches that "[o]ne infringes contributorily by intentionally inducing or encouraging direct infringement." 545 U.S. at 930, 125 S.Ct. 2764 (emphasis added). The requisite intent may, however, be presumed according to the "rules of fault-based liability derived from the common law." Id. at 934–35, 125 S.Ct. 2764. The most relevant of these common law rules is that if a person "knows that the consequences are certain, or substantially certain, to result from his act, and still goes ahead, he is treated by the law as if he had in fact desired to produce the result." See Restatement (Second) of Torts § 8A cmt. b (1965); Grokster, 545 U.S. at 932, 125 S.Ct. 2764 (a person "will be presumed to intend the natural consequences of his acts" (internal quotation marks and citation omitted)). . . . [¶¶]

It is well-established that one mental state slightly less demanding than actual knowledge—willful blindness—can establish the requisite intent for contributory copyright infringement. This is so because the law recognizes willful blindness as equivalent to actual knowledge. See Global-Tech Appliances, Inc. v. SEB S.A., 563 U.S. 754, 766, 131 S.Ct. 2060, 179 L.Ed.2d 1167 (2011) ("[P]ersons who know enough to blind themselves to direct proof of critical facts in effect have actual knowledge of those facts."); Aimster, 334 F.3d at 650 ("Willful blindness is knowledge, in copyright law . . . as it is in the law generally.").

Whether other mental states—such as negligence (where a defendant "should have known" of infringement)—can suffice to prove contributory copyright infringement presents a more difficult question.[FN4 omitted] The notion that contributory liability could be imposed based on something less than actual knowledge, or its equivalent, willful blindness, is not entirely without support. See Aimster, 334 F.3d at 650 ("[I]n copyright law . . . indeed it may be enough that the defendant should have known of the direct infringement . . . .") Nonetheless, we believe for several reasons, that, as Cox contends, negligence does not suffice to prove contributory infringement; rather, at least willful blindness is required.

First, Grokster's recitation of the standard—that "[o]ne infringes contributorily by intentionally inducing or encouraging direct infringement"—is on its face difficult to reconcile with a negligence standard. See 545 U.S. at 930, 125 S.Ct. 2764 (emphasis added). . . . [¶] In both Grokster and Sony, the Supreme Court adopted now-codified patent law doctrines—the staple article doctrine and the inducement rule. The Court did so because of "the historic kinship between patent law and copyright law," Sony, 464 U.S. at 439–42, 104 S.Ct. 774, and the similar need in both contexts to impose liability on "culpable expression and conduct" without "discouraging the development of technologies with lawful and unlawful potential," Grokster, 545 U.S. at 936–37, 125 S.Ct. 2764. We are persuaded that the Global-Tech rule developed in the patent law context, which held that contributory liability can be based on willful blindness but not on recklessness or negligence, is a sensible one in the copyright context. It appropriately targets culpable conduct without unduly burdening technological development.[FN5 omitted]

.... [¶] We therefore hold that proving contributory infringement requires proof of at least willful blindness; negligence is insufficient.

.... [¶¶] iii.

In sum, the district court erred in charging the jury that Cox could be found liable for contributory infringement if it "knew or should have known of such infringing activity." The formulation "should have known" reflects negligence and is therefore too low a standard. And because there is a reasonable probability that this erroneous instruction affected the jury's verdict, we remand for a new trial. See United States v. Wilson, 133 F.3d 251, 265 (4th Cir. 1997) ("[T]he instructions did not adequately impose ... the burden of proving knowledge .... For this reason, a new trial is required.").[FN6 omitted]

.... [¶¶] Put another way, the proper standard requires a defendant to have specific enough knowledge of infringement that the defendant could do something about it. On remand, therefore, the contributory infringement instruction should require that Cox knew of specific instances of infringement or was willfully blind to such instances.

.... [¶] D.

Although we have concluded that the district court incorrectly instructed the jury in some instances, we reject Cox's argument that with proper instructions, it is entitled to judgment as a matter of law. The district court's thoroughness and sure grasp of numerous complex issues provide a model of fair administration of justice. At trial, BMG offered powerful evidence from which a reasonable jury could find that Cox willfully blinded itself to specific instances of infringement by its subscribers, such as evidence that Cox prevented itself from receiving any of the more than one million notices Rightscorp sent on BMG's behalf. Indeed, that appears to be the primary theory for liability advanced by BMG. See Appellee Br. at 21 ("Cox was put on notice of—and willfully blinded itself to—millions of specific instances of unlawful sharing of BMG's works by its subscribers ...."). That determination, of course, must be made by a jury properly instructed as to the law. But the trial record provides no basis for judgment as a matter of law in Cox's favor.

.... [¶¶] V.

For the reasons stated above, we affirm the district court's grant of summary judgment to BMG on the § 512(a) DMCA safe harbor defense, but reverse and remand for a new trial. We also vacate the district court's grant of attorney's fees and costs to BMG and its denial of fees and costs to Cox.

LENZ V. UNIVERSAL MUSIC CORP.
815 F.3d 1145 (9th Cir. 2016)
(amending 801 F.3d 1126 and denying petition for rehearing)[2]

TALLMAN, CIRCUIT JUDGE:

OPINION

Stephanie Lenz filed suit under 17 U.S.C. § 512(f)—part of the Digital Millennium Copyright Act ("DMCA")—against Universal Music Corp., Universal Music Publishing, Inc., and Universal Music Publishing Group (collectively "Universal"). She alleges Universal misrepresented in a takedown notification that her 29-second home video (the "video") constituted an infringing use of a portion of a composition by the Artist known as Prince, which Universal insists was unauthorized by the law. Her claim boils down to a question of whether copyright holders have been abusing the extrajudicial takedown procedures provided for in the DMCA by declining to first evaluate whether the content qualifies as fair use. We hold that the statute requires copyright holders to consider fair use before sending a takedown notification, and that in this case, there is a triable issue as to whether the copyright holder formed a subjective good faith belief that the use was not authorized by law. We affirm the denial of the parties' cross-motions for summary judgment.

I

Founded in May 2005, YouTube (now owned by Google) operates a website that hosts user-generated content. About YouTube, YouTube.com, https://www.youtube.com/yt/about/ (last visited September 4, 2015). Users upload videos directly to the website. Id. On February 7, 2007, Lenz uploaded to YouTube a 29-second home video of her two young children in the family kitchen dancing to the song Let's Go Crazy by Prince. Available

---

[2]   Footnotes are omitted from this excerpt.

at https://www.youtube.com/watch?v=N1KfJHFWlhQ (last visited September 4, 2015). She titled the video " 'Let's Go Crazy' # 1." About four seconds into the video, Lenz asks her thirteen month-old son "what do you think of the music?" after which he bobs up and down while holding a push toy.

At the time Lenz posted the video, Universal was Prince's publishing administrator responsible for enforcing his copyrights. To accomplish this objective with respect to YouTube, Robert Allen, Universal's head of business affairs, assigned Sean Johnson, an assistant in the legal department, to monitor YouTube on a daily basis. Johnson searched YouTube for Prince's songs and reviewed the video postings returned by his online search query. When reviewing such videos, he evaluated whether they "embodied a Prince composition" by making "significant use of . . . the composition, specifically if the song was recognizable, was in a significant portion of the video or was the focus of the video." According to Allen, "[t]he general guidelines are that . . . we review the video to ensure that the composition was the focus and if it was we then notify YouTube that the video should be removed."

Johnson contrasted videos that met this criteria to those "that may have had a second or less of a Prince song, literally a one line, half line of Prince song" or "were shot in incredibly noisy environments, such as bars, where there could be a Prince song playing deep in the background . . . to the point where if there was any Prince composition embodied . . . in those videos that it was distorted beyond reasonable recognition." None of the video evaluation guidelines explicitly include consideration of the fair use doctrine.

When Johnson reviewed Lenz's video, he recognized Let's Go Crazy immediately. He noted that it played loudly in the background throughout the entire video. Based on these details, the video's title, and Lenz's query during the video asking if her son liked the song, he concluded that Prince's song "was very much the focus of the video." As a result, Johnson decided the video should be included in a takedown notification sent to YouTube that listed more than 200 YouTube videos Universal believed to be making unauthorized use of Prince's songs. The notice included a "good faith belief" statement as required by 17 U.S.C. § 512(c)(3)(A)(v): "We have a good faith belief that the above-described activity is not authorized by the copyright owner, its agent, or the law."

After receiving the takedown notification, YouTube removed the video and sent Lenz an email on June 5, 2007, notifying her of the removal. On June 7, 2007, Lenz attempted to restore the video by sending a counter-notification to YouTube pursuant to § 512(g)(3). After YouTube provided this counter-notification to Universal per § 512(g)(2)(B), Universal protested the video's reinstatement because Lenz failed to properly acknowledge that her statement was made under penalty of perjury, as required by § 512(g)(3)(C). Universal's protest reiterated that the video constituted infringement because there was no record that "either she or YouTube were ever granted licenses to reproduce, distribute, publicly perform or otherwise exploit the Composition." The protest made no mention of fair use. After obtaining pro bono counsel, Lenz sent a second counter-notification on June 27, 2007, which resulted in YouTube's reinstatement of the video in mid-July.

II

Lenz filed the instant action on July 24, 2007, and her Amended Complaint on August 15, 2007. After the district court dismissed her tortious interference claim and request for declaratory relief, Lenz filed her Second Amended Complaint on April 18, 2008, alleging only a claim for misrepresentation under § 512(f). The district court denied Universal's motion to dismiss the action.

On February 25, 2010, the district court granted Lenz's partial motion for summary judgment on Universal's six affirmative defenses, including the third affirmative defense that Lenz suffered no damages. Both parties subsequently moved for summary judgment on Lenz's § 512(f) misrepresentation claim. On January 24, 2013, the district court denied both motions in an order that is now before us. . . . [¶]

. . . . [¶] IV

Effective on October 28, 1998, the DMCA added new sections to existing copyright law by enacting five Titles, only one of which is relevant here: Title II—Online Copyright Infringement Liability Limitation Act— now codified in 17 U.S.C. § 512. Sections 512(c), (f), and (g) are at the heart of the parties' dispute. . . . [¶¶]

B

We must first determine whether 17 U.S.C. § 512(c)(3)(A)(v) requires copyright holders to consider whether the potentially infringing material is a fair use of a copyright under 17 U.S.C. § 107 before issuing a takedown notification. Section 512(c)(3)(A)(v) requires a takedown notification to include a "statement that the complaining party has a good faith belief that the use of the material in the manner complained of is not authorized by the copyright owner, its agent, or the law." The parties dispute whether fair use is an authorization under the law as contemplated by the statute— which is so far as we know an issue of first impression in any circuit across the nation. . . . . We agree with the district court and hold that the statute unambiguously contemplates fair use as a use authorized by the law.

Fair use is not just excused by the law, it is wholly authorized by the law. In 1976, Congress codified the application of a four-step test for determining the fair use of copyrighted works:

> Notwithstanding the provisions of sections 106 and 106A, *the fair use of a copyrighted work*, . . . for purposes such as criticism, comment, news reporting, teaching (including multiple copies for classroom use), scholarship, or research, *is not an infringement of copyright.* . . .

17 U.S.C. § 107 (emphasis added). The statute explains that the fair use of a copyrighted work is permissible because it is a non-infringing use. . . . [¶]

Universal's sole textual argument is that fair use is not "authorized by the law" because it is an affirmative defense that excuses otherwise infringing conduct. Universal's interpretation is incorrect as it conflates two different concepts: an affirmative defense that is labeled as such due to the procedural posture of the case, and an affirmative defense that excuses impermissible conduct. Supreme Court precedent squarely supports the conclusion that fair use does not fall into the latter camp: "[A]nyone who . . . makes a fair use of the work is not an infringer of the copyright with respect to such use." Sony Corp. of Am. v. Universal City Studios, Inc., 464 U.S. 417, 433, 104 S.Ct. 774, 78 L.Ed.2d 574 (1984).

[¶¶] . . . . That fair use may be labeled as an affirmative defense due to the procedural posture of the case is no different than labeling a license an affirmative defense for the same reason. Compare Campbell v. Acuff-Rose Music, Inc., 510 U.S. 569, 573 & n. 3, 590, 114 S.Ct. 1164, 127 L.Ed.2d 500 (1994) (stating that "fair use is an affirmative defense" where the district court converted a motion to dismiss based on fair use into a motion for summary judgment), with A & M Records, Inc. v. Napster, Inc., 239 F.3d 1004, 1025–26 (9th Cir.2001) ("Napster contends that . . . the district court improperly rejected valid affirmative defenses of . . . implied license. . . ."). Thus, Universal's argument that it need not consider fair use in addition to compulsory licenses rings hollow.

Even if, as Universal urges, fair use is classified as an "affirmative defense," we hold—for the purposes of the DMCA—fair use is uniquely situated in copyright law so as to be treated differently than traditional affirmative defenses. We conclude that because 17 U.S.C. § 107 created a type of non-infringing use, fair use is "authorized by the law" and a copyright holder must consider the existence of fair use before sending a takedown notification under § 512(c).

C

We must next determine if a genuine issue of material fact exists as to whether Universal knowingly misrepresented that it had formed a good faith belief the video did not constitute fair use. This inquiry lies not in whether a court would adjudge the video as a fair use, but whether Universal formed a good faith belief that it was not. Contrary to the district court's holding, Lenz may proceed under an actual knowledge theory, but not under a willful blindness theory.

1

Though Lenz argues Universal should have known the video qualifies for fair use as a matter of law, we have already decided a copyright holder need only form a subjective good faith belief that a use is not authorized. Rossi v. Motion Picture Ass'n of Am. Inc., 391 F.3d 1000 (9th Cir.2004). In Rossi, we explicitly held that "the 'good faith belief' requirement in § 512(c)(3)(A)(v) encompasses a subjective, rather than objective standard," and we observed that "Congress understands this distinction." Id. at 1004. We further held:

> When enacting the DMCA, Congress could have easily incorporated an objective standard of reasonableness. The fact that it did not do so indicates an intent to adhere to the subjective standard traditionally associated with a good faith requirement. . . .

> In § 512(f), Congress included an expressly limited cause of action for improper infringement notifications, imposing liability only if the copyright owner's notification is a knowing misrepresentation. A copyright owner cannot be liable simply because an unknowing mistake is made, even if the copyright owner acted unreasonably in making the mistake. Rather, there must be a demonstration of some actual knowledge of misrepresentation on the part of the copyright owner.

Id. at 1004–05 (citations omitted). Neither of these holdings are dictum. See United States v. Johnson, 256 F.3d 895, 914 (9th Cir.2001) (en banc). . . . We therefore judge Universal's actions by the subjective beliefs it formed about the video.

2

Universal faces liability if it knowingly misrepresented in the takedown notification that it had formed a good faith belief the video was not authorized by the law, i.e., did not constitute fair use. Here, Lenz presented evidence that Universal did not form any subjective belief about the video's fair use—one way or another—because it failed to consider fair use at all, and knew that it failed to do so. Universal nevertheless contends that its procedures, while not formally labeled consideration of fair use, were tantamount to such consideration. Because the DMCA requires consideration of fair use prior to sending a takedown notification, a jury must determine whether Universal's actions were sufficient to form a subjective good faith belief about the video's fair use or lack thereof.

To be clear, if a copyright holder ignores or neglects our unequivocal holding that it must consider fair use before sending a takedown notification, it is liable for damages under § 512(f). If, however, a copyright holder forms a subjective good faith belief the allegedly infringing material does not constitute fair use, we are in no position to dispute the copyright holder's belief even if we would have reached the opposite conclusion. A copyright holder who pays lip service to the consideration of fair use by claiming it formed a good faith belief when there is evidence to the contrary is still subject to § 512(f) liability. Cf. Disney Enters., Inc. v. Hotfile Corp., No. 11-cv-20427, 2013 WL 6336286, at *48 (S.D.Fla. Sept. 20, 2013) (denying summary judgment of § 512(f) counterclaim due to "sufficient evidence in the record to suggest that [Plaintiff] Warner intentionally targeted files it knew it had no right to remove") . . . .

3

We hold the willful blindness doctrine may be used to determine whether a copyright holder "knowingly materially misrepresent[ed]" that it held a "good faith belief" the offending activity was not a fair use. See 17 U.S.C. § 512(c)(3)(A)(v), (f). "[T]he willful blindness doctrine may be applied, in appropriate circumstances, to demonstrate knowledge or awareness of specific instances of infringement under the DMCA." Viacom Int'l, Inc. v. YouTube, Inc., 676 F.3d 19, 35 (2d Cir.2012) (interpreting how a party can establish the "actual knowledge"—a subjective belief—required by § 512(c)(1)(A)(i)) . . . . But, based on the specific facts presented during summary judgment, we reject the district court's conclusion that Lenz may proceed to trial under a willful blindness theory.

To demonstrate willful blindness a plaintiff must establish two factors: "(1) the defendant must subjectively believe that there is a high probability that a fact exists and (2) the defendant must take deliberate actions to avoid learning of that fact." Global-Tech Appliances, Inc. v. SEB S.A., 563 U.S. 754, 131 S.Ct. 2060, 2070, 179 L.Ed.2d 1167 (2011). "Under this formulation, a willfully blind defendant is one who takes deliberate actions to avoid confirming a high probability of wrongdoing and who can almost be said to have actually known the critical facts." Id. at 2070–71. To meet the Global-Tech test, Lenz must demonstrate a genuine issue as to whether—before sending the takedown notification—Universal (1) subjectively believed there was a high probability that the video constituted fair use, and (2) took deliberate actions to avoid learning of this fair use.

On summary judgment Lenz failed to meet a threshold showing of the first factor. To make such a showing, Lenz must provide evidence from which a juror could infer that Universal was aware of a high probability the video constituted fair use. See United States v. Yi, 704 F.3d 800, 805 (9th Cir.2013). But she failed to provide any such evidence. The district court therefore correctly found that "Lenz does not present evidence suggesting Universal subjectively believed either that there was a high probability any given video might make fair use of a Prince composition or her video in particular made fair use of Prince's song 'Let's Go Crazy.' " Yet the district court improperly denied Universal's motion for summary judgment on the willful blindness theory because Universal "has not shown that it lacked a subjective belief." By finding blame with Universal's inability to show that it "lacked a subjective belief," the district court improperly required Universal to meet its burden of persuasion, even though Lenz had failed to counter the initial burden of production that Universal successfully carried. See Celotex Corp. v. Catrett, 477 U.S. 317, 322, 106 S.Ct. 2548, 91 L.Ed.2d 265 (1986); Nissan Fire & Marine Ins. Co. v. Fritz Cos., Inc., 210 F.3d 1099, 1102 (9th Cir.2000). Lenz may not therefore proceed to trial on a willful blindness theory.

. . . . [¶ ¶] VI

Copyright holders cannot shirk their duty to consider—in good faith and prior to sending a takedown notification—whether allegedly infringing material constitutes fair use, a use which the DMCA plainly contemplates as authorized by the law. That this step imposes responsibility on copyright holders is not a reason for us to reject it. . . . We affirm the district court's order denying the parties' cross-motions for summary judgment.

AFFIRMED. Each party shall bear its own costs.

[M. SMITH, CIRCUIT JUDGE, concurred in part and dissented in part in a separate opinion that is omitted here.]

The next case also addresses the notice and takedown provisions of the DMCA as applied to music copyright infringement claims against third party ISPs whose users post copyrighted musical recordings on the web without permission. Veoh Networks ("Veoh") operated a free, public website that allowed users to share videos; Veoh earned revenue from ads displayed alongside videos on the site. Before they could share videos, users had to register with Veoh and agree to terms and conditions that included a prohibition on uploading material containing "infringing . . . or illegal content" and representations and warranties that they had all required rights, permissions and licenses to be able to permit Veoh to publish the videos. In addition, each time a user initiated an upload of a video to Veoh's website, a message appeared instructing the user to not upload videos that infringed copyright or otherwise violated Veoh's terms of use.

Users could provide titles or tags for their uploaded videos, which were automatically incorporated into the permalink established for the video by Veoh's system and none of which were screened or reviewed by Veoh employees. Users had the option of either streaming videos through the site, with temporary storage of the content on the user's computer, or downloading a copy of a video into a Veoh directory on the hard drive of the user's computer, which gave Veoh the ability to terminate access to the files.

Veoh implemented two main automatic technologies to attempt to prevent copyright infringement on its site. First, it adopted "hash filtering" software, which automatically disabled access to videos identical to any infringing videos to which Veoh might disable access. Second, it adopted a third-party filtering system produced by Audible Magic, which used audio fingerprints of video files and compared them to a database of copyright works provided by copyright owners and blocked files matching those of registered works. In addition, Veoh implemented a termination policy for users who repeatedly infringed on copyright and actually terminated thousands of users under that policy.

Universal Music Group ("UMG") sued for direct, vicarious and contributory copyright infringement, and for inducement of infringement, claiming that Veoh failed to adequately prevent its users from downloading videos containing sound recordings owned by UMG. The district court granted summary judgment to Veoh, finding that the DMCA safe harbor protected it from liability, and the Ninth Circuit affirmed that ruling.

UMG RECORDINGS, INC. V. SHELTER CAPITAL PARTNERS, LLC ("VEOH")

718 F.3d 1006 (9th Cir. 2013)[3]

FISHER, CIRCUIT JUDGE:

[¶¶] . . . . Although Congress was aware that the services provided by companies like Veoh are capable of being misused to facilitate copyright infringement, it was loath to permit the specter of liability to chill innovation that could also serve substantial socially beneficial functions. . . . [¶¶]

. . . UMG argues that genuine issues of fact remain about whether Veoh had actual knowledge of infringement, or was "aware of facts or circumstances from which infringing activity [wa]s apparent" under § 512(c)(1)(A). Finally, UMG argues that it presented sufficient evidence that Veoh "receive[d] a financial benefit directly attributable to . . . infringing activity" that it had "the right and ability to control" under § 512(c)(1)(B). We disagree on each count, and accordingly we affirm the district court.

[¶¶] . . . . UMG argues on appeal that the district court erred by improperly construing the knowledge requirement to unduly restrict the circumstances in which a service provider has "actual knowledge" under subsection (i) and setting too stringent a standard for what we have termed "red flag" awareness based on facts or circumstances from which infringing activity is apparent under subsection (ii). We hold that the district court properly construed these requirements.

1.

It is undisputed that, until the filing of this lawsuit, UMG "had not identified to Veoh any specific infringing video available on Veoh's system." UMG's decision to forgo the DMCA notice protocol "stripped it of the most powerful evidence of a service provider's knowledge—actual notice of infringement from the copyright holder." *Corbis Corp. v. Amazon.com, Inc.,* 351 F.Supp.2d 1090, 1107 (W.D.Wash.2004) (citing 3 M. Nimmer & D. Nimmer, Nimmer on Copyright § 12B.04(A)(3), at 12B-53 [hereinafter "Nimmer"]); *see also Io Grp.,* 586 F.Supp.2d at 1148. Nevertheless, UMG contends that Veoh hosted a category of copyrightable content—music—for which it had no license from any major music company. UMG argues Veoh thus must have known this content was unauthorized, given its general knowledge that its services could be used to post infringing material. UMG urges us to hold that this sufficiently demonstrates knowledge of infringement. We cannot, for several reasons.

---

[3]   Footnotes are omitted from this excerpt.

As an initial matter, contrary to UMG's contentions, there are many music videos that *could* in fact legally appear on Veoh. . . . [I]f merely hosting material that falls within a category of content capable of copyright protection, with the general knowledge that one's services could be used to share unauthorized copies of copyrighted material, was sufficient to impute knowledge to service providers, the § 512(c) safe harbor would be rendered a dead letter: § 512(c) applies only to claims of copyright infringement, yet the fact that a service provider's website could contain copyrightable material would remove the service provider from § 512(c) eligibility.

[¶¶] . . . . Requiring specific knowledge of particular infringing activity makes good sense in the context of the DMCA, which Congress enacted to foster cooperation among copyright holders and service providers in dealing with infringement on the Internet. *See* S.Rep. No. 105–190, at 20 (noting OCILLA was intended to provide "strong incentives for service providers and copyright owners to cooperate to detect and deal with copyright infringements"); H.R.Rep. No. 105–551, pt. 2, at 49 (1998) (same). Copyright holders know precisely what materials they own, and are thus better able to efficiently identify infringing copies than service providers like Veoh, who cannot readily ascertain what material is copyrighted and what is not. . . .

These considerations are reflected in Congress' decision to enact a notice and takedown protocol encouraging copyright holders to identify specific infringing material to service providers. . . . Congress made a considered policy determination that the "DMCA notification procedures [would] place the burden of policing copyright infringement—identifying the potentially infringing material and adequately documenting infringement—squarely on the owners of the copyright." *Perfect 10, Inc. v. CCBill LLC,* 488 F.3d 1102, 1113 (9th Cir.2007). In parsing § 512(c)(3), we have "decline[d] to shift [that] substantial burden from the copyright owner to the provider." *Id.*

UMG asks us to change course with regard to § 512(c)(1)(A) by adopting a broad conception of the knowledge requirement. We see no principled basis for doing so. We therefore hold that merely hosting a category of copyrightable content, such as music videos, with the general knowledge that one's services could be used to share infringing material, is insufficient to meet the actual knowledge requirement under § 512(c)(1)(A)(i).

We reach the same conclusion with regard to the § 512(c)(1)(A)(ii) inquiry into whether a service provider is "aware of facts or circumstances from which infringing activity is apparent." The district court's conception of this "red flag test" properly followed our analysis in *CCBill,* which reiterated that the burden remains with the copyright holder rather than the service provider. *See id.* at 1114. . . . [We] hold that Veoh's general knowledge that it hosted copyrightable material and that its services could be used for infringement is insufficient to constitute a red flag.

Of course, a service provider cannot willfully bury its head in the sand to avoid obtaining such specific knowledge. *See Viacom Int'l v. YouTube, Inc.,* 676 F.3d 19, 31 (2d Cir.2012). Even viewing the evidence in the light most favorable to UMG as we must here, however, we agree with the district court there is no evidence that Veoh acted in such a manner. Rather, the evidence demonstrates that Veoh promptly removed infringing material when it became aware of specific instances of infringement. Although the parties agree, in retrospect, that at times there was infringing material available on Veoh's services, the DMCA recognizes that service providers who do not locate and remove infringing materials they do not specifically know of should not suffer the loss of safe harbor protection.

[¶¶] . . . . A service provider is eligible for the § 512(c) safe harbor only if it "does not receive a financial benefit directly attributable to the infringing activity, in a case in which the service provider has the right and ability to control such activity." 17 U.S.C. § 512(c)(1)(B). UMG appeals the district court's determination that Veoh did not have the necessary right and ability to control infringing activity and thus remained eligible for safe harbor protection. We conclude the district court was correct, and therefore affirm.

[¶¶] . . . . We agree with Judge Matz that "Congress could not have intended for courts to hold that a service provider loses immunity under the safe harbor provision of the DMCA because it engages in acts that are specifically required by the DMCA" to obtain safe harbor protection. *UMG II,* 665 F.Supp.2d at 1113 (quoting *Hendrickson v. eBay, Inc.,* 165 F.Supp.2d 1082, 1093–94 (C.D.Cal.2001)) (internal quotation marks omitted); *see also Io Grp., Inc. v. Veoh Networks, Inc.,* 586 F.Supp.2d 1132, 1151 (N.D.Cal.2008) (same); Lee, *supra,* 32 Colum. J.L. & Arts at 247 ("A[ ] [service provider's] ability to remove materials posted by third parties does not satisfy the 'right and ability to control' prong, because such power is necessary for a[ ] [service provider] to satisfy the basic requirement of 'takedown' under the DMCA."). . . .

. . . Congress did not intend to exclude from § 512(c)'s safe harbor all service providers who would be vicariously liable for their users' infringing activity under the common law. [¶¶] . . . . First, Congress explicitly stated in three different reports that the DMCA was intended to "protect qualifying service providers from liability for all monetary relief for direct, *vicarious* and contributory infringement." H.R. Conf. Rep. No. 105–796, at 64, 1998 U.S.C.C.A.N. at 649 (emphasis added); S.Rep. No. 105–190, at 20, 40; H.R.Rep. No. 105–551, pt. 2, at 50. Under UMG's interpretation, however, *every* service provider subject to vicarious liability would be automatically excluded from safe harbor protection. Second, Congress made clear that it intended to provide safe harbor protection *not* by altering the common law vicarious liability standards, but rather by carving out permanent safe harbors to that liability for Internet service providers even while the common law standards continue to evolve. *See* S.Rep. No. 105–190, at 19 ("There have been several cases relevant to service provider liability for copyright infringement. Most have approached the issue from the standpoint of contributory and vicarious liability. Rather than embarking upon a wholesale clarification of these doctrines, the Committee decided to leave current law in its evolving state and, instead, to create a series of 'safe harbors,' for certain common activities of service providers. A service provider which qualifies for a safe harbor, receives the benefit of limited liability.").

Given Congress' explicit intention to protect qualifying service providers who would otherwise be subject to vicarious liability, it would be puzzling for Congress to make § 512(c) entirely coextensive with the vicarious liability requirements, which would effectively exclude all vicarious liability claims from the § 512(c) safe harbor. *See, e.g.,* Lee, *supra,* 32 Colum. J.L. & Arts at 236–37 (acknowledging that interpreting the DMCA to exclude service providers subject to vicarious liability would "undo the benefits of the safe harbors altogether" (quoting Mark A. Lemley, *Rationalizing Internet Safe Harbors,* 6 J. Telecomm. & High Tech. L. 101, 104 (2007)) (internal quotation marks omitted)). In addition, it is difficult to envision, from a policy perspective, why Congress would have chosen to exclude vicarious infringement from the safe harbors, but retain protection for contributory infringement. It is not apparent why the former might be seen as somehow worse than the latter. *See id.* at 243–44.

[¶¶] . . . . [B]ecause UMG has not created a triable issue regarding Veoh's right and ability to control infringing activity, we conclude that Veoh met all the § 512(c) requirements, and we affirm the entry of summary judgment in its favor.

NOTES AND QUESTIONS

1.   Both *Thomas* and *Cox* illustrate the various arguments that have been made regarding interpretation of the distribution and publication terms in the Copyright Act and the majority view of how those terms apply to "making available" claims. Which approach do you find the most compelling, and why? How far should liability extend for those who assist others in infringing protected works? If Congress takes action on this issue in the continuing copyright revision process after the enactment of the MMA in 2018, how do you think it should treat actions by individuals who make copyrighted works available for others to download? Should downloading P2P software be

sufficient, if that software automatically makes one's music and other files available through the file sharing software?

2.   The *Veoh, Cox* and *Lenz* cases provide some insight into the ongoing debate over proper interpretation and application of the notice and takedown provisions of the DMCA that are a prerequisite to the DMCA safe harbor protections for Internet service providers. What concerns do the facts and holdings of these cases raise from the perspective of copyright owners who seek to prevent unauthorized distribution of their works? What concerns do they raise from the perspective of Internet service providers in terms of the ability to comply with the DMCA?

3.   Given that more and more recordings and compositions are available online through more and more platforms, is the DMCA's notice and takedown mechanism (discussed in *Veoh*, as well as in *Cox* and *Lenz*) efficient and effective enough to protect both content owners and content users? If so, what leads you to that conclusion? If not, what solutions can you think of that would create a more effective/efficient means of protecting copyright owners while still permitting online platforms to operate efficiently? Do the current legal standards for secondary liability make sense in the context of digital transfers of copyrighted works via the Internet? Why or why not?

———————

D. CHALLENGES TO NEW DISTRIBUTION METHODS

This section provides a snapshot of some of the legal issues that have arisen in (relatively) recent cases in which content owners have challenged a new platform or distribution method as infringing. As you read the cases below, think about the themes that emerged from the earliest cases at the dawn of the music industry from the beginning of this textbook. Are the issues faced by those who seek to introduce new models for distributing music (or other copyrighted works) to the public distinct in the digital era? Or is it an example of "the more things change, the more they stay the same"?[4]

Although the first case discussed below, *Aereo*, does not directly relate to music but instead arose in the context of broadcast television, it provides insight and guidance regarding the challenges faced by developers of new distribution methods for any copyrighted work in the digital era—including musical works.

Aereo's technology allowed paid subscribers to access broadcast television programming via the Internet nearly simultaneously with the

———————

[4]   From an epigram by Jean-Baptiste Alphonse Karr in the January 1849 issue of his journal Les Guêpes ("The Wasps") ("plus ça change, plus c'est la même chose"); also appearing in lyrics to songs performed by Bon Jovi, Machine Head, Rush, Spin Doctors, Ludacris, Kenny Chesney, Kris Kristofferson, Jay-Z, They Might Be Giants, and Corrine Bailey Rae, among many, many others.

broadcasts. Aereo did not own the copyrights or hold public performance licenses from copyright owners to any of the copyrighted works that were broadcast. Aereo had a central warehouse of servers, transcoders, and dime-sized antennas. In order for a subscriber to watch a broadcast, the subscriber would access Aereo's website and select from the list of local programs, and Aereo's servers would dedicate an antenna to that subscriber and program.

The antenna would tune to and receive the selected broadcast and a transcoder would transmit the data over the internet to the subscriber. The Aereo system would create a subscriber-specific copy of the program in its hard drives and once several seconds of programming were saved, the streaming to the subscriber would begin.

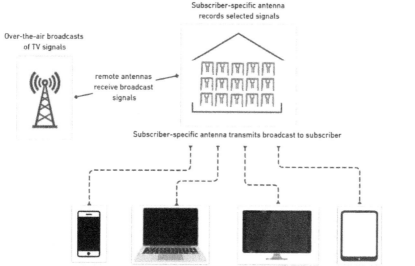

As you read *Aereo*, note that the issue before the Supreme court involved only whether Aereo's conduct constituted direct infringement— unlike the *Grokster*, *Cox*, and *Veoh* cases above, the issue of liability for secondary infringement under a theory of contributory liability, vicarious liability, or inducement was not before the Court.

AMERICAN BROADCASTING COMPANIES, INC. V. AEREO, INC.
573 U.S. 431 (2014)

BREYER, J., delivered the opinion of the Court, in which ROBERTS, C.J., and KENNEDY, GINSBURG, SOTOMAYOR, and KAGAN, JJ., joined. SCALIA, J., filed a dissenting opinion, in which THOMAS and ALITO, JJ., joined.

Opinion

JUSTICE BREYER delivered the opinion of the Court.

The Copyright Act of 1976 gives a copyright owner the "exclusive righ[t]" to "perform the copyrighted work publicly." 17 U.S.C. § 106(4). The Act's Transmit Clause defines that exclusive right as including the right to

> "transmit or otherwise communicate a performance . . . of the [copyrighted] work . . . to the public, by means of any device or process, whether the members of the public capable of receiving the performance . . . receive it in the same place or in separate places and at the same time or at different times." § 101.

We must decide whether respondent Aereo, Inc., infringes this exclusive right by selling its subscribers a technologically complex service that allows them to watch television programs over the Internet at about the same time as the programs are broadcast over the air. We conclude that it does.

[¶¶] . . . . Aereo emphasizes that the data that its system streams to each subscriber are the data from his own personal copy, made from the broadcast signals received by the particular antenna allotted to him. Its system does not transmit data saved in one subscriber's folder to any other subscriber. When two subscribers wish to watch the same program, Aereo's system activates two separate antennas and saves two separate copies of the program in two separate folders. It then streams the show to the subscribers through two separate transmissions—each from the subscriber's personal copy.

B

Petitioners are television producers, marketers, distributors, and broadcasters who own the copyrights in many of the programs that Aereo's system streams to its subscribers. They brought suit against Aereo for copyright infringement in Federal District Court. They sought a preliminary injunction, arguing that Aereo was infringing their right to "perform" their works "publicly," as the Transmit Clause defines those terms.

The District Court denied the preliminary injunction. 874 F.Supp.2d 373 (S.D.N.Y.2012). Relying on prior Circuit precedent, a divided panel of the Second Circuit affirmed. *WNET, Thirteen v. Aereo, Inc.*, 712 F.3d 676 (2013) (citing *Cartoon Network LP, LLLP v. CSC Holdings, Inc.*, 536 F.3d 121 (2008)). In the Second Circuit's view, Aereo does not perform publicly within the meaning of the Transmit Clause because it does not transmit "to the public." Rather, each time Aereo streams a program to a subscriber, it sends a *private* transmission that is available only to that subscriber. The Second Circuit denied rehearing en banc, over the dissent of two judges. *WNET, Thirteen v. Aereo, Inc.*, 722 F.3d 500 (2013). We granted certiorari.

II

This case requires us to answer two questions: First, in operating in the manner described above, does Aereo "perform" at all? And second, if so, does Aereo do so "publicly"? We address these distinct questions in turn.

Does Aereo "perform"? See § 106(4) ("[T]he owner of [a] copyright . . . has the exclusive righ[t] . . . to *perform* the copyrighted work publicly" (emphasis added)); § 101 ("To *perform* . . . a work 'publicly' means [among other things] to transmit . . . a performance . . . of the work . . . to the public . . ." (emphasis added)). Phrased another way, does Aereo "transmit . . . a performance" when a subscriber watches a show using Aereo's system, or is it only the subscriber who transmits? In Aereo's view, it does not perform. It does no more than supply equipment that "emulate[s] the operation of a home antenna and [digital video recorder (DVR)]." Brief for Respondent 41. Like a home antenna and DVR, Aereo's equipment simply responds to its subscribers' directives. So it is only the subscribers who "perform" when they use Aereo's equipment to stream television programs to themselves.

Considered alone, the language of the Act does not clearly indicate when an entity "perform[s]" (or "transmit[s]") and when it merely supplies equipment that allows others to do so. But when read in light of its purpose, the Act is unmistakable: An entity that engages in activities like Aereo's performs.

Ed. Note: The Court then discusses the 1976 amendment to the Copyright Act that was intended to overturn the Court's decisions in *Fortnightly Corp. v. United Artists Television, Inc.*, 392 U.S. 390 (1968) and *Teleprompter Corp. v. Columbia Broadcasting System, Inc.*, 415 U.S. 394 (1974). In *Fortnightly*, the Court held that a community antenna television (CATV) system that extended local television broadcasts to rural subscribers via antennas placed on the tops of hills—which amplified the signals, but did not edit or originate any programs—did not constitute a public performance. Thus, the CATV providers did not need to obtain licenses for the copyrighted programs that were broadcasted. The Court did not consider the CATV providers to be performing like broadcasters; rather they were more comparable to a viewer because they only "enhance[d] the viewer's capacity to receive the broadcaster's signals [by] provid[ing] a well-located antenna with an efficient connection to the viewer's television set." *Fortnightly*, 392 U.S. at 399. The Court reasoned that because an individual viewer using amplifying equipment to obtain a broadcast signal would not be considered a performer, nor should a CATV system for providing the same equipment. In *Teleprompter*, the Court found that a CATV provider's amplification of broadcast television programs to subscribers over hundreds of miles away still did not constitute a performance, despite the fact that an individual viewer might not be able to afford amplifying equipment of that strength.

Congress overturned the holdings of these cases by amending the Copyright Act to abolish the Court's distinction between broadcasters and viewers with respect to performing a work. The amended statute's new language included both broadcasters and viewers as performing a work because it defined "perform[ing]" an audiovisual work as "show[ing] its images in any sequence" or "mak[ing] the sounds accompanying it audible." § 101. Congress further enacted the Transmit Clause, which states that an entity publicly performs when "it transmit[s]. . .a performance. . .to the public," transmitting a performance being defined as "communicat[ing] it by any device or process whereby images or sounds are received beyond the place from which they are sent." § 101. Finally, Congress created a compulsory licensing scheme under a new section of the Act, § 111, to regulate the circumstances under which cable systems may publicly perform and retransmit broadcasts of copyrighted works.

[¶¶] . . . .

C

This history makes clear that Aereo is not simply an equipment provider. Rather, Aereo, and not just its subscribers, "perform[s]" (or "transmit[s]"). Aereo's activities are substantially similar to those of the CATV companies that Congress amended the Act to reach. See *id.*, at 89 ("[C]able systems are commercial enterprises whose basic retransmission operations are based on the carriage of copyrighted program material"). Aereo sells a service that allows subscribers to watch television programs, many of which are copyrighted, almost as they are being broadcast. . . .

Aereo's equipment may serve a "viewer function"; it may enhance the viewer's ability to receive a broadcaster's programs. It may even emulate equipment a viewer could use at home. But the same was true of the equipment that was before the Court, and ultimately before Congress, in *Fortnightly* and *Teleprompter*.

We recognize, and Aereo and the dissent emphasize, one particular difference between Aereo's system and the cable systems at issue in *Fortnightly* and *Teleprompter*. The systems in those cases transmitted constantly; they sent continuous programming to each subscriber's television set. In contrast, Aereo's system remains inert until a subscriber indicates that she wants to watch a program. Only at that moment, in automatic response to the subscriber's request, does Aereo's system activate an antenna and begin to transmit the requested program.

This is a critical difference, says the dissent. It means that Aereo's subscribers, not Aereo, "selec[t] the copyrighted content" that is "perform [ed]," *post,* at 2513 (opinion of SCALIA, J.), and for that reason they, not Aereo, "transmit" the performance. Aereo is thus like "a copy shop that provides its patrons with a library card." *Post,* at 2514. A copy shop is not directly liable whenever a patron uses the shop's machines to "reproduce" copyrighted materials found in that library. See § 106(1) ("exclusive righ[t] . . . to reproduce the copyrighted work"). And by the same token, Aereo should not be directly liable whenever its patrons use its equipment to "transmit" copyrighted television programs to their screens.

In our view, however, the dissent's copy shop argument, in whatever form, makes too much out of too little. Given Aereo's overwhelming likeness to the cable companies targeted by the 1976 amendments, this sole technological difference between Aereo and traditional cable companies does not make a critical difference here. The subscribers of the *Fortnightly* and *Teleprompter* cable systems also selected what programs to display on their receiving sets. Indeed, as we explained in *Fortnightly,* such a subscriber "could choose any of the . . . programs he wished to view by simply turning the knob on his own television set." 392 U.S., at 392, 88 S.Ct. 2084. The same is true of an Aereo subscriber. Of course, in *Fortnightly* the television signals, in a sense, lurked behind the screen, ready to emerge when the subscriber turned the knob. Here the signals pursue their ordinary course of travel through the universe until today's "turn of the knob"—a click on a website—activates machinery that intercepts and reroutes them to Aereo's subscribers over the Internet. But this difference means nothing to the subscriber. It means nothing to the broadcaster. We do not see how this single difference, invisible to subscriber and broadcaster alike, could transform a system that is for all practical purposes a traditional cable system into "a copy shop that provides its patrons with a library card."

In other cases involving different kinds of service or technology providers, a user's involvement in the operation of the provider's equipment and selection of the content transmitted may well bear on whether the provider performs within the meaning of the Act. But the many similarities between Aereo and cable companies, considered in light of Congress' basic purposes in amending the Copyright Act, convince us that this difference is not critical here. We conclude that Aereo is not just an equipment supplier and that Aereo "perform[s]."

III

Next, we must consider whether Aereo performs petitioners' works "publicly," within the meaning of the Transmit Clause. Under the Clause, an entity performs a work publicly when it "transmit[s] . . . a performance . . . of the work . . . to the public." § 101. Aereo denies that it satisfies this definition. It reasons as follows: First, the "performance" it "transmit[s]" is the performance created by its act of transmitting. And second, because each of these performances is capable of being received by one and only one subscriber, Aereo transmits privately, not publicly. Even assuming Aereo's first argument is correct, its second does not follow. . . .

[¶¶] . . . We assume *arguendo* that Aereo's first argument is correct. Thus, for present purposes, to transmit a performance of (at least) an audiovisual work means to communicate contemporaneously visible images and contemporaneously audible sounds of the work. Cf. *United States v. American Soc. of Composers, Authors and Publishers*, 627 F.3d 64, 73 (C.A.2 2010) (holding that a download of a work is not a performance because the data transmitted are not "contemporaneously perceptible"). When an Aereo subscriber selects a program to watch, Aereo streams the program over the Internet to that subscriber. Aereo thereby "communicate[s]" to the subscriber, by means of a "device or process," the work's images and sounds. § 101. And those images and sounds are contemporaneously visible and audible on the subscriber's computer (or other Internet-connected device). So under our assumed definition, Aereo transmits a performance whenever its subscribers watch a program.

But what about the Clause's further requirement that Aereo transmit a performance "to the public"? As we have said, an Aereo subscriber receives broadcast television signals with an antenna dedicated to him alone. Aereo's system makes from those signals a personal copy of the selected program. It streams the content of the copy to the same subscriber and to no one else. One and only one subscriber has the ability to see and hear each Aereo transmission. The fact that each transmission is to only one subscriber, in Aereo's view, means that it does not transmit a performance "to the public."

Aereo's miniature antenna (as pictured, about the size of a dime),
From Aereo's Answer and Counterclaim

In terms of the Act's purposes, these differences do not distinguish Aereo's system from cable systems, which do perform "publicly." Viewed in terms of Congress' regulatory objectives, why should any of these technological differences matter? They concern the behind-the-scenes way in which Aereo delivers television programming to its viewers' screens. They do not render Aereo's commercial objective any different from that of cable companies. Nor do they significantly alter the viewing experience of Aereo's subscribers. Why would a subscriber who wishes to watch a television show care much whether images and sounds are delivered to his screen via a large multisubscriber antenna or one small dedicated antenna, whether they arrive instantaneously or after a few seconds' delay, or whether they are transmitted directly or after a personal copy is made? And why, if Aereo is right, could not modern CATV systems simply continue the same commercial and consumer-oriented activities, free of copyright restrictions, provided they substitute such new technologies for old? Congress would as much have intended to protect a copyright holder from the unlicensed activities of Aereo as from those of cable companies.

The text of the Clause effectuates Congress' intent. Aereo's argument to the contrary relies on the premise that "to transmit . . . a performance" means to make a single transmission. But the Clause suggests that an entity may transmit a performance through multiple, discrete transmissions. That is because one can "transmit" or "communicate" something through a *set* of actions. . . . [¶] By the same principle, an entity may transmit a performance through one or several transmissions, where the performance is of the same work.

The Transmit Clause must permit this interpretation, for it provides that one may transmit a performance to the public "whether the members of the public capable of receiving the performance . . . receive it . . . at the same time or at different times." § 101. Were the words "to transmit . . . a performance" limited to a single act of communication, members of the public could not receive the performance communicated "at different times." Therefore, in light of the purpose and text of the Clause, we conclude that when an entity communicates the same contemporaneously perceptible images and sounds to multiple people, it transmits a performance to them regardless of the number of discrete communications it makes.

We do not see how the fact that Aereo transmits via personal copies of programs could make a difference. The Act applies to transmissions "by means of any device or process." *Ibid.* And retransmitting a television program using user-specific copies is a "process" of transmitting a performance. A "cop[y]" of a work is simply a "material objec[t] . . . in which a work is fixed . . . and from which the work can be perceived, reproduced, or otherwise communicated." *Ibid.* So whether Aereo transmits from the same or separate copies, it performs the same work; it shows the same images and makes audible the same sounds. Therefore, when Aereo streams the same television program to multiple subscribers, it "transmit[s] . . . a performance" to all of them.

Moreover, the subscribers to whom Aereo transmits television programs constitute "the public." . . . [¶¶] . . . "[T]he public" need not be situated together, spatially or temporally. For these reasons, we conclude that Aereo transmits a performance of petitioners' copyrighted works to the public, within the meaning of the Transmit Clause.

IV

Aereo and many of its supporting *amici* argue that to apply the Transmit Clause to Aereo's conduct will impose copyright liability on other technologies, including new technologies, that Congress could not possibly have wanted to reach. We agree that Congress, while intending the Transmit Clause to apply broadly to cable companies and their equivalents, did not intend to discourage or to control the emergence or use of different kinds of technologies. But we do not believe that our limited holding today will have that effect. . . .

[¶] . . . We cannot now answer more precisely how the Transmit Clause or other provisions of the Copyright Act will apply to technologies not before us. We agree with the Solicitor General that "[q]uestions involving cloud computing, [remote storage] DVRs, and other novel issues not before the Court, as to which 'Congress has not plainly marked [the] course,' should await a case in which they are squarely presented." Brief for United States as *Amicus Curiae* 34 (quoting *Sony, supra,* at 431, 104 S.Ct. 774 (alteration in original)). And we note that, to the extent commercial actors or other interested entities may be concerned with the relationship between the development and use of such technologies and the Copyright Act, they are of course free to seek action from Congress. Cf. Digital Millennium Copyright Act, 17 U.S.C. § 512.

* * *

In sum, having considered the details of Aereo's practices, we find them highly similar to those of the CATV systems in *Fortnightly* and

Teleprompter. And those are activities that the 1976 amendments sought to bring within the scope of the Copyright Act. Insofar as there are differences, those differences concern not the nature of the service that Aereo provides so much as the technological manner in which it provides the service. We conclude that those differences are not adequate to place Aereo's activities outside the scope of the Act.

For these reasons, we conclude that Aereo "perform[s]" petitioners' copyrighted works "publicly," as those terms are defined by the Transmit Clause. We therefore reverse the contrary judgment of the Court of Appeals, and we remand the case for further proceedings consistent with this opinion.

It is so ordered.

JUSTICE SCALIA, with whom JUSTICE THOMAS and JUSTICE ALITO join, dissenting.

This case is the latest skirmish in the long-running copyright battle over the delivery of television programming. . . . The Networks sued Aereo for several forms of copyright infringement, but we are here concerned with a single claim: that Aereo violates the Networks' "exclusive righ[t]" to "perform" their programs "publicly." 17 U.S.C. § 106(4). That claim fails at the very outset because Aereo does not "perform" at all. The Court manages to reach the opposite conclusion only by disregarding widely accepted rules for service-provider liability and adopting in their place an improvised standard ("looks-like-cable-TV") that will sow confusion for years to come. . . .

I.   Legal Standard

[¶¶] The Networks' claim is governed by a simple but profoundly important rule: A defendant may be held directly liable only if it has engaged in volitional conduct that violates the Act. See 3 W. Patry, Copyright § 9:5.50 (2013). . . . Although we have not opined on the issue, our cases are fully consistent with a volitional-conduct requirement. For example, we gave several examples of direct infringement in *Sony*, each of which involved a volitional act directed to the plaintiff's copyrighted material. See 464 U.S., at 437, n. 18, 104 S.Ct. 774.

The volitional-conduct requirement is not at issue in most direct-infringement cases; the usual point of dispute is whether the defendant's conduct is infringing (*e.g.*, Does the defendant's design copy the plaintiff's?), rather than whether the defendant has acted at all (*e.g.*, Did this defendant create the infringing design?). But it comes right to the fore when a direct-infringement claim is lodged against a defendant who does nothing more than operate an automated, user-controlled system. . . . The provider's system is "totally indifferent to the material's content," whereas courts require "some aspect of volition" directed at the copyrighted material before direct liability may be imposed. *CoStar,* 373 F.3d, at 550–551.[2] The defendant may be held directly liable only if the defendant *itself* "trespassed on the exclusive domain of the copyright owner." *Id.,* at 550. Most of the time that issue will come down to who selects the copyrighted content: the defendant or its customers. See *Cartoon Network, supra,* at 131–132.

A comparison between copy shops and video-on-demand services illustrates the point. A copy shop rents out photocopiers on a per-use basis. One customer might copy his 10-year-old's drawings—a perfectly lawful thing to do—while another might duplicate a famous artist's copyrighted photographs—a use clearly prohibited by § 106(1). Either way, *the customer* chooses the content and activates the copying function; the photocopier does nothing except in response to the customer's commands. Because the shop plays no role in selecting the content, it cannot be held directly liable when a customer makes an infringing copy. See *CoStar, supra,* at 550.

Video-on-demand services, like photocopiers, respond automatically to user input, but they differ in one crucial respect: *They choose the content.* . . .

The distinction between direct and secondary liability would collapse if there were not a clear rule for determining whether *the defendant* committed the infringing act. See *Cartoon Network,* 536 F.3d, at 132–133. The volitional-conduct requirement supplies that rule; its purpose is not to excuse defendants from accountability, but to channel the claims against them into the correct analytical track. See Brief for 36 Intellectual Property and Copyright Law Professors as *Amici Curiae* 7. Thus, in the example given above, the fact that the copy shop does not choose the content simply means that its culpability will be assessed using secondary-liability rules rather than direct-liability rules. See *Sony, supra,* at 434–442, 104 S.Ct. 774; *Cartoon Network, supra,* at 132–133.

II. Application to Aereo

So which is Aereo: the copy shop or the video-on-demand service? In truth, it is neither. Rather, it is akin to a copy shop that provides its patrons with a library card. Aereo offers access to an automated system consisting of routers, servers, transcoders, and dime-sized antennae. Like a photocopier or VCR, that system lies dormant until a subscriber activates it. When a subscriber selects a program, Aereo's system picks up the relevant broadcast signal, translates its audio and video components into digital data, stores the data in a user-specific file, and transmits that file's contents to the subscriber via the Internet—at which point the subscriber's

---

[2] Congress has enacted several safe-harbor provisions applicable to automated network processes, see, e.g., 17 U.S.C. § 512(a)–(b), but those provisions do not foreclose "any other defense," § 512(*l*), including a volitional-conduct defense.

laptop, tablet, or other device displays the broadcast just as an ordinary television would. The result of that process fits the statutory definition of a performance to a tee: The subscriber's device "show[s]" the broadcast's "images" and "make[s] the sounds accompanying" the broadcast "audible." § 101. The only question is whether those performances are the product of Aereo's volitional conduct.

They are not. Unlike video-on-demand services, Aereo does not provide a prearranged assortment of movies and television shows. Rather, it assigns each subscriber an antenna that—like a library card—can be used to obtain whatever broadcasts are freely available. Some of those broadcasts are copyrighted; others are in the public domain. The key point is that subscribers call all the shots: Aereo's automated system does not relay any program, copyrighted or not, until a subscriber selects the program and tells Aereo to relay it. Aereo's operation of that system is a volitional act and a but-for cause of the resulting performances, but, as in the case of the copy shop, that degree of involvement is not enough for direct liability. See *Grokster,* 545 U.S., at 960, 125 S.Ct. 2764 (BREYER, J., concurring) ("[T]he producer of a technology which *permits* unlawful copying does not himself *engage* in unlawful copying").

In sum, Aereo does not "perform" for the sole and simple reason that it does not make the choice of content. And because Aereo does not perform, it cannot be held directly liable for infringing the Networks' public-performance right.[3] That conclusion does not necessarily mean that Aereo's service complies with the Copyright Act. Quite the contrary. The Networks' complaint alleges that Aereo is directly *and* secondarily liable for infringing their public-performance rights (§ 106(4)) *and also* their reproduction rights (§ 106(1)). Their request for a preliminary injunction— the only issue before this Court—is based exclusively on the direct-liability portion of the public-performance claim (and further limited to Aereo's "watch" function, as opposed to its "record" function). See App. to Pet. for Cert. 60a–61a. Affirming the judgment below would merely return this case to the lower courts for consideration of the Networks' remaining claims.

III. Guilt By Resemblance

The Court's conclusion that Aereo performs boils down to the following syllogism: (1) Congress amended the Act to overrule our decisions holding that cable systems do not perform when they retransmit over-the-air

---

[3]   Because I conclude that Aereo does not perform at all, I do not reach the question whether the performances in this case are to the public. See ante, at 2507–2511.

broadcasts;[4] (2) Aereo looks a lot like a cable system; therefore (3) Aereo performs. *Ante,* at 2504–2507. That reasoning suffers from a trio of defects.

[¶] . . . [T]here are material differences between the cable systems at issue in *Teleprompter Corp. v. Columbia Broadcasting System, Inc.,* 415 U.S. 394, 94 S.Ct. 1129, 39 L.Ed.2d 415 (1974), and *Fortnightly Corp. v. United Artists Television, Inc.,* 392 U.S. 390, 88 S.Ct. 2084, 20 L.Ed.2d 1176 (1968), on the one hand and Aereo on the other. The former [CATVs] captured the full range of broadcast signals and forwarded them to all subscribers at all times, whereas Aereo transmits only specific programs selected by the user, at specific times selected by the user. . . .

. . . [M]ost importantly, even accepting that the 1976 amendments had as their purpose the overruling of our cable-TV cases, what they were meant to do and how they did it are two different questions—and it is the latter that governs the case before us here. The injury claimed is not violation of a law that says operations similar to cable TV are subject to copyright liability, but violation of § 106(4) of the Copyright Act. And whatever soothing reasoning the Court uses to reach its result ("this looks like cable TV"), the consequence of its holding is that someone who implements this technology *"perform[s]" under that provision.* That greatly disrupts settled jurisprudence which, before today, applied the straightforward, bright-line test of volitional conduct directed at the copyrighted work. If that test is not outcome determinative in this case, presumably it is not outcome determinative elsewhere as well. And it is not clear what the Court proposes to replace it. Perhaps the Court means to adopt (invent, really) a two-tier version of the Copyright Act, one part of which applies to "cable companies and their equivalents" while the other governs everyone else. *Ante,* at 2506–2507, 2510.

[¶] . . . Making matters worse, the Court provides no criteria for determining when its cable-TV-lookalike rule applies. Must a defendant offer access to live television to qualify? If similarity to cable-television service is the measure, then the answer must be yes. But consider the implications of that answer: Aereo would be free to do exactly what it is doing right now so long as it built mandatory time shifting into its "watch" function.[6] Aereo would not be providing *live* television if it made subscribers wait to tune in until after a show's live broadcast ended. A subscriber could watch the 7 p.m. airing of a 1-hour program any time after 8 p.m. Assuming the Court does not intend to adopt such a do-nothing rule

---

4   See *Teleprompter Corp. v. Columbia Broadcasting System, Inc.,* 415 U.S. 394, 94 S.Ct. 1129, 39 L.Ed.2d 415 (1974); *Fortnightly Corp. v. United Artists Television, Inc.,* 392 U.S. 390, 88 S.Ct. 2084, 20 L.Ed.2d 1176 (1968).

6   Broadcasts accessible through the "watch" function are technically not live because Aereo's servers take anywhere from a few seconds to a few minutes to begin transmitting data to a subscriber's device. But the resulting delay is so brief that it cannot reasonably be classified as time shifting.

(though it very well may), there must be some other means of identifying who is and is not subject to its guilt-by-resemblance regime.

Two other criteria come to mind. One would cover any automated service that captures and stores live television broadcasts at a user's direction. That can't be right, since it is exactly what remote storage digital video recorders (RS-DVRs) do, see *Cartoon Network*, 536 F.3d, at 124–125, and the Court insists that its "limited holding" does not decide the fate of those devices, *ante*, at 2510–2511. The other potential benchmark is the one offered by the Government: The cable-TV-lookalike rule embraces any entity that "operates an integrated system, substantially dependent on physical equipment that is used in common by [its] subscribers." Brief for United States as *Amicus Curiae* 20. The Court sensibly avoids that approach because it would sweep in Internet service providers and a host of other entities that quite obviously do not perform.

That leaves as the criterion of cable-TV-resemblance nothing but th'ol' totality-of-the-circumstances test (which is not a test at all but merely assertion of an intent to perform test-free, ad hoc, case-by-case evaluation). It will take years, perhaps decades, to determine which automated systems now in existence are governed by the traditional volitional-conduct test and which get the Aereo treatment. (And automated systems now in contemplation will have to take their chances.) . . . [¶¶]

I share the Court's evident feeling that what Aereo is doing (or enabling to be done) to the Networks' copyrighted programming ought not to be allowed. But perhaps we need not distort the Copyright Act to forbid it. As discussed at the outset, Aereo's secondary liability for performance infringement is yet to be determined, as is its primary and secondary liability for reproduction infringement. If that does not suffice, then (assuming one shares the majority's estimation of right and wrong) what we have before us must be considered a "loophole" in the law. It is not the role of this Court to identify and plug loopholes. It is the role of good lawyers to identify and exploit them, and the role of Congress to eliminate them if it wishes. Congress can do that, I may add, in a much more targeted, better informed, and less disruptive fashion than the crude "looks-like-cable-TV" solution the Court invents today.

[¶¶] . . . I respectfully dissent.

CAPITOL RECORDS, LLC V. REDIGI INC.
910 F.3d 649 (2d Cir. 2018)[5]

Decided: December 12, 2018

LEVAL, CIRCUIT JUDGE:

Defendant ReDigi, Inc. and its founders, Defendants Larry Rudolph and John Ossenmacher, appeal from the judgment of the United States District Court for the Southern District of New York (Richard J. Sullivan, J.) in favor of Plaintiffs, Capitol Records, LLC, Capitol Christian Music Group, Inc., and Virgin Records IR Holdings, Inc. ("Plaintiffs"), finding copyright infringement. Defendants had created an Internet platform designed to enable the lawful resale, under the first sale doctrine, of lawfully purchased digital music files, and had hosted resales of such files on the platform. The district court concluded that, notwithstanding the "first sale" doctrine, codified in the Copyright Act of 1976, 17 U.S.C. § 109(a), ReDigi's Internet system version 1.0 infringed the Plaintiffs' copyrights by enabling the resale of such digital files containing sound recordings of Plaintiffs' copyrighted music. We agree with the district court that ReDigi infringed the Plaintiffs' exclusive rights under 17 U.S.C. § 106(1) to reproduce their copyrighted works. We make no decision whether ReDigi also infringed the Plaintiffs' exclusive rights under 17 U.S.C. § 106(3) to distribute their works.

BACKGROUND

I. Facts

Plaintiffs are record companies, which own copyrights or licenses in sound recordings of musical performances. Plaintiffs distribute those sound recordings in numerous forms, of which the most familiar twenty years ago was the compact disc. Today, Plaintiffs also distribute their music in the form of digital files, which are sold to the public by authorized agent services, such as Apple iTunes, under license from Plaintiffs. Purchasers from the Apple iTunes online store download the files onto their personal computers or other devices.

ReDigi was founded by Defendants Ossenmacher and Rudolph in 2009 with the goal of creating enabling technology and providing a marketplace

---

5   Footnotes are omitted except where indicated.

for the lawful resale of lawfully purchased digital music files.[3] Ossenmacher served as ReDigi's Chief Executive Officer and Rudolph, who spent twelve years as a Principal Research Scientist at the Massachusetts Institute of Technology, served as ReDigi's Chief Technical Officer. During the period addressed by the operative complaint, ReDigi, through its system version 1.0, hosted resales of digital music files containing the Plaintiffs' music by persons who had lawfully purchased the files from iTunes.

Considering the evidence in the light most favorable to ReDigi, ReDigi's system version 1.0 operates as follows.

1.   *Music Manager:* A person who owns a digital music file lawfully purchased from iTunes and intends to employ ReDigi's system to resell it (the "user") must first download and install onto her computer ReDigi's "Music Manager" software program ("Music Manager"). Once Music Manager has been installed, it analyzes the digital file intended for resale, verifies that the file was originally lawfully purchased from iTunes, and scans it for indications of tampering. If the file was lawfully purchased, Music Manager deems it an "Eligible File" that may be resold.

2.   *Data Migration:* The ReDigi user must then cause the file to be transferred to ReDigi's remote server, known as the "Cloud Locker." To effectuate this transfer, ReDigi developed a new method that functions differently from the conventional file transfer. The conventional process is to reproduce the digital file at the receiving destination so that, upon completion of the transfer, the file exists simultaneously on both the receiving device and on the device from which it was transferred. If connectivity is disrupted during such a standard transfer, the process can be repeated because the file remains intact on the sender's device.

Under ReDigi's method—which it calls "data migration"—ReDigi's software "begins by breaking the [digital] music file into small 'blocks' [of data] of roughly four thousand bytes in length." Appellants Br. 24. Once the file has been broken into blocks of data ("packets"), ReDigi's system creates a "transitory copy" of each packet in the initial purchaser's computer buffer. *Id.* Upon copying (or "reading") a packet into the initial purchaser's computer buffer, ReDigi's software sends a command to delete that packet of the digital file from permanent storage on the initial purchaser's device. Rogel Decl. App'x 690–91. ReDigi's software then sends the packet to the ReDigi software to be copied into the buffer and deleted from the user's device. Rogel Decl. App'x 691. During the data migration process, the digital file cannot be accessed, played, or perceived. If connectivity is disrupted during the data migration process, the remnants

---

3   ReDigi was not making efforts in the shadows to infringe on copyrights. To the contrary, it invented a system designed in good faith to achieve a goal generally favored by the law of copyright, reasonably hoping the system would secure court approval as conforming to the demands of the Copyright Act.

of the digital file on the user's device are unusable, and the transfer cannot be re-initiated. In such circumstances, ReDigi (according to its brief) bears the cost of the user's loss. Appellants Br. 25.

Once all the packets of the source file have been transferred to ReDigi's server, the Eligible File has been entirely removed from the user's device. The packets are then re-assembled into a complete, accessible, and playable file on ReDigi's server.

ReDigi describes its primary technological innovation using the metaphor of a train (the digital file) leaving from one station (the original purchaser's device) and arriving at its destination (in the first instance, ReDigi's server). . . . In other words, as each packet "leaves the station," ReDigi deletes it from the original purchaser's device such that it "no longer exists" on that device. *Id.* As a result, the entire file never exists in two places at once. *Id.*

After the file has reached ReDigi's server but before it has been resold, the user may continue to listen to it by streaming audio from the user's Cloud Locker on ReDigi's server. If the user later re-downloads the file from her Cloud Locker to her computer, ReDigi will delete the file from its own server.

3.   Resale: Once an Eligible File has "migrated" to ReDigi's server, it can be resold by the user utilizing ReDigi's market function. If it is resold, ReDigi gives the new purchaser exclusive access to the file. ReDigi will (at the new purchaser's option) either download the file to the new purchaser's computer or other device (simultaneously deleting the file from its own server) or will retain the file in the new purchaser's Cloud Locker on ReDigi's server, from which the new purchaser can stream the music. ReDigi's terms of service state that digital media purchases may be streamed or downloaded only for personal use.

4.   Duplicates: ReDigi purports to guard against a user's retention of duplicates of her digital music files after she sells the files through ReDigi. To that end, Music Manager continuously monitors the user's computer hard drive and connected devices to detect duplicates. When a user attempts to upload an Eligible File to ReDigi's server, ReDigi "prompt[s]" her to delete any pre-existing duplicates that Music Manager has detected. If ReDigi detects that the user has not deleted the duplicates, ReDigi blocks the upload of the Eligible File. After an upload is complete, Music Manager continues to search the user's connected devices for duplicates. If it detects a duplicate of a previously uploaded Eligible File, ReDigi will prompt the user to authorize ReDigi to delete that duplicate from her personal device and, if authorization is not granted, it will suspend her account.

Plaintiffs point out, and ReDigi does not dispute, that these precautions do not *prevent* the retention of duplicates after resale through ReDigi. Suspension of the original purchaser's ReDigi account does not negate the fact that the original purchaser has both sold and retained the digital music file after she sold it. So long as the user retains previously-made duplicates on devices not linked to the computer that hosts Music Manager, Music Manager will not detect them. This means that a user could, prior to resale through ReDigi, store a duplicate on a compact disc, thumb drive, or third-party cloud service unconnected to the computer that hosts Music Manager and access that duplicate post-resale. While ReDigi's suspension of the original purchaser's ReDigi account may be a disincentive to the retention of sold files, it does not prevent the user from retaining sold files.

II. Proceedings Below

. . . . On June 6, 2016, the district court entered a stipulated final judgment awarding damages to Plaintiffs in the amount of three million five hundred thousand dollars ($3,500,000) and permanently enjoining Defendants from operating the ReDigi system. In the stipulation, Defendants reserved the right to appeal solely from the district court's finding of liability for reproduction and distribution as set forth in the summary judgment order. Defendants timely filed notice of this appeal on July 1, 2016. . . .

DISCUSSION

I.   The First Sale Doctrine

The primary issue on appeal is whether ReDigi's system version 1.0 lawfully enables resales of its users' digital files. Sections 106(1) and (3) of the Copyright Act respectively grant the owner of a copyright the exclusive right to control the reproduction and the distribution of the copyrighted work. 17 U.S.C. § 106(1) & (3). Under the first sale doctrine, codified in § 109(a), the rights holder's control *over the distribution* of any particular copy or phonorecord that was lawfully made effectively terminates when that copy or phonorecord is distributed to its first recipient. Section 109(a) provides:

> "Notwithstanding the provisions of section 106(3), the owner of a particular copy or phonorecord lawfully made under this title, or any person authorized by such owner, is entitled, without the authority of the copyright owner, to sell or otherwise dispose of the possession of that copy or phonorecord."

17 U.S.C. § 109(a).

Under this provision, it is well established that the lawful purchaser of a copy of a book is free to resell, lend, give, or otherwise transfer that copy without violating the copyright holder's exclusive right of distribution. The copy so resold or re-transferred may be re-transferred again and again without violating the exclusive distribution right. *See Kirtsaeng v. John Wiley & Sons, Inc.*, 568 U.S. 519, 530, 133 S.Ct. 1351, 185 L.Ed.2d 392

(2013); *Quality King Distribs. v. L'Anza Research Int'l, Inc.*, 523 U.S. 135, 152, 118 S.Ct. 1125, 140 L.Ed.2d 254 (1998); *Bobbs-Merrill Co. v. Straus*, 210 U.S. 339, 351, 28 S.Ct. 722, 52 L.Ed. 1086 (1908); *see also* 4 Patry on Copyright § 13:15 ("Placing a lawful copy of a work in commerce exhausts the distribution and display rights with respect to that particular copy . . . ."). It is undisputed that one who owns a digital file from iTunes of music that is fixed in a material object qualifies as "the owner of a particular . . . phonorecord lawfully made," 17 U.S.C. § 109(a), and is thus entitled under § 109(a) "to sell or otherwise dispose of the possession of *that* . . . phonorecord," *id.* (emphasis added), without violating § 106(3). On the other hand, § 109(a) says nothing about the rights holder's control under § 106(1) over *reproduction* of a copy or phonorecord.

The district court found that resales through ReDigi were infringing for two reasons. The first reason was that, in the course of ReDigi's transfer, the phonorecord has been reproduced in a manner that violates the Plaintiffs' exclusive control of *reproduction* under § 106(1); the second was that the digital files sold through ReDigi, being unlawful reproductions, are not subject to the resale right established by § 109(a), which applies solely to a "particular . . . phonorecord . . . lawfully made." 17 U.S.C. § 109(a). We agree with the first reason underlying the district court's finding of infringement. As that is a sufficient reason for affirmance of the judgment, we make no ruling on the district court's second reason.

ReDigi argues on appeal that its system effectuates transfer of the *particular* digital file that the user lawfully purchased from iTunes, that it should not be deemed to have reproduced that file, and that it should therefore come within the protection of 17 U.S.C. § 109(a). ReDigi makes two primary contentions in support of these arguments.

First, ReDigi asserts—as it must for its first sale argument to succeed—that the digital files should be considered "material objects" and therefore, under 17 U.S.C. § 101's definition of "phonorecords" as "material objects," should qualify as "phonorecords" eligible for the protection of § 109(a).

Second, ReDigi argues that from a technical standpoint, its process should not be seen as making a reproduction. ReDigi emphasizes that its system simultaneously "causes [packets] to be removed from the . . . file remaining in the consumer's computer" as those packets are copied into the computer buffer and then transferred to the ReDigi server, Appellants Br. 24, so that the complete file never exists in more than one place at the same time, and the "file on the user's machine continually shrinks in size while the file on the server grows in size." App'x 691. ReDigi points out that the "sum of the size of the data" stored in the original purchaser's computer and in ReDigi's server never exceeds the "size of the original file," which, according to ReDigi, "confirms that no reproductions are made during the transfer process." Appellants Br. 25.

As for ReDigi's first argument, that the digital file it transfers is a phonorecord protected by § 109(a), we do not decide this issue because we find that ReDigi effectuates an unlawful reproduction even if the digital file itself qualifies as a phonorecord.[10]

As for ReDigi's second argument, we reject it for the following reasons. The Copyright Act defines phonorecords as "material objects in which sounds . . . are fixed by any method now known or later developed, and from which the sounds can be perceived, reproduced, or otherwise communicated, either directly or with the aid of a machine or device." 17 U.S.C. § 101. Accordingly, when the purchaser of a digital music file from iTunes possesses that file, embodied "for a period of more than transitory duration" in a computer or other physical storage device, *Cartoon Network LP v. CSC Holdings, Inc.*, 536 F.3d 121, 127 (2d Cir. 2008) (quoting 17 U.S.C. § 101), that device—or at least the portion of it in which the digital music file is fixed (*e.g.*, the location on the hard drive)—becomes a phonorecord. *See London-Sire Records, Inc. v. Doe*, 542 F.Supp.2d 153, 171 (D. Mass. 2008) (holding that the segment of a hard disc on which an electronic music file is encoded is a "phonorecord" under the Copyright Act). In the course of transferring a digital music file from an original purchaser's computer, through ReDigi, to a new purchaser, the digital file is first received and stored on ReDigi's server and then, at the new purchaser's option, may also be subsequently received and stored on the new purchaser's device. At each of these steps, the digital file is fixed in a new material object "for a period of more than transitory duration." *Cartoon Network*, 536 F.3d at 127. The fixing of the digital file in ReDigi's server, as well as in the new purchaser's device, creates a new phonorecord, which is a reproduction. ReDigi version 1.0's process for enabling the resale of digital files thus inevitably involves the creation of new phonorecords by reproduction, even if the standalone digital file is deemed to be a phonorecord.

As for the argument that, as ReDigi copies a packet of data, it deletes the equivalent packet in the user's device so that the amount of data extant in the transfer process remains constant, this does not rebut or nullify the fact that the eventual receipt and storage of that file in ReDigi's server, as well as in the new purchaser's device (at his option), does involve the making of new phonorecords. Unless the creation of those new phonorecords is justified by the doctrine of fair use, which we discuss and reject in a later portion of this opinion, the creation of such new

---

[10]   A conclusion that a digital file cannot be a phonorecord would have decisive implications for a system functioning like ReDigi's version 2.0, as well as its version 1.0. Because our understanding of the technology is limited, as is our ability to appreciate the economic implications, we find it preferable to rule more narrowly.

phonorecords involves unauthorized reproduction, which is not protected, or even addressed, by § 109(a).

[¶¶] . . . . ReDigi further argues, citing *ABKCO Music, Inc. v. Stellar Records, Inc.*, 96 F.3d 60 (2d Cir. 1996),[6] that the computer hard drive into which the original purchaser's digital file is embedded cannot be her lawfully made phonorecord. A computer hard drive, ReDigi argues, cannot qualify as a phonorecord under § 101 because it contains more than a sound recording. This argument misinterprets *ABKCO*. We held in *ABKCO* that a license to publish a phonorecord did not authorize the publication of compact discs for use in karaoke that contained both sound recordings and visual depictions of song lyrics. 96 F.3d at 64. The *ABKCO* opinion undertook to construe the breadth of a compulsory license. The opinion does not support the conclusion that a compact disc that stores visual depictions of words as well as recorded music does not *contain* a phonorecord. To be sure, a license to distribute phonorecords of a particular song would not by its terms authorize the distribution of whatever other copyrighted content is contained in a computer hard drive that also contains the recording of the song. But it does not follow that a device or other "material object[ ] in which sounds . . . are fixed . . . and from which the sounds can be perceived, reproduced, or otherwise communicated," 17 U.S.C. § 101, is not a phonorecord, merely because it contains other matter as well. We reject ReDigi's argument.[13]

Finally, ReDigi argues that the district court's conclusion makes no sense because it would "require a customer to sell her [valuable] computer in order to be able to sell a[n] . . . iTunes music file" that was lawfully purchased for under $1.00. Appellants Br. 28. Of course it would make no economic sense for a customer to sell her computer or even a $5.00 thumb drive in order to sell "a[n] . . . iTunes music file" purchased for $1.00. But ReDigi far overstates its economic argument when it asserts that the "district court's ruling . . . eliminat[es] any meaningful competition from resellers" as "no secondary market . . . can ever develop if consumers are required to give away their computer hard disks as part of any resale." Appellants Br. 35. A secondary market can readily be imagined for first purchasers who cost-effectively place 50 or 100 (or more) songs on an inexpensive device such as a thumb drive and sell it. *See* U.S. Copyright Office, Library of Cong., Digital Millennium Copyright Act § 104 Report 78

---

6   [Ed. Note: The *ABKCO Music v. Stellar Records* case is addressed in Chapter 7, *infra*.]

13   ReDigi also draws our attention to the Ninth Circuit's decision in *Recording Industry Association of America v. Diamond Multimedia Systems, Inc.*, 180 F.3d 1072 (9th Cir. 1999). In *Diamond*, the Ninth Circuit held that "a hard drive is excluded from the definition of digital music recordings" under the Audio Home Recording Act ("AHRA") because § 1001(5)(B) expressly provides that a "digital music recording" does *not* include material objects "in which one or more computer programs are fixed," and "a hard drive is a material object in which one or more [computer] programs are fixed." *Id.* at 1076. Even if we were to accept the Ninth Circuit's construction of the term "digital music recording" under the AHRA, that would not alter the meaning of the term "phonorecord" under § 101 of the Copyright Act. *See id.* at 1077 n.4.

(2001) ("DMCA Report 2001") ("Physical copies of works in a digital format, such as CDs or DVDs, are subject to section 109 in the same way as physical copies of works in analog form."); 4 Patry on Copyright § 13:23 (observing that § 109 permits the sale of an iPod that contains lawfully made digital music files). Furthermore, other technology may exist or be developed that could lawfully effectuate a digital first sale.

We conclude that the operation of ReDigi version 1.0 in effectuating a resale results in the making of at least one unauthorized reproduction. Unauthorized reproduction is not protected by § 109(a). It violates the rights holder's exclusive reproduction rights under § 106(1) unless excused as fair use. For reasons explained below, we conclude that the making of such reproductions is not a fair use.

[¶¶] . . . . II. Fair Use

ReDigi argues that, regardless of whether what it does is protected by § 109(a), its actions are protected under the doctrine of fair use. We evaluate ReDigi's claim in accordance with the fair use statute. . . . 17 U.S.C. § 107.

ReDigi's argument for fair use in its opening brief did not address the statutory factors. Nonetheless, we consider each in turn.

A. Factor One

Factor One considers "the purpose and character of the use, including whether such use is of a commercial nature or is for nonprofit educational purposes." § 107(1). The Supreme Court has observed that this factor favors secondary uses that are transformative, meaning that the use "adds something new, with a further purpose or different character, altering the first with new expression, meaning, or message[,]" rather than merely superseding the original work. *Campbell v. Acuff-Rose Music, Inc.*, 510 U.S. 569, 579, 114 S.Ct. 1164, 127 L.Ed.2d 500 (1994). Uses that criticize, comment on, provide information about, or provide new uses for the copyrighted work are those likely to be deemed transformative. *See, e.g., Campbell*, 510 U.S. at 580–81, 114 S.Ct. 1164 ("Parody needs to mimic an original to make its point, and so has some claim to use the creation of its victim's . . . imagination, whereas satire can stand on its own two feet and so requires justification for the very act of borrowing.") (internal citations and footnote omitted). Similarly, a secondary use may be transformative if it provides information about the original, "or expands its utility." *Authors Guild v. Google, Inc.*, 804 F.3d 202, 214 (2d Cir. 2015) ("Google Books"). . . . . In *Sony*, the "apparent reasoning was that a secondary use may be a fair use if it utilizes technology to achieve the transformative purpose of improving the efficiency of delivering content without unreasonably encroaching on the commercial entitlements of the rights holder" because the improved delivery was to one entitled to receive the content. *Fox News Network, LLC v. TVEyes, Inc.*, 883 F.3d 169, 177 (2d Cir. 2018).

ReDigi makes no change in the copyrighted work. It provides neither criticism, commentary, nor information about it. Nor does it deliver the content in more convenient and usable form to one who has acquired an entitlement to receive the content. What ReDigi does is essentially to provide a market for the resale of digital music files, which resales compete with sales of the same recorded music by the rights holder. These characteristics of ReDigi's use favor Plaintiffs under Factor One.

In addition, while the mere fact of a commercial motivation rarely pushes the first factor determination against fair use (as so many of the canonical fair uses, such as book reviews; quotation of prominent figures in news reports, news commentary, and history books; the performance of parodic plays; and the sale of parodic books, are all commercial, *see Google Books*, 804 F.3d at 219), in some circumstances a commercial motive will weigh against a finding of fair use under Factor One. As noted in *Campbell*, the less a use provides transformative value, the more its commercialism will weigh against a finding of fair use. *See* 510 U.S. at 579, 114 S.Ct. 1164. Here, ReDigi hosts a remunerative marketplace that enables resale by purchasers of digital music files, which is a commercial purpose. Especially in view of the total absence (or at least very low degree) of transformative purpose, the commercial motivation here argues against ReDigi with respect to Factor One.

B.   Factor Two

The second fair use factor concerns "the nature of the copyrighted work." 17 U.S.C. § 107(2). Except to the extent that the nature of the copyrighted work is necessarily considered alongside the character and purpose of the secondary use in deciding whether the secondary use has a transformative purpose, it rarely, by itself, furnishes any substantial reasoning for favoring or disfavoring fair use. *See Google Books*, 804 F.3d at 220. This case is no exception.

C.   Factor Three

The third factor considers "the amount and substantiality of the portion [of the original] used in relation to the copyrighted work as a whole." 17 U.S.C. § 107(3). ReDigi's system makes identical copies of the whole of Plaintiffs' copyrighted sound recordings. Although use of the entirety of a digital file is not necessarily inconsistent with a finding of fair use, *see Google Books*, 804 F.3d at 221–22; *HathiTrust*, 755 F.3d at 98; *iParadigms*, 562 F.3d at 642; *Perfect 10*, 508 F.3d at 1165; *Arriba Soft*, 336 F.3d at 818–19, it tends to disfavor a finding of fair use.

D.   Factor Four

The fourth statutory factor is "the effect of the [copying] use upon the potential market for or value of the copyrighted work." § 107(4). When a secondary use competes in the rightsholder's market as an effective substitute for the original, it impedes the purpose of copyright to incentivize new creative works by enabling their creators to profit from them. For this reason, the Supreme Court in *Harper & Row Publishers, Inc. v. Nation Enterprises* described the fourth factor as "undoubtedly the single most important element of fair use." 471 U.S. 539, 566, 105 S.Ct. 2218, 85 L.Ed.2d 588 (1985) (relying on the Nimmer treatise). Factor Four "focuses on whether the copy brings to the marketplace a competing substitute for the original, or its derivative, so as to deprive the rights holder of significant revenues because of the likelihood that potential purchasers may opt to acquire the copy in preference to the original." *TVEyes*, 883 F.3d at 179 (quoting *Google Books*, 804 F.3d at 223). Factor Four is necessarily intertwined with Factor One; the more the objective of secondary use differs from that of the original, the less likely it will supplant the commercial market for the original. *See Google Books*, 804 F.3d at 223.

As Plaintiffs argue, ReDigi made reproductions of Plaintiffs' works for the purpose of resale in competition with the Plaintiffs' market for the sale of their sound recordings. ReDigi's replicas were sold to the same consumers whose objective in purchasing was to acquire Plaintiffs' music. It is also of possible relevance that there is a distinction between ReDigi's resales and resales of physical books and records. The digital files resold by ReDigi, although used, do not deteriorate the way printed books and physical records deteriorate. As the district court observed, the principal difference between the "product sold in ReDigi's secondary market" and that sold by Plaintiffs or their licensees in the primary market was its lower price. *Capitol Records, LLC v. ReDigi Inc.*, 934 F.Supp.2d 640, 654 (S.D.N.Y. 2013).

Factor Four weighs powerfully against fair use.

E.   *Four Factors Weighed Together*

The Supreme Court has instructed that, to ascertain whether there is fair use, all four of the statutory factors must be weighed together. *Campbell*, 510 U.S. at 577–78, 114 S.Ct. 1164. Our consideration is informed by our recent holding in *TVEyes*, 883 F.3d at 175. TVEyes copied all televised video programming throughout the nation, together with its accompanying closed-captioned text, into a database. It offered a commercial subscription service through which business and professional clients could search the transcripts, receive a list of video segments that mentioned the searched terms, and then view up to ten minutes of each video segment. *Id.* Fox News Network, a producer of televised content, sued, claiming that TVEyes's distribution of Fox's programming to TVEyes's subscribers infringed Fox's copyright. *Id.* We found that TVEyes's secondary use deployed modestly transformative technology (akin to the time shifting technology of *Sony*) in that "it enable[d] nearly instant access to a subset of material—and to information about the material—that would otherwise be irretrievable, or else retrievable only through prohibitively inconvenient or inefficient means." *Id.* at 177. As in *Sony*, it enabled its customers to view "programming they want at a time and place that is convenient to them, rather than at the time and place of broadcast." *Id.* at 177–78. Nonetheless, we held that TVEyes's use was not a fair use because it substantially competed with the rights holders' legitimate market. *Id.* at 180. By providing Fox's copyrighted programming to its clients "*without* payment to [the rights holder], TVEyes . . . usurped a market that properly belong[ed] to the copyright-holder." *Id.* (internal quotation marks and alteration omitted).

TVEyes is a substantial precedent for our holding here. The transformative purpose and character of TVEyes's use, while modest, was far more transformative than what ReDigi has shown here. TVEyes's transformative uses were nonetheless easily outweighed by the harm to the rights holders' market considered under Factor Four. *Id.* at 181. Even if ReDigi is credited with some faint showing of a transformative purpose, that purpose is overwhelmed by the substantial harm ReDigi inflicts on the value of Plaintiffs' copyrights through its direct competition in the rights holders' legitimate market, offering consumers a substitute for purchasing from the rights holders. We find no fair use justification.

* * * *

We conclude by addressing policy-based arguments raised by ReDigi and its amici. They contend that ReDigi's version 1.0 ought to be validated as in compliance with § 109(a) because it allows for realization of an economically beneficial practice, originally authorized by the courts in the common law development of copyright, *see Bobbs-Merrill Co. v. Straus*, 210 U.S. 339, 28 S.Ct. 722, 52 L.Ed. 1086 (1908), and later endorsed by Congress. They also contend that the Copyright Act must be read to vindicate purchasers' ability to alienate digital copyrighted works under the first sale doctrine—emphasizing that § 109(a) is styled as an entitlement rather than a defense to infringement—without regard to technological medium. *See* Copyright Law Professors Br. 4, 12, 14; *see also* Appellants Br. 38–41. On this score, they rely heavily on the breadth of the common law first sale doctrine, and on a purported imperative, described as the "principle of technological neutrality" by amici and the "equal treatment principle" by ReDigi, not to disadvantage purchasers of digital copyrighted works, as compared with purchasers of physical copyrighted works. *See* Copyright Law Professors Br. 14; Appellants Br. 36–42.

As for whether the economic consequences of ReDigi's program are beneficial and further the objectives of copyright, we take no position. Courts are poorly equipped to assess the inevitably multifarious economic consequences that would result from such changes of law. So far as we can see, the establishment of ReDigi's resale marketplace would benefit some, especially purchasers of digital music, at the expense of others, especially rightsholders, who, in the sale of their merchandise, would have to compete with resellers of the same merchandise in digital form, which, although second hand, would, unlike second hand books and records, be as good as new.

Furthermore, as to the argument that we should read § 109(a) to accommodate digital resales because the first sale doctrine protects a fundamental entitlement, without regard to the terms of § 109(a) (and incorporated definitions), we think such a ruling would exceed the proper exercise of the court's authority. The copyright statute is a patchwork, sometimes varying from clause to clause, as between provisions for which Congress has taken control, dictating both policy and the details of its execution, and provisions in which Congress approximatively summarized common law developments, implicitly leaving further such development to the courts. The paradigm of the latter category is § 107 on fair use. . . . In the provisions here relevant, Congress dictated the terms of the statutory entitlements. Notwithstanding the purported breadth of the first sale doctrine as originally articulated by the courts, *see Bobbs-Merrill Co.*, 210 U.S. at 350, 28 S.Ct. 722 . . .; *Bureau of Nat'l Literature v. Sells*, 211 F. 379, 381–82 (W.D. Wash. 1914) (finding no infringement, in light of first sale doctrine, where reseller re-bound used books and held them out as new books), Congress, in promulgating § 109(a), adopted a narrower conception, which negates a claim of unauthorized *distribution* in violation of the author's exclusive right under § 106(3), but not a claim of unauthorized *reproduction* in violation of the exclusive right provided by § 106(1). If ReDigi and its champions have persuasive arguments in support of the change of law they advocate, it is Congress they should persuade. We reject the invitation to substitute our judgment for that of Congress.

CONCLUSION

We have considered ReDigi's remaining arguments against the district court's ruling and find them to be without merit. The judgment of the district court is AFFIRMED.

NOTES AND QUESTIONS

1.   The District Court in *ReDigi* characterized the dispute as "a fundamental clash over culture, policy, and copyright law." What cultural, policy, and copyright law concerns do the *Aereo* and *ReDigi* cases raise in the context of emerging platforms for the music industry? What implications do these cases have on the ability of copyright owners to protect their works and on the possibilities for new platforms for discovering, exploiting, and promoting music to emerge? What impact might these cases have on consumers of music and the future options available to them for (legally) accessing music on multiple devices via the Internet?

2.   Based upon the description of how the Aereo system functions (or functioned, given the announcement of Aereo's bankruptcy filing not long after the Supreme Court opinion), do you find the reasoning of Justice Breyer or Justice Scalia more convincing regarding whether Aereo's transmission of broadcasts to its subscribers were "public performances" under the Copyright Act? Should "technical architecture" outweigh arguments based upon the purpose of the "transmit" clause of the Act? What are the potential implications of the ruling against Aereo for the music industry in terms of emerging platforms for music?

3.   Do you think that the Second Circuit's reasoning in *ReDigi* is consistent with the Supreme Court's reasoning in *Aereo*? Should similar analytical approaches govern the interpretation of the reproduction, distribution, and performance rights, or are the rights, purposes of Congress in protecting them, and language used in addressing them distinct enough that different interpretive approaches can/should be taken?

4.   How do you think courts (or Congress) should distinguish between direct and secondary liability in the context of infringement of musical works or sound recordings? Does it matter whether clear distinctions are drawn? Why do you suppose the plaintiffs in *Aereo* sought an injunction on the basis of direct infringement rather than focusing on secondary liability?

5.   Do you think the courts in *Lenz* and *ReDigi* properly weighed the fair use factors? Is fair use an effective defense for designers of new platforms? Why or why not? Can you think of alternative ways of evaluating whether the design of a new platform infringes on copyright or not? Should intent and effort to comply with the letter of the law matter?

6.   What do you think the best approach is for courts faced with applying statutory language to new uses of works that were not even remotely contemplated at the time the language was drafted? Given that copyright protection is purely a matter of statute, should the courts (as suggested by Justice Day in the 1908 Supreme Court White-Smith Music Publishing case) make it a matter of policy to refuse to extend protection to uses or transfers of works that do not readily fall into the existing statutory categories (i.e., reproduction, performance, etc.)? Why or why not? Should courts focus their

application of the statute's language more on the way that technology works behind the scenes or more on how it is used/experienced by the end-user?

7.   New platforms appear on a regular basis, aimed at giving consumers what they want in terms of access to music or providing an avenue for artists to offer exclusive content in exchange for higher royalties. What platforms do you favor, and why? Are there benefits to platforms that offer exclusive content? Are music platforms tied to other social media or online tools, such as Facebook and Amazon, more likely to be successful than stand-alone platforms? What advice do you have for record labels and artists seeing to capitalize on new platforms? Should the emphasis be more on promotion or on protection of copyrights? How can the law and the industry strike a balance between access to consumers and ensuring sufficient income from sales/licenses to promote the creation of musical works?

CHAPTER VI

INTRODUCTION TO MUSIC LICENSING AND STATUTORY LICENSES: *TICKET TO RIDE*[1]

■ ■ ■

This chapter provides an overview of statutory copyright licensing in one of the newest aspects of the music industry—Internet streaming services. The chapter concentrates especially on the first, early versions of Internet radio services providing "lean-back" programming with minimal user input. In Part A, we introduce the policies underlying, and arguments for and against, statutory licenses, and then focus specifically on the statutory license Congress created in 1995 for certain, non-interactive streaming services within section 114 of the Copyright Act. In addition, this section provides some of the details of the section 114 licensing provisions. In Part B, we provide an excerpt from one of the key, early cases addressing the features of services that qualify as "interactive" versus "non-interactive" for purposes of the statutory license. Finally, in Part C, we illustrate the complexities of the rate-setting process for the section 114 and 112 statutory licenses with a summary of the Copyright Royalty Board's 2016 "Web IV" determination of rates for webcasting services' use of the statutory license.

CONSIDER AS YOU READ . . .

- In what situations do you think imposition of a statutory (i.e., compulsory) licensing system is good policy? In what situations do you think it might not be good policy?

- Do you think that the section 114 statutory license is appropriately limited to "radio-like" streaming services, or should it be expanded to cover additional types of streaming activities? What are the pros and cons of expanding the scope of the statutory license?

---

[1] John Lennon & Paul McCartney (1965); released by the Beatles on HELP! (1965).

- What considerations do you think should be paramount in determining appropriate rates for statutory licenses? Is the "willing buyer/willing seller" standard in section 114 an effective guideline to use? Why or why not?

- Can you think of ways to simplify or streamline the statutory licensing provisions or rate-setting process?

A. INTRODUCTION TO STATUTORY LICENSING IN THE MUSIC INDUSTRY AND TO PERFORMANCE RIGHTS FOR STREAMING SOUND RECORDINGS

1. INTRODUCTION

Statutory licenses in the music industry have existed for over a century, dating back to 1909 with their first appearance in federal law as part of the major revision of the U.S. Copyright Law that year.[2] In the decades since that time, they have come to occupy an increasingly important part of the overall music industry. Developments in sound recording technology, manufacturing and distribution practices, and especially consumer usage habits have created a fertile ground for the creation and growth of statutory licenses. Indeed, such licenses can provide significant benefits to certain newer business models. Moreover, as legislation in the copyright arena increasingly becomes an exercise in negotiation among the various interest groups, statutory licenses offer a potential mechanism for compromising among the commercial interests in an effort to pass legislation.

There is no doubt that virtually all statutory licenses have both their supporters and detractors. For those whose intellectual property is mandatorily offered for licensing to any third party willing to meet the statutory conditions, it can be perceived as an unjustified incursion on their property rights that removes control over their product and provides below-market compensation. However, these content owners may nonetheless receive the financial benefits from an expanded industry that a statutory license enables, and they often receive other (sometimes unrelated) benefits as part of the "package" created by the relevant enacting legislation.

Conversely, those utilizing statutory licenses may view these licenses as extremely complex, sometimes-antiquated vehicles for gaining rights to particular intellectual property. However, these licenses provide them

---

[2]   Pub. L. No. 60–349, 35 Stat. 1075.

tremendous economies of scale, along with access to virtually all creative works ever published without the need to track down ownership and negotiate private licenses. These factors supply enormous commercial benefits to a variety of music licensees.

From a purely free-market perspective, statutory licensing is anathema to the concept of the invisible hand where arms-length negotiations theoretically result in maximum utility and maximum value. But such free-marketers must remember that intellectual property itself is a creation of government, pursuant to the directive of the U.S. Constitution that Congress shall "secure[ ] for limited Times to Authors and Inventors the exclusive Right to their respective Writings and Discoveries" to "promote the Progress of Science and useful Arts."[3] If statutory licenses serve the ultimate goal of promoting creative works, then they have a legitimate place in the order of the music industry under the primary foundations found in Article I.

Winston Churchill once described democracy as "the worst form of government, except for all others."[4] Perhaps statutory licenses could be viewed in a similar light, representing an imperfect method for comprehensive licensing that enables commerce in certain parts of the industry. They address some challenges in a necessarily imperfect market (is there really any such thing as a perfectly functioning market?), with fewer drawbacks than other available options. Despite their faults, statutory licenses serve an important purpose in an otherwise free-market regime.

Regardless of one's view, statutory licenses play an increasingly critical role in the music industry today. Consumers currently utilize music at more times and on more platforms than ever before. As technology ignites the modes for distribution and consumption, statutory licenses can help to render the engine of the modern music industry more efficient.

What Is a Statutory License?

In order to utilize another's intellectual property,[5] one must obtain permission, which is generally granted through a "license." In the music industry, that license is typically obtained in one of two ways: either (i) directly from the rights owner via a private contract, or (ii) indirectly from the federal government via a process codified in U.S. law that grants

---

[3]   U.S. Const, Art. I, Sec. 8.

[4]   444 Parl. Deb., H.C. (5th ser.) (1947) 206–207.

[5]   Naturally, the need to obtain permission from the owner applies only when all relevant rights are still fully vested with the owner and no legal exception applies. One need not get permission to utilize another entity's intellectual property when (i) it has fallen into the public domain, (ii) the rights have been curtailed from a legal perspective (e.g., abandonment, etc.), or (iii) some legal exception applies (e.g., fair use).

specific rights to those who meet the statutory requirements. It is the latter option that we refer to as a "statutory license."

When licensing via **_private contract_**, the potential user must locate the appropriate owner of the relevant rights (e.g., musical work, sound recording, etc.) in the relevant territory. This may be the original owner as filed with the Copyright Office, or it may be a licensee whom the owner has vested with authority to negotiate licenses. For instance, it is not unusual in today's industry for a sound recording owner (*i.e.*, a "master use owner") to outsource all digital licensing to a "digital licensing aggregator" (such as the Orchard, CDBaby, InGrooves or ReverbNation). Or a label or publisher might sub-license all rights for certain repertoires to a specific label or publisher in a particular foreign territory.

Once the proper licensing entity is determined, a licensee will approach that "owner" and negotiate the terms for use. These terms will cover a huge variety of issues[6] and are extremely flexible. For instance, modern licensing for a sound recording or musical work can apply to everything from usage of the sound recording/song on a compact disc, to an online streaming or download service, to a movie or television synchronization license, to a video game, to a greeting card, children's toys, musical toothbrushes, and beyond. The bounds of these negotiations are generally limited only by legal requirements that are not specific to music (e.g., antitrust, unfair trade practices, consumer protection) and—most importantly—rights owners have the ability to say "no" if they cannot negotiate satisfactory terms.

In contrast, a **_statutory license_** grants authority to a licensee *not* from the private rights owner, but rather from the federal government. It is a limitation on the property rights that Congress has otherwise provided for the intellectual product. Or, stated differently, it is a segment of the "bundle of rights" provided under the law that carries special conditions. The actual property "right" still resides with the private party, but federal law dictates the specific conditions and the price[7] under which the private party *must* offer the intellectual property. There is no ability to withhold the content; if a licensee is eligible and meets all conditions of the statutory license, it is entitled to use the property as a matter of law in the manner contemplated by the statutory license. It is for this reason that a statutory license is sometimes called a "compulsory license" (especially by the rights

---

[6]   The types of commercial terms that might be addressed in a modern sound recording license are extensive, and can include things such as: penny-rates, revenue shares, per-user minima, duration, promotional requirements, file type (e.g. AAP or mp3), digital rights management, bit-rate, reporting fields & format, publicity rights, limitation on bundling, advertising placements, etc.

[7]   The U.S. Code and accompanying regulations generally do not set the actual license rate that must be paid under the statutory license. Rather, they set up a process whereby rates and terms are set for specific time periods, and periodically adjusted at regular intervals. Many of the rates and terms in the music industry are currently determined by a three-judge panel called the Copyright Royalty Board, housed with the U.S. Library of Congress. *See* 17 U.S.C. § 801(a) & (b)(1).

owner who is being compelled to license its work). And unlike the flexibility that exists in private negotiations, a statutory license is extremely rigid. Statutory licenses are typically created for a very specific purpose and have very specific conditions that must be honored fully in order to receive protection under the license.

The real-world application of statutory licenses tends to be rather complex and requires some expertise to master. Statutory licenses are often implemented, or "administered," by organizations designed for this specific task (*e.g.*, SoundExchange for Section 114, the Mechanical Licensing Collective for Section 115, AARC for the Audio Home Recording Act, etc.). The complexity of these statutory regimes creates many benefits and challenges to parties on both sides of each license. We list below some of the pros and cons of statutory licenses as viewed from varying perspectives:

LICENSEE'S PERSPECTIVE—BENEFITS OF STATUTORY LICENSE

- Obviates the need to obtain individual licenses from thousands (or more) of rights owners, thereby significantly lowering transaction costs

- Permits creation of new products & services (including new business models) without the need to obtain direct licenses from the rights owners, avoiding negotiation and price uncertainty

- Likely results in lower rates than would occur in the free marketplace, at least for some works[8]

- Creates definite (if not always clear) rules around use that can be standardized across the industry

- Often administered through a single entity (e.g., SoundExchange, the Mechanical Licensing Collective, etc.)

---

[8]   The proposition that statutory licenses may result in below-market rates is controversial. Many statutory licenses direct the administrative rate-makers to set a "willing buyer-willing seller" rate. *See, e.g.,* 17 U.S.C. § 114(f)(2)(B). However, content owners generally argue that higher rates could be obtained through individual arms-lengths deals. (And licensees will generally complain that the statutory rate is too high.) At a minimum, private negotiations would allow price discrimination among different works in the same class, something that is virtually impossible in a statutory licensing construct.

LICENSEE PERSPECTIVE—DRAWBACKS OF STATUTORY LICENSE

- Often present extremely complex conditions for meeting terms of the statutory license

- Sometimes unclear whether license applies to certain types of uses (particularly new uses); leads to commercial uncertainty and/or litigation

- Unwieldy structure (and difficulty in seeking legislative amendment) makes it slow to adapt to new consumer or business-to-business uses

- Sometimes created to address very specific business circumstances that will change over time

- Creates a "one-size-fits-all" regime that limits business flexibility (including the ability to price discriminate)

RIGHTS OWNER'S PERSPECTIVE—BENEFITS OF STATUTORY LICENSE

- Provides an income stream without the accompanying need to dedicate significant licensing resources

- May enable certain business models that would otherwise be commercially impractical

- Often administered through a single entity that allows efficiency and cost-sharing

- Typically enables industry-wide collective rate-setting and enforcement

- Sometimes obtained as a *quid pro quo* for another industry benefit[9]

---

[9]   An example of this "benefit" to rights owners is the Digital Performance Right in Sound Recordings Act of 1995. Pub. L. 104–39, 109 Stat. 336 (1995). Prior to that date, there was no public performance right for sound recordings in the United States. As discussed previously, the sound recording industry had sought such a right for decades, and finally obtained a partial performance right for digital transmissions in 1995. However, although Congress chose to grant this right in 1995, it conditioned it on the creation of a statutory license for "non-interactive digital audio transmissions" that would ultimately apply to services such as Internet radio, satellite radio, and streaming music services over digital cable providers. A similar *quid pro quo* arose with one of the earliest statutory licenses in 1909, when Congress chose to vest a property right in the creation of mechanical reproductions of musical works, but did so within the context of a statutory license. As a result, the rights owners still lacked the ability to withhold the work from anyone but the first licensee, but they at least could receive compensation for use of the work.

RIGHTS OWNER'S PERSPECTIVE—DRAWBACKS OF STATUTORY LICENSE

- May result in lower rates than would occur in the free market place

- In any event, sets a "ceiling" on the value of the content for that purpose (a licensee may negotiate below the statutory license; but licensees would have no commercial incentive to pay above the statutory rate for the same use)

- Removes ability to withhold content (meaning content may be utilized in a manner, or associated with a product or service, to which the owner would otherwise object)

- Creates a "one-size-fits-all" regime that limits business flexibility (including the ability to price discriminate)

- Can have the effect of impacting/complicating commercial deals that happen "in the shadow" of the statutory provisions (i.e., with functionality very close to that covered by the statute)

The earliest iteration of a statutory license in the music world appeared when the sound recording industry was in its infancy, before the sound recording "technology" had evolved into a commercially viable platform.[10]

As of 2010, there were many statutory licenses within Title 17 of the U.S. Code available to the music industry that applied to a variety of platforms and uses. These licenses are administered in part by the Licensing Division of the Copyright Office, and include the following:

- Section 111: Statutory license for secondary transmissions by cable systems (17 U.S.C. § 111)

- Section 112: Statutory license for making ephemeral recordings (17 U.S.C. § 112)

- Section 114: Statutory license for the public performance of sound recordings by means of a digital audio transmission (17 U.S.C. § 114)

- Section 115: Statutory license for making and distributing phonorecords (17 U.S.C. § 115)

---

[10] See discussion *supra* in Chapter 2, discussing statutory licensing in the context of musical works, including the *White-Smith, Aeolian,* and *Standard Music Roll* cases, as well as the 1909 Copyright Act.

- Section 118: Statutory license for the use of certain works in connection with noncommercial broadcasting (17 U.S.C. § 118)

- Section 119: Statutory license for secondary transmissions by satellite carriers (17 U.S.C. § 119)

- Section 122: Statutory license for secondary transmissions by satellite carriers for local retransmissions (17 U.S.C. § 122)

- Section 1001: Statutory regime governing distribution of digital audio recording devices and media (AHRA, 17 U.S.C. § 1001 *et seq.*)

The bulk of this chapter is dedicated to the compulsory license related to the digital performance of sound recordings found in 17 U.S.C. § 114, which has grown in importance to the industry as music consumption has shifted from a sales to an access model. By the end of 2019, streaming (of all types) has come to represent approximately 80% of the U.S. recorded music industry revenue.

2. SUMMARY OF 17 U.S.C. § 114

The focus of this Chapter is Section 114 of the Copyright Act, 17 U.S.C. § 114, which provides a statutory license for "non-interactive" streaming of "digital audio transmissions." Section 114 is a complex piece of legislation, but we attempt to describe below at a very high level some of the key components of the statute. We also note that in October 2018, the Music Modernization Act made some changes to Sections 114 & 115 that are not fully addressed below. Key parts of that legislation will not be addressed until 2020 and beyond, as the Copyright Office implements the legislation based upon public notice and comment and further studies.

Outline of the Statutory License

In very general terms, Section 114 provides a statutory license for "non-interactive" streaming of sound recordings over digital audio services like SiriusXM satellite radio, Internet radio,[11] and cable radio channels (*i.e.,* the "music channels" offered by many digital cable providers, often branded as Music Choice, Stingray Music, etc.). The statutory license within 114 is intended to provide authorization for radio-like services[12] that offer users a mixed variety of sound recordings (the selection and order of which is chosen by the service) for general consumption by the public (whether it be an individual end-user or a business). The license does not cover "on-demand" streams or downloaded content, the functionality for which the licensee must obtain the rights directly from the master use owner.

Section 114 relates to the scope of rights originally afforded sound recording copyright owners within Section 106. Initially, by virtue of the Sound Recording Act of 1971 ("SRA"),[13] sound recordings were granted copyright protection under federal law[14] for three types of uses: (i) reproduction; (ii) adaptation (i.e., the creation of "derivative works" based on the sound recording); and (iii) distribution. Notably absent from this bundle of rights was a "public performance" right that existed at the time for virtually all other types of intellectual property.

---

[11] Section 114 is available both to straight "webcasters" (such as Pandora, Google, Deezer, SiriusXM (online), Slacker, and others) and to "simulcasters" (which are traditional radio broadcasters that stream their over-the-air signal simultaneously on the Internet). The statute is also utilized by the lone U.S. satellite digital audio radio service (SiriusXM satellite radio).

[12] S. Rep. No. 104–128, at 16 (1995).

[13] Pub. L. No. 140, 85 Stat. 39 (1971).

[14] Sound recordings fixed prior to the effective date of the SRA (specifically, prior to February 15, 1972) do not enjoy protection under U.S. federal law (although, since the 2018 Music Modernization Act, they are entitled to share in some revenues as if they were protected under federal law, thanks to the addition of 17 U.S.C. § 1401). However, until 2018, they were typically still protected under various state laws, which include state copyright laws, unauthorized duplication laws, and/or unfair trade practice laws. The Music Modernization Act of 2018 brought such recordings into the statutory licensing schema and allowed certain digital transmissions of pre-1972 sound recordings to be preempted from state law infringement claims if the federal statutory license is paid. Pub. L. No. 115–264, 132 Stat. 3676 (Oct. 11, 2018).

Nearly 25 years later, recognizing the need to ensure effective copyright protection for sound recordings as the proliferation of digital technologies began to impact the use of creative works in new ways, Congress created the Digital Performance Right in Sound Recordings Act of 1995 ("DPRA").[15] Through the DPRA, Congress added to § 106 a <u>limited</u> "public performance" right for sound recordings, but this right was significantly curtailed and did not include public performance over terrestrial radio or in most public venues such as arenas, bars, and restaurants.

Specifically, the new right applied only to performances by means of a "digital audio transmission"—i.e., certain types of streaming. Additionally, the DPRA created a system for compensating recording artists and copyright owners whose works are performed through certain types of "subscription" digital audio transmissions. Later, the Digital Millennium Copyright Act ("DMCA") clarified the scope of § 114 to include "nonsubscription" digital audio transmissions.

As part of the legislative tradeoff that enabled passage of the DPRA, Congress kept in place the exemption from a sound recording performance right that traditional terrestrial (i.e. over-the-air) radio had always enjoyed. Thus, with passage of the DPRA a performance right was extended only to "digital" transmissions.[16] In addition, Congress provided full property rights (*i.e.* rights subject to arms-length market negotiation) only to "interactive" digital transmission (such as on-demand streams and/or downloads), while simultaneously setting up a statutory license for the streaming of "non-interactive" digital audio transmissions (*e.g.,* Internet radio, and satellite radio).[17] By striking this compromise, Congress created the property right for the benefit of copyright owners, but ensured access to these works by licensees (in certain circumstances) through mandatory licensing via a statutory license.

In the below summary of § 114, we provide an explanation of the overall structure of the statute, paying particular attention to those key subparts that arguably make it one of the more complex provisions of the Copyright Act.

General Structure of Section 114

Section 114 can be best analyzed by focusing on three key sections of the statute:

---

[15]   Pub. L. No. 104–39, 109 Stat. 336 ("DPRA").

[16]   As a result of this exemption, the very same programming that requires a royalty payment for satellite radio and/or Internet webcasting requires *no* payment when broadcast via traditional "over-the-air" terrestrial radio stations.

[17]   It was unclear whether initial passage of the DPRA applied to typical non-subscription "webcasting" services. This ambiguity was clarified with passage of the Digital Millennium Copyright Act in 1998, which clearly extended the statutory license for "non-interactive" digital audio transmissions to Internet webcasting.

1. **Scope** of the exclusive rights provided to copyright owners: subparts (a) through (c), essentially define the scope of the initial bundle of exclusive rights assigned to copyright owners by virtue of the Sound Recording Act of 1971.

2. **Limitations** on that right: subpart (d) specifically sets forth the limitations on the public performance right now found in 106(6), including the creation of a statutory license for certain types of digital audio services making non-interactive public performances of sound recordings, and the exemption from a public performance right for traditional over-the-air radio.

3. **Implementation** of the right: subparts (e) through (j) address various considerations and procedures relating to the implementation of this new right, including:

   • setting forth the authority for negotiations of licenses;

   • outlining the procedures for setting rates and terms for certain digital audio services eligible for statutory licensing;

   • defining how licensing proceeds are to be divided;

   • putting limitations on licensing to affiliated entities; and

   • ensuring that compensation for this new "public performance" right for *sound recordings* would have no adverse effect on the licenses for the public performance of *musical works*.

First Part: Scope of the Right [Sections 114(a)–(c)]

As noted above, Sections 114(a)–(c) were created as part of the Sound Recording Act of 1971, where Congress limited federal copyright protection of sound recordings solely to the original three rights in the 1971 Act (reproduction, derivative works, and distribution). Congress also provided special exemptions for educational television and public broadcasting entities,[18] and made clear that it did not intend to limit in any way the public performance rights previously existing in those works identified in Section 106(4) (*i.e.*, literary, musical, dramatic, and choreographic works, pantomimes, motion pictures and other audio visual works).

Section 114(a) was amended by the DPRA to add the 106(6) sound recording performance right to the exclusive bundle of rights available to sound recordings.

---

[18] This exemption for public radio exists only if copies of the programs are not also commercially distributed to the public by public broadcasting entities. 17 U.S.C. § 114(b).

Second Part: The Statutory License [Section 114(d)]

One of the most complex provisions of Section 114 is 114(d). The DPRA added sections 114(d)–(j) to set specific limitations on the Section 106(6) right and procedures for implementing the right. Section 114(d) contains the core components of the statutory license for the public performance of sound recordings. It is a narrowly crafted provision that reflects Congress's intent at the time to address the potential impact of new digital subscription and interactive music services on the recorded music industry, without stifling technology, imposing unnecessary burdens on certain existing distribution services, or adversely affecting the public performance of musical works.[19] With these goals in mind, Section 114(d) contains four paragraphs that prescribe the scope of the sound recording public performance right by imposing several limitations.

114(d)(1)—Exemptions to the Performance Right

Section 114(d)(1) carves out certain transmissions that Congress believed, at the time, should not be subject to the performance right. These exempt transmissions are as follows:

- "Nonsubscription broadcast transmissions" (*e.g.*, traditional terrestrial radio and television) (§ 114(d)(1)(A)).

  — This section provides the noteworthy exemption that allows traditional over-the-air broadcast radio to avoid paying any royalties for the public performance of sound recordings. (They do pay for public performance of the underlying musical composition.)

- Most retransmissions of nonsubscription broadcast transmissions, including terrestrial retransmissions of public radio and television programming (*e.g.*, "repeater towers") (§ 114(d)(1)(B)(i)–(iv)).

- Transmissions that are incidental to exempt transmissions and are not intended for public reception (e.g., a radio station that receives a programming feed via satellite for broadcasting over its terrestrial signal; or a radio station that delivers a feed of its terrestrial transmission to a cable system for broadcasting) (§ 114(d)(1)(C)(i)).

- Transmissions *within* a "business establishment" (e.g., "storecasting" within a retail establishment) (§ 114(d)(1)(C)(ii)).

- Authorized retransmissions of transmissions that are already licensed (i.e., simultaneously retransmitting music programming provided by a licensed source; also referred to

---

[19]   S. Rep. No. 104–128, at 15–16 (1995); H.R. Rep. No. 104–274, at 14 (1995).

as the "through to the listener" exemption) (§ 114(d)(1)(C)(iii)).

- Transmissions *to* a "business establishment" (e.g., a service provider piping music into a retail establishment) (§ 114(d)(1)(C)(iv)).

  — As a result of this provision, the only royalty owed by "business establishments" is the accompanying "ephemeral right" that is required to create server copies. Thus, for example, Music Choice streaming statutory digital audio transmissions of sound recordings to a popular retail establishment (such as The Gap) is required to pay only for the server copies, and not for the performance right.

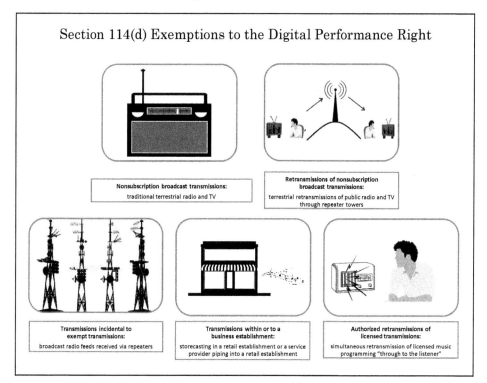

Section 114(d) Exemptions to the Digital Performance Right

Nonsubscription broadcast transmissions:
traditional terrestrial radio and TV

Retransmissions of nonsubscription broadcast transmissions:
terrestrial retransmissions of public radio and TV through repeater towers

Transmissions incidental to exempt transmissions:
broadcast radio feeds received via repeaters

Transmissions within or to a business establishment:
storecasting in a retail establishment or a service provider piping into a retail establishment

Authorized retransmissions of licensed transmissions:
simultaneous retransmission of licensed music programming "through to the listener"

Three things are particularly noteworthy about the Section 114(d)(1) exemptions.

First, the exemptions are *not available to so-called "interactive services"* that, for example, provide distinct recordings to listeners "on-demand." Congress believed that, among all of the transmission services that were available to the public at the time, interactive services were most likely to adversely affect music industry revenues. In other words, interactive services had the greatest potential to substitute for traditional music consumption and therefore the greatest potential to negatively impact sales. Because of this characteristic, Congress believed such services should not be eligible for these exemptions from the performance right.[20]

Second, the nonsubscription broadcast transmissions and retransmissions referred to in Section 114(d)(1)(A)&(B) reflect *Congress's intent to carve-out terrestrial "over-the-air" radio and television transmissions* (whether they are digital or analog) from the performance right, which Congress believed provided certain benefits to the recording industry that other new technologies did not (especially promotional benefits).[21] However, this exemption does not apply to "simulcast" retransmissions of broadcasts via the Internet, which the Copyright Office later determined (and the Third Circuit affirmed) are not eligible for the Section 114(d)(1)(A) exemption.[22] Thus, a traditional terrestrial radio broadcaster *does not* owe a performance royalty for analog broadcasts of sound recordings "over-the-air," but it *does* owe a performance royalty when it simultaneously transmits that same broadcast programming over the Internet.

Third, while the exemption within Section 114(d)(1)(C)(iv) carves out transmissions to a *business establishment* from public performance liability, a service that makes these exempt transmissions *would still need to obtain a license for the reproduction of the sound recordings that are made to facilitate these exempt transmissions* (i.e., "server copies" or "ephemeral recordings"). However, this can be obtained through the statutory license available to digital audio transmission services in Section 112(e).[23]

114(d)(2)—Categories & Requirements of the Statutory License

The hyper-technical provisions of Section 114(d)(2) establish the statutory license for certain digital audio transmissions. There are a host of different platforms and service types that are potentially covered by this

---

[20] S. Rep. No. 104–128, at 16 (1995).

[21] H.R. Rep. No. 104–274, at 13.

[22] 65 Fed. Reg. 77292 (Dec. 11, 2000); *Bonneville Int'l v. Peters*, 347 F.3d 485 (3d Cir. 2003).

[23] 17 U.S.C. § 112(e).

license. The types of services eligible for statutory licensing under 114(d)(2) include:

- *"eligible nonsubscription transmission"* services (e.g., nonsubscription "webcasting");

- *"new subscription services"* (e.g., subscription webcasting and music-only channels over cable and satellite television) (they are called "new" subscription services to distinguish them from "preexisting" services below);

- *"preexisting satellite digital audio radio services"* or "SDARS" (i.e., SiriusXM, which at the time the DPRA was enacted was two competing companies); and

- *"preexisting subscription services"* (i.e., subscription digital radio services over cable and satellite television that were grandfathered in when the DPRA was created, such MusicChoice and Muzak).

Each of these different "classes" of service may be subject to different royalty rates and conditions of the license. Some of them may pay a royalty fee on a "per performance" basis (*i.e.,* a certain payment for every stream to every user), on a percentage of revenue basis, on a "per subscriber" basis, or some other metric. Moreover, they are each subject to different license terms that typically last five years and have come up for renewal at different times.

Under the Section 114(d)(2) license, transmissions that meet certain eligibility requirements are essentially guaranteed a license (from the federal government) as long as the service complies with all other provisions of Section 114. Below are some of the key eligibility requirements of the Section 114(d)(2) license.

- the transmission is not part of an "interactive service";

- the transmission, if technically feasible, is accompanied by "metadata" that identifies, among other things, the title and artist of the sound recording;

- the transmission does not exceed the so-called "sound recording performance complement,"[24] which limits the number of selections within a 3-hour period to no more than 3 from a given album (no more than 2 consecutively) and no more than 4 from the same artist or a given compilation or box set (no more than 3 consecutively);

- the transmitting entity does not pre-publish the titles of specific sound recordings (e.g., by prior announcement or advance program schedule);

- "archived" programs (i.e., predetermined programs available on-demand to the listener) must be 5 or more hours in length and available for no more than 2 weeks;

- "continuous programs" (i.e., predetermined programs that are continuously "looped") must be 3 or more hours in length;

- the transmitting entity does not perform sound recordings as part of an audio-visual work that is likely to cause confusion as to the association of the copyright owner;

- the transmitting entity must take measures (to the extent feasible) to prevent "scanning" and "stream-ripping" (e.g., software that allows users to search for and make a copy of recordings streamed on Internet radio);

- the sound recordings used must be "commercially released" (i.e., released under the authority of the copyright owner);

- the transmitting entity does not interfere with sound recording copyright owners' measures to identify and protect the copyrighted work; and

---

[24] 17 U.S.C. § 114(j)(13).

- the transmitting entity must textually display to the listener the song title, album title (if any), and the featured artist on the recording.

These complex requirements are many and quite detailed. They were driven by a variety of motives considered by Congress when implementing the statutory license, including:

- Fostering "Radio-Like" Services: One of the main considerations in creating the license was a desire to reserve the statutory option only for services that were "radio-like" and/or functionally similar to traditional over-the-air radio. This effort was attributable in part to the belief that such services were less "substitutional"[25] than on-demand services, and it was therefore less troubling to Congress to authorize their use regardless of the copyright owner's permission.[26] Conversely, on-demand services were more substitutional, and should therefore require private licensing for this activity.[27] As evidence of this approach, a statutory service must be a streaming (*i.e.* not a download) "digital audio transmission" service,[28] it must be "non-interactive,"[29] it cannot transmit audio-visual works,[30] and it must mix up the selection of works (via the "sound recording performance complement") so that users receive an unpredictable variety of assorted works.[31] All of these served to make the service akin to traditional over-the-air radio.

- Reducing Online Piracy: Another strong motive driving enactment of the license was a desire to limit piracy online. Keep in mind that the DPRA was passed in 1995 when online piracy was just beginning to ravage the music industry. As a result, the license includes conditions that prohibit pre-publication of recordings before they stream,[32] that place limits on "archived" and "continuous" programming,[33] that require the service to take measures (if technically feasible)

---

[25] A service is considered "substitutional" if it provides an alternative way to consume music outside of the traditional sales model whereby a consumer purchases an album or CD. Thus, a user may turn to the service to satisfy the desire to hear particular music, leading to a corresponding decrease in sales.

[26] S. Rep. No. 104–128, at 24 (1995).

[27] *Id.*

[28] 17 U.S.C. § 101.

[29] 17 U.S.C. § 114(d)(2)(i).

[30] 17 U.S.C. § 114(d)(2)(vii).

[31] 17 U.S.C. § 114(d)(2)(iii).

[32] 17 U.S.C. § 114(d)(2)(iv).

[33] 17 U.S.C. § 114(d)(2)(v–vi).

to prevent scanning and "stream-ripping,"[34] and that preclude the service from impeding a copyright owner's attempt to protect the work.[35]

- Increasing Recognition of Individual Sound Recordings: Another justification for some of the § 114(d)(2) conditions was the desire to increase consumers' recognition of recordings that were streamed. The recording industry believed it was receiving decreasing benefit from over-the-air transmissions as broadcasters progressively lessened, or stopped altogether, "back announcement" of tracks played on traditional radio. Thus, the statute added requirements that a statutory licensee incorporate certain metadata in the stream (including the name and title of the song),[36] that the service cannot interfere with attempts to identify the recording,[37] and that the service must textually display information about the track to help the listener identify the recording.[38]

The lead requirement of Section 114(d)(2) (*i.e.*, that a service be non-interactive in order to qualify for the statutory license) is of particular importance. What constitutes an "interactive service"[39] was a controversial issue, and a source of much conflict, from the inception of the DPRA. There exists an almost infinite range of functionality among the thousands of digital music services. At one end of the spectrum, there are on-demand download services that are clearly "interactive" and outside the bounds of the statutory license. On the other end of the spectrum, there are "vanilla" webcasters that serve up regular streams with limited playlists and no user input, which are clearly "non-interactive" and eligible for the license. But at what point in the spectrum does a service switch from being "non-interactive" to "interactive"? How much variation and input are required to bump a service outside the statute?

---

[34]   17 U.S.C. § 114(d)(2)(viii).

[35]   17 U.S.C. § 114(d)(2)(x).

[36]   17 U.S.C. § 114(d)(2)(ii).

[37]   17 U.S.C. § 114(d)(2)(x).

[38]   17 U.S.C. § 114(d)(2)(xi).

[39]   An "interactive service" is defined as "one that enables a member of the public to receive a transmission of a program specially created for the recipient, or on request, a transmission of a particular sound recording, whether or not as part of a program, which is selected by or on behalf of the recipient. The ability of individuals to request that a particular sound recordings be performed for reception by the public at large, or in the case of a subscription service, by all subscribers of the service, does not make a service interactive, if the programming on each channel of the service does not substantially consist of sound recordings that are performed within 1 hour of the request or at a time designated by either the transmitting entity or the individual making such request. If an entity offers both interactive and noninteractive services (either concurrently or at different times), the noninteractive component shall not be treated as part of an interactive service." 17 U.S.C. § 114(j)(7).

This question is critical to both content owners and licensees, because it determines when a service can simply opt for the statutory license for all commercially released recordings, and when a service must negotiate individually for the rights to the content.

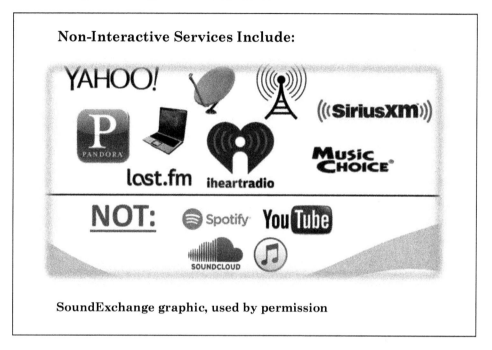

Non-Interactive Services Include:

NOT:

SoundExchange graphic, used by permission

The debate has become even more intense with the rise of music recommendation engines, which help mold programming of a station to the tastes of a particular user's preferences. The record industry argued for years that services like Yahoo's Launchcast Service (which allowed a user to indicate likes & dislikes for certain recordings, and then adjusted the subsequent streaming selections accordingly) were streams "specially created for the user"—and were therefore "interactive." This debate was resolved by the Second Circuit in *Arista Records, Inc. v. Launch Media, Inc.*, 578 F.3d 148 (2d Cir. 2009), which ruled that such functionality "does not provide sufficient control to users such that playlists are so predictable that users will choose to listen to the webcast in lieu of purchasing music."[40] As technology and creativity expand, there will surely be equally hard-fought debates in the future about the boundaries of this interactivity definition.

The debate over interactivity demonstrates the difficulty of creating a broad, "one-size-fits-all" statutory license that attempts to address the current technology while also accommodating future technology and business developments.

---

[40] *Arista Records, Inc. v. Launch Media, Inc.*, 578 F.3d 148, 162 (2d Cir. 2009).

114(d)(3)—Interactive Services

Section 114(d)(3) limits sound recording copyright owners' right to license to "interactive" services on an exclusive basis. Congress, in drafting this provision, was particularly concerned about hindering the growth of interactive services, thereby limiting the opportunities for performances of musical works.[41] So, Congress provided that the term of an exclusive license for interactive services is limited to a maximum of twelve months (24 months for small labels) and can only be renewed after at least an additional 13 months after expiration, unless the rights owner licenses a sufficient portion of its catalog to at least five different interactive services.

114(d)(4)—Savings Clause

Section 114(d)(4) is essentially a series of savings clauses making clear that, unless expressly provided by Section 114, nothing within the statute is intended to impair any of the existing rights available to musical works and sound recording copyright owners.

Third Part: Implementation Considerations and Procedures [Sections 114(e)–(j)]

As noted above, the provisions that follow Section 114(d) further define the procedures for licensing the public performance of sound recordings. Below is a high-level summary of each of the remaining provisions.

114(e)—Authority for Collective Negotiations

This provision affirms the copyright owner's ability to negotiate direct licenses with services for the public performance of the sound recording. In other words, the statutory license is a *non-exclusive* option; copyright owners may still directly license a service even for functionality that exactly mirrors the statutory license.

Additionally, Section 114(e) provides a limited antitrust exemption when negotiating rates and terms under the statutory license. Under this provision, any copyright owner and service may negotiate rates and terms under the license and designate common agents to do so on each of their behalves as long as the common agents do so on a nonexclusive basis.[42] This antitrust exemption is logical because joint discussions through collective agents is often the most practical way to negotiate and implement effective statutory licenses. Given the broad sweep of the statutory license, it promises to function most successfully when as many of the relevant players as possible are seated at the table.

---

[41] H.R. Rep. No. 104–274, at 14 (1995).

[42] However, when negotiating rates and terms for activity that falls outside of the scope of the 114(d) license, copyright owners and services may only designate common agents to perform a "clearinghouse function" on their behalf and not set rates on a collective basis.

114(f)—Licenses for Certain Nonexempt Transmissions

Section 114(f) establishes the procedures for setting rates and terms under the statutory license in the absence of negotiations. These procedures also include specific standards for setting statutory rates.

Pursuant to Section 114(f), statutory rates and terms (that are not otherwise settled by the parties) are set through a rate-setting proceeding before the Copyright Royalty Judges ("CRJs"), an administrative body within the Library of Congress.[43] Entities wishing to participate in such proceedings are required to file a petition to participate. Once the CRJs have set the rates and terms, such rates and terms become binding on all copyright owners and services using the statutory license and generally cover a 5-year period for each class of service.

The CRJs are instructed to set a rate that reflects the market value for the work. Specifically, in setting rates and terms the CRJs may consider the rates and terms for comparable types of services and must set rates that represent what would have been negotiated in the marketplace between a "willing buyer" and "willing seller" in the absence of a statutory license.

The "willing buyer—willing seller" standard is now the uniform rate standard for all services. However, prior to the passage of the MMA, Congress provided different treatment for services already in existence at the time the statute was passed (so-called "pre-existing" services), providing for a different rate standard for these services. This different treatment was justified because of the "business reliance" experienced by these groups. In other words, the "pre-existing" services had already invested substantial effort and capital into a business model based upon the previous laws. So, in altering the commercial landscape via the statutory license, Congress believed it should grandfather in these extant services and provide more flexibility in their rate structure in order to account for this business reliance. (For more detail, see Note 2 at the end of this chapter.)

Section 114(f) also gives the CRJs the authority to establish requirements for providing notice and maintaining and delivering records of the use (*i.e.*, playlists or "logs") of copyright owners' sound recordings by services operating under the statutory license.

114(g)—Proceeds from Licensing of Transmissions

Section 114(g) is a provision within the statute that makes clear Congress's intent "to ensure that a fair share of the digital sound recording performance royalties goes to performers."[44] It sets forth the "splits" in royalty payments that should be paid to the copyright owner, the featured

---

[43] Copyright Royalty and Distribution Reform Act of 2004, Pub. L. 108–419, 118 Stat. 2341.

[44] H.R. Rep. No. 104–274, at 24.

performer(s), and the non-featured performer(s),[45] as well as the permissible costs that the "designated agent" may deduct from the royalty stream. "Nonfeatured performers" (i.e., background vocalists and musicians) are entitled to a share of these royalties in accordance with the terms of the nonfeatured performers contract or some other collective bargaining agreement.

For performances subject to statutory licensing, Section 114(g)(2) sets forth the relevant "splits" as follows:

- **50%** to the sound recording **copyright owners**

- **45%** to the **"featured performer"**

- **2.5%** to **background musicians** (via to an escrow account managed by an administrator appointed by copyright owners and the American Federation of Musicians)

- **2.5%** to **background vocalists** (via an escrow account managed by an administrator appointed by copyright owners and the American Federation of Television and Radio Artists).

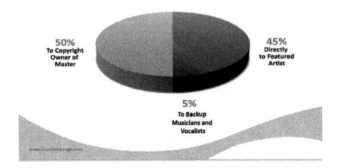

Under the DPRA as originally drafted, copyright owners were required to distribute the performers' half (45 + 2.5 + 2.5) of the royalty stream. The language within Section 114(g) was later modified to make clear that featured and non-featured performers are to be *directly* paid by a "designated agent" (i.e., SoundExchange) for statutory performances and not paid through the rights owner.

Section 114(g)(3) lists the types of administrative costs that may be permissibly deducted from any statutory royalty receipts received by the designated collecting agent prior to distribution.

---

[45] Under this provision, nonstatutory royalties received by copyright owners from performances of sound recordings are to be paid to featured artists in accordance with the terms of their contracts with the rights owner.

With the passage of the Music Modernization Act in 2018, Section 114 received some important additions meant to address how studio producers and engineers participate in the 114 process. Title III of the MMA, which embodies the Allocation for Music Producers (AMP) Act, codifies SoundExchange's longtime practice of honoring "Letters of Direction" ("LOD") from recording artists who want to direct a portion of their featured artist royalties to a creative participant in the sound recording (i.e., a producer, mixer, or sound engineer) . Beginning on January 1, 2020, the creative participant identified in the LOD will be considered the owner of the right to receive such payment for tax purposes, and the artist providing the LOD will be treated as having no interest in such payment.

In addition to codifying SoundExchange's LOD practice, the AMP Act provides for a default allocation payable to creative participants who participated in the creation of recordings made before November 1, 1995—the date the Digital Performance Right in Sound Recordings Act was passed. Under this provision of the AMP Act, SoundExchange will distribute to a creative participant a default 2% of the total royalties collected for the sound recording (deducted solely from the featured artists' share) as long as the creative participants and SoundExchange have undertaken specific, defined efforts to contact the featured artist. Because the right to payment ultimately rests with the featured artist, the featured artist has the ability to object to this payment at any point.[46]

To qualify to receive a default allocation under the AMP Act, the creative participant must be a producer, mixer or sound engineer of the sound recording and must have a written agreement with the sound recording rights owner or featured artist under which the creative participant is entitled to royalties related to the sound recording and that are payable to the featured artist. In addition, the creative participant must have made a creative contribution to the sound recording and must submit appropriate documents to SoundExchange. If more than one creative participant meets these requirements, SoundExchange will divide the 2% allocation equally among all such creative participants.

Separately, the AMP Act also revised Section 114 to make clear that the collection and distribution of royalties by SoundExchange is not subject to any State law (including common law) concerning escheatment or abandoned property.

114(h)—Licensing to Affiliates

Section 114(h) is a provision that is intended to prevent anticompetitive practices by requiring rights owners that are "affiliated"

---

[46] If, at any time, SoundExchange receives from a featured artist a written objection to the distribution of a default allocation under the AMP Act, SoundExchange must cease distribution of such royalties to the creative participant within 10 days of receipt of such written objection. Termination of the default allocation by the featured artist does not, however, entitle the featured artist to recoup any amounts already paid out to the creative participant.

with an entity seeking a public performance license to offer "no less favorable terms" to other nonaffiliated entities that offer similar services. In drafting this language, Congress made clear that licensors in these circumstances are permitted to offer different rate structures, terms and conditions based on material differences in the types of licenses requested. However, these differences should not be "based on arbitrary distinctions for monopolistic, discriminatory, or other anticompetitive purposes."[47]

114(i)—Effect on Royalties for Underlying Works (Repealed in 2018 as Part of the MMA)

Prior to the MMA, Section 114(i) specified that sound recording public performance licenses would have no effect on the public performance right in the musical work. More specifically, according to then-Section 114(i), royalties paid for the public performance of the sound recording "shall not be taken into account in any administrative, judicial, or other governmental proceeding" related to the royalties for the public performance of the musical work, nor should the sound recording public performance right diminish the musical works royalties in any way.[48]

This provision was originally included as a concession to the concerns of the songwriter and publisher communities, who worried at the time the statute was enacted that it could decrease performance income for musical works. Specifically, there was concern that lower rates for performance royalties in the Section 114 realm (for sound recordings) could be used as negative precedent in publishing rate setting proceedings, potentially leading to lower publishing rates. In the following years those fears proved to be unfounded—over the ensuing ten years, virtually all rate decisions for the Section 114 license across all categories resulted in significant rate increases for sound recording owners. As a result, the publishing community sought the ability to use these rates as *positive* benchmarks in their own rate setting proceedings, leading to the repeal of Section 114(i) by the MMA.

---

[47]   H.R. Rep. No. 104–274, at 32.

[48]   S. Rep. 104–128, at 32–33.

3. OVERVIEW OF SOUNDEXCHANGE

Since the creation of the performance right in sound recordings in 1995, all of the royalties paid under the statute have been collected and distributed by a company called SoundExchange. SoundExchange is a 501(c)(6) nonprofit performance rights organization originally established by the recording industry to help administer this new sound recording performance right. The board of SoundExchange represents the entirety of the recording industry, including artist and artists' representatives, unions, major and indie record labels, and industry trade groups—all split 50/50 between label and artist seats.

During the first fifteen years of its existence, the company was focused on the collection and distribution of royalties for the use of sound recordings over Internet, cable, satellite radio, and other digital audio transmission services. In more recent years, SoundExchange has branched out to provide other services into the industry, including music publishing administration, data services, and other payment administration.

SoundExchange has been the sole entity designated by the Library of Congress to collect and distribute royalties pursuant to the statutory licenses within Sections 112 and 114 of the Copyright Act since its founding. It thus tracks, collects and distributes digital performance royalties for sound recordings from more than 3,500 digital streaming services, including satellite radio (such as SiriusXM), Internet radio (such as Pandora & iHeart Radio) and cable television music channels (such as MusicChoice).

In addition to managing rights and royalties for digital radio offerings under the statutory license, SoundExchange also distributes performance royalties to artists for direct deals entered into by all the major record labels and more than 40 independent labels. The growth of SoundExchange's collections and payments is indicative of the explosive growth of digital streaming in the music industry. By 2020, SoundExchange had distribution over $7 billion to artist and labels from non-interactive streaming, and SoundExchange payments alone represented approximately 15% of all U.S. recorded music industry revenue (on a wholesale basis).[49] The chart below demonstrates the history of the company's distributions in recent years.

---

[49] RIAA 2019 Year-End Music Industry Revenue Report.

SoundExchange Growth in Payments

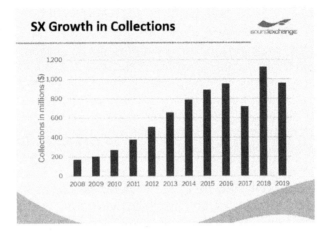

© 2019 SoundExchange, used with permission

NOTE

As noted above, the section 114 statutory license is only one of several such licenses authorized by the Copyright Act. As the above discussion illustrates, although one of the goals of a statutory licensing system is to make it easier for licensees to use protected works and for the owners of those works to be paid for that use, the statutory license provisions themselves create issues of interpretation that lead to disputes and leave those entities responsible for making rate determinations with complex issues to resolve. To give you a sense of how these disputes arise and are resolved, the materials that follow first provide an excerpt from one of the leading cases interpreting the statute's distinction between interactive and non-interactive services, followed by an introduction to how the complex issues surrounding rate setting are handled by the rate court that oversees these licenses: the Copyright Royalty Board.

B. DRAWING THE LINE BETWEEN INTERACTIVE AND NON-INTERACTIVE STREAMING SERVICES

ARISTA RECORDS, LLC v. LAUNCH MEDIA, INC.
578 F.3d 148 (2d Cir. 2009)[50]

Opinion

WESLEY, CIRCUIT JUDGE:

We are the first federal appellate court called upon to determine whether a webcasting service that provides users with individualized internet radio stations—the content of which can be affected by users' ratings of songs, artists, and albums—is an interactive service within the meaning of 17 U.S.C. § 114(j)(7). If it is an interactive service, the webcasting service would be required to pay individual licensing fees to those copyright holders of the sound recordings of songs the webcasting service plays for its users. If it is not an interactive service, the webcasting service must only pay a statutory licensing fee set by the Copyright Royalty Board. A jury determined that the defendant does not provide an interactive service and therefore is not liable for paying the copyright holders, a group of recording companies, a licensing fee for each individual song. The recording companies appeal claiming that as a matter of law the webcasting service is an interactive service . . . . We affirm; the webcasting service is not an interactive service as a matter of law.

Background

On May 24, 2001 Arista Records, LLC, Bad Boy Records, BMG Music, and Zomba Recording LLC (collectively, "BMG") brought suit against Launch Media, Inc. ("Launch") alleging that Launch violated provisions of . . . 17 U.S.C. § 114, by willfully infringing sound recording copyrights of BMG from 1999 to 2001. . . . The case was tried before a jury, and after the district court denied BMG's motion for judgment as a matter of law, the jury returned a verdict for Launch.

Launch operates an internet radio website, or "webcasting" service, called LAUNCHcast, which enables a user to create "stations" that play songs that are within a particular genre or similar to a particular artist or song the user selects. BMG holds the copyrights in the sound recordings of some of the songs LAUNCHcast plays for users. . . . [¶]

. . . . BMG has a right to demand that those who perform—i.e., play or broadcast—its copyrighted sound recording pay an individual licensing fee to BMG if the performance of the sound recording occurs through an "interactive service." See 17 U.S.C. § 114(d)(3)(C).

---

[50] Footnotes are omitted from this excerpt.

[¶¶] .... Discussion

.... [¶] [W]e agree with BMG that the central issue of this case—interactivity—presents an issue of law. The parties do not materially disagree on how LAUNCHcast works; their point of conflict centers on whether the program is "interactive" as defined by the statute—clearly an issue of law and therefore strictly under the purview of the courts. *See United States v. Nolan,* 136 F.3d 265, 271 (2d Cir.1998).

An "interactive service" according to the statute "is one that enables a member of the public to receive a transmission of a program specially created for the recipient, or on request, a transmission of a particular sound recording, whether or not as part of a program, which is selected by or on behalf of the recipient." 17 U.S.C. § 114(j)(7). The statute provides little guidance as to the meaning of its operative term "specially created." . . .

[¶].... BMG argues that any service that reflects user input is specially created for and by the user and therefore qualifies as an interactive service. But we should not read the statute so broadly. . . . The meaning of the phrase in question must significantly depend on the context in which Congress chose to employ it.

[¶¶].... The House report noted that the DPSR was enacted to address two related concerns. First, without "appropriate copyright protection in the digital environment, the creation of new sound recordings and musical works could be discouraged, ultimately denying the public some of the potential benefits of the new digital transmission technologies." H.R.Rep. No. 104–274, at 13. Second, "certain types of subscription and interaction audio services might adversely affect sales of sound recordings and erode copyright owners' ability to control and be paid for use of their work." *Id.* With regard to the latter concern, the House noted that "interactive services are most likely to have a significant impact on traditional record sales, and therefore pose the greatest threat to the livelihoods of those whose income depends upon revenues derived from traditional record sales." *Id.* at 14. . . .

The House also noted the importance of striking a balance between, on one hand, protecting sound recording copyright holders to promote sales, distribution, and development of new music, and, on the other hand, making development of new media and forms of distribution "economically [ ]feasible." H.R.Rep. No. 104–274, at 14. Congress attempted to address this concern by making the right "narrow"—limiting it to performance of digital audio transmissions and exempting nonsubscriber services. *See id.* . . .

Fairly soon after Congress enacted the DPSR, critics began to call for further legislation, charging that the DPSR was too narrowly drawn and did not sufficiently protect sound recording copyright holders from further internet piracy. . . . [¶] In light of these concerns, Congress enacted the current version of § 114 under the DMCA in 1998. The term "interactive service" was expanded to include "those that are specially created for a particular individual." H.R.Rep. No. 105–796, at 87 (1998) (Conf.Rep.). . . .

According to the House conference report,

> The conferees intend that the phrase "program specially created for the recipient" be interpreted reasonably in light of the remainder of the definition of "interactive service." For example, a service would be interactive if it allowed a small number of individuals to request that sound recordings be performed in a program specially created for that group and not available to any individuals outside of that group. In contrast, a service would not be interactive if it merely transmitted to a large number of recipients of the service's transmissions a program consisting of sound recordings requested by a small number of those listeners.

H.R.Rep. No. 105–796, at 87–88 (Conf.Rep.).

The House report continued that a transmission is considered interactive "if a transmission recipient is permitted to select particular sound recordings in a prerecorded or predetermined program." *Id.* at 88. "For example, if a transmission recipient has the ability to move forward and backward between songs in a program, the transmission is interactive. It is not necessary that the transmission recipient be able to select the actual songs that comprise the program." *Id.*

[¶¶]. . . . In sum, from the SRA to the DMCA, Congress enacted copyright legislation directed at preventing the diminution in record sales through outright piracy of music or new digital media that offered listeners the ability to select music in such a way that they would forego purchasing records.

Armed with the statute's text and context, we must examine the complex nature of the service LAUNCHcast provided. . . .

[A] LAUNCHcast user is able to create and modify personalized radio stations. First, the user is prompted to select artists whose music the user prefers. The user is then asked which music genres the user enjoys and asked to rate the genres on a scale. The user is also asked the percentage of new music—songs the user has not previously rated—the user would like to incorporate into the user's station (the "unrated quota") and whether the user permits playing songs with profane lyrics. The minimum unrated quota is 20%, meaning no less than 20% of the songs played can be unrated.

Once LAUNCHcast begins playing music based on the user's preferred artists and genres, the user rates the songs, artists, or albums LAUNCHcast plays between zero and 100, with 100 being the best rating. Below the rating field are hyperlinks termed "history," "share," and "buy." The history hyperlink allows the user to see a list of the songs previously played, and the buy hyperlink facilitates the user's purchase of the songs.

The share hyperlink allows the user to share the station with other users. This feature facilitates the "subscription" of one user to another user's station. . . . While a song is playing, the user has the ability to pause the song, skip the song, or delete the song from the station by rating the song zero. Notably, the user may not go back to restart the song that is playing, or repeat any of the previously played songs in the playlist.

Whenever the user logs into LAUNCHcast and selects a station, LAUNCHcast generates a playlist of fifty songs based on several variables. LAUNCHcast does not provide a list of the pool of songs or of the songs in the generated playlist, and therefore, the user does not know what songs might be played. LAUNCHcast selects the songs by first looking to the unrated quota and whether to exclude songs with profane lyrics or songs that cannot be transmitted over the user's bandwidth. Next LAUNCHcast creates a list of all the potential songs that can be put in the playlist (called a "hashtable"). LAUNCHcast then generates a list of all songs played for the user within the last thirty days, a list of all DJs, genres, and radio stations to which the user subscribes, and a list of all the ratings of all the songs, artists, and albums rated by either the user or any DJ to which the user subscribes. . . . All of these songs are initially added to the hashtable. LAUNCHcast then excludes: (1) all songs that the user, or a DJ to which the user subscribes, requests be skipped permanently (rated as zero) and (2) songs played within the last three hours for the user on any LAUNCHcast station. This yields approximately 4,000 songs.

LAUNCHcast then adds to the hashtable the 1,000 most popular songs—songs most highly rated by all LAUNCHcast users—in the bandwidth specified by the user, provided those songs are not already on the hashtable. LAUNCHcast then adds another 5,000 songs. . . . [¶] . . . LAUNCHcast picks the 5,000 songs randomly from its entire database, rather than solely from the user's selected genres.

At this point, the hashtable contains approximately 10,000 songs. All of the songs in the hashtable are then sorted according to rating: (1) explicitly rated; (2) implicitly rated; or (3) unrated. Based on these categories, LAUNCHcast determines which songs will be played from each category based on several criteria. . . .

Next, after determining what songs can be selected from the hashtable, LAUNCHcast picks songs from the hashtable to add to the playlist. To do this, LAUNCHcast first selects a song at random from one of the three categories, explicitly rated, implicitly rated, or unrated, but with some restrictions. . . . Although selection is random, according to Boulter the algorithm used to select songs for the playlist "[is] biased towards the top" of the list—i.e., choosing more highly rated songs—"but would pick randomly from there. So maybe the first time it picked No. 2

and then it picked 37. Then maybe it picked one and then it picked 300."
. . .

Finally, once all fifty songs are selected for the playlist, LAUNCHcast orders the playlist. The ordering of the songs is random, provided LAUNCHcast does not play more than two songs in the same album or three songs by the same artist consecutively.

It is hard to think of a more complicated way to "select songs," but this is the nature of webcast music broadcasting in the digital age. Given LAUNCHcast's format, we turn to the question of whether LAUNCHcast is an interactive service as a matter of law. As we have already noted, a webcasting service such as LAUNCHcast is interactive under the statute if a user can either (1) request—and have played—a particular sound recording, or (2) receive a transmission of a program "specially created" for the user. 42 U.S.C. § 114(j)(7). A LAUNCHCAST user cannot request and expect to hear a particular song on demand; therefore, LAUNCHcast does not meet the first definition of interactive. But LAUNCHcast may still be liable if it enables the user to receive a transmission of a program "specially created" for the user. It comes as no surprise to us that the district court, the parties, and others have struggled with what Congress meant by this term.

[¶]. . . . Contrary to BMG's contentions, Congress was clear that the statute sought to prevent further decreases in revenues for sound recording copyright holders due to significant reductions in record sales, perceived in turn to be a result of the proliferation of interactive listening services. If the user has sufficient control over the interactive service such that she can predict the songs she will hear, much as she would if she owned the music herself and could play each song at will, she would have no need to purchase the music she wishes to hear. Therefore, part and parcel of the concern about a diminution in record sales is the concern that an interactive service provides a degree of predictability—based on choices made by the user—that approximates the predictability the music listener seeks when purchasing music.

[¶¶]. . . . [I]n expanding the definition of interactive service to include the transmission of programs specially created for the user, Congress intended to include bodies of pre-packaged material, such as groups of songs or playlists specially created for the user. Given this definition, we turn to the ultimate issue of whether the LAUNCHcast playlists, uniquely generated for the user each time the user selects a station, are specially created and therefore interactive.

Launch does not deny that each playlist generated when a LAUNCHcast user selects a radio station is unique to that user at that particular time. However, this does not necessarily make the LAUNCHcast playlist specially created for the user. Based on a review of how

LAUNCHcast functions, it is clear that LAUNCHcast does not provide a specially created program within the meaning of § 114(j)(7) because the webcasting service does not provide sufficient control to users such that playlists are so predictable that users will choose to listen to the webcast in lieu of purchasing music, thereby—in the aggregate—diminishing record sales.

First, the rules governing what songs are pooled in the hashtable ensure that the user has almost no ability to choose, let alone predict, which specific songs will be pooled in anticipation for selection to the playlist. At least 60% of the songs in the hashtable are generated by factors almost entirely beyond the user's control. The playlist—a total of fifty songs—is created from a pool of approximately 10,000 songs, at least 6,000 of which (1,000 of the most highly rated LAUNCHcast songs among all users and 5,000 randomly selected songs) are selected without any consideration for the user's song, artist, or album preferences. The user has control over the genre of songs to be played for 5,000 songs, but this degree of control is no different from a traditional radio listener expressing a preference for a country music station over a classic rock station. . . .

Second, the selection of songs from the hashtable to be included in the playlist is governed by rules preventing the user's explicitly rated songs from being anywhere near a majority of the songs on the playlist. At minimum, 20% of the songs played on the station are unrated—meaning the user has never expressed a preference for those songs. If the user attempts to increase her chances of hearing a particular song by rating only a small number of songs—making the user's list of explicitly and implicitly rated songs smaller than 100—90% of the songs LAUNCHcast selects for the playlist will be unrated, flooding the playlist with songs for which the user has never expressed a preference.

Even the ways in which songs are rated include variables beyond the user's control. . . . Even if a user logs off LAUNCHcast then logs back on and selects the same station, the user will still hear the remainder of the playlist to which she had previously been listening with its restrictions still in operation, provided there were at least eight songs left to be played on the playlist—or, in other words, until the user listens to at least forty-two of the playlist's songs.

Finally, after navigating these criteria to pool a hashtable and generate a playlist, LAUNCHcast randomly orders the playlist. This randomization is limited by restrictions on the consecutive play of artists or albums, which further restricts the user's ability to choose the artists or albums they wish to hear. LAUNCHcast also does not enable the user to view the unplayed songs in the playlist, ensuring that a user cannot sift through a playlist to choose the songs the user wishes to hear.

It appears the only thing a user can predict with certainty—the only thing the user can control—is that by rating a song at zero the user will not hear that song on that station again. But the ability not to listen to a particular song is certainly not a violation of a copyright holder's right to be compensated when the sound recording is played.

In short, to the degree that LAUNCHcast's playlists are uniquely created for each user, that feature does not ensure predictability. Indeed, the unique nature of the playlist helps Launch ensure that it does not provide a service so specially created for the user that the user ceases to purchase music. LAUNCHcast listeners do not even enjoy the limited predictability that once graced the AM airwaves on weekends in America when "special requests" represented love-struck adolescents' attempts to communicate their feelings to "that special friend." Therefore, we cannot say LAUNCHcast falls within the scope of the DMCA's definition of an interactive service created for individual users.

When Congress created the sound recording copyright, it explicitly characterized it as "narrow." There is no general right of performance in the sound recording copyright. There is only a limited right to performance of digital audio transmission with several exceptions to the copyright, including the one at issue in this case. We find that LAUNCHcast is not an interactive service within the meaning of 17 U.S.C. § 114(j)(7).

NOTES AND QUESTIONS

1. Before the *Launch Media* case was decided, there was a great deal of uncertainty in the marketplace regarding how much functionality a service could offer and still remain within the bounds of the Section 114 statutory license. One controversial point with early "personal radio stations" related to how much control a user could exercise over the music she received through the service (i.e. what level of engagement could a service provide and still be considered "non-interactive" under the statute). Even if a digital service attempted to meet the requirement of the statute, and paid appropriate licensee fees to SoundExchange, the service could still be found liable for copyright infringement if it did not actually meet the statute's requirements for non-interactivity. While the *Launch Media* case did not definitively indicate exactly where the interactivity vs. non-interactivity line fell, it did provide greater clarity that certain "customizable" stations could nonetheless be eligible for the statutory license.

2. How might you revise the statute's definition of "interactive" to incorporate the *Launch Media* holding and to add more clarity regarding what types of services "count" as interactive vs. non-interactive? Is it better for the language of the statute to remain more general, giving more uncertainty but perhaps more flexibility to future services? Do the rationales for limiting the

statutory license to "radio-like" services discussed in part A, above, continue to have relevance in today's music marketplace, or should the compulsory license be expanded to encompass other types of streaming services? If you think it should be expanded, how broadly should it apply? Conversely, do the rationales for creating the compulsory license apply with less force today, and should copyright owners have greater control over the use of their works in the streaming marketplace?

C. DIGITAL PERFORMANCE LICENSES FOR SOUND RECORDINGS: RATE-SETTING

1. WEBCASTING AND SATELLITE DIGITAL RADIO SERVICES PROCEEDINGS: INTRODUCTION

Whenever a compulsory rate is created by statute, a key component of the process is obviously the actual rate that licensees must pay for use of the content. To be clear, the regulations that implement the statutory license include many aspects besides payment, including reporting obligations, data requirements, timing of the payment, late fees, etc. But entities looking to construct a business around the content that is offered by the license are intently focused on the cost of this input for their business.

There are two critical aspects to the actual rate. First is the "rate structure" which determines the type of metric used for assessing a royalty payment. There are many different potential rate structures, which can be set up in a variety of ways. Some examples include:

- percentage of overall revenue
- percentage of a subset of revenue
- "per performance" (which applies a rate for each stream to each listener)
- "per spin" (which applies a rate for each use of a recording, regardless of audience size)
- "per subscriber minimum" (which is a minimum fee based on each user)

And these structures can be set up based upon a single metric, or they can be constructed as a "greater of" across multiple metrics.

Second, the statutory license must be set for a specific rate, which is the most heavily-fought issue in proceedings around the license. The content owner will naturally attempt to gain the highest rate possible, while the potential licensees will try to minimize the rate.

Currently under the U.S. system, these battles over the rate and the rate structure take place before the CRJ, a three-judge panel housed within the Library of Congress. Each of these judges is appointed by the Librarian of Congress (upon recommendation of the Register of Copyrights) to staggered six-year terms. They currently oversee virtually all of the statutory licenses set forth in the U.S. Copyright Act and are constantly involved in one or more of these rate proceedings.

Proceedings to set the rates are typically very complex trials, involving many parties, a variety of expert witnesses, and significant legal fees. Each side will support its rate proposal using a battery of experts opining on things such as business models, economic forecasting, industry projections, and high-level economic theory. The judges are often tasked with analyzing tens-of-thousands of pages of testimony, dozens of witnesses, and a significant set of filings in their ultimate quest to set rates and terms for the next license period. As an example of the scale of these proceedings, in one recent webcasting case there were initially over 40 participants (*i.e.,* parties). The Webcasting III trial leading up to the tribunal's 2011 ruling involved 50 witnesses during 48 days of hearings that totaled over 13,000 pages of transcripts. Over the course of the case, 192 exhibits were admitted, and the docket contained 475 entries of pleadings, motions and orders.

We provide below, in section 2, a summary of the Webcasting decision ("Webcasting IV") that the Copyright Royalty Judges published in May 2016. This decision covered the rates and terms for statutory webcasting for the period 2016–2020. As you review the summary of this decision, it is not necessary to understand and absorb all aspects of the opinion, but it will provide some insight into the range of arguments asserted by the parties, the complexity of the arguments and the process that is inevitable when setting a "one-size-fits-all" rate for a statutory license.

2. SUMMARY OF WEB IV COPYRIGHT ROYALTY BOARD DETERMINATION

Introduction

The Copyright Act provides a statutory license for the public performance of sound recordings by means of digital transmissions for non-interactive services that operate over the Internet ("webcasters"), and it directs the Copyright Royalty Judges ("CRJs") to set rates and terms for this license that "most clearly represent the rates and terms that would have been negotiated in the marketplace between a willing buyer and a willing seller." 17 U.S.C. §§ 114(f)(2), 112(e). Over 2,500 webcasters currently take advantage of the statutory license for streaming sound recordings, representing hundreds of millions of dollars in royalties to recording artists and record labels. The setting of statutory rates, therefore, is a significantly important component to overall industry revenue.

On May 2, 2016, the Librarian of Congress published the CRJs' Final Determination in the *Web IV* proceeding, a proceeding to set the statutory license's rates and terms for webcasting performances for the 2016–2020 rate period.[51] The CRJs adopted a minimum fee of $500 annually per station or channel operated by a webcaster, as well as these rates, which they will adjust annually to account for inflation:

Commercial Subscription Services:	$0.0022 per performance
Commercial Nonsubscription Services:	$0.0017 per performance
Noncommercial Services:	$500 annually per station or channel for up to 159,140 aggregate tuning hours each month; $0.0017 per performance thereafter.[52]

Below is a **summary** of the key issues that affected the CRJs' adoption of these rates in the *Web IV* Final Determination.

Matters Identified by the CRJs as Threshold Issues

A. Benchmarking

When trying to set "willing buyer-willing seller" prices through a judicial proceeding in the case, there are various approaches that might be taken by a court. One popular approach is "benchmarking," where a court might look to the most analogous types of deals found in the free market

---

[51] Determination of Royalty Rates and Terms for Ephemeral Recording and Webcasting Digital Performance of Sound Recordings (Web IV), 81 Fed. Reg. 26,316 (May 2, 2016).

[52] These rates do not apply to noncommercial services that separately settled with SoundExchange, including college radio broadcasters and NPR affiliates.

and then adjust the price to account for differences from the target market. But there are other potential methods a court might use as well, including customer surveys, financial modeling, and/or complex statistical analysis.

In *Web IV* (as in past proceedings), the CRJs decided to follow a "benchmarking" approach. Benchmarking involves two steps: First, the CRJs attempt to identify voluntary license agreements that they believe are comparable to the statutory license. Second, the CRJs make adjustments to the rates reflected in these voluntary license agreements to account for any differences between these so-called "benchmark" licenses and the statutory license. In making such adjustments, the CRJs' goal is to determine the rates that willing buyers and willing sellers would negotiate for the statutory license.

In *Web IV*, the CRJs relied on three principal benchmarks: [1] the "interactive benchmark" proposed by SoundExchange, based on license agreements negotiated between copyright owner record companies and interactive, on-demand streaming services like Spotify; [2] the Pandora-Merlin benchmark, based on an agreement between Pandora and an organization, Merlin, that negotiates digital rights on behalf of a set of independent record companies; and [3] the iHeart Media-Warner benchmark, based on an agreement between iHeart Media (formerly known as Clear Channel) and Warner Music Group.

B. Financial Circumstances

During the *Web IV* proceedings, webcasters introduced evidence regarding their financial circumstances, their asserted inability to generate profits, and the difficulties faced by the webcasting industry. SoundExchange introduced countervailing evidence, but its principal argument on this issue was that such evidence is ultimately irrelevant to the statutory standard.

The CRJs agreed that, to the extent rates are set under a benchmarking approach, it is not necessary to examine evidence of the financial performance of webcasters. In the CRJs' view, these factors were already "baked into" the benchmark agreements they considered because rational copyright owners and services would already have taken these factors into account in negotiating these benchmark agreements.

C. Promotion & Substitution

The Copyright Act directs the CRJs to consider, in adopting rates and terms, the extent to which webcasting promotes or interferes with a copyright owner's other streams of revenues, such as the sale of albums. *See* 17 U.S.C. § 114(f)(2)(B)(i). During *Web IV*, certain webcasters attempted to show that their services were promotional to the sales of sound recordings, or, at the very least, more promotional than interactive services. These webcasters argued that the greater promotional value of their services justified a lower statutory rate. The CRJs concluded, however, that the available evidence did not support the view that webcasting was more promotional than other services.

D. Simulcaster Segmentation

The National Association of Broadcasters (the "NAB") argued that simulcasters (terrestrial radio broadcasters that simultaneously stream their radio broadcasts) should pay a lower rate for performing sound recordings than other webcasters. According to the NAB, simulcasters are materially different from other webcasters because of their local focus, their on-air personalities and hosts, FCC licensing requirements, and their heavy use of non-music content.

SoundExchange argued otherwise, and the CRJs agreed that simulcasters and other webcasters were sufficiently similar to each other and competed for the same pool of listeners, such that willing buyers and willing sellers would not negotiate a separate lower rate for simulcasters than for other webcasters.

E. Rate Structure

SoundExchange and Pandora proposed a "greater of" royalty structure under which webcasters would pay the greater of a royalty calculated on a per performance basis and a royalty calculated as a percentage of revenue. Other webcasters, including the NAB, argued against the inclusion of a prong based on a percentage of revenue. During the proceeding, SoundExchange presented evidence that voluntary license agreements invariably include a "greater of" structure, and that such a structure allows copyright owners and artists to share in a successful service's ability to monetize their creative contributions.

The CRJs did not adopt a "greater of" structure for several reasons and, instead, adopted a flat per-performance rate structure. *First*, the CRJs noted that the percentage-of-revenue prongs in most marketplace agreements have never been triggered.[53]

Second, the CRJs were not persuaded that the evidence in the record showed that willing buyers and willing sellers would agree to a "greater of" structure.

Third, the CRJs found the notion "that record companies should share in the upside if the Services monetize their models at a faster rate" to be "wholly unconvincing."

---

[53] Critics of this decision have noted that the CRJs did not explain why this fact is relevant; by analogy, the fact that an employee's stock options are not currently "in the money" does not suggest that the employee would attach no value to additional option grants.

Commercial Rates

SoundExchange proposed a uniform rate for all commercial webcasters, but the CRJs adopted separate per performance rates for subscription services and non-subscription services.

A. Per Performance Rates for Subscription Services

SoundExchange's rate proposal for all commercial services was based on the interactive benchmark. A SoundExchange expert calculated the rates paid by interactive services to record companies and then applied a downwards adjustment (approximately a 50% reduction) to account for differences in functionality between interactive and non-interactive services (e.g. the ability to select a specific song). In other words, because the statutory service offered less functionality than the on-demand benchmark, it would therefore provide less value to the consumer and should therefore be priced lower than the benchmark market.

SoundExchange argued that interactive license agreements were the best available evidence of what willing buyers and willing sellers would negotiate as these agreements were least influenced by the "statutory shadow"—the distortionary effect the existence of the statutory license has on agreements. This "statutory shadow" concept argues that the existence of the statutory license has a deflationary impact on any arms-length pricing that would otherwise occur with the non-interactive services. Because *interactive* services are ineligible for the statutory license, these services and copyright owners must voluntarily agree on rates and terms. By contrast, a *non-interactive* service can simply resort to the statutory rate if a copyright owner demands more than the statutory rate; this is the "shadow" effect. Accordingly, an agreement between a non-interactive service and a copyright owner does not necessarily reveal the rate the parties would agree upon absent the compulsory statutory license (i.e. in a truly free market).

The CRJs relied on the interactive benchmark with respect to commercial *subscription* services only. The CRJs were persuaded by evidence in the record that interactive services are generally comparable to statutory services because the two types of services are "converging" in the marketplace—their functionality is becoming increasingly similar. The CRJs also concluded that, at least with respect to subscription services, SoundExchange's expert had adequately accounted for any differences between interactive and non-interactive services.

But the CRJs also concluded that SoundExchange's interactive benchmark did not adequately describe the *non-subscription* portion of the non-interactive market. According to the CRJs, the record showed that there are two distinct subgroups of music consumers: (1) consumers willing to pay for music and (2) consumers unwilling to pay anything for music. Because many interactive services are primarily subscription-based, the

CRJs concluded that the interactive benchmark accurately compared to only non-interactive *subscription* services, which cater to the first subgroup of music consumers, and not non-interactive non-subscription services, which cater to the second subgroup.

B. Per Performance Rates for Non-Subscription Services

In adopting per performance rates for non-subscription services, the CRJs turned to two benchmarks based on non-interactive license agreements between webcasters and copyright owners. First, the CRJs concluded that the Pandora-Merlin benchmark was a reasonable proxy for the rate that would be agreed upon by a willing webcaster and a willing *independent* record label. Second, the CRJs concluded that the iHeart Media-Warner benchmark was a reasonable proxy for the rate that a willing *major* record label would agree to. The CRJs rejected arguments that the Pandora-Merlin and iHeart Media-Warner benchmarks should be adjusted to account for the effect of the "statutory shadow," as well as arguments that the benchmarks should be adjusted to reflect additional consideration provided for in those agreements that was not assigned a specific value, such as the promise of advertising slots or guarantees.

Once the CRJs derived benchmark rates from the Pandora-Merlin agreement and the iHeart Media-Warner agreement, they calculated a weighted average of these rates based on an estimate of the relative market shares of repertoire owned by independent labels and repertoire owned by major labels.

Non-Commercial Rates

Though the CRJs' determination focused largely on the reasoning supporting rates for commercial webcasters, the determination also set the rates applicable to performances by noncommercial webcasters.[54] The CRJs agreed with SoundExchange that, beyond a certain threshold of usage of sound recordings, commercial and non-commercial services are competitors. While noncommercial stations may have served a different niche at lower levels of listenership, once a noncommercial station grew to a significant size and popularity, it had the potential to cannibalize listenership that would have otherwise gone to large, commercial stations. As a result, the CRJs concluded that, beyond this usage threshold, commercial and noncommercial services should pay the same statutory rates that commercial webcasters pay for non-subscription performances. In continuing the same 159,140 aggregate tuning hours usage threshold adopted in prior proceedings, the Judges relied on (a) evidence presented by SoundExchange that the overwhelming majority of noncommercial webcasters operated well below this usage threshold and (b) the

---

[54] This rate did not apply to certain categories of noncommercial webcasters, such as NPR public radio stations or noncommercial college radio broadcasters, which reached separate voluntary settlements with SoundExchange.

SoundExchange-CBI settlement, which included a similar threshold. Based on the record evidence, it was expected that the vast majority of noncommercial webcasters would only pay a royalty fee of $500 annually per station or channel—a rate that is the equivalent of the minimum statutory fee applicable to all non-interactive webcasters, whether commercial or non-commercial.

<hr />

NOTES AND QUESTIONS

1. You will note in the webcasting decision regarding rate-setting under the section 114 statutory license that the judges are directed to set a rate that reflects what would naturally occur between a **"willing buyer and a willing seller"** in a working market. However, as mentioned previously, other digital music platforms operated for years under a different rate standard to which the judges adhered when selecting a rate. Specifically, some "pre-existing" services (i.e. that were already in existence at the time of the implementing legislation in 1995) operated under a multi-prong rate standard set forth in 17 U.S.C. § 801(b)(1). This different standard applied to services such as satellite radio (SiriusXM) and traditional "music supply" companies like Muzak and MusicChoice. The 801(b)(1) standard directed the court to consider the following factors when setting a rate for a particular platform:

(A) To maximize the availability of creative works to the public.

(B) To afford the copyright owner a fair return for his or her creative work and the copyright user a fair income under existing economic conditions.

(C) To reflect the relative roles of the copyright owner and the copyright user in the product made available to the public with respect to relative creative contribution, technological contribution, capital investment, cost, risk, and contribution to the opening of new markets for creative expression and media for their communication.

(D) To minimize any disruptive impact on the structure of the industries involved and on generally prevailing industry practices.

In what way is this "801(b) standard" different from the "willing buyer/willing seller standard? Or is it that different? This older construct was removed from the music industry's statutory license with passage of the MMA in 2018, which set all the industry statutory rate standards at the "willing buyer/willing seller" standard.

2. In the *Web IV* summary above, you will note that the Copyright Royalty Board differentiated between "subscription" and "non-subscription" webcasting services. The relationship between these two types of services is a hotly discussed topic in the music industry. In general, record labels and publishers tend to prefer subscription services because they are typically more profitable and generate more revenue than non-subscription offerings. Much

of the business strategy of content owners and the digital service providers revolves around attempts to drive consumers to the subscription models. However, non-subscription services continue to be some of the most popular services in the marketplace. They can sometimes act as a "funnel" through which services can eventually "upsell" to the subscription product. But as a policy matter, there are proponents who believe we will always need to have non-subscription options available to consumers. The CRB asserts that these are very different markets with very different consumers, and therefore that in setting rates for these two markets they should look to different benchmarks. Do you agree with this assessment? Is there an argument that these markets are substitutional for one another, and should that influence the assessment of the rate? Or do you believe they are wholly distinct and therefore justifiably treated separately?

3.   It is undeniably a difficult task to set a price for all products covered in a statutory license. The Copyright Royalty Board must find a "one-size-fits-all" solution that applies, in some cases, to hundreds of companies employing dozens of business models that utilize countless recordings. What are some of the different rate structures that might be used to set the royalty fee (*e.g.*, revenue share, per-subscriber minimum, etc.)? What are the benefits and drawbacks of each? Can you think of any unconventional models for pricing a statutory license?

4.   In the webcasting cases discussed above, there were extreme differences between the rate proposals of the various groups of participants. Of additional note are (i) the economic complexity of the arguments, (ii) the speculative nature of the arguments, and (iii) the need to create a generic rate that applies to all relevant licensees. Do you think this process is a good method for determining the value of the statutory license? Can you think of any other different approaches that Congress could have taken for administering the statutory license? Think back to the Ringer Report's recommendations for a compulsory license from Chapter 4. Would Register Ringer's recommended approach be better, if only for its relative simplicity? Why or why not?

5.   One of the biggest challenges in determining a statutory rate is selecting the economic theory that underlies the decision. How do you go about determining actual value of the sound recording in a statutory license, especially when there is no corresponding free market for the court to use as a reference point? What types of arguments would you use to try to value the work? What are some analogs that you might point to, and how would you adjust them to fit the Section 114 license?

6.   Almost all statutory licenses set rates for a moderately long term (often at least five years or longer). What are the challenges of determining such rates in advance of the term? Do you think there is a need to adjust rates at points over the length of the license term? If so, how would you do it? Or is the rate setting process really a type of "rough justice" that should be occasionally corrected only through periodic proceedings?

CHAPTER VII

MECHANICAL LICENSING AND THE 2018 MUSIC MODERNIZATION ACT: *GETTING BETTER*[1]

■ ■ ■

This chapter focuses on modern issues relating to the Section 115 mechanical license for use of compositions in recordings and other mechanical means of fixing a composition. As you saw in earlier chapters, Section 115 provides the earliest example of a statutory license for use of a copyrighted work, having been adopted as a means of dealing with "new" technology that allowed compositions to be reproduced through mechanical means by fixing them in a piano roll or record for playback by a machine (the player piano or gramophone/phonograph).

Other than a handful of small increases in the statutory rate for the mechanical license and some clarifications regarding the types of recordings that would trigger the license and the right of the composer/publisher to control new arrangements, this section of the Copyright Act remained largely unchanged after the 1976 revision. As the technology for mechanically reproducing compositions changed dramatically with the advent of digital technology, Section 115 was amended in 1995 to address "digital phonorecord deliveries" (also known as "DPDs"). Still, the law had difficulty keeping pace with technology.

As noted above in Chapter 3, in February of 2015, the Copyright Office issued a lengthy report on "Copyright and the Music Marketplace" that made wide-ranging recommendations for modernizing copyright law, focusing in particular on problems in the application of outdated copyright provisions to the digital music world. In October of 2018, the Music Modernization Act ("MMA") was signed into law, with a substantial revision to the mechanical licensing provisions. Most significantly, the MMA established a new, blanket license system for providing mechanical reproduction rights to digital music providers, as well as a new collective for administering that system. The MMA was enacted in the wake of a multi-year review process, both by Congress and by the Copyright Office, and with the participation of many industry entities.

---

[1] John Lennon & Paul McCartney (1967); released by the Beatles on SGT. PEPPER'S LONELY HEARTS CLUB BAND (1967).

331

This chapter begins with excerpts from several cases that illustrate some of the issues that have arisen in the modern era regarding the scope and implementation of the statutory mechanical license. Next, we provide a 2004 statement of the Register of Copyrights with recommendations for modernizing the law governing mechanical licensing, which summarizes the history of Section 115 and makes recommendations for updating the law to address technological change in the industry. The Register's statement identifies some of the debates occurring in the early days of music streaming regarding how the mechanical license might or should apply to different types of online music transmissions. The chapter also includes excerpts from the 2015 Copyright Office Report on Copyright and the Music Marketplace in order to provide more context regarding what the MMA did and did not address, and its likely success in solving the stated problems. This chapter concludes with Copyright Office summaries of the changes to Section 115 put into motion by the MMA—the most significant of which still remain the subject of ongoing rulemaking as of the date of this text—and a summary of litigation regarding the potential for continued liability exposure for digital music providers even after the MMA's enactment.

CONSIDER AS YOU READ . . .

- How broadly should the mechanical license apply? What sorts of uses should fall under its purview?

- Does it make sense to have different mechanical licensing systems for digital phonorecord deliveries and all other types of mechanical reproductions of compositions? Are there simpler solutions to the problems described in the materials below regarding mechanical licensing that you might propose?

- The mechanical license was created to address new technology (piano rolls, records) and its impact on income to composers and publishers. Does the MMA do an adequate job of addressing the interests of composers/publishers and the interests of digital licensees? Why or why not?

A. CASE LAW INTERPRETING THE SCOPE AND APPLICATION OF SECTION 115 AT THE DAWN OF THE DIGITAL ERA

ABKCO MUSIC, INC. V. STELLAR RECORDS, INC.

96 F.3d 60 (2d Cir. 1996)

Opinion

OWEN, DISTRICT JUDGE:

This is an appeal from an order of the District Court for the Southern District of New York (Batts, *J.*), entered on August 10, 1995, preliminarily enjoining defendant-appellant Performance Tracks, Inc. ("Tracks")[FN2 omitted] from publishing without authority the lyrics to copyrighted songs owned by plaintiffs-appellees ABKCO Music Inc. and ABKCO Music and Records Inc. ("ABKCO"), thus prohibiting Tracks from distributing its compact discs containing the copyrighted songs. We affirm.

Although this presents a case of first impression in terms of the technology at issue, the applicable legal principles are well-settled. ABKCO owns the copyrights to seven musical compositions by Mick Jagger and Keith Richards of the Rolling Stones, including the rock-and-roll classics "Satisfaction (I Can't Get No)," "Jumping Jack Flash," and "Brown Sugar." Despite many requests, ABKCO has never licensed these famous songs for use in the "karaoke" or "sing-along" industry.

Tracks, a newcomer in the music field, is in the sing-along industry. It uses a new technology to encode on a compact disc ("CD") not only the audio rendition of a song, but also the contemporaneous video display of a song's lyrics. Thus, for a user who has a CD player with a video output, the lyrics of the songs can be displayed on a video screen in "real time" as the songs are playing so that the viewer can sing the lyrics along with the recorded artist. No other image or information appears, and the user cannot print the lyrics from the screen or control the speed of the music or lyrics. The Tracks discs, called "Compact Discs + Graphics" ("CD+G's"), will provide audio playback alone when played on standard CD players. . . . The primary difference between traditional karaoke discs and CD+G's is that CD+G's display only the lyrics, whereas karaoke discs display some video image, such as a sun-drenched beach, behind the song lyrics. Under the

Copyright Act of 1976, 17 U.S.C. § 101 *et seq.,* the producers and distributors of karaoke versions of songs must acquire synchronization or "synch" licenses[4] from the copyright owners of the songs to legally manufacture karaoke discs; a copyright owner may negotiate, if so disposed, the karaoke use of a song and the terms of the authorizing synch license with a karaoke maker.

Tracks did not secure synchronization licenses from ABKCO, but instead, viewing its products as "phonorecords," obtained "compulsory licenses" for the compositions, pursuant to the Copyright Act, 17 U.S.C. § 115, which permits the manufacture and distribution of new "cover" versions of copyrighted musical works as long as the licensee follows the statutory notice requirements and pays the proper royalty fees. Section 115 of the Copyright Act provides in part:

Compulsory license for making and distributing phonorecords

In the case of nondramatic musical works, the exclusive rights . . . to make and to distribute *phonorecords* of such works, are subject to compulsory licensing under the conditions specified by this section.

(a) Availability and Scope of Compulsory License.—

(1) When *phonorecords* of a nondramatic musical work have been distributed to the public in the United States under the authority of the copyright owner, any other person . . . may, by complying with the provisions of this section, obtain a compulsory license to make and distribute *phonorecords* of the work. A person may obtain a compulsory license only if his or her primary purpose in making *phonorecords* is to distribute them to the public for private use. . . . [¶]

17 U.S.C. § 115 (emphasis added).

Under the Copyright Act, "phonorecords" are defined as

material objects in which *sounds, other than those accompanying a motion picture or other audiovisual work,* are fixed by any method now known or later developed, and from which the sounds can be perceived, reproduced, or otherwise communicated, either

---

4   A synchronization license is required if a copyrighted musical composition is to be used in "timed-relation" or synchronization with an audiovisual work. 4 Melville B. Nimmer & David Nimmer, *Nimmer on Copyright* § 24.02[f] (1995) (hereinafter "Nimmer"). Most commonly, synch licenses are necessary when copyrighted music is included in movies and commercials. *See* 4 Nimmer § 24.04[C][1]. The "synch" right is a right exclusively enjoyed by the copyright owner. *Buffalo Broadcasting Co., Inc. v. ASCAP,* 744 F.2d 917, 920 (2d Cir.1984), *cert. denied,* 469 U.S. 1211, 105 S.Ct. 1181, 84 L.Ed.2d 329 (1985). The Copyright Act does not explicitly confer synchronization rights, but courts have held that the synch right is derived from the exclusive right of a copyright owner, under 17 U.S.C. § 106(1), to reproduce his work. *Agee v. Paramount Communications, Inc.,* 853 F.Supp. 778, 786 (S.D.N.Y.1994), *aff'd in part, rev'd in part,* 59 F.3d 317 (2d Cir.1995); *Angel Music, Inc. v. ABC Sports, Inc.,* 631 F.Supp. 429, 433 n. 4 (S.D.N.Y.1986).

directly or with the aid of a machine or device. The term "phonorecords" includes the material object in which the sounds are first fixed.

17 U.S.C. § 101 (emphasis added). "Audiovisual works" are defined as

works that consist of *a series of related images* which are intrinsically *intended to be shown by the use of machines* or devices such as projectors, viewers, or electronic equipment, *together with accompanying sounds,* if any, regardless of the nature of the material objects, such as films or tapes, in which the works are embodied.

17 U.S.C. § 101 (emphasis added).

Tracks sent ABKCO a CD+G entitled "Songs of the Rolling Stones" containing the compositions, as well as notices of its intention to obtain compulsory licenses for the compositions. ABKCO thereupon informed Tracks that the Rolling Stones CD+G infringed on its copyrights of the compositions, and shortly thereafter initiated this action.

On July 5, 1995, ABKCO obtained a temporary restraining order. Thereafter, on August 10, 1995, Judge Deborah A. Batts, ruling from the bench, granted a preliminary injunction enjoining Tracks from "further publishing the lyrics of plaintiff's copyrighted Rolling Stones songs without authorization to do so," concluding that the visual depiction of the lyrics constituted an unauthorized publication of the lyrics, infringing ABKCO's copyrights. Tracks appeals pursuant to 28 U.S.C. § 1292(a)(1).

* * * *

Tracks asserts as error, first, the district court's conclusion that the CD+G's visual display of song lyrics constitutes an unauthorized reproduction in violation of 17 U.S.C. § 106[FN5 omitted] because the visual feature of the CD+G's is not within the ambit of the compulsory license provisions of 17 U.S.C. § 115, and second, the court's holding that the irreparable harm requirement had been satisfied.

In granting the preliminary injunction, the court below properly found that Tracks' compulsory licenses do not give it the right to publish the compositions' lyrics on a screen. Song lyrics enjoy independent copyright protection as "literary works," 1 Nimmer § 2.05[B], and the right to print a song's lyrics is exclusively that of the copyright holder under 17 U.S.C. § 106(1). Thus, while a compulsory license permits the recording of a "cover" version of a song, it does not permit the inclusion of a copy of the lyrics. That requires the separate permission of the copyright holder.

* * * *

A time-honored method of facilitating singing along with music has been to furnish the singer with a printed copy of the lyrics. Copyright holders have always enjoyed exclusive rights over such copies. While projecting lyrics on a screen and producing printed copies of the lyrics, of course, have their differences, there is no reason to treat them differently for purposes of the Copyright Act.

While we hardly need go further to affirm, we deal briefly with Tracks' contention that the court below, applying *Bourne*, was in error because its CD+G's are "phonorecords," not copies,[6] within the meaning of the Copyright Act, and therefore its compulsory licenses include the right to its limited video display. While the court below did not reach this contention, we do so hereafter and conclude that it is both factually and legally flawed.

Tracks' contention that CD+G's are "phonorecords" and thus the video aspect is within the grant of its compulsory licenses can be disposed of quickly. The plain language of the Copyright Act refutes Tracks' view. Phonorecords are defined as objects on which "sounds" are fixed; CD+G's, however, are objects on which sounds *and* visual representations of song lyrics are fixed. Moreover, the term phonorecord expressly excludes "audiovisual works," yet CD+G's constitute "audiovisual works," since they "consist of a series of related images"—the lyrics—"together with accompanying sounds"—the music. 17 U.S.C. § 101.

Tracks does not claim that the actual definition of "phonorecord" in Section 101 includes the visual capabilities of its CD+G's, but rather contends that the Copyright Act has not kept pace with new technology, and that Congress, in view of its definition of "digital music recording" in the Audio Home Recording Act of 1992, 17 U.S.C. § 1001 et seq. ("AHRA"),[7] would include Tracks' entire CD+G capability within the definition of "phonorecords" if it were to redefine "phonorecord" today. It would, however, seem to be a sufficient answer to Tracks' contention to observe that Tracks' product is *not* within the statutory definition of "phonorecord," and what Congress may or may not do in the future to redefine the term is not for us to speculate.

* * * *

Although the court below did not directly address Tracks' contention dealt with above, its observations implicitly—and correctly—rejected Tracks' interpretation of the AHRA:

> It seems to me that Congress at the time it passed the Audio Home Recording Act . . . was aware of the provision of the Copyright Act and the definitions of the Copyright Act, and that if Congress had

---

[6]   Copies are defined as "material objects, *other than phonorecords,* in which a work is fixed by any method now known or later developed. . . ." 17 U.S.C. § 101 (emphasis added).

[7]   The AHRA was enacted to address the problem of private copying of music using new digital recording devices. Primarily, the AHRA limits the ability of individuals to make digital copies of audio recordings, and provides for royalty payments to copyright holders. H.R.Rep. No. 873, 102d Cong., 2d Sess., pt. 1, at 8–26 (1992), *reprinted in* 1992 U.S.C.C.A.N. 3578, 3579–3596.

intended to amend the Copyright Act, or had it intended that its 1992 Audio Home Recording Act was to have some impact on the Copyright Act, I'm sure that Congress would have said so. . . .

J.A. at A211.

* * * *

CONCLUSION

For the foregoing reasons, the order of the district court granting the preliminary injunction is affirmed.

THE RODGERS AND HAMMERSTEIN ORG. v. UMG RECORDINGS, INC.
2001 WL 1135811 (S.D.N.Y. Sept. 26, 2001)

MEMORANDUM OPINION AND ORDER

MARTIN, DISTRICT J.

The Rogers and Hammerstein Organization, together with other songwriters and music publishers (collectively "Plaintiffs"), bring this action for copyright infringement of various musical compositions against UMG Recordings, Inc. ("UMG") and The Farm Club Online, Inc. ("Farmclub") (collectively "Defendants"). Defendants now move for summary judgment on the ground that they are licensed to make recordings of the musical compositions at issue, or in the alternative, for a stay pending resolution of a Copyright Office proceeding regarding online music services. Plaintiffs cross-move for partial summary judgment. For the reasons set forth below, Defendants' motion is denied in all respects and Plaintiffs' motion is granted.

BACKGROUND

Plaintiffs are music publishers and songwriters that own or control the copyrights of famous musical compositions such as "White Christmas" and "These Boots are Made for Walking." (Comp.¶¶ 17–25.) UMG is in the business of making and distributing phonorecords[1] through its various music labels, including MCA Records, A & M Records, Polygram Records, and Mercury Records. When making and distributing a phonorecord of a musical composition for which they do not own the copyright, UMG must obtain a license from the copyright owner. *See* 17 U.S.C. § 115.

---

[1] " 'Phonorecords' are material objects in which sounds, other than those accompanying a motion picture or other audiovisual work, are fixed by any method now known or later developed, and from which the sounds can be perceived, reproduced, or otherwise communicated, either directly or with the aid of a machine or device. The term 'phonorecords' includes the material object in which the sounds are first fixed." 17 U.S.C. § 101.

Owners of copyrighted musical compositions are required to grant licences under certain circumstances pursuant to the Copyright Act of 1976 (the "Copyright Act"), 17 U.S.C. § 115 ("Section 115"). Section 115(a)(1) provides:

> When phonorecords of a non-dramatic musical work have been distributed to the public in the United States under the authority of the copyright owner, any other person, including those who make phonorecords or digital phonorecord deliveries, may, by complying with the provisions of this section, obtain a compulsory license to make and distribute phonorecords of the work. A person may obtain a compulsory license only if his or her primary purpose in making phonorecords is to distribute them to the public for private use, including by means of a digital phonorecord delivery.

The notice requirements and royalty rates for these "compulsory licences"[2] [sic] are also set forth in Section 115 and its related regulations. *See id.* § 115(b) & (c); 37 C.F.R. §§ 201.18, 255.3(j). Failure to conform to the notice provisions of the statute "forecloses the possibility of a compulsory license and, in the absence of a negotiated license, renders the making and distribution of phonorecords actionable as acts of infringement." 17 U.S.C. § 115(b)(2).

Section 115 also provides an alternative to the statutory notice and royalty requirements by allowing copyright owners and persons seeking compulsory licenses to negotiate the terms and rates of royalty payments. *See id.* § 115(c)(3)(B). The statute also authorizes the use of common agents to negotiate licenses, receive notices, and pay and collect royalty payments. *See id.*

Most music publishers, including Plaintiffs, employ the Harry Fox Agency, Inc. ("HFA") as their agent to receive notice of the intention to obtain a compulsory license, and to collect and distribute royalties. Acting on behalf of their clients, HFA waives the statutory notice requirements, negotiates royalty rates at or below the statutory level, and substitutes a quarterly accounting and payment schedule for the monthly schedule prescribed by Section 115.

When a potential licensee notifies HFA of its intention to obtain a compulsory mechanical license, HFA issues a document that sets out the agreed-upon variance of the statutory terms. The parties dispute whether this document is the license itself or merely a confirmation of receipt of notice. The top of the document lists the name and address of the licencee [sic], a licence [sic] number, and the date. (Goodman Aff. Ex. 1.) Each

---

[2]   Compulsory licenses for the use of musical compositions are often referred to as "mechanical licenses" because Section 115 allows the act of "mechanically" recording a song on fixed media. *See Staggers v. Real Authentic Sound,* 77 F.Supp.2d 57, 64 n. 10 (D.D.C.1999).

document contains the following language: "Refer to the provisions hereof reproduced on reverse side varying terms of compulsory license provision of Copyright Act. The following is supplementary thereto: . . . ." The document then contains information about the musical composition at issue, including a song code, title, writer, publisher, a record number, a format code such as "CD" for compact disc, an artist, and the royalty rate stated as a percentage of the statutory royalty rate. The reverse side of the document contains the following language:

> You have advised us, in our capacity as Agent for the Publisher(s) . . . that you wish to obtain a compulsory license to make and to distribute phonorecords of the copyrighted work referred to [on the front of the document], under the compulsory license provision of Section 115 of the Copyright Act.
>
> Upon doing so, you shall have all the rights which are granted to, and all the obligations which are imposed upon, users of said copyrighted work under the compulsory license provision of the Copyright Act, after phonorecords of the copyrighted work have been distributed to the public in the United States under the authority of the copyright owner by another person, except that with respect to phonorecords thereof made and distributed hereunder:
>
> 1. You shall pay royalties and account to us as Agent for and on behalf of said Publishers quarterly, within forty-five days after the end of each calendar quarter, on the basis of phonorecords made and distributed;
>
> 2. For such phonorecords made and distributed, the royalty shall be the statutory rate in effect at the time the phonorecord is made, except as otherwise stated [on the front of the document];
>
> 3. This compulsory license covers and is limited to one particular recording of said copyrighted work as performed by the artist and on the phonorecord number identified [on the front of the document]; and this compulsory license does not supersede nor in any way affect any prior agreements now in effect respecting phonorecords of said copyrighted work;
>
> 4. In the event you fail to account to us and pay royalties as herein provided for, said Publisher(s) or his Agent may give written notice to you that, unless the default is remedied within 30 days from the date of the notice, this compulsory license will be automatically terminated. Such termination shall render either the making or the distribution, or both, of all phonorecords for which royalties have not been paid, actionable as acts of infringement under, and fully subject to the remedies provided by the Copyright Act;

5. You need not serve or file the notice of intention to obtain a compulsory license required by the Copyright Act. . . .

Defendants have submitted HFA documents for each of the musical compositions identified in the complaint. The documents indicate specific record numbers and configurations, such as "CD", "cassette tape" and/or "LP".

On or about October 23, 2000, Farmclub, a subsidiary of UMG, began operating an Internet music service website located at http://www.farm club.com. Farmclub "streams" Universal recordings over the Internet. The source files used for streaming are sound recordings contained on magnetic disks of computer file servers. Although the magnetic computer media on which the server copies reside is not distributed to the public, the Farmclub service allows consumers to access sound recordings of Plaintiffs' copyrighted compositions on demand. Defendants reproduced sound recordings of Plaintiffs' works onto their computer servers in order to offer the Farmclub service. Plaintiffs assert that they never authorized the use of their works on the website and are not being paid any royalties for the use of their works on the Farmclub site.

On or about October 26, 2000, Edward P. Murphy ("Murphy"), the president and Chief Executive Officer of the National Music Publishers' Association, Inc. (the "NMPA"),[3] spoke to Lawrence Kenswil of UMG and informed him that the Internet music service was unlicenced and urged UMG to take copyrighted songs for which it had no licenses off the service. (Murphy Decl. ¶ 6.) During a subsequent telephone call with Mr. Zach Horowitz, President of UMG, on November 2, 2000, Murphy repeated that the Internet music service was not licensed and again advised that UMG should remove the musical compositions for which it did not have licenses from the service.

On November 20, 2000, UMG sent a letter to HFA seeking licenses to use Plaintiffs' copyrighted music on an Internet music subscription service. (Panos Decl. Ex. 12.) The letter noted that:

> [A]pplication of the mechanical license provisions of the Copyright Act (17 U.S.C. § 115) to the Service remains unresolved. Among other things, it is not clear whether operation of the Service might involve making and distributing [digital phonorecord deliveries ("DPDs")]. Submission of this application does not express or imply our agreement that a license is required for the operation of the [Internet] Service. We expect these issues to be addressed by industry negotiation or, if necessary, a Copyright Office proceeding. If it is determined that the operation of the Service involves the making and distribution of DPDs, we

---

[3] The NMPA is the principal trade association of music publishers in the United States. HFA is a wholly-owned subsidiary of NMPA.

commit promptly to pay applicable royalties retroactive to the inception of the Service.

On November 22, 2000, UMG and other record labels, acting through the Recording Industry Association of America ("RIAA"), filed a petition with the Copyright Office to commence a rule-making proceeding in order to determine the applicability of Section 115 to streaming music through online services and the royalty rates to be paid for such activities.

On December 8, 2000, Plaintiffs commenced this litigation, arguing that Defendants' unauthorized copying of the musical compositions named in the complaint onto the Farmclub server was as infringing use of their copyrights. Defendants contend that they hold compulsory mechanical licenses for each work listed in the complaint as evidenced by HFA documents for each song and therefore have an absolute defense to the infringement claim. Plaintiffs respond that the licenses held by Defendants are limited to the express configurations and record numbers identified on the HFA documents.

DISCUSSION

Defendants argue that Section 115 "automatically" confers a license when notice is timely served. In Defendants' view, the "automatic" nature of the license renders the piece of paper prepared by HFA nothing more than a confirmation of a compulsory license and a variance of the statutory requirements of notice, accounting, and royalty payments for a particular phonorecord number. Thus, Defendants assert that by giving HFA notice of the intention to obtain a compulsory license for a particular song, they obtained compulsory licenses for all of the works relevant to this litigation for *all* configurations, and the record number limitations contained in the HFA documents only apply to the variances for the statutory royalty and accounting terms. Plaintiffs respond that each HFA document is a license limited by its express terms to a particular phonorecord number and configuration.

The problem with the Defendant's argument is that it ignores the fact that Defendant never served a notice of intent to acquire a compulsory license. Rather it submitted to the Harry Fox Agency a document entitled: "Mechanical License Request" on which it listed the catalogue number and format of the recording for which the license was sought. In response to this application, Defendant received a document entitled "License" which identified a specific "Record Number" and specific configuration for which the license was issued, e.g., "CD". The license stated, "Refer to provisions on reverse side varying terms of compulsory license provision of Copyright Act." As noted above one of those limitations is:

> 3. This compulsory license covers and is limited to one particular recording of said copyrighted work as performed by the artist and on the phonorecord number identified [on the front of

the document]; and this compulsory license does not supersede nor in any way affect any prior agreements now in effect respecting phonorecords of said copyrighted work . . . .

Defendants contend that because the portion of the license which they signed stated "We acknowledge receipt of a copy hereof", they did not bind themselves to the terms set forth on the form. However, what they were acknowledging was that they received the license and were aware of its limitations. Since they received no broader license from any other source, their rights were limited to those contained in the license they acknowledged receiving.

Even if one were to consider this licensing process in strict contract terms, Defendants' application for the license would constitute an offer which defendants accepted by sending the Harry Fox license. By signing the license acknowledging receipt of the terms upon which it was granted and, thereafter using the license, Defendants clearly manifested their assent to the terms on which the license was issued.

Defendants' argument that the Harry Fox Agency had no authority to limit the license that could be obtained had they submitted a proper notice of intention to obtain a compulsory license is without merit. While this would be true had they chosen to submit such a notice, they did not do so; they submitted an application for a license to the Agency and they were bound by the terms of the license granted in response to that application. Nothing in Section 115 suggests that Congress intended to limit the ability of either copyright holders or prospective licensees to enter into private agreements that would contain different terms and conditions of the license. Indeed, Section 115(b)(2) expressly provides:

> Failure to serve or file notice required by clause (1) forecloses the possibility of a compulsory license and, in the absence of a negotiated license, renders the making and distribution of phonorecords actionable as acts of infringement . . . .

See also § 115(c)(3)(B).

Thus Congress clearly recognized that those like Defendants who wished to obtain a license to include a copyrighted work in a phonorecord had a choice either to serve the notice required to obtain a compulsory license or to obtain a "negotiated license." Congress manifested no preference for either of these licensing methods. By choosing to submit a license application to Harry Fox rather than serve the statutorily required notice, Defendants exercised the option Congress granted them to obtain a "negotiated license." They are, therefore, bound by the terms they negotiated.

Defendants' contention that the Harry Fox license is not limited to the particular album and configuration listed thereon is refuted by the document itself, as well as by the practice of the parties. Defendants do not dispute that they often obtained multiple HFA licenses for a particular composition. (Goodman Aff. Exs. 32–38.) Defendants argue that they notified HFA of the intent to distribute a new use of each composition in order to (1) obtain the variances for each use, (2) create a paper trail for royalty tracking purposes, and (3) accommodate HFA. One difficulty with this argument is that each of the HFA documents, received and acknowledged by Defendants with a signature, has a license number in the top right corner. The license number is different for each use of the song. Defendants dismiss this fact by pointing to the statute and the "automatic" nature of the license. According to Defendants, Plaintiffs could have put whatever they wanted on the HFA document and Defendants were under no obligation to object because all of the rights of the parties are governed by the statute. This argument is particularly difficult to digest because the HFA documents obviously benefit Defendants in many ways, such as by making accounting and royalty payments due on a quarterly rather than monthly basis. More importantly, in many instances, the HFA documents set a royalty rate below the statutory rate. (Goodman Aff. Ex. 16.) Under Defendants' view, they were free to disregard any language on the HFA documents that they found contrary to the statute, but at the same time they could benefit from the variance from the statutory royalty rate and accounting requirements. Furthermore, under this theory Defendants could rely upon the HFA documents to prove that they had obtained a compulsory license for a particular musical composition, but Plaintiffs would be unable to rely on the document to establish the scope of the license. Such an argument defies common sense and finds no support in the statute.

* * * *

Even if it were not clear that Defendants' licenses are limited by the particulars set forth in the Harry Fox license, it appears that even a compulsory license would not permit Defendants to stream these copyrighted works over the Internet.

Section 115 states that "[a] person may obtain a compulsory license only if his or her primary purpose in making phonorecords is to distribute them to the public for private use." 17 U.S.C. § 115(a)(1). Thus, while it may be that a compulsory license would permit Defendants to sell copies of the phonorecords at issue over the Internet, that is not what Defendants are purporting to do. Defendants place copies of various albums on the Internet and then allow computer users to listen to whatever songs on those albums they choose. They do not sell copies of the records to their users. Indeed, the user agreement which the Defendants require users of their service to accept, states: "you can't reproduce copy or distribute the Content by any means (including but not limited to downloading or saving such Content to a computer hard drive) . . . ."

Thus the Defendants' server copies of the copyrighted works are not analogous to master recordings made in the course of the process of making phonorecords to be distributed to the public. Defendants concede that their server copies themselves are not for distribution to the public. (Def. Reply Mem. at 13.) Since Defendants' server copies are neither intended for distribution to the public nor part of a process for distributing digital copies of the existing phonorecords, Section 115 would not give the Defendants a right to a compulsory license for the server copies.

* * * *

CONCLUSION

. . . . It is obvious that Defendants do not want to pay the Plaintiffs the license fee for a record every time one of their customers listens to recording on the Internet. However, the only license that Defendants rely on here is one that is limited to the distribution of records to the public for which there is an established fee. Defendants' choice is to obtain a license for that purpose and pay the fee or cease their infringing activity. They cannot avoid that liability by relying on the strained arguments they have asserted here.

For the reasons set forth above, Defendants' motion for summary judgement or to stay the proceedings is denied and Plaintiffs' cross-motion for partial summary judgment is granted.

SO ORDERED.

NOTES AND QUESTIONS

1. As a drafting matter, if you wanted to propose an amendment to the language of Section 115 to have the mechanical license include visual representation of a song's lyrics in products like the CD+G, how might you craft the language to avoid overbroad application of the compulsory license? Similarly, if you wanted to propose revised language in the Harry Fox voluntary mechanical license that was at issue in the *Rodgers & Hammerstein* case that would extend the license to the digital reproductions at issue in that case, how might you do so?

2. Do you think the *Stellar Records* case reached the correct decision in narrowly interpreting the mechanical license provisions of the Copyright Act? When a copyrighted composition includes both lyrics and music, does it make sense to apply the statutory license only to the recorded lyrics and music but not to embedded information, like the lyrics, if the technology makes it possible for them to be visually displayed when the mechanical device (here, the CD+G) is played? Why or why not?

3. The *Rodgers & Hammerstein* case also gave a narrow interpretation of the scope of the mechanical license, this time with a focus not on what material is

covered by the license, but instead with a focus on the application of the license to new forms of reproduction and distribution in the digital era. It provides a nice preview of the challenges presented by the song-by-song nature of the statutory mechanical license and voluntary mechanical licensing service provided by Harry Fox when applied to the context of online delivery of entire catalogs of sound recordings, which are discussed more fully in the materials below.

B. COPYRIGHT OFFICE ANALYSIS AND RECOMMENDATIONS REGARDING MECHANICAL LICENSING

STATEMENT OF MARYBETH PETERS, THE REGISTER OF COPYRIGHTS, BEFORE THE SUBCOMMITTEE ON COURTS, THE INTERNET AND INTELLECTUAL PROPERTY OF THE HOUSE COMMITTEE ON THE JUDICIARY

U.S. House of Representatives, 108th Congress, 2d Session
(March 11, 2004): Section 115 Compulsory License[2]

Mr. Chairman, Mr. Berman, and distinguished members of the Subcommittee, I appreciate the opportunity to appear before you to testify on the Section 115 compulsory license, which allows for the making and distribution of physical phonorecords and digital phonorecord deliveries. The compulsory license to allow for the use of nondramatic musical works has been with us for 95 years and has resulted in the creation of a multitude of new works for the pleasure and consumption of the public, and in the creation of a strong and vibrant music industry which continues to flourish to this day. Nevertheless, the means to create and provide music to the public has changed radically in the last decade, necessitating changes in the law to protect the rights of copyright owners while at the same time balancing the needs of the users in a digital world.

Background

1. *Mechanical Licensing under the 1909 Copyright Act*

In 1909, Congress created the first compulsory license to allow anyone to make a mechanical reproduction (known today as a phonorecord) of a musical composition[1] without the consent of the copyright owner provided that the person adhered to the provisions of the license. . . . Although the

---

[2]   Available at https://www.copyright.gov/docs/regstat031104.html.

[1]   The music industry construed the reference in Section 1(e) of the 1909 Act as referring only to a nondramatic musical composition as opposed to music contained in dramatico-musical compositions. See Melville B. Nimmer, Nimmer on Copyright, § 16.4 (1976). This interpretation was expressly incorporated into the law by Congress with the adoption of the 1976 Act. 17 U.S.C. § 115(a)(1).

focus at the time was on piano rolls, the mechanical reproduction right also applied to the nascent medium of phonograph records as well.

Congress, however, was concerned that the right to make mechanical reproductions of musical works might become a monopoly controlled by a single company. Therefore, it decided that rather than provide for an exclusive right to make mechanical reproductions, it would create a compulsory license in Section 1(e) of the 1909 Act which would allow any person to make "similar use" of the musical work upon payment of a royalty of two cents for "each such part manufactured." However, no one could take advantage of the license until the copyright owner had authorized the first mechanical reproduction of the work. Moreover, the initial license placed notice requirements on both the copyright owners and the licensees. Section 101(e). The copyright owner had to file a notice of use with the Copyright Office—indicating that the musical work had been mechanically reproduced—in order to preserve his rights under the law, whereas the person who wished to use the license had to serve the copyright owner with a notice of intention to use the license and file a copy of that notice with the Copyright Office. The license had the effect of capping the amount of money a composer could receive for the mechanical reproduction of this work. The two cent rate set in 1909 remained in effect until January 1, 1978, and acted as a ceiling for the rate in privately negotiated licenses.

Such stringent requirements for use of the compulsory license did not foster wide use of the license. It is my understanding that the "mechanical" license as structured under the 1909 Copyright Act was infrequently used until the era of tape piracy in the late 1960s. When tape piracy was flourishing, the "pirates" inundated the Copyright Office with notices of intention, many of which contained hundreds of song titles. The music publishers refused to accept such notices and any proffered royalty payments since they did not believe that reproduction and duplication of an existing sound recording fell within the scope of the compulsory license. After this flood of filings passed, the use of the license appears to have again became almost non-existent; up to this day, very few notices of intention are filed with the Copyright Office.

2.   *The Mechanical License under the 1976 Copyright Act*

The music industry adapted to the new license and, by and large, sought its retention, opposing the position of the Register of Copyrights in 1961 to sunset the license one year after enactment of the omnibus revision of the copyright law. Music publishers and composers had grown accustomed to the license and were concerned that the elimination of the license would cause unnecessary disruptions in the music industry. Consequently, the argument shifted over time away from the question of whether to retain the license and, instead, the debate focused on reducing the burdens on copyright owners, clarifying ambiguous provisions, and setting an appropriate rate. The House Judiciary Committee's approach reflected this trend and in its 1976 report on the bill revising the Copyright Act, it reiterated its earlier position 'that a compulsory licensing system is still warranted as a condition for the rights of reproducing and distributing phonorecords of copyrighted music," but "that the present system is unfair and unnecessarily burdensome on copyright owners, and that the present statutory rate is too low." H. Rep. No. 94–1476, at 107 (1976), citing H. Rep. No. 83, at 66–67 (1967).

To that end, Congress adopted a number of new conditions and clarifications in Section 115 of the Copyright Act of 1976, including:

- The license becomes available only after a phonorecord has been distributed to the public in the United States with the authority of the copyright owner (§ 115(a)(1));

- The license is only available to someone whose primary intent is to distribute phonorecords to the public for private use (§ 115(a)(1));

- A licensee cannot duplicate a sound recording embodying the musical work without the authorization of the copyright owner of the sound recording (§ 115(a)(1));

- A musical work may be rearranged only "to the extent necessary to conform it to the style or manner of the interpretation of the performance involved," without "chang[ing] the basic melody or fundamental character of the work," (§ 115(a)(2));

- A licensee must still serve a Notice of Intention to obtain a compulsory license on the copyright owner or, in the case where the public records of the Copyright Office do not identify the copyright owner and include an address, the licensee must file the Notice of Intention with the Copyright Office (§ 115(b)(1));

- A licensee must serve the notice on the copyright owner "before or within thirty days after making, and before distributing any phonorecords of the work." Otherwise, the licensee loses the opportunity to make and distribute phonorecords pursuant to the compulsory license (§ 115(b)(1));

- A copyright owner is entitled to receive copyright royalty fees only on those phonorecords made[3] and distributed[4] after the copyright owner is identified in the registration or other public records of the Copyright Office (§ 115(c)(1));[5]

- The rate payable for each phonorecord made and distributed is adjusted by an independent body which, prior to 1993, was the Copyright Royalty Tribunal.[6]

- A compulsory license may be terminated for failure to pay monthly royalties if a user fails to make payment within 30 days of the receipt of a written notice from the copyright owner advising the user of the default (§ 115(c)(6)).

The Section 115 compulsory license worked well for the next two decades, but the use of new digital technology to deliver music to the public required a second look at the license to determine whether it continued to meet the needs of the music industry. During the 1990s, it became apparent that music services could offer options for the enjoyment of music in digital formats either by providing the public an opportunity to hear any sound recording it wanted on-demand or by delivering a digital version of the work directly to a consumer's computer. In either case, there was the possibility that the new offerings would obviate the need for mechanical reproductions in the forms heretofore used to distribute musical works and sound recordings in a physical format, e.g., vinyl records, cassette tapes and most recently audio compact discs. Moreover, it was clear that digital transmissions were substantially superior to analog transmissions. . . .

3.   *The Digital Performance Right in Sound Recordings Act of 1995*

By 1995, Congress recognized that "digital transmission of sound recordings [was] likely to become a very important outlet for the performance of recorded music." S. Rep. No. 104–128, at 14 (1995). Moreover, it realized that '[t]hese new technologies also may lead to new systems for the electronic distribution of phonorecords with the authorization of the affected copyright owners." *Id.* For these reasons,

---

[3]   Congress intended the term "made" "to be broader than 'manufactured' and to include within its scope every possible manufacturing or other process capable of reproducing a sound recording in phonorecords." H. Rep. No. 1476, at 110 (1976).

[4]   For purposes of Section 115, "the concept of 'distribution' comprises any act by which the person exercising the compulsory license voluntarily relinquishes possession of a phonorecord (considered as a fungible unit), regardless of whether the distribution is to the public, passes title, constitutes a gift, or is sold, rented, leased, or loaned, unless it is actually returned and the transaction cancelled." *Id.*

[5]   This provision replaced the earlier requirement in the 1909 law that a copyright owner must file a notice of use with the Copyright Office in order to be eligible to receive royalties generated under the compulsory license.

[6]   In 1993, Congress passed the Copyright Royalty Tribunal Reform Act of 1993, Pub. L. 103–198, 107 Stat. 2304, which eliminated the Copyright Royalty Tribunal and replaced it with a system of *ad hoc* Copyright Arbitration Royalty Panels (CARPs) administered by the Librarian of Congress.

Congress made changes to Section 115 to meet the challenges of providing music in a digital format when it enacted the Digital Performance Right in Sound Recordings Act of 1995 ("DPRA"), Pub. L. 104–39, 109 Stat. 336, which also granted copyright owners of sound recordings an exclusive right to perform their works publicly by means of a digital audio transmission, 17 U.S.C. § 106(6), subject to certain limitations. *See* 17 U.S.C. § 114. The amendments to Section 115 clarified the reproduction and distribution rights of music copyright owners and producers and distributors of sound recordings, especially with respect to what the amended Section 115 termed "digital phonorecord deliveries." Specifically, Congress wanted to reaffirm the mechanical rights of songwriters and music publishers in the new world of digital technology. It is these latter amendments to Section 115 that are of particular interest today.

First, Congress expanded the scope of the compulsory license to include the making and distribution of a digital phonorecord and, in doing so, adopted a new term of art, the "digital phonorecord delivery" ("DPD"), to describe the process whereby a consumer receives a phonorecord by means of a digital transmission, the delivery of which requires the payment of a statutory royalty under Section 115. The precise definition of this new term reads as follows:

> A "digital phonorecord delivery" is each individual delivery of a phonorecord by digital transmission of a sound recording which results in a specifically identifiable reproduction by or for any transmission recipient of a phonorecord of that sound recording, regardless of whether the digital transmission is also a public performance of the sound recording or any nondramatic musical work embodied therein. A digital phonorecord delivery does not result from a real-time, nonintegrated subscription transmission of a sound recording where no reproduction of the sound recording or the musical work embodied therein is made from the inception of the transmission through to its receipt by the transmission recipient in order to make the sound recording audible.

17 U.S.C. § 115(d). What is noteworthy about the definition is that it includes elements related to the right of public performance and the rights of reproduction and distribution with respect to both the musical work and the sound recording. The statutory license, however, covers only the making of the phonorecord, and only with respect to the musical work. The definition merely acknowledges that the public performance right and the reproduction and distribution rights may be implicated in the same act of transmission and that the public performance does not in and of itself implicate the reproduction and distribution rights associated with either the musical composition or the sound recording. In fact, Congress included a provision to clarify that "nothing in this Section annuls or limits the exclusive right to publicly perform a sound recording or the musical work

embodied therein, including by means of a digital transmission." 17 U.S.C. § 115(c)(3)(K). [¶] . . .

* * * *

The difficult issue, however, is identifying those reproductions that are subject to compensation under the statutory license, a subject I will discuss in greater detail.

Regulatory Responses

* * * *

2. *Consideration of what constitutes an "incidental digital phonorecord delivery"*

In 1995 when Congress passed the DPRA, its intent was to extend the scope of the compulsory license to cover the making and distribution of a phonorecord in a digital format—what Congress referred to as the making of a digital phonorecord delivery. Since that time, what constitutes a "digital phonorecord delivery" has been a hotly debated topic. Currently, the Copyright Office is in the midst of a rulemaking proceeding to examine this question, especially in light of the new types of services being offered in the marketplace, e.g. "on-demand streams" and "limited downloads." *See* 66 FR 14099 (March 9, 2001).

The Office initiated this rulemaking proceeding in response to a petition from the Recording Industry Association of America ("RIAA"), asking that we conduct such a proceeding to resolve the question of which types of digital transmissions of recorded music constitute a general DPD and which types should be considered an incidental DPD. RIAA made the request after it became apparent that industry representatives found it difficult, if not impossible, to negotiate a rate for the incidental DPD category, as required by law, when no one knew which types of prerecorded music were to be included in this category.

Central to this inquiry are questions about two types of digital music services: "on-demand streams" and "limited downloads." For purposes of the inquiry, the music industry has defined an "on-demand stream" as an "on-demand, real-time transmission using streaming technology such as Real Audio, which permits users to listen to the music they want when they want and as it is transmitted to them," and a "limited download" as an "on-demand transmission of a time-limited or other use-limited (i.e., non-permanent) download to a local storage device (e.g., the hard drive of the user's computer), using technology that causes the downloaded file to be available for listening only either during a limited time (e.g., a time certain or a time tied to ongoing subscription payments) or for a limited number of times.". . .

The perspective of music publishers appears to be clear. They have taken the position that both on-demand streams and limited downloads implicate their mechanical rights. Moreover, they maintain that copies made during the course of a digital stream or in the transmission of a DPD are for all practical purposes reproductions of phonorecords that are covered by the compulsory license. The recording industry supports this view, recognizing that while certain reproductions of a musical work are exempt under Section 112(a), other reproductions do not come within the scope of the exemption. For that reason, the recording industry has urged the Office to interpret the Section 115 license in such a way as to cover all reproductions of a musical work necessary to operate such services; and, we are considering their arguments. In the meantime, certain record companies and music publishers have worked out a marketplace solution.

a. Marketplace solution

In 2001, the RIAA, the National Music Publishers' Association, Inc. ("NMPA"), and the Harry Fox Agency, Inc. ("HFA") entered into an agreement concerning the mechanical licensing of musical works for new subscription services on the Internet. Licenses issued under the RIAA/NMPA/HFA agreement are nonexclusive and cover all reproduction and distribution rights for delivery of on-demand streams and limited downloads and include the right to make server copies, buffer copies and other related copies used in the operation of a covered service. . . .

The industry approach to resolving the problems associated with mechanical licensing for digital music services is both innovative and comprehensive. . . . The Office welcomes the industry's initiative and creativity, and fully supports marketplace solutions to what really are commercial transactions between owners and users.

However, parties should not need to rely upon privately negotiated contracts exclusively to clear the rights needed to make full use of a statutory license, or need to craft an understanding of the legal limits of the compulsory license within the provisions of the private contract. The scope of the license and any limitations on its use should be clearly expressed in the law. . . . [¶]

. . . . Section 115 does not provide a definition for incidental DPDs, so what constitutes an "incidental DPD" is not always clear. While some temporary copies made in the course of a digital transmission, such as buffer copies made in the course of a download, may qualify, others—such as buffer copies made in the course of a transmission of a performance (e.g., streaming)—are more difficult to fit within the statutory definition. In either case, it is clear that such copies need to comply with the statutory definition in order to be covered by the compulsory license. In other words, the copies must result in an "individual delivery of a phonorecord which results in a *specifically identifiable reproduction* by or for any transmission recipient of a phonorecord of that sound recording." 17 U.S.C. § 115(d) (emphasis added), Similar questions can be raised with respect to cache copies and intermediate server copies made in the course of (1) downloads and (2) streaming of performances.

* * * *

The critical question to be decided is whether an on-demand stream results in reproductions that reasonably fit the statutory definition of a DPD, and creates a "phonorecord by digital transmission of a sound recording which results in a specifically identifiable reproduction by or for any transmission recipient," as required by law. Unless it does so, such reproductions cannot be reasonably considered as DPDs for purposes of Section 115, no matter what position private parties take within the four corners of their own agreement. What is more clear is that the delivery of a digital download, whether limited or otherwise, for use by the recipient appears to fit the statutory definition, since it must result in an identifiable reproduction in order for the recipient to listen to the work embodied in the phonorecord at his leisure.

b.   Possible legislative solutions

. . . . [¶] At this point in time, I do not have any specific legislative recommendations, but I would like to outline a number of possible options for legislative action. I must emphasize that these are not recommendations, but rather they constitute a list of options that should be explored in the search for a comprehensive resolution of issues involving digital transmission of musical works. . . .

The options that should be considered fall into two distinct categories: (1) legal questions concerning the scope of the Section 115 license, and (2) technical problems associated with service of notice and payment of royalty fees under the Section 115 license.

Among the options that should be considered relating to the scope of the license are:

- **Elimination of the Section 115 statutory license.** Although the predecessor to Section 115 served as a model for similar provisions in other countries, today all of those countries, except for the United States and Australia, have eliminated such compulsory licenses from their copyright laws. A fundamental principle of copyright is that the author should have the exclusive right to exploit the market for his work, except where this would conflict with the public interest. A compulsory license limits an author's bargaining power. It deprives the author of determining with whom and on what terms he wishes to do business. In fact, the Register of Copyrights' 1961 Report on the General Revision of the

U.S. Copyright Law favored elimination of this compulsory license.

I believe that the time has come to again consider whether there is really a need for such a compulsory license. Since most of the world functions without such a license, why should one be needed in the United States? Is a compulsory license the only or the most viable solution? Should the United States follow the lead of many other countries and move to a system of collective administration in which a voluntary organization could be created (perhaps by a merger of the existing performing rights organizations and the Harry Fox Agency) to license all rights related to making musical works available to the public? Should we follow the model of collective licenses in which, subject to certain conditions, an agreement made by a collective organization would also apply to the works of authors or publishers who are not members of the organization? Will the creation of new digital rights management systems make such collective administration more feasible?

In fact, we already have a very successful model for collective administration of similar rights in the United States: performing rights organizations (ASCAP, BMI and SESAC) license the public performance of musical works—for which there is no statutory license—providing users with a means to obtain and pay for the necessary rights without difficulty. A similar model ought to work for licensing of the rights of reproduction and distribution.

As a matter of principle, I believe that the Section 115 license should be repealed and that licensing of rights should be left to the marketplace, most likely by means of collective administration. But I recognize that many parties with stakes in the current system will resist this proposal and that there would be many practical difficulties in implementing it. The Copyright Office would be pleased to study the issue and prepare a report for you with recommendations, if appropriate. Meanwhile, there are a number of other options for legislative action that merit consideration.

- **Clarification that all reproductions of a musical work made in the course of a digital phonorecord delivery are within the scope of the Section 115 compulsory license. . . .** [C]onsideration should be given to amending Section 115 to provide expressly that all reproductions that are incidental to the making of a digital phonorecord delivery, including buffer and cache copies and server copies,[9] are included within the scope of the Section 115 compulsory license. Consideration should also be given to clarifying that

---

[9] Technically, these are phonorecords rather than copies. See 17 U.S.C. § 101 (definitions of "copies" and "phonorecords"), but terms such as "buffer copy" and "server copy" have entered common parlance.

no compensation is due to the copyright owner for the making of such copies beyond the compensation due for the ultimate DPD.

- **Amendment of the law to provide that reproductions of musical works made in the course of a licensed public performance are either exempt from liability or subject to a statutory license.** When a webcaster transmits a public performance of a sound recording of a musical composition, the webcaster must obtain a license from the copyright owner for the public performance of the musical work, typically obtained from a performing rights organization such as ASCAP, BMI or SESAC. At the same time, webcasters find themselves subject to demands from music publishers or their representatives for separate compensation for the reproductions of the musical work that are made in order to enable the transmission of the performance. . . . [I]t is inconsistent to provide broadcasters with an exemption in Section 112(a) for ephemeral recordings of their transmission programs but to subject webcasters to a statutory license for the functionally similar server copies that they must make in order to make licensed transmissions of performances. DMCA Section 104 Report, U.S. Copyright Office 144 n. 434 (2001). In this respect, the playing field between broadcasters and webcasters should be leveled, either by converting the Section 112(a) exemption into a statutory license or converting the Section 112(e) statutory license into an exemption.

I can also see no justification for providing a compulsory license which covers ephemeral reproductions of sound recordings needed to effectuate a digital transmission and not providing a similar license to cover intermediate copies of the musical works embodied in these same sound recordings, but that is what Section 112 does in its current form. Parallel treatment should be offered for both the sound recordings and the musical works embodied therein which are part of a digital audio transmission.

- **Expansion of the Section 115 DPD license to include both reproductions and performances of musical works in the course of either digital phonorecord deliveries or transmissions of performances,** *e.g.,* in the course of streaming on the Internet. As noted above, many of the problems faced by online music services arise out of the distinction between reproduction rights and performance rights, and the fact that demands are often made upon services to pay separately for the exercise of each of these rights whether the primary conduct is the delivery of a DPD or the transmission of a performance. Placing both uses under a single license requiring a single payment—a form of "one-stop shopping" for rights—might be a more rational and workable solution.

Among the options that have been proposed relating to service of notice and payment of royalty fees under the Section 115 license are suggestions by users who have expressed their frustration with the cumbersome process involved in securing the Section 115 license, including:

- **Adoption of a model similar to that of the Section 114 webcasting license, requiring services using the license to file only a single notice with the Copyright Office stating their intention to use the statutory license with respect to all musical works.** Section 115 currently requires the licensees to serve notices identifying each musical work for which they intend to make and distribute copies under the compulsory license. This system has worked fairly well and is sensible with respect to the traditional mechanical license, but do such requirements make sense for services offering DPDs of thousands of musical works? The current system does have the virtue of giving a copyright owner notice when one of its works is being used under the compulsory license. Removing that requirement would mean that a copyright owner would find it much more difficult to ascertain whether a particular work owned by that copyright owner is being used by a particular licensee under the compulsory license. . . .

- **Establishment of a collective to receive and disburse royalties under the Section 115 license.** Again, Section 114 may provide a useful model. . . . While such a scheme offers obvious benefits to licensees, copyright owners (and, in particular, those copyright owners who are readily identifiable under the current system) might find themselves receiving less in royalties than they receive under the current system, since administrative costs of the receiving and disbursing entity presumably would be deducted from the royalties and the allocation of royalties might result in some copyright owners receiving less than they would receive under the current system, which requires that each copyright owner be paid precisely (and directly) the amount of royalties derived from the use of that copyright owner's musical works.

- **Designation of a single entity, like the Copyright Office, upon which to serve notices and make royalty payments.** I am skeptical of the benefits of this approach, which would shift to the Copyright Office the burden of locating copyright owners and making payments to them. The administrative expense and burden would likely be considerable, and giving a government agency the responsibility to receive such funds, identify copyright owners and make the appropriate payments to each copyright owner is probably not the most efficient means of getting the royalties to the persons entitled to them.

- **Creation of a complete and up-to-date electronic database of all musical works registered with the Copyright Office. . . .** Determining who owns the copyright in a particular work is not always a simple matter. Someone reviewing the current Copyright Office records to determine ownership of a particular work would have to search both the registration records and the records of documents of transfer that are recorded with the Office. While basic information about post-1977 registrations and documents of transfer is available through the Office's online indexing system, in any case where ownership of all or some of the exclusive rights in a work have been transferred it would be necessary to review the copy of the actual document of transfer maintained at the Copyright Office (and not available online) to ascertain exactly what rights have been transferred to whom. Chain of title can often be complicated. . . . While the registration and recordation system works reasonably well when a person is seeking information on ownership of a particular work, such information must usually be interpreted by a lawyer (especially if there have been transfers of ownership). The system is not well-suited for the type of large-scale licensing of thousands of works in a single transaction that is desired by online music services.

- **Shifting the burden of obtaining the rights to the sound recording copyright owner.** Online music services generally transmit performances or DPDs of sound recordings that have already been released by record companies. The record company already will have obtained a license—either directly from the copyright owner of the musical work that has been recorded or by means of the section 115 statutory license—for use of the musical work. . . . Because record companies already have substantial incentives and presumably have greater ability to clear the rights to the musical works that they record, consideration should be given to permitting online music services ... to stand in the shoes of the record company as beneficiaries of the compulsory license for DPDs. The online music company could make royalty payments to the record company for the DPDs of the musical works, and the record company (which might charge the online music company an administrative fee for the service) could pass the royalty on to the copyright owner of the musical work. . . .

* * * *

- **Provision for payment of royalties on a quarterly basis rather than a monthly basis**. It is my understanding that most licenses *negotiated* with copyright owners under Section 115 (e.g., the licenses given by the Harry Fox Agency in lieu of actual statutory licenses) provide for quarterly payments rather than the monthly payments required under the compulsory license. . . . Amending Section 115 to require quarterly payments might lead many more licensees to elect to obtain statutory licenses rather than deal directly with publishers or their agents. Consideration should be given to whether that would be desirable.

* * * *

In general, I do support the music industry's attempt to simplify the requirements for obtaining the compulsory license and its desire to create a seamless licensing regime under the law to allow for the making and distribution of phonorecords of sound recordings containing musical works.

However, the need for extensive revisions is difficult to assess. Prior to the passage of the DPRA, each year the Copyright Office received fewer than twenty notices of intention from those seeking to obtain the Section 115 license. Last year, two hundred and fourteen (214) notices were filed with the Office, representing a significant jump in the number of notices filed with the Office over the pre-1995 era. Yet, the noted increase represents only 214 song titles, a mere drop in the bucket when considered against the thousands, if not hundreds of thousands, of song titles that are being offered today by subscription music services. While we acknowledge that this observation may merely reflect the reluctance of users to use the license in its current form to clear large numbers of works, as well as the fact that users may file with the Office only when our records do not provide the identity and current address of the copyright owner, it may also represent the success of viable marketplace solutions.

Certainly we have heard few complaints about the operation of Section 115 in the context of the traditional mechanical license. To the extent that reform of the license is needed, it may be that the traditional mechanical license should be separated from the license for DPDs, and that two different regimes be created, each designed to meet the needs of both copyright owners and the persons using the two licenses.

COPYRIGHT OFFICE REPORT: COPYRIGHT AND THE MUSIC MARKETPLACE (FEB. 2015)

In February, 2015, the Copyright Office issued a study on Copyright and the Music Marketplace that addressed many of the issues raised in the preceding materials and suggested specific amendments to the Copyright Act and related statutes. Below are excerpts from that Report relating to mechanical licenses. As you read these excerpts and the subsequent discussion of the Music Modernization Act, consider how these recommendations evolved from the Register of Copyright's 2004 statement above, as well as how the Music Modernization Act of 2018 addressed (or failed to address) the issues raised in this study.

In its introduction to the issue of mechanical rights licensing, the report reiterated many of the points raised in the 2004 Peters Statement and summarized issues raised by music industry participants, noting:

- Broad dissatisfaction with royalty rates established by the CRB and recommendations by some parties that a "willing buyer/willing seller" standard be adopted so that rates might better "reflect the fair market value of musical works"

- "[N]ear universal concern about the inefficiencies of the mechanical licensing process," particularly with respect to

  o the existing per-work licensing model in the context of digital music services

  o "lack of readily available data concerning musical work ownership" and

  o Section 115's detailed accounting and payment requirements

- Arguments by publishers and songwriters regarding perceived unfairness in the absence of audit rights

Below are excerpts from the report's summary of the parties' proposals and the Copyright Office's analysis and recommendation for legislative action relating to mechanical rights licensing.

UNITED STATES COPYRIGHT OFFICE

COPYRIGHT AND THE MUSIC MARKETPLACE

A REPORT OF THE REGISTER OF COPYRIGHTS   FEBRUARY 2015

. . . Mechanical Rights Licensing

* * * *

d.   Parties' Proposals

Elimination of Statutory License

Songwriters and publishers appear almost universally to favor the elimination of the section 115 statutory license, albeit with an appropriate phase-out period.[FN584 omitted] They assert that the statutory regime creates an artificial *status quo* that precludes a private market from developing.[FN585 omitted] Musical work owners predict that the elimination of a license would allow "a functioning licensing market . . . [to] flourish."[586]

Digital music services, however, assert that the section 115 license is both important and fair, as it "provides an *essential counter-balance to the unique market power of copyright rights owners* . . . by providing a mechanism for immediate license coverage, thereby negating the rights owner's prerogative to withhold the grant of a license."[587] Thus, some licensees view section 115 as a protection against monopoly power that allows the public to enjoy musical works while still compensating copyright owners.[588] Spotify argued that the free market is not stifled by the statutory license, but that section 115 instead acts as "an indispensable component to facilitating a vibrant marketplace for making millions of

---

[586]   NMPA & HFA First Notice Comments at 7; *see also* IPAC First Notice Comments at 6.

[587]   DiMA First Notice Comments at 19 (emphasis in original).

[588]   Modern Works Music Publishing Second Notice Comments at 3 (explaining that section 115 is "an *antitrust provision* that accelerates the entry of musical works into the public sphere, while ensuring that copyright holders are paid.") (emphasis in original).

sound recordings available to the public on commercially reasonable terms."[589]

Blanket Licensing

In light of the widely perceived inefficiencies of song-by-song licensing of mechanical rights—particularly as compared to the collective approach of the PROs—a wide range of stakeholders suggested that a blanket system would be a superior means of licensing mechanical rights.[FN590 omitted] As RIAA noted, blanket licensing avoids the administrative costs associated with negotiating and managing large numbers of licenses of varying terms and provides a way for legitimate services to avoid infringement risk.[591] Similarly, the publisher ABKCO opined that blanket license agreements would facilitate the use of music and would help licensees fulfill notification and reporting obligations.[592] IPAC[3] suggested that blanket licensing could be implemented through the creation of one or more licensing agencies.[593]

To highlight the complexity of licensing in the modern music marketplace, RIAA described the experience of one of its members, which had released "a very successful album," and "had to obtain for that album 1481 licenses for the release of three physical products, the 92 digital products, the 27 songs across the 51 songwriters" with a total of "89 shares."[594] One of those shares "represented [a] 1.5 percent interest in a song, and there were two publishers for that."[595] According to the RIAA, apart from multiple songwriter interests, one of the reasons for this explosion in licensing complexity is the increased complexity of the releases themselves—whereas in the past a record label release consisted of "a disk and some liner notes," today it comprises multiple digital formats, different kinds of audiovisual presentations, and different kinds of music services.[596]

In light of its belief that these problems "cannot be solved by piecemeal efforts," RIAA proposed fundamentally restructuring performance and mechanical licensing for musical works.[597] Under the RIAA proposal, record labels would receive a compulsory blanket license covering all rights (performance, mechanical, and synch) necessary for what RIAA calls "modern music products," including audiovisual products like music videos,

---

[589] Spotify First Notice Comments at 3.

[591] RIAA Second Notice Comments at 13.

[592] ABKCO First Notice Comments at 1–2.

[3] Ed. Note: At page 19 of the Copyright and the Music Marketplace Report, the Copyright Office noted: "Interested Parties Advancing Copyright ('IPAC'), was established in Nashville in 2014 and includes independent publishers, administrators, business managers, and entertainment attorneys."

[593] IPAC First Notice Comments at 6–7.

[594] Tr. 25:11–16 (June 4, 2014) (Steven Marks, RIAA).

[595] *Id. at* 25:16–18.

[596] *Id. at* 24:04–26:18.

[597] RIAA First Notice Comments at 15–17.

videos with album art or liner notes, and lyric videos.[598] The rate court and CRB would be eliminated. Instead, the record labels and publishers would agree upon splits of revenues received by the record labels from their sale and licensing of recorded music. The record companies would have sole responsibility to sell and license those products; those deals would be negotiated by the labels in the marketplace (except for uses falling under the section 112 and 114 licenses).[FN599 omitted] RIAA believed that its proposal would achieve fair market rates for publishers and songwriters while retaining the benefits of a collective licensing system, such as simplified licensing and lower administrative costs.[FN600 omitted]

But publishers and songwriters vigorously resisted RIAA's proposal, arguing that it would merely shift control over musical works from songwriters and music publishers to record labels—since the labels would then be in charge of licensing decisions and royalty rates.[601] They also expressed concern about bringing audiovisual works or other rights currently outside of the compulsory system under a statutory blanket license.[602] NMPA characterized the RIAA's proposal as "seeking to expand the scope of the Sec. 115 compulsory license to authorize almost all forms of exploitation of a sound recording, including, among other things, record label created videos, and 'first use' rights."[603]

* * * *

IV. Analysis and Recommendations

It may be the very power of music that has led to its disparate treatment under the law. The songs we enjoy in our early years resonate for the rest of our lives. Human beings have a deep psychological attachment to music that often seems to approach a sense of ownership; people want to possess and share the songs they love. Perhaps this passion is one of the reasons music has been subject to special treatment under the law.

Regardless of what has animated our century-old embrace of government regulation of music, the Copyright Office believes that the time is ripe to question the existing paradigm and consider meaningful change.

. . . . [¶] As a number of commenters remarked during the course of this study, if we were to do it all again, we would never design the system that we have today. But as tempting as it may be to daydream about a new

---

[598] *Id.* at 16. RIAA made clear that its proposed blanket license would not cover other uses of musical works, like synch rights for movie, television, and advertising, performances within live venue, stand-alone lyrics, and sheet music. *Id.* at 17.

[601] NMPA Second Notice Comments at 32–33; *see also* Tr. at 245:12–20 (June 24, 2014) (Peter Brodsky, Sony/ATV).

[602] LaPolt Second Notice Comments at 14; NMPA Second Notice Comments at 32–35; NSAI Second Notice Comments at 8; *see also* Tr. at 214:14–20 (June 16, 2014) (John Barker, IPAC); Tr. at 246:21–247:09 (June 24, 2014) (Peter Brodsky, Sony/ATV).

[603] NMPA Second Notice Comments at 32.

model built from scratch, such a course would seem to be logistically and politically unrealistic. We must take the world as we find it, and seek to shape something new from the material we have on hand.

. . . . The recommendations below seek to capitalize on the value that existing institutions and methods could continue to provide under an updated framework.

Rather than presenting a detailed plan, the Office's recommendations should be understood as high-level and preliminary in nature—more of a sketch than a completed picture. . . .

A. *Guiding Principles*

The Copyright Office appreciates and agrees with the four grounding principles that were articulated by many during the course of this study, as discussed above. These are:

- Music creators should be fairly compensated for their contributions
- The licensing process should be more efficient
- Market participants should have access to authoritative data to identify and license sound recordings and musical works
- Usage and payment information should be transparent and accessible to rightsowners

As much as there may be consensus on these points, however, the opposite could be said of stakeholders' views as to how best to achieve them. Having considered the plethora of issues that plague our current licensing system—and how they might practically be addressed—the Office has identified some additional principles that it believes should also guide any process of reform. These are:

- Government licensing processes should aspire to treat like uses of music alike
- Government supervision should enable voluntary transactions while still supporting collective solutions
- Ratesetting and enforcement of antitrust laws should be separately managed and addressed
- A single, market-oriented ratesetting standard should apply to all music uses under statutory licenses

Each of these principles is explored below in the context of the Office's overall recommendations.

* * * *

3. Mechanical Licensing and Section 115

As sales of CDs continue to slip away, mechanical licensing revenues for the reproduction and distribution of musical works under section 115—once the primary source of income for publishers and songwriters—likewise continue to decline.[FN839 omitted] Although sales of digital downloads through services like Apple iTunes have bolstered mechanical royalties in recent years, even DPD sales have fallen off with the rise of streaming services such as Spotify. Even so, mechanical revenues still currently represent about 23% of income for musical works (as compared to 52% generated by performances, 20% by synch uses, and 5% by other uses).[FN840 omitted] Of the mechanical share, a small amount is generated by the server and other reproductions of musical works required for online providers to operate interactive streaming services which, as noted above, also pay performance royalties.

Commenting parties have focused on two primary areas of concern with respect to the 106-year old compulsory license embodied in section 115. The first, put forth by music publishers and songwriters, is that the compulsory license does not permit them to control the use of their works or seek higher royalties. Relatedly, rightsowners also complain about the lack of an audit right under section 115 and practical inability to enforce reporting or payment obligations against recalcitrant licensees.

The second overarching concern with respect to section 115 is its song-by-song licensing requirement, which dates back to the original incarnation of the compulsory license in 1909. Song-by-song licensing is viewed by music users as an administratively daunting—if not sisyphean—task in a world where online providers seek licenses for millions of works.

a. Free Market Negotiation Versus Collective Administration

One of the most challenging issues to arise in this study has been whether musical work owners should be liberated from the section 115 compulsory licensing regime. Citing the significantly higher rates paid to sound recording owners for uses where musical work owners are regulated and sound recording owners are not—and the contrasting example of the unregulated synch licensing market, where in many cases licensing fees are evenly apportioned—music publishers and songwriters have made a convincing case that government regulation likely yields rates below those they would enjoy in a free market. Motivated by concerns similar to those raised in connection with the consent decrees, many musical work owners would like to see an end to section 115. The Office—which, as noted, believes that compulsory licensing should exist only when clearly needed to address a market failure—is sympathetic to these claims.

On the other hand, in comparison to the record industry—where three major companies can issue licenses for much of the most sought-after content, with independent labels representing the balance[841]—U.S. musical work ownership is more diffusely distributed over a greater number of entities and self-published songwriters.[842] Unlike sound recordings—which are typically wholly owned by an individual label— many musical works are controlled by two, three or even more publishers. Notwithstanding the default rules of joint copyright ownership, publishers and songwriters frequently have understandings that they are not free to license each other's respective shares.[FN843 omitted] And there are millions of musical works in the marketplace. Spotify, for instance, reports that it offers some 30 million songs on its service.[FN844 omitted]

Understandably, as described above, digital music providers are intensely opposed to a system that would require individual licensing negotiations with thousands of musical work owners. Even publisher proponents of the proposal to sunset section 115 do not deny that it would be extraordinarily difficult for services to negotiate with myriad small copyright owners for all of the mechanical licenses they seek, and concede that there needs to be some sort of collective system to facilitate licensing from smaller rightsowners.[FN845 omitted] But apart from the optimistic view that should section 115 be retired, new entities will spring forth to meet this need, publisher participants offered little detail concerning how a collective solution would reliably be implemented.

The difficulty, then, is how to reconcile the competing values of free market negotiation and collective management of rights. Each represents an express goal of reform: fair compensation to creators, on the one hand, and licensing efficiency, on the other. A middle path may provide the best answer.

Publisher Opt-Out Right

The Office believes that rather than eliminating section 115 altogether, section 115 should instead become the basis of a more flexible collective licensing system that will presumptively cover all mechanical uses except to the extent individual rightsowners choose to opt out. At least initially, the mechanical opt-out right would extend to the uses that could

---

[841] Although three record companies dominate, independent record labels enhance the market with a rich variety of content, including well-known hit recordings. A2IM First Notice Comments at 1 ("Billboard Magazine, using Nielsen SoundScan data, identified the Independent music label sector as 34.6 percent of the music industry's U.S. recorded music sales market in 2013."). Many independent labels are represented by organizations that aggregate repertoire for collective licensing, such as the U.K.-based Merlin, which issues licenses to digital services such as YouTube and Spotify on a global basis. *Merlin Strikes Licensing Deal with YouTube*, MERLIN (Oct. 19, 2011), http://www.merlinnetwork.org/news/post/merlin-strikes-licensing-deal-with-youtube.

[842] In recent years, as with recorded music, there has been significant consolidation in the music publishing industry, such that the three major publishers now represent some 63% of the market—approaching the record company figure of 65%. *See* Christman, *First-Quarter Music Publishing Rankings: SONGS Surges Again*; Bruce Houghton, *Indie Labels Now Control 34.6% Of U.S. Market*, HYPEBOT (Jan. 16, 2014), http://www.hypebot.com/hypebot/2014/01/indie-labels-now-control-346-of-us-market.html.

be withdrawn from blanket performance licenses—that is, to interactive streaming rights—as well as to downloading activities[FN846 omitted] (which, by judicial interpretation, do not implicate the public performance right[FN847 omitted]). To reiterate, these are uses where sound recording owners operate in the free market but publishers do not.[FN848 omitted]

* * * *

b.   Shift to Blanket Licensing

Regardless of its scope or whether it includes an opt-out right, the Office believes that section 115 should be updated to better meet the needs of the digital age. Congress attempted to do this in 2006 with the proposed SIRA legislation, which would have created a blanket mechanical license for digital uses. Although that bill got as far as passing the relevant House subcommittee,[862] it faced a degree of resistance from certain industry participants and ultimately foundered.

Based on stakeholders' sentiments, however—especially those of the digital services—the time seems ripe to revisit the concept of blanket mechanical licensing. Users have made a strong case in pointing out the inefficiencies of a system that requires multiple licensees to ascertain song-by-song licensing information and maintain it in redundant databases. At the same time, they have repeatedly expressed a willingness to pay royalties in cases where they are unable to track down licensing information for particular songs in order to mitigate their potential liability for unmatched works.[863]

But while considerably more user-friendly for licensees, blanket licensing cannot be viewed as a panacea. It does not cure the problem of bad or missing data, or the inability to match sound recordings with the musical works they embody. In any situation where a licensed transaction takes place, in order for a royalty to be paid to the rightsowner, there must

---

[862] *See* SIRA, H.R. 5553. In 2006, the House Judiciary Committee's Subcommittee on Courts, the Internet, and Intellectual Property forwarded SIRA to the full Judiciary Committee by unanimous voice vote. *See H.R. 5553*, CONGRESS.GOV (June 8, 2006), https://www.congress.gov/bill/109th-congress/house-bill/5553.

[863] Notably, section 115 has, since its inception, provided a mechanism to file a notice of intent to use a musical work with the Copyright Office if the owner of the work cannot be found in Copyright Office records. *See* 17 U.S.C. § 115(b)(1). Under section 115, no royalties are required to be collected by the Office in connection with these filings. *See id.* It is the Office's understanding, however, that this provision does little to ameliorate concerns of digital services in light of the filing fees that the Office must charge to administer such song-by-song notices, which may number in the thousands or perhaps even the millions for a large service. *See* DiMA First Notice Comments at 20 ("[T]o the extent that a service chooses to file statutory license notices with the Copyright Office for the many musical works for which the relevant rightsowners cannot be identified, the costs can be overwhelming given the volume of works at issue."). Under its current fee schedule, the Office charges a fee of $75 for a notice of intention covering a single title, and for notices incorporating additional titles, a fee of $20 per 10 additional titles submitted on paper, and $10 per 100 additional titles submitted electronically. 37 C.F.R. § 201.3(e). Moreover, due to IT constraints within the Library of Congress, the Office is still not able to accept such submissions in bulk electronic form.

be a link between the work used and the owner of that work. Especially in the case of lesser known works, it can be challenging to match a sound recording with the musical work it embodies, and that musical work to its owner.

Today, under section 115, the burden of identifying the song and its owners is on the licensee (or sometimes a third-party agent retained by the licensee); the link is made in the song-specific license that issues. Blanket licensing merely kicks this responsibility down the road for another actor to address. Under a blanket system, the obligation to make the match between the exploited work and its owner falls on the licensing organization—for example, the PRO—which must identify the use and connect it to the owner.

Nonetheless, the Office believes that on the whole, the benefits of a blanket licensing approach clearly outweigh the conceded challenges of matching reported uses with copyright owners. Throughout this study, the Office has heard consistent praise for the efficiencies of blanket licensing by SoundExchange and the PROs, and widespread frustration with the song-by-song process required under section 115—including from publishers who find themselves burdened with deficient notices and accountings.

Ultimately, it is in the interest of music owners as well as licensees to improve the licensing process so it is not an obstacle for paying services. To further facilitate the rights clearance process and eliminate user concerns about liability to unknown rightsowners, the Office believes that mechanical licensing, like performance licensing, should be offered on a blanket basis by those that administer it. This would mean that a licensee would need only to file a single notice to obtain a repertoire-wide performance and mechanical license from a particular licensing entity. Song-by-song licensing is widely perceived as a daunting requirement for new services and an administrative drag on the licensing system as a whole. The move to a blanket system would allow marketplace entrants to launch their services—and begin paying royalties—more quickly.

c. Ratesetting

As explained above, the Office supports integration of mechanical with performance rights administration to simplify the licensing process, especially where both rights are implicated, as in the case of interactive streaming.[FN864 omitted] Even if both rights are not implicated—as in the case of DPD licensing—it would still appear to make sense to combine licensing resources into unified MROs ["Music Rights Organizations"], especially in a world of declining mechanicals. In order to reap the rewards of a more unified licensing structure, the Office further recommends that the ratesetting procedures for mechanical and performance also be combined.

"As-Needed" Ratesetting

The CRB establishes mechanical rates for the various categories of use that fall under section 115.[865] The Office believes this responsibility should continue, though with an important modification: as is now the case with performance rights, rather than establish rates across the board every five years, the CRB should set rates for particular uses only on an as-needed basis when an MRO and licensee are unsuccessful in reaching agreement.

* * * *

Use of Benchmarks

Throughout the study, there has been significant debate concerning the ratesetting standard that should be employed by the CRB . . . . [¶] As noted above, the Office believes that all potentially informative benchmarks should be reviewed and evaluated in the ratesetting process. An advantage of the proposed opt-out system is that there would be a greater likelihood that actual market benchmarks would exist to inform the ratesetting tribunal. . . .

* * * *

d. Audit Right

Publishers and songwriters have long complained about the lack of an audit right under section 115.[FN869 omitted] In addition to monthly statements of use, the statute provides that each licensee must provide to the copyright owner a cumulative annual statement that is certified by a CPA.[870] But section 115 confers no express right for a copyright owner to audit a licensee's statements.[871]

Although section 114 does not include such an express audit right, it does provide that the CRB shall "establish requirements by which copyright owners may receive reasonable notice of the use of their sound recordings under [section 114], and under which records of such use shall be kept and made available by entities performing sound recordings."[872] Based on this authority, the CRB has promulgated regulations to permit

---

[865] A section 115 license is only available after phonorecords of the work in question have first been distributed to the public in the United States under the authority of the copyright owner. 17 U.S.C. § 115(a)(1). The Office is not recommending any change to this aspect of the statutory system, which permits musical work owners to control the so-called "first use" (or initial recording) of their works.

[870] In a notable departure from the terms of section 115, HFA, which licenses mechanical rights on behalf of numerous publishers, does not rely upon the submission of certified annual statements but instead conducts royalty examinations of significant licensees to verify their payments.

[871] By contrast, the section 111 and 119 cable and satellite compulsory licenses, as well as the Audio Home Recording Act ("AHRA"), provide for a royalty verification process for the benefit of copyright owners. *See* 17 U.S.C. §§ 111(d)(6) (cable licensees), 119(b)(2) (satellite licensees), 1003(c)(2) (manufacturers of digital audio recording devices and media).

[872] *Id.* § 114(f)(4)(A).

audits of royalty payments of statutory licensees by SoundExchange.[873] Notably, there is parallel language in section 115, though it is limited to reporting in connection with the making of DPDs, and no equivalent royalty verification rules have been promulgated by the CRB under that provision.[874]

Regardless of any other potential adjustments to section 115, the Office believes that the mechanical licensing system should be amended to provide for an express audit right covering the full range of uses under section 115, with the particular logistics of the audit process to be implemented by regulation.[FN875 omitted]

* * * *

NOTES AND QUESTIONS

1.   The Copyright Office materials excerpted above raise a host of issues faced by participants in the industry in the context of mechanical licensing of compositions. As both the Register's Statement and the 2015 Report noted, although there was agreement across constituencies regarding the problems with the current licensing system, there was a great disparity of views about the best legal solutions to those problems. What do you think about the respective parties' positions and arguments about possible "fixes" to the mechanical licensing system that were excerpted above? Which did you find most compelling?

2.   Consider the Guiding Principles stated by the Copyright Office in the 2015 Report in the excerpt above. Do you agree with them as appropriate general principles for considering amendments to the Copyright Act? Do the recommendations by the Copyright Office in the above excerpt seem consistent with those principles? Why or why not? Keep these Guiding Principles in mind, as well as the more specific recommendations by the Copyright Office in the excerpts above, as you read the following materials about the Music Modernization Act's changes to the mechanical licensing provisions of the Copyright Act. Do you think that the final amendments are consistent with the Guiding Principles? Are there recommendations that you believe the MMA should have addressed but did not?

---

[873]   37 C.F.R. §§ 380.6, 380.15, 380.25.

[874]   17 U.S.C. § 115(c)(3)(D).

C. THE MUSIC MODERNIZATION ACT OF 2018 AND CURRENT LAW GOVERNING MECHANICAL LICENSING: COPYRIGHT OFFICE CIRCULARS 73A AND 73B RE 17 U.S.C. § 115

As the prior sections demonstrate, there was no shortage of challenges involving the law relating to mechanical licensing in the digital age. Interest groups on all sides of the issue, as well as multiple Registers of Copyright and studies going back decades, all pointed to the shortcomings of attempts to apply the antiquated rules surrounding Section 115 in the digital age. This history, as well as the shared belief by virtually all parties that the system needed to change in order to accommodate the scale and technical realities of the digital age, led to passage of the seminal Music Modernization Act in 2018.

The Music Modernization Act is long and complex; some provisions took effect immediately and others were designed to be rolled in over a longer time period. Some key categories of changes to the Copyright Act that were the focus of the MMA include:

(1) adoption of a blanket statutory mechanical license for compositions used by digital music providers, to be administered by a newly-established "Mechanical Licensing Collective";

(2) amendment to the rate-setting standards to adopt a uniform, "willing buyer, willing seller" standard in the context of statutory performance licenses across all digital music platforms;

(3) addressing procedures for PRO rate court proceedings in the S.D.N.Y., including provisions for randomized assignment of judges to decide rate disputes regarding ASCAP and BMI;

(4) allowing rate court judges to consider royalty rates for sound recordings when setting rates for performances of compositions;

(5) providing for congressional oversight of future changes to the ASCAP and BMI consent decrees;

(6) provision of some federal protection for pre-1972 sound recordings and limitation of state law protections for those recordings in the context of digital streaming services;

(7) creating mechanisms for producers, mixers, and sound engineers to participate more fully in royalties from statutory licenses.

This section deals with the first, and most complicated, change in music licensing that resulted from the MMA. (Previous chapters, including Chapters 3, 4, and 6, have addressed the other listed changes made by the MMA.)

Since the MMA became law, the Copyright Office has published several online circulars and FAQs to explain how the compulsory mechanical license will work under the amended law.

Circular 73A[4] deals with the compulsory license for making and distributing phonorecords *other than* digital phonorecord deliveries—and the process remains essentially unchanged from the prior procedure for obtaining a mechanical license for use of a composition in a sound recording. Once a phonorecord of a composition has been distributed to the public under the authority of the copyright owner of the work within the United States or one of its territories, the compulsory license is available to anyone who wishes to record the composition and who meets the conditions of the license. This license is a "per-work, song-by-song" license; it does not operate as a blanket license and it does not preclude direct negotiation with the owner of the composition. The Section 115 license permits licensees who satisfy its requirements to make and distribute phonorecords "only if the primary purpose in making phonorecords of the musical work is to distribute them to the public for private use."[5] The most common use of this type of mechanical license relates to the distribution of physical records and compact discs.

Circular 73B[6] addresses new procedure for the compulsory license of ***digital phonorecord deliveries (DPDs)*** enacted in October of 2018:

> Under section 115 of the Copyright Act, an individual or entity, subject to certain terms and conditions, may make digital phonorecord deliveries (DPDs) of nondramatic musical works if they have already been distributed as phonorecords to the public in the United States under the authority of the copyright owner. When this condition does not exist, a digital music provider may still make and distribute a DPD of a musical work if it satisfies three criteria:
>
> 1. the first fixation of the sound recording embodied in the DPD was made under the authority of the musical work copyright owner;
>
> 2. the sound recording copyright owner has the authority of the musical work copyright owner to make and

---

[4]   Available at https://www.copyright.gov/circs/circ73a.pdf.

[5]   17 U.S.C. § 115(a)(1)(A).

[6]   Available at https://www.copyright.gov/circs/circ73b.pdf.

distribute digital phonorecord deliveries of such musical work to the public; and

3. the sound recording copyright owner authorizes the digital music provider to make and distribute digital phonorecord deliveries of the sound recording to the public.

NOTE: A nondramatic musical work is an original work of authorship consisting of music—the succession of pitches and rhythm—and any accompanying lyrics not created for use in a motion picture or dramatic work.

On October 11, 2018, the Orrin G. Hatch-Bob Goodlatte Music Modernization Act updated section 115 to establish a new blanket license for **digital** music providers to engage in specific covered activities, namely, permanent downloads, limited downloads, and interactive streaming.

This blanket license is not yet available. However, the Office will no longer accept Notices of Intention to Obtain a Compulsory License (NOIs) for making a DPD of a musical work, such as in the form of a permanent download, limited download, or interactive stream. During the current transition period, set to end on the license availability date of January 1, 2021, licensees may still serve NOIs directly on copyright owners and, as discussed further below, may in certain circumstances enjoy a limitation of liability for activity covered by section 115.

After the transition period, users will be able to obtain a blanket license covering all musical works available for compulsory licensing for DPDs by submitting a notice of license to the Mechanical Licensing Collective (MLC). Designated by the Register of Copyrights, the MLC's duties will include collecting and distributing royalties from digital musical providers, establishing a musical works database, and administering a process by which copyright owners can claim ownership of musical works (and shares of musical works).

* * * *

What Is a Digital Phonorecord Delivery?

A digital phonorecord delivery (DPD), is the individual digital transmission of a sound recording resulting in a specifically identifiable reproduction by or for a recipient, regardless of whether the digital transmission is also a public performance of the sound recording or any underlying nondramatic musical work. The reproduction must be sufficiently permanent or stable to permit it to be perceived, reproduced, or otherwise communicated for a period of more than transitory duration. The reproduction may be permanent or available to the recipient for a limited period of time or for a specified number of performances. A DPD includes all phonorecords that are made for the purpose of making the delivery. Permanent downloads, limited downloads, and interactive streams are DPDs.

What Can I Do under a Compulsory License or Limitation on Liability?

If you meet the statutory requirements, including payment of required royalties, you may engage in the following activities, known as "covered activities":

- Make and distribute DPDs of the eligible nondramatic musical work, including in the form of a permanent download, limited download, or interactive stream, where the primary purpose is distribution to the public for private use.

- Make a musical arrangement of the work to the extent necessary to conform it to the style or manner of interpretation of the performance involved.

You cannot engage in the following activities. You will need to seek permission from the copyright owner to:

- Make, reproduce, or distribute a sound recording publicly distributed in phonorecords.

- Distribute phonorecords intended for use in background music systems, jukeboxes, broadcasting, or any other public use (such as a concert).

- Change the basic melody or fundamental character of the work in the arrangement.

- Claim copyright protection in your arrangement as a derivative work.

Does "Covered Activity" Include Making and Reproducing a Sound Recording?

No. Section 115 does not cover sound recordings. Rather, it covers the reproduction and distribution of nondramatic musical works.

A musical work and a sound recording are two separate works for copyright purposes. The author of a musical work is generally the composer and any lyricist. A sound recording, on the other hand, is the fixation of a series of musical, spoken, or other sounds, often of a musical work. The author(s) of a sound recording is generally the performer(s) whose performance is fixed and/or the producer(s) who captures and processes the performance to make the final recording.

Licenses generally must be obtained separately from the copyright owners of the sound recording and the underlying musical work. Copyright in a sound recording is not the same as, or a substitute for, copyright in the underlying musical work.

For more general information about these works, see *Copyright Registration for Musical Compositions* (**Circular 50**), *Copyright Registration for Sound Recordings* (**Circular 56**), and *Copyright Registration of Musical Compositions and Sound Recordings* (**Circular 56A**).

D. COPYRIGHT OFFICE 2019 FINAL RULEMAKING

After the MMA was signed into law in the fall of 2018, the Copyright Office sought public comment on that process and issued a final rulemaking in July 2019, designating a mechanical licensing collective (MLC) and digital licensee coordinator (DLC) in 37 C.F.R. § 210.1, with an explanation in the publication of the final rule in 84 Fed. Reg. 32274–01 (July 8, 2019). Below are excerpts from the Copyright Office explanation of the process and final rule, available in full through its web page devoted to implementation of the MMA at https://www.copyright.gov/rulemaking/mma-designations/. The Copyright Office web page provides the full record of materials in the rulemaking proceeding, including public comments, ex parte materials, and the Federal Register notice setting forth the Register's analysis and conclusions.

DESIGNATION OF MUSIC LICENSING COLLECTIVE AND DIGITAL LICENSEE COORDINATOR
84 Fed. Reg. 32274–01 (July 8, 2019)[7]

Summary: Pursuant to the Musical Works Modernization Act, title I of the Orrin G. Hatch-Bob Goodlatte Music Modernization Act (MMA), the U.S. Copyright Office has designated a mechanical licensing collective (MLC) and a digital licensee coordinator (DLC) to carry out key functions under the statute.

Title I of the MMA modified the existing section 115 "mechanical" license for reproduction and distribution of musical works in phonorecords

---

[7]   Footnotes are omitted from this excerpt.

(which was previously obtained by licensees on a per-work, song-by-song basis) to establish a new blanket license for digital music providers to engage in specific covered activities (namely, permanent downloads, limited downloads, and interactive streaming).

The MMA directs the Register of Copyrights to designate an entity as the MLC to administer the blanket license and distribute collected royalties to songwriters and music publishers. The MLC is tasked with developing and maintaining a comprehensive database of musical works and sound recordings, which will be publicly available. The MMA also allows the Register to designate a DLC, which will represent digital music services in the administration of the license and in the determination of the administrative assessment fee paid by digital music providers for the reasonable costs of establishing and operating the new MLC. Both entities will be subject to a redesignation process commencing in January 2025.

In December 2018, the Office issued a notice of inquiry soliciting proposals from entities seeking to be designated as the MLC or DLC. Following submission of proposals, the Office also received over 600 comments from members of the public regarding these submissions.

Based on the submissions received and the selection criteria provided in the statute, the Register designated the **Mechanical Licensing Collective, Inc.** as the MLC, and the **Digital Licensee Coordinator, Inc.** as the DLC, with the Librarian's approval.

* * * *

* * * * *A.   MLC Designation Requirements, Duties, and Functions*

The entity designated as the MLC must be:

- A single nonprofit entity that is created by copyright owners to carry out its statutory responsibilities;

- "endorsed by, and enjoy[ ] substantial support from, musical work copyright owners that together represent the greatest percentage of the licensor market for uses of such works in covered activities, as measured over the preceding 3 full calendar years;"

- able to demonstrate to the Copyright Office that, by the license availability date, it will have the administrative and technological capabilities to perform the required functions; and

- governed by a board of directors and include committees that are composed of a mix of voting and non-voting members as directed by the statute.

If no single entity meets each of these statutory criteria, the Register must designate as the MLC the entity that most nearly fits these qualifications. After five years, the Register will commence a periodic review of this designation.

The MMA enumerates a number of required functions for the MLC. A core aspect of the MLC's responsibilities includes identifying musical works and copyright owners, matching them to sound recordings (and addressing disputes), and ensuring that a copyright owner gets paid as he or she should. To that end, the MLC will create and maintain a free, public database of musical work and sound recording ownership information. The MLC will administer processes by which copyright owners can claim ownership of musical works (and shares of such works), and by which royalties for works for which the owner is not identified or located are equitably distributed to known copyright owners on a market share basis after a required holding period. The MLC will participate in proceedings before the CRJs to establish the administrative assessment that will fund the MLC's activities, as well as proceedings before the Copyright Office with respect to the foregoing activities.

The board of the MLC shall consist of fourteen voting members and three nonvoting members. Ten voting members shall be representatives of music publishers that have been assigned exclusive rights of reproduction and distribution of musical works with respect to covered activities, and four other voting members shall be professional songwriters who have retained and exercise exclusive rights of reproduction and distribution for musical works they have authored. There are also three nonvoting members that will represent the interests of songwriters, music publishers, and digital licensees via representatives of relevant trade associations or, in the case of licensees, the DLC, if one has been designated. Within one year of designation, the MLC must establish publicly available bylaws relating to the governance of the collective, following statutory criteria.

By statute, the MLC board must establish three committees. First, an operations advisory committee will make recommendations concerning the operations of the collective, "including the efficient investment in and deployment of information technology and data resources." Second, an unclaimed royalties oversight committee will establish policies and procedures necessary to undertake a fair distribution of unclaimed royalties. Third, a dispute resolution committee will establish policies and procedures for copyright owners to address disputes relating to ownership interests in musical works, including a mechanism to hold disputed funds pending the resolution of the dispute.

B. *DLC Designation Criteria and Functions*

Similar to the MLC, the DLC must:

- Be a single nonprofit entity created to carry out certain statutory responsibilities;

- be endorsed by digital music service providers and significant nonblanket licensees that together represent the greatest percentage of the licensee market for uses of musical works in covered activities, as measured over the preceding 3 calendar years; and

- possess the administrative and technological capabilities necessary to carry out a wide array of authorities and functions.

The Register is directed to designate the DLC following substantially the same procedure described for designation of the MLC. Unlike the MLC, in the event the Register is unable to identify an entity that fulfills the criteria for the DLC, the Register may decline to designate a DLC; in that event, the statutory references to the DLC go without effect unless or until a DLC is designated.

The DLC is tasked with coordinating the activities of the licensees. The DLC shall make reasonable, good faith efforts to assist the MLC in its efforts to locate and identify copyright owners of unmatched musical works (and shares of such works) by encouraging digital music providers to publicize the existence of the collective and the ability of copyright owners to claim unclaimed accrued royalties, including by posting contact information for the collective at reasonably prominent locations on digital music provider websites and applications, and conducting in-person outreach activities with songwriters. The DLC is authorized to participate in proceedings before the CRJs to determine the administrative assessment to be paid by digital music providers, and before the Copyright Office with respect to the blanket mechanical license.

* * * *

C. *Conclusion*

* * * *

As the legislative history amply documents, this historic music copyright legislation was enacted only in the wake of significant consensus-building and cooperation across a wide berth of industry stakeholders. Now that it is time to roll up sleeves, sustained dedication to these worthy goals will be critical as the MLC and DLC turn to the many tasks involved in preparation for the license availability date.

The Copyright Office looks forward to working with the MLC, DLC, and other interested parties on next steps in MMA implementation. As noted, the MLC and DLC, along with the Copyright Office, are asked to facilitate education and outreach regarding the new blanket licensing system to the broader songwriting community. In the coming months, the Office will initiate additional regulatory activities required under the statute and begin planning its public policy study regarding best practices, which the MLC may implement to identify musical work copyright owners with unclaimed accrued royalties and reduce the incidence of unclaimed royalties. Future information regarding those activities will be made available at: https://www.copyright.gov/music-modernization/.

＊ ＊ ＊ ＊

NOTES AND QUESTIONS

1.   Compare the practical workings of the section 114 statutory license and the section 115 mechanical license for *non-digital* phonorecord reproductions of sound recordings (described in the Copyright Office's Circular 73A). For these traditional 115 mechanical licenses, the statutory rate often serves as a ceiling, with actual rates paid under agreements with the Harry Fox Agency being lower than the statutory rate and the Harry Fox licenses serving as an alternative to the statutory license process. Why do you think such a practice developed? Is it that different from the negotiation process that exists for the section 114 license? What makes the latter potentially more complicated?

2.   What are your thoughts about the effectiveness of the Music Modernization Act in addressing the concerns raised in the Register's 2004 Statement and Copyright Office's 2015 report on the music marketplace? Did it go far enough, too far, or get it just right? Are there important issues that should have been addressed but were not? Are there additional constituencies whose voices should have been heard in the process?

3.   One of the most striking things about the enactment of the MMA was the fact that it was unanimously approved in both the House and Senate at a time when the federal legislature was fractured and after many previous versions of some parts of the Act died in committee. What do you think was the motivating force behind the success of this version?

4.   What issues do you see arising in the context of establishing a new blanket licensing system for digital distribution of musical compositions? At the time this text was published, the process still ongoing. We recommend a review of the updates on the Copyright Office web page dedicated to implementation of the MMA: https://www.copyright.gov/music-modernization/.

5.   The Copyright Office has outlined the next steps for implementation of the MMA's mechanical licensing revisions to the Copyright Act as follows in its *Frequently Asked Questions on the Designation of the Mechanical Licensing Collective and the Digital Licensee Coordinator*, available at https://www.copyright.gov/rulemaking/mma-designations/faq.html:

What are the Copyright Office's next steps in implementing the MMA?

While the designation of the MLC and DLC allows these entities to begin performing many of their statutory functions, the MMA also requires additional activities of the Copyright Office and, separately, the Copyright Royalty Board. The Copyright Office is directed to promulgate regulations related to the license and operation of the MLC, including requirements for notices of license and non-blanket activity, usage reporting, handling of confidential information, and operational aspects of the MLC database. The Copyright Office will also engage in education and outreach activities to inform the public of important changes under the law, including by educating songwriters and others about the process by which they may claim ownership of musical works in the MLC database and receive royalties for uses of these works. The Office will also conduct a policy study regarding best practices for the MLC.

Separately, the Copyright Royalty Judges have initiated a proceeding to determine the administrative assessment that digital music providers and any significant nonblanket licensees must pay to fund the operations of the MLC. The Copyright Office's inquiry and process for designating the MLC and DLC was separate and without prejudice to the Copyright Royalty Judges' administrative assessment proceeding.

6.   As the Copyright Office has proceeded with the process of proposing new rules for the reporting obligations of the MLC and seeking public comment on aspects of the new digital mechanical licensing system, the MLC has begun its own work in education and outreach. Its website includes the following graphic[8] about the manner in which the MLC will operate:

---

8   https://www.themlc.com/how-it-works (used by permission of the MLC).

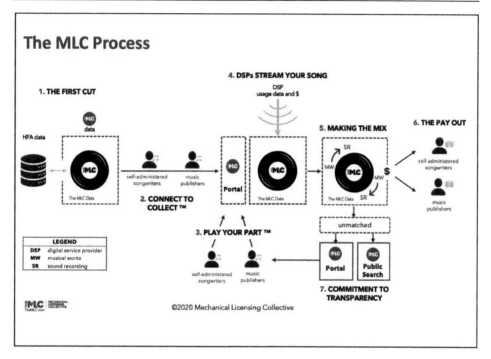

The MLC Process

©2020 Mechanical Licensing Collective

E. MUSIC PUBLISHER DISPUTES WITH SPOTIFY OVER MECHANICAL LICENSING

In December 2015, class action suits were filed in federal court—one led by musician and songwriter David Lowery and one by songwriter Melissa Ferrick, which were later consolidated into a single action—alleging that Spotify USA had failed to comply with the Section 115 notice and payment requirements for reproductions of compositions in sound recordings made in connection with Spotify's streaming services. The dispute centered around so-called "unmatched" royalties, where Spotify could not identify or locate the author of a composition for which a mechanical royalty was owed. Although Spotify filed notices of intent under Section 115 with respect to those songs that it included in its streaming services for whom composers were identified, it had publicly noted the difficulty in identifying the co-authors of each of the tens of millions of copyrighted musical works included in its streaming platform. The class action plaintiffs asserted that Spotify did not make a reasonable effort to identify owners of thousands of songs and that their identities could have been readily found. The litigation focused attention on the inherent problems faced by services like Spotify that wanted to make a huge catalog of works available for streaming but that lacked sufficient information to obtain all of the required licenses for doing so.

By this time, with consumer preferences moving from ownership of music (through downloads or CD purchases) to access to music (through subscription or free streaming services), the music industry was both literally and figuratively invested in Spotify's success. Both record companies and music publishers were interested in negotiating a solution to the problem of mechanical licensing in the context of digital streaming. The National Music Publishers Association (NMPA) reached an agreement with Spotify in 2016, with a three-month opt-in period for any of its member publishers to share in a $30 million pool in exchange for a limitation of Spotify's liability for unmatched royalties for a two-year period. This settlement also provided a set of "best practices" for future efforts by Spotify to match royalties to publishers and songwriters.

In the consolidated class actions by Lowery and Ferrick, the district court certified the settlement class and approved a settlement totaling more than $112 million in 2018. Below are excerpts from the opinion approving the class action settlement, Ferrick v. Spotify USA, Inc., 2018 WL 2324076 (S.D.N.Y. May 22, 2018). First, in finding class settlement certification appropriate, the court reasoned:

* * * *

Here, the settlement addresses a question common to all class members. As the class is defined, all class members will have a certificate of registration for a musical composition that Spotify made available for streaming or downloading without Spotify having a license to do so. Indeed, as the Central District of California explained in its decision granting the motion to consolidate in this case, Spotify is alleged to have infringed class members' copyrights by "reproduc[ing] and/or distribut[ing] . . . copyrighted musical compositions using Spotify's streaming service and offline listening service, without identifying and/or locating the owners of those compositions for payment or a notice of intent to reproduce." Dkt. No. 72 at 3. Whether Spotify's alleged conduct constitutes copyright infringement is "a common contention . . . capable of classwide resolution" whose "truth or falsity will resolve an issue that is central to the validity of each one of the claims in one stroke." *Wal-Mart Stores, Inc.*, 564 U.S. at 350. As for typicality, the named Class Plaintiffs are Melissa Ferrick (individually and doing business as Nine Two One Music and Right On Records/Publishing), Jaco Pastorius, Inc., and Gerencia 360 Publishing, Inc. According to the Consolidated Complaint, Ferrick has over 150 copyrighted musical compositions, and her songs have been streamed one million times by Spotify without a license; Jaco Pastorius, Inc. is a corporation that owns the songs of Jaco Pastorius, songs that have been streamed millions of times by Spotify without a license; and

Gerencia 360 Publishing, Inc. is a company that owns copyrights to the songs of artists who are signed to the Gerencia 360 record label, and its songs have been streamed millions of times by Spotify without a license. *See* Dkt. No. 75 (Consolidated Complaint) ¶¶ 8–11. Thus the named Class Plaintiffs have claims that are likely typical of the claims of other class members.

     * * * *

The court also ruled that the settlement itself was fair, reasonable, and adequate, both procedurally and substantively, noting "it is far from clear that they would have been able to establish liability or damages—or damages as significant as the recovery established in the settlement."[9]

Another hurdle for Spotify and other digital phonorecord delivery services in their efforts to streamline mechanical licensing and limit liability is ongoing litigation filed by musician Eminem's publishing company, Eight Mile Style, against Spotify in federal court in Nashville, Tennessee, in August of 2019. Eight Mile Style asserted that Spotify's failure to take reasonable steps to identify, notify, and pay Eight Mile Style for the Eminem songs it streams was a willful copyright infringement. In addition, it specifically challenged the MMA's limitation of liability set out in Section 115(d)(10), which retroactively eliminated any damages other than actual unpaid royalties, claiming it to be a violation of both substantive and procedural due process and of the takings clauses of the Constitution.[10]

---

[9] Some related litigation followed this settlement, in which parties who opted out of the settlement sought damages arising from similar claims. Lawsuits were filed by Wixen Music Publishing, Bob Guadio, and Bluewater Music Services Corp. near the end of 2017, just as the Music Modernization Act was in its draft stages. The MMA, enacted a little over ten months later, included a limitation of liability for digital phonograph delivery services like Spotify for any lawsuits filed after January 1, 2018:

> A copyright owner that commences an action under section 501 on or after January 1, 2018, against a digital music provider for the infringement of the exclusive rights provided by paragraph (1) or (3) of section 106 arising from the unauthorized reproduction or distribution of a musical work by such digital music provider in the course of engaging in covered activities prior to the license availability date, shall, as the copyright owner's sole and exclusive remedy against the digital music provider, be eligible to recover the royalty prescribed under subsection (c)(1)(C) and chapter 8, from the digital music provider, provided that such digital music provider can demonstrate compliance with the requirements of subparagraph (B), as applicable. In all other cases the limitation on liability under this subparagraph shall not apply.

17 U.S.C.A. § 115(d)(10). These additional lawsuits all settled by mid-2019 on undisclosed terms. *See, e.g.,* Jem Aswad, *Spotify Settles $1.6 Billion Lawsuit From Wixen Publishing,* VARIETY (Dec. 20, 2018), *available at* https://variety.com/2018/biz/news/spotify-settles-1-6-billion-lawsuit-from-wixen-publishing-1203093990/. It is thought that this series of lawsuits was instrumental in the willingness of Spotify and other digital music services to come to the table and ultimately facilitate the passage of the MMA. Their main goal in doing so was to end the "notice of intent" process in Section 115 in favor of a blanket licensing system and a music licensing entity that could create and administer a comprehensive database—ultimately leading to the music licensing collective established by the MMA.

[10] *See* Complaint in *Eight Mile Style, LLC v. Spotify USA, Inc.,* Case No. 3:19-cv-00736 (M.D. Tenn. August 21, 2019), available at 2019 WL 4017301. In May 2020, Spotify filed a third party

As of the date of this writing, the litigation was still in the early procedural stages and had not addressed any of the substantive issues raised by the parties, including the constitutional challenge to the Section 115(d)(10) limitation of liability enacted as part of the MMA.

NOTES AND QUESTIONS

1.   The Copyright Office, Congress, and courts have all pointed to the difficulty in balancing an interest in streamlining the licensing process with an interest in allowing copyright owners to both control and be compensated for uses of their intellectual property. Do you think that the MMA has properly struck this balance?

2.   Is it necessary or appropriate to limit liability for past, unlicensed uses of a work in order to facilitate a more modern, streamlined system moving forward? Why or why not?

---

complaint for indemnification against Kobalt Music Publishing America, Inc., which has an administration deal with Eight Mile Style. Spotify's complaint alleges that Kobalt led it to believe that Eight Mile Style's catalog was included in its direct licensing agreement with Kobalt, and that it had been paying royalties to Kobalt for streams of the catalog for years. In its original complaint, Eight Mile Style had alleged that although it granted Kobalt "the right to receive income arising from licenses issued by Eight Mile," it did not grant "the right or ability to license Eight Mile compositions for digital mechanical licenses, unless consented to by Eight Mile." *See* Third Party Complaint in *Eight Mile Style, LLC v. Spotify USA, Inc.*, Case No. 3:19-cv-00736 (M.D. Tenn. May 29, 2020), available at https://www.bloomberglaw.com/product/blaw/document/ X2AIEH8A5P28TJR4I8TJ30VIR90/download?imagename=1.

CHAPTER VIII

SUBSTANTIAL SIMILARITY AND SAMPLING IN MUSIC COPYRIGHT DISPUTES: *YOU CAN'T DO THAT*[1]

■ ■ ■

Just as compositions and sound recordings are treated differently in terms of the nature and scope of protections they receive under U.S. copyright law, so are they sometimes treated differently with respect to the standards for evaluating claims of copyright infringement. In part, this is a function of the nature of the works themselves. Compositions can be unlawfully copied in many ways—for example, the lyrics or sheet music could be literally copied and distributed; a later composer could publish a work that contains similar musical elements or lyrics to a prior work; a sound recording that embodies the composition could be made without compliance with the statutory mechanical license; a sound recording that embodies the composition could be "pirated." However, sound recordings can only be unlawfully copied by reproduction of the actual sounds fixed in the work without permission. Creating a "sound-alike" recording, for example, is expressly permitted under section 114(b), which provides that the exclusive rights to sound recordings "do not extend to the making or duplication of another sound recording that consists entirely of an independent fixation of other sounds, even though such sounds imitate or simulate those in the copyrighted sound recording."

This chapter provides excerpts or summaries of some of the most famous copyright disputes involving claims that an earlier work has been infringed by the release of a later work.[2] We first address compositions, as infringement claims for compositions involve a variety of complex issues that courts have wrestled with for many years. Then, we address sound

---

[1]   John Lennon & Paul McCartney (1964); released by the Beatles on A HARD DAY'S NIGHT (1964).

[2]   Because this textbook presumes some familiarity with U.S. copyright law, we have not included foundational cases on the elements of proof and applicable legal standards for proving copyright infringement that would be discussed in the typical copyright law textbook or treatise. You will see that many such cases (which often relate to copyrighted works other than those specific to the music industry) are cited in the excerpts below for the underlying legal tests applied by the courts, and we refer you to those often-cited authorities if you are interested in more background on the manner in which these legal tests have been developed and applied.

recording infringement in the context of use of a sound recording in a subsequent creative work.

A. COPYRIGHT INFRINGEMENT OF COMPOSITIONS: ACCESS, SUBSTANTIAL SIMILARITY, AND STYLE

The cases below all involve allegations that the combinations of notes and chords and/or lyrics in a song are "substantially similar" to those in an earlier song owned by the plaintiff. Because it is so difficult to prove that the defendant copied the prior work, courts look to whether the two works are *substantially similar* and whether the defendant had *access* to the plaintiff's prior work. As you will see in the cases below, both of these questions are fraught with difficulty in the context of musical works. Even if substantially similar, the portion of a song alleged to be infringing must be the plaintiff's original work, rather than a common element of musical works that has been used in many prior compositions. Like cases involving claims of copyright infringement of most other works, the role of the judge and jury is to determine whether a sufficient amount of the prior work has been used in the later work for an infringement to have occurred. What constitutes a "sufficient amount" will depend on how significant the alleged infringing segment is when compared to the work as a whole. Relatedly, *de minimis* copying is an affirmative defense—i.e., an assertion that the piece taken is so insignificant that it will not be deemed a violation.

In addition to substantial similarity, there is also the question of access by the defendant. Some courts have found that access can be presumed if the prior work was widely distributed, as is the case with popular songs. Below, we provide a cross-section of cases that have addressed these issues in the context of musical compositions. As you read them, note how the standards for evaluating substantial similarity in and access to musical works have evolved over time and how the courts have wrestled with the fact that what appears similar in written musical notation might not sound at all similar to the average listener.

Ira Arnstein

Cole Porter

ARNSTEIN V. PORTER
154 F.2d 464 (2d Cir. 1946)[3]

Opinion by CIRCUIT JUDGE FRANK.

* * * *

2.   The principal question on this appeal is whether the lower court, under Rule 56, properly deprived plaintiff of a trial of his copyright infringement action. The answer depends on whether 'there is the slightest doubt as to the facts.' . . . In applying that standard here, it is important to avoid confusing two separate elements essential to a plaintiff's case in such a suit: (a) that defendant copied from plaintiff's copyrighted work and (b) that the copying (assuming it to be proved) went to far as to constitute improper appropriation.

As to the first—copying—the evidence may consist (a) of defendant's admission that he copied or (b) of circumstantial evidence—usually evidence of access—from which the trier of the facts may reasonably infer copying. Of course, if there are no similarities, no amount of evidence of access will suffice to prove copying. If there is evidence of access and

---
3   Footnotes omitted.

similarities exist, then the trier of the facts must determine whether the similarities are sufficient to prove copying. On this issue, analysis ('dissection') is relevant, and the testimony of experts may be received to aid the trier of the facts. If evidence of access is absent, the similarities must be so striking as to preclude the possibility that plaintiff and defendant independently arrived at the same result.

If copying is established, then only does there arise the second issue, that of illicit copying (unlawful appropriation). On that issue (as noted more in detail below) the test is the response of the ordinary lay hearer; accordingly, on that issue, 'dissection' and expert testimony are irrelevant.

In some cases, the similarities between the plaintiff's and defendant's work are so extensive and striking as, without more, both to justify an inference of copying and to prove improper appropriation. But such double-purpose evidence is not required; that is, if copying is otherwise shown, proof of improper appropriation need not consist of similarities which, standing alone, would support an inference of copying.

Each of these two issues—copying and improper appropriation—is an issue of fact. . . . But a case could occur in which the similarities were so striking that we would reverse a finding of no access, despite weak evidence of access (or no evidence thereof other than the similarities); and similarly as to a finding of no illicit appropriation.

3. We turn first to the issue of copying. After listening to the compositions as played in the phonograph recordings submitted by defendant, we find similarities; but we hold that unquestionably, standing alone, they do not compel the conclusion, or permit the inference, that defendant copied. The similarities, however, are sufficient so that, if there is enough evidence of access to permit the case to go to the jury, the jury may properly infer that the similarities did not result from coincidence.

Summary judgment was, then, proper if indubitably defendant did not have access to plaintiff's compositions. Plainly that presents an issue of fact. On that issue, the district judge, who heard no oral testimony, had before him the depositions of plaintiff and defendant. The judge characterized plaintiff's story as 'fantastic'; and, in the light of the references in his opinion to defendant's deposition, the judge obviously accepted defendant's denial of access and copying. Although part of plaintiff's testimony on deposition (as to 'stooges' and the like) does seem 'fantastic,' yet plaintiff's credibility, even as to those improbabilities, should be left to the jury. . . .

But even if we were to disregard the improbable aspects of plaintiff's story, there remain parts by no means 'fantastic.' On the record now before us, more than a million copies of one of his compositions were sold; copies of others were sold in smaller quantities or distributed to radio stations or band leaders or publishers, or the pieces were publicly performed. If, after hearing both parties testify, the jury disbelieves defendant's denials, it can, from such facts, reasonably infer access. It follows that, as credibility is unavoidably involved, a genuine issue of material fact presents itself. . . . With all that in mind, we cannot now say—as we think we must say to sustain a summary judgment—that at the close of a trial the judge could properly direct a verdict.

We agree that there are cases in which a trial would be farcical. . . . But where, as here, credibility, including that of the defendant, is crucial, summary judgment becomes improper and a trial indispensable. . . .

* * * *

4.   Assuming that adequate proof is made of copying, that is not enough; for there can be 'permissible copying,' copying which is not illicit. Whether (if he copied) defendant unlawfully appropriated presents, too, an issue of fact. The proper criterion on that issue is not an analytic or other comparison of the respective musical compositions as they appear on paper or in the judgment of trained musicians. The plaintiff's legally protected interest is not, as such, his reputation as a musician but his interest in the potential financial returns from his compositions which derive from the lay public's approbation of his efforts. The question, therefore, is whether defendant took from plaintiff's works so much of what is pleasing to the ears of lay listeners, who comprise the audience for whom such popular music is composed, that defendant wrongfully appropriated something which belongs to the plaintiff.

[¶] . . . We should not be taken as saying that a plagiarism case can never arise in which absence of similarities is so patent that a summary judgment for defendant would be correct. Thus suppose that Ravel's 'Bolero' or Shostakovitch's 'Fifth Symphony' were alleged to infringe 'When Irish Eyes Are Smiling.' But this is not such a case. For, after listening to the playing of the respective compositions, we are, at this time, unable to conclude that the likenesses are so trifling that, on the issue of misappropriation, a trial judge could legitimately direct a verdict for defendant.

At the trial, plaintiff may play, or cause to be played, the pieces in such manner that they may seem to a jury to be inexcusably alike, in terms of the way in which lay listeners of such music would be likely to react. The plaintiff may call witnesses whose testimony may aid the jury in reaching its conclusion as to the responses of such audiences. Expert testimony of musicians may also be received, but it will in no way be controlling on the issue of illicit copying, and should be utilized only to assist in determining the reactions of lay auditors. The impression made on the refined ears of musical experts or their views as to the musical excellence of plaintiff's or defendant's works are utterly immaterial on the issue of misappropriation;

for the views of such persons are caviar to the general—and plaintiff's and defendant's compositions are not caviar.

* * * *

Modified in part; otherwise reversed and remanded.

CLARK, CIRCUIT JUDGE (dissenting).

While the procedure followed below seems to me generally simple and appropriate, the defendant did make one fatal tactical error. In an endeavor to assist us, he caused to be prepared records of all the musical pieces here involved, and presented these transcriptions through the medium of the affidavit of his pianist. Though he himself did not stress these records and properly met plaintiff's claims as to the written music with his own analysis, yet the tinny tintinnabulations of the music thus canned resounded through the United States Courthouse to the exclusion of all else, including the real issues in the case. Of course, sound is important in a case of this kind, but it is not so important as to falsify what the eye reports and the mind teaches. Otherwise plagiarism would be suggested by the mere drumming of repetitious sound from our usual popular music, as it issues from a piano, orchestra, or hurdy-gurdy— particularly when ears may be dulled by long usage, possibly artistic repugnance or boredom, or mere distance which causes all sounds to merge. . . .

. . . . In our former musical plagiarism cases we have, naturally, relied on what seemed the total sound effect; but we have also analyzed the music enough to make sure of an intelligible and intellectual decision. Thus in *Arnstein v. Edward B. Marks Music Corp.*, 2 Cir., 82 F.2d 275, 277, Judge L. Hand made quite an extended comparison of the songs, concluding, inter alia: '* * * the seven notes available do not admit of so many agreeable permutations that we need be amazed at the re-appearance of old themes, even though the identity extend through a sequence of twelve notes.' See also the discussion in *Marks v. Leo Feist, Inc.*, 2 Cir., 290 F. 959, and *Darrell v. Joe Morris Music Co.*, 2 Cir., 113 F.2d 80, where the use of six similar bars and of an eight-note sequence frequently repeated were respectively held not to constitute infringement, and *Wilkie v. Santly Bros.*, 2 Cir., 91 F.2d 978, affirming D.C.S.D.N.Y., 13 F.Supp. 136, certiorari denied *Santly Bros. v. Wilkie*, 302 U.S. 735, 58 S.Ct. 120, 82 L.Ed. 568, where use of eight bars with other similarities amounting to over three-quarters of the significant parts was held infringement.

. . . . Music is a matter of the intellect as well as the emotions; that is why eminent musical scholars insist upon the employment of the intellectual faculties for a just appreciation of music.

Consequently I do not think we should abolish the use of the intellect here even if we could. When, however, we start with an examination of the written and printed material supplied by the plaintiff in his complaint and exhibits, we find at once that he does not and cannot claim extensive copying, measure by measure, of his compositions. He therefore has resorted to a comparative analysis . . . to support his claim of plagiarism of small detached portions here and there, the musical fillers between the better known parts of the melody. And plaintiff's compositions, as pointed out in the cases cited above, are of the simple and trite character where small repetitive sequences are not hard to discover. It is as though we found Shakespeare a plagiarist on the basis of his use of articles, pronouns, prepositions, and adjectives also used by others. The surprising thing, however, is to note the small amount of even this type of reproduction which plaintiff by dint of extreme dissection has been able to find.

Though it is most instructive, it will serve no good purpose for me to restate here this showing as to each of the pieces in issue. . . . The usual claim seems to be rested upon a sequence of three, of four, or of five—never more than five—identical notes, usually of different rhythmical values. Nowhere is there anything approaching the twelve-note sequence of the Marks case, supra. . . .

. . . So far as I have been able to discover, no earlier case approaches the holding that a simple and trite sequence of this type, even if copying may seem indicated, constitutes proof either of access or of plagiarism. . . . [¶]

* * * *

Of course it is error to deny trial when there is a genuine dispute of facts; but it is just as much error . . . to deny or postpone judgment where the ultimate legal result is clearly indicated. . . . Here I think we ought to assume the responsibility of decision now. If, however, we are going to the other extreme of having all decisions of musical plagiarism made by ear, the more unsophisticated and musically I the better, then it seems to me we are reversing our own precedents to substitute chaos, judicial as well as musical.

NOTES AND QUESTIONS

1.   Consider the debate between the majority opinion and dissenting opinion in the *Arnstein v. Porter* excerpt above in light of the historical summary in Chapter 1 regarding the shift in society's view of music from one of divine inspiration to a form of "intellectual property" attributable to a human author. What do you think is the proper balance to strike between claims of authorship/ownership and common themes or combinations of notes that have been a part of musical culture for generations? How much of a composition must be substantially similar to a prior work for that composition to be

infringing? How should judges and juries evaluate compositions—by how they sound, or by how the sheet music appears?

2. This theme regarding the conflict between the sound of a composition and how it is represented in written notation has been repeated in numerous subsequent cases, and you will see in some of the excerpts below that courts are still citing to *Arnstein v. Porter* for basic propositions of law in the context of claims of infringement of musical works. The themes introduced by the dissent are also ones that you will see have survived in current-day disputes over ownership and infringement of elements of musical compositions.

3. One way that disputes over how much a prior work has influenced a subsequent work have been resolved is through the granting of shared songwriting credits for the later work, so that the prior composer receives a continuing piece of the revenues from the later work over time. For example, when Brian Wilson wrote "Surfin' U.S.A." for the Beach Boys in 1963, he had Chuck Berry's 1958 song "Sweet Little Sixteen" in mind and intended his song to be a tribute. After Berry sued for infringement, the case was settled by giving publishing rights to the song to Berry and crediting him as a songwriter starting in 1966.[4] Similarly, Radiohead ended up giving writing credits on their song "Creep" to the writers of the Hollies' 1974 hit "The Air I Breathe," Albert Hammond and Mike Hazlewood, after they complained of infringement.[5]

4. Another high-profile example is the dispute between The Verve and The Rolling Stones relating to the use in The Verve's 1997 *Bittersweet Symphony* of a sample from the orchestral version of *The Last Time* by the Stones. The symphony version was recorded by The Andrew Loog Oldham Orchestra in the 1960s and apparently owned by Decca, the Rolling Stones' original record company. The Verve and Decca had agreed in advance to The Verve's use of the sample, and in exchange The Verve had agreed to pay Decca royalties. However, the manager of the Rolling Stones from 1967 to 1970, Allen Klein, sued The Verve on behalf of the songwriters (through his holding company, ABKCO Records), claiming that the band had used more of "The Last Time" than agreed upon, thus infringing on the songwriters' rights. In settling Allen Klein's suit, The Verve gave writing credits to the Rolling Stones' Mick Jagger and Keith Richards and publishing royalties to ABKCO.[6]

> To complicate matters even further, Andrew Loog Oldham, who produced for the Rolling Stones in the 1960s, claimed to own the composition that The Verve had licensed, rather than Decca. In 1999, Oldham sued The Verve for $1.7 million in mechanical royalties—

---

[4] *See Parker v. Winwood*, 938 F.3d 833 (6th Cir. 2019) (Judge Bernice Bouie Donald, dissenting).

[5] *See* Jordan Runtagh, *Songs on Trial: 12 Landmark Music Copyright Cases*, ROLLING STONE MAGAZINE (June 8, 2016), *available at* https://www.rollingstone.com/politics/politics-lists/songs-on-trial-12-landmark-music-copyright-cases-166396/the-verve-vs-the-rolling-stones-1997-60961/.

[6] *Id.* Ironically, the piece of the orchestral arrangement that had been sampled was actually the work of orchestra arranger David Whitaker—who was not credited on any of the recordings. *Id.*

resulting in all mechanical royalties from *Bittersweet Symphony* going to Rolling Stones' members Oldham, Jagger, and Klein.[7] In 2019, however, Mick Jagger and Keith Richards signed over their publishing rights in *Bittersweet Symphony* to The Verve—finally ending the two-decade controversy surrounding the song.[8]

5.   Such disputes are sometimes resolved through contractual agreements in which a popular artist is obligated to record and release covers of a composer's past works. For example, the Beatles often cited Chuck Berry's legendary guitar work as an influence in their own compositions and recordings. Chuck Berry recorded "You Can't Catch Me" in 1956, and when the Beatles recorded "Come Together" in 1969, John Lennon of the Beatles said he used Berry's song as inspiration for his work but maintained that the songs were nothing alike despite their similar lyrics.[9] Morris Levy, who owned the copyright to "You Can't Catch Me," sued, arguing that the Beatles song was the same tune played 1.5 times slower than the original tempo. Ultimately, John Lennon agreed to record other songs owned by Levy on Lennon's next music project to resolve the issue—but new litigation arose over that agreement when Lennon's subsequent album did not include the promised songs. In *Big Seven Music Corp. v. Lennon*, 554 F.2d 504, 506 (2d Cir. 1977), the court described the dispute as being about "alleged broken promises and acrimony between supposed friends in the recording industry." *Id.* At 506–07, 514.

6.   In the excerpt below, you will see another case involving a former Beatle that has had a significant impact in music copyright litigation. In explicitly recognizing that unconscious copying of a widely-distributed song is actionable, it introduced a new layer to the debate about how much composers are able to build upon the works that precede them.

---

[7]   *See* John Willcock, Who's Suing Whom: *Bitter symphony as The Verve is sued by Oldham,* INDEPENDENT, *available at* https://www.independent.co.uk/news/business/whos-suing-whom-bitter-symphony-as-the-verve-is-sued-by-oldham-1046409.html; Anastasia Tsioulcas, *Not Bitter, Just Sweet: The Rolling Stones Give Royalties To The Verve,* NATIONAL PUBLIC RADIO (May 23, 2019), *available at* https://www.npr.org/2019/05/23/726227555/not-bitter-just-sweet-the-rolling-stones-give-royalties-to-the-verve.

[8]   *See* Anastasia Tsioulcas, *Not Bitter, Just Sweet: The Rolling Stones Give Royalties To The Verve,* NATIONAL PUBLIC RADIO (May 23, 2019), *available at* https://www.npr.org/2019/05/23/726 227555/not-bitter-just-sweet-the-rolling-stones-give-royalties-to-the-verve.

[9]   The Beatles Bible: Not Quite as Popular as Jesus, *You Can't Catch Me* (quoting David Sheff, ALL WE ARE SAYING) (the Beatles sang, "Here come old flat-top, he come groovin' up slowly" while Berry sang "Here come a flat-top, he was moving up with me"), *available at* https://www. beatlesbible.com/people/john-lennon/songs/you-cant-catch-me/.

George Harrison, performing in Japan in 1991
Bartek311d [CC BY-SA 4.0
(https://creativecommons.org/
licenses/by-sa/4.0)]

BRIGHT TUNES MUSIC CORP. V. HARRISONGS MUSIC, LTD.
420 F. Supp. 177 (S.D.N.Y. 1976)

OPINION AND ORDER

OWEN, DISTRICT JUDGE.

This is an action in which it is claimed that a successful song, My
Sweet Lord, listing George Harrison as the composer, is plagiarized from
an earlier successful song, He's So Fine, composed by Ronald Mack,
recorded by a singing group called the "Chiffons," the copyright of which is
owned by plaintiff, Bright Tunes Music Corp.

He's So Fine, recorded in 1962, is a catchy tune consisting essentially
of four repetitions of a very short basic musical phrase, "sol-mi-re,"
(hereinafter motif A),[1] altered as necessary to fit the words, followed by
four repetitions of another short basic musical phrase, "sol-la-do-la-do,"
(hereinafter motif B).[2] While neither motif is novel, the four repetitions of
A, followed by four repetitions of B, is a highly unique pattern.[3] In addition,

1

2

3   All the experts agreed on this.

in the second use of the motif B series, there is a grace note inserted making the phrase go "sol-la-do-la-re-do."[4]

My Sweet Lord, recorded first in 1970, also uses the same motif A (modified to suit the words) four times, followed by motif B, repeated three times, not four. In place of He's So Fine's fourth repetition of motif B, My Sweet Lord has a transitional passage of musical attractiveness of the same approximate length, with the identical grace note in the identical second repetition.[5] The harmonies of both songs are identical.[6]

George Harrison, a former member of The Beatles, was aware of He's So Fine. In the United States, it was No. 1 on the billboard charts for five weeks; in England, Harrison's home country, it was No. 12 on the charts on June 1, 1963, a date upon which one of the Beatle songs was, in fact, in first position. For seven weeks in 1963, He's So Fine was one of the top hits in England.

According to Harrison, the circumstances of the composition of My Sweet Lord were as follows. Harrison and his group, which include an American black gospel singer named Billy Preston,[7] were in Copenhagen, Denmark, on a singing engagement. There was a press conference involving the group going on backstage. Harrison slipped away from the press conference and went to a room upstairs and began "vamping" some guitar chords, fitting on to the chords he was playing the words, "Hallelujah" and "Hare Krishna" in various ways.[8] During the course of this vamping, he was alternating between what musicians call a Minor II chord and a Major V chord.

At some point, germinating started and he went down to meet with others of the group, asking them to listen, which they did, and everyone began to join in, taking first "Hallelujah" and then "Hare Krishna" and putting them into four part harmony. Harrison obviously started using the "Hallelujah," etc., as repeated sounds, and from there developed the lyrics, to wit, "My Sweet Lord," "Dear, Dear Lord," etc. In any event, from this

---

4

⁵   This grace note, as will be seen infra, has a substantial significance in assessing the claims of the parties hereto.

⁶   Expert witnesses for the defendants asserted crucial differences in the two songs. These claimed differences essentially stem, however, from the fact that different words and number of syllables were involved. This necessitated modest alterations in the repetitions or the places of beginning of a phrase, which, however, has nothing to do whatsoever with the essential musical kernel that is involved.

⁷   Preston recorded the first Harrison copyrighted recording of My Sweet Lord, of which more infra, and from his musical background was necessarily equally aware of He's So Fine.

⁸   These words ended up being a "responsive" interjection between the eventually copyrighted words of My Sweet Lord. In He's So Fine the Chiffons used the sound "dulang" in the same places to fill in and give rhythmic impetus to what would otherwise be somewhat dead spots in the music.

very free-flowing exchange of ideas, with Harrison playing his two chords and everybody singing "Hallelujah" and "Hare Krishna," there began to emerge the My Sweet Lord text idea, which Harrison sought to develop a little bit further during the following week as he was playing it on his guitar. Thus developed motif A and its words interspersed with "Hallelujah" and "Hare Krishna."

Approximately one week after the idea first began to germinate, the entire group flew back to London because they had earlier booked time to go to a recording studio with Billy Preston to make an album. In the studio, Preston was the principal musician. Harrison did not play in the session. He had given Preston his basic motif A with the idea that it be turned into a song, and was back and forth from the studio to the engineer's recording booth, supervising the recording "takes." Under circumstances that Harrison was utterly unable to recall, while everybody was working toward a finished song, in the recording studio, somehow or other the essential three notes of motif A reached polished form.

"Q. (By the Court): . . . you feel that those three notes . . . the motif A in the record, those three notes developed somewhere in that recording session?

"Mr. Harrison: I'd say those three there were finalized as beginning there."

"Q. (By the Court): Is it possible that Billy Preston hit on those (notes comprising motif A)?

"Mr. Harrison: Yes, but it's possible also that I hit on that, too, as far back as the dressing room, just scat singing."

Similarly, it appears that motif B emerged in some fashion at the recording session as did motif A. This is also true of the unique grace note in the second repetition of motif B.

"Q. (By the Court): All I am trying to get at, Mr. Harrison, is if you have a recollection when that (grace) note popped into existence as it ends up in the Billy Preston recording.

"Mr. Harrison: . . . (Billy Preston) might have put that there on every take, but it just might have been on one take, or he might have varied it on different takes at different places."

The Billy Preston recording, listing George Harrison as the composer, was thereafter issued by Apple Records. The music was then reduced to paper by someone who prepared a "lead sheet" containing the melody, the words and the harmony for the United States copyright application.[9]

---

9   It is of interest, but not of legal significance, in my opinion, that when Harrison later recorded the song himself, he chose to omit the little grace note, not only in his musical recording but in the printed sheet music that was issued following that particular recording. The genesis of

Seeking the wellsprings of musical composition why a composer chooses the succession of notes and the harmonies he does whether it be George Harrison or Richard Wagner is a fascinating inquiry. It is apparent from the extensive colloquy between the Court and Harrison covering forty pages in the transcript that neither Harrison nor Preston were conscious of the fact that they were utilizing the He's So Fine theme.[10] However, they in fact were, for it is perfectly obvious to the listener that in musical terms, the two songs are virtually identical except for one phrase. There is motif A used four times, followed by motif B, four times in one case, and three times in the other, with the same grace note in the second repetition of motif B.[11]

What happened? I conclude that the composer,[12] in seeking musical materials to clothe his thoughts, was working with various possibilities. As he tried this possibility and that, there came to the surface of his mind a particular combination that pleased him as being one he felt would be appealing to a prospective listener; in other words, that this combination of sounds would work. Why? Because his subconscious knew it already had worked in a song his conscious mind did not remember. Having arrived at this pleasing combination of sounds, the recording was made, the lead sheet prepared for copyright and the song became an enormous success. Did Harrison deliberately use the music of He's So Fine? I do not believe he did so deliberately. Nevertheless, it is clear that My Sweet Lord is the

---

the song remains the same, however modestly Harrison may have later altered it. Harrison, it should be noted, regards his song as that which he sings at the particular moment he is singing it and not something that is written on a piece of paper.

[10] Preston may well have been the "composer" of motif B and the telltale grace note appearing in the second use of the motif during the recording session, for Harrison testified:

"The Court: To be as careful as I can now in summing this up, you can't really say that you or Billy Preston or somebody else didn't somewhere along the line suggest these; all you know is that when Billy Preston sang them that way at the recording session, you felt they were a successful way to sing this, and you kept it?

"The Witness: Yes, I mean at that time we chose what is a good performance.

"The Court: And you felt it was a worthy piece of music?

"The Witness: Yes . . . ."

[11] Even Harrison's own expert witness, Harold Barlow, long in the field, acknowledged that although the two motifs were in the public domain, their use here was so unusual that he, in all his experience, had never come across this unique sequential use of these materials. He testified:

"The Court: And I think you agree with me in this, that we are talking about a basic three-note structure that composers can vary in modest ways, but we are still talking about the same heart, the same essence?

"The Witness: Yes.

"The Court: So you say that you have not seen anywhere four A's followed by three B's or four?

"The Witness: Or four A's followed by four B's."

The uniqueness is even greater when one considers the identical grace note in the identical place in each song.

[12] I treat Harrison as the composer, although it appears that Billy Preston may have been the composer as to part. (See fn. 10 supra). Even were Preston the composer as to part, this is immaterial. Peter Pan Fabrics, Inc. v. Dan River Mills, Inc., 295 F.Supp. 1366, 1369 (S.D.N.Y.), aff'd, 415 F.2d 1007 (2d Cir. 1969).

very same song as He's So Fine with different words,[13] and Harrison had access to He's So Fine. This is, under the law, infringement of copyright, and is no less so even though subconsciously accomplished. Sheldon v. Metro-Goldwyn Pictures Corp., 81 F.2d 49, 54 (2d Cir. 1936); Northern Music Corp. v. Pacemaker Music Co., Inc., 147 U.S.P.Q. 358, 359 (S.D.N.Y.1965).

Given the foregoing, I find for the plaintiff on the issue of plagiarism, and set the action down for trial on November 8, 1976 on the issue of damages and other relief as to which the plaintiff may be entitled. The foregoing constitutes the Court's findings of fact and conclusions of law.

So Ordered.

NOTES AND QUESTIONS

1.   After a hearing on damages, Judge Owen concluded that damages for the infringement exceeded $1.5 million, although the judgment for the plaintiff offset those damages due to a finding of breach of fiduciary duty by the entity that acquired the interests of Bright Tunes Music during the pendency of the case. Judge Owen's ruling as to liability was upheld on appeal in *ABKCO Music, Inc. v. Harrisongs Music, Ltd.*, 722 F.2d 988 (2d Cir. 1983). The Second Circuit addressed the argument advanced by Harrison that permitting liability for subconscious copying under the facts of this case would be "unsound policy":

> It is not new law in this circuit that when a defendant's work is copied from the plaintiff's, but the defendant in good faith has forgotten that the plaintiff's work was the source of his own, such "innocent copying" can nevertheless constitute an infringement. *See Sheldon v. Metro-Goldwyn Pictures Corp.*, 81 F.2d at 54; *see also* 3 M. Nimmer, *Nimmer on Copyright* § 13.08 (1983). We do not find this stance in conflict with the rule permitting independent creation of copyrighted material. It is settled that "[i]ntention to infringe is not essential under the [Copyright] Act," *Buck v. Jewel-LaSalle Realty Co.*, 283 U.S. 191, 198, 51 S.Ct. 410, 411, 75 L.Ed. 971 (1931); *see also Plymouth Music Co. v. Magnus Organ Corp.*, 456 F.Supp. 676, 680 (S.D.N.Y.1978); 3 M. Nimmer, *Nimmer on Copyright,* § 13.08 (1983) ("Innocent intent should no more constitute a defense in an infringement action than in the case of conversion of tangible personalty."). Moreover, as a practical matter, the problems of proof inherent in a rule that would permit innocent intent as a defense to copyright infringement could substantially undermine the protections Congress intended to afford to copyright holders. We therefore see no reason to retreat from this

---

[13]   Harrison himself acknowledged on the stand that the two songs were substantially similar. This same conclusion was obviously reached by a recording group called the "Belmonts" who recorded My Sweet Lord at a later time. With "tongue in cheek" they used the words from both He's So Fine and My Sweet Lord interchangeably at certain points.

circuit's prior position that copyright infringement can be subconscious.

722 F.2d at 998–99. What do you think about the merits of Harrison's policy argument? If a defendant is able to make a convincing showing of independent creation of a composition, should the fact that a prior work was widely publicized many years before the defendant's work was created be given significant weight? In other words, does the subconscious copying doctrine eviscerate a defendant's ability to prove independent creation when the prior work was popular?

2.   The next case, *Fantasy Records, Inc. v. Fogerty*, took the subconscious copying doctrine a step further. Fogerty, the sole songwriter and lead singer for the band Creedence Clearwater Revival ("CCR"), transferred all of the copyrights in his CCR songs to publishing companies affiliated with the band's record label, Fantasy Records. After a falling out with Fantasy that involved years of litigation, Fogerty negotiated a release from his recording contract. However, when he released his first single album with his new label, Warner Brothers Records, Fantasy sued both Fogerty and Warner, claiming that the song "Old Man Down the Road" on the Warner-released *Centerfield* album infringed upon the song "Run Through the Jungle," which Fogerty had composed for CCR while under contract with Fantasy. Thus, this case involved self-plagiarism—access was easily established, and if Fogerty could have subconsciously copied one of his prior compositions, even his intent to create an original composition could be disregarded.

Although many of Fogerty's compositions for CCR shared similar components to one another, including those at issue in the lawsuit, the court found a trial warranted because substantial similarity was a question of fact. Similarly, the court found Fogerty's fair use defense was a question of fact that could not be decided on summary judgment, but the court rejected Fogerty's argument that the First Amendment protected him against infringement claims based upon his "style" and that allowing Fantasy's suit to proceed would serve to deprive him of the ability to make a living as a songwriter. As you read the opinion in the *Fogerty* case below, consider what circumstances might make summary judgment appropriate in cases such as these; when will a trial *not* be necessary to determine substantial similarity or fair use? How can copyright law adequately distinguish between protectable expression and style in the context of music; is the idea/expression dichotomy an adequate tool?

John Fogerty performing in Italy in 2009
Photo by Marco Annunziata (CC BY 2.0)

FANTASY, INC. V. FOGERTY
664 F. Supp. 1345 (N.D. Cal. 1987)

ORDER RE PLAINTIFF'S MOTION TO STRIKE AND MOTIONS FOR SUMMARY JUDGMENT AND FOGERTY'S MOTION FOR SUMMARY JUDGMENT

CONTI, DISTRICT JUDGE.

Plaintiff brings this action against defendants John C. Fogerty and Wenaha Music Co., (collectively "Fogerty") and Fogerty's licensees, defendants WEA International, Inc. ("WEA") and Warner Bros. Records, Inc. ("WBR") (collectively "Warner") for copyright infringement. Plaintiff also sues Fogerty for declaratory relief. In turn, Fogerty asserts various counterclaims against plaintiff.

In 1970, Fogerty wrote the song "Run Through the Jungle" ("Jungle"). Fogerty subsequently granted the exclusive rights in the Jungle copyright to plaintiff's alleged predecessors, Cireco Music and Galaxy Records. In return, Fogerty received a sales percentage and other royalties derived from the exploitation of Jungle. In 1984, Fogerty wrote the song "The Old Man Down the Road" ("Old Man"). Fogerty registered a copyright to Old Man and then authorized Warner to distribute copies of Fogerty's performance of Old Man. Plaintiff claims Old Man is Jungle with new words and has sued for infringement.

Several motions bring this matter presently before the court.... Second, plaintiff moves for summary judgment establishing defendants' liability for copyright infringement or, in the alternative, an order specifying that certain facts appear without substantial controversy. Warner joins Fogerty's opposition to this motion. . . .

II. *Motions for Summary Judgment.*

* * * *

A. *Plaintiff's Motion for Summary Judgment Re Copyright Infringement.*

Plaintiff moves for summary judgment concerning defendants' liability for copyright infringement. In addition, plaintiff requests summary judgment regarding defendants' fair use and 1st Amendment defenses. . . . In the alternative, plaintiff seeks an order specifying that certain facts appear without substantial controversy. Warner joins Fogerty's opposition to plaintiff's motion.

1. *Summary Judgment as to Infringement.*

The Ninth Circuit has recently reviewed the elements necessary for a successful claim of copyright infringement.

> To establish a successful claim for copyright infringement, a plaintiff must prove (1) ownership of the copyright, and (2) "copying" of a protectible expression by defendant. [citations omitted] Because direct evidence of copying is rarely available, a plaintiff may establish copying by circumstantial evidence of: (1) defendant's access to the copyrighted work prior to the creation of defendant's work, and (2) substantial similarity of both general ideas and expression between the copyrighted work and the defendant's work.

Baxter v. MCA, 812 F.2d 421, 423 (9th Cir.1987). Once a plaintiff proves access and substantial similarity, the burden shifts to the defendant to disprove copying. *Transgo, Inc. v. Ajac Transmissions Parts Corp.,* 768 F.2d 1001, 1018 (9th Cir.1985).

Addressing the first element, plaintiff has established its chain of title to the Jungle copyright. . . .

The court also finds that plaintiff has satisfied the registration and recordation requirements of the Copyright Act. . . . [¶] Accordingly, plaintiff has proved the first element establishing copyright infringement. The court finds plaintiff the legal owner of the Jungle copyright.

Turning to the second element, plaintiff must prove that defendants copied a protectible expression. As previously explained, plaintiff may show this circumstantially (1) by demonstrating that Fogerty had access to Jungle prior to the creation of Old Man and (2) by providing evidence that establishes a substantial similarity of both general idea and expression between Jungle and Old Man. *See, Baxter,* 812 F.2d at 423.

The court finds that Fogerty had access to Jungle prior to the creation of Old Man. Fogerty admits that at the time he wrote Old Man, he had knowledge of Jungle. . . . In any event, the court finds it self-evident that Fogerty had access to Jungle prior to the creation of Old Man. Fogerty composed Jungle prior to his composing Old Man.

As to substantial similarity, plaintiff maintains that substantial similarity exists between Jungle and Old Man as a matter of law. After reviewing the papers and exhibits submitted by the parties, the court finds that reasonable minds could differ as to the absence or existence of substantial similarity between Jungle and Old Man. *See e.g., Baxter,* 812 F.2d at 424–25.

Accordingly, the court denies plaintiff's motion for summary judgment concerning copyright infringement. The court however does find that plaintiff's ownership of the Jungle copyright and Fogerty's access to Jungle prior to the creation of Old Man are without substantial controversy. Fed.R.Civ.P. 56(d).

2.   *Summary Judgment Re Defendants' Fair Use and 1st Amendment Defenses.*

(a) *Fair Use Defense:*

After reviewing the parties' papers, the court finds that disputed issues of material fact exist concerning defendants' fair use defense. The court therefore denies plaintiff's motion for summary judgment concerning defendants' fair use defense.

(b) *1st Amendment Defense:*

Defendants claim that the 1st Amendment protects them from plaintiff's infringement claim. . . . More specifically, defendants argue that the 1st Amendment protects Fogerty's songwriting style; consequently, a finding of infringement would impair Fogerty's right to earn a livelihood. *Id.*

In *Sid & Marty Krofft Television v. McDonald's Corp.,* 562 F.2d 1157 (9th Cir.1977), the Ninth Circuit found that the "idea/expression" dichotomy of the substantial similarity test serves to accommodate the competing interests of copyright and the 1st Amendment. *Id.,* at 1170. As the Ninth Circuit noted, a party cannot copyright ideas which may be of public interest; but, a party can copyright an idea's specific form of expression. *Id.* Accordingly, the Ninth Circuit observed that:

> [w]ith the law of copyright permitting the free use of ideas, it is not surprising that the few courts addressing the issue have not permitted defendants who copy a work's expression to hide behind the first amendment.

Id.

Therefore, the court grants plaintiff's motion for summary judgment as to defendants' 1st Amendment defense. The "idea/expression" dichotomy serves to accommodate any 1st Amendment concerns expressed by defendants. *See e.g., Fisher v. Dees,* 794 F.2d 432, 434 n. 2 (9th Cir.1986).

* * * *

NOTES AND QUESTIONS

1.   How should courts and juries distinguish between style and protected expression? This is a question that arises not only in music copyright infringement cases, as you see in this chapter, but also in other contexts, such as the right of publicity (addressed in the next chapter).

2.   The *Fogerty* case went to trial, at which Fogerty testified about how he composed "Old Man Down the Road." The jury ruled in Fogerty's favor, finding no infringement. Both the District Court and the Ninth Circuit refused Fogerty's request for attorneys' fees as the prevailing party under Section 505 of the Copyright Act, applying the existing rule in the Ninth Circuit that required a prevailing defendant to prove that the suit was frivolous or brought in bad faith. The United States Supreme Court later reversed the denial of fees, finding that an even-handed standard governs Section 505 awards because prevailing defendants can advance the underlying purposes of the Copyright Act as much as prevailing plaintiffs can. *Fogerty v. Fantasy,* 510 U.S. 517 (1994). The Supreme Court did not address the merits of the infringement claim.

3.   During the *Fogerty* trial, expert witnesses testified as to the originality of the claimed similarities between the two works, with Fogerty's expert noting that many of Fogerty's compositions shared similar chord progressions. One issue that arose during that litigation was that Fogerty composed his songs for CCR by playing/singing them into a tape recorder—he did not write music using musical notation. When it came time to register the songs for copyright, the publishing company that took ownership of the copyrights hired someone to transcribe the music by listening to the completed recording of each song, and the resulting sheet music was what Fantasy registered with the Copyright Office as the copyrighted musical composition. For some songs, including *Run Through the Jungle,* the written version of the composition was different, in places, from the actual song, and a dispute arose over what the copyrighted work actually was—the written composition that was registered with the Copyright Office, or the composition performed in the master recording that was released to the public. The distinction could be significant if the portion of the song alleged to have been infringed appears only in one version (the written notation or the sound recording).

4.   The question of whether the written notation of the composition deposited with the Copyright Office ("deposit copy") or a recorded version of the composition by the composer "counts" as the copyrighted musical work is most

pertinent to compositions covered by the 1909 Copyright Act, as the 1976 Act provided that public distribution of a recording of a composition is considered a publication of that composition. 17 U.S.C. § 101. Thus, composers of musical works published after 1978 may submit either sheet music or a recording as the deposit copy for registration purposes. The deposit copy question was also an issue in the next case, *Williams v. Gaye*, but the Ninth Circuit declined to decide the issue. However, in 2019, the Ninth Circuit granted an *en banc* rehearing in a copyright dispute filed by the estate of Spirit guitarist and composer Randy Wolfe against Led Zeppelin for allegedly copying a riff from the song "Taurus" in "Stairway to Heaven." Although the original jury had ruled in Led Zeppelin's favor, a three-judge panel granted a new trial, finding, *inter alia*, that the deposit copy of the sheet music governed the scope of the protected work, not the original sound recording of the work by the composer. In March 2020, the *en banc* panel affirmed that the deposit copy of the composition "circumscribes the scope of the copyright" and thus that, for compositions published prior to 1978, the sheet music deposited with the Copyright Office would be considered to be the copyrighted work for purposes of substantial similarity analysis even if the composer's intended work as it appears in a recording is different in material respects.[10]

WILLIAMS V. GAYE

895 F.3d 1106 (9th Cir. 2018)

OPINION

M. SMITH, CIRCUIT JUDGE:

After a seven-day trial and two days of deliberation, a jury found that Pharrell Williams, Robin Thicke, and Clifford Harris, Jr.'s song "Blurred Lines," the world's best-selling single in 2013, infringed Frankie Christian Gaye, Nona Marvisa Gaye, and Marvin Gaye III's copyright in Marvin Gaye's 1977 hit song "Got To Give It Up." Three consolidated appeals followed.

Appellants and Cross-Appellees Williams, Thicke, Harris, and More Water from Nazareth Publishing, Inc. (collectively, Thicke Parties) appeal

---

[10] *Skidmore as Tr. for Randy Craig Wolfe Tr. v. Zeppelin*, 952 F.3d 1051, 1064 (9th Cir. 2020).

from the district court's judgment. They urge us to reverse the district court's denial of their motion for summary judgment and direct the district court to enter judgment in their favor. In the alternative, they ask us to vacate the judgment and remand the case for a new trial, on grounds of instructional error, improper admission of expert testimony, and lack of evidence supporting the verdict. If a new trial is not ordered, they request that we reverse or vacate the jury's awards of actual damages and infringer's profits, and the district court's imposition of a running royalty. Finally, they seek reversal of the judgment against Harris, challenging the district court's decision to overturn the jury's general verdict finding in Harris's favor.

Appellants and Cross-Appellees Interscope Records, UMG Recordings, Inc., Universal Music Distribution, and Star Trak, LLC (collectively, Interscope Parties) appeal from the district court's judgment. They urge us to reverse the judgment against them, challenging the district court's decision to overturn the jury's general verdict finding in their favor.

. . . . The Gayes also protectively cross-appeal the district court's ruling limiting the scope of the Gayes' compositional copyright to the four corners of the sheet music deposited with the United States Copyright Office. In the event a new trial is ordered, the Gayes urge us to hold that Marvin Gaye's studio recording of "Got To Give It Up," rather than the deposit copy, establishes the scope of the Gayes' copyright under the Copyright Act of 1909.

* * * *

FACTUAL AND PROCEDURAL BACKGROUND

A. "Got To Give It Up"

In 1976, Marvin Gaye recorded the song "Got To Give It Up" in his studio. "Got To Give It Up" reached number one on Billboard's Hot 100 chart in 1977, and remains popular today.

In 1977, Jobete Music Company, Inc. registered "Got To Give It Up" with the United States Copyright Office and deposited six pages of handwritten sheet music attributing the song's words and music to Marvin Gaye. Marvin Gaye did not write or fluently read sheet music, and did not prepare the deposit copy. Instead, an unidentified transcriber notated the sheet music after Marvin Gaye recorded "Got To Give It Up."

The Gayes inherited the copyrights in Marvin Gaye's musical compositions.

B. "Blurred Lines"

In June 2012, Pharrell Williams and Robin Thicke wrote and recorded "Blurred Lines." Clifford Harris, Jr., known popularly as T.I., separately wrote and recorded a rap verse for "Blurred Lines" that was added to the track seven months later. "Blurred Lines" was the best-selling single in the world in 2013.

Thicke, Williams, and Harris co-own the musical composition copyright in "Blurred Lines." Star Trak and Interscope Records co-own the sound recording of "Blurred Lines." Universal Music Distribution manufactured and distributed "Blurred Lines."

C.   The Action

The Gayes made an infringement demand on Williams and Thicke after hearing "Blurred Lines." Negotiations failed, prompting Williams, Thicke, and Harris to file suit for a declaratory judgment of non-infringement on August 15, 2013.

The Gayes counterclaimed against the Thicke Parties, alleging that "Blurred Lines" infringed their copyright in "Got To Give It Up,"[FN1 omitted] and added the Interscope Parties as third-party defendants.

D.   The District Court's Denial of Summary Judgment

The district court denied Williams and Thicke's motion for summary judgment on October 30, 2014.

1.   The District Court's Interpretation of the Copyright Act of 1909

The district court ruled that the Gayes' compositional copyright, which is governed by the Copyright Act of 1909, did not extend to the commercial sound recording of "Got To Give It Up," and protected only the sheet music deposited with the Copyright Office. The district court accordingly limited its review of the evidence to the deposit copy, and concluded there were genuine issues of material fact.

* * * *

E.   Trial

The case proceeded to a seven-day trial. The district court ruled before trial that the Gayes could present sound recordings of "Got To Give It Up" edited to capture only elements reflected in the deposit copy. Consequently, the commercial sound recording of "Got To Give It Up" was not played at trial.

Williams and Thicke testified, each acknowledging inspiration from Marvin Gaye and access to "Got To Give It Up."

Finell [the plaintiffs' expert musicologist] testified that "Blurred Lines" and "Got To Give It Up" share many similarities, including the bass lines, keyboard parts, signature phrases, hooks, "Theme X," bass melodies, word painting, and the placement of the rap and "parlando" sections in the two songs. She opined that nearly every bar of "Blurred Lines" contains an element similar to "Got To Give It Up." Although the district court had filtered out "Theme X," the descending bass line, and the keyboard rhythms as unprotectable at summary judgment, Finell testified that those elements were in the deposit copy.

Dr. Monson [another expert witness for the plaintiffs] played three audio-engineered "mash-ups" she created to show the melodic and harmonic compatibility between "Blurred Lines" and "Got To Give It Up." She testified that the two songs shared structural similarities on a sectional and phrasing level.

Wilbur [defendants' expert witness] opined that the two songs are not substantially similar and disputed Finell and Dr. Monson's opinions. Wilbur prepared and played a sound recording containing her rendition of the deposit copy of "Got To Give It Up." . . .

On March 10, 2015, after two days of deliberation, the jury returned mixed general verdicts.[FN4 omitted] The jury found that Williams, More Water from Nazareth Publishing,[FN5 omitted] and Thicke infringed the Gayes' copyright in "Got To Give It Up." In contrast, the jury found that Harris and the Interscope Parties were not liable for infringement. The jury awarded the Gayes $4 million in actual damages, $1,610,455.31 in infringer's profits from Williams and More Water from Nazareth Publishing, and $1,768,191.88 in infringer's profits from Thicke.

* * * *

ANALYSIS

A. Elements of a Copyright Infringement Claim

To prevail on a copyright infringement claim, a plaintiff must show that (1) he or she owns the copyright in the infringed work, and (2) the defendant copied protected elements of the copyrighted work. *Swirsky v. Carey*, 376 F.3d 841, 844 (9th Cir. 2004). A copyright plaintiff may prove copying with circumstantial, rather than direct, evidence. *Three Boys Music Corp. v. Bolton*, 212 F.3d 477, 481 (9th Cir. 2000). "Absent direct evidence of copying, proof of infringement involves fact-based showings that the defendant had 'access' to the plaintiff's work and that the two works are 'substantially similar.' " *Id.* (quoting *Smith v. Jackson*, 84 F.3d 1213, 1218 (9th Cir. 1996)).

We use a two-part test for substantial similarity: an extrinsic test and an intrinsic test. *Swirsky*, 376 F.3d at 845. For a jury to find substantial similarity, there must be evidence on both the extrinsic and intrinsic tests. *Id.* (citing *Rice v. Fox Broad. Co.*, 330 F.3d 1170, 1174 (9th Cir. 2003)). A district court applies only the extrinsic test on a motion for summary judgment, as the intrinsic test is reserved exclusively for the trier of fact. *Benay v. Warner Bros. Entm't, Inc.*, 607 F.3d 620, 624 (9th Cir. 2010).

The extrinsic test is objective. *Swirsky*, 376 F.3d at 845. It "considers whether two works share a similarity of ideas and expression as measured by external, objective criteria." *Id.* Application of "[t]he extrinsic test requires 'analytical dissection of a work and expert testimony.'" *Id.* (quoting *Three Boys Music*, 212 F.3d at 485). An analytical dissection, in turn, "requires breaking the works 'down into their constituent elements, and comparing those elements for proof of copying as measured by "substantial similarity."'" *Id.* (quoting *Rice v. Fox Broad. Co.*, 148 F.Supp.2d 1029, 1051 (C.D. Cal. 2001)).

The intrinsic test, on the other hand, is subjective. *Three Boys Music*, 212 F.3d at 485. It "asks 'whether the ordinary, reasonable person would find the total concept and feel of the works to be substantially similar.'" *Id.* (quoting *Pasillas v. McDonald's Corp.*, 927 F.2d 440, 442 (9th Cir. 1991)).

* * * *

B.   The Standard of Similarity for Musical Compositions

We have distinguished between "broad" and "thin" copyright protection based on the "range of expression" involved. *Mattel, Inc. v. MGA Entm't, Inc.*, 616 F.3d 904, 913–14 (9th Cir. 2010). "If there's a wide range of expression . . ., then copyright protection is 'broad' and a work will infringe if it's 'substantially similar' to the copyrighted work." *Id.* (citation omitted). On the other hand, "[i]f there's only a narrow range of expression . . ., then copyright protection is 'thin' and a work must be 'virtually identical' to infringe." *Id.* At 914 (citation omitted). To illustrate, there are a myriad of ways to make an "aliens-attack movie," but "there are only so many ways to paint a red bouncy ball on blank canvas." *Id.* At 913–14. Whereas the former deserves broad copyright protection, the latter merits only thin copyright protection. *See id.*

We reject the Thicke Parties' argument that the Gayes' copyright enjoys only thin protection. Musical compositions are not confined to a narrow range of expression.[7] . . . They are unlike a page-shaped computer desktop icon, *see Apple Computer, Inc. v. Microsoft Corp.*, 35 F.3d 1435, 1444 (9th Cir. 1994), or a "glass-in-glass jellyfish sculpture," *Satava v. Lowry*, 323 F.3d 805, 810 (9th Cir. 2003). Rather, as we have observed previously, "[m]usic . . . is not capable of ready classification into only five or six constituent elements," but is instead "comprised of a large array of elements, some combination of which is protectable by copyright." *Swirsky*, 376 F.3d at 849. As "[t]here is no one magical combination of . . . factors that will automatically substantiate a musical infringement suit," and as "each allegation of infringement will be unique," the extrinsic test is met,

---

[7]   Even the *de minimis* exception, which renders insignificant copying inactionable, does not require a standard of similarity as exacting as virtual identity. *See VMG Salsoul, LLC v. Ciccone*, 824 F.3d 871, 878 (9th Cir. 2016) ("A 'use is *de minimis* only if the average audience would not recognize the appropriation.'" (quoting *Newton v. Diamond*, 388 F.3d 1189, 1193 (9th Cir. 2004))).

"[s]o long as the plaintiff can demonstrate, through expert testimony . . ., that the similarity was 'substantial' and to 'protected elements' of the copyrighted work." *Id.* We have applied the substantial similarity standard to musical infringement suits before, *see id.*; *Three Boys Music*, 212 F.3d at 485, and see no reason to deviate from that standard now. Therefore, the Gayes' copyright is not limited to only thin copyright protection, and the Gayes need not prove virtual identity to substantiate their infringement action.

C.   The Copyright Act of 1909

Marvin Gaye composed "Got To Give It Up" before January 1, 1978, the effective date of the Copyright Act of 1976. Accordingly, the Copyright Act of 1909 governs the Gayes' compositional copyright. *See Twentieth Century Fox Film Corp. v. Entm't Distrib.*, 429 F.3d 869, 876 (9th Cir. 2005); *Dolman v. Agee*, 157 F.3d 708, 712 n.1 (9th Cir. 1998).

While the Copyright Act of 1976 protects "works of authorship" fixed in "sound recordings," 17 U.S.C. § 102, the 1909 Act did not protect sound recordings. It is well settled that "[s]ound recordings and musical compositions are separate works with their own distinct copyrights."[FN8 omitted] *See VMG Salsoul, LLC v. Ciccone*, 824 F.3d 871, 877 (9th Cir. 2016) (quoting *Erickson v. Blake*, 839 F.Supp.2d 1132, 1135 n.3 (D. Or. 2012)). It remains unsettled, however, whether copyright protection for musical compositions under the 1909 Act extends only to the four corners of the sheet music deposited with the United States Copyright Office, or whether the commercial sound recordings of the compositions are admissible to shed light on the scope of the underlying copyright. Here, the district court ruled that the 1909 Act protected only the deposit copy of "Got To Give It Up," and excluded the sound recording from consideration.

. . . . For purposes of this appeal, we accept, without deciding, the merits of the district court's ruling that the scope of the Gayes' copyright in "Got To Give It Up" is limited to the deposit copy.

* * * *

1.   Jury Instruction 42

The Thicke Parties argue that Instruction 42 allowed the jury to place undue weight on Williams and Thicke's statements claiming inspiration from "Got To Give It Up" and Marvin Gaye. The district court instructed the jurors:

> In order to find that the Thicke Parties copied either or both of the Gaye Parties' songs, it is not necessary that you find that the Thicke Parties consciously or deliberately copied either or both of these songs. It is sufficient if you find that the Thicke Parties subconsciously copied either or both of the Gaye Parties' songs.

Because direct evidence is rare, copying is usually circumstantially proved by a combination of access and substantial similarity. *See Swirsky*, 376 F.3d at 844. As the Thicke Parties acknowledge, access may be "based on a theory of widespread dissemination and subconscious copying." *Three Boys Music*, 212 F.3d at 483. In short, there is no scienter requirement. *See id.* At 482–85. Instruction 42 stated as much.

The Thicke Parties argue that Instruction 42 was nonetheless inappropriate, because the issue of access was not at issue. Not so. The Thicke Parties take an unduly narrow view of Instruction 42 in isolation. The instructions as a whole make plain that a circumstantial case of copying requires not just access, but also substantial similarity. Instructions 28 and 41 provide that copying may be proven by demonstrating access plus substantial similarity.[11] Instruction 43 further underscores that the Gayes "must show that there is both substantial 'extrinsic similarity' and substantial 'intrinsic similarity' as to that pair of works." Looking to the jury instructions as a whole, *see Dang*, 422 F.3d at 805, it is clear that the district court properly instructed the jury to find both access and substantial similarity.

In light of the foregoing, we conclude that the district court did not err in giving Jury Instruction 42.

* * * *

C.   The Verdict Was Not Against the Clear Weight of the Evidence.

The Thicke Parties argue that the verdict is against the clear weight of the evidence, maintaining that there is no extrinsic or intrinsic similarity between the two songs.

We are bound by the " 'limited nature of our appellate function' in reviewing the district court's denial of a motion for a new trial." *Lam*, 869 F.3d at 1084 (quoting *Kode*, 596 F.3d at 612). So long as "there was some 'reasonable basis' for the jury's verdict," we will not reverse the district court's denial of a motion for a new trial. *Id.* (quoting *Molski*, 481 F.3d at 729). . . . Of note, we are "reluctant to reverse jury verdicts in music cases"

---

11   Instruction 28 provides: "The Gaye Parties may show the Thicke Parties copied from the work by showing by a preponderance of the evidence that the Thicke Parties had access to the Gaye Parties' copyrighted work and that there are substantial similarities between the Thicke Parties' work and original elements of the Gaye Parties' work." That the instruction uses the permissive "may" presents no problem. It simply reflects the fact that the Gayes may, but are not required to, prove copying by way of a circumstantial theory, rather than a direct one.

Instruction 41 provides: "If you conclude that the Thicke Parties had access to either or both of the Gaye Parties' works before creating either or both of their works, you may consider that access in connection with determining whether there is substantial similarity between either or both pairs of works." Instruction 41's use of "may" is not problematic either. Instruction 41 merely reiterates that the Gayes may choose to prove infringement by using a circumstantial theory.

on appeal, "[g]iven the difficulty of proving access and substantial similarity."[16] *Three Boys Music*, 212 F.3d at 481.

The Thicke Parties face significant, if not unsurmountable, hurdles. First, we are generally reluctant to disturb the trier of fact's findings, and have made clear that "[w]e will not second-guess the jury's application of the intrinsic test." *Id.* At 485. Second, our review is necessarily deferential where, as here, the district court, in denying the Rule 59 motion, concluded that the verdict was not against the clear weight of the evidence. Finell testified that nearly every bar of "Blurred Lines" contains an area of similarity to "Got To Give It Up." Even setting aside the three elements that trouble the Thicke Parties ("Theme X," the bass line, and the keyboard parts), [plaintiffs' experts] testified to multiple other areas of extrinsic similarity, including the songs' signature phrases, hooks, bass melodies, word painting, the placement of the rap and "parlando" sections, and structural similarities on a sectional and phrasing level. Thus, we cannot say that there was an absolute absence of evidence supporting the jury's verdict.

We conclude that the district court did not abuse its discretion in denying the Thicke Parties' motion for a new trial.

* * * *

VIII. You Can't Get There from Here: The Dissent Ignores Governing Law that We Must Apply Given the Procedural Posture of the Case.

The dissent's position violates every controlling procedural rule involved in this case. The dissent improperly tries, after a full jury trial has concluded, to act as judge, jury, and executioner, but there is no there there, and the attempt fails.

. . . . The dissent attempts to sidestep these obstacles: It finds that the Thicke Parties are entitled to judgment as a matter of law, but fails to explain the procedural mechanism by which this could be achieved. Given this flawed premise, it is perhaps unsurprising how little the dissent mirrors the majority opinion, and how far it veers into analysis untethered from the procedural posture of this case.

* * * *

Two of our conclusions in *Swirsky* are particularly relevant here. First, we held that the district court erred in discounting the expert's musical methodology on technical grounds. *See id.* At 846–47. For example, the district court rejected the expert's "selective" choice to "discount[ ] notes

---

[16]   Our conclusion in *Three Boys Music* provides an example of the deference we must apply in reviewing the jury's verdict. Although that case presented "a weak case of access and a circumstantial case of substantial similarity," we held that "neither issue warrants reversal of the jury's verdict." 212 F.3d at 486.

that he characterize[d] as 'ornamental,' " and discredited the expert's opinion that, "even though measure three of both choruses were not identical in numerical pitch sequence or note selection," they emphasized the same scale degree and resolved similarly. *Id.* We observed that "[t]here is nothing inherently unsound about [the expert's] musicological methodology," *id.* At 846, and we similarly decline to conclude otherwise in this case.

Second, we held in *Swirsky* that the district court "erred by basing its comparison of the two choruses almost entirely on a measure-by-measure comparison of melodic note sequences from the full transcriptions of the choruses." *Id.* At 847. In so holding, we reiterated our case law. We stressed that "substantial similarity can be found in a combination of elements, even if those elements are individually unprotected." *Id.* At 848; *see also Three Boys Music*, 212 F.3d at 485 ("It is well settled that a jury may find a combination of unprotectible elements to be protectible under the extrinsic test because ' "the over-all impact and effect indicate substantial appropriation." ' ") (quoting *Krofft*, 562 F.2d at 1169)). In fact, "[e]ven if a copied portion be relatively small in proportion to the entire work, if qualitatively important, the finder of fact may properly find substantial similarity." *Swirsky*, 376 F.3d at 852 (alteration in original) (quoting *Baxter v. MCA, Inc.*, 812 F.2d 421, 425 (9th Cir. 1987)). Thus, even "an arrangement of a limited number of notes can garner copyright protection." *Id.* At 851. If taken to its logical conclusion, the dissent's musicological analysis and approach would sound the death knell for these governing legal principles.

Consider the principle that, at summary judgment, so long as the Gayes "presented '*indicia* of a sufficient disagreement concerning the substantial similarity of [the] two works,' then the case *must* be submitted to a trier of fact." *Id.* At 844 (alteration in original) (emphasis added) (quoting *Brown Bag Software v. Symantec Corp.*, 960 F.2d 1465, 1472 (9th Cir. 1992)). To require that a case be submitted to a trier of fact if there is any "indicia" of a disagreement regarding substantial similarity, only to impose on the district court the task of independently scrutinizing the expert testimony presented at trial, would turn our law on its head. Worse still, to require a district court to do so in the absence of a Rule 50 motion defies law and logic.

Moreover, the expert review conducted by the dissent does not provide a workable standard for district courts to follow. It is unrealistic to expect district courts to possess even a baseline fluency in musicology, much less to conduct an independent musicological analysis at a level as exacting as the one used by the dissent. After all, we require parties to present expert testimony in musical infringement cases for a reason. *See id.* At 845.

The dissent has failed to take into account another wrinkle that would ensue from vacating the judgment and remanding the case for a new trial. The Gayes have cross-appealed protectively, challenging the district court's interpretation of the 1909 Act, in the event a new trial is ordered. Even though a vacatur and remand would trigger the Gayes' protective cross-appeal, the dissent does not wrestle with the merits of this issue. While the dissent is adamant that the scope of the Gayes' copyright is limited to the four corners of the deposit copy, it provides no statutory interpretation or legal analysis supporting its assertion.

Lastly, the dissent prophesies that our decision will shake the foundations of copyright law, imperil the music industry, and stifle creativity. It even suggests that the Gayes' victory will come back to haunt them, as the Gayes' musical compositions may now be found to infringe any number of famous songs preceding them. Respectfully, these conjectures are unfounded hyperbole.[FN26 omitted] Our decision does not grant license to copyright a musical style or "groove." Nor does it upset the balance Congress struck between the freedom of artistic expression, on the one hand, and copyright protection of the fruits of that expression, on the other hand. Rather, our decision hinges on settled procedural principles and the limited nature of our appellate review, dictated by the particular posture of this case and controlling copyright law. Far from heralding the end of musical creativity as we know it, our decision, even construed broadly, reads more accurately as a cautionary tale for future trial counsel wishing to maximize their odds of success.

CONCLUSION

We have decided this case on narrow grounds. Our conclusions turn on the procedural posture of the case, which requires us to review the relevant issues under deferential standards of review. For the foregoing reasons, we reverse the district court's entry of judgment against Harris and the Interscope Parties, and affirm the remainder of the district court's judgment, and its order denying attorney's fees and apportioning costs.

The parties shall bear their own costs on appeal.

AFFIRMED IN PART, REVERSED IN PART.

NGUYEN, CIRCUIT JUDGE, dissenting:

The majority allows the Gayes to accomplish what no one has before: copyright a musical style. "Blurred Lines" and "Got to Give It Up" are not objectively similar. They differ in melody, harmony, and rhythm. Yet by refusing to compare the two works, the majority establishes a dangerous precedent that strikes a devastating blow to future musicians and composers everywhere.

While juries are entitled to rely on properly supported expert opinion in determining substantial similarity, experts must be able to articulate facts upon which their conclusions—and thus the jury's findings—logically rely. Here, the Gayes' expert, musicologist Judith Finell, cherry-picked brief snippets to opine that a "constellation" of individually unprotectable elements in both pieces of music made them substantially similar. That might be reasonable if the two constellations bore any resemblance. But Big and Little Dipper they are not. The only similarity between these "constellations" is that they're both compositions of stars.

I.

When a court, with the assistance of expert testimony, is able to determine substantial similarity (or lack thereof) under the extrinsic test, judgment must be given as a matter of law. *See Benay v. Warner Bros. Entm't, Inc.*, 607 F.3d 620, 624 (9th Cir. 2010). If, for example, the defendant copied verbatim most of the plaintiff's work, then the plaintiff is entitled to a finding of substantial similarity as a matter of law. *See Calhoun v. Lillenas Publ'g*, 298 F.3d 1228, 1232 (11th Cir. 2002) ("[E]ven a casual comparison of the two compositions compels the conclusion that the two compositions are practically identical."). Conversely, if the objective similarities between the two pieces are merely trivial, then a verdict for the plaintiff could not stand. *See Peters v. West*, 692 F.3d 629, 636 (7th Cir. 2012) (affirming dismissal of infringement suit where the two songs "share[d] only small cosmetic similarities"); *Newton v. Diamond ("Newton II")*, 388 F.3d 1189 (9th Cir. 2004) (affirming grant of summary judgment to defendants who appropriated a *de minimis* portion of the plaintiff's musical composition and used it throughout their own work).

The majority, like the district court, presents this case as a battle of the experts in which the jury simply credited one expert's factual assertions over another's. To the contrary, there were no material factual disputes at trial. Finell testified about certain similarities between the deposit copy of the "Got to Give It Up" lead sheet and "Blurred Lines." Pharrell Williams and Robin Thicke don't contest the existence of these similarities. Rather, they argue that these similarities are insufficient to support a finding of substantial similarity as a matter of law. The majority fails to engage with this argument.

Finell identified a few superficial similarities at the "cell" level by focusing on individual musical elements, such as rhythm or pitch, entirely out of context. Most of these "short ... pattern[s]" weren't themselves protectable by copyright, and Finell ignored both the other elements with which they appeared and their overall placement in each of the songs. Her analysis is the equivalent of finding substantial similarity between two pointillist paintings because both have a few flecks of similarly colored paint. A comparison of the deposit copy of "Got to Give it Up" and "Blurred Lines" under the extrinsic test leads to only one conclusion. Williams and Thicke were entitled to judgment as a matter of law.

II.

A.

The purpose of copyright law is to ensure a robust public domain of creative works. *See Sony Corp. of Am. V. Universal City Studios, Inc.*, 464 U.S. 417, 429, 104 S.Ct. 774, 78 L.Ed.2d 574 (1984). While the Constitution authorizes Congress to grant authors monopoly privileges on the commercial exploitation of their output, *see* U.S. Const. art. I, § 8, cl. 8, this "special reward" is primarily designed to motivate authors' creative activity and thereby "allow the public access to the products of their genius." *Sony Corp.*, 464 U.S. at 429, 104 S.Ct. 774. Accordingly, copyrights are limited in both time and scope. *See* U.S. Const. art. I, § 8, cl. 8 (providing copyright protection only "for limited Times"); *Sony Corp.*, 464 U.S. at 432, 104 S.Ct. 774 ("This protection has never accorded the copyright owner complete control over all possible uses of his work."); *see also Berlin v. E.C. Publ'ns, Inc.*, 329 F.2d 541, 544 (2d Cir. 1964) ("[C]ourts in passing upon particular claims of infringement must occasionally subordinate the copyright holder's interest in a maximum financial return to the greater public interest in the development of art, science and industry.").

An important limitation on copyright protection is that it covers only an author's expression—as opposed to the idea underlying that expression. *See* 17 U.S.C. § 102(a) ("Copyright protection subsists . . . in original works of authorship fixed in any tangible medium of expression . . . from which they can be perceived, reproduced, or otherwise communicated. . . ."); *id.* § 102(b) ("In no case does copyright protection . . . extend to any idea, procedure, process, system, method of operation, concept, principle, or discovery, regardless of the form in which it is described, explained, illustrated, or embodied in [the author's original] work."). Copyright "encourages others to build freely upon the ideas and information conveyed by a work." *Feist Publ'ns, Inc. v. Rural Tel. Serv. Co.*, 499 U.S. 340, 349–50, 111 S.Ct. 1282, 113 L.Ed.2d 358 (1991) (citing *Harper & Row Publishers, Inc. v. Nation Enters.*, 471 U.S. 539, 556–57, 105 S.Ct. 2218, 85 L.Ed.2d 588 (1985)).

The idea/expression dichotomy, as this principle is known, "strikes a definitional balance between the First Amendment and the Copyright Act." *Bikram's Yoga Coll. Of India, L.P. v. Evolation Yoga, LLC*, 803 F.3d 1032, 1037 (9th Cir. 2015) (quoting *Harper & Row*, 471 U.S. at 556, 105 S.Ct. 2218) (alteration in *Harper & Row* omitted). Because "some restriction on expression is the inherent and intended effect of every grant of copyright," *Golan v. Holder*, 565 U.S. 302, 327–28, 132 S.Ct. 873, 181 L.Ed.2d 835 (2012), the idea/expression dichotomy serves as one of copyright law's "built-in First Amendment accommodations." *Eldred v. Ashcroft*, 537 U.S. 186, 219, 123 S.Ct. 769, 154 L.Ed.2d 683 (2003) (citing *Harper & Row*, 471 U.S., at 560, 105 S.Ct. 2218).

Such accommodations are necessary because "in art, there are, and can be, few, if any, things, which in an abstract sense, are strictly new and original throughout." *Campbell v. Acuff-Rose Music, Inc.*, 510 U.S. 569, 575, 114 S.Ct. 1164, 127 L.Ed.2d 500 (1994) (quoting *Emerson v. Davies*, 8 F.Cas. 615, 619 (C.C.D. Mass. 1845) (Story, J.)). Every work of art "borrows, and must necessarily borrow, and use much which was well known and used before." *Id.* (quoting *Emerson*, 8 F.Cas. at 619); *see* 1 Melville D. Nimmer & David Nimmer, *Nimmer on Copyright* § 2.05[B] (rev. ed. 2017) ("In the field of popular songs, many, if not most, compositions bear some similarity to prior songs.").[1] But for the freedom to borrow others' ideas and express them in new ways, artists would simply cease producing new works—to society's great detriment.

B.

"Blurred Lines" clearly shares the same "groove" or musical genre as "Got to Give It Up," which everyone agrees is an unprotectable idea. *See, e.g.*, 2 William F. Patry, *Patry on Copyright* § 4:14 (2017) ("[T]here is no protection for a communal style. . . ."). But what the majority overlooks is that two works in the same genre must share at least some protectable expression in order to run afoul of copyright law.

Not all expression is protectable. Originality, the *"sine qua non* of copyright," accommodates authors' need to build on the works of others by requiring copyrightable expression to be "independently created by the author" and have "at least some minimal degree of creativity." *Feist*, 499 U.S. at 345, 348, 111 S.Ct. 1282. If an author uses commonplace elements that are firmly rooted in the genre's tradition, the expression is unoriginal and thus uncopyrightable. *See id.* At 363, 111 S.Ct. 1282.

Even original expression can be so intimately associated with the underlying idea as to be unprotectable. Under the doctrine of 414ample à faire, "expressions that are standard, stock, or common to a particular subject matter or medium are not protectable under copyright law." *Satava v. Lowry*, 323 F.3d 805, 810 (9th Cir. 2003) (citing *See v. Durang*, 711 F.2d 141, 143 (9th Cir. 1983)). The doctrine of merger provides that "where an idea contained in an expression cannot be communicated in a wide variety of ways," the "idea and expression may merge . . . [such] that even verbatim reproduction of a factual work may not constitute infringement." *Allen v. Acad. Games League of Am., Inc.*, 89 F.3d 614, 617 (9th Cir. 1996); *see also*

---

[1]   As an example, Williams and Thicke attempted to show the jury a video demonstrating how a common sequence of four chords serves as the harmonic backbone of innumerable songs. *See* Axis of Awesome, *4 Chord Song (with song titles)*, YouTube (Dec. 10, 2009) https://www. youtube.com/watch?v=5pidokakU4I (singing 38 popular songs over the same chord progression, ranging from "Let It Be" by the Beatles to "If I Were a Boy" by Beyoncé). "Blurred Lines" employs only two chords—the first two from this sequence. The district court prevented the jury from hearing this evidence. However, the court allowed the jury to hear mashups of "Blurred Lines" played together with "Got to Give It Up," which the Gayes used to show that the two songs were harmonically similar.

Rice v. Fox Broad. Co., 330 F.3d 1170, 1175 (9th Cir. 2003) ("[S]imilarities derived from the use of common ideas cannot be protected; otherwise, the first to come up with an idea will corner the market." (quoting *Apple Computer, Inc. v. Microsoft Corp.*, 35 F.3d 1435, 1443 (9th Cir. 1994))).

. . . "[T]he mere fact that a work is copyrighted does not mean that every element of the work may be protected." *Feist*, 499 U.S. at 348, 111 S.Ct. 1282. Application of the extrinsic test "requires breaking the [copyrighted and allegedly infringing] works down into their constituent elements, and comparing those elements for proof of copying as measured by substantial similarity." *Swirsky v. Carey*, 376 F.3d 841, 845 (9th Cir. 2004) (internal quotation marks omitted). "Because the requirement is one of substantial similarity to *protected* elements of the copyrighted work, it is essential to distinguish between the protected and unprotected material. . . ." *Id.* We then "apply the limiting doctrines, subtracting the unoriginal elements," to determine how "broad" or "thin" the remaining copyright is. *Ets-Hokin v. Skyy Spirits, Inc.*, 323 F.3d 763, 766 (9th Cir. 2003) (citing *Apple Computer*, 35 F.3d at 1442).

The majority doesn't explain what elements are protectable in "Got to Give It Up," which is surprising given that our review of this issue is de novo. *See Mattel, Inc. v. MGA Entm't, Inc.*, 616 F.3d 904, 914 (9th Cir. 2010). But by affirming the jury's verdict, the majority implicitly draws the line between protectable and unprotectable expression "so broadly that future authors, composers and artists will find a diminished store of ideas on which to build their works." *Oravec v. Sunny Isles Luxury Ventures, L.C.*, 527 F.3d 1218, 1225 (11th Cir. 2008) (quoting *Meade v. United States*, 27 Fed.Cl. 367, 372 (Fed. Cl. 1992)).

The issue here isn't whether Williams and Thicke copied "Got to Give It Up"—there's plenty of evidence they were attempting to evoke Marvin Gaye's style. Rather, the issue is whether they took too much.

Copying in and of itself "is not conclusive of infringement. Some copying is permitted." *Newton II*, 388 F.3d at 1193 (quoting *West Publ'g Co. v. Edward Thompson Co.*, 169 F. 833, 861 (E.D.N.Y. 1909) (Hand, J.)). Copying will only have legal consequences if it "has been done to an unfair extent." *Id.* (quoting *West Publ'g*, 169 F. at 861). In determining liability for copyright infringement, the critical and ultimate inquiry is whether "the copying is substantial." *Id.*

Requiring similarities to be substantial is of heightened importance in cases involving musical compositions. Sound recordings have "unique performance elements" that must be "filter[ed] out . . . from consideration." *Newton II*, 388 F.3d at 1194. Thus, the range of musical expression is necessarily more circumscribed when music is written down than when it is performed. "Given the limited number of musical notes (as opposed to words in a language), the combination of those notes and their phrasing, it is not surprising that a simple composition of a short length might well be susceptible to original creation by more than one composer." *Calhoun*, 298 F.3d at 1232 (footnote omitted).

* * * *

C.   Overall Lack of Similarity

Even considering all of these individually unprotectable elements together, *see Metcalf*, 294 F.3d at 1074, there is no evidentiary basis to conclude that the two works are substantially similar. *See Guzman v. Hacienda Records & Recording Studio, Inc.*, 808 F.3d 1031, 1040 (5th Cir. 2015) (finding no similarity where "the alleged compositional similarities running between the songs in their entirety, *i.e.*, their melodies, rhythmic patterns, lyrical themes, and instrumental accompaniment, were either common to the . . . genre or common in other songs").

The two pieces have different structures. [Plaintiffs' expert] acknowledged that "Got to Give It Up" lacks a chorus whereas "Blurred Lines" has a "pretty common structure for a popular song" in that it consists of a verse, pre-chorus, and chorus. The two songs' harmonies share no chords.

The discrete elements identified by [plaintiffs' expert] don't occur at the same time within the musical theme or phrase in each piece. And with the exception of parlando, the various themes and phrases she identified don't occur in corresponding places in each piece. Thus, whether considered micro- or macroscopically, "Got to Give It Up" and "Blurred Lines" are objectively dissimilar. Williams and Thicke are entitled to judgment as a matter of law.

* * * *

V.

The Gayes, no doubt, are pleased by this outcome. They shouldn't be. They own copyrights in many musical works, each of which (including "Got to Give It Up") now potentially infringes the copyright of any famous song that preceded it.[13]

That is the consequence of the majority's uncritical deference to music experts.

Admittedly, it can be very challenging for judges untrained in music to parse two pieces of sheet music for extrinsic similarity. But however difficult this exercise, we cannot simply defer to the conclusions of experts about the ultimate finding of substantial similarity.[FN14 omitted] While experts are invaluable in identifying and explaining elements that appear in both works, judges must still decide whether, as a matter of law, these

---

[13]   "Happy Birthday to You" was still copyright protected when Marvin Gaye wrote Theme X. *See Eldred*, 537 U.S. at 262, 123 S.Ct. 769 (2003) (Breyer, J., dissenting).

elements collectively support a finding of substantial similarity. Here, they don't, and the verdict should be vacated.

I respectfully dissent.

SKIDMORE AS TR. FOR RANDY CRAIG WOLFE TR. V. ZEPPELIN

952 F.3d 1051, 1064 (9th Cir. 2020) (en banc)[11]

MCKEOWN, CIRCUIT JUDGE . . . :

Stairway to Heaven has been called the greatest rock song of all time. Yet, hyperbole aside, nearly 40 years after the English rock band Led Zeppelin released its hit recording, the song is not impervious to copyright challenges. The estate of guitarist Randy Wolfe claims that Led Zeppelin and its guitarist Jimmy Page and vocalist Robert Plant copied portions of *Taurus,* a song written by Wolfe and performed by his band Spirit.

This appeal stems from the jury's verdict in favor of Led Zeppelin and a finding that the two songs are not substantially similar. Like the jury, we don't need to decide whether *Stairway to Heaven* has a place in the annals of iconic rock songs. Instead, we address a litany of copyright issues, including the interplay between the 1909 and 1976 Copyright Acts, the inverse ratio rule, the scope of music copyright, and the standards for infringement.

The 1909 Copyright Act, which does not protect sound recordings, controls our analysis. The copyright at issue is for the unpublished musical composition of *Taurus*, which was registered in 1967. The unpublished work is defined by the deposit copy, which in the case of *Taurus* consists of

---

[11] Footnotes are omitted from this excerpt.

only one page of music. We also join the majority of circuits in rejecting the inverse ratio rule and overrule our precedent to the contrary. Finally, we are not persuaded by the challenges to jury instructions and various other evidentiary and trial rulings. We affirm the district court's entry of judgment in favor of Led Zeppelin and related parties.

BACKGROUND

Randy Wolfe, professionally known as Randy California, wrote the instrumental song *Taurus* in 1966 or 1967. He was a guitarist in the band Spirit. Spirit signed a recording contract in August 1967 and released its first eponymous album—which included *Taurus*—a few months later. . . .

Around the same time, across the Atlantic, another rock band, Led Zeppelin, was formed by Jimmy Page, Robert Plant, John Paul Jones, and John Bonham. Led Zeppelin released its fourth album in late 1971. The untitled album, which became known as "Led Zeppelin IV," contained the now iconic song *Stairway to Heaven*. *Stairway to Heaven* was written by Jimmy Page and Robert Plant.

It is undisputed that Spirit and Led Zeppelin crossed paths in the late 1960s and the early 1970s. The bands performed at the same venue at least three times between 1968 and 1970. Led Zeppelin also performed a cover of a Spirit song, *Fresh Garbage*. But there is no direct evidence that the two bands toured together, or that Led Zeppelin band members heard Spirit perform *Taurus*. [¶] . . . .

Fast forward forty-three years from the release of *Stairway to Heaven* to May 2014. Skidmore filed a suit alleging that *Stairway to Heaven* infringed the copyright in *Taurus*. . . .

Skidmore alleged direct, contributory, and vicarious copyright infringement. . . . Skidmore's claims are not based on the entire *Taurus* composition. Rather, Skidmore claims that the opening notes of *Stairway to Heaven* are substantially similar to the eight-measure passage at the beginning of the *Taurus* deposit copy:

The claimed portion includes five descending notes of a chromatic musical scale. These notes are represented on the piano as a set of adjacent black and white keys, from right to left. The beginning of *Stairway to Heaven* also incorporates a descending chromatic minor chord progression in A minor. However, the composition of *Stairway to Heaven* has a different ascending line that is played concurrently with the descending chromatic line, and a distinct sequence of pitches in the arpeggios, which are not present in *Taurus*.

Led Zeppelin disputed ownership, access, and substantial similarity. Led Zeppelin also alleged affirmative defenses, including independent creation, unclean hands, and laches.... [¶¶]

... [T]he trial lasted five days. Two key issues predominated: access to *Taurus* by Led Zeppelin band members and substantial similarity.

[¶¶] .... At the close of trial, the district court discussed with counsel the intended jury instructions. The district court did not give the proposed instructions on the inverse ratio rule and the selection and arrangement of unprotectable elements. Skidmore objected to the district court's decision to omit an inverse ratio instruction but did not do so as to the omitted selection and arrangement instruction.

The jury returned a verdict for Led Zeppelin. In special interrogatories, the jury found that Skidmore owned the copyright to *Taurus* and that Led Zeppelin had access to *Taurus*, but that the two songs were not substantially similar under the extrinsic test..... [¶¶]

.... [¶¶] A panel of our court vacated the amended judgment in part and remanded for a new trial. We granted rehearing en banc.... [¶¶]

IV. THE JURY INSTRUCTION CHALLENGES

Three jury instructions are at issue in this appeal: (1) the failure to give an inverse ratio rule instruction. . . .

A. THE INVERSE RATIO RULE

Copyright infringement cases often boil down to the crucial question of substantial similarity. We have stated that "substantial similarity is inextricably linked to the issue of access," and have adhered to "what is known as the 'inverse ratio rule,'" which requires "a lower standard of proof of substantial similarity when a high degree of access is shown." *Three Boys Music*, 212 F.3d at 485 (quoting *Smith v. Jackson*, 84 F.3d 1213, 1218 (9th Cir. 1996)). That is, "the stronger the evidence of access, the less compelling the similarities between the two works need be in order to give rise to an inference of copying." *Rentmeester*, 883 F.3d at 1124.

Skidmore proposed an inverse ratio rule instruction, but the court chose not to give the instruction. The court reaffirmed this decision when Skidmore raised the question again after the close of testimony: "We're not going to give that instruction." Because the inverse ratio rule, which is not part of the copyright statute, defies logic, and creates uncertainty for the courts and the parties, we take this opportunity to abrogate the rule in the Ninth Circuit and overrule our prior cases to the contrary. *See e.g.*, *Three Boys Music*, 212 F.3d at 485–86; *Shaw v. Lindheim*, 919 F.2d 1353, 1361–62 (9th Cir. 1990).

The circuits are split over the inverse ratio rule, but the majority of those that have considered the rule declined to adopt it. The Second, Fifth, Seventh, and Eleventh Circuits have rejected the rule. . . . Only our circuit and the Sixth Circuit have endorsed it. . . .

But even within our circuit, our embrace and application of the rule have had a "checkered application." 4 Nimmer § 13.03[D]. The very nature of the rule spawned uncertainty in its application. We first articulated the rule in 1977, holding that the high "degree of access" present in that case "justifie[d] a lower standard of proof to show substantial similarity," though "[n]o amount of proof of access will suffice to show copying if there are no similarities." *Sid & Marty Krofft Television Prods., Inc. v. McDonald's Corp.*, 562 F.2d 1157, 1172 (9th Cir. 1977), *superseded on other grounds by* 17 U.S.C. § 504(b). In its next breath, the court in *Krofft* admitted that "it is impossible to quantify this standard," so it is unsurprising that the court was unclear—failing to explain whether the rule applied to the actual copying or unlawful appropriation prong of the infringement analysis. *Id.*; *see* David Aronoff, *Exploding the "Inverse Ratio Rule*," 55 J. Copyright Soc'y U.S.A. 125, 136 (2008) ("[T]he court [in *Krofft*] was confused as to whether the [inverse ratio rule] applied to the element of actual copying or unlawful appropriation . . . .").

A decade later, we reversed course and distanced ourselves from *Krofft*, relying on the Second Circuit's rejection of the inverse ratio rule in *Arc Music* . *See Aliotti v. R. Dakin & Co.*, 831 F.2d 898, 902 (9th Cir. 1987). According to *Aliotti*, because the rule "ha[d] been employed by no Ninth Circuit case since *Krofft* and had been earlier criticized for 'confus[ing] and even conceal[ing]' the requirement of substantial similarity," the court declined to "address the continuing viability of" the rule. *Id.* (alteration in original) (quoting *Arc Music*, 296 F.2d at 187–88). But *Aliotti* was a momentary detour. We later returned to the inverse ratio rule and, in a series of cases throughout the 1990s and early 2000s, applied it in confusing ways. [¶] . . .

The lack of clear guidance is likely due in no small part to our use of the term "substantial similarity," both in the context of copying and unlawful appropriation, muddying the waters as to what part of the infringement analysis the rule applies. . . . [¶¶]

Our jurisprudence in recent years brought additional uncertainty. In 2000, we circumscribed the rule by explaining that it is not a two-way street: while the rule "requires a lesser showing of substantial similarity if there is a strong showing of access," it does not mean that "a weak showing of access requires a stronger showing of substantial similarity." *Three Boys Music*, 212 F.3d at 486. In 2018, it seems, the rule goes both ways: it also provides that the "more compelling the similarities supporting an inference of copying, the less compelling the evidence of access need be." *Rentmeester*, 883 F.3d at 1124. In the face of tangled precedent, the *Rentmeester* panel tried to carefully thread the needle, but ended up adding another indecipherable stitch.

Just two years ago, we again sowed doubt whether the rule ought to apply at all. In *Williams v. Gaye*, which dealt with the song *Blurred Lines*, the majority initially defended use of the rule against the dissent's criticism because the rule is "binding precedent" that "we are bound to apply." 885 F.3d 1150, 1163 n.6 (9th Cir. 2018). But in an amended opinion, the court deleted all references to the rule. *Williams v. Gaye*, 895 F.3d 1106 (9th Cir. 2018). One commentator posited the rule was excised because it "is so controversial." Edwin F. McPherson, *Crushing Creativity: The* Blurred Lines *Case and Its Aftermath*, 92 S. Cal. L. Rev. Postscript 67, 75 n.22 (2018).

As we struggled with the inverse ratio rule over the years, the Second Circuit rejected it as early as 1961, describing the idea as a "superficially attractive apophthegm which upon examination confuses more than it clarifies." *Arc Music*, 296 F.2d at 187. . . . Importantly, the Second Circuit noted that there is "no such principle" in "the federal law of copyright." *Id.* At 187.

The Second Circuit also identified the problematic implications of this principle where access is very high and similarity very low: "[t]he logical outcome of the claimed principle is obviously that proof of actual access will render a showing of similarities entirely unnecessary." *Id.* However, "it does not follow that 'more' access increases the likelihood of copying." Aronoff, *supra*, at 126. Yet that is what the rule compels. Complete access without any similarity should never result in infringement liability because there *is* no infringement. Even so, the rule suggests that liability may be imposed in such a case. "There is," however, "simply no logic in presupposing that the mid-points of [the rule] give rise to a 'ratio' of access to similarity constituting proof of" infringement. *Id.* At 141. Indeed, even "[w]hen the inverse ratio rule is applied, we still don't know how much similarity is required." Patry § 9.91. [¶¶] . . . .

As a practical matter, the concept of "access" is increasingly diluted in our digitally interconnected world. Access is often proved by the wide dissemination of the copyrighted work. *See Loomis v. Cornish*, 836 F.3d 991, 995 (9th Cir. 2016). Given the ubiquity of ways to access media online, from YouTube to subscription services like Netflix and Spotify, access may be established by a trivial showing that the work is available on demand. *See* Brooks Barnes, *The Streaming Era Has Finally Arrived. Everything Is About to Change.*, N.Y. Times, Nov. 18, 2019 (In addition to Netflix, which "entertain[s] more than 158 million subscribers worldwide," there are currently "271 online video services available in the United States").

To the extent "access" still has meaning, the inverse ratio rule unfairly advantages those whose work is *most* accessible by lowering the standard of proof for similarity. Thus the rule benefits those with highly popular works, like *The Office*, which are also highly accessible. But nothing in copyright law suggests that a work deserves stronger legal protection simply because it is more popular or owned by better-funded rights holders.

Finally, the inverse ratio rule improperly dictates how the jury should reach its decision. The burden of proof in a civil case is preponderance of the evidence. Yet this judge-made rule could fittingly be called the "inverse burden rule."

Although we are cautious in overruling precedent—as we should be— the constellation of problems and inconsistencies in the application of the inverse ratio rule prompts us to abrogate the rule. Access does not obviate the requirement that the plaintiff must demonstrate that the defendant actually copied the work. By rejecting the inverse ratio rule, we are not suggesting that access cannot serve as circumstantial evidence of actual copying in all cases; access, however, in no way can prove substantial similarity. We join the majority of our sister circuits that have considered the inverse ratio rule and have correctly chosen to excise it from copyright analysis. In light of this holding, the district court did not err in failing to instruct the jury on the inverse ratio rule. [¶¶] . . . .

CONCLUSION

This copyright case was carefully considered by the district court and the jury. Because the 1909 Copyright Act did not offer protection for sound recordings, Skidmore's one-page deposit copy defined the scope of the copyright at issue. In line with this holding, the district court did not err in limiting the substantial similarity analysis to the deposit copy or the scope of the testimony on access to *Taurus*. As it turns out, Skidmore's complaint on access is moot because the jury found that Led Zeppelin had access to the song. We affirm the district court's challenged jury instructions. We take the opportunity to reject the inverse ratio rule, under which we have permitted a lower standard of proof of substantial similarity where there is a high degree of access. This formulation is at odds with the copyright statute and we overrule our cases to the contrary. Thus the district court did not err in declining to give an inverse ratio instruction. Nor did the district court err in its formulation of the originality instructions, or in excluding a selection and arrangement instruction. Viewing the jury instructions as a whole, there was no error with respect to the instructions. Finally, we affirm the district court with respect to the remaining trial issues and its denial of attorneys' fees and costs to Warner/Chappell.

The trial and appeal process has been a long climb up the *Stairway to Heaven*. The parties and their counsel have acquitted themselves well in presenting complicated questions of copyright law. We affirm the judgment that Led Zeppelin's *Stairway to Heaven* did not infringe Spirit's *Taurus*.

AFFIRMED.

Steve Winwood performing in
Hamburg, Germany in 1973

PARKER V. WINWOOD
938 F.3d 833 (6th Cir. 2019)

GRIFFIN, J., delivered the opinion of the court in which BERTELSMAN, D.J., joined. DONALD, J. delivered a separate dissenting opinion.

OPINION

GRIFFIN, CIRCUIT JUDGE.

Plaintiffs Willia Dean Parker and Rose Banks sued defendants Mervyn Winwood, Steve Winwood, and Kobalt Music Publishing for copyright infringement. The district court found that plaintiffs failed to submit admissible evidence showing that Steve copied plaintiffs' protected work—one element of an infringement claim—so it granted judgment in his and Kobalt's favor. . . . We affirm.

I.

In 1965, in Memphis, Tennessee, Willia Dean Parker and Homer Banks wrote the song *Ain't That a Lot of Love* and registered it with the United States Copyright Office. The very next year, in London, England, brothers Mervyn and Steve Winwood wrote the song *Gimme Some Lovin'*. They were members of the Spencer Davis Group, a band that contracted with Island Records to market its music. Island registered the song with the Copyright Office as well.

Ain't That a Lot of Love fell flat. But *Gimme Some Lovin'* roared up the charts, reaching the second spot in the United Kingdom and later the seventh spot in the United States.

Fifty-one years later, Parker and Banks's wife, Rose, sued the Winwoods and Kobalt Music Publishing—the company that exploits Steve's copyright interest in *Gimme Some Lovin'*—in the United States District Court for the Middle District of Tennessee. When writing *Gimme Some Lovin'*, plaintiffs claimed, the Winwoods lifted the bass line from *Ain't That a Lot of Love*. And that move, plaintiffs asserted, entitled them to statutory damages for copyright infringement under 17 U.S.C. § 504, as well as other relief.

Steve Winwood and Kobalt moved for summary judgment, arguing that Steve had not infringed plaintiffs' copyright because no one in the Spencer Davis Group had heard *Ain't That a Lot of Love* before writing *Gimme Some Lovin'*. In response, plaintiffs asked the district court to consider several documents they claimed contained direct evidence of copying. They also argued that there was a twenty-one-day window—between *Ain't That a Lot of Love*'s debut in the United Kingdom and the commercial release of *Gimme Some Lovin'*—during which the Spencer Davis Group could have copied the bass line. In reply, Steve and Kobalt claimed that plaintiffs' direct evidence of copying was inadmissible under the rule against hearsay. *See* Fed. R. Evid. 802. The district court granted the motion. It noted that Steve and Kobalt had submitted affidavits in support of their claim that no one in the band had heard *Ain't That a Lot of Loving* before writing *Gimme Some Lovin'*. The court also ruled that the documents plaintiffs sought to rely on to show direct evidence of copying were inadmissible under the rule against hearsay, *see* Fed. R. Evid. 801, 802, which meant they failed to produce any evidence showing that Steve copied *Ain't That a Lot of Love*. . . .

II.

We begin with the district court's grant of summary judgment in favor of Steve Winwood and Kobalt, which we review de novo. *S.E.C. v. Zada*, 787 F.3d 375, 380 (6th Cir. 2015). Summary judgment is appropriate if there is no genuine dispute as to any material fact and the movant is entitled to judgment as a matter of law. Fed. R. Civ. P. 56(a).

Because plaintiffs brought a copyright-infringement claim, to make it to trial they needed to create factual disputes over two things: whether they owned a copyrighted creation and whether Steve copied it. *Jones v. Blige*, 558 F.3d 485, 490 (6th Cir. 2009). Only the second is at issue.

"Direct evidence of copying is rare," and in its absence, a plaintiff can create an inference of copying if she can show both that the defendant had access to the work and that the original and allegedly infringing work are *substantially* similar. *Ellis v. Diffie*, 177 F.3d 503, 506 (6th Cir. 1999). And even when a plaintiff is unable to prove access, she can establish copying by showing a "*striking* similarity" between her work and the allegedly infringing one. *Murray Hill Publ'ns, Inc. v. Twentieth Century Fox Film Corp.*, 361 F.3d 312, 317 (6th Cir. 2004) (emphasis added).

A.

On appeal, plaintiffs argue that the district court erred when it ruled that four documents they sought to rely on were inadmissible under the rule against hearsay. . . .

The first document plaintiffs claim is admissible is a one-page excerpt from Timothy White's 1990 book, titled *Rock Lives: Profiles and Interviews*. That excerpt, plaintiffs assert, contains portions of an interview with Spencer Davis in which Davis said *Gimme Some Lovin'* used *Ain't That a Lot of Loving*'s bass riff. . . . [W]e find that the district court correctly excluded the document as hearsay.

The second document plaintiffs seek to rely on is more difficult to describe. Plaintiffs characterize it as "Timothy White's 1988 *Billboard Magazine* interview with Spencer Davis . . . as republished . . . on SteveWinwood.com." That description appears at least partially accurate. The document includes the phrase "By Timothy White," contains the date "November 23, 1988," and has the type of exposition one might find in a magazine. It also purports to quote Spencer Davis. Yet the document is obviously not just a copy of a magazine article. . . . Perhaps the best way to describe the document, then, is to call it a scan, of a printout, of the webpage www.stevewinwood.com/news/1414, as it appeared on February 28, 2017, that seems to include a reproduction of an article, by Timothy White, that itself appeared in the November 1988 copy of *Musician* magazine (not *Billboard* magazine). Like the first document, this document seems to include portions of an interview with Spencer Davis in which Davis said *Gimme Some Lovin'* used *Ain't That a Lot of Loving*'s bass riff.

[¶¶] . . . . But as the Supreme Court has noted, "[m]erely hosting a document on a Web site does not indicate that the hosting entity adopts the document as its own statement or exercises control over its content." *Janus Capital Grp., Inc. v. First Derivative Traders*, 564 U.S. 135, 148 n.12, 131 S.Ct. 2296, 180 L.Ed.2d 166 (2011). . . .

Because plaintiffs have not shown that the webpage, Timothy White's purported article, and Spencer Davis's statements were not hearsay or fell under exceptions to the rule against hearsay, and because they seek to use Davis's statement for its truth, the district court correctly excluded the document as hearsay. *See* Fed. R. Evid. 801, 802, 805.

The third and fourth documents plaintiffs claim were admissible are similar to the second. One appears to be a scan, of a printout, of the webpage www.stevewinwood.com/news/5765, as it appeared on February 13, 2017, that seems to include a reproduction of an article, by Johnny Black, that itself appeared in the May 1997 copy of *Mojo* magazine. And the other appears to be a scan, of a printout, of the webpage www.steve winwood.com/news/1421, as it appeared on February 28, 2017, that seems to include a reproduction of an article, by Patrick Humphries, that itself appeared in the June 1994 copy of *RH* magazine. Like the second document, they contain statements—one from Spencer Davis and another from Jim Capaldi (a member of Steve Winwood's subsequent band, Traffic)—suggesting that the bass riff in *Gimme Some Lovin'* came from *Ain't That a Lot of Loving*. Again, plaintiffs contend that the documents are admissible as party-opponent statements. But because plaintiffs seek to use Davis's and Capaldi's statements for their truth, because Steve Winwood did not make those statements, and because one does not manifest adoption of a statement or belief in it simply by hosting it on a website, the district court correctly excluded the documents as hearsay.

In short, plaintiffs presented no admissible evidence that created a genuine issue of material fact over whether Steve Winwood copied *Ain't That a Lot of Loving*. Thus, he and Kobalt were entitled to judgment as a matter of law. *See* Fed. R. Civ. P. 56(a).

* * * *

IV.

For these reasons, we affirm the judgment in favor of Steve Winwood and Kobalt Music Publishing, and the dismissal of all claims against Mervyn Winwood.

DISSENT

BERNICE BOUIE DONALD, CIRCUIT JUDGE, dissenting.

Before this Court is a tune nearly as old as song—an allegation of copyright infringement. Such claims span across the decades of modern music, and notable ones include:

- Chuck Berry v. The Beach Boys (1963): Beach Boys composer Brian Wilson wrote the band's 1963 song "Surfin' U.S.A." with Chuck Berry's 1958 song "Sweet Little Sixteen" in mind. Although Wilson said he wrote the song as tribute to the black guitarist, Berry's lawyers sued for plagiarism, making this dispute one of the first of its kind in rock history. The Beach Boys' manager agreed to hand over publishing rights to the song, and Berry was credited as a songwriter beginning in 1966.[1]

---

[1] *See Jordan Runtagh, Songs on Trial: 12 Landmark Music Copyright Cases,* ROLLING STONE MAGAZINE (June 8, 2016), https://www.rollingstone.com/politics/politics-lists/songs-on-trial-12-landmark-music-copyright-cases-166396/the-beach-boys-vs-chuck-berry-1963-65098/.

- The Chiffons v. George Harrison (1976): Ronald Mack, writer for the female R&B group the Chiffons' 1962 hit "He's So Fine," sued Beatles member George Harrison for plagiarism over Harrison's 1970 song "My Sweet Lord." The suit went to trial, where the judge ruled that Harrison had "subconsciously" plagiarized the song. Harrison was eventually ordered to pay over $500,000 in damages, and later admitted that the songs were similar in his autobiography, *I Me Mine*.[2]

- Marvin Gaye v. Robin Thicke and Pharrell Williams (2015): In one of the most widely-publicized copyright infringement suits in recent memory, the family of Marvin Gaye claimed singer Robin Thicke's and producer Pharrell Williams' 2013 song "Blurred Lines" was a rip off of Gaye's 1977 song "Got to Give It Up." During litigation, Gaye's family cited to an interview in which Thicke said he told Williams they should write a song with the same "groove" as Gaye's classic. A jury found that Thicke and Williams infringed on the song's copyright, and the Ninth Circuit affirmed the $5.3 million judgment awarded to Gaye's family.[3]

This small sampling of cases illustrates how artists must sometimes fight to protect their creative work, and how the courts must sometimes intervene to uphold the integrity of the creative process.

Out of the transatlantic music exchange in the mid 1960s, which brought British Rock to the United States and American Rhythm & Blues to Britain, came two songs: "Ain't That a Lot of Love," by Black Americans Willia Dean Parker and Homer Banks, and "Gimme Some Lovin,' " by British band The Spencer Davis Group. Many British bands—including the Beatles[4] and the Rolling Stones[5]—have been inspired by the works of black R&B artists. However, there is a fine line between inspiration and infringement, and evidence in the record below supports a finding that the

---

[2]   *See Bright Tunes Music Corp. v. Harrisongs Music, Ltd.*, 420 F. Supp. 177 (S.D.N.Y. 1976); Runtagh, supra note 1.

[3]   *See Williams v. Gaye*, 895 F.3d 1106 (9th Cir. 2018); Kory Grow, *Robin Thicke, Pharrell Lose Multi-Million Dollar 'Blurred Lines' Lawsuit*, ROLLING STONE MAGAZINE (Mar. 10, 2015), https://www.rollingstone.com/music/music-news/robin-thicke-pharrell-lose-multi-million-dollar-blurred-lines-lawsuit-35975/.

[4]   *See* Bill Crandall, *Motown Really Had A Hold On The Beatles*, CBS NEW YORK (Jan. 24, 2014), https://newyork.cbslocal.com/2014/01/24/motown-really-had-a-hold-on-the-beatles/ (describing how the Beatles were inspired by black musicians upon their "U.S. invasion," as evidenced by their second album's feature of "one Chuck Berry cover . . . and a whole lot of Motown").

[5]   *See* Adam Theisen, *The Rolling Stones and Motown: A musical fascination*, DETROIT METRO TIMES (July 1, 2015), https://www.metrotimes.com/detroit/the-rolling-stones-and-motown/Content?oid=2353522 (detailing how black musicians influenced the Rolling Stones, and how Motown music "proved to be a cover song bank from which the group could continuously withdraw").

Defendants crossed this line. . . . Because I respectfully disagree with the majority's opinion concerning both issues on appeal, I dissent, and would reverse the findings of the district court.

I.

The majority concludes that the district court did not err when it ruled that four documents Plaintiffs sought to admit as proof of copying were inadmissible hearsay. Even if this were true, the majority neglects other evidence in the record—Dan Dixon's expert report, submitted by Plaintiffs—that points to a genuine issue of material fact. Accordingly, the district court's grant of summary judgment should be reversed.

Defendants' assertion that Plaintiffs have not submitted evidence of striking similarity must be dismissed in the interests of justice. Defendants argue that the expert report should not be considered because it was not submitted in response to their motion for summary judgment—but instead was submitted in response to Mervyn's motion to dismiss. . . .

. . . For copying to be actionable, a plaintiff must prove that the copied elements are original, meaning that the elements were "independently created by the author (as opposed to copied from other works), and that it possesses at least some minimal degree of creativity." *Feist Publications, Inc. v. Rural Tel. Serv. Co.*, 499 U.S. 340, 345, 111 S.Ct. 1282, 113 L.Ed.2d 358 (1991). In the usual infringement case, the copy element proves problematic, as there is often no objective evidence that shows the process by which the defendant copied the work. *See Murray Hill Publ'ns, Inc. v. Twentieth Century Fox Film Corp.*, 361 F.3d 312, 316 (6th Cir. 2004). Recognizing this, where there is no direct evidence of copying, courts allow a plaintiff to establish an inference of copying in one of two ways: (1) by establishing defendants had access to the allegedly-infringed work and that the two works are substantially similar, *Ellis v. Diffie*, 177 F.3d 503, 506 (6th Cir. 1999); or, (2) when access cannot be proven, by establishing that the two works are "strikingly similar," *Murray Hill*, 361 F.3d at 317. A finding of "striking similarity" requires the similarities at issue be "so striking as to preclude the possibility that the defendant independently arrived at the same result. In other words, as a matter of logic, the only explanation for the similarities between the two works must be 'copying rather than . . . coincidence, independent creation, or prior common source.'" 4 Melville B. Nimmer & David Nimmer, Nimmer on Copyright § 13.02[B]. For a plaintiff to show that two musical works are strikingly similar, however, expert testimony is often required due to the technical nature of musical compositions. *See id.*

Defendants are not entitled to summary judgment because Dixon's expert report clearly establishes a triable issue of fact as to whether Defendants copied Plaintiffs' song. . . .

The expert report concludes that "the two works [ ] exhibit a clear and unmistakable overall similarity of sound . . . primarily due to the fact that the two works prominently feature identical bass lines, nearly identical piano patterns, and similar harmonic, melodic, and lyrical materials." Notably, the identical base lines and nearly identical piano patterns "constitute clear and obvious similarly between the two works," and are referenced more than once in the report. According to the report, "this combination of identical and similar compositional features . . . is extremely unlikely to have been the result of independent creation." The report further concludes that the two songs "exhibit strikingly similar compositional features, that there is clear objective musicological evidence that strongly suggests copying of protectable musical expression . . ., and that the amount of musical expression at issue is substantial and constitutes the 'heart' of both works."

These conclusions indicate that the two songs are strikingly similar. Notwithstanding the expert report, anyone with a listening ear, including a jury, could reasonably conclude that the two songs contain a strikingly similar musical composition. Thus, there is an issue of material fact as to whether Defendants copied Plaintiffs' song, and Defendants are therefore not entitled to summary judgment. *See Murray Hill*, 361 F.3d at 317. The majority chooses to overlook this evidence simply because Plaintiffs presented it after briefing was complete, despite our ability on appeal to consider the entire record. This Court should not be in the business of punishing litigants for their attorney's misdeeds or failure to take the preferred course of action. . . . Regrettably, the majority has denied Plaintiffs their deserved opportunity to present their case to a jury, which is a grave injustice.

* * * *

III.

For the foregoing reasons, I respectfully dissent.

NOTES AND QUESTIONS

1.   The verdict and the Ninth Circuit's subsequent opinion affirming the jury's finding of liability of copyright infringement in the "Blurred Lines" case were widely reported and debated. As the dissenting opinion excerpted above noted, "there's plenty of evidence [Williams and Thicke] were attempting to evoke Marvin Gaye's style. Rather, the issue is whether they took too much." That issue was not easily resolved, as is illustrated by the lengthy majority and dissenting opinions by the Ninth Circuit panel, the conflicting expert testimony, and the need for a seven-day trial to address whether parts of the four minute, twenty-five second "Blurred Lines" composition infringed Gaye's earlier composition. Although it received less publicity, the *Winwood* case also

produced a strong dissenting opinion that raised important equitable issues and highlighted the importance of expert testimony. How should the line be drawn between unprotected "style" and protectable components of a musical work? How can "style" of a performer be separated from protectable components of a song, given that recorded performances and musical compositions are distinct copyrightable works? And who should decide these questions—courts, juries, experts?

2.   Given the difficulty of evidentiary proof of copying, how do you think courts should deal with claims of copying of musical works? Are the rules of evidence adequately designed to deal with the difficulties in proving infringement in this context? Are courts the best venue for deciding these difficult issues?

3.   Can the reasoning and results in the Blurred Lines case be reconciled with those in the *Winwood* case? Where do you think they diverge—is it a purely factual issue as to the available evidence, or are the courts' approaches different?

4.   In another widely reported case finding infringement of a composition in 2019, *Gray v. Hudson*, a jury in federal court in Los Angeles found that a six-note sequence in the song "Dark Horse," released by Katy Perry in 2013, infringed the copyright of Marcus Gray, a Christian hip-hop artist known as "Flame," in the 2008 song "Joyful Noise." The plaintiffs argued that the defendants infringed their copyright to "Joyful Noise," and also tarnished the message and reputation of the original composition and its authors by associating it with imagery of paganism and witchcraft in the artwork and videos for Perry's recording of "Dark Horse." Although all of the five songwriters for "Dark Horse" denied ever hearing "Joyful Noise," the plaintiffs' attorneys argued that the song had been included in a Grammy-nominated album (for best rock or rap gospel album) and had been successful enough that any of the "Dark Horse" composers could have heard it. The plaintiffs were awarded more than $2.7 million in damages by the jury. However, in March of 2020, the district court granted Perry's motion for judgment as a matter of law notwithstanding the jury's verdict. Judge Synder found that none of the individual elements of the sequence were protectable, and concluded that the combination of musical elements comprising the 8-note ostinato in 'Joyful Noise' were not "numerous enough" or " 'arranged' in a sufficiently original manner to warrant copyright protection." *Gray v. Perry*, No. 215-CV-05642-CASJCX, 2020 WL 1275221, at *10 (C.D. Cal. Mar. 16, 2020). The district court also found that, even if protectable, the sequence in question was not similar enough to the challenged sequence in "Dark Horse" to meet the extrinsic test for substantial similarity. As of this writing, the time to appeal the district court's judgment had not yet expired, and there was a strong indication that the plaintiffs would appeal.

5.   Some in the industry had expressed concern that the recent, widely-publicized verdicts in the Blurred Lines case (and the Katy Perry case prior to the district court's judgment as a matter of law in Perry's favor) might lead to

a rush to litigation over the copyrights to musical compositions, particularly given how much easier it is to prove access in the Internet era. Do you think that the recent *Zeppelin* case in which the Ninth Circuit abandoned the inverse ratio rule (where greater proof of access meant a reduced burden in proving substantial similarity) will serve as a disincentive for future litigants? Do you agree with the Ninth Circuit's reasoning in abrogating that rule? Even if the rule should not work two ways, is it reasonable to presume that a high degree of similarity requires less evidence of access? Why or why not?

6.   The cases discussed above cost millions of dollars to litigate to a verdict, making a trial on the merits financially impractical for many composers and publishers. Settlements in which credit (and publishing income) is shared are more common than court verdicts and receive less public attention. Are such settlements a good way of resolving the difficult question of how much a composer may borrow from those who preceded him or her?

7.   In providing examples from the Chuck Berry, Chiffons, and Marvin Gaye cases, the dissent in the *Winwood* case alludes to a longstanding debate among critics and legal scholars regarding race, cultural appropriation, and originality of authorship. Dating back to the early days of the popular music industry in America, there were sometimes objections by black composers that white composers and artists were appropriating elements of their preexisting works, or elements of cultural songs passed down from generation to generation in African American families. Early publishers and record companies in the industry often borrowed from the African American ragtime and blues musical traditions. Despite that influence, "[u]ltimately, no African Americans appear to have worked as staff songwriters or arrangers in any of the leading Tin Pan Alley firms before the 1920s, and some moreover experienced outright theft of their work by whites, some of whom sold songs they heard in African American clubrooms as their own."[12] Although much of what gave American music its unique sound and worldwide appeal at the dawn of the music industry had its roots in African American music, the industry largely excluded African Americans from the ranks of its early composers, recording artists, and company executives. A detailed discussion of race in the American music industry can be found in many excellent sources, several of which we cite below.[13] Considerations of race and cultural appropriation are typically absent from courts' legal analysis of copyright infringement claims, as illustrated by the excerpts above. Do you think these considerations should

---

[12]   DAVID SUISMAN, SELLING SOUNDS: THE COMMERCIAL REVOLUTION IN AMERICAN MUSIC 38–39 (Harvard University Press 2009).

[13]   *See, e.g.,* DAVID SUISMAN, SELLING SOUNDS: THE COMMERCIAL REVOLUTION IN AMERICAN MUSIC ch. 7 (Harvard University Press 2009) (discussing African American musicians' role in the early years of the music industry in the context of the hurdles faced by the first major black-owned record company, Black Swan Records, led by Harry H. Pace in 1921); TIM BROOKS, LOST SOUNDS: BLACKS AND THE BIRTH OF THE RECORDING INDUSTRY, 1890–1919 (Univ. of Illinois Press 2005) (detailing the varying roles of black artists in the first three decades of the recording industry); K.J. Greene, *Copyright, Culture & Black Music: A Legacy of Unequal Protection*, 21 HASTINGS COMM. & ENT L.J. 339, 340 (1999) (exploring how African-American musical artists, as a group, were "routinely deprived of legal protection for creative works under the copyright regime").

play a more express role in evaluating liability for infringement of musical compositions? Why or why not? How?

The next case gives you an introduction into how claims of infringement of musical compositions are treated in the context of **sampling**.

NEWTON V. DIAMOND

388 F.3d 1189 (9th Cir. 2004)

Opinion by CHIEF JUDGE SCHROEDER; Dissent by JUDGE GRABER.

ORDER AMENDING OPINION AND DENYING REHEARING AND AMENDED OPINION AND AMENDED DISSENT

* * * *

SCHROEDER, CHIEF JUDGE.

This appeal raises the difficult and important issue of whether the incorporation of a short segment of a musical recording into a new musical recording, i.e., the practice of "sampling," requires a license to use both the performance and the composition of the original recording. The particular sample in this case consists of a six-second, three-note segment of a performance of one of his own compositions by plaintiff, and accomplished jazz flutist, James W. Newton. The defendants, the performers who did the sampling, are the members of the musical group Beastie Boys. They obtained a license to sample the sound recording of Newton's copyrighted performance, but they did not obtain a license to use Newton's underlying composition, which is also copyrighted.

The district court granted summary judgment to the defendants. In a scholarly opinion, it held that no license to the underlying composition was required because, as a matter of law, the notes in question—C-D flat-C, over a held C note—lacked sufficient originality to merit copyright protection. Newton v. Diamond, 204 F.Supp.2d 1244, 1256 (C.D.Cal.2002). The district court also held that even if the sampled segment of the composition were original, Beastie Boys' use of a brief segment of the sound recording of "Choir" was a de minimis use of the "Choir" composition and therefore was not actionable. Id. At 1259. We affirm on the ground that the use was de minimis.

Background and Procedural History

The plaintiff and appellant in this case, James W. Newton, is an accomplished avant-garde jazz flutist and composer. In 1978, he composed the song "Choir," a piece for flute and voice intended to incorporate elements of African-American gospel music, Japanese ceremonial court music, traditional African music, and classical music, among others. According to Newton, the song was inspired by his earliest memory of music, watching four women singing in a church in rural Arkansas. In 1981, Newton performed and recorded "Choir" and licensed all rights in the sound recording to ECM Records for $5000.[1] The license covered only the sound recording, and it is undisputed that Newton retained all rights to the composition of "Choir." Sound recordings and their underlying compositions are separate works with their own distinct copyrights. 17 U.S.C. § 102(a)(2), (7).

The defendants and appellees include the members of the rap and hip-hop group Beastie Boys, and their business associates. In 1992, Beastie Boys obtained a license from ECM Records to use portions of the sound recording of "Choir" in various renditions of their song "Pass the Mic" in exchange for a one-time fee of $1000.[2] Beastie Boys did not obtain a license from Newton to use the underlying composition.

The portion of the composition at issue consists of three notes, C-D flat-C, sung over a background C note played on the flute. The score to "Choir" also indicates that the entire song should be played in a "largo/senza-misura" tempo, meaning "slowly/without-measure." . . . .

The dispute between Newton and Beastie Boys centers around the copyright implications of the practice of sampling, a practice now common to many types of popular music. Sampling entails the incorporation of short segments of prior sound recordings into new recordings. The practice originated in Jamaica in the 1960s, when disc jockeys (DJs) used portable sound systems to mix segments of prior recordings into new mixes, which they would overlay with chanted or "scatted" vocals. See Robert M. Szymanski, Audio Pasitiche: Digital Sampling, Intermediate Copying, Fair Use, 3 U.C.L.A. Ent. L. Rev. 271, 277 (Spring 1996). Sampling migrated to the United States and developed throughout the 1970s, using the analog

---

[1]   In relevant part, the license reads as follows: 1) [Newton] herewith grants, transfers and assigns to ECM without limitations and restrictions whatsoever the exclusive rights to record his performances and to exploit these recordings in perpetuity throughout the world in any manner whatsoever. . . . 3) The grant of rights according to section 1) especially, includes the rights to manufacture in quantity [sic], to distribute, to license to others, as well as to perform the recordings in public and to utilize it in radio, TV, or in other ways without any restrictions.

[2]   In relevant part, the license reads as follows:[ECM Records], as owner of the applicable sound recording rights, including but not limited to recording, reproduction, synchronization and performing rights, grants to Beastie Boys, its licensees, assigns, employees and agents (the "Licensed Parties"), the irrevocable non-exclusive license and right to copy portions (if any) of the sound recording entitled "Choir" performed by James Newton (the "Sample"); to embody the sample in some or all versions of the selection entitled "Pass the Mic" by the Beastie Boys (all versions of "Pass the Mic" which contain the Sample are referred to as the "Selection"); to reproduce, distribute and otherwise exploit the Sample as part of the Selection in all media, whether now known or hereinafter developed, including, without limitation, all record formats throughout the world in perpetuity.

technologies of the time. Id. The digital sampling involved here developed in the early 1980s with the advent of digital synthesizers having MIDI (Musical Instrument Digital Interface) keyboard controls. These digital instruments allowed artists digitally to manipulate and combine sampled sounds, expanding the range of possibilities for the use of pre-recorded music. Whereas analog devices limited artists to "scratching" vinyl records and "cutting" back and forth between different sound recordings, digital technology allowed artists to slow down, speed up, combine, and otherwise alter the samples. See id.

Pursuant to their license from ECM Records, Beastie Boys digitally sampled the opening six seconds of Newton's sound recording of "Choir." Beastie Boys repeated or "looped" this six-second sample as a background element throughout "Pass the Mic," so that it appears over forty times in various renditions of the song. In addition to the version of "Pass the Mic" released on their 1992 album, "Check Your Head," Beastie Boys included the "Choir" sample in two remixes, "Dub the Mic" and "Pass the Mic (Pt. 2, Skills to Pay the Bills)." It is unclear whether the sample was altered or manipulated, though Beastie Boys' sound engineer stated that alterations of tone, pitch, and rhythm are commonplace, and Newton maintains that the pitch was lowered slightly.

Newton filed the instant action in federal court on May 9, 2000, alleging violations of his copyright in the underlying composition, as well as Lanham Act violations for misappropriation and reverse passing off. The district court dismissed Newton's Lanham Act claims on September 12, 2000, and granted summary judgment in favor of Beastie Boys on the copyright claims on May 21, 2002. Newton v. Diamond, 204 F.Supp.2d 1244 (C.D.Cal.2002). The district court held that the three-note segment of the "Choir" composition could not be copyrighted because, as a matter of law, it lacked the requisite originality. 204 F.Supp.2d at 1256. The court also concluded that even if the segment were copyrightable, Beastie Boys' use of the work was *de minimis* and therefore not actionable. Id. At 1259. Newton appealed.

Whether Defendants' Use was De Minimis

We may affirm the grant of summary judgment on any basis supported by the record and need not reach each ground relied upon by the district court. See Venetian Casino Resort L.L.C. v. Local Joint Executive Bd. Of Las Vegas, 257 F.3d 937, 941 (9th Cir.2001), cert. denied, 535 U.S. 905, 122 S.Ct. 1204, 152 L.Ed.2d 142 (2002). Assuming that the sampled segment of the composition was sufficiently original to merit copyright protection, we nevertheless affirm on the ground that Beastie Boys' use was *de minimis* and therefore not actionable.

For an unauthorized use of a copyrighted work to be actionable, the use must be significant enough to constitute infringement. See Ringgold v.

Black Entm't Television, Inc., 126 F.3d 70, 74–75 (2d Cir.1997). This means that even where the fact of copying is conceded, no legal consequences will follow from that fact unless the copying is substantial. See Laureyssens v. Idea Group, Inc., 964 F.2d 131, 140 (2d Cir.1992); 4 Melville B. Nimmer & David Nimmer, Nimmer on Copyright § 13.03 [A], at 13–30.2. The principle that trivial copying does not constitute actionable infringement has long been a part of copyright law. Indeed, as Judge Learned Hand observed over 80 years ago: "Even where there is some copying, that fact is not conclusive of infringement. Some copying is permitted. In addition to copying, it must be shown that this has been done to an unfair extent." West Publ'g Co. v. Edward Thompson Co., 169 F. 833, 861 (E.D.N.Y.1909). This principle reflects the legal maxim, *de minimis non curatlex* (often rendered as, "the law does not concern itself with trifles"). See Ringgold, 126 F.3d at 74–75.

A leading case on *de minimis* infringement in our circuit is Fisher v. Dees, 794 F.2d 432 (9th Cir.1986), where we observed that a use is *de minimis* only if the average audience would not recognize the appropriation. See id. At 434 n. 2 ("[A] taking is considered *de minimis* only if it is so meager and fragmentary that the average audience would not recognize the appropriation."). This observation reflects the relationship between the *de minimis* maxim and the general test for substantial similarity, which also looks to the response of the average audience, or ordinary observer, to determine whether a use is infringing. See, e.g., Cavalier v. Random House, Inc., 297 F.3d 815, 822 (9th Cir.2002); Castle Rock Entm't, Inc. v. Carol Publ'g Group, Inc., 150 F.3d 132 (2d Cir.1998) ("Two works are substantially similar where 'the ordinary observer, unless he set out to detect the disparities, would be disposed to overlook them, and regard [the] aesthetic appeal [of the two works] as the same.' " (quoting Arica Inst., Inc. v. Palmer, 970 F.2d 1067, 1072 (2d Cir.1992) (quoting Peter Pan Fabrics, Inc. v. Martin Weiner Corp., 274 F.2d 487, 489 (2d Cir.1960) (L. Hand, J.)))). To say that a use is *de minimis* because no audience would recognize the appropriation is thus to say that the use is not sufficiently significant. [¶]. . . .

This case involves not only use of a composition, . . . but also use of a sound recording of a particular performance of that composition. Because the defendants were authorized to use the sound recording, our inquiry is confined to whether the unauthorized use of the composition itself was substantial enough to sustain an infringement claim. Therefore, we may consider only Beastie Boys' appropriation of the song's compositional elements and must remove from consideration all the elements unique to Newton's performance. Stated another way, we must "filter out" the licensed elements of the sound recording to get down to the unlicensed elements of the composition, as the composition is the sole basis for Newton's infringement claim. See Cavalier, 297 F.3d at 822; Apple Computer, Inc. v. Microsoft Corp., 35 F.3d 1435, 1446 (9th Cir.1994).

[¶] . . . . Newton licensed the recording at issue to ECM Records over twenty years ago, and ECM Records in turn licensed the interest in the recording to the Beastie Boys. Newton's copyright extends only to the elements that he fixed in a tangible medium—those that he wrote on the score. Thus, regardless of whether the average audience might recognize the "Newton technique" at work in the sampled sound recording, those performance elements are beyond consideration in Newton's claim for infringement of his copyright in the underlying composition.

Once we have isolated the basis of Newton's infringement action—the "Choir" composition, devoid of the unique performance elements found only in the sound recording—we turn to the nub of our inquiry: whether Beastie Boys' unauthorized use of the composition, as opposed to their authorized use of the sound recording, was substantial enough to sustain an infringement action. In answering that question, we must distinguish between whether there is a high enough degree of similarity between the works to establish copying, and whether that copying is substantial enough to constitute infringement. Cf. Ringgold, 126 F.3d at 74–75; 4 Nimmer § 13.03[A][2], at 13–45. The practice of music sampling will often present cases where the degree of similarity is high. Indeed, unless the sample has been altered or digitally manipulated, it will be identical to the sampled portion of the original recording. Yet as Nimmer explains, "[if] the similarity is only as to nonessential matters, then a finding of no substantial similarity should result." 4 Nimmer § 13.03[A][2], at 13–48; cf. Warner Bros. v. Am. Broad. Cos., 720 F.2d 231, 242 (2d Cir.1983). This reflects the principle that the substantiality requirement applies throughout the law of copyright, including cases of music sampling, even where there is a high degree of similarity.

The high degree of similarity between the works here (i.e., "Pass the Mic" and "Choir"), but the limited scope of the copying, place Newton's claim for infringement into the class of cases that allege what Nimmer refers to as "fragmented literal similarity." 4 Nimmer § 13.03[A][2], at 13–45. Fragmented literal similarity exists where the defendant copies a portion of the plaintiff's work exactly or nearly exactly, without appropriating the work's overall essence or structure. Id. Because the degree of similarity is high in such cases, the dispositive question is whether the copying goes to trivial or substantial elements. Substantiality is measured by considering the qualitative and quantitative significance of the copied portion in relation to the plaintiff's work as a whole. See, e.g., Worth v. Selchow & Righter Co., 827 F.2d 569, 570 n. 1 (9th Cir.1987) ("[T]he relevant inquiry is whether a substantial portion of the protectable material in the plaintiff's work was appropriated—not whether a substantial portion of defendant's work was derived from plaintiff's work."); Jarvis v. A & M Records, 827 F.Supp. 282, 289–90 (D.N.J.1993); 4 Nimmer § 13.03[A][2], at 13–47 to 48 & n. 97. This focus on the sample's relation to the plaintiff's work as a whole embodies the fundamental question in any infringement action, as expressed more than 150 years ago by Justice Story: whether "so much is taken[ ] that the value of the original is sensibly diminished, or the labors of the original author are substantially to an injurious extent appropriated by another." Folsom v. Marsh, 9 F.Cas. 342, 348 (C.C.D.Mass.1841) (No. 4901). . . . Thus, as the district court properly concluded, the fact that Beastie Boys "looped" the sample throughout "Pass the Mic" is irrelevant in weighing the sample's qualitative and quantitative significance. See Newton, 204 F.Supp.2d at 1257.

On the undisputed facts of this record, no reasonable juror could find the sampled portion of the composition to be a quantitatively or qualitatively significant portion of the composition as a whole. Quantitatively, the three-note sequence appears only once in Newton's composition. It is difficult to measure the precise relationship between this segment and the composition as a whole, because the score calls for between 180 and 270 seconds of improvisation. When played, however, the segment lasts six seconds and is roughly two percent of the four-and-a-half-minute "Choir" sound recording licensed by Beastie Boys. Qualitatively, this section of the composition is no more significant than any other section. Indeed, with the exception of two notes, the entirety of the scored portions of "Choir" consist of notes separated by whole and half-steps from their neighbors and is played with the same technique of singing and playing the flute simultaneously; the remainder of the composition calls for sections of improvisation that range between 90 and 180 seconds in length.

The Beastie Boys' expert, Dr. Lawrence Ferrara, concludes that the compositional elements of the sampled section do not represent the heart or the hook of the "Choir" composition, but rather are "simple, minimal and insignificant." . . . [¶] Dr. Ferrara stated that the sampled excerpt from the "Choir" composition "is merely a common, trite, and generic three-note sequence, which lacks any distinct melodic, harmonic, rhythmic or structural elements." He described the sequence as "a common building block tool" that "has been used over and over again by major composers in the 20th century, particularly in the '60s and '70s, just prior to James Newton's usage."

Because Newton conceded that "Choir" and "Pass the Mic" "are substantially dissimilar in concept and feel, that is, in [their] overall thrust and meaning" and failed to offer any evidence to rebut Dr. Ferrara's testimony that the sampled section is not a quantitatively or qualitatively significant portion of the "Choir" composition, the Beastie Boys are entitled to prevail on summary judgment. On the undisputed facts of this case, we conclude that an average audience would not discern Newton's hand as a composer, apart from his talent as a performer, from Beastie Boys' use of the sample. The copying was not significant enough to constitute infringement. Beastie Boys' use of the "Choir" composition was *de minimis*. There is no genuine issue of material fact, and the grant of summary judgment was appropriate.

Conclusion

Because Beastie Boys' use of the sound recording was authorized, the sole basis of Newton's infringement action is his remaining copyright interest in the "Choir" composition. We hold that Beastie Boys' use of a brief segment of that composition, consisting of three notes separated by a half-step over a background C note, is not sufficient to sustain a claim for infringement of Newton's copyright in the composition "Choir". We affirm the district court's grant of summary judgment on the ground that Beastie Boys' use of the composition was *de minimis* and therefore not actionable.

AFFIRMED.

GRABER, CIRCUIT JUDGE, dissenting:

I respectfully dissent. The majority has laid out correctly the legal principles that apply in this case, and I agree with the majority's assumption that the sampled portion of "Choir" qualifies as "original" and therefore is copyrightable. Maj. Op. at 1192. However, on the record before us, a finder of fact reasonably could find that Beastie Boys' use of the sampled material was not *de minimis*. Therefore, summary judgment is inappropriate.

As the majority observes, a use is *de minimis* only if an average audience would not recognize the appropriation. Fisher v. Dees, 794 F.2d 432, 434 n. 2 (9th Cir.1986). The majority is correct that James Newton's considerable skill adds many recognizable features to the performance sampled by Beastie Boys. Even after those features are "filtered out," however, the composition, standing alone, is distinctive enough for a fact-finder reasonably to conclude that an average audience would recognize the appropriation of the sampled segment and that Beastie Boys' use was therefore not *de minimis*.

[¶] . . . . Because Newton has presented evidence establishing that reasonable ears differ over the qualitative significance of the composition of the sampled material, summary judgment is inappropriate in this case. Newton should be allowed to present his claims of infringement to a fact-finder. I therefore dissent from the majority's conclusion to the contrary.

NOTES AND QUESTIONS

The *Newton* analysis dealt with copyright infringement when a musical composition is sampled without the composer or publisher's permission. In the next section, you will see how the analysis of copyright infringement of a sound recording through sampling differs in important ways from that in the context of musical compositions, at least in some jurisdictions. As you read the opinions and notes below, consider how and why the analysis diverges and whether you agree with the *Bridgeport Music* case's different treatment of compositions and sound recordings or the *Ciccone* case's determination that the two types of works should be evaluated by similar standards in the context of sampling.

B. DISPUTES REGARDING SOUND RECORDINGS: SAMPLING

The prior cases focus on claims that one composition infringed parts of another composition, but allegations of copying can also occur with regard to the sound recording itself. Copyright infringement disputes regarding use of a sound recording in a subsequent creative work typically involve the practice of sampling—taking a small piece of a prior recording and integrating it into a new song in a variety of ways. Because sound recordings can only be unlawfully copied by reproduction of the actual sounds fixed in the work without permission, nothing precludes a recording artist from making his/her own version of a prior sound recording (assuming compliance with the mechanical license for the underlying composition) and using it in a new song. However, the hip-hop and R&B music genres grew out of a long tradition of sampling, and as those genres became popular and commercially successful, record labels struggled with the copyright and licensing implications of releasing records that included samples from prior works. The *Bridgeport Music* case excerpted below provides both background on the practice of sampling and an illustration of how courts initially treated claims of infringement of a sound recording via sampling, with particular emphasis on the availability of the *de minimis* use defense. The *Ciccone* case, decided more than a decade later, rejects the reasoning of the *Bridgeport Music* case, leading to a circuit split on the question that remains unresolved at the time of this writing.

American funk musician George Clinton
and his band Parliament Funkadelic
performing Virginia in 2007,
Photo by Joe Loong (CC-SA-2.0)

BRIDGEPORT MUSIC, INC. V. DIMENSION FILMS
410 F.3d 792 (6th Cir. 2005)

AMENDED OPINION ON REHEARING

RALPH B. GUY, JR., CIRCUIT JUDGE.

[¶] . . . This action arises out of the use of a sample from the composition and sound recording "Get Off Your Ass and Jam" ("Get Off") in the rap song "100 Miles and Runnin' " ("100 Miles"), which was included in the sound track of the movie *I Got the Hook Up* (*Hook Up*). Specifically, Westbound appeals from the district court's decision to grant summary judgment to defendant on the grounds that the alleged infringement was *de minimis* and therefore not actionable. . . . For the reasons that follow, we reverse the district court's grant of summary judgment to No Limit on Westbound's claim of infringement of its sound recording copyright . . . .

I.

The claims at issue in this appeal were originally asserted in an action filed on May 4, 2001, by the related entities Bridgeport Music, Southfield Music, Westbound Records, and Nine Records, alleging nearly 500 counts against approximately 800 defendants for copyright infringement and various state law claims relating to the use of samples without permission in new rap recordings. . . .

The claims in this case were brought by all four plaintiffs: Bridgeport and Southfield, which are in the business of music publishing and exploiting musical composition copyrights, and Westbound Records and Nine Records, which are in the business of recording and distributing sound recordings. . . .

Bridgeport and Westbound claim to own the musical composition and sound recording copyrights in "Get Off Your Ass and Jam" by George

Clinton, Jr. and the Funkadelics. We assume, as did the district court, that plaintiffs would be able to establish ownership in the copyrights they claim. There seems to be no dispute either that "Get Off" was digitally sampled or that the recording "100 Miles" was included on the sound track of *I Got the Hook Up*. Defendant No Limit Films, in conjunction with Priority Records, released the movie to theaters on May 27, 1998. . . . .

Westbound's claims are for infringement of the sound recording "Get Off."[FN3 omitted] Because defendant does not deny it, we assume that the sound track of *Hook Up* used portions of "100 Miles" that included the allegedly infringing sample from "Get Off." The recording "Get Off" opens with a three-note combination solo guitar "riff" that lasts four seconds. According to one of plaintiffs' experts, Randy Kling, the recording "100 Miles" contains a sample from that guitar solo. Specifically, a two-second sample from the guitar solo was copied, the pitch was lowered, and the copied piece was "looped" and extended to 16 beats. Kling states that this sample appears in the sound recording "100 Miles" in five places; specifically, at 0:49, 1:52, 2:29, 3:20 and 3:46. By the district court's estimation, each looped segment lasted approximately 7 seconds. As for the segment copied from "Get Off," the district court described it as follows:

> The portion of the song at issue here is an arpeggiated chord-that is, three notes that, if struck together, comprise a chord but instead are played one at a time in very quick succession-that is repeated several times at the opening of "Get Off." The arpeggiated chord is played on an unaccompanied electric guitar. The rapidity of the notes and the way they are played produce a high-pitched, whirling sound that captures the listener's attention and creates anticipation of what is to follow.

Bridgeport, 230 F.Supp.2d at 839. No Limit Films moved for summary judgment, arguing (1) that the sample was not protected by copyright law because it was not "original"; and (2) that the sample was legally insubstantial and therefore does not amount to actionable copying under copyright law.

Mindful of the limited number of notes and chords available to composers, the district court explained that the question turned not on the originality of the chord but, rather, on "the use of and the aural effect produced by the way the notes and the chord are played, especially here where copying of the sound recording is at issue." *Id.* (citations omitted). The district court found, after carefully listening to the recording of "Get Off," "that a jury could reasonably conclude that the way the arpeggiated chord is used and memorialized in the 'Get Off' sound recording is original and creative and therefore entitled to copyright protection." *Id.* (citing *Newton v. Diamond*, 204 F.Supp.2d 1244, 1249–59 (C.D.Cal.2002)) (later affirmed on other grounds at 349 F.3d 591 (9th Cir.2003)). No Limit Films does not appeal from this determination.

Turning then to the question of *de minimis* copying in the context of digital sampling, the district court concluded that, whether the sampling is examined under a qualitative/quantitative *de minimis* analysis or under the so-called "fragmented literal similarity" test, the sampling in this case did not "rise to the level of a legally cognizable appropriation." 230 F.Supp.2d at 841. Westbound argues that the district court erred both in its articulation of the applicable standards and its determination that there was no genuine issue of fact precluding summary judgment on this issue.

On October 11, 2002, the district court granted summary judgment to No Limit Films on the claims of Bridgeport and Westbound; dismissed with prejudice the claims of Southfield and Nine Records; denied as moot the motion of Bridgeport and Westbound for partial summary judgment on the issue of copyright ownership; and entered final judgment accordingly. Bridgeport and Westbound appealed. . . .

II.

[¶] . . . In granting summary judgment to defendant, the district court looked to general *de minimis* principles and emphasized the paucity of case law on the issue of whether digital sampling amounts to copyright infringement. Drawing on both the quantitative/qualitative and "fragmented literal similarity" approaches, the district court found the *de minimis* analysis was a derivation of the substantial similarity element when a defendant claims that the literal copying of a small and insignificant portion of the copyrighted work should be allowed. After listening to the copied segment, the sample, and both songs, the district court found that no reasonable juror, even one familiar with the works of George Clinton, would recognize the source of the sample without having been told of its source. This finding, coupled with findings concerning the quantitatively small amount of copying involved and the lack of qualitative similarity between the works, led the district court to conclude that Westbound could not prevail on its claims for copyright infringement of the sound recording.[4]

Westbound does not challenge the district court's characterization of either the segment copied from "Get Off" or the sample that appears in "100 Miles." Nor does Westbound argue that there is some genuine dispute as to any material fact concerning the nature of the protected material in the two works. The heart of Westbound's arguments is the claim that no substantial similarity or *de minimis* inquiry should be undertaken at all when the defendant has not disputed that it digitally sampled a

---

[4]   Were we to follow the analysis used by the district judge, we would agree with the result he reached.

copyrighted sound recording. We agree and accordingly must reverse the grant of summary judgment.

A. Digital Sampling of Copyrighted Sound Recordings

At the outset it is important to make clear the precise nature of our decision. Our conclusions are as follows:

1.   The analysis that is appropriate for determining infringement of a musical composition copyright, is not the analysis that is to be applied to determine infringement of a sound recording. We address this issue only as it pertains to sound recording copyrights.[FN5 omitted]

2.   Since the district court decision essentially tracked the analysis that is made if a musical composition copyright were at issue, we depart from that analysis.[6]

3.   We agree with the district court's analysis on the question of originality. On remand, we assume that Westbound will be able to establish it has a copyright in the sound recording and that a digital sample from the copyrighted sound recording was used in this case.

4.   This case involves "digital sampling" which is a term of art well understood by the parties to this litigation and the music industry in general. Accordingly, we adopt the definition commonly accepted within the industry.

5.   Because of the court's limited technological knowledge in this specialized field, our opinion is limited to an instance of digital sampling of a sound recording protected by a valid copyright. If by analogy it is possible to extend our analysis to other forms of sampling, we leave it to others to do so.

6.   Advances in technology[7] coupled with the advent of the popularity of hip hop or rap music have made instances of digital sampling extremely common and have spawned a plethora of copyright disputes and litigation.

7.   The music industry, as well as the courts, are best served if something approximating a bright-line test can be established. Not

---

[6]   "In most copyright actions, the issue is whether the infringing work is substantially similar to the original work. . . . The scope of inquiry is much narrower when the work in question is a sound recording. The only issue is whether the actual sound recording has been used without authorization. Substantial similarity is not an issue . . . ." Bradley C. Rosen, Esq., 22 CAUSES OF ACTION § 12 (2d ed.2003).

[7]   "E.g., Terry Fryer, *Sampling Jargon Illustrated*, KEYBOARD, June 1988, at 66–73. First, the cost barrier to enter into the audio production arena is low due to the influx of affordable digital recording equipment. The combination of a microphone, digital audio equipment, consumer audio equipment and an album or compact disc collection are the only tools needed to produce commercial rap music. Second, utilizing samples as the musical element of the song enables the producer to create commercial rap music without any original musical accompaniment prior to recording the vocals. Third, using music samples saves a considerable amount of time when compared to the traditional recording methods because another artist already recorded the underlying music. . . ." Stephen R. Wilson, *Music Sampling Lawsuits: Does Looping Music Samples Defeat the De Minimis Defense?*, 1 Journal of High Technology Law (JHTL) 179 n. 9 (2002) (citations omitted).

necessarily a "one size fits all" test, but one that, at least, adds clarity to what constitutes actionable infringement with regard to the digital sampling of copyrighted sound recordings.

B. Analysis

We do not set forth the arguments made by Westbound since our analysis differs somewhat from that offered by the plaintiff. Our analysis begins and largely ends with the applicable statute. Section 114(a) of Title 17 of the United States Code provides:

> The exclusive rights of the owner of copyright in a sound recording are limited to the rights specified by clauses (1), (2), (3) and (6) of section 106, and do not include any right of performance under section 106(4).

Section 106 provides:

> Subject to sections 107 through 122, the owner of copyright under this title has the exclusive rights to do and to authorize any of the following:
>
> (1) to reproduce the copyrighted work in copies or phonorecords;
>
> (2) to prepare derivative works based upon the copyrighted work . . .

Section 114(b) states:

> (b) The exclusive right of the owner of copyright in a sound recording under clause (1) of section 106 is limited to the right to duplicate the sound recording in the form of phonorecords or copies that directly or indirectly recapture the actual sounds fixed in the recording. The exclusive right of the owner of copyright in a sound recording under clause (2) of section 106 is limited to the right to prepare a derivative work in which the actual sounds fixed in the sound recording are rearranged, remixed, or otherwise altered in sequence or quality. The exclusive rights of the owner of copyright in a sound recording under clauses (1) and (2) of section 106 do not extend to the making or duplication of another sound recording that consists entirely of an independent fixation of other sounds, even though such sounds imitate or simulate those in the copyrighted sound recording. . . .

Before discussing what we believe to be the import of the above quoted provisions of the statute, a little history is necessary. The copyright laws attempt to strike a balance between protecting original works and stifling further creativity. The provisions, for example, for compulsory licensing make it possible for "creators" to enjoy the fruits of their creations, but not to fence them off from the world at large. 17 U.S.C. § 115. Although musical compositions have always enjoyed copyright protection, it was not until 1971 that sound recordings were subject to a separate copyright. If one were to analogize to a book, it is not the book, i.e., the paper and binding, that is copyrightable, but its contents. There are probably any number of reasons why the decision was made by Congress to treat a sound recording differently from a book even though both are the medium in which an original work is fixed rather than the creation itself. None the least of them certainly were advances in technology which made the "pirating" of sound recordings an easy task. The balance that was struck was to give sound recording copyright holders the exclusive right "to duplicate the sound recording in the form of phonorecords or copies that directly or indirectly recapture the actual sounds fixed in the recording." 17 U.S.C. § 114(b). This means that the world at large is free to imitate or simulate the creative work fixed in the recording so long as an actual copy of the sound recording itself is not made.[FN8 omitted] That leads us directly to the issue in this case. If you cannot pirate the whole sound recording, can you "lift" or "sample" something less than the whole. Our answer to that question is in the negative.[9]

Section 114(b) provides that "[t]he exclusive right of the owner of copyright in a sound recording under clause (2) of section 106 is limited to the right to prepare a derivative work in which the actual sounds fixed in the sound recording are rearranged, remixed, or otherwise altered in sequence or quality." Further, the rights of sound recording copyright holders under clauses (1) and (2) of section 106 "do not extend to the making or duplication of another sound recording that consists *entirely* of an independent fixation of other sounds, even though such sounds imitate or simulate those in the copyrighted sound recording." 17 U.S.C. § 114(b) (emphasis added). The significance of this provision is amplified by the fact that the Copyright Act of 1976 added the word "entirely" to this language. Compare Sound Recording Act of 1971, Pub.L. 92–140, 85 Stat. 391 (Oct. 15, 1971) (adding subsection (f) to former 17 U.S.C. § 1) ("does not extend to the making or duplication of another sound recording that is an independent fixation of other sounds"). In other words, a sound recording owner has the exclusive right to "sample" his own recording. We find much to recommend this interpretation.[10]

---

[9]   A question arises as to whether the copying of a single note would be actionable. Since that is not the fact situation in this case, we need not provide a definitive answer. We note, however, that under the Copyright Act, the sound recording must "result from the fixation of a series of musical, spoken, or other sounds . . . ." 17 U.S.C. § 101 (definition of "sound recording").

[10]   "[B] by clarifying the rights of a sound recording copyright owner in regard to derivative works, Section 114(b) makes it clear that the digital sampling of a copyrighted sound recording must typically be licensed to avoid an infringement. . . . The import of this language is that it does not matter how much a digital sampler alters the actual sounds or whether the ordinary lay observer can or cannot recognize the song or the artist's performance of it. Since the exclusive right encompasses rearranging, remixing, or otherwise altering the actual sounds, the statute by its own terms precludes the use of a substantial similarity test." Susan J. Latham, *Newton v. Diamond:*

To begin with, there is ease of enforcement. Get a license or do not sample. We do not see this as stifling creativity in any significant way. It must be remembered that if an artist wants to incorporate a "riff" from another work in his or her recording, he is free to duplicate the sound of that "riff" in the studio. Second, the market will control the license price and keep it within bounds.[11] The sound recording copyright holder cannot exact a license fee greater than what it would cost the person seeking the license to just duplicate the sample in the course of making the new recording. Third, sampling is never accidental. It is not like the case of a composer who has a melody in his head, perhaps not even realizing that the reason he hears this melody is that it is the work of another which he had heard before. When you sample a sound recording you know you are taking another's work product.[12]

This analysis admittedly raises the question of why one should, without infringing, be able to take three notes from a musical composition, for example, but not three notes by way of sampling from a sound recording. Why is there no *de minimis* taking or why should substantial similarity not enter the equation.[13] Our first answer to this question is what we have earlier indicated. We think this result is dictated by the applicable statute. Second, even when a small part of a sound recording is sampled, the part taken is something of value.[14] No further proof of that is necessary than the fact that the producer of the record or the artist on the record intentionally sampled because it would (1) save costs, or (2) add something to the new recording, or (3) both. For the sound recording copyright holder,

---

Measuring the Legitimacy of Unauthorized Compositional Sampling—A Clue Illuminated and Obscured, 26 Hastings Comm. & Ent. L.J. 119, 125 (2003) (footnotes omitted).

[11] "Samplers should apply for the appropriate licenses, respect the rights of copyright holders, and be respected in turn as equal creators, Responsibility for obtaining clearance should fall to either the artist, the label, or both. Samplers realize that in the litigious environment of the United States, there is nothing to be gained and much money potentially to be lost by being a renegade. Surely some obscure materials will be sampled and overlooked, but the process should proceed devoid of recrimination and with the opportunity for money to be made by both the sampler and those whom he samples." David Sanjek, *"Don't Have to DJ No More": Sampling and the "Autonomous" Creator*, 10 Cardozo Arts & Ent. L.J. 607, 621 (1992).

[12] The opinion in *Grand Upright Music Ltd. v. Warner Bros. Records, Inc.*, 780 F.Supp. 182 (S.D.N.Y.1991), one of the first cases to deal with digital sampling, begins with the phrase, " 'Thou shalt not steal.' " *Id.* at 183 (quoting Exodus 20:15).

[13] "Thus, it seems like the only way to infringe on a sound recording is to re-record sounds from the original work, which is exactly the nature of digital sound sampling. Then the only issue becomes whether the defendant re-recorded sound from the original. This suggests that the substantial similarity test is inapplicable to sound recordings." Jeffrey R. Houle, *Digital Audio Sampling, Copyright Law and the American Music Industry: Piracy or Just a Bad "RAP"?*, 37 Loy. L. Rev. 879, 896 (1992).

[14] "(A)ll samples from a record appropriate the work of the musicians who performed on that record. This enables the sampler to use a musical performance without hiring either the musician who originally played it or a different musician to play the music again. Thus sampling of records . . . allows a producer of music to save money (by not hiring a musician) without sacrificing the sound and phrasing of a live musician in the song. This practice poses the greatest danger to the musical profession because the musician is being replaced with himself." Christopher D. Abramson, *Digital Sampling and the Recording Musician: A Proposal for Legislative Protection*, 74 N.Y.U. L. Rev. 1660, 1668 (1999) (footnote omitted).

it is not the "song" but the sounds that are fixed in the medium of his choice. When those sounds are sampled they are taken directly from that fixed medium. It is a physical taking rather than an intellectual one.

This case also illustrates the kind of mental, musicological, and technological gymnastics that would have to be employed if one were to adopt a *de minimis* or substantial similarity analysis. The district judge did an excellent job of navigating these troubled waters, but not without dint of great effort. When one considers that he has hundreds of other cases all involving different samples from different songs, the value of a principled bright-line rule becomes apparent. We would want to emphasize, however, that considerations of judicial economy are not what drives this opinion. If any consideration of economy is involved it is that of the music industry. As this case and other companion cases make clear, it would appear to be cheaper to license than to litigate.[15]

Since our holding arguably sets forth a new rule, several other observations are in order. First, although there were no existing sound recording judicial precedents to follow,[16] we did not pull this interpretation out of thin air.[17] Several law review and text writers, some of whom have

---

[15] "The current lack of bright-line rules leads to unpredictability, which may be one reason that so few sampling cases are brought to trial . . . . A cost-benefit analysis generally indicates that it is less expensive for a sampler to purchase a license before sampling (or settle a post-sampling lawsuit) rather than take his chances in an expensive trial, the outcome of which . . . is nearly impossible to predict with any degree of certainty." Stephen R. Wilson, *Music Sampling Lawsuits: Does Looping Music Samples Defeat the De Minimis Defense*, 1 Journal of High Technology Law (JHTL) 179, 187 n. 97 (2002).

[16] Two prior cases are worthy of mention, however, as they are often cited in discussions of digital sampling. These cases are *Grand Upright Music Ltd. v. Warner Bros. Records, Inc.*, 780 F.Supp. 182 (S.D.N.Y.1991), and *United States v. Taxe*, 540 F.2d 961 (9th Cir.1976). Although *Grand Upright* applied a bright-line test in a sampling case, we have not cited it as precedent for several reasons. First, it is a district court opinion and as such has no binding precedential value. Second, although it appears to have involved claims for both sound recording and musical composition copyright infringement, the trial judge does not distinguish which he is talking about in his ruling, and appears to be addressing primarily the musical composition copyright. Third, and perhaps most important, there is no analysis set forth to indicate how the judge arrived at his ruling, which has resulted in the case being criticized by commentators. Although often cited in later cases, there appears to be no case involving only the digital sampling of sound recordings that has relied on that decision. Nonetheless, it did precipitate a significant increase in licensing requests and changes in the way some artists and recording companies approached the issue of digital sampling.

Taxe involved a criminal prosecution of sound recording "pirates." The defendants were convicted in the district court and on appeal the court held that a jury instruction that characterized "any and all re-recordings as infringements" went too far, but nonetheless found the instructions as a whole to be free of any error requiring reversal. Like *Grand Upright*, there was no analysis to support this conclusion. This is understandable because the court was upholding the instructions given and had no need to dwell on that portion of the instruction the court "believed" "went beyond the law." *Taxe*, 540 F.2d at 965. Although *Taxe* has been cited frequently, it has not been cited for the pronouncement relative to the nature of the copyright protection afforded to sound recordings. It has been cited, however, for the proposition that infringement occurs even though the unauthorized recording makes changes in the sounds duplicated. *Id.* at n. 2.

[17] We have not addressed several of the cases frequently cited in music copyright cases because in the main they involve infringement of the composition copyright and not the sound recording copyright or were decided on other grounds. . . . *Newton v. Diamond*, 349 F.3d 591 (9th

been referenced in this opinion, have suggested that this is the proper interpretation of the copyright statute as it pertains to sound recordings.[18] Since digital sampling has become so commonplace and rap music has become such a significant part of the record industry, it is not surprising that there are probably a hundred articles dealing with sampling and its ramifications. It is also not surprising that the viewpoint expressed in a number of these articles appears driven by whose ox is being gored. As is so often the case, where one stands depends on where one sits. For example, the sound recording copyright holders favor this interpretation as do the studio musicians and their labor organization. On the other hand, many of the hip hop artists may view this rule as stifling creativity. The record companies and performing artists are not all of one mind, however, since in many instances, today's sampler is tomorrow's samplee. The incidence of "live and let live" has been relatively high, which explains why so many

---

Cir.2003), amended 388 F.3d 1189 (9th Cir.2004), cert. denied, ___ U.S. ___, 125 S.Ct. 2905, ___ L.Ed.2d ___, 2005 WL 585458, 73 U.S.L.W. 3557 (U.S. Jun. 13, 2005) (No. 04–1219). We note that in *Newton*, the matter at issue was infringement of the composition copyright. The alleged infringer had secured a license for use of the sound recording.

[18] "Certain provisions of the copyright law, however, do suggest that broader protection against unauthorized sampling may be available for owners of sound recordings than for the owners of musical compositions that may be embodied in those sound recordings. For example, the copyright act states that, 'The exclusive rights of the owner of copyright in a sound recording . . . do not extend to the making or duplication of another sound recording that consists entirely of an independent fixation of other sounds, even though such sounds imitate or simulate those in the copyrighted sound recording' [17 U.S.C. § 114(b)] (emphasis added). By using the words ' entirely of an independent fixation' in referring to sound recordings which may imitate or simulate the sounds of another, Congress may have intended that a recording containing any sounds of another recording would constitute infringement. Thus, it would appear that any unauthorized use of a digital sample taken from another's copyrighted recording would be an infringement of the copyrighted recording.

In fact, the copyright law specifically provides that the owner of copyright in a sound recording has the exclusive right to prepare a derivative work 'in which the actual sounds fixed in the sound recording are rearranged, remixed, or otherwise altered in sequence or quality.' A recording that embodies samples taken from the sound recording of another is by definition a 'rearranged, remixed, or otherwise altered in sequence or quality.'

It has been suggested that the strong protection implied by the foregoing provisions could be mitigated by a judicially applied standard which permits some degree of *de minimis* copying or copying where the sampled portion of the resulting work is not substantially similar to the copied work. For example, a court could determine that the taking of a millisecond of sound from another's copyrighted recording, or the taking of a more extensive portion that has been modified to the point of being completely unrecognizable or impossible to associate with the copied recording, does not constitute infringement. It is believed, however, that the courts should take what appears to be a rare opportunity to follow a 'bright line' rule specifically mandated by Congress. This would result in a substantial reduction of litigation costs and uncertainty attending disputes over sampling infringement of sound recordings and would promote a faster resolution of these disputes.

While the question whether an unauthorized use of a digital sample infringes a musical composition may require a full substantial similarity analysis, the question whether the use of a sample constitutes infringement of a sound recording could end upon a determination that the sampler physically copied the copyrighted sound recording of another. If the sampler physically copied any portion of another's copyrighted sound recording, then infringement should be found. If the sampler did not physically copy, then there could be no infringement (even if the resulting recording substantially simulates or imitates the original recording)." AL KOHN & BOB KOHN, KOHN ON MUSICLICENSING 1486–87 (Aspen Law & Business 3d ed.2002) (footnotes omitted).

instances of sampling go unprotested and why so many sampling controversies have been settled.

Second, to pursue further the subject of stifling creativity, many artists and record companies have sought licenses as a matter of course.[19] Since there is no record of those instances of sampling that either go unnoticed or are ignored, one cannot come up with precise figures, but it is clear that a significant number of persons and companies have elected to go the licensing route. Also there is a large body of pre-1972 sound recordings that is not subject to federal copyright protection.[20] Additionally, just as many artists and companies choose to sample and take their chances, it is likely that will continue to be the case.

Third, the record industry, including the recording artists, has the ability and know-how to work out guidelines, including a fixed schedule of license fees, if they so choose.

Fourth, we realize we are announcing a new rule and because it is new, it should not play any role in the assessment of concepts such as "willful" or "intentional" in cases that are currently before the courts or had their genesis before this decision was announced.

Finally, and unfortunately, there is no Rosetta stone for the interpretation of the copyright statute. We have taken a "literal reading" approach. The legislative history is of little help because digital sampling wasn't being done in 1971. If this is not what Congress intended or is not what they would intend now, it is easy enough for the record industry, as they have done in the past, to go back to Congress for a clarification or change in the law. This is the best place for the change to be made, rather than in the courts, because as this case demonstrates, the court is never aware of much more than the tip of the iceberg. To properly sort out this type of problem with its complex technical and business overtones, one needs the type of investigative resources as well as the ability to hold hearings that is possessed by Congress.

---

[19] "As a result of actual, as well as threatened, litigation in the area of digital sampling infringement, several developments have occurred. Sampling clearinghouses serve as one recent outgrowth. These companies are similar to publisher clearinghouses in that they are authorized by member copyright owners to clear samples for use on albums according to an agreed upon fee structure. In addition, record companies and most music publishers have instituted certain licensing policies as more and more artists routinely seek clearance for their samples with the hope of avoiding litigation." A. Dean Johnson, *Music Copyrights: The Need for an Appropriate Fair Use Analysis in Digital Sampling Infringement Suits*, 21 FLA. ST. U.L. REV. 135, 163 (1993) (footnote omitted).

[20] We speak as to federal copyright protection only, and recognize that the Copyright Act provides that: "With respect to sound recordings fixed before February 15, 1972, any rights or remedies under the common law or statutes of any State shall not be annulled or limited by this title until February 15, 2067. The preemptive provisions of subsection (a) shall apply to any such rights and remedies pertaining to any cause of action arising from undertakings commenced on and after February 15, 2067. Notwithstanding the provisions of section 303, no sound recording fixed before February 15, 1972, shall be subject to copyright under this title before, on, or after February 15, 2067." 17 U.S.C. § 301(c) (1998).

These conclusions require us to reverse the entry of summary judgment entered in favor of No Limit Films on Westbound's claims of copyright infringement. Since the district judge found no infringement, there was no necessity to consider the affirmative defense of "fair use." On remand, the trial judge is free to consider this defense and we express no opinion on its applicability to these facts.

VMG SALSOUL, LLC V. CICCONE
824 F.3d 871 (9th Cir. 2016)[14]

OPINION

GRABER, CIRCUIT JUDGE:

In the early 1990s, pop star Madonna Louise Ciccone, commonly known by her first name only, released the song *Vogue* to great commercial success. In this copyright infringement action, Plaintiff VMG Salsoul, LLC, alleges that the producer of *Vogue*, Shep Pettibone, copied a 0.23-second segment of horns from an earlier song, known as *Love Break*, and used a modified version of that snippet when recording *Vogue*. Plaintiff asserts that Defendants Madonna, Pettibone, and others thereby violated Plaintiff's copyrights to *Love Break*. The district court applied the longstanding legal rule that "de minimis" copying does not constitute infringement and held that, even if Plaintiff proved its allegations of actual copying, the claim failed because the copying (if it occurred) was trivial. The district court granted summary judgment to Defendants and awarded them attorney's fees under 17 U.S.C. § 505. Plaintiff timely appeals.

[¶]. . . . We hold that the "de minimis" exception applies to infringement actions concerning copyrighted sound recordings, just as it applies to all other copyright infringement actions. Accordingly, we affirm the summary judgment in favor of Defendants.

[¶]. . . . FACTUAL AND PROCEDURAL HISTORY [¶]. . . .

In the early 1980s, Pettibone recorded the song *Ooh I Love It (Love Break)*, which we refer to as *Love Break*. In 1990, **Madonna** and Pettibone recorded the song *Vogue*, which would become a mega-hit dance song after its release on **Madonna**'s albums. Plaintiff alleges that, when recording *Vogue*, Pettibone "sampled" certain sounds from the recording of *Love Break* and added those sounds to *Vogue*. . . .

[¶]. . . . Plaintiff now asserts a sole theory of infringement: When creating two commercial versions of *Vogue*, Pettibone sampled a "horn hit"

---

14   Footnotes are omitted from this excerpt.

from *Love Break*, violating Plaintiff's copyrights to both the composition and the sound recording of *Love Break*.

[¶]. . . . The alleged source of the sampling is the "instrumental" version of *Love Break*, which lasts 7 minutes and 46 seconds. The single horn hit occurs 27 times, and the double horn hit occurs 23 times. The horn hits occur at intervals of approximately 2 to 4 seconds in two different segments: between 3:11 and 4:38, and from 7:01 to the end, at 7:46. The general pattern is single-double repeated, double-single repeated, single-single-double repeated, and double-single repeated. Many other instruments are playing at the same time as the horns.

[¶]. . . . The two commercial versions of *Vogue* that Plaintiff challenges are known as the "radio edit" version and the "compilation" version. The radio edit version of *Vogue* lasts 4 minutes and 53 seconds. The single horn hit occurs once, the double horn hit occurs three times, and a "breakdown" version of the horn hit occurs once. They occur at 0:56, 1:02, 3:41, 4:05, and 4:18. The pattern is single-double-double-double-breakdown. As with *Love Break*, many other instruments are playing at the same time as the horns.

The compilation version of *Vogue* lasts 5 minutes and 17 seconds. The single horn hit occurs once, and the double horn hit occurs five times. They occur at 1:14, 1:20, 3:59, 4:24, 4:40, and 4:57. The pattern is single-double-double-double-double-double. Again, many other instruments are playing as well.

[¶]. . . . In a written order, the district court granted summary judgment to Defendants on two alternative grounds. First, neither the composition nor the sound recording of the horn hit was "original" for purposes of copyright law. Second, the court ruled that, even if the horn hit was original, any sampling of the horn hit was "de minimis or trivial." . . .

DISCUSSION

[¶]. . . . Taking the facts in the light most favorable to Plaintiff, Plaintiff has demonstrated actual copying. Accordingly, our analysis proceeds to the next step.

Our leading authority on actual copying is *Newton*, 388 F.3d 1189. We explained in *Newton* that proof of actual copying is insufficient to establish copyright infringement:

For an unauthorized use of a copyrighted work to be actionable, the use must be significant enough to constitute infringement. *See Ringgold v. Black Entm't Television, Inc.*, 126 F.3d 70, 74–75 (2d Cir. 1997). This means that even where the fact of copying is conceded, no legal consequences will follow from that fact unless the copying is substantial. . . . This principle reflects the legal maxim, *de minimis non curat lex* (often rendered as, "the law does not concern itself with trifles"). *See Ringgold*, 126 F.3d at 74–75.

Newton, 388 F.3d at 1192–93. In other words, to establish its infringement claim, Plaintiff must show that the copying was greater than de minimis.

Plaintiff's claim encompasses two distinct alleged infringements: infringement of the copyright to the *composition* of *Love Break* and infringement of the copyright to the *sound recording* of Love Break. . . . We squarely held in *Newton*, 388 F.3d at 1193, that the de minimis exception applies to claims of infringement of a copyrighted composition. But it is an open question in this circuit whether the exception applies to claims of infringement of a copyrighted sound recording.

* * * *

B. *The De Minimis Exception and Sound Recordings*

Plaintiff argues, in the alternative, that even if the copying here is trivial, that fact is irrelevant because the de minimis exception does not apply to infringements of copyrighted sound recordings. Plaintiff urges us to follow the Sixth Circuit's decision in *Bridgeport Music, Inc. v. Dimension Films*, 410 F.3d 792 (6th Cir. 2005), which adopted a bright-line rule: For copyrighted sound recordings, any unauthorized copying—no matter how trivial—constitutes infringement.

The rule that infringement occurs only when a substantial portion is copied is firmly established in the law. The leading copyright treatise traces the rule to the mid-1800s. 4 Melville B. Nimmer & David Nimmer, *Nimmer on Copyright* § 13.03[A][2][a], at 13-56 to 13-57, 13-57 n.102 (2013) . . . . We recognized the rule as early as 1977: "If copying is established, then only does there arise the second issue, that of illicit copying (unlawful appropriation). On that issue the test is the response of the ordinary lay hearer. . . ." *Sid & Marty Krofft Television Prods., Inc. v. McDonald's Corp.*, 562 F.2d 1157, 1164 (9th Cir. 1977) (alteration and internal quotation marks omitted), *superseded in other part by* 17 U.S.C. § 504(b); *see Fisher*, 794 F.2d at 434 n.2 (using the term "de minimis" to describe the concept). The reason for the rule is that the "plaintiff's legally protected interest [is] the potential financial return from his compositions which derive from the lay public's approbation of his efforts." *Krofft*, 562 F.2d at 1165 (quoting *Arnstein v. Porter*, 154 F.2d 464, 473 (2d Cir. 1946)). If the public does not recognize the appropriation, then the copier has not benefitted from the original artist's expressive content. Accordingly, there is no infringement.

Other than *Bridgeport* and the district courts following that decision, we are aware of no case that has held that the de minimis doctrine does not apply in a copyright infringement case. Instead, courts consistently have applied the rule in *all* cases alleging copyright infringement. Indeed, we stated in dictum in *Newton* that the rule "applies *throughout the law of copyright*, including cases of music sampling." 388 F.3d at 1195 (emphasis added).

Plaintiff nevertheless argues that Congress intended to create a special rule for copyrighted sound recordings, eliminating the de minimis exception. [¶¶]. . . . Plaintiff's statutory argument hinges on the third sentence of 17 U.S.C. § 114(b), which states:

> The exclusive rights of the owner of copyright in a sound recording under clauses (1) and (2) of section 106 do not extend to the making or duplication of another sound recording that consists entirely of an independent fixation of other sounds, even though such sounds imitate or simulate those in the copyrighted sound recording.

[¶]. . . . A straightforward reading of the third sentence in § 114(b) reveals Congress' intended limitation on the rights of a sound recording copyright holder: A new recording that mimics the copyrighted recording is not an infringement, even if the mimicking is very well done, so long as there was no actual copying. That is, if a band played and recorded its own version of *Love Break* in a way that sounded very similar to the copyrighted recording of *Love Break*, then there would be no infringement so long as there was no actual copying of the recorded *Love Break*. But the quoted passage does not speak to the question that we face: whether Congress intended to eliminate the longstanding de minimis exception for sound recordings in all circumstances even where, as here, the new sound recording as a whole sounds nothing like the original.

Even if there were some ambiguity as to congressional intent with respect to § 114(b), the legislative history clearly confirms our analysis on each of the above points. [¶]. . . . With respect to § 114(b) specifically, a House Report stated:

> Subsection (b) of section 114 makes clear that statutory protection for sound recordings extends only to the particular sounds of which the recording consists, and would not prevent a separate recording of another performance in which those sounds are imitated. Thus, infringement takes place whenever all *or any substantial portion* of the actual sounds that go to make up a copyrighted sound recording are reproduced in phonorecords by repressing, transcribing, recapturing off the air, or any other method, or by reproducing them in the soundtrack or audio portion of a motion picture or other audiovisual work. Mere imitation of a recorded performance would not constitute a copyright infringement even where one performer deliberately sets out to simulate another's performance as exactly as possible.

Id. at 106, *reprinted in* 1976 U.S.C.C.A.N. at 5721 (emphasis added). That passage strongly supports the natural reading of § 114(b), discussed above. [¶]. . . . Perhaps more importantly, the quoted passage articulates the principle that "infringement takes place whenever all *or any substantial portion* of the actual sounds . . . are reproduced." *Id.* (emphasis added).

That is, when enacting this specific statutory provision, Congress clearly understood that the de minimis exception applies to copyrighted sound recordings, just as it applies to all other copyrighted works. In sum, the statutory text, confirmed by the legislative history, reveals that Congress intended to maintain the de minimis exception for copyrighted sound recordings.

In coming to a different conclusion, the Sixth Circuit reasoned as follows:

> [T]he rights of sound recording copyright holders under clauses (1) and (2) of section 106 "do not extend to the making or duplication of another sound recording that consists *entirely* of an independent fixation of other sounds, even though such sounds imitate or simulate those in the copyrighted sound recording." 17 U.S.C. § 114(b) (emphasis added). The significance of this provision is amplified by the fact that the Copyright Act of 1976 added the word "entirely" to this language. *Compare* Sound Recording Act of 1971, Pub. L. 92–140, 85 Stat. 391 (Oct. 15, 1971) (adding subsection (f) to former 17 U.S.C. § 1) ("does not extend to the making or duplication of another sound recording that is an independent fixation of other sounds"). In other words, a sound recording owner has the exclusive right to "sample" his own recording.

Bridgeport, 410 F.3d at 800–01.

We reject that interpretation of § 114(b). *Bridgeport* ignored the statutory structure and § 114(b)'s express *limitation* on the rights of a copyright holder. *Bridgeport* also declined to consider legislative history on the ground that "digital sampling wasn't being done in 1971." 410 F.3d at 805. But the state of technology is irrelevant to interpreting Congress' intent as to statutory structure. Moreover, as Nimmer points out, *Bridgeport*'s reasoning fails on its own terms because contemporary technology plainly allowed the copying of small portions of a protected sound recording. Nimmer § 13.03[A][2][b], at 13-62 n.114.16. [¶]. . . . A statement that rights do not extend to a particular circumstance does not automatically mean that the rights extend to all other circumstances. In logical terms, it is a fallacy to infer the inverse of a conditional from the conditional. *E.g.*, Joseph G. Brennan, *A Handbook of Logic* 79–80 (2d ed. 1961).

The Sixth Circuit also looked beyond the statutory text, to the nature of a sound recording, and reasoned:

> [E]ven when a small part of a sound recording is sampled, the part taken is something of value. No further proof of that is necessary than the fact that the producer of the record or the artist on the record intentionally sampled because it would (1) save costs, or (2)

add something to the new recording, or (3) both. For the sound recording copyright holder, it is not the "song" but the sounds that are fixed in the medium of his choice. When those sounds are sampled they are taken directly from that fixed medium. It is a physical taking rather than an intellectual one.

Bridgeport, 410 F.3d at 801–02 (footnote omitted).

We disagree for three reasons. *First*, the possibility of a "physical taking" exists with respect to other kinds of artistic works as well, such as photographs, as to which the usual de minimis rule applies. *See, e.g.*, *Sandoval v. New Line Cinema Corp.*, 147 F.3d 215, 216 (2d Cir. 1998) (affirming summary judgment to the defendant because the defendant's use of the plaintiff's photographs in a movie was de minimis). A computer program can, for instance, "sample" a piece of one photograph and insert it into another photograph or work of art. We are aware of no copyright case carving out an exception to the de minimis requirement in that context, and we can think of no principled reason to differentiate one kind of "physical taking" from another. *Second*, even accepting the premise that sound recordings differ qualitatively from other copyrighted works and therefore *could warrant* a different infringement rule, that theoretical difference does not mean that Congress *actually adopted* a different rule. *Third*, the distinction between a "physical taking" and an "intellectual one," premised in part on "sav[ing] costs" by not having to hire musicians, does not advance the Sixth Circuit's view. The Supreme Court has held unequivocally that the Copyright Act protects only the expressive aspects of a copyrighted work, and *not* the "fruit of the [author's] labor." *Feist Publ'ns, Inc. v. Rural Tel. Serv. Co.*, 499 U.S. 340, 349, 111 S.Ct. 1282, 113 L.Ed.2d 358 (1991). Indeed, the Supreme Court in *Feist* explained at length why, though that result may seem unfair, protecting only the expressive aspects of a copyrighted work is actually a key part of the design of the copyright laws. *Id.* At 349–54, 111 S.Ct. 1282 (explaining how "the 'sweat of the brow' doctrine flouted basic copyright principles"). Accordingly, all that remains of *Bridgeport*'s argument is that the second artist has taken some expressive content from the original artist. But that is always true, regardless of the nature of the work, and the de minimis test nevertheless applies. *See* Nimmer § 13.03[A][2][b], at 13-63 to 13-64 (providing a similar critique of *Bridgeport*'s physical/intellectual distinction and concluding that it "seems to be built on air").

Because we conclude that Congress intended to maintain the "de minimis" exception for copyrights to sound recordings, we take the unusual step of creating a circuit split by disagreeing with the Sixth Circuit's contrary holding in *Bridgeport*. We do so only after careful reflection because, as we noted in *Seven Arts Filmed Entertainment Ltd. v. Content Media Corp.*, 733 F.3d 1251, 1256 (9th Cir. 2013), "the creation of a circuit split would be particularly troublesome in the realm of copyright. Creating inconsistent rules among the circuits would lead to different levels of protection in different areas of the country, even if the same alleged infringement is occurring nationwide." (Citation, internal quotations marks, and brackets omitted.) We acknowledge that our decision has consequences. But the goal of avoiding a circuit split cannot override our independent duty to determine congressional intent. Otherwise, we would have no choice but to blindly follow the rule announced by whichever circuit court decided an issue first, even if we were convinced, as we are here, that our sister circuit erred.

[¶]. . . . Additionally, as a practical matter, a deep split among the federal courts *already exists*. Since the Sixth Circuit decided *Bridgeport*, almost every district court not bound by that decision has declined to apply *Bridgeport*'s rule. . . . Although we are the first circuit court to follow a different path than *Bridgeport*'s, we are in well-charted territory.

[¶]. . . . Finally, Plaintiff advances several reasons why *Bridgeport*'s rule is superior *as a matter of policy*. For example, the Sixth Circuit opined that its bright-line rule was easy to enforce; that "the market will control the license price and keep it within bounds"; and that "sampling is never accidental" and is therefore easy to avoid. *Bridgeport*, 410 F.3d at 801. Those arguments are for a legislature, not a court. They speak to what Congress *could decide*; they do not inform what Congress *actually decided*.

We hold that the "de minimis" exception applies to actions alleging infringement of a copyright to sound recordings.

NOTES AND QUESTIONS

1.   Do you agree with the reasoning in the *Bridgeport* opinion for why a "bright line" test applies to sampling of sound recordings but not to sampling of compositions? Or do you agree with the *Ciccone* opinion's rejection of Bridgeport's refusal to apply the *de minimis* use test to samples of sound recordings? Do you think the *de minimis* rule makes sense in one context but not the other? Why or why not?

2.   The prevalence of mixtapes in the industry, particularly as both a method of promoting new artists (with labels commonly sending recordings to DJs as an incentive to including new artists in mixtapes and stimulating public interest) and as an alleged vehicle for infringement of copyright, led to a number of disputes in recent decades.[15] Today, mixtapes have largely moved

---

[15]   *See, e.g.*, Samantha M. Shapiro, *Hip-Hop Outlaw (Industry Version)*, The New York Times Magazine *2 (Feb. 18, 2007), *available at* https://www.nytimes.com/2007/02/18/magazine/18dj drama.t.html (discussing arrest of DJ Drama and DJ Don Cannon relating to their production of mixtapes); Hillary Crosley & Ed Christman, *Mixed Messages: DJ Drama's Bust Leaves Future of Mixtapes Uncertain*, 1/27/07 Billboard 8, 2007 WLNR 1525354; Jeff Leeds, *Cautiously, Big Labels Confront the Mixtape*, New York Times (Dec. 15, 2007), *available at* http://www.nytimes.com/2007/

from distribution and sale of physical CDs to online streaming through sites like Soundcloud and Mixcloud. These online sites allow users to stream content posted by other users and essentially follow DMCA guidelines with posted policies against infringement and procedures for notifying the sites of infringements, relying on the safe harbors of the DMCA for protection against infringement claims under U.S. law. The notice and takedown system established by the DMCA provides perhaps more of a safety net for distributors of mixtapes and more of a hurdle for copyright owners who seek to prevent unauthorized exploitation of samples from their sound recordings—but online streaming sites can also provide a means of capturing a share of revenues from exploitation of sampled works that can replace expensive litigation or the need for law enforcement intervention. It does not, however, resolve the recurring question of how much today's artists may borrow from—or be inspired by—yesterday's artists.

3.   Do you think that DJs who incorporate tracks sent to them by labels to promote new releases into mixtapes should be protected under the fair use doctrine or an equitable estoppel doctrine? As you consider this question, recall the fair use factors laid out in Section 107: "(1) the purpose and character of the use, including whether such use is of a commercial nature or is for nonprofit educational purposes; (2) the nature of the copyrighted work; (3) the amount and substantiality of the portion used in relation to the copyrighted work as a whole; and (4) the effect of the use upon the potential market for or value of the copyrighted work." Would such an argument be any different from that made in *Harms v. Cohen* in Chapter 3, where the movie theater argued that sending promotional copies of sheet music to movie theater pianists should be deemed as giving consent to perform the compositions? Why or why not?

4.   As indicated at the end of the *Bridgeport* opinion, the Sixth Circuit did not reach any determination as to the application of the fair use defense to the claims in the case, and the case was settled after remand without any resolution of how the fair use defense might apply to sampling. Do you think that the fair use defense should apply differently to sampling of sound recordings than to sampling of compositions? Would it make sense for a sampler to have engaged in fair use of a composition but not in fair use of the sound recording of that composition? Why or why not?

5.   In a context different from sampling, but also involving the use of a sound recording in a subsequent creative work, the fair use defense has been found in some cases to permit use of sound recordings in audiovisual works without a synchronization license from the recording's owner. For example, in *Threshold Media Corp. v. Relativity Media, LLC*, 2013 WL 12331550 (C.D. Cal. March 19, 2013), the court analyzed the four fair use factors in connection with a film's use of the plaintiff's sound recording as a plot device in the film's story, finding the film's use of the recording to be transformative: "[T]o hold that [defendants'] use of [plaintiff's] music was not fair would be to grant Plaintiff

12/15/arts/music/15dram.html; Hillary Crosley, *All Mixed Up: Legal Questions Surrounding Charting Mixtapes*, 5/3/08 Billboard 8, 2008 WLNR 9749030.

not just a copyright but—in effect—a veto over a new, transformative work." Similarly, in *Lennon v. Premise Media Corp.*, 556 F.Supp.2d 310 (S.D.N.Y. 2008), the court ruled in favor of the defendants based on their fair use defense, permitting the defendants' use of a 15-second clip of John Lennon's song "Imagine" in a nationally released feature film. The court found the use "highly transformative" and fair where Lennon's "secular utopian vision" was paired with "Cold War-era images" as a form of criticism and commentary. How might a recording artist's use of an unlicensed sample or a DJ's mixtape be argued to be a "transformative use," similar to the unlicensed uses of recordings in the audiovisual works in the *Threshold Media* and *Lennon* cases? How might the use of samples in sound recordings be differentiated from the use of samples in films, given the fact that courts must balance all of the fair use factors to reach a result?

6.   Of course, relying on a fair use or *de minimis* use defense is fraught with uncertainty in light of the balancing of different factors and the fact-specific nature of the inquiry. As a result, many record labels are unwilling to include unlicensed samples in their releases even where a fair use or *de minimis* use defense could be asserted. There are still many instances in which copyright owners are unwilling to grant permission for a sound recording to be sampled, causing some to argue for creation of a statutory licensing system for samples of sound recordings.[16] What do you think is the most appropriate way to address licensing of samples? Should sampling be permitted as a matter of law as long as a statutory license fee is paid, or should owners of sound recordings retain control over sampling of their works, or should some middle ground be found in which some types of uses are statutorily permitted and others require individual licensing? Or is it more appropriate to simply maintain the regime of fair use as an affirmative defense to such sampling?

---

[16]   *See, e.g.,* Michael L. Baroni, *A Pirate's Palette: The Dilemmas of Digital Sound Sampling and A Proposed Compulsory License Solution*, 11 U. MIAMI ENT. & SPORTS L. REV. 65, 66 (1993) (describing the "struggle between the rights of artists to control uses of their own work, and the creative opportunities inherent in the new technology of sampling" and proposing a compulsory licensing system to balance these competing interests).

CHAPTER IX

USE OF AN ARTIST'S NAME, LIKENESS, AND VOICE: *YOU KNOW MY NAME (LOOK UP THE NUMBER)*[1]

■ ■ ■

A. INTRODUCTION TO THE RIGHT OF PUBLICITY

In addition to the products of their creative efforts, musical artists possess another form of quasi-intellectual property: the right of publicity. A creation of state law, the right of publicity has its roots in the right of privacy, which most states have interpreted to provide a cause of action for misappropriation of one's name and likeness for commercial purposes. As it became more and more common over the last decades of the 20th century for celebrities to earn income from licensing their names and images for commercial purposes, the tort shifted in focus from its privacy roots to a more property-like conception of the right.[2] As noted by the U.S. Supreme Court in *Zacchini v. Scripps-Howard Broadcasting Co.*,[3] a case in which the Court decided that the First Amendment did not preclude an award of damages for a news broadcast of a performer's entire performance under a state's recognized right of publicity, the interest protected by the right of publicity is "one of preventing unjust enrichment by the theft of good will. No social purpose is served by having the defendant get free some aspect of the plaintiff that would have market value and for which he would normally pay."[4] The right has been expressly recognized in most states within the U.S., many of which have enacted statutes to define the contours of the right.[5]

---

[1] John Lennon & Paul McCartney (1969); released by the Beatles as the B-side of the single *Let It Be* (1970).

[2] Haelan Laboratories v. Topps Chewing Gum, 202 F.2d 866 (2d Cir. 1953) (coining the term "right of publicity" in a case recognizing a baseball player's right to grant an exclusive license for the use of his name and likeness for commercial purposes).

[3] 433 U.S. 562 (1977).

[4] *Id.* at 576 (quoting Kalven, *Privacy in Tort Law: Were Warren and Brandeis Wrong?*, 31 LAW & CONTEMP. PROB. 326, 331 (1966)).

[5] For example, the following states have enacted right of publicity or misappropriation of name and likeness statutes: California, Cal. Civ. Code §§ 3344, 3344.1 (West 1997 & Supp. 2009); Florida, Fla. Stat. Ann. § 540.08 (West 2007 & Supp. 2009); Illinois, 765 Ill. Comp. stat. 1075/1–60 (2009); Indiana, Ind. Code Ann. § 32–36–1–1 to –20 (West 2002 & Supp. 2009); Kentucky, Ky. Rev. Stat. Ann. § 391.170 (West 1999 & Supp. 2009); Massachusetts, Mass. Gen. Laws ch. 214, § 3A (2005 & Supp. 2009); Nebraska, Neb. Rev. Stat. § 20–202 (2007); Nevada, Nev. Rev. Stat. § 597.770–810 (2007); New York, N.Y. Civ. Rights Law §§ 50, 51 (McKinney 2009); Ohio, Ohio Rev.

Because it is a creature of state law (there is no federal right of publicity), the scope of the right of publicity varies from state to state, with some states providing broad protection to include all aspects of a celebrity's persona that might have commercial value and others providing more limited protection to only one's name and image. In general, the right allows a person to prohibit others from using his or her name, likeness, and often other aspects of his or her persona (e.g., the distinctive sound of a voice or singing style), for commercial purposes without prior consent. The right is limited by First Amendment considerations, with most jurisdictions balancing the nature and purpose of the challenged use against the limitations on free expression that enforcement of the right would create in the particular case. Typically, the more clearly the commercial purpose of the use of a celebrity's persona, the less likely it will be that the First Amendment would bar a right of publicity claim. Conversely, uses that are less closely tied to a commercial or advertising purpose are more likely to be protected by the First Amendment and to bar right of publicity claims.[6]

Federal law also provides a related avenue of relief for many celebrities who believe that their identity is being used without their permission in a way that may be confusing to the public. The Lanham Act, which governs federal trademark law, prohibits "false designations of origin" of goods or services or uses of names or symbols that are likely to cause confusion as to the affiliation with or sponsorship of the product by the plaintiff.[7] Although both right of publicity and Lanham Act claims are often asserted in situations involving the use of a celebrity's name or identity in connection with the unlicensed sale of a product or service, a Lanham Act claim differs from a right of publicity claim in several respects.

Code Ann. §§ 2741.01–09, 99 (West 2006 & Supp. 2009); Oklahoma, Okla. Stat. Ann. tit. 12, §§ 1448, 1449 (West 2002 & Supp. 2010); Pennsylvania, 42 Pa. Cons. Stat. Ann. § 8316 (West 2007 & Supp. 2009); Rhode Island, R.I. Gen. Laws § 9–1–28.1 (1997 & Supp. 2009); Tennessee, Tenn. Code Ann. § 47–25–1101 to –1108 (2001 & Supp. 2009); Texas, Tex. Prop. Code Ann. § 26.001–015 (2000 & Supp. 2009); Utah, Utah Code Ann. § 45–3–1 to –6 (2008); Virginia, Va. Code Ann. § 8.01–40 (2007 & Supp. 2009); Washington, Wash. Rev. Code § 63.60.010–080 (2008); Wisconsin, Wis. Stat. § 995.50 (2007).

6   For example, the uses of a celebrity sound-alike in the *Midler* and *Waits* cases, excerpted below, were clearly commercial uses, as the sound-alikes recorded songs for purposes of commercial advertisements of the defendants' products, and thus there were no First Amendment concerns about imposing liability for those uses. In contrast, the First Amendment can be a potential bar to liability in cases in which a celebrity's image is used in a transformative way in an expressive work such as a comic strip, *see* Winter v. D.C. Comics, Inc., 30 Cal.4th 881 (2003), or a celebrity's name is used for expressive purposes rather than commercial purposes, *see* Parks v. LaFace Records, 329 F.3d 437 (6th Cir. 2003) (reversing summary judgment for defendants on right of publicity claim where plaintiff's name was used in defendant's song title, because there were issues of fact as to the relevance of the plaintiff's name to the content of the song at issue that barred summary judgment on defendant's First Amendment defense).

7   The Lanham Act also protects against "dilution" or "tarnishment" of one's trademark. 15 U.S.C. § 1125(c). Most claims brought by musicians under the Lanham Act are based upon a likelihood of consumer confusion as to the artists' affiliation with or sponsorship of the defendant's product, and thus the discussion here focuses on § 1125(a) and cases applying it in the music industry.

In some ways, the Lanham Act provides narrower protection because it requires proof of a likelihood of consumer confusion resulting from the use, whereas a right of publicity claim can be established even if there is no likelihood of consumer confusion as to the celebrity's association with or endorsement of the product. In other ways, the Lanham Act provides broader protection than some states' right of publicity laws because it has been interpreted to apply to many aspects of a celebrity's "persona" that may not be protected by the right of publicity in a particular jurisdiction, such as imitations of an artist's voice in product advertisements.

In the music industry, the Lanham Act and right of publicity come into play in two important areas: lawsuits by musical artists against entities that use the artists' names, images, or voices without their permission for commercial purposes, and contractual provisions in recording agreements that permit record labels and their assignees to use the recording artists' names and images in connection with the licensed recordings. The materials that follow will introduce you first to the most relevant provisions of the Lanham Act and the state statutes in California and New York that recognize the right of publicity and then to specific cases in which the right has been asserted in the context of the music industry. As you read through the provisions of each statute, take note of the different nature and scope of protection that each provides.

CONSIDER AS YOU READ . . .

- How much control should performing artists have over how recordings of their voices are used? Should this be left to contractual negotiations with the record labels, or should the law step in to provide additional protection?

- Is it best for the law to protect voice and band names as a property-like interest or to focus on the likelihood of consumer confusion from a use—or both? Why?

- Does it matter whether the law is consistent from state to state with respect to the existence of a right to prevent one's voice from being exploited for commercial purposes without permission?

- Should political campaigns be given special treatment regarding use of musical works and sound recordings? How might the interests of individual composers and recording artists be balanced with First Amendment concerns? Does current law appropriately balance those concerns?

- What advice would you give to members of a band regarding contractual or other arrangements (e.g., formation of a corporation to own and control band assets like its name) for future use of the band's name?

B. STATUTES PROTECTING AN ARTIST'S NAME, LIKENESS, AND VOICE FROM UNAUTHORIZED COMMERCIAL USE

15 U.S.C. § 1125 (LANHAM ACT SECTION 43). FALSE DESIGNATIONS OF ORIGIN, FALSE DESCRIPTIONS, AND DILUTION FORBIDDEN

(a) Civil action

(1) Any person who, on or in connection with any goods or services, or any container for goods, uses in commerce any word, term, name, symbol, or device, or any combination thereof, or any false designation of origin, false or misleading description of fact, or false or misleading representation of fact, which—

(A) is likely to cause confusion, or to cause mistake, or to deceive as to the affiliation, connection, or association of such person with another person, or as to the origin, sponsorship, or approval of his or her goods, services, or commercial activities by another person, or

(B) in commercial advertising or promotion, misrepresents the nature, characteristics, qualities, or geographic origin of his or her or another person's goods, services, or commercial activities,

shall be liable in a civil action by any person who believes that he or she is or is likely to be damaged by such act.

CALIFORNIA CIVIL CODE § 3344. USE OF ANOTHER'S NAME, VOICE, SIGNATURE, PHOTOGRAPH, OR LIKENESS FOR ADVERTISING OR SELLING OR SOLICITING PURPOSES

(a)   Any person who knowingly uses another's name, voice, signature, photograph, or likeness, in any manner, on or in products, merchandise, or goods, or for purposes of advertising or selling, or soliciting purchases of, products, merchandise, goods or services, without such person's prior consent, or, in the case of a minor, the prior consent of his parent or legal guardian, shall be liable for any damages sustained by the person or persons injured as a result thereof. In addition, in any action brought under this section, the person who violated the section shall be liable to the injured party or parties in an amount equal to the greater of seven hundred fifty dollars ($750) or the actual damages suffered by him or her as a result of the unauthorized use, and any profits from the unauthorized use that are attributable to the use and are not taken into account in computing the actual damages. . . . Punitive damages may also be awarded to the injured party or parties. The prevailing party in any action under this section shall also be entitled to attorney's fees and costs. . . . [¶¶]

(d)   For purposes of this section, a use of a name, voice, signature, photograph, or likeness in connection with any news, public affairs, or sports broadcast or account, or any political campaign, shall not constitute a use for which consent is required under subdivision (a). . . . [¶¶]

(g)   The remedies provided for in this section are cumulative and shall be in addition to any others provided for by law.

CALIFORNIA CIVIL CODE § 3344.1. DECEASED PERSONALITY'S NAME, VOICE, SIGNATURE, PHOTOGRAPH, OR LIKENESS; UNAUTHORIZED USE; DAMAGES AND PROFITS FROM USE; PROTECTED USES; PERSONS ENTITLED TO EXERCISE RIGHTS; SUCCESSORS IN INTEREST OR LICENSEES; REGISTRATION OF CLAIM

(a) (1)   Any person who uses a deceased personality's name, voice, signature, photograph, or likeness, in any manner, on or in products, merchandise, or goods, or for purposes of advertising or selling, or soliciting purchases of, products, merchandise, goods, or services, without prior consent from the person or persons specified in subdivision (c), shall be liable for any damages sustained by the person or persons injured as a result thereof. In addition, in any action brought under this section, the person who violated the section shall be liable to the injured party or parties in an amount equal to the greater of seven hundred fifty dollars ($750) or the actual damages suffered by the injured party or parties, as a result of the unauthorized use, and any profits from the unauthorized use that are attributable to the use and are not taken into account in computing the actual damages. . . . Punitive damages may also be awarded to the injured party or parties. The prevailing party or parties in any action under this section shall also be entitled to attorney's fees and costs.

(2)   For purposes of this subdivision, a play, book, magazine, newspaper, musical composition, audiovisual work, radio or television program, single and original work of art, work of political or newsworthy value, or an advertisement or commercial announcement for any of these works, shall not be considered a product, article of merchandise, good, or service if it is fictional or nonfictional entertainment, or a dramatic, literary, or musical work.

(3)   If a work that is protected under paragraph (2) includes within it a use in connection with a product, article of merchandise, good, or service, this use shall not be exempt under this subdivision, notwithstanding the unprotected use's inclusion in a work otherwise exempt under this subdivision, if the claimant proves that this use is so directly connected with a product, article of merchandise, good, or service as to constitute an act of advertising, selling, or soliciting purchases of that product, article of merchandise, good, or service by the deceased personality without prior consent from the person or persons specified in subdivision (c).

(b) The rights recognized under this section are property rights, freely transferable or descendible, in whole or in part, by contract or by means of any trust or any other testamentary instrument, executed before or after January 1, 1985. The rights recognized under this section shall be deemed to have existed at the time of death of any deceased personality who died prior to January 1, 1985, and, except as provided in subdivision (o), shall vest in the persons entitled to these property rights under the testamentary instrument of the deceased personality effective as of the date of his or her death. . . . The rights established by this section shall also be freely transferable or descendible by contract, trust, or any other testamentary instrument by any subsequent owner of the deceased personality's rights as recognized by this section. . . .

(c) The consent required by this section shall be exercisable by the person or persons to whom the right of consent, or portion thereof, has been transferred in accordance with subdivision (b), or if no transfer has occurred, then by the person or persons to whom the right of consent, or portion thereof, has passed in accordance with subdivision (d).

(d) Subject to subdivisions (b) and (c), after the death of any person, the rights under this section shall belong to . . . and may be exercised, on behalf of and for the benefit of all of those persons, by those persons who, in the aggregate, are entitled to more than a one-half interest in the rights [list of surviving relatives of the decedent and their respective ownership interests in the absence of a will, such as spouse, children, etc., based upon Cal. Probate Code provisions, is omitted]. . . . [¶¶]

(e) If any deceased personality does not transfer his or her rights under this section by contract, or by means of a trust or testamentary instrument, and there are no surviving persons as described in subdivision (d), then the rights set forth in subdivision (a) shall terminate.

(f) (1) A successor in interest to the rights of a deceased personality under this section or a licensee thereof shall not recover damages for a use prohibited by this section that occurs before the successor in interest or licensee registers a claim of the rights under paragraph (2).

(2) Any person claiming to be a successor in interest to the rights of a deceased personality under this section or a licensee thereof may register that claim with the Secretary of State on a form prescribed by the Secretary of State and upon payment of a fee . . . .

(3) Upon receipt and after filing of any document under this section, the Secretary of State shall post the document along with the entire registry of persons claiming to be a successor in interest to the rights of a deceased personality or a registered licensee under this section upon the Secretary of State's Internet Web site. . . .

(4) Claims registered under this subdivision shall be public records.

(g) An action shall not be brought under this section by reason of any use of a deceased personality's name, voice, signature, photograph, or likeness occurring after the expiration of 70 years after the death of the deceased personality.

(h) As used in this section, "deceased personality" means any natural person whose name, voice, signature, photograph, or likeness has commercial value at the time of his or her death, or because of his or her death, whether or not during the lifetime of that natural person the person used his or her name, voice, signature, photograph, or likeness on or in products, merchandise, or goods, or for purposes of advertising or selling, or solicitation of purchase of, products, merchandise, goods, or services. A "deceased personality" shall include, without limitation, any such natural person who has died within 70 years prior to January 1, 1985. [¶]. . . .

(j) For purposes of this section, the use of a name, voice, signature, photograph, or likeness in connection with any news, public affairs, or sports broadcast or account, or any political campaign, shall not constitute a use for which consent is required under subdivision (a). . . . [¶¶]

(m) The remedies provided for in this section are cumulative and shall be in addition to any others provided for by law. . . . [¶¶]

(p) The rights recognized by this section are expressly made retroactive, including to those deceased personalities who died before January 1, 1985.

NEW YORK CIVIL RIGHTS LAW § 50. RIGHT OF PRIVACY

A person, firm or corporation that uses for advertising purposes, or for the purposes of trade, the name, portrait or picture of any living person without having first obtained the written consent of such person, or if a minor of his or her parent or guardian, is guilty of a misdemeanor.

NEW YORK CIVIL RIGHTS LAW § 51. ACTION FOR INJUNCTION AND FOR DAMAGES

Any person whose name, portrait, picture or voice is used within this state for advertising purposes or for the purposes of trade without the written consent first obtained as above provided [See § 50] may maintain an equitable action in the supreme court of this state against the person, firm or corporation so using his name, portrait, picture or voice, to prevent and restrain the use thereof; and may also sue and recover damages for any injuries sustained by reason of such use and if the defendant shall have knowingly used such person's name, portrait, picture or voice in such manner as is forbidden or declared to be unlawful by section fifty of this article, the jury, in its discretion, may award exemplary damages. But nothing contained in this article shall be so construed as to prevent any person, firm or corporation from selling or otherwise transferring any material containing such name, portrait, picture or voice in whatever medium to any user of such name, portrait, picture or voice, or to any third party for sale or transfer directly or indirectly to such a user, for use in a manner lawful under this article; . . . and nothing contained in this article shall be so construed as to prevent any person, firm or corporation from using the name, portrait, picture or voice of any manufacturer or dealer in connection with the goods, wares and merchandise manufactured, produced or dealt in by him which he has sold or disposed of with such name, portrait, picture or voice used in connection therewith; or from using the name, portrait, picture or voice of any author, composer or artist in connection with his literary, musical or artistic productions which he has sold or disposed of with such name, portrait, picture or voice used in connection therewith. Nothing contained in this section shall be construed to prohibit the copyright owner of a sound recording from disposing of, dealing in, licensing or selling that sound recording to any party, if the right to dispose of, deal in, license or sell such sound recording has been conferred by contract or other written document by such living person or the holder of such right. Nothing contained in the foregoing sentence shall be deemed to abrogate or otherwise limit any rights or remedies otherwise conferred by federal law or state law.

NOTES AND QUESTIONS

1.   Read the language of the above statutory provisions carefully and consider the following hypotheticals:[8]

a.   The potential plaintiff, BA, is now a successful, well-known actor. Before he found success, he played a minor role in a film that went straight to video, appearing on-screen for only two minutes of the 90-minute film. He has just discovered that the film has been re-issued on DVD with new packaging that prominently features his picture (from the film footage) and his name on the cover of the DVD. When he appeared in the film, he signed a contract that gave the production company permission to use his name and likeness in connection with the film. BA believes that the packaging misrepresents the scope of his involvement in the film and wants to know whether he can successfully assert a claim under the Lanham Act, the California right of publicity statute, or the New York right of publicity statute.

b.   A famous musician and environmental activist, JD, agreed to appear in and narrate a documentary about the Alaskan wilderness, signing a contract that gave the production company permission to use his name and likeness in connection with the documentary. He also licensed several of his most famous recordings to be used in the background of the documentary. After production of the documentary, the producers sold the rights to the documentary to a soft drink company. In a version of the documentary created for television syndication, M embedded two commercials in the documentary that television networks were required to include with the broadcast of the documentary, each of which followed an appearance by JD in the documentary and each of which used a sound-alike recording in the background of the commercial that mimicked the style and distinctive voice of JD for purposes of advertising M's soft drink. JD wants to know whether he can successfully assert a claim under the Lanham Act, the California right of publicity statute, or the New York right of publicity statute. Would your answer be any different if JD is no longer alive, and his heirs are considering a lawsuit? Can you think of language that could have been used in the grant of permission to use JD's name and likeness in

---

8   Thanks to Vincent Chieffo for early versions of some of the following hypotheticals, which are modified versions of actual disputes.

connection with the documentary that would clearly make M's conduct permissible or impermissible?

c.   A very positive, but knowingly fictionalized, newspaper article about a well-known musical artist, SC, appears in a gossip magazine. No reference is made to the article on the cover of the magazine and no photographs are used. The magazine is sold by subscription only. Does SC have a possible claim under the Lanham Act, the California right of publicity statute, or the New York right of publicity statute? Would your answer change if the cover of the magazine included a large picture of SC with the headline, "SC Reveals All—Read Story on Page 15"? Would it make any difference in your analysis if the magazine is sold primarily in newsstands next to supermarket check-out lines rather than by subscription?

2.   Based upon your answers to the hypotheticals in Note 1, above, consider the following questions: How does the federal Lanham Act provision excerpted above differ from the California and New York right of publicity statutes? How do California's right of publicity statutes differ from those of New York? How do California's right of publicity protections for living celebrities differ from those of the heirs of deceased celebrities?

3.   If you represented a celebrity whose image had been used in a commercial advertisement without her permission, (a) would you prefer to have California or New York law govern the claim, and (b) would you include a Lanham Act claim along with your right of publicity claim? Why? What factors would be relevant to your decision? If you represented a company that had used a celebrity's image in a commercial advertisement without her permission, which jurisdiction's law would you prefer to have govern the claim: California, New York, or federal Lanham Act? Why? What factors would be relevant to your decision?

4.   Although you should carefully compare the nature and scope of the rights created by the above statutes, even a cursory comparison of the California and New York statutes governing the right of publicity (or even just the California statute governing the rights of living celebrities versus deceased celebrities) demonstrates one of the difficulties in advising clients about the right of publicity. With fifty (fifty-one, counting the District of Columbia) different sets of state legislatures and courts in addition to the federal legislature and courts, lawyers representing clients who have dealings in more than one state will often face difficult issues regarding both what law governs a transaction and how that law is likely to be interpreted. These materials introduce you to some of the general issues that arise in the right of publicity arena and a few of the specific statutory and common law claims that have been recognized, but each state will have its own interpretation of the scope of the right afforded to individuals to protect against the unauthorized use of their names, likenesses, voices, or identities.

C. JUDICIAL DEVELOPMENT OF RIGHT OF PUBLICITY AND PROTECTIONS FOR MISAPPROPRIATION OF AN ARTIST'S VOICE

As the right of publicity became more widely recognized, one issue that was heavily litigated and that was decided differently from state to state was whether that right died with the person whose name or likeness was at issue, or whether the heirs of that person could continue to control the commercial use of the decedent's name and likeness and thus preclude others from profiting from them. The right of privacy, from which the right of publicity evolved, was most commonly viewed as non-descendible because of the personal nature of the right, and thus those seeking to exploit a deceased celebrity's name and likeness argued that, like the right of privacy, the right of publicity should not descend to one's heirs. Those seeking to preserve control over a deceased relative's name and likeness argued that the right was more like an intellectual property right that could be freely assigned and transferred and thus that should survive the death of the original owner/creator.

This debate was vividly highlighted in a series of cases arising out of efforts by the Estate of Elvis Presley to preserve the right to control (and profit from) the use of his name and likeness after his death in 1977.

Elvis Presley promoting Jailhouse Rock,
Metro-Goldwyn-Mayer, Inc.
Reproduction Number: LC-USZ6-2067
Location: NYWTS–BIOG / Public domain

Right of Publicity: Descendibility of the Right in Tennessee
Although the marketing of celebrities' names and images is a common practice today, Elvis Presley (or at least his manager, Col. Tom Parker, who owned 56% of the corporation that marketed Elvis Presley's persona) was one of the first to recognize and tap into the potential profits from licensing the rights to items containing Presley's name and likeness. During Presley's lifetime, a Tennessee corporation established by Parker and Presley called Boxcar Enterprises issued licenses for the use of Presley's name and likeness, and two days after his death, Boxcar gave an exclusive license to commercially exploit Presley's name and likeness to a company called Factors Etc., Inc. ("Factors").

Also within days of Presley's death, other individuals and entities sought to profit from the sale of memorabilia containing Presley's name and likeness. Some of those items were sold in New York, and Factors filed a lawsuit in federal court in New York to enjoin the continued sale of items containing Presley's name and likeness by some of these competitors and to recover damages for past sales. Similarly, Factors filed suit in federal court in Tennessee to enjoin another company from selling statuettes bearing Presley's likeness. Among other issues, all of the courts involved in these lawsuits had to address the question of whether Elvis Presley's right of publicity survived his death or whether anyone was free to commercially exploit his name and likeness after his death.

The first of these cases to reach a federal circuit court was the *Memphis Development Foundation*[9] case in the Sixth Circuit Court of Appeals, which resolves appeals from federal trial courts in Tennessee. The Sixth Circuit ruled that the right was not descendible, stating:

> This appeal raises the interesting question: Who is the heir of fame? The famous have an exclusive legal right during life to control and profit from the commercial use of their name and personality. We are called upon . . . to determine whether, under Tennessee law, the exclusive right to publicity survives a celebrity's death. We hold that the right is not inheritable. After death the opportunity for gain shifts to the public domain, where it is equally open to all.[10]

After the Sixth Circuit issued its ruling that, under Tennessee law, the right of publicity is not descendible and thus that the unlicensed defendant was permitted to commercially exploit Elvis Presley's name and likeness after his death, the Second Circuit Court of Appeals (which resolves appeals from cases decided by federal trial courts in New York) issued its opinion in the New York case.[11] In that case, the federal trial court had

---

[9]   *Memphis Development Foundation v. Factors Etc., Inc.*, 616 F.2d 956 (6th Cir. 1980).

[10]   *Id.* at 957.

[11]   *Factors Etc., Inc. v. Pro Arts, Inc.*, 652 F.2d 278 (2d Cir. 1981).

granted an injunction that precluded the defendant from exploiting Presley's name and likeness, in spite of the defendant's arguments that the Sixth Circuit had decided that Presley's right of publicity did not survive his death. The Second Circuit reversed the trial court's decision, giving deference to the Sixth Circuit's interpretation of what Tennessee law might be if the Tennessee Supreme Court were to address the issue, over the strong dissent of one member of the three-judge panel.

After both the Sixth Circuit and Second Circuit had issued rulings finding that the right of publicity was not descendible in Tennessee, the intermediate court of appeals in Tennessee, which is not bound by decisions of federal courts on issues of state law, dealt with the issue of descendibility of the right of publicity in the *Elvis Presley International Memorial Foundation* case.[12] The Tennessee court concluded that the state law right of publicity was, in fact, descendible in spite of the two prior federal decisions, noting:

> It would be difficult for any court today, especially one sitting in Music City U.S.A. practically in the shadow of the Grand Ole Opry, to be unaware of the manner in which celebrities exploit the public's recognition of their name and image. The stores selling Elvis Presley tee shirts, Hank Williams, Jr. bandannas or Barbara Mandrell satin jackets are not selling clothing as much as they are selling the celebrities themselves. We are asked to buy the shortening that makes Loretta Lynn's pie crusts flakier or to buy the same insurance that Tennessee Ernie Ford has or to eat the sausage that Jimmy Dean makes.
>
> There are few every day activities that have not been touched by celebrity merchandising. . . . Celebrity endorsements are extremely valuable in the promotion of goods and services. *Carson v. Here's Johnny Portable Toilets, Inc.,* 698 F.2d 831, 834 (6th Cir.1983). They increase audience appeal and thus make the commodity or service more sellable. *Uhlaender v. Hendricksen,* 316 F.Supp. 1277, 1278 (D.Minn.1970). These endorsements are of great economic value to celebrities and are now economic reality.[13]

The Tennessee court based its conclusion as to the descendibility of the right of publicity in Tennessee on a variety of important policy considerations recognized by the state, including the state's expansive common law view of property, the recognition of the right of testamentary distribution as an essential right, and the value of the contract rights of those who acquired the right to use the celebrity's name and likeness

---

[12] *State ex rel. The Elvis Presley International Memorial Foundation,* 733 S.W.2d 89 (Ct. App. Tenn. 1987).

[13] *Id.* at 94.

during his lifetime.[14] The court also noted the 1984 enactment of a right of publicity statute by the Tennessee legislature that not only recognized an individual's "property right in the use of his name, photograph or likeness in any medium in any manner," but also made the right descendible.[15] The court expressly recognized a common law right of publicity in addition to the statutory right created by the legislature in 1984, stating:

> Our decision concerning the descendibility of Elvis Presley's right of publicity is not based upon Tenn.Code Ann. § 47–25–1101 *et seq.* but rather upon our recognition of the existence of the common law right of publicity. We note, however, that nothing in Tenn.Code Ann. § 47–25–1101 *et seq.* should be construed to limit vested rights of publicity that were in existence prior to the effective date of the act. To do so would be contrary to Article I, Section 20 of the Tennessee Constitution. A statute cannot be applied retroactively to impair the value of a contract right in existence when the statute was enacted.[16]

Right of Publicity: Scope of the Right in California Versus New York: As expressly stated in California Civil Code Sections 3344 and 3344.1, the California right of publicity statute exists side by side with the common law right that had previously been recognized by the California courts, and thus plaintiffs may assert both a common law and a statutory claim in the same action. The elements of proof for the common law and statutory claims are slightly different. The statutory claim requires knowing conduct, whereas the common law claim does not, and the statutory claim is limited to use of name, voice, signature, photograph, or likeness, whereas the common law claim has been more broadly construed to apply to any identifying aspects of a celebrity's identity.[17] The statutory claim also has a minimum damage provision and allows recovery of attorney's fees, whereas the common law claim does not.

In contrast to California's recognition of both a common law and statutory claim and Tennessee's recognition of a common law right of publicity predating its statutorily-created right, New York courts have expressly stated that there is no common law right of publicity under New York law. In New York jurisprudence, any claim must arise exclusively

---

[14]   *Id.* at 97–99.

[15]   *Id.* at 99 (citing Tenn. Code Ann. § 47–25–1104(a) & (b)(1)).

[16]   *Id.* at 99.

[17]   *See generally Eastwood v. Superior Court*, 149 Cal. App. 3d 409 (Ct. App. 1983). For example, in *White v. Samsung Electronics*, 971 F.2d 1395 (9th Cir. 1992), the common law right of publicity in California was extended to protect the invocation of plaintiff Vanna White's identity in an advertisement that incorporated a robot in a blond wig and evening gown on the set of *Wheel of Fortune*, even though the advertisement did not use White's name, likeness, or photograph. Similarly, in the *Midler v. Ford Motor Co.* case excerpted below, 849 F.2d 460 (9th Cir. 1988), the use of a sound-alike was found to violate California's common law right of publicity even though Midler's actual singing voice was not used on the commercial at issue.

under the New York Civil Rights Law.[18] As a result, right of publicity claims arising under New York law have generally been more narrowly construed than those arising under California law.

Protection of an Artist's Voice: Although the right of publicity is generally a valuable right for musical artists to exploit, with many artists using it to protect against sales of unauthorized merchandise, the protection of the unique sound of an artist's voice is of particular interest to those in the music industry. The Lanham Act does not list individual features of an artist that are protected under the law, but instead applies more generally to any false designation of origin or endorsement that creates a likelihood of consumer confusion, and thus it has been applied by the courts to protect against the use of sound-alikes to create the impression that a celebrity endorses a particular product.[19]

Until 1995, the New York statute provided protection only for unauthorized uses of an individual's name, portrait, or picture, and thus claims based upon misappropriation of one's voice were repeatedly rejected prior to 1995.[20] The New York legislature then amended Section 51 to include "voice" among the personal attributes that could not be used for commercial purposes without permission.[21] In California, both the right of publicity statute and the common law tort have been found to provide protection to individuals against the commercial use of their voice, and the protection of the common law right has been extended not only to use of the individual's actual voice, but also to the use of sound-alikes to evoke the celebrity's persona in endorsing a product.[22] The two cases that follow—involving claims by Bette Midler and Tom Waits, respectively—illustrate the comparative scope of the protection of an individual's voice under California law and the Lanham Act.

---

[18]   *E.g., Maxwell v. N.W. Ayer, Inc.*, 605 N.Y.S.2d 174, 176 (N.Y. Sup. Ct. 1993).

[19]   *E.g., Waits v. Frito-Lay, Inc.*, 978 F.2d 1093 (9th Cir. 1992) (excerpted below).

[20]   *Maxwell*, 605 N.Y.S.2d at 176.

[21]   Only a few cases have addressed claims for misappropriation of voice under Section 51 of the New York statute, and thus there has been little development of the nature and scope of that provision. *See, e.g., Robinson v. Snapple Beverage Corp.*, 2000 WL 781079, 55 U.S.P.Q.2d 150 (S.D.N.Y., June 19, 2000) (entering judgment under Section 51 in favor of members of The Sugar Hill Gang for use of their images and voices while singing "Rappers Delight" in a Snapple commercial without their written consent). *But see Costanza v. Seinfeld*, 279 A.D.2d 255, 719 N.Y.S.2d 29 (S.Ct. App. Div. 2001) (which did not involve a claim of misappropriation of voice but came up in a search of cases interpreting Section 51 and is now our favorite case name ever and perhaps your reward for reading the footnotes).

[22]   *E.g., Midler v. Ford Motor Co.*, 849 F.2d 460 (9th Cir. 1988) (excerpted below). Other jurisdictions have also afforded protection to one's voice under the right of publicity. *See, e.g.*, Ind. Code Ann. § 32–36–1–6 (West 2002 & Supp. 2009); Nev. Rev. Stat. § 597.790 (2007); Ohio Rev. Code Ann. §§ 2741.01 (West 2006 & Supp. 2009); Okla. Stat. Ann. tit. 12, § 1449 (West 2002 & Supp. 2010); 42 Pa. Cons. Stat. Ann. § 8316 (West 2007 & Supp. 2009); Tex. Prop. Code Ann. § 26.011 (2000 & Supp. 2009); Wash. Rev. Code § 63.60.050 (2008).

Bette Midler in a 1973 publicity photo
Creative Management Associates/
AEC-Aaron Russo (management)

MIDLER V. FORD MOTOR CO.
849 F.2d 460 (9th Cir. 1988)

Before HUG, TANG and NOONAN, CIRCUIT JUDGES.

NOONAN, CIRCUIT JUDGE:

This case centers on the protectibility of the voice of a celebrated chanteuse from commercial exploitation without her consent. Ford Motor Company and its advertising agency, Young & Rubicam, Inc., in 1985 advertised the Ford Lincoln Mercury with a series of nineteen 30 or 60 second television commercials in what the agency called "The Yuppie Campaign." The aim was to make an emotional connection with Yuppies, bringing back memories of when they were in college. Different popular songs of the seventies were sung on each commercial. The agency tried to get "the original people," that is, the singers who had popularized the songs, to sing them. Failing in that endeavor in ten cases the agency had the songs sung by "sound alikes." Bette Midler, the plaintiff and appellant here, was done by a sound alike.

Midler is a nationally known actress and singer. She won a Grammy as early as 1973 as the Best New Artist of that year. Records made by her since then have gone Platinum and Gold. . . . Time hailed her in its March 2, 1987 issue as "a legend" and "the most dynamic and poignant singer-actress of her time."

When Young & Rubicam was preparing the Yuppie Campaign it presented the commercial to its client by playing an edited version of Midler singing "Do You Want To Dance," taken from the 1973 Midler album, "The Divine Miss M." . . . [T]he agency contacted Midler's manager, Jerry Edelstein. The conversation went as follows: "Hello, I am Craig Hazen from Young and Rubicam. I am calling you to find out if Bette Midler would be interested in doing . . .? Edelstein: "Is it a commercial?" "Yes." "We are not interested."

Undeterred, Young & Rubicam sought out Ula Hedwig whom it knew to have been . . . a backup singer for Midler for ten years. Hedwig was told by Young & Rubicam that "they wanted someone who could sound like Bette Midler's recording of [Do You Want To Dance]." . . .

. . . . She was told to "sound as much as possible like the Bette Midler record," leaving out only a few "aahs" unsuitable for the commercial. Hedwig imitated Midler to the best of her ability.

After the commercial was aired Midler was told by "a number of people" that it "sounded exactly" like her record of "Do You Want To Dance." Hedwig was told by "many personal friends" that they thought it was Midler singing the commercial. . . .

Neither the name nor the picture of Midler was used in the commercial; Young & Rubicam had a license from the copyright holder to use the song. At issue in this case is only the protection of Midler's voice. The district court described the defendants' conduct as that "of the average thief." They decided, "If we can't buy it, we'll take it." The court nonetheless believed there was no legal principle preventing imitation of Midler's voice and so gave summary judgment for the defendants. Midler appeals.

The First Amendment protects much of what the media do in the reproduction of likenesses or sounds. A primary value is freedom of speech and press. Time, Inc. v. Hill, 385 U.S. 374, 388, 87 S.Ct. 534, 542, 17 L.Ed.2d 456 (1967). The purpose of the media's use of a person's identity is central. If the purpose is "informative or cultural" the use is immune; "if it serves no such function but merely exploits the individual portrayed, immunity will not be granted." Felcher and Rubin, "Privacy, Publicity and the Portrayal of Real People by the Media," 88 Yale L.J. 1577, 1596 (1979). Moreover, federal copyright law preempts much of the area. "Mere imitation of a recorded performance would not constitute a copyright infringement even where one performer deliberately sets out to simulate another's performance as exactly as possible." Notes of Committee on the Judiciary, 17 U.S.C.A. § 114(b). It is in the context of these First Amendment and federal copyright distinctions that we address the present appeal.

Nancy Sinatra once sued Goodyear Tire and Rubber Company on the basis of an advertising campaign by Young & Rubicam featuring "These Boots Are Made For Walkin'," a song closely identified with her; the female singers of the commercial were alleged to have imitated her voice and style and to have dressed and looked like her. The basis of Nancy Sinatra's complaint was unfair competition; she claimed that the song and the arrangement had acquired "a secondary meaning" which, under California law, was protectible. This court noted that the defendants "had paid a very substantial sum to the copyright proprietor to obtain the license for the use of the song and all of its arrangements." To give Sinatra damages for their use of the song would clash with federal copyright law. Summary judgment for the defendants was affirmed. Sinatra v. Goodyear Tire & Rubber Co., 435 F.2d 711, 717–718 (9th Cir.1970), cert. denied, 402 U.S. 906, 91 S.Ct. 1376, 28 L.Ed.2d 646 (1971). If Midler were claiming a secondary meaning to "Do You Want To Dance" or seeking to prevent the defendants from using that song, she would fail like Sinatra. But that is not this case. Midler does not seek damages for Ford's use of "Do You Want To Dance," and thus her claim is not preempted by federal copyright law. Copyright protects "original works of authorship fixed in any tangible medium of expression." 17 U.S.C. § 102(a). A voice is not copyrightable. The sounds are not "fixed." What is put forward as protectible here is more personal than any work of authorship.

Bert Lahr once sued Adell Chemical Co. for selling Lestoil by means of a commercial in which an imitation of Lahr's voice accompanied a cartoon of a duck. Lahr alleged that his style of vocal delivery was distinctive in pitch, accent, inflection, and sounds. The First Circuit held that Lahr had stated a cause of action for unfair competition, that it could be found "that defendant's conduct saturated plaintiff's audience, curtailing his market." Lahr v. Adell Chemical Co., 300 F.2d 256, 259 (1st Cir.1962). That case is more like this one. But we do not find unfair competition here. One-minute commercials of the sort the defendants put on would not have saturated Midler's audience and curtailed her market. Midler did not do television commercials. The defendants were not in competition with her. See Halicki v. United Artists Communications, Inc., 812 F.2d 1213 (9th Cir.1987).

California Civil Code section 3344 is also of no aid to Midler. The statute affords damages to a person injured by another who uses the person's "name, voice, signature, photograph or likeness, in any manner." The defendants did not use Midler's name or anything else whose use is prohibited by the statute. The voice they used was Hedwig's, not hers. The term "likeness" refers to a visual image not a vocal imitation. The statute, however, does not preclude Midler from pursuing any cause of action she may have at common law; the statute itself implies that such common law causes of action do exist because it says its remedies are merely "cumulative." Id. § 3344(g).

The companion statute protecting the use of a deceased person's name, voice, signature, photograph or likeness states that the rights it recognizes are "property rights." Id. § 990(b). By analogy the common law rights are also property rights. Appropriation of such common law rights is a tort in California. Motschenbacher v. R.J. Reynolds Tobacco Co., 498 F.2d 821 (9th Cir.1974). In that case what the defendants used in their television commercial for Winston cigarettes was a photograph of a famous professional racing driver's racing car. The number of the car was changed and a wing-like device known as a "spoiler" was attached to the car; the car's features of white pinpointing, an oval medallion, and solid red coloring were retained. The driver, Lothar Motschenbacher, was in the car but his features were not visible. Some persons, viewing the commercial, correctly inferred that the car was his and that he was in the car and was therefore endorsing the product. The defendants were held to have invaded a "proprietary interest" of Motschenbacher in his own identity. Id. at 825.

Midler's case is different from Motschenbacher's. He and his car were physically used by the tobacco company's ad; he made part of his living out of giving commercial endorsements. But, as Judge Koelsch expressed it in Motschenbacher, California will recognize an injury from "an appropriation of the attributes of one's identity." Id. at 824. It was irrelevant that Motschenbacher could not be identified in the ad. The ad suggested that it was he. The ad did so by emphasizing signs or symbols associated with him. In the same way the defendants here used an imitation to convey the impression that Midler was singing for them.

Why did the defendants ask Midler to sing if her voice was not of value to them? Why did they studiously acquire the services of a sound-alike and instruct her to imitate Midler if Midler's voice was not of value to them? What they sought was an attribute of Midler's identity. Its value was what the market would have paid for Midler to have sung the commercial in person.

A voice is more distinctive and more personal than the automobile accouterments protected in Motschenbacher. A voice is as distinctive and personal as a face. The human voice is one of the most palpable ways identity is manifested. We are all aware that a friend is at once known by a few words on the phone. At a philosophical level it has been observed that with the sound of a voice, "the other stands before me." D. Ihde, Listening and Voice 77 (1976). A fortiori, these observations hold true of singing, especially singing by a singer of renown. The singer manifests herself in the song. To impersonate her voice is to pirate her identity. See W. Keeton, D. Dobbs, R. Keeton, D. Owen, Prosser & Keeton on Torts 852 (5th ed. 1984).

We need not and do not go so far as to hold that every imitation of a voice to advertise merchandise is actionable. We hold only that when a distinctive voice of a professional singer is widely known and is deliberately imitated in order to sell a product, the sellers have appropriated what is not theirs and have committed a tort in California. Midler has made a showing, sufficient to defeat summary judgment, that the defendants here for their own profit in selling their product did appropriate part of her identity.

REVERSED AND REMANDED FOR TRIAL.

———————

Tom Waits during an interview in
Buenos Aires, Argentina, April 2007
Photo by Theplatypus (CC-SA-2.0)

WAITS V. FRITO-LAY, INC.
978 F.2d 1093 (9th Cir. 1992)

Before: BROWNING, BOOCHEVER, and REINHARDT, CIRCUIT JUDGES.

OPINION

BOOCHEVER, CIRCUIT JUDGE:

Defendants Frito-Lay, Inc., and Tracy-Locke, Inc., appeal a jury verdict and award of $2.6 million in compensatory damages, punitive damages, and attorney's fees, in favor of singer Tom Waits. Waits sued the snack food manufacturer and its advertising agency for voice misappropriation and false endorsement following the broadcast of a radio commercial for SalsaRio Doritos which featured a vocal performance imitating Waits' raspy singing voice. On appeal, the defendants mount attacks on nearly all aspects of the judgment.

In challenging the judgment on Waits' voice misappropriation claim, the defendants first contend that our decision in Midler v. Ford Motor Co., 849 F.2d 460 (9th Cir.1988), cert. denied, 503 U.S. 951, 112 S.Ct. 1513, 1514, 117 L.Ed.2d 650 (1992), recognizing voice misappropriation as a California tort, is no longer good law. Next, they contend that the district court erred in instructing the jury on the elements of voice misappropriation. . . .

In challenging the judgment on Waits' false endorsement claim under section 43(a) of the Lanham Act, the defendants contend that Waits lacks standing to sue because he is not in competition with the defendants. . . .

Because it is duplicative, we vacate the award of damages under the Lanham Act. We affirm in all other respects.

BACKGROUND

Tom Waits is a professional singer, songwriter, and actor of some renown. Waits has a raspy, gravelly singing voice, described by one fan as "like how you'd sound if you drank a quart of bourbon, smoked a pack of cigarettes and swallowed a pack of razor blades. . . . Late at night. After not sleeping for three days." Since the early 1970s, when his professional singing career began, Waits has recorded more than seventeen albums and has toured extensively, playing to sold-out audiences throughout the United States, Canada, Europe, Japan, and Australia. Regarded as a "prestige artist" rather than a musical superstar, Waits has achieved both commercial and critical success in his musical career.... Waits has appeared and performed on such television programs as "Saturday Night Live" and "Late Night with David Letterman," and has been the subject of numerous magazine and newspaper articles appearing in such publications as Time, Newsweek, and the Wall Street Journal. Tom Waits does not, however, do commercials. He has maintained this policy consistently during the past ten years, rejecting numerous lucrative offers to endorse major products. Moreover, Waits' policy is a public one: in magazine, radio, and newspaper interviews he has expressed his philosophy that musical artists should not do commercials because it detracts from their artistic integrity.

Frito-Lay, Inc. is in the business of manufacturing, distributing, and selling prepared and packaged food products, including Doritos brand corn chips. Tracy-Locke, Inc. is an advertising agency which counts Frito-Lay among its clients. In developing an advertising campaign to introduce a new Frito-Lay product, SalsaRio Doritos, Tracy-Locke found inspiration in a 1976 Waits song, "Step Right Up." Ironically, this song is a jazzy parody of commercial hucksterism, and consists of a succession of humorous advertising pitches.[1] The commercial the ad agency wrote echoed the rhyming word play of the Waits song. In its presentation of the script to Frito-Lay, Tracy-Locke had the copywriter sing a preliminary rendition of the commercial and then played Waits' recorded rendition of "Step Right Up" to demonstrate the feeling the commercial would capture. Frito-Lay approved the overall concept and the script.

The story of Tracy-Locke's search for a lead singer for the commercial suggests that no one would do but a singer who could not only capture the feeling of "Step Right Up" but also imitate Tom Waits' voice.... [¶] A recording engineer who was acquainted with Carter's work had recommended him to Tracy-Locke as someone who did a good Tom Waits imitation. Carter was a professional musician from Dallas and a Tom Waits fan.... When Carter auditioned, members of the Tracy-Locke creative team "did a double take" over Carter's near-perfect imitation of Waits, and remarked to him how much he sounded like Waits. In fact, the commercial's musical director warned Carter that he probably wouldn't get the job because he sounded too much like Waits, which could pose legal problems. Carter, however, did get the job.

---

[1]   Waits characterizes the song as an indictment of advertising. It ends with the line, "What the large print giveth, the small print taketh away." See Murray Ohio Mfg. Co. v. Continental Ins. Co., 705 F.Supp. 442, 444 (N.D.Ill.1989) (quoting "Tom Waits' noted maxim" in interpreting insurance contract).

. . . . After the session, Carter remarked to Brenner that Waits would be unhappy with the commercial because of his publicly avowed policy against doing commercial endorsements and his disapproval of artists who did. Brenner acknowledged he was aware of this, telling Carter that he had previously approached Waits to do a Diet Coke commercial and "you never heard anybody say no so fast in your life." Brenner conveyed to Robert Grossman, Tracy-Locke's managing vice president and the executive on the Frito-Lay account, his concerns that the commercial was too close to Waits' voice. As a precaution, Brenner made an alternate version of the commercial with another singer.

On the day the commercial was due for release to radio stations across the country, Grossman had a ten-minute long-distance telephone consultation with Tracy-Locke's attorney, asking him whether there would be legal problems with a commercial that sought to capture the same feeling as Waits' music. The attorney noted that there was a "high profile" risk of a lawsuit in view of recent case law recognizing the protectability of a distinctive voice. Based on what Grossman had told him, however, the attorney did not think such a suit would have merit, because a singer's style of music is not protected. Grossman then presented both the Carter tape and the alternate version to Frito-Lay, noting the legal risks involved in the Carter version. He recommended the Carter version, however, and noted that Tracy-Locke would indemnify Frito-Lay in the event of a lawsuit. Frito-Lay chose the Carter version.

The commercial was broadcast in September and October 1988 on over 250 radio stations located in 61 markets nationwide. . . . Waits heard it during his appearance on a Los Angeles radio program, and was shocked. He realized "immediately that whoever was going to hear this and obviously identify the voice would also identify that [Tom Waits] in fact had agreed to do a commercial for Doritos."

In November 1988, Waits sued Tracy-Locke and Frito-Lay, alleging claims of misappropriation under California law and false endorsement under the Lanham Act. The case was tried before a jury in April and May 1990. The jury found in Waits' favor, awarding him $375,000 compensatory damages and $2 million punitive damages for voice misappropriation, and $100,000 damages for violation of the Lanham Act. The court awarded Waits attorneys' fees under the Lanham Act. This timely appeal followed.

DISCUSSION

I.   Voice Misappropriation

In Midler v. Ford Motor Co., 849 F.2d 460, 463 (9th Cir.1988), cert. denied, 503 U.S. 951, 112 S.Ct. 1513, 1514, 117 L.Ed.2d 650 (1992), we held that "when a distinctive voice of a professional singer is widely known and is deliberately imitated in order to sell a product, the sellers have appropriated what is not theirs and have committed a tort in California."

The Midler tort is a species of violation of the "right of publicity," the right of a person whose identity has commercial value—most often a celebrity—to control the commercial use of that identity. See Motschenbacher v. R.J. Reynolds Tobacco Co., 498 F.2d 821, 824–25 (9th Cir.1974). See generally J.T. McCarthy, The Rights of Publicity and Privacy (1987) (hereafter Publicity and Privacy). We recognized in Midler that when voice is a sufficient indicia of a celebrity's identity, the right of publicity protects against its imitation for commercial purposes without the celebrity's consent. See Midler, 849 F.2d at 463.

The jury found that the defendants had violated Waits' right of publicity by broadcasting a commercial which featured a deliberate imitation of Waits' voice. In doing so, the jury determined that Waits has a distinctive voice which is widely known. . . .

A.   Continuing Viability of *Midler*

As a threshold matter, the defendants ask us to rethink Midler, and to reject it as an inaccurate statement of California law. Midler, according to the defendants, has been "impliedly overruled" by the Supreme Court's decision in Bonito Boats, Inc. v. Thunder Craft Boats, Inc., 489 U.S. 141, 109 S.Ct. 971, 103 L.Ed.2d 118 (1989). Additionally, they argue that the Midler tort is preempted by the federal Copyright Act.

. . . [¶] . . . Bonito Boats itself cautions against reading Sears and Compco for a "broad pre-emptive principle" and cites subsequent Supreme Court decisions retreating from such a sweeping interpretation. "[T]he Patent and Copyright Clauses do not, by their own force or by negative implication, deprive the States of the power to adopt rules for the promotion of intellectual creation." Bonito Boats, 489 U.S. at 165, 109 S.Ct. at 985 (citing, inter alia, Goldstein v. California, 412 U.S. 546, 552–61, 93 S.Ct. 2303, 2307–08, 37 L.Ed.2d 163 (1973) and Kewanee Oil Co. v. Bicron Corp., 416 U.S. 470, 478–79, 94 S.Ct. 1879, 1885, 40 L.Ed.2d 315 (1974)). Instead, the Court reaffirmed the right of states to "place limited regulations on the use of unpatented designs in order to prevent consumer confusion as to source." Id. Bonito Boats thus cannot be read as endorsing or resurrecting the broad reading of Compco and Sears urged by the defendants, under which Waits' state tort claim arguably would be preempted.

Moreover, the Court itself recognized the authority of states to protect entertainers' "right of publicity" in Zacchini v. Scripps-Howard Broadcasting Co., 433 U.S. 562, 97 S.Ct. 2849, 53 L.Ed.2d 965 (1977). In Zacchini, the Court endorsed a state right-of-publicity law as in harmony with federal patent and copyright law, holding that an unconsented-to television news broadcast of a commercial entertainer's performance was not protected by the First Amendment. Id. at 573, 576–78, 97 S.Ct. at 2856, 2858–59. . . . In sum, our holding in Midler, upon which Waits' voice misappropriation claim rests, has not been eroded by subsequent authority.

The defendants ask that we rethink Midler anyway, arguing as the defendants did there that voice misappropriation is preempted by section 114 of the Copyright Act. Under this provision, a state cause of action escapes Copyright Act preemption if its subject matter "does not come within the subject matter of copyright . . . including works or authorship not fixed in any tangible medium of expression." 17 U.S.C. § 301(b)(1). We rejected copyright preemption in Midler because voice is not a subject matter of copyright: "A voice is not copyrightable. The sounds are not 'fixed.' " Midler, 849 F.2d at 462. As a three-judge panel, we are not at liberty to reconsider this conclusion, and even if we were, we would decline to disturb it.

Waits' claim, like Bette Midler's, is for infringement of voice, not for infringement of a copyrightable subject such as sound recording or musical composition. Moreover, the legislative history of section 114 indicates the express intent of Congress that "[t]he evolving common law rights of 'privacy,' 'publicity,' and trade secrets . . . remain unaffected [by the preemption provision] as long as the causes of action contain elements, such as an invasion of personal rights . . . that are different in kind from copyright infringement." H.R.Rep. No. 1476, 94th Cong., 2d Sess. 132, reprinted in 1976 U.S.C.C.A.N. 5659, 5748. Waits' voice misappropriation claim is one for invasion of a personal property right: his right of publicity to control the use of his identity as embodied in his voice. . . . The trial's focus was on the elements of voice misappropriation, as formulated in Midler: whether the defendants had deliberately imitated Waits' voice rather than simply his style and whether Waits' voice was sufficiently distinctive and widely known to give him a protectable right in its use. These elements are "different in kind" from those in a copyright infringement case challenging the unauthorized use of a song or recording. Waits' voice misappropriation claim, therefore, is not preempted by federal copyright law.

B.   Jury Instructions

The defendants next contend that the district court committed prejudicial error by rejecting their proposed jury instructions on three elements of the Midler tort: the deliberate misappropriation for commercial purposes of (1) a voice, that is (2) distinctive and (3) widely known. . . .

(1) "Voice" vs. "Style"

The defendants argued at trial that although they had consciously copied Tom Waits' style in creating the Doritos commercial, they had not deliberately imitated his voice. They accordingly proposed a jury instruction which distinguished in detail between voice, which is protected under Midler, and style, which is not.[2] The district court rejected this instruction. Instead, its instructions on voice misappropriation track closely the elements of the tort as formulated in Midler. The court's instruction directed the jury to decide whether Waits' voice is distinctive, whether his voice is widely known, and whether the defendants had deliberately imitated his voice.

The defendants argue that their proposed "style" instruction was crucial because of the deliberate stylistic similarities between the Doritos commercial and "Step Right Up" and because in instructing the jury on Waits' Lanham Act claim, the court told the jury that it could consider Waits' singing style, songwriting style, and manner of presentation. In failing to give their proposed instruction, the defendants contend, the court misled the jury into believing that it could also consider the defendants' admitted imitation of Waits' style in determining liability for voice misappropriation.

We disagree because, read as a whole, the instructions were not misleading. In charging the jury, the court repeatedly noted that two claims were presented for determination and gave separate instructions on each claim. The court's voice misappropriation instructions limited the jury's consideration to voice, and in no way implied that it could consider style. Indeed, in addressing the jury in closing argument, Waits' attorney agreed with the defendants that style was not protected. Moreover, the court included an additional instruction that effectively narrowed the jury's focus to Waits' voice and indicated that style imitation alone was insufficient for tort liability. For the defendants to be liable for voice misappropriation, the court stated, the imitation had to be so good that "people who were familiar with plaintiff's voice who heard the commercial believed plaintiff performed it. In this connection it is not enough that they were reminded of plaintiff or thought the singer sounded like plaintiff. . . ."[3] (Emphasis added.) Even if the jury were initially confused about whether the defendants could be liable simply for imitating Waits' style, this instruction would have disabused them of this notion.

---

[2]   The proposed instruction read in pertinent part: Style is the way, manner or method of carrying out an activity. . . . In contemporary music, there are a great many styles or "sounds," for example . . . blues, dixieland, country and western, rock, rap, rhythm and blues, etc.

Style is how a song is sung, how the music is delivered, how the words of a song are expressed. Style includes mood, phrasing, and timing, whether a selection is performed loudly or quietly, whether the song is expressed in singing, talking, or a combination of the two.

Style is not subject to ownership. No singer can appropriate for himself any style and exclude others from performing in the same style. Any singer is free to sing in the same style as any other singer. That is why we have a great many opera singers, blues singers, country-western singers, etc.

Defendants could not be held liable to plaintiff merely because the singer in their commercial performed in the same style as plaintiff has performed in.

[3]   This instruction effectively added an additional element to Midler's formulation of voice misappropriation: actual confusion. The validity of this instruction is not before us in this appeal and we express no opinion on this issue.

(2)   Definition of "Distinctive"

The defendants next argue that the court's instruction concerning the meaning of "distinctive" was an unfair and inaccurate statement of the law because it confuses the "distinctiveness" of a voice with its identifiability or recognizability. The instruction given states in part: "A voice is distinctive if it is distinguishable from the voices of other singers. . . . if it has particular qualities or characteristics that identify it with a particular singer." At trial the defendants' experts testified that identifiability depends, not on distinctiveness, but on the listener's expectations; that distinctiveness and recognizability are not the same thing; and that recognizability is enhanced by style similarity. The defendants argue that these theories were inadequately dealt with by the court's instruction and that because anyone's voice is identifiable by someone, it was error for the court not to make clear the difference between distinctiveness and identifiability. We disagree.

The defendants' technical argument that distinctiveness is a separate concept from identifiability, while supported by their experts' testimony, has no basis in law. Identifiability is properly considered in evaluating distinctiveness, for it is a central element of a right of publicity claim. See Publicity and Privacy § 3.4[A] & n. 1 (citing cases). Our Midler holding is premised on the fact that a person is as identifiable by voice as by any other indicia of identity previously recognized as protectable. Although we did not define "distinctiveness" in Midler, we stated: "A voice is as distinctive and personal as a face. The human voice is one of the most palpable ways identity is manifested. We are all aware that a friend is at once known by a few words on the phone. . . . [T]hese observations hold true of singing. . . ." Midler v. Ford, 849 F.2d at 463 (emphasis added). See also Motschenbacher, 498 F.2d at 826–27 (rejecting trial court's ruling that because plaintiff's face was not recognizable in advertisement photograph, his identity had not been misappropriated, and finding that plaintiff was identifiable from distinctive decorations on race car).

The court's "distinctiveness" instruction informed the jury that it could consider the recordings of Waits' voice introduced into evidence and the testimony of expert and other witnesses. The court thus invited members of the jury to use their common sense in determining whether Waits has a distinctive enough voice to warrant protection, and to consider as well what the experts had to say. This was entirely appropriate. . . . The court was not required to formulate instructions endorsing expert opinions which lacked legal foundation. Finally, we are unpersuaded by the defendants' argument that the court's instruction would have allowed the jury to hold them liable for imitation of a voice that was identifiable by only a small number of people, inasmuch as Midler also requires that the plaintiff's voice be "widely known."

(3) Definition of "Widely Known"

The defendants next object to the district court's instruction concerning the element of "widely known" on the ground that it was too vague to guide the jury in making a factual determination of the issue. The court instructed the jury: "A professional singer's voice is widely known if it is known to a large number of people throughout a relatively large geographic area." (Emphasis added.) The court rejected an instruction proposed by the defendants, which reflected their contention at trial that Tom Waits is a singer known only to music insiders and to a small but loyal group of fans: "A singer is not widely known if he is only recognized by his own fans, or fans of a particular sort of music, or a small segment of the population."

The legal underpinnings of this proposed instruction are questionable. The defendants assert that because Waits has not achieved the level of celebrity Bette Midler has, he is not well known under the Midler standard. We reject this crabbed interpretation of Midler. The defendants' proposed instruction would have excluded from legal protection the voices of many popular singers who fall short of superstardom. "Well known" is a relative term, and differences in the extent of celebrity are adequately reflected in the amount of damages recoverable. See Motschenbacher, 498 F.2d at 824 n. 11 ("Generally, the greater the fame or notoriety of the identity appropriated, the greater will be the extent of the economic injury suffered."). Moreover, even were these instructions inadequate in some regard the error would be harmless, for we agree with the district court that the "great weight of evidence produced at trial indicates that Tom Waits is very widely known."

In sum, we find no error in the instructions given to the jury on Waits' voice misappropriation claim. [¶] . . . .

II. Lanham Act Claim

Section 43(a) of the Lanham Act, 15 U.S.C. § 1125(a), prohibits the use of false designations of origin, false descriptions, and false representations in the advertising and sale of goods and services. Smith v. Montoro, 648 F.2d 602, 603 (9th Cir.1981). Waits' claim under section 43(a) is premised on the theory that by using an imitation of his distinctive voice in an admitted parody of a Tom Waits song, the defendants misrepresented his association with and endorsement of SalsaRio Doritos. The jury found in Waits' favor and awarded him $100,000 in damages. The district court also awarded him attorneys' fees under section 35 of the Lanham Act. On appeal, the defendants argue that Waits lacks standing to bring a Lanham Act claim, that Waits' false endorsement claim fails on its merits, that the damage award is duplicative, and that attorneys' fees are improper. Before we address these contentions, however, we turn to the threshold issue of whether false endorsement claims are properly cognizable under section

43(a) of the Lanham Act,[5] a question of first impression in this circuit.[FN6 omitted]

A.   False Endorsement

At the time of the broadcast of the Doritos commercial, section 43(a) provided in pertinent part:

Any person who shall affix, apply, or annex, or use in connection with any goods or services ... a false designation of origin, or any false designation or representation ... shall be liable to a civil action ... by any person who believes that he is or is likely to be damaged by the use of any such false designation or representation.

15 U.S.C. § 1125 note (Amendments) (1988). Courts in other jurisdictions have interpreted this language as authorizing claims for false endorsement. E.g., Better Business Bureau v. Medical Directors, Inc., 681 F.2d 397 (5th Cir.1982); Jackson v. MPI Home Video, 694 F.Supp. 483 (N.D.Ill.1988); Wildlife Internationale, Inc. v. Clements, 591 F.Supp. 1542 (S.D.Oh.1984); Geisel v. Poynter Prods., Inc., 283 F.Supp. 261, 267 (S.D.N.Y.1968). Moreover, courts have recognized false endorsement claims brought by plaintiffs, including celebrities, for the unauthorized imitation of their distinctive attributes, where those attributes amount to an unregistered commercial "trademark." See Dallas Cowboys Cheerleaders, Inc. v. Pussycat Cinema, Ltd., 604 F.2d 200, 205 (2d Cir.1979) (recognizing claim under § 43(a) because uniform worn by star of X-rated movie was confusingly similar to plaintiffs' trademark uniforms, falsely creating impression that plaintiffs "sponsored or otherwise approved the use" of the uniform); Allen v. Men's World Outlet, Inc., 679 F.Supp. 360, 368 (S.D.N.Y.1988) (celebrity states a claim under § 43(a) by showing that advertisement featuring photograph of a look-alike falsely represented that advertised products were associated with him); Allen v. National Video, Inc., 610 F.Supp. 612, 625–26 (S.D.N.Y.1985) (recognizing celebrity's false endorsement claim under § 43(a) because celebrity has commercial investment in name and face tantamount to interests of a trademark holder in distinctive mark); see also Lahr v. Adell Chemical Co., 300 F.2d 256, 258 (1st Cir.1962) (imitation of unique voice actionable as common law unfair competition); cf. Sinatra v. Goodyear Tire & Rubber Co., 435 F.2d 711, 716 (9th Cir.1970) (rejecting common law unfair competition claim because plaintiff's voice not sufficiently unique to be protectable), cert. denied, 402 U.S. 906, 91 S.Ct. 1376, 28 L.Ed.2d 646 (1971).

---

[5]   Although we agree with the defendants that the damage award is duplicative and vacate it, the underlying issues of the cognizability of false endorsement actions, Waits' standing to sue, and the merits of his Lanham Act claim are not moot, inasmuch as the judgment on this claim also supports an award of attorneys' fees.

The persuasiveness of this case law as to the cognizability of Waits' Lanham Act claim is reinforced by the 1988 Lanham Act amendments. See Trademark Law Revision Act of 1988, Pub.L. 100–667, § 132, 102 Stat. 3935, 3946. The legislative history states that the amendments to section 43(a) codify previous judicial interpretation given this provision. S.Rep. No. 515, 100th Cong., 2d Sess., at 40, reprinted in 1988 U.S.C.C.A.N. 5577, 5603. Although these amendments did not take effect until November 1989, approximately a year after the broadcast of the defendants' Doritos commercial, as a codification of prior case law and in the absence of controlling precedent to the contrary, they properly inform our interpretation of the previous version of section 43(a). Specifically, we read the amended language to codify case law interpreting section 43(a) to encompass false endorsement claims. Section 43(a) now expressly prohibits, inter alia, the use of any symbol or device which is likely to deceive consumers as to the association, sponsorship, or approval of goods or services by another person.[FN7 omitted] Moreover, the legislative history of the 1988 amendments also makes clear that in retaining the statute's original terms "symbol or device" in the definition of "trademark," Congress approved the broad judicial interpretation of these terms to include distinctive sounds and physical appearance. See S.Rep. No. 101–515 at 44, 1988 U.S.C.C.A.N. at 5607. In light of persuasive judicial authority and the subsequent congressional approval of that authority, we conclude that false endorsement claims, including those premised on the unauthorized imitation of an entertainer's distinctive voice, are cognizable under section 43(a).

B.   Standing

According to the defendants, however, Waits lacks standing to sue for false endorsement. They assert that because he is not in competition with the defendants, he cannot sue under the Lanham Act. Common sense contradicts this argument, for the purported endorser who is commercially damaged by the false endorsement will rarely if ever be a competitor, and yet is the party best situated to enforce the Lanham Act's prohibition on such conduct. . . .

[¶. . .] A false endorsement claim based on the unauthorized use of a celebrity's identity is a type of false association claim, for it alleges the misuse of a trademark, i.e., a symbol or device such as a visual likeness, vocal imitation, or other uniquely distinguishing characteristic, which is likely to confuse consumers as to the plaintiff's sponsorship or approval of the product. Standing, therefore, does not require "actual competition" in the traditional sense; it extends to a purported endorser who has an economic interest akin to that of a trademark holder in controlling the commercial exploitation of his or her identity. See Allen v. National Video, 610 F.Supp. at 625, 628 (celebrity's interest in the marketing value of his identity is similar to that of a trademark holder, and its misuse through evocation of celebrity's persona that creates likelihood of consumer confusion as to celebrity's endorsement is actionable under Lanham Act). Moreover, the wrongful appropriator is in a sense a competitor of the celebrity, even when the celebrity has chosen to disassociate himself or herself from advertising products as has Waits. They compete with respect to the use of the celebrity's name or identity. They are both utilizing or marketing that personal property for commercial purposes. Accordingly, we hold that a celebrity whose endorsement of a product is implied through the imitation of a distinctive attribute of the celebrity's identity, has standing to sue for false endorsement under section 43(a) of the Lanham Act.[10] Tom Waits, therefore, need not be a competitor in the traditional sense to sue under the Lanham Act for the imitation of his voice on the theory that its use falsely associated him with Doritos as an endorser. Rather, his standing was sufficiently established by the likelihood that the wrongful use of his professional trademark, his unique voice, would injure him commercially.

C.   Merits

The defendants next argue that Waits' false endorsement claim must fail on its merits because the Doritos commercial "did not represent that . . . [Waits] sponsored or endorsed their product." We disagree. The court correctly instructed the jury that in considering Waits' Lanham Act claim, it must determine whether "ordinary consumers . . . would be confused as to whether Tom Waits sang on the commercial . . . and whether he sponsors or endorses SalsaRio Doritos." The jury was told that in making this determination, it should consider the totality of the evidence, including the distinctiveness of Waits' voice and style, the evidence of actual confusion as to whether Waits actually sang on the commercial, and the defendants' intent to imitate Waits' voice. See generally, Clamp Mfg. Co. v. Enco Mfg. Co., 870 F.2d 512, 517 (9th Cir.) (discussing factors to be considered in determining likelihood of confusion, including strength of mark, similarity of marks, evidence of actual confusion, marketing channels used, and intent in selecting marks), cert. denied, 493 U.S. 872, 110 S.Ct. 202, 107 L.Ed.2d 155 (1989).

---

[10]   In reaching this conclusion, we are mindful that Midler, on facts similar to those involved here, disapproved the plaintiff's unfair competition claim because she "did not do television commercials. The defendants were not in competition with her." Midler, 849 F.2d 460, 462–63. Midler, however, did not involve a Lanham Act claim, but rather a common law unfair competition claim. Nor were we called upon there to examine standing in the specific context of a false endorsement claim, for Midler had not grounded her unfair competition claim on such a theory. Notably, Midler had sought in the district court to amend her complaint to include a claim under section 43(a) of the Lanham Act on a theory of false endorsement. The district court denied her request, not because she lacked standing as the defendants there had argued, but because her delay in seeking to amend was prejudicial. See Midler v. Ford Motor Co., No. 86–2683 (C.D.Cal.), Record at 7, 43, 48. Our statement in Midler, therefore, is dicta as it relates to Lanham Act standing and is not controlling here.

At trial, the jury listened to numerous Tom Waits recordings, and to a recording of the Doritos commercial in which the Tom Waits impersonator delivered this "hip" endorsement of SalsaRio Doritos: "It's buffo, boffo, bravo, gung-ho, tally-ho, but never mellow. . . . try 'em, buy 'em, get 'em, got 'em." The jury also heard evidence, relevant to the likelihood of consumer confusion, that the Doritos commercial was targeted to an audience which overlapped with Waits' audience, males between the ages of 18 to 35 who listened to the radio. Finally, there was evidence of actual consumer confusion: the testimony of numerous witnesses that they actually believed it was Tom Waits singing the words of endorsement.

This evidence was sufficient to support the jury's finding that consumers were likely to be misled by the commercial into believing that Waits endorsed SalsaRio Doritos. See Allen v. Men's World Outlet, 679 F.Supp. at 368–69 (likelihood of consumer confusion established where advertiser intentionally used a look-alike of well-known celebrity and where audience to whom commercial was directed intersected with celebrity's audience); Allen v. National Video, 610 F.Supp. at 626–27 & n. 8 (use of celebrity look-alike in pose of product spokesperson sufficient to indicate endorsement). The jury's verdict on Waits' Lanham Act claim must therefore stand.

[¶] . . . . CONCLUSION

Waits' voice misappropriation claim and his Lanham Act claim are legally sufficient. The court did not err in instructing the jury on elements of voice misappropriation. The jury's verdict on each claim is supported by substantial evidence, as are its damage awards. Its award of damages on Waits' Lanham Act claim, however, is duplicative of damages awarded for voice misappropriation; accordingly we vacate it. Finally, the court did not abuse its discretion in awarding attorneys' fees under the Lanham Act.

NOTES AND QUESTIONS

1. In both *Midler* and *Waits*, there was strong evidence that the defendants had intentionally sought to have voices that sounded indistinguishable from the plaintiffs' voices in their advertisements. There was also evidence that both of the plaintiffs were personally opposed to using their singing voices in commercial advertisements. As noted by the Supreme Court in the *Zacchini* case, one of the policies underlying recognition of the right of publicity is to prevent unjust enrichment—to prevent advertisers from profiting from the value of associating a celebrity's goodwill with their product without compensating the celebrity. Should the intent of the defendant to imitate the plaintiff's voice or the failure of a celebrity to exploit the commercial value of his or her voice be relevant considerations in determining liability? What if a defendant had no intent to evoke a plaintiff's identity, but the similarity in

voice was simply a coincidence—should that lack of intent make a difference in whether a right of publicity violation is found? And what if a plaintiff's voice has been used in many commercial advertisements? Should it make a difference in determining liability for violation of the right of publicity whether the celebrity has exploited the right in the past or not? Is there an inherent value in lack of exploitation, such that a plaintiff should have the right and ability to control the "first use" in that manner? Or are the policy implications here different from those in the copyright law "first use" context?

2.   The discussion in the *Waits* case regarding the distinction between an imitation of one's "voice" and one's singing "style" highlights one of the problems created by creating a property right in one's voice that includes imitations as well as uses of one's actual voice. Why do you think it might matter in terms of the policies underlying recognition of a right of publicity whether it is a plaintiff's voice or style of singing that is imitated? If listeners are reminded of the celebrity, associating the imitation with the celebrity and thus associating the celebrity with the product, should a right of publicity violation be recognized to avoid the problem of unjust enrichment recognized by the *Zacchini* court? How should the celebrities' rights be balanced against the interests of the "substitute" performers in commercializing their own voices or likenesses?

3.   The *Waits* case illustrates some of the differences (and similarities) in the approaches that courts take to the right of publicity and the Lanham Act. In *Waits*, the circumstances of the case were sufficient to support a jury verdict for both causes of action, because Waits' voice was found to be distinctive and widely recognized and because the use of the sound-alike in the commercial was found to be likely to confuse those who heard the commercial. Suppose for a moment that the commercial at issue in the Waits case had included a voice-over disclaimer, stating that the singing voice used in the commercial was not that of Tom Waits. Do you think that Waits could still have succeeded on a common law right of publicity claim for misappropriation of his voice? What about a Lanham Act claim for false endorsement? The *Waits* court notes in footnote 3 that it was not asked to address, and thus was not ruling upon, the jury instruction that included an element of "actual confusion" in the right of publicity claim. If a sound-alike voice is used in a commercial, but listeners are not actually confused as to whether the voice is that of the plaintiff, what are some of the arguments why the plaintiff should nonetheless be able to recover for violation of the right of publicity?

4.   In the context of challenged uses of a celebrity look-alike, the courts have generally permitted recovery for uses that merely "evoke" a celebrity's image or persona, with the Ninth Circuit going so far as to allow Vanna White to recover on a right of publicity claim for the use of a robot with a blond wig, turning letters on a futuristic "Wheel of Fortune" set in a Samsung commercial, because the robot evoked White's persona. *White v. Samsung Electronics*, 971 F.2d 1395 (9th Cir. 1992). In *White*, the court stated: "It is not important *how* the defendant has appropriated the plaintiff's identity, but *whether* the defendant has done so. *Motschenbacher, Midler,* and *Carson* teach the

impossibility of treating the right of publicity as guarding only against a laundry list of specific means of appropriating identity. A rule which says that the right of publicity can be infringed only through the use of nine different methods of appropriating identity merely challenges the clever advertising strategist to come up with the tenth." *Id.* at 1398. Even in New York, where the right of publicity is more narrowly interpreted to apply only to the listed attributes in Section 51 of the Civil Rights Law, the protection of one's "portrait or picture" has been interpreted as extending to "a representation which conveys the essence and likeness of an individual, not only in actuality, but the close and purposeful resemblance to reality." *Onassis v. Christian Dior-New York, Inc.*, 122 Misc. 2d 603, 611 (Sup. Ct. N.Y. 1984) (granting an injunction to plaintiff Jacqueline Kennedy Onassis against use of a look-alike in a Dior advertisement). What arguments might you make that a celebrity's "voice" should receive the same breadth of protection? What arguments might you make that a celebrity's voice should be treated differently from his or her likeness?

D. COPYRIGHT PREEMPTION AND CONTRACTUAL LICENSING

The issue of copyright preemption is one that frequently arises in misappropriation of voice cases, as both the *Midler* and *Waits* excerpts above illustrate. As mentioned within the *Waits* excerpt and in Chapter 4, *supra*, Section 301 of the Copyright Act[23] preempts state causes of action that are "equivalent to any of the exclusive rights within the general scope of copyright" under Section 106 in works that are fixed in a tangible medium of expression and "come within the subject matter of copyright" under Sections 102 and 103 of the Copyright Act. Any preemption inquiry thus involves an analysis of whether the state cause of action—here, the right of publicity—is "equivalent" to any exclusive rights under the Copyright Act and whether the work in question "comes within the subject matter of copyright" as specified in Sections 102 and 103.

Because copyright protects a recording of one's voice, such as the recordings of Midler's original version of "Do You Want to Dance" and Waits' original version of "Step Right Up," the right of publicity (in those jurisdictions in which it extends to voice) may be preempted when a celebrity complains about the use of his or her previously-recorded voice, particularly under those circumstances in which the defendant has obtained a license from the celebrity's record company to use the recording. As discussed in more detail in Chapter 10, dealing with contractual agreements in the music industry, a record company typically owns the copyright to sound recordings made under contract with the record company and thus the record company can license the use of a recording that it owns for commercial purposes.[24] The person or entity wanting to use that recording would also need to obtain copyright permission from the composer of the song to use the song in the commercial.

Typically, the recording agreement between the record label and the artist would have a provision covering the artist's right of publicity, and typically such a provision would grant the record label permission to use and to license the use of an artist's name, likeness, and voice in connection with the sound recordings. Some artists are able to negotiate approval rights over uses of their recordings in advertisements or commercials and thus to exercise some level of control over what products their recordings might be used to promote, but complaints that advertisements using a licensed sound recording are a misappropriation of the voice of the original artist on the sound recording will rarely have the "extra element" necessary to avoid preemption if the sound recording is one that was made after 1972,

---

[23]   17 U.S.C. § 301.

[24]   Indeed, such licensing of these sound recordings in various commercial products and platforms has traditionally been one of the core business functions of a record label (although the "standard" record label business model is experiencing rapid changes in modern times, as is discussed in Chapter 10).

when federal copyright protection was granted to sound recordings. In such cases, the artist's claim amounts to unauthorized use of the sound recording on which the artist's voice was fixed, and the existence of a valid license for the use from the owner of the copyright to the sound recording will typically defeat the right of publicity claim.

The issue has been raised in several cases, the results of which demonstrate the seemingly inconsistent manner in which courts have treated right of publicity claims and Lanham Act claims with respect to the use of copyrighted sound recordings and copyrighted musical compositions and the difficulty of determining what the "extra element" that could avoid preemption might be in cases where misappropriation of voice is alleged.

The Romantics v. Activision Publishing, Inc.: Members of the musical group *The Romantics* sued (among other defendants) Activision Publishing, Inc., the makers of the "Guitar Hero" video game, in November of 2007 in the Eastern District of Michigan, and sought a preliminary injunction prohibiting the defendant from distributing the "Guitar Hero Encore: Rock's the 80s" game.[25] The game included thirty songs from the 1980s, one of which was "What I Like About You," a song originally recorded and made popular by the Romantics. The defendant had obtained a synchronization license for use of the composition in the game and commissioned a new recording of the song that was incorporated into the game. When playing the game, if the player reached the advanced level of play, s/he would encounter the song, which was identified by its title and the words, "as made famous by the Romantics." Neither the song nor the band's name were used in advertising or marketing the game, nor were they used in the game's packaging. The plaintiffs alleged that consumers would be likely to be confused as to the plaintiffs' sponsorship or endorsement of the game and asserted claims under the Lanham Act and under Michigan common law for violation of the right of publicity.[26]

The court denied the motion for preliminary injunction in its entirety, finding that the plaintiff was unlikely to succeed on the merits of either its state right of publicity or federal Lanham Act claims. With respect to the right of publicity, the court found that Michigan had never recognized a right of publicity in one's voice and that, even if it did, the Copyright Act preempted any right of publicity claim:

> Here, Plaintiffs' "identity" claims to the sound of the Song are essentially claims regarding the licensing of a copyrighted work, falling squarely within the "subject matter" of the Copyright Act. Moreover, Plaintiffs' right of publicity claim, as pleaded, arises from Defendants' arrangement and production of musical and vocal performances that allegedly sound similar to those

---

[25] *The Romantics v. Activision Publishing, Inc.*, 532 F. Supp. 2d 884 (E.D. Mich. 2008).

[26] *Id.*

embodied and reflected in a copyrighted sound recording released by The Romantics in 1980, as distinct from the sound of any individual's voice or musical performance existing separate and apart from a copyrighted work. Thus, the rights asserted by Plaintiffs are "rights equivalent" to those protected by the Copyright Act under Michigan law.[27]

In addition, the court noted that sections 106 and 114(b) of the Copyright Act permit the copyright owner of a musical composition to license others to use the composition, which "expressly allows third parties such as Defendants to make a sound-alike recording of a song. Further, the Copyright Act, 17 U.S.C. § 114(b), expressly disallows any recourse for such sound-alike recordings of a song."[28] Because the defendant had a valid synchronization license for use of the composition in the Guitar Hero game, the court found that it was permissible to make a new recording of the composition and integrate it into the game and that plaintiffs could not succeed on a right of publicity claim.

Similarly, the court found that the plaintiffs were unlikely to succeed on their Lanham Act false endorsement claim, relying on the fact that the defendant only used the name "The Romantics" to accurately identify the group that made the song famous and thus was protected from trademark liability under the "nominative use" doctrine that permits uses of trademarks to accurately identify a product or service or a person's past association with a service, such as identifying a musician as "formerly a member" of a popular group.[29] The court also noted that use of the song in the Guitar Hero game did not mislead consumers as to the content or source of the game.[30]

***Laws v. Sony Music Entertainment, Inc.*:** In *Laws v. Sony Music Entertainment, Inc.*,[31] the defendant, Sony Music Entertainment, obtained a license from the owner of a sound recording made by the plaintiff, Debra Laws, to use a sample of the recording in a song recorded by Jennifer Lopez and L.L. Cool J. Laws sued Sony, asserting a claim for misappropriation of voice.

The Ninth Circuit affirmed the district court's grant of summary judgment in favor of the defendants on the plaintiff's California right of publicity claim, finding that the claim was preempted by the Copyright Act. The court distinguished its holdings in *Midler* and *Waits* (excerpted above)

---

[27] *Id.* at 889.

[28] *Id.*

[29] *Id.* at 890 (citing *New Kids on the Block v. News America Publ., Inc.*, 971 F.2d 302 (9th Cir. 1992).

[30] *Id.*

[31] 448 F.3d 1134 (9th Cir. 2006).

by emphasizing the difference between soundalike recordings and the use of an actual, licensed recording of the artist's voice:

> What Midler sought was relief from an unauthorized vocal imitation for advertising purposes, and that was not the subject of copyright. . . . Although California law recognizes an assertable interest in the publicity associated with one's voice, we think it is clear that federal copyright law preempts a claim alleging misappropriation of one's voice when the entirety of the allegedly misappropriated vocal performance is contained within a copyrighted medium. Our conclusion is consistent with our holdings in *Midler* and *Waits*, where we concluded that the voice misappropriation claim was not preempted, because the alleged misappropriation was the imitation of the plaintiffs' voices.[32]

In addition to concluding that use of a recording of an artist's voice is subject to copyright whereas imitation of an artist's voice is not, the court also found that, in the context of the use of sound recordings of an artist's voice, the "extra element" required to avoid preemption was not present:

> The mere presence of an additional element ("commercial use") in section 3344 is not enough to qualitatively distinguish Laws's right of publicity claim from a claim in copyright. The extra element must transform the nature of the action. Although the elements of Laws's state law claims may not be identical to the elements in a copyright action, the underlying nature of Laws's state law claims is part and parcel of a copyright claim. *See Fleet*, 58 Cal.Rptr.2d at 649. Under the Act, a copyright owner has the exclusive right "to reproduce the copyrighted work." 17 U.S.C. § 106(1). Laws's claims are based on the premise that Sony reproduced a sample of "Very Special" for commercial purposes without her permission. But Sony obtained a limited license from the copyright holder to use the copyrighted work for the Lopez album. The additional element of "commercial purpose" does not change the underlying nature of the action.[33]

In concluding that the right of publicity claim was preempted, the Ninth Circuit stated:

> Both copyright and the right of publicity are means of protecting an individual's investment in his or her artistic labors. As the Court said of copyright:
>
>> The economic philosophy behind the clause empowering Congress to grant patents and copyrights is the conviction that encouragement of individual effort by personal gain is

---

[32] *Id.* at 1140–41.

[33] *Id.* at 1144–45.

the best way to advance public welfare through the talents of authors and inventors in "Science and useful Arts." Sacrificial days devoted to such creative activities deserve rewards commensurate with the services rendered.

Mazer v. Stein, 347 U.S. 201, 219, 74 S.Ct. 460, 98 L.Ed. 630 (1954). Similarly, the Supreme Court has said that the

> right of publicity . . . rests on more than a desire to compensate the performer for the time and effort invested in his act; the protection provides an economic incentive for him to make the investment required to produce a performance of interest to the public.

Zacchini v. Scripps-Howard Broad. Co., 433 U.S. 562, 576, 97 S.Ct. 2849, 53 L.Ed.2d 965 (1977). On the one hand, we recognize that the holder of a copyright does not have "a license to trample on other people's rights." *See* J. Thomas McCarthy, The Rights of Publicity and Privacy § 11:60, at 788 (2d ed.2005). On the other hand, however, the right of publicity is not a license to limit the copyright holder's rights merely because one disagrees with decisions to license the copyright. We sense that, left to creative legal arguments, the developing right of publicity could easily supplant the copyright scheme. This, Congress has expressly precluded in § 301. Were we to conclude that Laws's voice misappropriation claim was not preempted by the Copyright Act, then virtually every use of a copyrighted sound recording would infringe upon the original performer's right of publicity. We foresaw this distinct possibility in *Sinatra:*

> An added clash with the copyright laws is the potential restriction which recognition of performers' "secondary meanings" places upon the potential market of the copyright proprietor. If a proposed licensee must pay each artist who has played or sung the composition and who might therefore claim unfair competition-performer's protection, the licensee may well be discouraged to the point of complete loss of interest.

Sinatra, 435 F.2d at 718. It is hard to imagine how a copyright would remain meaningful if its licensees were potentially subject to suit from any performer anytime the copyrighted material was used.

To be clear, we recognize that not every right of publicity claim is preempted by the Copyright Act. Our holding does not extinguish common law or statutory rights of privacy, publicity, and trade secrets, as well as the general law of defamation and fraud (or any other similar causes of action), so long as those causes of action do not concern the subject matter of copyright and contain qualitatively different elements than those contained in a copyright infringement suit. Elektra copyrighted Laws's performance of "Very Special" and licensed its use to Sony. If Laws wished to retain control of her performance, she should (and may) have either retained the copyright or contracted with the copyright holder, Elektra, to give her control over its licensing. In any event, her remedy, if any, lies in an action against Elektra, not Sony.

We therefore agree with the district court's conclusion that Laws's right of publicity claims are preempted by the Copyright Act.[34]

The result in *Laws* is consistent with that reached in the *Romantics* case and several other cases that have addressed right of publicity claims involving the use of licensed sound recordings. However, the Third Circuit has distinguished *Laws* based on both the nature of the contractual agreement between the artist and the owner of the sound recording and on the nature of the work alleged to violate the right of publicity (i.e., an artistic work in *Laws* as compared to a product advertisement).

Facenda v. N.F.L. Films, Inc.: In *Facenda v. N.F.L. Films, Inc.*,[35] the estate of John Facenda, a well-known Philadelphia broadcaster who had narrated a series of documentaries for the N.F.L., sued N.F.L. Films, Inc. and other N.F.L.-related entities after they used clips from Facenda's narrations in a televised documentary about the making of a football video game called "The Making of Madden NFL '06." The court described the relevant claims and defenses as follows:

> The Estate claims that the program's use of Facenda's voice falsely suggested that Facenda endorsed the video game, violating the federal Lanham Act, which deals with trademarks and related theories of intellectual property. The Estate also claims that the program was an unauthorized use of Facenda's name or likeness in violation of Pennsylvania's "right of publicity" statute. In its defense the NFL argued, among other things, that its copyrights in the original NFL Films productions that Facenda narrated gave it the exclusive right to use portions of those productions' soundtracks as it saw fit, including in the television piece at issue.[36]

The district court had granted the plaintiff's motions for summary judgment on both the Lanham Act and right of publicity claims, concluding that the defendants used Facenda's voice for commercial purposes in a way

---

34   *Id.* at 1145–46.

35   542 F.3d 1007 (3d Cir. 2008).

36   *Id.* at 1011.

that was likely to confuse consumers as to his sponsorship or endorsement of the Madden NFL video game. The Third Circuit affirmed the grant of summary judgment to the plaintiff on the state right of publicity claim but found that the "likelihood of confusion" determination under the Lanham Act was a question of fact that should not have been decided on summary judgment and remanded that claim for trial.

The court found that the documentary was purely promotional, and thus commercial, in nature, with the sole purpose of promoting sales of the Madden NFL video game, and thus rejected a First Amendment defense to the plaintiff's Lanham Act claim because the allegations of the likelihood of consumer confusion, if proved to be true, took the claim outside of the protection of the First Amendment.[37] The court also rejected a defense based on the standard release form signed by Facenda when he provided his narration services to the NFL:

> The contract states that the NFL can use its recordings featuring Facenda's voice as it sees fit, "provided, however, such use does not constitute an endorsement of any product or service." . . . In the contract, Facenda waived his rights with regard to any uses that were not endorsements. But if the Estate succeeds in proving the elements of its false-endorsement claim, such a finding by the District Court will demonstrate that the NFL's use of Facenda's voice was an endorsement, falling outside the contract's waiver clause. On the other hand, if the Estate's false-endorsement claim were to fail, meaning that the use was not an endorsement, the contract's waiver would apply to that claim. Thus, what falls inside the Lanham Act's prohibitions defines what is outside the contract's waiver. This renders further analysis of the contract as an independent defense moot. The significance of the contract is that Facenda did not waive the right to bring a claim under the Lanham Act for false endorsement.[38]

In affirming the district court's grant of summary judgment to the plaintiff on the Pennsylvania right of publicity claim, the Third Circuit expressly rejected the defendants' argument that the right of publicity claim was preempted by the Copyright Act. First, the court found that the requirement of the Pennsylvania right of publicity statute that the plaintiff's voice have "commercial value" provides an "additional element" beyond what a copyright infringement claim would require.[39] Second, the court concluded that although one's voice can be fixed "in a tangible medium by recording it, one cannot divorce his distinctive voice from [his]

---

[37]   *Id.* at 1018.

[38]   *Id.* at 1022–23.

[39]   *Id.* at 1027.

identity (or persona)" and thus that one's voice is outside the subject matter of copyright.[40]

After finding that the right of publicity claim was not expressly preempted by Section 301 of the Copyright Act, the court went on to analyze whether the claim was impliedly preempted under the doctrine of conflict preemption that arises pursuant to the Supremacy Clause of the U.S. Constitution, which requires that state laws that directly conflict with the purposes and policies underlying a federal law be given no effect. In fact, some courts "have found conflict preemption where state laws interfere with federal copyright law's goal of leaving some works, or uses of works, in the public domain. For example, these concerns might arise with respect to state laws offering protection for 'sound-alike' sound recordings, which copyright does not protect."[41] The court relied on Nimmer on Copyright[42] in stating a two-part framework for evaluating a case that presents a potential conflict between copyright, the right of publicity, and contract, first focusing on the manner in which the copyrighted work is used and then focusing on the nature of the contractual agreement by which the plaintiff initially assigned the copyright. If the copyrighted work is used for advertising purposes it is less likely to be preempted than if it is used for expressive purposes, and if the plaintiff initially consented to commercial uses of the work in his assignment of copyright or production agreement it is more likely to be preempted than if the plaintiff did not consent to producing a work that would be used for advertising purposes.[43]

Applying that test, the court in *Facenda* ruled that conflict preemption did not bar the plaintiff's right of publicity claims, because the copyrighted works at issue—the recordings of Facenda's voice—were used for promotional purposes and his underlying contract did not consent to such uses of his voice, but in fact expressly prohibited any endorsement use. In so ruling, the court stated:

> The NFL argues that Facenda's only remedy should lie in contract. While we agree that Facenda could state a claim for breach of contract, we believe that he also retained his tort-derived remedy for violation of Pennsylvania's right-of-publicity statute. Parties may waive tort remedies via contract. It follows that they may also preserve them. While performing artists should have the burden of reserving publicity rights when contracting away any rights under copyright law they might have,

---

[40]   *Id.* at 1027–28.

[41]   *Id.* at 1028 (citations omitted).

[42]   *Id.* at 1029 (citing 1 Nimmer on Copyright § 1.01[B][3][b][iv][I], at 1–88.2(9)–(11)).

[43]   *Id.* at 1029–30.

we hold that Facenda successfully bore that burden here and preserved his state-law right-to-publicity claims.

Despite our holding, we emphasize that courts must circumscribe the right of publicity so that musicians, actors, and other voice artists do not get a right that extends beyond commercial advertisements to other works of artistic expression. If courts failed to do so, then every record contract or movie contract would no longer suffice to authorize record companies and movie studios to distribute their works. In addition to copyrights, entertainment companies would need additional licenses for artists' rights of publicity in every case.

Thus, we believe that *Laws* was rightly decided—Debra Laws sought to enforce a right that she had contracted away. We do not intend to express any disagreement with the Ninth Circuit Court of Appeals by distinguishing the facts of our case from those of *Laws*. Our case simply presents a different scenario than *Laws*. Just as Facenda did not, in the standard release contract, waive the right to bring a false-endorsement claim, see *supra* Section V.B.1, he did not grant the NFL the right to use his voice in a promotional television program. This contrasts with the situation in Laws. Debra Laws's voice was not used in an endorsement, but in a work of artistic expression.

In the endorsement context, an individual's identity and credibility are put directly on point. Advertisements are special in the way they implicate an individual's identity. Precisely what Pennsylvania's right of publicity is meant to protect is a citizen's prerogative *not* to have his or her name, likeness, voice, or identity used in a commercial advertisement, whether that citizen is a celebrity or not.

In our case, we have no precedent to hold that the right of publicity in an individual's voice is analogous to the public domain. In this void, we believe state-law protection of an individual's voice will not upset copyright law's balance as long as the state law is not construed too broadly. Pennsylvania's section 8316 focuses solely on the commercial-advertising context. It is targeted at endorsements, not the full universe of creative works. The Estate's claim lies at the heart of the statute's focus. For these reasons, the state-law right of publicity does not conflict with federal copyright law in this case.[44]

---

[44]   *Id.* at 1031–32 (citations and footnote omitted).

NOTES AND QUESTIONS

1.   In *Laws*, the Ninth Circuit distinguished *Midler* and *Waits* by stating that unlike a sound recording of a voice, which is the subject of copyright, the imitation of a voice is not the subject of copyright. How might you reconcile this finding with the reasoning of the court in the *Romantics* case, in which the district court concluded that sections 106 and 114(b) of the Copyright Act expressly permit sound-alike recordings of a composition and disallow any recourse for sound-alike recordings? Section 114(b) provides in pertinent part: "The exclusive rights of the owner of copyright in a sound recording under clauses (1) and (2) of section 106 do not extend to the making or duplication of another sound recording that consists entirely of an independent fixation of other sounds, even though such sounds imitate or simulate those in the copyrighted sound recording."

2.   In a preemption analysis, do you think it should matter, as the court suggests in *Facenda*, whether a challenged use of a copyrighted work is in another artistic work or in a product advertisement? Is there always a clear distinction that can be made between art and product advertisements, or can some advertisements be art and some art be a product advertisement? Additionally, should it matter, as the court also suggests in *Facenda*, whether the artist who created the original sound recording had a contractual provision prohibiting the use of the sound recording in commercials? Why or why not?

3.   Note that preemption is not an issue with respect to Lanham Act claims, because Section 301 of the Copyright Act preempts only state law claims that are equivalent to copyright, not competing claims that might be asserted under federal law.[45] Thus, even a licensed use of a copyrighted sound recording or musical composition could potentially run afoul of the Lanham Act if it were found to be likely to confuse consumers as to the sponsorship, endorsement, or source of a product.

4.   Given the reasoning in the preemption cases discussed above, do you think that a right of publicity claim arising out of an *unlicensed* use of a sound recording in an advertising context should be preempted by federal copyright law? Imagine, for example, that a musical artist created many successful sound recordings, but under his recording contract the record label owns all copyrights in the sound recordings. If the record label licensed the sound recording for use, the artist's ability to pursue a right of publicity claim challenging that use would likely (at least under the reasoning of the *Facenda* court) depend upon whether the recording contract included a grant of rights to use the recording for endorsement purposes and whether the licensed use was for expressive or commercial purposes. But what if the record label did not license the sound recording for use, but the defendant simply inserted the recording in its new expressive work (i.e., sampled it as in the *Laws* case) or in an advertisement (as in the *Facenda* case) without any authorization by the

---

[45]   Section 301 provides in pertinent part: "[N]o person is entitled to any such right or equivalent right in any such work under the common law or statutes of any State." 17 U.S.C. § 301(a).

copyright owner—should the same analysis apply, or should the defendant's failure to obtain a license from the copyright owner preclude it from taking advantage of the preemption provision of the Copyright Act? Why or why not?

E. USE OF MUSIC IN POLITICAL CAMPAIGNS

Use of compositions and sound recordings in the context of political campaigns raises its own set of questions. For example, during the 2008 presidential campaign, Ann and Nancy Wilson, the members of Heart, issued public complaints about the use of their song, *Barracuda* (both written and recorded by them), during the Republican National Convention in connection with vice-presidential nominee Sarah Palin's convention speech. Their press release asked that the McCain-Palin campaign cease playing their song, and their publisher and record label sent cease and desist letters to the campaign.[46] The Wilsons' objection was based upon their disagreement with the political views of the campaign, but other artists such as Van Halen and Sam Moore have complained about the use of their recordings and compositions in political campaigns simply because they do not want their music associated with any political campaign, regardless of their agreement with the political positions of the candidates.[47]

The 2016 presidential campaigns also inspired their share of complaints by recording artists relating to political uses of their records by candidates. For example, the Texas band Explosions in the Sky objected to inclusion of their 2003 song *Your Hand in Mine* in a video clip that announced Texas Governor Greg Abbott's endorsement of Ted Cruz.[48] After the video was taken down from YouTube, the band's label, Temporary Residence, issued a statement saying:

> Temporary Residence and Explosions In The Sky issued an
> immediate takedown of the Ted Cruz campaign video, as it

---

[46] *See* Christopher Sprigman & Siva Vaidhyanathan, *In Music and Politics, Let Freedom Sing,* The Star-Ledger (Newark, New Jersey) October 14, 2008.

[47] *Id.* For example, in 2008, Sam Moore wrote to President Obama, asking that his campaign stop playing the Sam and Dave song "Hold On, I'm Comin'" at campaign rallies. The letter graciously noted that it was "thrilling, in my lifetime, to see that our country has matured to the place where it is no longer an impossibility for a man of color to really be considered as a legitimate candidate for the highest office in our land." However, it asked that the campaign not use his song: "I have not agreed to endorse you for the highest office in our land. . . . My vote is a very private matter between myself and the ballot box." Following receipt of the letter, President Obama's campaign stopped using the song. *See* Stephen Davis, *Do Rock Stars Dislike Democrats, Too?,* Browbeat Culture Blog, SLATE (June 30, 2011) at http://www.slate.com/blogs/browbeat/2011/06/30/has_a_rock_star_ever_sued_a_democrat_for_using_a_song_in_a_campa.html.

[48] Chris Payne, *Ted Cruz Used Explosions in the Sky for Campaign Video and the Band is Not Happy,* BILLBOARD (Feb. 25, 2016), available at http://www.billboard.com/articles/columns/rock/6890288/ted-cruz-explosions-sky-video-campaign-greg-abbott-your-hand-mine-texas (last visited March 13, 2016).

violates the artist and label's copyrights. No attempt was made by Ted Cruz's campaign to seek permission to use this song. All uses of Explosions In The Sky's music in Ted Cruz's campaign are illegal and in direct violation of U.S. Copyright law.[49]

Use of a variety of songs at rallies during Donald Trump's 2016 campaign inspired public complaints from R.E.M., Adele, Neil Young, Aerosmith, Smashing Pumpkins, Elton John, and Speedy Ortiz, among others.

When the complaints relate to performance of compositions or recordings at events like the national convention or campaign rallies held in large venues, however, until recently composers and artists have had little or no legal standing to complain. Almost without exception, the blanket ASCAP and BMI licenses held by many venues in the campaign years mentioned above typically permitted performance of the composition, and copyright law currently does not recognize a performance right in sound recordings that extends to music played for crowds at arenas or other venues.

In recent years, however, publishers and songwriters have taken steps in their agreements with some of the PROs to try to limit political uses of their works. In the 2020 presidential campaign, for example, the Trump campaign was put on notice by BMI that its Political Entities License— which permits millions of musical works to be performed wherever campaign events occur, whether or not the particular venue has a blanket license—excludes works by songwriters or publishers who object to their use by a campaign. The relevant provision of the BMI 2019 license states:

> BMI hereby grants to LICENSEE a non-exclusive license to perform, present or cause the live and/or recorded performance during Events or Functions, or by means of internet or intranet transmissions from LICENSEE's website, of all musical works of which BMI shall have the right to grant public performance licenses during the Term hereof. Notwithstanding the foregoing, one or more work(s) or catalog(s) of works by one or more BMI songwriter(s) may be excluded from this license if notice is received by BMI that such BMI songwriter(s) objects to the use of their copyrighted work(s) for the intended uses by LICENSEE. BMI shall provide written notice to LICENSEE of any such exclusion. Any performance by LICENSEE of any excluded work(s) or catalog(s) of works at any Event or Function following receipt of such notice shall not be covered by the grant under, and shall be deemed a material breach of, this Agreement, even if the venue or establishment at which the Event or Function takes

---

[49] Susie Garrard, *Explosions in the Sky are "Not Okay" With Soundtracking Ted Cruz's Campaign*, HOWL & ECHOS (Feb. 26, 2016), available at http://howlandechoes.com/2016/02/explosions-in-the-sky-ted-cruz/.

place is separately licensed to publicly perform the work(s) or catalog(s) of works. LICENSEE shall not rely on, or use as a defense, any such separate license in any legal action or claim arising out of any performance of such excluded work(s).[50]

In late June of 2020, BMI informed the Trump campaign that it had received such an objection from the Rolling Stones and thus that works by the Rolling Stones had been removed from the campaign license, making any further use a breach of the license agreement. As of the date of this writing, the Trump campaign had not responded to BMI's notice,[51] and it remains to be seen whether the contractual limitation of rights by PROs provides an enforceable remedy that would otherwise be unavailable to songwriters and publishers for objectionable public performances of their works in political campaign events.

Aside from the limitations recently included in the PROs licenses for political entities with respect to composition performances at political events, the right of publicity is unlikely to provide relief. This is both because of copyright preemption and because some state right of publicity statutes are interpreted to exclude liability for use of an artist's identity—including voice—in connection with political speech, based upon both First Amendment concerns and state law policies (for example, review the language of California Civil Code section 3344(d) above).

Use in political advertisements might give composers and recording artists a clearer likelihood of an available legal remedy (although not under the California right of publicity statute), particularly if a synchronization license was not obtained from the copyright holders for use in the advertisement or if the composer or artist retained contractual approval rights over promotional or political uses of the work. In another example arising out of the 2008 presidential campaign, Jackson Browne sued the McCain campaign, the Republican National Committee, and the Ohio Republican Party over the use of his song *Running on Empty* in an advertisement that criticized then-presidential candidate Obama's energy policy. No synchronization license had been obtained for inclusion of the recording in the ad, and Browne sued under the Lanham Act false endorsement provisions and the California common law right of publicity. The complaint survived an initial motion to dismiss on First Amendment grounds, because the court found that the use was primarily commercial,

---

[50]   BMI, *Music License for Political Entities or Organizations*, § 2(a), available at https://pmc deadline2.files.wordpress.com/2020/06/political-entities_pol1.2019.pdf. ASCAP also now has a similar license provision in its Political Campaign License agreement. *See* ASCAP, *Using Music in Political Campaigns: What You Should Know*, at https://www.ascap.com/~/media/files/pdf/advocacy-legislation/political_campaign.pdf.

[51]   *See* Chris Willman, *Rolling Stones Working with BMI to Stop Trump's Use of "You Can't Always Get What You Want" at Rallies*, VARIETY (June 27, 2020), at https://variety.com/2020/music/news/rolling-stones-trump-rallies-bmi-stop-use-cant-always-get-what-you-want-12346923 81/.

and the case was subsequently settled.[52] In another widely reported dispute, in 2010, *Talking Heads* lead singer and songwriter David Byrne sued then-Florida Governor Charlie Crist and his senatorial campaign for $1 million in damages for copyright infringement and Lanham Act violations in connection with the use of the song "Road to Nowhere" in a website and YouTube ad attacking Crist's then-Republican primary opponent, Marco Rubio.[53] The case was settled, with Gov. Crist posting a video apology on YouTube stating "Mr. Byrne has never permitted his songs to be used for advertising of any kind," and that his campaign's use of the song in the ad "was wrong and should not have occurred."[54]

NOTES AND QUESTIONS

1.   What do you think about the merits of Browne's and Byrne's right of publicity and Lanham Act claims, given the above cases, materials, and notes? Is there a difference between using a musician's name/likeness in a political ad and using a musician's voice to promote a political candidate? Is that use the kind that is contemplated under the exception in the California statute (even though Browne did not assert a claim under the statute and Byrne's claim arose in Florida)? Should it be?

2.   How effective do you think the recent changes to the BMI and ASCAP political use license limitations will be in preventing compositions from being publicly performed at campaign events if the songwriter or publisher objects? What possible arguments might campaigns have regarding the enforceability of those provisions? Should sound recording owners and performers have similar rights? If so, how might those rights be created?

---

[52]   *Browne v. McCain*, 612 F. Supp. 2d 1125 (C.D. Cal. 2009); *see also Henley v. DeVore*, 733 F. Supp. 2d 1144 (C.D. Cal. 2010) (rejecting fair use defense for use of modified versions of Don Henley's compositions in campaign advertisements without permission, distinguishing between satire and parody; but also finding that Henley could not maintain a Lanham Act claim because trademark law does not protect performances of artists and there was no attempt to mimic Henley's voice or likelihood of consumer confusion).

[53]   *See* Complaint, *Byrne v. Crist*, No. 8:10-CV1187-T26, 2010 WL 2833809 (M.D.Fla. May 24, 2010).

[54]   NPR, All Things Considered: *Crist Apologizes for Using Talking Heads Song* (Aug. 13, 2011), at https://www.npr.org/2011/04/13/135386575/crist-apologizes-for-using-talking-heads-song.

F. DISPUTES OVER BAND NAMES

Disputes over the use of band names have been common in the music industry, largely because of the failure of members of a band to enter into contractual agreements that clearly specify who will own or be permitted to use a band name after the band breaks up or when there are significant changes in the band's membership. While disputes regarding the use of an artist's voice (or a simulation of the artist's voice) typically raise issues under both the right of publicity and the Lanham Act, disputes regarding the use of a band name typically raise issues under the Lanham Act and state laws governing contract interpretation (if a band agreement exists) or joint ventures and partnerships (if a band agreement does not exist). The right of publicity is usually not implicated because it is viewed in most jurisdictions as an individual right, protecting an individual's name, rather than as a right that extends to business entities as well as individuals.

Just as it is at the beginning of a marriage, when couples generally do not discuss how they will divide their assets in the event that the marriage fails, when bands are first starting out, they generally do not want to sit down and discuss what will happen to one of the band's most important assets—its name—if the band ultimately breaks up or if members leave the band. However, as the cases excerpted below demonstrate, failing to do so in a clear, written agreement can lead to very difficult-to-resolve disputes, as the courts must typically weigh both general principles of partnership law and the general policies underlying the Lanham Act regarding the likelihood of consumer confusion.

The first case excerpted below involved the group "The Kingsmen," who did not have a written agreement governing the use of the band's name by members after they left the band. The second case involved the band "Lynyrd Skynyrd" and the use of the band name after the tragic deaths of members of the original band, where the band had formed a corporation that owned the name, but the surviving members of the band and the heirs of the deceased members had a verbal agreement not to use the band name. As you will see, the courts weigh the application of the Lanham Act to these situations somewhat differently, looking at both the nature of the relevant agreements, whether oral or written, governing use of the band name and the effect of the challenged use on the public.

The Kingsmen, from a May 28, 1966 Billboard ad (p. 19) (Scandore/Shayne)

THE KINGSMEN V. K-TEL INTERNATIONAL LTD.
557 F. Supp. 178 (S.D.N.Y. 1983)

SAND, DISTRICT JUDGE.

The plaintiffs in this action are a group of musicians who claim ownership of the name "The Kingsmen," a popular band of the 1960's. They seek to restrain the defendants, several music production and record companies, from selling or distributing a long-playing album entitled "60's Dance Party," which contains a selection that purports to be a "re-recording" by the original Kingsmen of probably their most popular hit, "Louie, Louie." . . .

FACTS

Lynn Easton, Michael Mitchell, Norman Sundholm, Richard Peterson and Barry Curtis, the plaintiffs, claim that they comprise a rock and roll band known as The Kingsmen. The original Kingsmen were formed in 1962. While the members of the band were still in high school, they recorded a demonstration tape of a song entitled "Louie, Louie." The lead vocalist on that recording was Jack Ely who, along with Easton, was an original member of the group.

Ely left the group in 1964 after his recording of Louie, Louie but before it became popular on the record charts. In 1964, Louie, Louie became the second best selling record in the United States, and The Kingsmen were off to a successful music career. They recorded a number of albums after their initial success with Louie, Louie, and made numerous concert tours and television appearances. The five named plaintiffs comprised The Kingsmen during this period. Although Ely had originally recorded Louie, Louie, he did not tour with the band, did not perform on their subsequent albums, and did not participate in any fashion with the other members of the band after his 1964 departure. The Kingsmen ceased performing and disbanded in 1967 after three years of relative success.

In 1976, after nearly a decade in which no member of the group performed as The Kingsmen, S.J. Productions, one of the defendants in this action, communicated with Easton and Ely and made a proposal to "re-record" songs originally performed by The Kingsmen. These recordings were to be included on records produced by the defendant highlighting the most popular dance songs of the 1960's. Easton recorded a version of the song "Jolly Green Giant," The Kingsmen's second most popular hit, and a song on which he had been the original lead vocalist. Ely recorded Louie, Louie. In neither case did the original members of The Kingsmen or any of the plaintiffs herein participate in the recording sessions (except for Easton and Ely).[1]

Defendants contend that both Ely and Easton represented at the time they entered into the contracts with S.J. Productions that they were authorized and entitled to use the name Kingsmen with regard to their individual performances. Affidavit of Stanley J. Shulman ("Shulman Affidavit"), ¶ 4. The contracts themselves do not fully support this contention. Easton's contract does indeed describe him as "Lynn Easton, a/k/a Kingsmen," and it is arguable that this constitutes an effort on his part to grant the right to defendants to use the name The Kingsmen in the marketing of his recording of "Jolly Green Giant." Shulman Affidavit, Ex. A. Ely's contract, by contrast, makes no mention of the name Kingsmen. Affidavit of Robert W. Cinque, Ex. B. There are no other affidavits or evidence suggesting that Ely authorized the use of the name Kingsmen. In the absence of any contractual representations to the contrary, and when viewed in contrast to the Easton contract, we conclude that it is likely that Ely made no representations that he was authorized to use the name Kingsmen.[FN2 omitted]

Ely's most recent recording of Louie, Louie now appears on defendant ERA Records, Inc.'s "60's Dance Party" album, which was released in October, 1982. This record contains songs identified with a number of groups popular during the 1960's. The title "Louie, Louie ... The Kingsmen" appears in bold black letters on the back of the album cover. In small print below the listing of the contents of the album is the notation, "These selections are re-recordings by the original artists."

DISCUSSION

The plaintiffs seek to enjoin the defendants from representing that the version of Louie, Louie appearing on the 60's Dance Party album is

---

[1]   It appears from the papers presented that plaintiffs Peterson and Curtis were not original members of the Kingsmen, but replaced Gary Abbott and Don Gallucci at some point prior to the time the band became popular and signed their first recording contracts. See Affidavit of Stanley J. Shulman, ¶ 4.

recorded by the group known to the public as The Kingsmen. They point out that none of the other members of the band that toured and recorded as The Kingsmen between 1964 and 1967 participated with Mr. Ely in this recording of Louie, Louie. Even though Ely was the lead vocalist on the original recording of the song, plaintiffs assert that the use of the name Kingsmen, together with the notation that the song is a "re-recording by the original artists," creates the false impression to consumers that they are getting a recording of Louie, Louie as performed by those five persons associated by the consumer with the band The Kingsmen. Instead, plaintiffs argue, they are receiving a recording by Mr. Ely, the lead vocalist on Louie, Louie, in conjunction with musicians who have no relation whatsoever with The Kingsmen.

The defendants argue that Mr. Ely has as great a right as anyone else associated with The Kingsmen at any point in its existence to use the name Kingsmen, and that they are not, therefore, infringing any type of statutory or common law trademark. Moreover, defendants suggest that Mr. Ely has every right to record Louie, Louie under the name The Kingsmen, given the undisputed fact that he was the lead singer on the original version. . . .

Plaintiffs assert protection for the name "Kingsmen" under Section 43(a) of the Lanham Act, 15 U.S.C. § 1125(a), the federal common law of misappropriation and unfair competition, and Sections 368–d and 133 of New York General Business Law.

Section 43(a) of the Lanham Act . . . has been broadly construed, *Warner Brothers Inc. v. Gay Toys, Inc.,* 658 F.2d 76 (2d Cir.1981); *Geisel v. Poynter Products, Inc.,* 283 F.Supp. 261, 267 (S.D.N.Y.1968), and has been applied to protect the name of popular musical recording groups, *see, e.g., Noone, p/k/a Herman of Herman's Hermits v. Banner Talent Associates, Inc.,* 398 F.Supp. 260 (S.D.N.Y.1975); *Rare Earth, Inc. v. Hoorelbeke,* 401 F.Supp. 26 (S.D.N.Y.1975).

Section 43(a) provides relief against the type of unfair competition analogous to the misappropriation of trade names. *Noone v. Banner Talent Associates,* 398 F.Supp. at 263. It protects against the use of a false description or designation of origin. *Rare Earth, Inc. v. Hoorelbeke,* 401 F.Supp. at 38. . . . The essence of a complaint under the Lanham Act is an allegation that the consuming public is being deceived as to the origin of the product, which may arise from a misleading representation that a product was produced, manufactured or authorized by a particular person. *See Rare Earth, Inc. v. Hoorelbeke,* 401 F.Supp. at 38 (citations omitted).

To obtain preliminary injunctive relief under the statute, the plaintiff must make a clear showing of probable success on the merits, and the likelihood of irreparable harm in the absence of such relief. *Sonesta International Hotels Corp. v. Wellington Associates,* 483 F.2d 247, 250 (2d Cir.1973). To show probability of success on the merits in the context of a

Section 43(a) suit under the Lanham Act, the plaintiff need only show the likelihood that consumers will be deceived by the actions of the defendant. *Warner Brothers Inc. v. Gay Toys, Inc.*, 658 F.2d at 79; *Dallas Cowboys Cheerleaders, Inc. v. Pussycat Cinema, Ltd.*, 604 F.2d 200 (2d Cir.1979). Actual confusion need not be proved on a motion for preliminary relief. *DC Comics, Inc. v. Powers*, 465 F.Supp. 843, 848 (S.D.N.Y.1978).

It is clear that the plaintiffs meet the requirements of standing, probable success on the merits, and likelihood of irreparable harm necessary to bring suit for preliminary relief under the Lanham Act. Throughout the entire period from 1964 through 1967, when The Kingsmen were at the height of their popularity, these five plaintiffs toured and recorded as The Kingsmen and were known to the public as The Kingsmen. Plaintiffs have submitted numerous newspaper clippings from this period that identify these plaintiffs both pictorially and by caption with the group The Kingsmen. See Plaintiffs' Exhibits 15, 18–20, 22–23. None of these pictures shows or refers to Mr. Ely as a member of the group. More importantly, it is these five plaintiffs that contracted with Jerden Music, Inc. and Scepter Records, Inc. under the name The Kingsmen for royalties from the sale of original recordings of The Kingsmen, including royalties from the sale of the original recording of Louie, Louie. Supplemental Affidavit of Charles Rubin, Ex. 6, 7. These plaintiffs continue to this day to receive royalties from the sale of compositions recorded by the Kingsmen in the 1960's. Supplemental Affidavit of Charles Rubin, ¶ 4, Ex. 8; Affidavit of Charles Rubin, Exhibit 1.

Moreover, having listened to the recordings by The Kingsmen submitted as exhibits to the Court, including the original recording of Louie, Louie, we stress the ensemble nature of The Kingsmen's music. Although the listener can discern the lead singer from the background vocals and music on a number of Kingsmen songs, the group's "sound" is clearly a collective one. No one member of the group can be singled out as representing the essence of The Kingsmen's performing style. Given the evidence referred to above and the nature of The Kingsmen's recordings to which we have listened, we find as a fact for purposes of this preliminary proceeding that the five plaintiffs herein constitute the band known to the public as The Kingsmen and therefore have standing to sue under the Lanham Act.

Plaintiffs have also made the necessary showing of the likelihood of irreparable harm. Plaintiffs have submitted a number of record albums that are collections of popular dance music of the 1960's. These albums appear to compete directly with the "60's Dance Party" album produced by the defendants. One such album is entitled "Original Rock N' Roll Hits of the 60's" and contains the *original* recording of Louie, Louie by The Kingsmen. Plaintiff's Exhibit 2. Another is entitled "Oldies But Goodies, Original Recordings of the Greatest Rock N' Roll Hits of All Time." Volume

11 of the series also contains the original recording of Louie, Louie. Plaintiffs' Ex. 26. The plaintiffs have authorized the use of Louie, Louie on these albums and receive royalties from their sale. Supplemental Affidavit of Charles Rubin, ¶ 4 and Ex. 8. It is clear from these facts that the defendants' record directly competes with original recordings by The Kingsmen for which plaintiffs continue to receive royalties and that preliminary injunctive relief is therefore appropriate.

There is also little question that defendants' labelling of its 60's Dance Party album is likely to cause confusion in the mind of the public with respect to the origin of the album's contents. The clear import of the notation "Re-recordings by the original artists" is that those persons known in the public consciousness as The Kingsmen assembled in a studio to re-record Louie, Louie—an event that all parties agree did not occur. Finally, there is little doubt that this confusion will cause financial harm to the plaintiffs. The plaintiffs continue to receive royalties from the sale of albums containing Louie, Louie. Every time a consumer purchases one of defendants' records, thinking he is getting a recording of Louie, Louie by The Kingsmen, the royalties owed the plaintiffs are reduced.

For all these reasons, we find that the plaintiffs have established their right to assert protection for the name Kingsmen. We also find that plaintiffs have shown a likelihood of confusion on the part of consumers that purchase defendants' album and the danger that plaintiffs will suffer economic damages in the absence of injunctive relief. *See Eden Toys, Inc. v. Florelee Undergarment Co.,* 526 F.Supp. 1187, 1193 (S.D.N.Y.1981) ("The crucial [standing] question is whether the prospective plaintiff has a reasonable interest that requires protection from the defendant's false representations.") (citation omitted). Defendants should therefore be enjoined from representing on their album, "60's Dance Party," that "Louie, Louie" was "rerecorded" by the original Kingsmen.

[¶¶] There are a number of other important questions we do not decide in this case. As we noted above, we do not suggest that Mr. Ely (or, for that matter, Mr. Easton or any other present or former member of The Kingsmen) is restrained from recording Louie, Louie or any other Kingsmen song. Nor do we suggest that the defendants are barred from selling such a recording to the public. It is the misleading labelling of defendants' album that is the gist of this action. For example, we would see no objection to defendants' marketing of this particular recording of Louie, Louie under the name of Jack Ely with the caption, "formerly of the Kingsmen" or "Jack Ely, lead singer on the original Kingsmen recording of Louie, Louie." It is the representation that the rendition of Louie, Louie appearing on defendants' album was re-recorded by the individuals collectively known as The Kingsmen that we find likely to confuse and therefore objectionable under the Lanham Act. . . . [¶]

Plaintiffs' motion for a preliminary injunction restraining the defendants from selling their album "60's Dance Party" with a representation that the recording of Louie, Louie contained therein was performed by the original Kingsmen is hereby granted. . . .

1973 Trade Ad featuring Lynyrd Skynyrd
(Billboard Magazine)

VAN ZANT GRONDIN V. ROSSINGTON
690 F. Supp. 200 (S.D.N.Y. 1988)

SWEET, DISTRICT JUDGE.

Plaintiff Judith Van Zant Grondin ("Grondin") has moved for a preliminary injunction pursuant to Rule 65, Fed.R.Civ.P., enjoining defendants Gary R. Rossington ("Rossington"), Leon R. Wilkeson ("Wilkeson"), William N. Powell ("Powell"), Artimus Pyle ("Pyle"), Ed King ("King"), Randal Hall ("Hall"), Johnny Van Zant ("Johnny"), and Charlie Brusco ("Brusco") from performing as a musical group under the name Lynyrd Skynyrd (the new group referred to herein as the "87–88 Skynyrd" or the "new band"), and enjoining defendant MCA Records, Inc. ("MCA") from marketing a record album entitled "Lynyrd Skynyrd Live" (the "album" or "Live"). For the reasons set forth below, preliminary relief will be granted in part and denied in part, and an early trial date will be set. . .
[¶]

Facts

This controversy centers around the use of the name Lynyrd Skynyrd, the name of a rock and roll band that was quite popular in the 1970's,[1] to describe a current version of that group and to market the new band's record album. The plaintiff is the widow of Ronnie Van Zant ("Ronnie"), the mother of his children and the representative of his estate. The individual

---

[1]   From here forward when the name Lynyrd Skynyrd is used in this opinion it is meant to refer to the band as it existed before October 20, 1977, inclusive of members Ronnie Van Zant and Steven Gaines.

defendants are past and current members or affiliates of the new band. MCA is currently marketing the Live album.

The group Lynyrd Skynyrd was formed in the early 1970's. Its founding members were Ronnie and Rossington. The name Lynyrd Skynyrd was chosen as a spoof on the name of their highschool gym teacher and is pronounced Leonard Skinnerd. Soon after, Allen Collins ("Collins"), and defendants Wilkeson and Powell joined the band.

After several years of hard work Lynyrd Skynyrd began to achieve a reasonable amount of success, and by 1974, had entered into an exclusive artists recording agreement with MCA. By 1975, the group decided to form a corporation known as Lynyrd Skynyrd Productions, Inc. ("LSPI") to hold, among other things, all rights to the trade name, trade marks or service marks. The shareholders agreement setting forth these rights was dated September 15, 1975, and was signed by Rossington, Ronnie, Wilkeson, Powell, and Collins.

Over the course of the next two years, Lynyrd Skynyrd achieved great commercial success. The group by then included guitarist Steven Gaines, Pyle, and backup singers. They had six record albums on the market by 1977 including an album recording live performances. The albums had sold millions of copies and the band had toured the country, performing in various cities. However, on October 20, 1977, while on tour, the plane in which the group was flying ran out of gas, crashed and Ronnie, Gaines and two others were killed. According to all parties, the survivors were physically and emotionally devastated.

A few months after the crash, Grondin—Ronnie's personal representative and beneficiary—Rossington, Collins, and the widow of Steven Gaines, now Teresa Gaines Rapp ("Rapp") were present in Grondin's home. At that time Grondin, Rossington and Collins agreed orally never to use the name Lynyrd Skynyrd again in an effort not to capitalize on the tragedy that had befallen the group. According to Grondin's testimony, that agreement (the "non-use agreement" or "blood oath") was restated on several occasions.

The blood oath was memorialized in several forms. First, it is in writing in the corporate minutes of a March 14, 1978 LSPI shareholders' meeting. Grondin, as a shareholder, was present at that meeting. A written agreement reflecting the nonuse agreement was signed simultaneously. That agreement purported to be a modification of the September 15, 1975 shareholders' agreement. It restricted the use of the name Lynyrd Skynyrd to material produced with Ronnie before his death.

For the ten years following the crash, the non-use agreement was observed by all concerned. The individual defendants continued to perform but did so under other names and with only limited success. . . . However, during this period materials recorded by Lynyrd Skynyrd prior to the crash were continually released yielding profits for all involved. The materials consisted of three albums that Grondin was aware of and consented to and one compilation of previously released material put out by MCA of which she was unaware. During this period Grondin and Rapp remarried, Grondin to another musician.

After hotly debating the subject, on September 1, 1987, the survivors of the crash, along with Grondin, elected to conduct a tribute tour to Lynyrd Skynyrd.[FN3 omitted] An agreement was entered into whereby LSPI would form a corporation known as "The Tribute, Inc." ("Tribute") and would enter into a licensing agreement with Tribute allowing it to conduct a tour to be completed by December 31, 1987, produce videos of the tour, sell merchandise in connection with the tour, and produce a live album of the tour ("Tribute Agreement"). An accompanying agreement ("Licensing Agreement") actually giving Tribute license to perform the above mentioned acts, including a license to use the name Lynyrd Skynyrd, was entered into simultaneously. Grondin and Rapp, who were to receive 28.57% of the net proceeds from merchandising, were signatories to the Tribute Agreement, but not to the Licensing Agreement which was executed by LSPI. Both agreements contain clauses stating that nothing in the agreement constitutes a waiver of rights relative to the name Lynyrd Skynyrd. On October 1, 1987, Tribute entered into an agreement with MCA, authorizing MCA to produce an album from tour performances.

According to Grondin's testimony, she agreed to the tour under pressure and after rejecting various drafts of the agreement. She testified that the rejected drafts expressly referred to the touring band as Lynyrd Skynyrd. Grondin claims not to have permitted use of the name Lynyrd Skynyrd for the new band. . . .

The concerts took place in the fall of 1987. The 1987 tour ran from September 23, 1987 through November 1 of that year, and covered twenty-nine cities. The tour was conducted as a tribute to Lynyrd Skynyrd. Lacy Van Zant, the father of Ronnie and Johnny, began each show by introducing himself as the father of these men and by introducing the band. References to those killed in the crash are made throughout the show, particularly by Johnny, and videos of past performances with the late band members are displayed on a screen behind the musicians.

The record was produced from those performances. The final product is entitled, "Lynyrd Skynyrd Live." These words appear in large, bold, bright blue lettering across the top of the jacket, and they are outlined in white. They stand out starkly against a dark background depicting a concert audience waiving a confederate flag. At the bottom of the jacket front in much smaller, muted gold lettering are the words "Lynyrd Skynyrd Tribute Tour 1987." On the jacket back in red lettering are the words "Southern By The Grace of God." This latter title also appears on the spine of the album. Grondin did not approve the jacket design or the album's title. She testified that she learned of it by reading various trade publications in March 1988 and by seeing it in a record store.

Grondin testified that she first learned of the 1988 tour in February of that year, when she was contacted by an attorney for Powell. She was told that the tour was intended to promote the live album. She did not at that time consent to the tour. She testified that soon thereafter she spoke with Allen Collins expressing her displeasure with the impending concerts. Collins agreed to complain to Rossington about the tour and to thus halt its progress. By April, Grondin testified that she had been contacted by Larkin Collins, Allen's father, who claimed that Rossington had agreed to Allen's demands and had cancelled the tour.

From Ronnie's death through April 1988, Grondin had been a 20% shareholder in LSPI, as well as a director. She essentially stood in Ronnie's shoes. In that month she received notice of a special shareholders meeting. The notice includes the statement: "Following the special meeting of the stockholders, the persons elected to the board of directors will meet to discuss plans for the continuation of the tribute concert tour and will take all appropriate corporate action related thereto." That, Grondin testified, was the first she had heard of the tour since Larkin Collins' claim that it had been cancelled.

On April 21, 1988, Grondin attended the meeting. At that time she was ousted from the corporation. By-laws, which had never before existed, were introduced. In fact, the corporation existed rather informally, there having been only two previous meetings since the crash, the March 1978 meeting and a 1982 meeting regarding merchandise. After failing to reach agreements on the tour and the album, the corporation voted to remove Grondin as a director and to take her stock. Grondin is still a shareholder of Tribute. However, she has not received any financial information regarding that concern.

The 1988 tour, which defendants claim is similar in format to the 1987 tour, began on May 10, 1988. It is to run through July 4, 1988 and cover thirty-six cities and a second leg of the tour is to commence August 4, 1988 and end September 15, 1988. The tour is presently underway.

Conclusions

The standard for granting a preliminary injunction in this Circuit is 1) irreparable injury and 2) either (a) a likelihood of success on the merits or (b) sufficiently serious questions going to the merits to make them a fair ground for litigation and a balance of hardships tipping in favor of the movant. Jackson Dairy, Inc. v. H.P. Hood & Sons, 596 F.2d 70, 72 (2d Cir.1979). In this case, Grondin has established irreparable injury and will probably succeed on the merits. She thus may win permanent injunctive relief. However, her injury is abated by the fact that she delayed in seeking relief regarding the tour, and thus the individual defendants may continue to conduct the tour that is already under way. Nevertheless, limited injunctive relief will be granted with respect to the album.

Grondin claims that she will be irreparably injured as a result of the tour's continuance and the album's distribution. Her claim first is that she had a valid non-use agreement through which she sought to protect her late husband's memory and Lynyrd Skynyrd's reputation. Moreover, she claims that even if she was not able to contract successfully to protect the Lynyrd Skynyrd name, the Lanham Act provides her with a remedy by prohibiting the use of a protected mark in such a way as to cause consumer confusion.

Indeed, if in this case confusion or a valid contract can be shown, irreparable injury follows. The number of consumers who would attend a concert of the 87–88 Lynyrd Skynyrd and thereafter would be less inclined to purchase previously released Lynyrd Skynyrd albums is incalculable. Also incalculable is the number of consumers who would purchase the Live album under the impression they were purchasing previously released material, or who would be less inclined to purchase old Lynyrd Skynyrd materials based on their impression of the Live album. Additionally, to the extent Grondin entered into a contract motivated by the desire to preserve her husband's memory, her emotional damages are difficult to quantify. A review of the merits clarifies the issue of injury.

The Non-Use Agreement

Grondin testified that she was a party, along with Rossington and Collins, to an oral non-use agreement entered into several months after the October 1977 plane crash. Her testimony was corroborated by Rapp, who was present when the original blood oath was entered into, and by others who claim to have heard the agreement restated by the defendants on other occasions. None of the defendants who were present when the oath was taken have denied that the agreement existed. They merely contest the contract's enforceability. Thus, Grondin's testimony as to the existence of the agreement is credible and this court holds that the agreement did, in fact, exist.

[¶¶]. . . Grondin can make out no colorable contract claim against MCA however. MCA was not a party to the non-use agreement. Moreover, Grondin authorized Tribute to make arrangements for the production of an album from the 1987 tour by signing the Tribute Agreement. Her only complaint about the album is its title and its reference to the band performing on it as Lynyrd Skynyrd. She has no quarrel with the marketing of the album under a different name. However, MCA was authorized to use the Live title by Tribute, and the artwork for the jacket was also approved by that organization. Since MCA was acting pursuant to the orders of an organization with apparent authority to approve Live, and since it was not in contractual [relations] with Grondin, it cannot be held accountable to her for breach of the non-use agreement.

Thus, Grondin has not shown a likelihood of success on the merits on this claim as against MCA. Nor has she set forth sufficient questions going to the merits to make them a fair ground for litigation.

The Lanham Act

Section 43(a) of the Lanham Act, 15 U.S.C. § 1125(a) provides that:

> [a]ny person who shall affix, apply, or annex, or use in connection with any goods or services . . . a false designation of origin, or any false description or representation, including words or other symbols tending falsely to describe or represent the same, and shall cause such goods or services to enter into commerce . . . shall be liable to a civil action . . . by any person who believes that he is or is likely to be damaged by the use of any such false description or representation.

Grondin asserts that by touring under the name Lynyrd Skynyrd, the individual defendants are in violation of the Lanham Act, and that by marketing the Live album, all the defendants are in violation of this provision.

The Lanham Act protects names of popular musical recording groups even though that name is not a registered trademark. See Kingsmen v. K-Tel International, Ltd., 557 F.Supp. 178 (S.D.N.Y.1983); Rare Earth, Inc. v. Hoorelbeke, 401 F.Supp. 26 (S.D.N.Y.1975). The Act "provides relief against the type of unfair competition analogous to the misappropriation of trade names . . . [and] protects against the use of a false description or designation of origin." Kingsmen, supra, 557 F.Supp. at 181 (citations omitted). Thus, Grondin's claim against use of the name Lynyrd Skynyrd is properly brought pursuant to the Lanham Act.

The question to be addressed when seeking equitable relief under the Lanham Act is whether consumers are likely to be confused as to the source or sponsorship of the product in question. See Dallas Cowboys Cheerleaders, Inc. v. Pussycat Cinema, Ltd., 604 F.2d 200, 204–05 (2d Cir.1979); Kingsmen, supra, 557 F.Supp. at 181; CBS Inc. v. Springboard International Records, 429 F.Supp. 563, 567 (S.D.N.Y.1976). Actual confusion need only be proven in an action for damages. Warner Brothers, Inc. v. Gay Toys, Inc., 658 F.2d 76, 79 (2d Cir.1981).

Grondin's Lanham Act claim as it pertains to the tour is not as strong as her contract claim. She claims that there is a likelihood that by holding themselves out to be Lynyrd Skynyrd, the defendants will deceive the concert going public into believing that they are buying tickets for the group that achieved popularity a decade ago, even though the band's lead singer and main attraction is dead. In making this assertion, she relies primarily on two cases from this district, Kingsmen, supra, and Springboard, supra.

Kingsmen centered around a musical group that achieved popularity in the 1960's with the song "Louie, Louie." . . . The court held that there was a likelihood of confusion as this was not a recording by the Kingsmen, a group that continued to exist, perform and sell albums after the departure of Ely.

Springboard involved recordings by different artists. In one case, the performer Charlie Rich, who early in his career had been associated with the defendants, achieved popularity while under contract to CBS Inc. After Rich became popular and was no longer involved with the defendant, the defendant produced an album of early Rich songs and marketed it with a photograph of Rich as he looked not at the time the early material was recorded but at the time of the record's production. Similarly, the band LaBelle, which had formerly been known as Patti LaBelle and the Bluebelles but had drastically changed their image and style, sued to prevent the defendant from marketing an album of Bluebelle songs bearing a recent photograph of that group. The court in the Rich case held that the record buying public was likely to be deceived by the picture on the album cover, because while it would see a picture of the old Rich, it would be buying a substantially different product. The court found the defendant's actions regarding LaBelle even more egregious since the Patti LaBelle and the Bluebelles and LaBelle were vastly different bands selling vastly different products. Injunctions thus issued in both cases.

Although these cases may be persuasive in the context of the Live album, which will be discussed below, they are not so compelling with regard to the concerts in issue here. First the October 1977 tragedy was highly publicized. Both parties submitted numerous news articles reporting the crash of Lynyrd Skynyrd and the deaths of Ronnie, Gaines and the others. The fact that the death of Ronnie has received much attention in the media is not contested. Thus, although possible, it is improbable that sophisticated fans of the original Lynyrd Skynyrd will be led to believe that the 87–88 Skynyrd included Ronnie Van Zant by virtue of the use of the name Lynyrd Skynyrd. Consumers here are thus unlike consumers in the Kingsmen case, a case where the individual performers did not achieve attention or prominence. Additionally, unlike Springboard, promotional advertising for the tour does not present old photographs of the band[8] but bills the concerts as a tribute to Lynyrd Skynyrd and to those who perished in the crash.[9]

---

[8]   Programs available for purchase at the concert do contain photographs of the original Lynyrd Skynyrd. However, the program contains a history of the band as well as photographs entitled "Then & Now."

[9]   Contrary to the defendant's assertion, the fact that Lacy Van Zant, Ronnie and Johnny's father, introduces the band and introduces himself as the father of the Van Zants, does not

Nonetheless, there are minor ways in which this tour might deceive the unsophisticated concert goer. For example, there is promotional material that uses a logo similar to that displayed on an older album featuring Ronnie. However, the logo also sets forth the names of the members of the new band. Additionally, potential consumers may hear of the tour without hearing promotional advertising pertaining to the tribute and thus think they will hear the same band that recorded the previously released songs. Thus, Grondin has presented sufficiently serious questions going to the merits to present a fair ground for litigation.[10]

However, the balance of hardships tips in favor of the individual defendants on this score. The 1988 tour has not only already been scheduled, but it is already underway. Tickets have been sold. The expense to defendants to undo what has been and is being done weighs in their favor. Thus, the tour will not be enjoined on Lanham Act grounds.

Similarly, the tour will not be enjoined based on the contract rights set forth above. The 1987 and 1988 tours are substantially similar in format in that the new band, calling itself Lynyrd Skynyrd, conducts a tribute to the original band while performing the original selections. However, Grondin did not object to the 1987 tour. In fact, she received a percentage of the merchandising profits from those concerts. She did not object until the 1988 tour was about to get underway. She now objects to both tours. While she is not guilty of laches and thus may ultimately prevail after a trial and be granted a permanent injunction, her delay in seeking relief indicates "an absence of the kind of irreparable harm required to support a preliminary injunction." Citibank, N.A. v. Citytrust, 756 F.2d 273, 275 (2d Cir.1985).

Likelihood of confusion is greater with respect to the album. While seasoned concert goers are unlikely to believe Ronnie Van Zant has risen from the grave to perform on tour, they have no way of knowing whether a record company has decided to release recordings of his live performances recorded before his death. This is especially so in light of the fact that Lynyrd Skynyrd albums were continually released after 1977. The prominent logo on the album jacket, as described above, is the wording

---

alleviate the likelihood of confusion. Nor does Johnny's introduction of the song "Free Bird," during which he states that "no one can sing this song like my brother Ronnie" and in which he dedicates the number to the memory of those who died, cure the problem. Ignoring the fact that Lacy's acknowledgment of paternity does not reveal that one son is dead, a statement captured on Live as well, a concert goer would have had to spend his money on a ticket before he would hear any of these proclamations.

[10] This is especially so in light of the fact that tours under consideration in this opinion are the tribute tours only, where the new band performs old Lynyrd Skynyrd material and promotes itself as honoring the dead. The results might change if the band continued to perform as Lynyrd Skynyrd without holding itself out to be in tribute Ronnie and the others. The court is particularly mindful of this in light of recently proposed changes to the Lanham Act that would increase protection under its auspices. See N.Y.L.J., May 27, 1988, at 3.

"Lynyrd Skynyrd Live." The words "Lynyrd Skynyrd Tribute Tour 1987" are so small in comparison as to be nearly meaningless.

First, the small lettering does not adequately explain that the record in the jacket does not contain recordings of the original group packaged in a 1987 context, or in addition to 1987 recordings. This is especially deceiving to those who are not familiar with the existence of the 1987 tour and who think Lynyrd Skynyrd has not performed live since 1977, even though records have been released since then. Nothing on the jacket cover dispels that confusion. The back of the jacket sheds no light and only lists some, but not all, solo performers on some selections. It is only after one purchases the album and removes its plastic wrapper that the dedication to the victims of the crash is revealed-and then in type size barely visible without eye strain.

Moreover, the small gold lettering appears at the very bottom of the jacket face. Thus, when the album is on display in those record stores in which records appear behind a low barrier that keeps the record in place, the small lettering is not visible at all.[11] This situation is at least as compelling as the LaBelle case set forth above. In that case there was a notation on the album cover setting forth that these were "LaBelle and the Bluebelles Early Hits."[12] However, other things about the cover, mainly the photograph, rendered the album deceptive thus warranting a grant of injunctive relief.

In sum, Grondin has set forth a colorable claim under the Lanham Act with respect to the Live album by showing a likelihood of confusion.[FN13 omitted] Although she has not presented evidence of actual confusion thus showing a likelihood of success on the merits, she has presented sufficiently serious questions going to the merits to make them a fair ground for litigation and a balance of hardships tipping in her favor.

Grondin did not delay in objecting to the distribution of Live in its present jacket. She first saw the offending jacket in March 1988, and she filed this action in May. The Live album could, as is discussed above, cause confusion among consumers. "A record album's cover ... is one of the primary means of advertisement for a record album, particularly when, in the normal retail situation, 'a customer has no way of hearing the record prior to purchase.'" PPX Enterprises, Inc. v. Audiofidelity Enterprises, Inc., 818 F.2d 266, 272 (2d Cir.1987) (quoting CBS, Inc. v. Gusto Records, Inc., 403 F.Supp. 447, 449 (M.D.Tenn.1974)). Since a consumer could see Live in a record store and think he was purchasing a compilation of live performances of the original Lynyrd Skynyrd, and since this could decrease

---

[11]   The compact disc version is contained in similar packaging, except that there appears thereon a picture of some, but not all, members of the new band along with guest performers.

[12]   The band was originally called Patti LaBelle and the Bluebelles where as the new band was simply LaBelle.

sales of previously released albums unquantifiably,[14] Grondin is entitled to injunctive relief.

The balance of hardship tips decidedly in Grondin's favor because the relief granted will be limited in scope thus reducing any hardship MCA might suffer. MCA will not be required to recall all records currently in the marketplace. Additionally, MCA may utilize the jackets already manufactured. Grondin approved the release of a recording of the 1987 tour and thus must have expected that some fans of the original Lynyrd Skynyrd would purchase the Live album. Moreover, MCA has produced this jacket at great expense. Thus, relief will be more narrowly tailored to fit the exigencies of the situation. See Spring Mills v. Ultracashmere House, Ltd., 724 F.2d 352 (2d Cir.1983). MCA will be required to affix, or have affixed to the jacket a label explicitly conveying that this is a recording of the new band recorded in 1987 and not the original Lynyrd Skynyrd. See Springboard, supra, 429 F.Supp. at 569 (granting similar relief). The exact wording of the label should be mutually agreeable to the parties; however, the court will intervene if the parties are unable to agree.

Conclusion

In sum, Grondin's motion for a preliminary injunction pursuant to Rule 65, Fed.R.Civ.P. is denied with respect to the tour and the individual defendants but is granted insofar as MCA will be required to affix to all Live albums a sticker representing the album as a recently recorded performance of the new band. An early trial date will be set. Settle order on notice.

IT IS SO ORDERED.

NOTES AND QUESTIONS

1.   In the context of band name disputes, how important is the issue of potential consumer confusion if there is a valid license to use the name? Should the owners of band names be permitted to license them for uses that are likely to confuse consumers even if the former band members are all in agreement about such a license? For example, in another band name dispute, *Brother Records, Inc. v. Jardine*, 318 F.3d 900 (9th Cir. 2003), former members of the Beach Boys disputed the use of the name "Beach Boys Family and Friends" for a touring group led by former Beach Boy Alan Jardine. In that case, the corporation had offered the use of the name so long as the corporation's pre-approved promotors were used and a large license fee was paid by Jardine, but Jardine refused. What if Jardine had simply taken advantage of the offered non-exclusive license to tour as "The Beach Boys" (i.e., using the approved

---

[14]   In fact, Lynyrd Skynyrd produced a live album in 1976 entitled "One More From the Road." That album is still available in record stores.

promoters and paying the required license fee) and both Mike Love and Alan Jardine simultaneously engaged in separate tours as "The Beach Boys"— should such an arrangement be permitted even if it would cause actual consumer confusion? Why or why not?

2.   Note the different issues that arise when there is no contractual agreement between band members versus when there is an express agreement covering use of the name, and when any such agreement is written versus oral. How should band members protect themselves in light of the discussion in these cases? If you were advising members of a band entering into a band agreement, would you recommend a majority approval for licenses of the band name, a provision that the name cannot be used at all by any combination of the band members after the band breaks up, a unanimous approval requirement for uses of the band name, or some other alternative? Why?

CHAPTER X

MUSIC INDUSTRY CONTRACTS PART 1: *WE CAN WORK IT OUT*[1]

■ ■ ■

As was discussed in the overview of the music industry in Chapter 1, contracts in the music industry cover a wide range of relationships throughout the timeline from creation of a musical work (and even before its creation) to the consumer's enjoyment of that work through any one of a wide variety of distribution or performance platforms. You saw in previous chapters how the licensing process for using a composition or sound recording in the host of modern contexts—online streaming on personal devices, stores, elevators, radio, film, television, gaming, live concerts, sporting events, bars, restaurants, etc.—can be complex and involves a variety of entities depending on the nature of the work and the nature of the use. In this chapter and the next, we focus not on license agreements for use of existing works, but on agreements between songwriters/composers or recording artists and the entities that typically play an important role in releasing their creative works into the stream of commerce.[2]

> ### CONSIDER AS YOU READ . . .
>
> • Are there any governing principles that you think should guide all contracts between composers/songwriters/performing artists and music publishers/record labels? What are they? Why are they important?
>
> • Individual provisions of contracts are not interpreted in isolation, and thus disputes over one provision of a contract often involve consideration of the contract as a whole. Where do you see the most overlap between different types of provisions in the courts' analysis of the legal issues in the cases that follow?

---

[1]   John Lennon & Paul McCartney (1965); released by the Beatles as a double A-side with *Day Tripper* (1965).

[2]   We intentionally omit discussion of the role of unions in the music industry (e.g., AFTRA, AFM), although they continue to play an important role—particularly with respect to orchestral musicians, non-featured musicians on sound recordings, health and instrument insurance and other benefits, and advocacy. A discussion of labor relations within the music industry is beyond the scope of this text.

A. OVERVIEW

We will initially focus below on contracts between publishers and songwriters and contracts between record labels and performing artists, with a brief introduction to some provisions specific to each category of agreements below.[3] In Part B, we address some of the categories of provisions that are typically included in these types of agreements, interspersed with relevant excerpts of cases that illustrate some of the issues that have arisen in these contractual relationships. These categories include ownership of the works created pursuant to or covered by songwriting and recording contracts; duration of the agreement; and compensation provisions, including royalties and accounting rights. Chapter 11 will address additional categories of provisions commonly addressed in music industry contracts, including obligations to exploit or promote the works covered by the agreement; creative control and control over uses of the works; permitted uses of the artist's name and likeness under the agreement; the nature of the legal relationship established by the contract; and choice of governing law.

Songwriter Agreements

As you saw in Chapters 1 and 3, music publishing companies started out as entities that published compositions in the form of music books or sheet music, sold them, and distributed royalties to composers based on those sales. Today's music publishers do much more, having evolved with the music industry as a whole to identify up-and-coming songwriters and composers; to support their writers as they create new songs (usually through some sort of advance payment and a percentage of revenues earned from exploiting the songs); to document the copyrights in the works and enforce those copyrights if necessary; to promote and license the works for a variety of uses, including for use in sound recordings, in live and virtual public performances, and in audiovisual works; and to collect, account for, and distribute revenues from licensed uses.

The three largest U.S. music publishers are Sony/ATV Music Publishing, Universal Music Publishing, and Warner/Chappell Music, which together own more than seven million songs. There are also many smaller, independent music publishers, and quite a few singer-songwriters

---

[3]   For those interested in more detail on songwriting and recording agreements, or several examples of these and other types of contractual agreements between publishers, record labels, and contributors to the creative process (e.g., producers' agreements), we recommend the following sources: BOB KOHN, KOHN ON MUSIC LICENSING, 5th ed. (Wolters Kluwer 2018); DONALD S. PASSMAN, ALL YOU NEED TO KNOW ABOUT THE MUSIC BUSINESS, 9th ed. (Simon & Schuster 2105) (10th ed. forthcoming October 2019); Practicing Law Institute, *Counseling Clients in the Entertainment Industry* (annual series of publications), 2019 version *available at* https://legacy. pli.edu/Content/CourseHandbook/Counseling_Clients_in_the_Entertainment_Industry/_/N-4mZ1 z0zgg4?ID=356316. In addition, although we have not included it in this text because of its length, we recommend *Gordy Co. v. Mary Jane Girls, Inc.*, 1989 WL 149290 (S.D.N.Y. 1989), *as substantively amended in Gordy Co. v. Mary Jane Girls, Inc.*, 1990 WL 47684 (S.D.N.Y. April 12, 1990) as a wonderful case study of a dispute over recording, producing, and publishing agreements.

who have formed their own music publishing companies. Among the common sources of music publishing revenue are public performance royalties, mechanical royalties, synchronization licenses (uses of the composition in "timed synchronization" with images, as in films, television shows, commercials, music videos, etc.), and other sources such as sales of sheet music. Typically, a music publisher will play a role with respect to at least some of these revenue sources, although its role will shift in prominence depending upon the nature of the agreement it has with an individual songwriter and the nature of the revenue source.

Songwriter agreements between composers and music publishers can take many forms. In a typical *exclusive songwriting agreement*, the composer assigns the copyright in musical compositions created during the term of the agreement to the publisher, and the publisher covenants to promote the songs, license uses of the compositions, collect revenues from those licenses, and distribute a share of those revenues to the composer. Typically, the publisher shares most revenue 50–50 with the composer, but different types of revenue can be divided in different percentages. In the context of the performance right, the 50 percent share of the songwriter is often viewed as inviolate—it is typically paid directly to songwriters, rather than paid through the accounting department of the music publisher, and thus it is one source of revenue that goes to songwriters without deduction of the publisher's expenses. Some exclusive songwriting agreements require delivery of a specified number of songs rather than requiring a specified number of years of exclusive writing services. Typically, these agreements provide for a perpetual and worldwide grant of copyright to the publisher. In exclusive songwriting agreements, as compared with other options discussed below, the publisher takes on a greater role in seeking out artists to record the composition—because without a recorded version of the song to exploit, the song is less likely to earn significant revenues for either the publisher or composer.

Distinct from the exclusive songwriting agreement is the *co-publishing agreement*, which involves shared copyright ownership. Typical co-publishing deals involve 50-50 ownership of the copyright by the composer and publisher, with the composer thus often receiving 75% of royalties—the 50% writer's share, plus half of the publisher's share. The co-publishing deal has become more common in recent decades as composers have become more sophisticated about retaining the copyright in their works if at all possible.

If a songwriter is well-known, and thus in demand, or if she is a singer-songwriter who will be recording her own compositions without the need to find artists to record them, the songwriter might instead opt for an *administration agreement*. In this type of songwriting agreement, the songwriter retains the copyright, with the publisher taking on purely administrative functions in licensing rights and collecting and distributing proceeds without any obligation to promote the works. In administration deals, the publisher's fee is typically 15–25% of revenues from exploitation of the compositions subject to the agreement.

Other options for music publishing deals include a *collection agreement*, which is much like an administration agreement except that the publisher takes on no licensing role other than to collect and distribute revenues from uses of the compositions. With these reduced publisher responsibilities comes a reduced fee—typically around 10%. Finally, some composers who manage their own publishing may use a larger music publisher to handle only the *foreign sub-publishing* of their works. Administration, collection, and foreign sub-publishing deals typically have relatively short terms, often not exceeding three years.

Of course, publishing agreements can run the gamut between the examples described above, depending on the interests and negotiating power of the individual parties.

Recording Agreements

Just as changes in the industry led to shifts in the role of music publishers and thus in the scope of rights and obligations assumed by the parties to songwriter agreements, so, too, have changes in the industry led to shifts in the role of recording companies and in the scope of rights and obligations assumed by the parties to recording agreements. The product containing sound recordings for public consumption has progressed from wax cylinders or 78 rpm discs with a single composition (and later one on each side), to 45 rpm discs with an "A-side" song and a "B-side" song, to 33–1/3 rpm long-playing albums, to cassette tapes, to 8-track tapes, then compact discs, digital audio tape, MP3s, and now digital streams. This progression tracked the development of innovative technology—particularly new devices and software—that could hold more minutes of a recording, capture and replay a richer complexity of sound, take up less and less physical space, and become more and more portable. Each new product—at least until the digital revolution and advent of digital downloads and streams—required specialized recording equipment and a manufacturing and distribution system, giving record labels an important role to play.

The stage for what became the "standard" recording agreement was set in the formative years of the industry, with Caruso's 1902 exclusive recording contract with Victor (mentioned in Chapter 2) as a leading example. Over the course of his two-decade contractual relationship with Victor, Caruso was paid a large (at the time) "advance" fee for his exclusive recording services and a royalty from the sale of records. Although his income from live performances exceeded his income from recording, Victor's promotion of Caruso's recordings served to enhance his performance fees. In the middle of his career in 1915–1916, he was earning more than $78,000 per year in royalties from sales of recordings in the U.S.; in 1919, his new contract with Victor guaranteed him $100,000 per year plus ten percent of retail sales of his recordings[4]—in 2019 dollars, that would be equivalent to an advance guarantee of more than $1.5 million a year even without royalties. Although Caruso was paid more than any other recording artist of his time, the practice of paying artists a guaranteed fee plus a share of the royalties from record sales in exchange for their exclusive recording services became the common model in the industry for almost a century, at least for the larger labels—i.e. the largest of the recording companies, typically with ties to other aspects of the industry, such as device manufacturers (Victor, Columbia, RCA) or film companies (Warner, Universal).

The rock-n-roll era, lasting from the late 1950s through the mid-1970s, was a time of expansive growth for the recording industry, both in terms of sales and in terms of the number and variety of record labels that sprang into existence. As the market for sales of recorded music began to contract in the 1970s, the industry began a trend of consolidation that ultimately led to the current landscape, with only three major labels remaining— Universal Music Group, Sony Music Entertainment, and Warner Music Group. Each of these "majors" has many different sub-labels or "imprints," often corresponding to well-known labels that were acquired by each company (e.g., the Capitol, Mercury, Geffen, and Motown labels are all part of the Universal Music Group). In addition, there are many smaller, independent (or "indie") labels that make up a vibrant part of the recording industry—but the three majors together encompass the vast majority of the market.

Like publishing agreements, recording contracts between musical performing artists and record labels can also take many forms, and shifts in how recordings are distributed have had an impact on the scope and nature of the parties' rights and obligations. The "standard" recording contract of past decades has evolved into a more fluid contractual relationship that may cover just the artist's recordings during the term of the contract or that may extend to other aspects of the artist's work and "brand," such as touring, merchandizing, and/or commercial endorsements. Recording contracts covering aspects of an artist's career beyond creation and distribution, sale and performance of sound recordings are commonly referred to as "360" deals. Some early examples of expansive 360 deals include Madonna's and Jay-Z's contracts with Live Nation in 2007 and 2008, respectively, in which Live Nation made a huge investment in all aspects of each superstar's career, receiving a share in virtually all revenues earned by each in exchange of guaranteed payments of over $10 million per year for ten years. However, 360 deals containing this

---

[4]   DAVID SUISMAN, SELLING SOUNDS: THE COMMERCIAL REVOLUTION IN AMERICAN MUSIC 130 (Harvard Univ. Press 2009).

expansive coverage are more the exception than the rule; many of these deals in today's recording industry are not truly "360" in that they do not encompass the entirety of a recording artist's earnings from all sources. The specific revenue sources encompassed within individual deals will depend, as always, upon the interests and negotiating power of the individual parties to the deal.

A common provision of many recording contracts is the obligation of the artist to deliver a specified number of master recordings to the record label during the term of the agreement in exchange for the payment of specified artist royalties and other sums. Labels typically request option(s) to renew the contract, giving them flexibility to keep successful artists under contract while letting go of less successful artists. Before paying any royalty share to the artist, the label is typically permitted to deduct a range of costs from revenues, often calculated as a percentage of the revenue rather than based on actual costs. Royalties typically vary based upon the nature of the use of the sound recording—e.g., for sales of recordings, the artist's percentage might range from 9% to 20% or more depending on the stature of the artist; for master use licenses in films, the artist often will get 50% of the license fee. Many recording contracts include royalty escalation provisions, in which royalties increase when contractually-stated sales targets are reached.

As noted above, another common feature of recording agreements is the payment by the label of an advance guarantee to the artist, with the accompanying right by the label to recoup the advance payment from revenues before any royalty payments are made to artists. As a result, many of the more successful artists are able to negotiate a (relatively) large sum of money up front from the label but then do not receive any share of revenues from sales and licenses of the recordings for quite some time after release of the recording, if ever. Record labels report that less than twenty percent of record releases break even for them; far more often than not, the advance guarantee and costs invested in recording and promoting a record will not be recouped by the label.

Recording contracts often provide great detail about the manner in which royalties will be calculated—both in terms of the royalty rate that will apply to different types of licenses/uses for the recordings and in terms of the specific deductions from revenue that labels will be permitted to make before royalties are determined. Some common deductions from revenues that are included in recording agreements, besides the advance guarantee, include: recording costs, production costs for music videos, and (for physical phonorecords) deductions for packaging costs, breakage, and a reserve against returns. In addition, many recording contracts include cross-collaterization provisions, allowing a record label to charge unrecouped costs for prior projects as costs for subsequent projects. For example, if a recording artist's first album did not earn sufficient revenues for the label to recoup its advance, the unrecouped amount of that advance could be recouped from the next album's revenues before the artist's royalties would be paid.

Within the popular music world, the advent of the singer-songwriter in the 1960s eventually led to incorporation of what are known as "controlled composition" clauses in recording agreements, and they still commonly appear in today's recording contracts. Such clauses are designed to give recording companies a discount on mechanical royalties when a recording artist is also the songwriter; they sometimes also limit the number of "covers" that recording artists may include on an album or place a cap on total mechanical royalties for an album. Another type of provision often found in recording agreements with multi-member performing groups addresses what happens when individuals leave the group, with labels seeking what are known as "leaving member clauses" that give them the option of signing (or not signing) individual band members when members leave the band or the entire band dissolves.[5]

In the section below and continuing into Chapter 11, we introduce common provisions of both songwriter/publisher and artist/record label agreements. The materials below also highlight some of the past and current disputes over typical provisions in these types of agreements within the music industry.

---

[5]   *See, e.g., Forrest RB Enterprises v. Capricorn Records*, 430 F. Supp. 847 (S.D.N.Y. 1977) (finding language of Allman Brothers recording agreement only addressed circumstance where individual band member left and did not contemplate dissolution of the band as a whole, permitting individual band member to sign with a different label upon dissolution).

B. KEY PROVISIONS OF SONGWRITER AND RECORDING AGREEMENTS

Both songwriter and recording contracts share provisions that are common to most types of contracts, although the substance of each type of provision will vary quite a bit depending on conventions in the industry, relative bargaining power of each party to the agreement, and the specific needs and interests of the parties. There are contracts as short as a single page that give basic terms in bullet points and contracts as long as 150 pages that include complex royalty provisions and artist approval requirements for every conceivable use.

Typical contractual provisions, some of which are heavily negotiated and some of which have led to litigation in the past, include:

    (1)   ownership/assignment of copyright;

    (2)   the duration of the agreement;

    (3)   the manner in which compensation is calculated and distributed;

    (4)   the respective obligations of the parties to the agreement regarding promotion or other efforts to exploit the works covered by the agreement;

    (5)   control over the content of the works covered by the agreement;

    (6)   permissions and limitations of use of name and likeness;

    (7)   the nature of the legal relationship between the parties; and

    (8)   choice of governing law.

These issues are almost always interrelated—if copyright ownership is shared, for example, then the calculation of compensation will almost always be different than if copyright were to vest in just one of the parties, as will the level of control that the parties exercise over the works.

Below are introductions to the first three of these general topics, with excerpts of relevant cases and points for you to consider regarding each. The remaining general topics are covered in Chapter 11.[6]

---

[6]   Note that contract negotiation and drafting are both skills that are worthy of their own courses; we only give a brief introduction and overview of the issues here and encourage all students interested in practicing in this area to take courses in both negotiation theory and contract drafting. Typical songwriting and recording deals also include many other types of provisions—some common to many business contracts. Here, we intentionally focus on provisions that highlight some of the contractual issues that have been the subject of debate as the industry has evolved, but we do not want to suggest that these should be the only focus in contract negotiations between songwriters/artists and publishers/labels.

1. OWNERSHIP/ASSIGNMENT OF COPYRIGHT

Who will own the copyright in the works created under the agreement? The more negotiating power that the composer or recording artist has, the greater the chance that the copyrights can be retained or co-owned. The value of having a publisher or record label, though, is in the expertise those entities bring in promoting and distributing the works; the greater the interest that the publisher or label holds in the works created under the agreement, the stronger its interest will be in promoting the works and creating income streams from the exploitation of those works. For new composers or artists, it may not be possible to get a deal in which they retain ownership of the works—but it is always a topic of discussion and both publishing and recording contracts will include a provision that deals with who will own the copyright in works that fall under the contract's purview. Even when authors are able to retain or share copyright ownership in the works they produce under an agreement with a publisher or label, the contract will still need to detail the manner in which the parties are to administer/exploit the rights and the scope of rights licensed to the publisher/label.

> SAMPLE GRANT OF RIGHTS (RECORDING AGREEMENT)
>
> *Company shall be exclusively entitled to and shall own all right, title, and interest throughout the universe in and to the results and proceeds of Artist's services hereunder including, but not limited to, any and all Recordings (as hereinafter defined) and all Masters (collectively, "Works") whether or not completed, and any and all sound recording copyrights therein. The Works shall be entirely and exclusively Company's property, free of any claims whatsoever by Artist or any other person or entity. Company and its designees shall have the exclusive rights, in perpetuity, to manufacture, sell, reproduce, adapt, distribute, transmit, broadcast, cable cast, stream, and/or otherwise exploit the Works, throughout the universe, in any manner, in any form, in any and all languages, in whole or in part, in any and all media, and by any method now known or hereafter discovered or conceived.*

One complexity in provisions granting or licensing copyrights in both publishing and recording agreements is identifying the works that will fall under the grant or assignment of rights. Often, those works have not yet been created, and it is the obligation of the composer or recording artist to "deliver" either a specified number of works or all works created during the time period covered by the agreement. Some agreements will include works created before the contract was signed (e.g., songs or demo recordings that gained the author the publishing or recording deal in the first place) as well as any works created during some time window following expiration of the contract (e.g., six months after the end of the contract). For works created but not delivered during the duration of contracts that require delivery of a certain number of works, exclusivity provisions will often prevent publication/release of those works during a specified time period without express, written approval of the publisher or label. For composers or artists who wish to enter into collaborations with others who are signed to different companies, these provisions can create potential hurdles to such creative collaborations.

Encompassed within any provision dealing with assignment or ownership of copyright in the works covered by an agreement will be the duration of the copyright grant, the scope of the rights assigned or licensed, and any geographic limitations on those rights.

SAMPLE CO-PUBLISHING GRANT OF RIGHTS

Writer hereby irrevocably and absolutely assigns, transfers and grants to Publisher, its successors, and assigns, all rights and interests of every kind and nature in and to any revenues generated from Writer's songwriting during the Term, including, without limitation, the Compositions, and the copyrights therein; provided, however, that Publisher and Writer shall jointly own, in equal shares, Writer's share in and to the Compositions, so that fifty percent (50%) of the copyright to the Compositions shall be owned by Publisher and fifty percent (50%) shall be owned by Writer, with Publisher being the exclusive administrator throughout the Territory with respect to one hundred percent (100%) of Publisher's and Writer's respective interests in and to the Compositions. The Compositions shall, at Publisher's election, be registered for copyright by Publisher in the names of Publisher and Writer in the United States Copyright Office. If any of the Compositions have heretofore been registered for copyright in the name of Writer, Writer shall promptly execute and deliver to Publisher such instruments of transfer and other documents regarding the rights of Publisher in the Compositions as Publisher may reasonably request to carry out the purposes of this Agreement.

The default for publishers and labels is a ***perpetual grant of rights***, lasting as long as the copyright lasts under governing law. The duration of the copyright itself will depend in part upon where the work was created, when the work was created, whether the work was created by an individual author or several authors, and whether it qualifies as a work made for hire.

For example, for works created after the effective date of the 1976 Copyright Act in the U.S. and its territories, the statutory duration ranges from life of the author plus 70 years for individual authors to 120 years from creation or 95 years after publication (whichever is first) for works made for hire.[7] Prior to 1976, U.S. copyright law set forth a series of "renewal" requirements that must be undertaken in order for a copyright owner to retain ownership.[8] However, the 1976 Copyright Act replaced this renewal system with a right to terminate assignments (usually after 35 years) that is not subject to assignment at the time of the grant of rights.[9] Termination rights under the Copyright Act are discussed in more detail in Chapter 12, but outside of the statutory termination right, some songwriters and performing artists will seek a contractual right to terminate, or a reversion right, if the publisher or label does not release or publish a work delivered under the agreement within a contractually-specified time.

The default in the scope of rights assigned or transferred in recording and publishing agreements is typically a ***broad grant of all rights***, often specifying that such rights may be exercised through all means "now or hereinafter discovered." As noted in Chapter 1 and illustrated by the ongoing debate about collective licensing of performance rights, because copyright is viewed as a "bundle" of separate rights, grants or assignments of rights can be limited to only specific activities. For example, a grant of rights may provide control over only reproduction, or only performance, or only distribution—or narrowed down even more specifically to the right to publish in print format or distribute through interactive streaming.

For major publishers and labels with a worldwide distribution and licensing network, the default in the geographic reach of a publishing or recording agreement is typically ***throughout the world*** (and since the Space Age, can often be "throughout the universe"). However, songwriters and artists with pre-existing relationships with entities in other countries—which is common for those who are "discovered" in other countries and have already granted non-U.S. rights to other companies— often enter into initial agreements with a more limited geographic scope. Similarly, smaller publishing houses or independent labels may only be interested in exploiting rights in the U.S. market and thus may take a more limited geographic scope in a grant or license of rights.

Note that most contracts in which the copyright is assigned, rather than simply licensed, will expressly indicate that the grant of rights survives the expiration of the agreement; even when the songwriter or

---

[7] *See* 17 U.S.C. §§ 302–304.

[8] Often, contracts entered into for works subject to the 1909 Copyright Act's renewal provisions would include express assignments of all renewal rights by the authors of the works to the publisher or label.

[9] 17 U.S.C. § 203.

artist is no longer under contract with a publisher/label, all works as to which copyright was granted under the agreement will remain with the grantee. The following case illustrates how important clarity in drafting can be in determining the nature of the rights retained or granted in a recording or songwriting agreement.

A Day to Remember singer Jeremy McKinnon and
bassist Joshua Woodard live in concert, 2014
Photo by Will Fisher (CC-ASA-2.0)

WOODARD V. VICTORY RECORDS, INC.

2016 WL 1270423 (N.D. Ill. March 31, 2016)

MEMORANDUM OPINION AND ORDER

JOHN Z. LEE, UNITED STATES DISTRICT JUDGE

Plaintiffs Joshua Woodard, Neil Westfall, Alex Shelnutt, and Jeremy McKinnon are members of the band "A Day to Remember." They entered into a recording agreement with Defendant Victory Records, Inc. in 2006, but terminated the agreement some years later, believing that all of their obligations had been fulfilled. Victory disagreed, and this dispute ensued.

For their part, Plaintiffs seek a judgment declaring that they have performed their obligations under the recording agreement and that they (rather than Victory) own the copyrights to songs recorded under the agreement. Plaintiffs also assert claims for breach of contract and accounting, as well as for violations of the Tennessee Consumer Protection Act, the Illinois Consumer Fraud Act, the Illinois Right of Publicity Act, and the Lanham Act. In response, Defendants Victory Records and Another Victory, Inc., filed a counterclaim seeking declaratory judgment on the same issues as Plaintiffs (although, of course, requesting the opposite result) and assert claims for breach of contract.

Both sides have filed motions for summary judgment. For the reasons provided below, Plaintiffs' motion for partial summary judgment [327] is denied, and Victory's motion for summary judgment [324] is granted in part and denied in part.

Factual Background

Plaintiffs Joshua Woodard, Neil Westfall, Alex Shelnutt, and Jeremy McKinnon are members of the rock band A Day to Remember ("ADTR"). In 2006, ADTR entered into an exclusive recording agreement with Victory Records. See Defs.' LR 56.1(a)(3) Stmt. ¶ 1, ECF No. 325. The agreement, labeled a "Deal Memo," provided for the production of five "albums." See Deal Memo at 1, Second Am. Compl., Ex. A, ECF No. 216.

For each album, the Deal Memo set out a royalty rate that increased if the album sold more than a certain number of units. See id. These royalty rates ranged from 11.5 percent to 15.5 percent. In addition, the parties agreed to split equally any revenue from third-party licenses. See id.

The crux of this dispute is whether ADTR has met its obligation to deliver five albums to Victory, as that term appears in the Deal Memo. There are thirteen recording projects by ADTR, three of which Victory concedes are, in fact, "albums": For Those Who Have Heart; Homesick; and What Separates Me From You. See Defs.' LR 56.1(a)(3) Stmt. ¶¶ 5, 27, 47.

Of the remaining ten recording projects, four relate in some fashion to For Those Who Have Heart: (1) a recording of a live concert in Florida of songs from the album; (2) a combination consisting of the studio-recorded audio tracks with video footage, For Those Who Have Heart—Reissue (CD/DVD); (3) a digital version of the reissue; and (4) a vinyl version. See Defs.' LR 56.1(a)(3) Stmt. ¶¶ 5–17; Pls.' LR 56.1(b)(3)(B) Stmt. ¶¶ 5–17, ECF No. 362.

Three of the remaining projects relate to Homesick: (1) a recording of a live concert in Switzerland; (2) Homesick—Special Edition, which includes the studio-recorded audio tracks from the qualifying album along with acoustic versions of two songs; and (3) a combination of the studio-recorded audio tracks and video footage, Homesick—Special Edition Deluxe (CD/DVD). See Defs.' LR 56.1(a)(3) Stmt. ¶¶ 27–40; Pls.' LR 56.1(b)(3)(B) Stmt. ¶¶ 27–40.

The remaining three projects in dispute are—for lack of a better term—free-standing: an EP titled Attack of the Killer B Sides, which consisted of four songs; a single titled "All I Want" containing two versions of the song from What Separates Me from You; and a record titled Old Record, which was a re-release of an album entitled And Their Name Was Treason that the band had recorded for a previous label. See Defs.' LR 56.1(a)(3) Stmt. ¶¶ 18–26, 41–46, 54–57; Pls.' LR 56.1(b)(3)(B) Stmt. ¶¶ 18–26, 41–46, 54–57.

. . . . [¶]

<u>Analysis</u>

I.   Ownership of the Copyrights

In Count II of their complaint, ADTR seeks a declaratory judgment that they are the owners of all copyrights arising from songs that were recorded pursuant to the Deal Memo. See Second Am. Compl. ¶¶ 18–19. When it comes to musical recordings, there are two types of copyrights at play: (1) copyrights in the actual recordings of the performance of the songs, and (2) copyrights in the composition for each song, meaning the musical notes and lyrics that make up the song. See id.; Johnson v. Cypress Hill, 641 F.3d 867, 870 n.5 (7th Cir. 2011). A copyright owner is entitled to a bundle of six different exclusive rights . . . . 17 U.S.C. § 106. "These rights are divisible, meaning that the owner may convey each one of them to a different person." HyperQuest, Inc. v. N'Site Solutions, Inc., 632 F.3d 377, 382 (7th Cir. 2011) (citing 17 U.S.C. § 201(d)(2)). Furthermore, pursuant to the Copyright Act, "[a] transfer of copyright ownership, other than by operation of law, is not valid unless an instrument of conveyance, or a note or memorandum of the transfer, is in writing and signed by the owner of the rights conveyed or such owner's duly authorized agent." 17 U.S.C. § 204(a).[1]

"The interpretation of an unambiguous contract is a question of law, and therefore a dispute over the terms of an unambiguous contract is suited to disposition on summary judgment." Util. Audit, Inc. v. Horace Mann Serv. Corp., 383 F.3d 683, 687 (7th Cir. 2004). A contract is deemed ambiguous if its language is susceptible to more than one reasonable interpretation. Guerrant v. Roth, 777 N.E.2d 499, 503 (Ill. App. Ct. 2002). Under Illinois law, there are two different kinds of ambiguity. Home Ins. Co. v. Chi. & Nw. Transp. Co., 56 F.3d 763, 768 (7th Cir. 1995). "A contract may be internally unclear or inconsistent as when it is 'reasonably and fairly susceptible to more than one meaning,' and thus, intrinsically ambiguous." Id. "Or it may be extrinsically ambiguous, being clear on its face but someone who knows the context of the contract would know that the contract means something other than what it seems to mean." Id.

[¶]. . . . A.   Copyrights in the Recordings

ADTR argues that it has all copyrights in the recordings and never transferred any rights to Victory. See Pls.' Mem. Supp. Mot. Summ. J. at 1. Victory, on the other hand, contends that the Deal Memo gave it an exclusive license to reproduce, distribute, and perform the work publicly by

---

[1]   The phrase "transfer of copyright ownership" is defined as "an assignment, mortgage, exclusive license, or any other conveyance, alienation, or hypothecation of a copyright or of any of the exclusive rights comprised in a copyright, whether or not it is limited in time or place of effect, but not including a nonexclusive license." 17 U.S.C. § 101.

means of audio transmission. See Defs.' Mot. Summ. J. at 3 (citing § 106(1), (3), and (6)).[2]

The main provision of the Deal Memo states:

[Victory] hereby engages your exclusive personal services as a recording artists in connection with the production of Records and you hereby accept such engagement and agree to exclusively render such services for [Victory] in the Territory during the Term and all extensions and renewals thereof.

Exclusive, 5 Album deal with option on second, third, fourth and fifth album. . . .

An Album is a of reproduction, transmission or communication of Recordings, not or hereafter known, manufactured, distributed, transmitted or communicated in any format. [ADTR] agrees to and allows [Victory] to sell music, images and anything else relating to the Artist via mobile technologies consisting of ringtones, ringbacks, mastertones, wallpapers and any other format or method now or hereafter known.

Deal Memo at 1.

Based upon the language in the Deal Memo, the Court concludes that it unambiguously gives Victory an exclusive license to distribute the "albums" created as part of the agreement. The parties are not required to use specific terms, such as the word "copyright" or "right to distribute," to evince a transfer of rights and comply with § 204(a). See ITOFCA, 322 F.3d at 931. Instead, as in other instances of contract interpretation, courts must look at the intent of the parties as expressed in the written contract. See Kennedy v. Nat'l Juvenile Detention Ass'n, 187 F.3d 690, 694 (7th Cir. 1999) ("Normal rules of contract construction are generally applied in construing copyright agreements."). Here, the contract makes clear that Victory was acquiring the right to distribute the music ADTR produced as part of the Deal Memo. The agreement envisions that ADTR would produce up to five albums and Victory would then sell those albums and pay ADTR a recording advance and royalties based on how well each album sold. In order for this arrangement to make economic sense, Victory had to receive an exclusive license to distribute the albums. The alternative explanation, which ADTR espouses, is that Victory had a nonexclusive license to distribute the albums. But this argument fails on two counts.

First, it completely ignores the fact that the agreement calls for an "exclusive" deal, both in the band's provision of services and in its delivery

---

[2]   For copyrights in sound recordings, the bundle of rights that a copyright owner has is limited to § 106(1) (right to reproduce), § 106(2) (right to prepare derivative works), § 106(3) (right to distribute by sale), and § 106(6) (right to perform publicly by means of digital audio transmission). See 17 U.S.C. § 114(a).

of the five albums to Victory. Second, under the band's interpretation of the Deal Memo, ADTR would be able to collect the recording advance ($20,000) and then immediately enter into another agreement to distribute with a competing recording company—or, for that matter, distribute the album themselves. The Court need not accept this perverse reading of the Deal Memo. "When a contractual interpretation makes no economic sense, that's an admissible and, in the limit, a compelling reason for rejecting it." Dispatch Automation, Inc. v. Richards, 280 F.3d 1116, 1119 (7th Cir. 2002). . . .

Victory limits its motion for summary judgment on Count II to the exclusive right to distribute the recordings (§ 106(3)). See Defs.' Mot. Summ. J. at 3 n.3. Accordingly, the Court grants Victory's motion for Count II as to rights listed in § 106(3) for the copyrights in the recordings. Because Victory has, at a minimum, exclusive rights to distribute the albums, the Court denies ADTR's motion seeking declaratory judgment as to all copyrights in the recordings.

B.   Copyrights in the Compositions

Unlike with the copyrights in the recordings, the Deal Memo is ambiguous as to the transfer of copyrights in the compositions.[3] The Deal Memo states in relevant part:

> 5.   Publishing
>
> $15,000 fully recoupable advance, for publishing deal with Another Victory Inc. (ASSCAP). The publishing advance will be paid half upon signing of this Deal Memo and the balance on commencement of Recording of Album 1.

Deal Memo at 2.

Based on this language, the Court holds that the Deal Memo is ambiguous as to whether it transfers the copyrights in the compositions to Victory. On the one hand, the Deal Memo may be contemplating that ADTR and Another Victory—Victory's publishing affiliate—will enter into a separate publishing deal. Under this reading, because the publishing deal was never finalized, there was never a transfer of copyrights in the compositions. On the other hand, the parties may have considered section 5 of the Deal Memo was sufficient to give Another Victory publishing rights, and any separate agreement would merely expound on the terms of that transfer. After all, according to the terms of the Deal Memo, ADTR was to receive half of the publishing advance at the time the Deal Memo was signed. This suggests that it is at least plausible that the parties

---

[3]   The term "publishing" is used by both parties to refer to the exploitation of copyrights in the compositions. See Pls.' Mem. Supp. Mot. Summ. J. at 3 n.2.

considered the Deal Memo itself to be a transfer of the copyrights in the compositions.

In fact, there is evidence in the record from which a reasonable jury could find that the Deal Memo in fact transferred the copyrights in the compositions. In a discussion with the band's manager over a negotiation with Victory's president, one of the band members wrote "Give us our publishing. . .," suggesting that the publishing rights were Victory's to provide. Defs.' LR 56.1(b)(3)(B) Stmt. ¶ 33, ECF No. 374.[4] Taking this evidence in the light most favorable to Victory, a fact-finder could find that the parties intended section 5 of the Deal Memo to transfer the publishing rights to Victory.

Accordingly, the Court denies both ADTR's and Victory's motions for summary judgment on Count II as they relate to the copyrights in the compositions. . . .

NOTES AND QUESTIONS

1. After considering the court's analysis of the short-form agreement in the *Woodard* case, what advice do you have for parties to agreements that involve a grant of rights in intellectual property? How might you rewrite the provisions at issue to avoid ambiguity?

2. Two main areas of dispute relating to the grant of rights in songwriter and recording agreements are (a) efforts by authors to revoke the grant of rights as a remedy for a material breach of the contract and (b) claims that certain rights were not included in the grant and were retained by the authors. The cases below address both issues, and the results are illustrative of how many of these disputes are resolved.

The first two cases below deal with efforts to rescind a grant of rights— something often sought by artists who wish to regain control over their works after leaving their publisher or label or when the relationship sours. Not surprisingly, since record labels and publishers usually seek and obtain language intended to make grants of rights irrevocable and limit remedies for breach to damages, the courts usually find that the contracts' language precludes rescission as a remedy, as illustrated in the *Nolan* case below, unless the defendant label or publisher has completely abandoned its contractual obligations, as in the *Peterson* case below. Similarly, labels and publishers often include broad language granting rights in the works subject to these agreements, making it difficult for authors to demonstrate that specific rights

---

[4]   ADTR argues that the band member could have been asking that Victory pay the publishing advance for What Separates Me From You, which the band claims was not paid on time. See Pls.' Resp. Defs.' LR 56.1(b)(3)(B) Stmt. ¶ 33, ECF No. 386. Even under ADTR's interpretation of the email, the band member is asking for the publishing advance. Presumably ADTR is receiving a publishing advance because Another Victory received the copyrights in the compositions.

were retained by them unless the contract clearly specifies a more limited grant. The third case below, *Silvester*, provides an illustration of the difficulties faced by authors seeking to prove only a limited grant of rights in a publishing or recording agreement.

NOLAN V. SAM FOX PUB. CO., INC.

499 F.2d 1394 (2d Cir. 1974)

WATERMAN, CIRCUIT JUDGE:

These are cross-appeals by the plaintiff Nolan and one of the defendants below, Sam Fox Publishing Company, from a judgment of the United States District Court for the Southern District of New York, David N. Edelstein, Chief Judge, entered after a trial by the court without a jury. . . .

Robert Nolan composed the song 'Tumbling Tumbleweeds' (the 'song') in 1929, and thereafter assigned the song and the copyright on it to the Sam Fox Publishing Co. ('Fox'). Subsequently, in an agreement dated January 28, 1946, Fox in turn assigned all of its right and interest in and to the song to Williamson Music, Inc. ('Williamson'). On March 1, 1960, the plaintiff assigned the renewal term of the copyright to Fox which then assigned that renewal term, as it had all its previous rights and interests in the song, to Williamson.

In 1963 plaintiff Nolan sought to rescind the assignment to Fox of the original and renewal copyright on the musical composition. The plaintiff also sought injunctive relief protecting his claimed interest in the song. He sought the return of the copyright renewal, an accounting for royalties, and damages for alleged infringement of the copyright. He stated he had rescinded all his contractual arrangements with Fox and sought a judicial declaration confirming the rescission. Although Chief Judge Edelstein found divers [sic] breaches of the contract by Fox he found that none of them were substantial enough or were so material as to justify rescission by Nolan, maintaining that Nolan could 'be rendered whole by an award of monetary damages.' 300 F.Supp. at 1317–1318. As Chief Judge Edelstein viewed the suit as being one based upon breach of contract he ordered an accounting by a Special Master to determine the amount of damages Nolan should recover for such a breach, which damages consisted principally of past royalty payments owed by Fox to Nolan. . . .

After the Special Master had issued his findings of fact, the court below determined that Fox was liable to Nolan in the amount of $94,148, including interest and taxable costs. This figure included royalties on money earned by Williamson but not paid over to Fox. . . . The plaintiff appeals from the judgment insofar as it denied him the other and additional relief he sought.

The defendant Sam Fox Publishing Company, Inc. cross-appeals from that part of the judgment granting Nolan an accounting and computing the award of damages. . . .

We now turn to our discussion of the merits of the appeals. All parties to this action agree that rescission of a contract is an extraordinary remedy which should not be granted whenever there is only an inconsequential breach of the contract. Rather, before rescission will be permitted the breach must be found to be 'material and willful, or, if not willful, so substantial and fundamental as to strongly tend to defeat the object of the parties in making the contract.' Callanan v. Powers, 199 N.Y. 268, 284, 92 N.E. 747, 752 (1910). . . .

A showing of fraud would certainly be grounds for rescission. Adams v. Gillig, 199 N.Y. 314, 92 N.E. 670 (1910). It is plaintiff Nolan's contention here that the facts presented below demonstrate the existence of fraud, and that Chief Judge Edelstein erred in his conclusion that they do not. Nolan's principal claim of fraud is that Fox's relationship with Williamson was fraudulently concealed from the plaintiff. In support of this claim Nolan relies on the facts that he was never given actual notice of Fox's assignment of the copyright to Williamson, and that he was totally ignorant of the arrangement whereby Fox would turn over the copyright renewal to Williamson. Nevertheless, these facts do not demonstrate that fraud existed. Fox had the right to assign the copyright, In re Waterson, Berlin & Snyder co., supra, and Chief Judge Edelstein was unable to discern any effort by either Fox or Williamson to conceal their relationship from Nolan. We therefore do not believe that Chief Judge Edelstein was clearly erroneous in finding that 'the reliable evidence fails to demonstrate fraud.' 300 F.Supp. at 1316.

In 1946, an advertisement appeared in the widely circulated trade newspaper *Variety* stating:

Important Announcement.

WILLIAMSON MUSIC, INC. By special arrangement with

SAM FOX PUBLISHING COMPANY

Have Acquired The SENSATIONAL WESTERN SONG TUMBLING TUMBLEWEEDS By BOB NOLAN

This public announcement is, of course, patently inconsistent with the theory that Fox and Williamson were intent on concealing their relationship. Moreover, Williamson's name was displayed on all the sheet music copies of the song published by it. Nolan argues, however, that nowhere in the *Variety* announcement or on the sheet music was

Williamson identified as the 'publisher.' This omission, in and of itself, surely would not demonstrate fraud. In addition, it is significant that the assignment from Fox to Williamson was recorded at the Copyright Office. Inasmuch as that assignment was recorded, we need not even reach the question of whether Nolan can be charged with knowledge of the assignment because of that recording, for it suffices to say here that this recordation further illustrates that Williamson and Fox had no intention whatsoever of concealing their relationship from Nolan or from anyone else.... [¶]

In addition to his claim that there was fraud, plaintiff Nolan argues that Fox's failure to pay a substantial percentage of the royalties later determined to be owing to him by the Special Master is such a substantial breach of the contract by Fox as to justify rescission by Nolan. Nolan did not receive 74% of the royalties due him for the applicable six-year period from 1957 until 1963. Fox failed to pay any royalties on income from foreign sources, royalties on income from licensing of the song for public performances, and royalties on income from printed material other than piano copies. At the trial below, Fox advanced several defenses that it argued relieved it of the obligation to pay these royalties. The court found that, with the exception of the statute of limitations claim, cutting off liability for failure to pay any royalties due prior to 1957, all the defenses raised were without merit. Chief Judge Edelstein attributed Fox's failure to pay to 'oversight, negligence and less than meticulous bookkeeping ....' 300 F.Supp. at 1320.

Although the existence of fraud is a sufficient ground for permitting rescission it is not a necessary one. Rescission has also been allowed, despite the absence of any showing of fraud, in cases in which a publisher has made none of the royalty payments. The rationale of these decisions is, of course, that an essential objective of a contract between a composer and publisher is the payment of royalties, and a complete failure to pay means this objective has not been achieved. Here, however, Fox did pay 26% of the royalties due to Nolan for the applicable six-year period, and this partial payment of royalties due distinguishes this case from cases where there was total failure to pay the required royalties. See Driver-Harris Co. v. Industrial Furnace Corp., 12 F.Supp. 918 (WDNY 1935); Broadcast Music, Inc. v. Taylor, 10 Misc.2d 9, 55 N.Y.S.2d 94 (Sup.Ct.1945); DeMille Co. v. Casey, 115 Misc. 646, 189 N.Y.S. 275 (Sup.Ct.1921).

* * * *

Affirmed.

The Kingsmen, from a May 28, 1966 Billboard ad (p. 19) (Scandore/Shayne)

PETERSON V. HIGHLAND MUSIC, INC.
140 F.3d 1313 (9th Cir. 1998)

As Amended on Denial of Rehearing and Suggestion for Rehearing En Banc June 15, 1998.* . . .

Opinion

FLETCHER, CIRCUIT JUDGE:

This case involves an attempt by the Kingsmen, a musical group, to secure a rescission of the contract by which they assigned to others the rights to their popular recording of the hit song, "Louie, Louie." We review three actions consolidated on appeal. In the first, the parties litigated the right to rescind. In the second, the defendants sought a declaratory judgment to limit the effect of the judgment of rescission.[1] In the third, the district court imposed contempt sanctions upon the defendants for their refusal to comply with the judgment of rescission. We affirm the district court in all respects.

I.

The facts of this procedurally convoluted case are relatively simple. The members of the Kingsmen seek to secure their rights to the master recordings (the "Masters") of their hit song, "Louie, Louie." The group made the recording over thirty years ago. They then sold the Masters to one Specter Records (first through their agent, Jerden Records, but ultimately on their own behalf) in return for nine per cent of any profits or licensing

---

*   Judges FLETCHER and Nelson vote to reject the suggestion for rehearing en banc, and Judge Magill so recommends.

[1]   For simplicity's sake, we will refer to the Kingsmen as "plaintiffs" and Gusto et al. as "defendants" throughout this opinion, although the parties technically switched roles in the declaratory action.

fees that the recording might generate. The Kingsmen and Specter entered into their contract in 1968. Specter's interest in the Masters was eventually transferred to Gusto Records and GML, who were the named defendants in the rescission action. The parties do not dispute that the Kingsmen have never received a single penny of the considerable royalties that "Louie, Louie" has produced over the past thirty years.

In 1993, the Kingsmen brought suit in federal district court in California for rescission of the contract, basing their claim entirely on actions (or inactions) by the defendants that fell within the four-year statutory limitations period. After a full trial, the district court ruled in plaintiffs' favor and granted the rescission, restoring possession of the Masters to the Kingsmen. Defendants refused to comply with that judgment, however, instead filing a declaratory action in federal district court in Tennessee. In the Tennessee action, defendants asked for a declaration that plaintiffs were not entitled to any of the income that continued to be generated by those licenses that pre-existed the rescission. In the meantime, defendants steadfastly refused to comply with the first judgment and to return possession of the Masters to the Kingsmen.

The district court in Tennessee transferred the declaratory action to the Central District of California, returning it to the district judge who had handled the original action. The judge ruled, on summary judgment, that the rescission enforced in the original action was effective as of the date when the Kingsmen formally declared their intention to rescind—the date of the filing of the complaint—and that defendants must pay to the Kingsmen any royalties or profits that accrued thereafter, whether from licenses entered into after the date of rescission or from licenses that preexisted that date. . . . Defendants appeal all of these rulings.

* * * *

II. The Rescission Action

* * * *

B.

[¶]. . . In analyzing requests for rescission where there have been multiple breaches under an installment contract, California courts have held that each breach starts the clock afresh for statute of limitations purposes. In Conway v. Bughouse, Inc., 105 Cal.App.3d 194, 164 Cal.Rptr. 585 (1980), for example, a California appeals court looked to the manner in which money would be paid under a pension contract in determining how a party's failure to make any given payment should affect the tolling of the statute of limitations.

> [T]he total amount of money to be paid to [the pensioner] is not a fixed sum which is to be paid out over a period of time. To the contrary, the total amount owed is unascertainable until the date

of [the pensioner's] death because each payment is separate and contingent upon [the survival of the pensioner and his adherence to the terms of the contract]. As each payment is separable from the others and is not a part of a total payment, the agreement should logically be considered an installment contract for purposes of determination of the application of the statute of limitations.

Id. at 199–200, 164 Cal.Rptr. 585. The same holds true in the present case: There is no fixed amount to be paid out over time under the Kingsmen's contract, but rather a continuing obligation to pay a portion of the profits and royalties on "Louie, Louie" as the recording gets used over time.

The district court in this case made it clear that, in determining whether rescission was warranted and appropriate, it was relying upon breaches that had occurred within the limitations period. To find for defendant under these circumstances would be to hold that California law forever bars a party from seeking a remedy of rescission after it has once passed up the opportunity to do so, regardless of the nature of any future breaches of the other party's obligations. We have found no authority that would support such a reading of California law. We therefore affirm the district court's conclusion that the statute of limitations does not bar rescission of the contract in this case.

C.

Defendants have raised a host of arguments on appeal concerning prejudice they claim they will suffer as a result of the rescission, alleged threats to the rights of third parties, and actions allegedly taken by the Kingsmen's former agent that, defendants claim, raise an equitable bar to rescission. They failed to raise any of these arguments before the district court. . . . Defendants' newly minted arguments are all inherently factual in nature; none depends upon a change in the law applicable to this dispute; and none must be heard in order to prevent a miscarriage of justice. We therefore find that defendants have waived these arguments, and we will not consider them.

III. The Declaratory Action

The district court issued a declaration that the judgment of rescission entitles plaintiffs to all post-rescission licensing income from the Masters, even post-rescission income from licenses originally granted before the date of rescission. . . . [¶]

On the merits, the district court found that the rescission of the Kingsmen's contract was effective as of the date of the filing of the Kingsmen's complaint. We agree. Under California law, "a party to a contract [can] rescind it and . . . such rescission [can] be accomplished by the rescinding party by giving notice of the rescission and offering to restore everything of value which [the rescinding party has] received." *Runyan v. Pacific Air Indus.,* 2 Cal.3d 304, 311, 85 Cal.Rptr. 138, 466 P.2d 682 (1970); see also id. at 311–13, 85 Cal.Rptr. 138, 466 P.2d 682. When a party gives notice of rescission, it has effected the rescission, and any subsequent judicial proceedings are for the purpose of confirming and enforcing that rescission. See id. at 311–12, 85 Cal.Rptr. 138, 466 P.2d 682. Thus, when the Kingsmen filed suit in 1993, they rescinded the contract and became owners of the Masters. The lawsuit that followed confirmed that their rescission was a proper one and resulted in an order enforcing that rescission. The district court correctly ruled that, as the owners of the Masters, the Kingsmen are entitled to all income derived from the exploitation of the recordings following September 29, 1993, the date of the notice of rescission.

* * * *

CONCLUSION

The district court's rulings in these consolidated actions are well-reasoned and supported by ample evidence in the record. We affirm in all respects.

> The next case excerpt is from a case that raised numerous legal theories. Here, we provide the court's discussion and analysis of the **scope of the grant of rights**, but we will return to other aspects of the court's opinion in one of the following subsections.

SILVESTER V. TIME WARNER, INC.
1 Misc.3d 250, 763 N.Y.S.2d 912 (N.Y. Sup. Ct. 2003)

HELEN E. FREEDMAN, J.

This is a motion pursuant to CPLR 3211(a)(1),(a)(2) and (a)(7) to dismiss the Complaint and the claims set forth therein based on documentary evidence and on jurisdictional and statutory grounds, including time limitations. As class representatives, plaintiffs seek to recover a share of the proceeds of defendants' successful prosecution of the *RIAA v. MP3.com* litigation in the United States District Court for the Southern District of New York. The latter concerned distribution over the internet of digital audio files.

Parties

Plaintiffs are individual recording artists who, as long ago as the 1950's, signed recording contracts with defendant companies or their predecessors, which granted master recording and licensing rights to defendants or their assignors. Plaintiff Tony Silvester d/b/a the Main Ingredient, is a citizen of New York who has recording contracts with RCA Records, as predecessor to defendant BMG Entertainment, Inc., dated 1969, 1972, 1980 and 1981, and one or more record contracts with Polydor Records, as predecessor to defendant Universal Music Group, Inc., dated 1989. Silvester and the other plaintiffs were primarily members of the named groups, and still hold rights to perform under those names. . . .

Defendants Time Warner Inc, Universal Music Group, Inc. ("UMG"), Sony Music Entertainment, Inc. ("Sony"), and BMG Entertainment, Inc ("BMG") are successors in interest to companies with which plaintiffs have recording contracts and are all either incorporated in New York or have principal places of business in New York.

* * * *

Plaintiffs' Claims

Plaintiffs claim to represent a class of thousands of recording artists and their heirs, executors, successors and assignees who, at various times between 1956 and February 1, 1996, signed master recording agreements with defendants or their predecessors in interest. The gist of the complaint is that the recording contracts gave defendants no right to exploit plaintiffs' work in digital format. Plaintiffs allege that they and other proposed class members have no agreements with any defendant which authorize or entitle defendants to exploit plaintiffs' sound recordings in any form other than as phonograph records or other "analog media". Plaintiffs claim that their contracts, for which they receive trailing royalties for previously recorded works, did not confer rights on defendants to exploit the sound recordings through digital media including compact discs ("CD's") and digital audio files that can be distributed over the internet and across computer networks. Plaintiffs also claim that their contracts do not constitute the full agreements between the parties because they are subject to the terms and provisions of the National Codes of Fair Practice for Sound Recordings of the American Federation of Television and Radio Artists, (the "Phono Codes"), a series of collective bargaining agreements between the American Federation of Television and Radio Artists ("AFTRA") and record producers, which plaintiffs contend provide that the sound recordings could not be used in any medium other than phonograph records.

Plaintiffs aver that the new digital mastering technology that record companies adopted in the early 1980's enabled recordings to be copied without the loss of sound quality or distortions associated with the copying of analog recordings; thus digitalization was not permitted by the contracts or Phono Codes. Before the release of CD's in digital form, sound recordings could only be distributed in fixed tangible analog media (vinyl records or tapes). In or about 1999, an audio format, "MP3," was developed, allowing digital audio files to be compressed into much smaller files with little degradation of sound quality, which in turn made distribution over the Internet and across computer networks much easier (and permitted consumers to download digital audio files containing plaintiffs' and other class members' recordings at low or no cost). Plaintiffs also claim that various members of the recording industry, by prosecuting claims against MP3.com and Napstar, Inc. obtained settlements of approximately $15 to $20 million and warrants to purchase shares of MP3.com common stock and licensing fees of at least $6 million in exchange for releases. Plaintiffs claim that defendants had no right to enter into any agreements with MP3.com or Napster licensing the right to distribute sound recordings in digital form over the Internet.

Specifically, plaintiffs and putative class members seek compensatory and punitive damages for the following allegations. Plaintiffs allege defendants breached express and implied provisions of the recording contracts, as modified by the "Phono Codes", by digitalizing recordings and allowing or facilitating distribution of recordings over the internet, without protecting plaintiffs' rights to royalties and licensing fees. . . . Additionally, plaintiffs claim that defendants negligently and recklessly exposed class members to the risk of music piracy by releasing sound recordings in digital audio files on CDs, and that defendants breached both implied covenants of good faith and fair dealing and a fiduciary obligation to protect plaintiffs' beneficial interests or property rights in their sound recordings.

Defendants' Claims

Defendants move to dismiss on the basis that the plain language of each of the recording agreements in question provided that in exchange for royalties, plaintiffs gave all of their rights in the sound recordings to the record companies. . . .

[¶]. . . DISCUSSION

Motion to dismiss [¶] . . . *Breach of Contract Claims*

Based on the submissions contained here, it appears that all of the original agreements contain provisions that conveyed full ownership rights to the master recordings to the defendant companies or their predecessors. While there is some variation among the contracts, they all contain language identical or similar to the following:

> All recordings, phonograph record masters and reproductions made therefrom, together with the performances embodied therein, shall be entirely [the Record Company's] property. [The Record Company] shall have the unrestricted right to manufacture, use, distribute and sell sound productions of the

performances recorded hereunder made by any method now known, or hereafter to become known. . .

(Atlantic Contract) See also Columbia Contract, RCA Contract, PolyGram Contract, aff. of Katherine B. Forrest.

Such contracts have been interpreted according to their plain meaning. The words by any method now or hereafter known or to become known, which are contained in these contracts clearly anticipate development of new technologies. See discussion in *Greenfield v. Philles Records Inc.,* 98 N.Y.2d 562, 750 N.Y.S.2d 565, 780 N.E.2d 166 (2002).

In *Greenfield v. Philles Records Inc.,* 98 N.Y.2d 562, 750 N.Y.S.2d 565, 780 N.E.2d 166 (2002), the Court of Appeals, interpreting a recording artist's contract transfer of ownership rights to a record company, held that in the absence of "an explicit contractual reservation of rights by the artists," the "artists' transfer of full ownership rights to the master recordings of musical performances carried with it the unconditional right of the producer to redistribute those performances in any technological format." 98 N.Y.2d at 566, 750 N.Y.S.2d 565, 780 N.E.2d 166. That case involved the right of Philles Records to license master recordings for synchronization and redistribution of domestic licenses in 1987 based on a 1963 contract. The Court found that, despite the technological innovations that are revolutionizing the recording industry, long settled common-law contract law governed. The broad contractual provisions of the agreements conveying to the defendants the "right to make phonograph records, tape recordings or other reproductions of the performances embodied in such recordings by any method now or hereafter known", *id.* at 568–69, 750 N.Y.S.2d 565, 780 N.E.2d 166, was a clear and unambiguous provision that authorized defendants to license performances for use in all visual media, i.e., television or movies. The Court stated that "a written agreement that is complete, clear and unambiguous on its face must be enforced according to the plain meaning of its terms," *Id.* at 569, 750 N.Y.S.2d 565, 780 N.E.2d 166.

The conclusion reached by the Court of Appeals in *Greenfield,* supra, mirrored that reached by Judge Rakoff, in the Southern District action when he stated

> This language (and the equivalent language in the other contracts) is clear. Without limitation it conveys all of plaintiffs' rights in these recordings to the [r]ecord [c]ompanies, including the right to exploit the recordings by any method whatsoever, whether known at the time or 'hereafter to become known.' *Chambers,* 123 F.Supp.2d at 200.

Plaintiff's claim that, somehow, the fact that the recording contracts here were subject to AFTRA union contracts or "Phono Codes" distinguishes their situation from that of the Ronettes in *Greenfield* is not persuasive.

The Phono Codes are a series of fair practices agreements between AFTRA and the record companies which govern minimum wage and fee compensation and terms, including minimal payments for benefits to welfare funds and conditions for the engagement of artists making phonograph recordings. They do not affect the broader contractual provisions that convey the artists' property rights to the record companies. In fact, the language of some of the AFTRA agreements or the Phono Codes specifically permits copying of master recordings on "microgroove recordings or tape or any other similar or dissimilar device now or hereafter devised." (Provision 8 of the 1962 AFTRA contract) *See also Chambers,* 123 F.Supp.2d at 201, rejecting the claim that AFTRA contracts affect the recording contracts. Thus the breach of contract claims must be dismissed.

* * * *

Negligence Claim

Plaintiffs also assert that defendants negligently failed to protect plaintiffs' rights to maximize royalties by releasing digital files that were subject to piracy. However, such claim is unavailing because the contractual rights specifically provide for the right to exploit the copyrighted Sound Recordings in "future technologies", which clearly includes compact discs and other digital media. A plaintiff cannot transform a claim for breach of contract into a negligence claim by merely alleging a breach of due care. ". . . A simple breach of contract is not to be considered a tort unless a legal duty independent of the contract itself has been violated." *Clark-Fitzpatrick, Inc. v. Long Island R. Co.,* 70 N.Y.2d 382, 389, 521 N.Y.S.2d 653, 516 N.E.2d 190 (1987). The only possible claim for negligence is the creation of digital audio files that were subject to piracy. Compact discs were first created or distributed some twenty years ago (1983) and, therefore, a claim arising from that act is time barred under CPLR 214(6). The piracy occurred many years later in 1999 and 2000, and, in fact, defendants aggressively pursued claims against the wrongdoers in the Napster and MP.3 litigations; the injunctions obtained in those lawsuits will accrue to the benefit of plaintiffs.

* * * *

Based on the foregoing, the claims set forth, are hereby dismissed and the clerk is directed to ENTER Judgment for defendants.

_____

NOTES AND QUESTIONS

1.   Should an "irrevocable" grant of rights be subject to rescission, even for a material breach of contract? Entities that exploit creative works build their business on licensing of and long-term investment in the works. Are there monetary damages that could compensate for a material breach (e.g. continuing payments of revenues from exploitation) without reversion of copyright? Or should authors be able to reclaim their works if their assignees have not complied with their end of the bargain? Do the policies underlying the renewal provisions in the 1909 Copyright Act and termination provisions of the 1976 Act have any import in this debate, or should it solely be a matter of state contract law?

2.   Broad or ambiguous grants of rights in recording and publishing agreements will inevitably lead to claims based on unfairness or lack of mutual intent to assign/convey rights that were not in existence at the time of the agreement. Should the relative knowledge/experience of the parties to the agreement be a consideration in interpreting these clauses? Should the court consider the fairness of consideration for a grant of as-yet-unknown rights in hindsight, after it is clear what those rights were worth once they came into existence, or should the parties be held to the risks inherent in the language to which they agree? Why or why not?

2. DURATION OF THE CONTRACT

Distinct from provisions governing the duration of any grant or license of rights to the works covered by the agreement, recording and songwriting agreements will include express provisions addressing the duration of the contract itself—i.e., how long the relationship between the songwriter and publisher or recording artist and label will last. The following questions will typically be addressed:

- Will the contract last for a specified period of time? If so, when does it become effective, and when will it end?

- Alternatively, does the contract require delivery of a certain number of songs or master recordings? If so, what counts as "delivery" and who decides whether the work is acceptable?

- Will there be any options to renew the agreement once the initial period (whether it be defined by a specified time or a specified number of works) has expired? If so, who holds those options? How many option periods does that party hold?

SAMPLE RECORDING CONTRACT PROVISION RE DURATION

The term of this Agreement shall commence on the date hereof and shall continue until six (6) months following delivery by Artist to Company of the first LP (defined herein) featuring the performances of Artist ("Initial Period"). Artist hereby grants to Company four (4) separate and consecutive options to extend the term of this Agreement under the same terms and conditions for additional periods (each an "Option Period") commencing upon the expiration of the Initial Period or the immediately preceding Option Period, if any, and expiring six (6) months after Artist's delivery to Company of the requisite LP for the respective Option Period. Each Option Period shall be deemed automatically exercised by Company unless Company sends Artist written notice to the contrary no later than thirty (30) days prior to the end of the then current Option Period, if any.

> **SAMPLE EXCLUSIVE SONGWRITING CONTRACT
> PROVISION RE DURATION**
>
> *The term of this Agreement (the "Term") shall begin on the date hereof
> and continue through the initial commercial release by a major record
> Company of a Qualifying Album in the United States (referred to
> herein as the "Commercial Release"). During the Term, Writer shall
> deliver to Publisher one (1) Album. An album ("Album") shall mean
> one (1) or more compact discs, or the equivalent, embodying at least
> thirty-five (35) minutes of music and no fewer than ten (10) musical
> compositions, which is Commercially Released during the Term.*

a. Duration Disputes and California's Seven-Year Statute, Cal. Lab. Code § 2855

Given the nature of the creative process in both songwriting and
recording, it is perhaps not surprising that the duration of many publishing
and recording contracts is tied to delivery of a specified number of songs or
master recordings—typically a number sufficient to make up an album,
although as the market increasingly moves away from album sales to
single-song digital streaming, the number of deliverable works called for
by these agreements is more subject to individual negotiation. Exclusive
songwriting agreements for songwriters who are not also performing
artists, and thus who are not producing albums from the songs that they
compose, are more often likely to include a term of years rather than
recording agreements—as well as options in favor of the publisher.

Although contracts that last until a specified number of works are
delivered can take pressure off of creators to produce songs or recordings
on an arbitrary timeline, they also can stretch out over many years—
particularly if options are exercised to extend them beyond the original
number of works. During that time, the nature of the relationship between
the parties can change drastically; executives who worked with a creator
might leave, the company might change ownership and switch its
emphasis, a writer or performer might change her musical interests, public
interest in the genre might wane, etc. When the relationship between a
company and an author sours, there are significant commercial challenges
that arise on both sides. On the one hand, companies that have made a
substantial, up-front investment in the author will want to reap the
benefits of their agreements should the author produce commercially
successful work in the period covered by the agreement. On the other hand,
composers and artists who do not want to remain in an unproductive
relationship with a publisher or label are unable to leave and pursue their
livelihood elsewhere without breaching their contracts.

One widely-publicized example of this conflict is the litigation between the band 30 Seconds to Mars and its label, EMI/Virgin, in 2008, which highlights how some state law protections against long-term personal services contracts apply in the music industry. In 2008, EMI/Virgin filed a lawsuit against Jared and Shannon Leto, alleging breach of contract in connection with the recording agreement entered into between the parties for the defendants' band, 30 Seconds to Mars. As Jared Leto explained the lawsuit on the band's web page:

> We had been signed to our record contract for 9 years. Basically, under California law, where we live and signed our deal, one cannot be bound to a contract for more than 7 years. . . . It is a law that protects people from lengthy, unfair, career-spanning contracts. . . . That, and other issues, like the new regime at EMI. . . made it easy to not want to continue as is.[10]

The California Labor Code provision referenced in Leto's statement as the grounds for termination of the band's recording agreement, **Cal. Lab. Code § 2855**, provided in pertinent part as follows:

(a) Except as otherwise provided in subdivision (b), a contract to render personal service . . . may not be enforced against the employee beyond seven years from the commencement of service under it. . . .

(b) Notwithstanding subdivision (a):

(1) Any employee who is a party to a contract to render personal service in the production of phonorecords in which sounds are first fixed, as defined in Section 101 of Title 17 of the United States Code, may not invoke the provisions of subdivision (a) without first giving written notice to the employer . . . specifying that the employee from and after a future date certain specified in the notice will no longer render service under the contract by reason of subdivision (a). . . .

(3) If a party to a contract described in paragraph (1) is, or could contractually be, required to render personal service in the production of a specified quantity of the phonorecords and fails to render all of the required service prior to the date specified in the notice provided in paragraph (1), the party damaged by the

---

<hr>

[10]   Jared Leto, A Letter from the Front: 30 Seconds to Mars/EMI (the Lawsuit) (8/18/2008), *originally available at* http://thirtysecondstomars.forumsunlimited.com/index.php?showtopic=312 534. For those who are interested in more about this dispute, a one-sided but detailed view of the dispute from the band's perspective is preserved in the documentary *Artifact*, filmed by the band from the start of the litigation through its ultimate settlement.

> failure shall have the right to recover damages for each phonorecord as to which that party has failed to render service in an action that, notwithstanding paragraph (2), shall be commenced within 45 days after the date specified in the notice.

Thus, Leto's characterization of the protections afforded under the California statute did not consider that performing artist contracts with record labels are an exception to the broad terms of California's seven-year statute. The statute was passed in response to concerns raised by film actors during the decades when they were required to sign exclusive personal services contracts with film studios that required them to perform in a specified number of films and precluded them from working for any other studio during the term of their contracts. However, the exception for recording artists was added in 1987 after a lobbying effort by the recording industry.

Songwriters who sign contracts with terms tied to delivery of a certain number of songs may take advantage of the California statute and terminate their publishing agreements, but performing artists may only do so if they are willing and able to pay damages to their former record label as a result of their nondelivery of the required number of recordings—the calculation of which is left unspecified and uncertain. To date, all of the disputes that have arisen between labels and recording artists regarding application of the California seven-year statute—including the one between 30 Seconds to Mars and Virgin/EMI—have been settled, with no judicial resolution of the question of how damages for failure to deliver the specified number of recordings are to be calculated under the statute.[11]

b. Disputes over Delivery Requirements

In the context of songwriter agreements, the product that must be delivered is often described as follows:

---

[11] Another widely-publicized dispute between a recording artist and her record label in which the California seven-year statute was invoked occurred in 2000 between Courtney Love and Vivendi Universal Music Group. Vivendi Universal sued Love, alleging she had failed to deliver five albums under her recording contract; Love countersued, alleging unfair conduct by the label and seeking to terminate the recording contract, in part based upon section 2855. At one point, Love vowed she would never settle, but in 2002 a settlement was announced in which her band, Hole, recovered ownership of their unreleased masters and Hole gave Universal rights to release new albums from her deceased husband's band, Nirvana. *See* Anthony Breznican, *Courtney Love Settles Lawsuit*, CBS NEWS (Sept. 27, 2002).

EXCLUSIVE SONGWRITING CONTRACT
SAMPLE PROVISION RE DELIVERY

Each Composition delivered shall be commercially satisfactory in the sole discretion of Publisher. Publisher shall advise Writer of any Compositions Publisher deems unsatisfactory by written notice within forty-five (45) days after delivery.

In the context of recording agreements, the "delivery" requirement typically has an additional layer, as illustrated by the sample provision below:

RECORDING CONTRACT SAMPLE PROVISION RE DELIVERY

A Master shall not be deemed delivered hereunder unless and until it is technically and commercially satisfactory to Company.

The "technically and commercially satisfactory to Company" language presents both an objective and a subjective standard for the label to apply. The "technically satisfactory" requirement is based on standards in the industry for quality of a recording for commercial release; compliance with this provision is governed by easily-discernible practices in the industry and has become easier and less expensive as technology has improved. The "commercially satisfactory" requirement, however, is much more subjective in nature and gives labels a great deal of discretion in determining whether a master recording "counts" in the required number of works delivered under the contract. How much discretion a label will be given will depend on the precise wording of the agreement; at the very least, though, such determinations must be grounded in good faith.

Although there have been many reported disputes between artists and labels regarding the scope of a label's discretion in refusing delivery of masters for failure to meet the "commercially satisfactory" requirement, they are typically settled before courts are asked to weigh in on whether a particular recording meets the requirement. Some of the most publicized disputes involving a recording artist's delivery of "commercially satisfactory" masters include the following:

- **Neil Young and Geffen Records**:[12] Young left Reprise Records, with whom he had been signed since his debut album in 1968, to go to Geffen Records in 1982 with a promise of a $1 million advance per album and complete creative control. The first album he recorded under his agreement with Geffen was *Trans*, an electronic album with heavy synthesizers that was a big stylistic shift from his previous work—a blend of country, folk, and rock recordings. Geffen accepted the album, but it met with widespread criticism and poor sales. The next album that Young delivered to Geffen, called *Old Ways*, was pure country. Geffen rejected it as commercially unsatisfactory, informing Young that it wanted his next album to be a rock and roll album. In response, Young delivered *Everybody's Rockin'*—a collection of rockabilly songs, some of which were covers and some of which he had written years before but never recorded. Although he intended to make it a concept album, with two additional songs, when he delivered the first ten songs to Geffen, Geffen canceled his remaining recording sessions and released it as a 25-minute album. It was critically panned and a commercial failure. In December, 1983, Geffen sued Young for $3.3 million for making music that was not "commercial" and "unrepresentative" of himself, and Young countersued for $21 million, claiming that Geffen had breached its obligation to give him complete creative control. Ultimately, the parties dismissed their claims after Geffen apologized; Young recorded two more albums with Geffen before returning to Reprise.

- **Tom Petty and MCA Records**: Tom Petty had earned a reputation for standing up to his label by the time he delivered *Into the Great Wide Open* to MCA in 1991. Upon learning of MCA's acquisition of Shelter Records, he sought to exercise a clause in the band's contract with Shelter that gave the band members approval over assignments of the contract to another label; when MCA sued him for breach of contract, he self-funded the recording of his third album and then declared bankruptcy when MCA would not let him distribute it. "To pay for their legal bills, the Heartbreakers went on a short tour, the 'Lawsuit Tour.' They wore T-shirts that said, 'Why MCA?' "[13] They settled this dispute, with

---

[12]   For an interview with Neil Young that details, from his perspective, this dispute, see Chris Clancy, *From the Vault: Neil Young*, MONEY, September 2, 2010.

[13]   Gary Jules, *Op Ed: That Time Tom Petty Wouldn't Back Down*, LOS ANGELES TIMES (Oct. 9, 2017), *available at* https://www.latimes.com/opinion/op-ed/la-oe-jules-how-tom-petty-took-on-the-music-industry-20171010-story.html.

Petty and the Heartbreakers signing with one of MCA's labels, but the relationship was not an easy one. When Petty delivered the masters for *Full Moon Fever*, his first solo album, to MCA in 1988, MCA initially rejected it as commercially unsatisfactory, stating that they "didn't hear a single."[14] In response, Petty turned his focus to his ongoing projects with the Traveling Wilburys, and MCA eventually agreed to release *Full Moon Fever* in 1989, excluding two of the songs recorded in the original sessions for the album and adding three later-recorded songs.[15] The album ended up producing five singles, one of which, *Free Fallin'*, was Petty's highest charting Billboard single, selling more than five million copies.

In 1991, Petty reunited with the Heartbreakers and released *Into the Great Wide Open* through MCA. The title song included the lines:

> *The papers said "Ed always played from the heart"*
> *He got an agent and a roadie named Bart*
> *They made a record and it went in the chart*
> *The sky was the limit*
>
> *His leather jacket had chains that would jingle*
> *They both met movie stars, partied and mingled*
> *Their A&R man said, "I don't hear a single"*
> *The future was wide open*[16]

- **Fiona Apple and Epic Records**: Fiona Apple delivered her third album, *Extraordinary Machine*, to Epic Records in 2003. The first recording of the album was produced by Jon Brion, and Epic initially rejected it for lack of commercial appeal. Apple ultimately rerecorded the tracks with the help of producer Mike Elizondo and Epic agreed to release the revamped version in the fall of 2005. "It's rumored that Epic only gave Apple enough money to re-record one track at a time, and the doe-eyed singer's loyal fans were stirring an already bubbling pot. One such fan, Dave Muscato, launched the site FreeFiona.com, a campaign to petition Epic and owner Sony Music Entertainment for the long-awaited release of *Machine*. Fans sent boxes of foam apples to express their impatient displeasure in the label's withholding the

---

[14] *See* PAUL ZOLLO, CONVERSATIONS WITH TOM PETTY 118–19 (Omnibus Press 2005).

[15] *See 100 Best Albums of the Eighties: 92, Tom Petty, "Full Moon Fever,"* ROLLING STONE (Nov. 16, 1989), *available at* https://www.rollingstone.com/music/music-lists/100-best-albums-of-the-eighties-150477/tom-petty-full-moon-fever-56934/.

[16] Tom Petty, INTO THE GREAT WIDE OPEN (MCA Records 1991).

album."[17] The album went on to being certified as gold by the RIAA, selling more than a million copies. Apple did not release a fourth album with Epic until 2012.

• **Wilco and Reprise Records**:[18] Wilco's dispute with Reprise, like the dispute between 30 Seconds to Mars and Virgin/EMI referred to above, is a prime example of how the rapid consolidation of the recording industry impacted ongoing contractual relationships between artists and labels that changed leadership. In 2001, Wilco completed its *Yankee Hotel Foxtrot* album, right around the time that Time Warner merged with AOL. The merger resulted in termination of 600 employees, one of whom was Reprise Records President Howie Klein, who had been Wilco's strong supporter during the band's relationship with the label. Reprise's newly appointed executives who oversaw Wilco's contract did not see any singles in *Yankee Hotel Foxtrot* and declared it not commercially satisfactory. After Wilco declined repeated requests by the label's new management to rework the album, it was officially rejected by Reprise. Wilco was ultimately able to negotiate buyout terms with Reprise, acquiring the rights to the album and streaming it on their website. Eventually, the band signed with another AOL/Time Warner imprint, Nonesuch Records, which released the album in 2002 to both critical acclaim and commercial success.

NOTES AND QUESTIONS

1.   How do you think courts should interpret the damage provision of Cal. Labor Code Section 2855? Should lost revenues be a part of that calculation, or should recording artists simply have to reimburse labels for unrecouped advances and expenses as a condition for termination under the statute?

2.   What policy rationales might support the exception to California's seven-year statute for recording artists as compared to other entertainers/creators who enter into personal services contracts in California?

3.   Is a grant of complete creative control over an album consistent with a requirement of delivery of a "commercially satisfactory" recording? Why or why not?

---

[17]   Neph Basedow, *Top Six Artist Vs. Record Label Feuds*, THE HOUSTON PRESS (Jan. 7, 2011), available at https://www.houstonpress.com/music/top-six-artist-vs-record-label-feuds-6507606.

[18]   For more detail about this dispute, see Neph Basedow, *Top Six Artist Vs. Record Label Feuds*, The Houston Press (Jan. 7, 2011), available at https://www.houstonpress.com/music/top-six-artist-vs-record-label-feuds-6507606.

4. How do you think courts should evaluate whether a recording meets the "commercially satisfactory" requirement under a contract if the issue is ever presented to them? Given that only one out of five albums will typically break even for record labels, how much weight should their subjective evaluation be given? If applying a more objective standard, what sort of evidence should courts consider in evaluating the likely commercial success of a recording?

5. How should the change of personnel at a record label or publisher impact the contractual relationship of the parties? It's understandable that "relationships matter," and that certain individuals inside a label or publisher become a significant influencer on the creator's experience. But it is also typical and natural that companies have changes in personnel. How should the parties anticipate and account for this challenge when initially setting forth their commercial relationship?

6. What are the arguments in favor of and against allowing ownership of recordings to revert to recording artists if they are rejected by a record label as unsatisfactory? Giving the policies underlying the Copyright Clause of the U.S. Constitution, should labels be able to prevent release of recordings it deems "commercially unsatisfactory"? Why or why not?

3. DEFINITION/CALCULATION/ DISTRIBUTION OF COMPENSATION

The first issue that is typically addressed regarding compensation is whether the composer or performing artist will be paid a specified, up-front fee; earn royalties from revenues earned from exploiting the song or record; or some combination of the two. Most exclusive songwriting agreements and recording agreements include what is called an ***advance***—a specified sum of money that is paid to the composer or performing artist by the publisher or label at the start of the contractual relationship that the publisher or label then gets to recoup from earnings before any additional payments are made to the composer/artist. ***Royalties*** are typically a specified percentage of net revenues received by the publisher/label from exploitation of the works—and the percentage can vary widely depending upon the nature of the use and the negotiating power of the composer/artist. Composers often get both an advance and royalties; lead performers (especially well-known performers) on a sound recording also often receive both. Backup singers and studio musicians usually only receive a fixed, up-front payment for their participation in the recording, plus whatever benefits they are entitled to through union negotiations (mainly for studio musicians) and statutory provisions (for example, digital performances of sound recordings require that a percentage of revenues be paid to non-featured artists and musicians).

Whether any royalties are ultimately paid under contracts that give a percentage of net revenue to the composer/artist will greatly depend on both the amount of the advance and the success of the work—for example, high-advance deals may net very little in the way of royalties regardless of the royalty percentage, but hugely successful compositions or sound recordings with a relatively low advance may end up paying out significant royalties to the composer/artist. Viewed from the publisher's or label's perspective, advances are an investment in an uncertain future product; most record deals, for example, do not break even on the advance paid to recording artists. Viewed from a composer or artist's perspective, advances are essentially an interest-free, guaranteed payment against future royalties—money that they are guaranteed to keep, but that reduces the royalties they receive in the future from revenues earned through exploiting their works.

Disputes over the calculation of royalties are commonplace in the industry. Many factors contribute to such disputes, including (a) ambiguous contractual language regarding how royalties will be calculated; (b) when and how accountings for royalties may be audited and challenged; (c) exploitation of new uses for works that do not fall clearly into an existing category for revenue sharing; and (d) difficulty in attributing income from equity deals or settlements that involve entire catalogs or multiple works.

a. Ambiguous Contractual Language Regarding Royalty Calculation

Even when parties agree upon language for how royalties are to be calculated, misunderstandings frequently arise regarding how payments from different sources of revenues are to be divided and what costs may be deducted by the publisher/label before the songwriter's/artist's share is calculated. The case below is illustrative of how these disputes often play out.

War Original Lineup, 1976,
Source: Lee Oskar and Harold Brown
(Wardrums)

BROWN V. GOLDSTEIN
34 Cal. App. 5th 418 (2019)

ZELON, J.

Former and current members of the band WAR filed a breach of contract action alleging that their music publisher had failed to pay them a share of the royalties generated from public performances of the band's songs.

The publisher filed a motion for summary judgment arguing that the parties' music publishing agreement did not require it to pay the band any royalties derived from song performances. Plaintiffs, however, argued the agreement was ambiguous, and filed extrinsic evidence in support of their interpretation. The trial court concluded the agreement was not reasonably susceptible to the plaintiffs' proposed interpretation, and granted judgment in the publisher's favor. We reverse.

FACTUAL BACKGROUND

A. Background Information Regarding the Music Publishing Industry

. . . . Under the traditional form of music publishing agreement, the songwriter assigns his or her copyright interest in the composition to the publisher. In return, the publisher agrees to promote and exploit the composition on the market, and pay the songwriter his or her share of royalties. (See generally Broadcast Music, Inc. v. Roger Miller Music, Inc. (6th Cir. 2005) 396 F.3d 762, 765 (Roger Miller) [describing the "basics of the music industry"].)

There are four primary categories of royalty income generated from music publishing: (1) "mechanical royalties," consisting of income from the sale of records, audio cassettes, compact discs, etc.; (2) "synchronization royalties," consisting of income from music that is synchronized with a visual image, such as a movie, television show or commercial; (3) "song book and folio royalties," consisting of income from the sale of printed music; and (4) "public performance royalties," consisting of income from public performances of the music composition. . . .

In standard publishing agreements, the publisher is responsible for collecting the first three categories of royalties from third parties who have licensed the composition, and then paying the songwriter his or her contracted share of those royalties, typically 50 percent. However, the writer and publisher normally agree to affiliate with a "performing rights organization" (PRO) to collect and distribute public performance royalties (hereafter performance royalties or performance income). . . . (Roger Miller, supra, 396 F.3d at p. 765.) "Commonly, writers and publishers agree to be paid their respective shares of performing rights royalties directly by the [PRO]." (Ibid.) As with most other forms of music publishing income, the songwriter is typically entitled to 50 percent of the performance royalties, and the publisher is entitled to the remaining 50 percent.

B. Summary of the Parties' Agreements

1. The 1970 Agreement

In 1970, each member of the band WAR entered into an identically-worded music publishing agreement with Far Out Music (FOM), then owned by Gerald Goldstein and his now-deceased partner, Stephen Gold. In exchange for each band member's copyrights to the music compositions he had written (or co-authored), FOM agreed to pay the following royalties, set forth in paragraph 9: (1) 4 cents per copy of sheet music, and 10 percent of income generated from sale of music folios; and (2) 50 percent of the net sums received from mechanical royalties, synchronization royalties and foreign income (income generated from the sale or license of the compositions outside the United States). Paragraph 9(d) of the Agreement, however, directed that the writer "shall receive his public performance royalties . . . directly from his own affiliated performing rights society and shall have no claim whatsoever against publisher for any royalties received by publisher as a distribution from any performing right society which makes payment directly . . . to writers authors and composers."[FN2 omitted]

The 1970 Agreement did not entitle the band members to any form of payment other than the royalties set forth in paragraph 9.

2. The 1972 Memorandum of Understanding

Following the publication of a successful album in 1971, the band retained attorney Nicholas Clainos to represent them in litigation against FOM and several FOM-related entities. As part of the litigation, the band sought to terminate the 1970 Agreement, and negotiate a new agreement that included more favorable terms.

After extensive negotiations between Clainos and Stephen Gold, the parties signed a "Memorandum of Agreement" on August 22, 1972 (the MOA) that included the following preface: "Prior to the preparation of formal contracts between [the band members] and [FOM], this memorandum of agreement will confirm the agreements we have reached with respect to the subject matter contained herein." The MOA further provided that each band member would "enter into an exclusive songwriter agreement upon the terms and conditions hereinafter set forth, as well as those standard terms which are customary in the entertainment industry in the agreements of this type."

Paragraph 3(b) of the MOA described the royalties FOM had agreed to pay the band, which were essentially identical to the royalties set forth in paragraph 9 of the 1970 Agreement. . . .

In addition to the royalties described in paragraph 3(b), however, the MOA included a new provision, set forth at paragraph 3(e), that entitled the band to a share of the income FOM received from the exploitation of the compositions: "In addition to the foregoing, the writer shall receive with respect to those songs which he has written, a sum equal to 30% . . . share of publisher's income (after deduction for collection fees, direct costs and administration fees)."

The final paragraph of the MOA reiterated that the terms set forth therein "correctly reflect[ed] [the signatories'] mutual understanding. . . . Until formal contracts are entered into . . . reflecting the agreements set forth above, this memorandum of agreement shall for all purposes govern and bind the parties hereto."

3.   The 1972 Agreement

Shortly after signing the MOA, the parties signed the 1972 Agreement, which was to take effect as of August 22, 1972, the same date the MOA was signed.[FN3 omitted]

Paragraph 7 of the 1972 Agreement set forth the royalties FOM agreed to pay the band, which were the same amounts set forth in paragraph 3(b) of the MOA. The 1972 Agreement however, contained modified language regarding the payment of performance royalties. Paragraph 7(c), for example, stated that the writer was to receive "50% of any and all net sums actually received by the Publisher from the mechanical rights, electrical transcriptions, . . . synchronization and . . . and all other rights (except as otherwise specifically provided for herein) . . ., except that the Writer shall not be entitled to share in any sum or sums received by the Publisher from [a PRO]." Paragraph 7(d) similarly provided that band members were entitled to 50 percent of the net sum of any foreign income "other than public performance uses for which Writer is paid by any [PRO]."

Finally, paragraph 7(f) confirmed that "the publisher shall not be required to pay royalties earned by reasons of the public performances of the composition; said royalties being payable only by the [PRO] with which Writer is or may in the future become affiliated."

As with the MOA, the 1972 Agreement included an additional provision, set forth at paragraph 22, that entitled the writer to receive a 30 percent share of FOM's revenue after the deduction of certain administrative costs and fees:

> "22. In addition to the royalties provided for in Paragraph 7 above, all monies actually earned and received from the sale, lease, license, disposition or other turning to account of rights in the Compositions, including all monies received in connection with the infringement by third parties of rights in the Compositions ("Composition Gross Receipts") shall be treated as follows:
>
> > (a) Publisher shall be entitled first to deduct any and all administration and related fees from the Composition Gross receipts. . . .;
> >
> > (b) Publisher shall then deduct from Composition Gross Receipts . . . the royalties due to the composers of the composition in accordance with any agreement the Publisher may have with such composers;
> >
> > (c) From the balance of the Composition Gross Receipts remaining . . ., Publisher shall be entitled to deduct and retain amounts equal to the following direct costs actually advanced or incurred by Publisher in realizing Composition Gross Receipts (Composition Costs): All costs of copyrighting

the composition; ... legal fees [relating to any claim of copyright infringement]; Accounting fees. . . . [etc.];

(d) 30% of the balance of the Composition Gross Receipts remaining after the deductions provided for in Paragraphs 22(a), 22(b) or 22(c) hereof . . . shall belong to Writer and be paid to Writer. . . ."

4. The 1975 Agreement and subsequent litigation

In 1975, FOM and the band members signed a new agreement (the 1975 Agreement) that modified the payout formula set forth in paragraph 22 of the 1972 Agreement. The new revenue sharing provision provided that, after the deductions of certain administrative costs and fees, FOM would be entitled to 25 percent of the Composition Gross Receipts, and the writer would be entitled to the remaining balance. . . .

In 2009 and 2011, several band members brought multiple lawsuits in connection with FOM's payment of royalties under the parties' publishing agreements. The litigation resulted in two settlement agreements, both of which contained language confirming that the 1972 Agreement and 1975 Agreement remained in effect.

C. The Current Litigation

1. Summary of plaintiffs' claims

In October 2014, several current and former band members (or their successors-in-interest) (collectively plaintiffs or the band) filed the current breach of contract action against FOM, Gerald Goldstein and numerous FOM-related entities (collectively FOM). The complaint alleged FOM had violated the terms of the 1972 Agreement by excluding public performance royalties from "Composition Gross Receipts" described in paragraph 22, denying plaintiffs their right to share in that category of income.

The complaint alleged paragraph 22 defined Composition Gross Receipts to include "all moneys" FOM had received from the sale, lease or license of the compositions, which necessarily included any performance royalties FOM had received from its PRO. The complaint further alleged FOM had consistently "paid [plaintiffs] royalties on [its share] of 'performance income' without fail for nearly four decades." In December of 2013, however, FOM "suddenly . . ., [and] without any basis for doing so, eliminated [its] share of public performance as a category of income for which [it] w[as] paying participant royalties. . . ."

In their prayer for relief, plaintiffs sought a declaration that FOM's "share of public performance revenue is to be included in the revenue base upon which [FOM] account[s] to and pay[s] Plaintiffs pursuant . . . to paragraph 22 of the [1972 Agreement]." They also sought contract damages for any accounting period during which FOM had excluded its performance royalties from Composition Gross Receipts.[FN4 omitted]

2.   FOM's motion for summary judgment

a.   Summary of FOM's motion

FOM filed a motion for summary judgment arguing that the plain and unambiguous language of the 1972 Agreement made clear that the publisher's performance royalties were to be excluded from paragraph 22's revenue-sharing provision. . . .

FOM further asserted that paragraph 22 could not be read to "grant rights [to plaintiffs] that [were] specifically excluded by Paragraph 7." FOM explained that the revenue-sharing payment described in paragraph 22 was to be made "in addition to" whatever royalties were due under paragraph 7, which expressly excluded any type of payment for performance royalties. FOM contended that because paragraph 7 excluded performance royalties, such royalties were necessarily excluded from paragraph 22. According to FOM, any other interpretation would render paragraph 7's exclusion of performance royalties meaningless.

* * * *

b.   Plaintiffs' opposition and extrinsic evidence

Plaintiffs, however, argued the 1972 Agreement should be interpreted to require FOM to include performance royalties in the base amount used to calculate the revenue-sharing payment due under paragraph 22. Plaintiffs noted that paragraph 22 specifically defined Composition Gross Receipts to include "all moneys" FOM had received from the sale or lease of the compositions, and contained no language excluding performance royalties. Plaintiffs further asserted the language FOM had cited in paragraph 7 was merely intended to clarify that FOM had no duty to pay plaintiffs royalties for performance revenue because the band was to receive all of its performance royalties directly from its PRO. Paragraph 22, in contrast, described a separate and distinct type of payment consisting of a share of all revenue FOM received from the exploitation of the music, including performance royalties.

In support of their opposition, plaintiffs submitted copies of all the parties' prior written agreements, and declarations from several witnesses. . . .

i.   Declaration of Nicholas Clainos

Nicholas Clainos's declaration stated that his primary contact at FOM during the negotiation of the 1972 Agreement was Steven Gold, who Clainos described as a co-owner of the company. Clainos asserted that he had told Gold the band would drop its legal claims regarding the 1970 Agreement if FOM agreed to enter into a new agreement that contained a provision entitling the band to participate in "the pool of the publisher's share of money," which was to include "the entire pot of money collected by the publisher for all sources, including the publisher's share of public performance monies." [¶] . . . .

Clainos further stated that before the parties signed the 1972 MOA, he reaffirmed with Gold that the band's 30 percent participation in FOM's share of revenue "was to include 100% of all revenue the publisher received, including the publisher's public performance revenue. [Gold] acknowledged that such was the agreement. . . ." Clainos also asserted that when drafting the 1972 Agreement, he and Gold "specifically . . . discuss[ed]" that paragraph 22 was intended to apply to all forms of revenue that FOM actually received, "including the publisher's share of public performance revenues, less only specifically delineated deductions."

ii. Declaration of Michael Perlstein

Michael Perlstein's declaration stated that he had over 50 years of experience representing clients in the music industry, and was "very familiar" with "the standard music publishing industry practices of [the 1970s], the customs and practices in connection with such contracts . . . and the customary usage of terminology in such contracts." . . . .

According to Perlstein, the plaintiffs' 1970 and 1972 Agreements reflected the favorable changes that more successful songwriters were able to impose on publishers during that era. Specifically, Perlstein explained that the original 1970 Agreement merely provided the band members traditional royalty payments, while the 1972 Agreement, negotiated after the band had become more successful, contained a new and additional paragraph entitling them to "receive from FOM, a portion of the publisher's share [of revenue]." [¶] . . . .

Perlstein contended that in his "nearly 50 years of experience of drafting and negotiating music publishing agreement[s] and evaluating them for [his] publishing catalogue clients . . ., [he had] never seen a music publishing contract which provided for songwriters to be paid a portion of the publisher's share of . . . income that did not include in its base amount, the publisher's share of public performance income."

iii. Declaration of Frederick Wolinsky

Frederick Wolinsky's declaration stated that he had "more than 35 years of experience in royalty and forensic accounting in the music industry," and had personally participated in an audit between the parties in 2007. Wolinsky further asserted that he had reviewed the parties' prior publishing agreements, and "at least 30 years of statements issued by defendants." Based on his review of those materials, Wolinsky concluded that until May of 2014, FOM had "consistently included [its] share of . . .

public performance revenue in . . . calculat[ing] . . . and pay[ing] Plaintiffs' . . . 'participant's share' under paragraph 22 of the 1972 [Agreement]."

[¶] . . . . Wolinsky further stated that in May of 2014, FOM sent plaintiffs a letter asserting that they were "not entitled to share in the publisher's share of performance royalties," and that some prior statements reflected an "overpayment in connection with performance royalties." The letter further explained that FOM intended to offset those overpayments against future royalty payments owed to plaintiffs. According to Perlstein, "[t]his reversed [FOM's] decades-old course of performance," and was "inconsistent with at least 30 years of prior statements."

3.   FOM's reply brief

In its reply brief, FOM reasserted that "the words of the [1972 Agreement] plainly and clearly manifest the intentions of the parties in 1972 that the publisher's public performance royalties would not be included in the calculation of royalties to plaintiffs." FOM further asserted that the trial court should not consider any of the plaintiffs' extrinsic evidence because the 1972 Agreement was not reasonably susceptible to their proposed interpretation. According to FOM, the extrinsic evidence was instead admitted for an improper purpose: "to create for the parties a contract which they did not make and . . . insert language which one party now wishes were there." . . . [¶]

D.   The Trial Court's Ruling and Judgment

After a hearing, the trial court issued an order granting FOM's motion for summary judgment. In its analysis, the court agreed with FOM that paragraph 7 impliedly excluded performance royalties from the payment due under paragraph 22: "The language of paragraph 7 . . . specifically excludes, in three separate subparagraphs, public performance royalties from being shared with the 'writer,' i.e., plaintiffs. It would be difficult to imagine a more clear mutual intention of the parties at that time. Nothing in the more general language of [paragraph] 22 of this agreement modifies this exclusion." . . . [¶]

On September 16, 2016, the court entered judgment in FOM's favor.

DISCUSSION

Plaintiffs argue that the trial court erred in concluding the 1972 Agreement is not reasonably susceptible to their proposed interpretation. Plaintiffs assert that the text of the document and the uncontroverted extrinsic evidence demonstrate that their proposed interpretation is not only reasonable, but also the correct interpretation of the parties' agreement.

A. Standard of Review and Applicable Law

* * * *

2. Rules governing the interpretation of contracts

"The rules governing the role of the court in interpreting a written instrument are well established. The interpretation of a contract is a judicial function. [Citations.] In engaging in this function, the trial court 'give[s] effect to the mutual intention of the parties as it existed' at the time the contract was executed. [Citation.] Ordinarily, the objective intent of the contracting parties is a legal question determined solely by reference to the contract's terms. [Citation.]" (Wolf v. Walt Disney Pictures & Television (2008) 162 Cal.App.4th 1107, 1125–1126, 76 Cal.Rptr.3d 585 (Wolf).)

"The court generally may not consider extrinsic evidence of any prior agreement or contemporaneous oral agreement to vary or contradict the clear and unambiguous terms of a written, integrated contract. [Citations.] Extrinsic evidence is admissible, however, to interpret an agreement when a material term is ambiguous. [Citations.]" (Wolf, supra, 162 Cal.App.4th at p. 1126, 76 Cal.Rptr.3d 585; see also Pacific Gas & Electric Co. v. G.W. Thomas Drayage & Rigging (1968) 69 Cal.2d 33, 39–40, 69 Cal.Rptr. 561, 442 P.2d 641 [if extrinsic evidence reveals that apparently clear language in the contract is, in fact, "susceptible to more than one reasonable interpretation," then extrinsic evidence may be used to determine the contracting parties' objective intent].)

"The interpretation of a contract involves 'a two-step process: First the court provisionally receives (without actually admitting) all credible evidence concerning the parties' intentions to determine "ambiguity," i.e., whether the language is "reasonably susceptible" to the interpretation urged by a party. If in light of the extrinsic evidence the court decides the language is "reasonably susceptible" to the interpretation urged, the extrinsic evidence is then admitted to aid in the second step—interpreting the contract. [Citation.]' [Citation.]" (Wolf v. Superior Court (2004) 114 Cal.App.4th 1343, 1351, 8 Cal.Rptr.3d 649 (Wolf II). . . .

"When there is no material conflict in the extrinsic evidence, the trial court interprets the contract as a matter of law. . . . [¶]

B. The 1972 Agreement is Reasonably Susceptible to Plaintiffs' Interpretation

The first question we must address is whether the 1972 Agreement "is 'reasonably susceptible' to the interpretation urged by [plaintiffs.] If it is not, the case is over. [Citation.]" (Southern Cal. Edison Co. v. Superior Court (1995) 37 Cal.App.4th 839, 847, 44 Cal.Rptr.2d 227 (Southern Cal. Edison).) After provisionally receiving plaintiffs' extrinsic evidence (except for those portions to which objections were sustained), the trial court concluded that the revenue-sharing provision in paragraph 22 could not be reasonably interpreted to include income FOM had received from performance royalties. In support, the court relied on language in paragraph 7 stating that plaintiffs were not entitled to share in any sums FOM had received from a PRO for performance royalties.

We disagree with the trial court's threshold determination. As the plaintiffs note, paragraph 22 of the agreement does not contain any language indicating that performance royalties are to be excluded from "Composition Gross Receipts," which defines the pool of income that is subject to plaintiffs' revenue sharing rights. Instead, paragraph 22 states that Composition Gross Receipts consists of "all monies actually earned and received from the sale, lease, license, disposition or other turning to account of rights in the Compositions. . . ." FOM does not dispute that performance royalties are a form of "money . . . earned" from the sale or license of the compositions that are subject to the 1972 Agreement. Thus, considered in isolation, the language of paragraph 22 supports the plaintiffs' interpretation of the agreement. [¶] . . . .

The language in paragraph 7 does not render plaintiffs' proposed interpretation of the 1972 Agreement unreasonable. Paragraph 7 and paragraph 22 address two distinct types of payments that FOM must pay to plaintiffs: royalty payments (paragraph 7) and a revenue-sharing payment (paragraph 22). The language in paragraph 7 that precludes plaintiffs from sharing in FOM's "performance income" can be reasonably interpreted as applying only to the type of payment described in paragraph 7, namely royalty payments. Paragraph 7 does not include any language stating that the exclusion of "performance fees" extends to paragraph 22's revenue-sharing provision. Moreover, the first clause of paragraph 22 directs that the revenue-sharing payment described therein is to be paid "In addition to the royalties provided for in Paragraph 7." The fact that plaintiffs are not entitled to receive royalty payments on FOM's performance income does not necessarily preclude them from receiving a portion of FOM's performance income based on the revenue-sharing payment described in paragraph 22, which is to be paid "in addition to" whatever royalties are due under paragraph 7.

FOM argues that plaintiffs' proposed interpretation of paragraph 22 would render "paragraph 7's specific exclusion of . . . public performance royalties . . . meaningless." As explained above, however, under plaintiffs' interpretation, the exclusionary language in paragraph 7 serves to clarify that while FOM must pay plaintiffs a 50 percent royalty on most forms of income, the performance income FOM receives from its PRO is not subject to that requirement. Paragraph 22, in turn, provides that "in addition to" the royalties described in paragraph 7, plaintiffs are entitled to a certain share (30 percent after various administrative costs and fees are deducted) of "all monies [FOM] actually earned and received" from the sale or licensing of the music compositions. Thus, the language in paragraph 7 and

22 are both given effect: the former provision establishes that FOM does not have to pay plaintiffs a 50 percent royalty on the performance income it receives from its PRO, while the latter provision establishes that such income is nonetheless subject to the revenue-sharing formula set forth in paragraph 22.

Plaintiffs' proposed interpretation is also supported by their extrinsic evidence. First, as explained in Clainos's declaration, prior to signing the 1972 Agreement, the parties entered into a MOA that summarized the terms of what they had agreed to. The MOA expressly states that the signatories agreed that it "reflect[ed]" the terms of the agreement that were to be included in their "formal contract[ ]." Paragraph 3(b) of the MOA sets forth the royalties FOM agreed to pay plaintiffs, and includes language clarifying that plaintiffs were to obtain "any and all performance moneys" from ASCAP, and not from FOM. Paragraph 3(e) of the MOA sets forth the revenue participation payment, directing that "in addition to the foregoing, the writer shall receive . . . 30% of [FOM's] share of publisher income (after deduction for collection fees, direct costs and administration fees.)" Paragraph 3(e) has no language excluding income that FOM received from performance royalties. Considered together, paragraph 3(b) and 3(e) support plaintiffs' assertion that the parties intended FOM would not be required to pay royalties on performance income, but would nonetheless be required to include such income when calculating the revenue-sharing payment.

Nicholas Clainos's declaration lends further support to plaintiffs' interpretation. . . .

Michael Perlstein's expert testimony regarding industry usage and custom also provides support for plaintiffs' interpretation. According to Perlstein, at the time the 1972 Agreement was negotiated, it was customary in the music publishing industry that a provision entitling a writer to a share of the publisher's income would include income generated from performance royalties. . . . This testimony suggests plaintiffs' proposed interpretation accords with the industry customs and practices that were in effect at the time the contract was negotiated.[FN7 omitted]

Finally, the plaintiffs submitted accounting statements showing that, as recently as 2011 and 2013, FOM had paid plaintiffs a share of the income it derived from performance royalties.[FN8 omitted] These accounting statements provide circumstantial evidence that FOM believed the 1972 Agreement entitled plaintiffs to share in performance royalties, which again accords with plaintiffs' proposed interpretation. . . . .

In sum, contrary to the trial court's conclusion, the language of the 1972 Agreement, considered in conjunction with plaintiffs' extrinsic evidence, demonstrates that the contract is reasonably susceptible to the plaintiffs' proposed interpretation.

C. Plaintiffs' Interpretation Is More Reasonable than the Interpretation FOM Has Proposed

Having concluded that the parties' agreement is reasonably susceptible to plaintiffs' proposed interpretation, we move to the "second step—interpreting the contract." [citations omitted] Because the parties' summary judgment materials do not contain any conflicting extrinsic evidence (FOM having elected not to submit any extrinsic evidence), we interpret the contract as a "question of law subject to our independent construction." [citations omitted]

" 'The goal of contractual interpretation is to determine and give effect to the mutual intention of the parties. [Citations.]' [Citation.] Thus, 'a "court's paramount consideration . . . is the parties' objective intent when they entered into [the contract]." ' . . .

Based on the language of the parties' agreement, and aided by the extrinsic evidence in the record, we conclude that plaintiffs' interpretation of the 1972 Agreement is the most reasonable. As explained above, paragraph 22 does not include any language indicating that income derived from performance royalties is to be excluded from "Composition Gross Receipts," the base amount used to determine plaintiffs' revenue sharing payment. Instead, Composition Gross Receipts is specifically defined to include "all monies actually earned and received" in connection with the sale and licensing of the music compositions. Had the parties intended to exclude performance royalties from Composition Gross Receipts, we expect that they would have included language to that effect.

Paragraph 7's exclusion of performance-based income from FOM's royalty payment requirements does not compel a different result. . . . The fact that the parties expressly excluded performance-based revenue from the royalty payments described in paragraph 7, but did not include any such exclusion in paragraph 22, suggests that they intended to include performance royalties in the revenue-sharing provision.

This interpretation is consistent with the plaintiffs' uncontroverted extrinsic evidence . . . .

For the purposes of summary judgment, FOM chose not to submit any extrinsic evidence that contradicted or otherwise responded to plaintiffs' extrinsic evidence. Instead, FOM relied solely on the text of the 1972 Agreement, asserting that it unambiguously excluded performance royalties from the revenue-sharing provision described in paragraph 22. For the reasons discussed above, we reject that assertion, and conclude that the text of the 1972 Agreement, interpreted with the aid of the extrinsic evidence currently in the record, shows that the parties intended that performance royalties would be included in paragraph 22's revenue-sharing provision. We therefore reverse the trial court's judgment.

---

b.   Accounting for Royalties and Audit Rights

In any agreement that provides a royalty from revenue, it is common to see terms addressing both provision of a regular accounting of revenues and procedures for challenging any accounting. Often, a music publisher or record label will seek to limit the period within which an accounting may be challenged to a time that is shorter than the pertinent state's statute of limitations—e.g., whereas a state statute of limitations might be six years, a contractual limitation for challenging a particular accounting might be six or eighteen months, thereby limiting the company's exposure to claims of misreporting of revenue. As you will see in the cases summarized below, even a contractual limitations period does not preclude equitable claims based on the "discovery" rule, where the conduct of the defendant impedes a plaintiff's ability to discover the misreporting.

Composers and recording artists will typically also seek to obtain the right to audit, so that they can confirm the accuracy of accountings received by them from publishers and labels. Audit rights are also typically limited in time and scope, and most agreements call for the costs of any audit to be borne by the composer/recording artist unless the audit discovers a specified level of error in the accountings (typically 10%). Audits can be expensive, and thus even though the right might be provided in a contract, only the most successful composers and recording artists are typically able to exercise contractual audit rights.

SAMPLE AUDIT PROVISION FROM RECORDING CONTRACT

Artist shall have the right to audit Company's books and records with respect to each accounting statement provided to Artist by Company, to object to any such accounting statement, and to institute legal action against Company in connection with any such accounting statement within one (1) year after receipt thereof.

SAMPLE AUDIT PROVISION FROM SONGWRITING CONTRACT

Within ninety (90) days after the end of each of Publisher's semi-annual accounting periods, Publisher shall compute the total royalties earned by Writer pursuant to this Agreement and will submit to Writer the detailed royalty statement for each such period together with the Net Amount of such royalties, if any, that shall be payable under this Agreement. "Net Amount," shall mean the total royalties earned by Writer after deducting from such royalties any and all unrecouped Advances and other chargeable costs under this Agreement. All royalty statements shall be binding upon Writer unless specific written objection, stating the basis thereof, is submitted by Writer to Publisher within 180 days from the date such statement is received by Writer. An independent certified public accountant, on Writer's behalf, may, at Writer's sole cost and expense, not more than once per year, examine Publisher's books and records only as they concern royalties due to Writer, during Publisher's usual business hours and upon thirty (30) days prior written notice, for the sole purpose of verifying the accuracy of any statement rendered to Writer hereunder. In the event such examination discovers a discrepancy of greater than ten percent (10%), Publisher shall, in addition to promptly paying Writer the amount owed, reimburse Writer the costs for such examination.

Below, we provide a brief excerpt of a case illustrating a dispute over the obligation to account and the contractual limitation period for challenging an accounting or seeking an audit.

WALL STREET ENTERTAINMENT, LLC v. BuVISION, LLC

2014 WL 6471706 (S.D.N.Y. Oct. 31, 2014)

REPORT AND RECOMMENDATION

JAMES C. FRANCIS IV, UNITED STATES MAGISTRATE JUDGE.

TO THE HONORABLE LEWIS A. KAPLAN, U.S.D.J.

This case concerns the breach of a Co-Publishing Agreement between the plaintiff, Wall Street Entertainment, LLC ("Wall Street"), a New York based music publisher and producer, and the defendant, BuVision, LLC ("BuVision"), a Georgia based limited liability company. (Complaint ("Compl."), ¶¶ 2–3). The CoPublishing Agreement, which was entered into on June 11, 2009, required BuVision to render semi-annual statements and provide corresponding semi-annual royalty payments to Wall Street, an obligation that the defendant allegedly failed to meet. (Compl., ¶¶ 15–18).[FN1 omitted]

Wall Street filed the instant motion for summary judgment on July 15, 2014. . . .

For the reasons set forth below, I recommend that partial summary judgment be granted on liability but denied with respect to damages. . . .

Background[FN2 omitted]

A. The Exclusive Producer Agreement

On July 25, 2007, Wall Street entered into an Exclusive Producer Agreement with songwriters Melvin Hough, II and Rivelino Wouter (the "Writers"). . . . The Exclusive Producer Agreement obligated Wall Street to pay the Writers fifty percent of any negotiated sum from any third party co-publishing agreement entered into between Wall Street and a co-publisher with respect to the Songs. (Compl., ¶ 9).

B. The Co-Publishing Agreement

On June 11, 2009, Wall Street and BuVision entered into the Co-Publishing Agreement that is at issue. (Co-Publishing Agreement by and between BuVision, LLC and Wall Street Entertainment, LLC dated June 11, 2009 ("Co-Publishing Agreement"), attached as Exh. 2 to Pl. Memo., at 1). This contract made the parties joint owners in the Songs for a specified term, which continued until three full compositions, or the fractional equivalent thereof, were completed by the Writers and released on any album by any major record label or distributor. (Co-Publishing Agreement at 1–2). In consideration for receiving a fifty percent interest in the Songs, the Co-Publishing Agreement required BuVision to submit semi-annual royalty statements to Wall Street on or before September 30 and March 31 of each year, accompanied by payments of any royalties due in connection with the Songs for the preceding semi-annual period ending June 30 and December 31, respectively. (Pl. Memo. at 3; Co-Publishing Agreement at 4).

As of January, 2011, BuVision had not rendered any royalty statements or payments to Wall Street. (Reply Memorandum in Support of Plaintiff's Motion for Summary Judgment ("Pl. Reply Memo.") at 2). On January 14, 2011, the plaintiff sent a letter to the defendant, asserting that BuVision had failed to perform its accounting obligations under the Co-Publishing Agreement. (Letter of Louise C. West dated Jan. 14, 2011 ("West Letter"), attached as Exh. 4 to Pl. Reply Memo.). This letter notified the defendant that failing to remit a royalty statement within thirty days of the letter's receipt would result in "material breach" of the parties' agreement. (West Letter; Pl. Reply Memo. at 2). The defendant neither responded to the letter nor submitted any statements or payment to the plaintiff prior to the filing of the instant complaint. (Pl. Reply Memo. at 2).

C. Procedural History

On Feb. 25, 2013, Wall Street filed its complaint against BuVision for breach of contract, money damages, and attorneys' fees and costs. BuVision filed an answer on May 15, 2013, acknowledging its failure to submit any royalty statements to Wall Street. (Answer ("Ans."), ¶ 17). . . .

. . . . [¶] Discussion

* * * *

B. BuVision's Affirmative Defenses

There is no dispute that there was a valid agreement between the parties and that the defendant breached it. (Pl. Memo. at 2–4; Def. Memo. at 1). Instead, BuVision contends that Wall Street's claims are barred by . . . the limitations provision in paragraph 8(b). (Def. Memo. at 3–4).

. . . . [¶] 2.   Limitations Period

Paragraph 8(b) of the Co-Publishing Agreement contains the following provision:

> You shall be foreclosed from maintaining any action, claim or proceeding against Company in any forum or tribunal with respect to any statement or accounting rendered hereunder unless such action, claim or proceeding is commenced against Company in a court of competent jurisdiction within two (2) years after the due date of such statement or accounting.

(Co-Publishing Agreement at 4).

It is undisputed that BuVision failed to render any accounting statements to Wall Street. (Pl. Reply at 4; Def. Memo. at 1). Accordingly, the limitations period on which the defendant seeks to rely has not begun to run. See Drum Major Music, 2012 WL 423350, at *3 (finding contractual provision that barred claims "eighteen months after the date such statement or accounting is rendered" to apply only to statements actually "completed and delivered" to plaintiff). A contract may provide for a limitations period to run from the due date of an accounting, even if the accounting is never actually delivered. See Malmsteen v. Universal Music Group, Inc., No. 10 Civ. 3955, 2012 WL 2159281, at *7–8 (S.D.N.Y. June 14, 2012) (finding limitations period to run from due date of accounting when contract provided that "all statements hereunder will be deemed conclusively to have been rendered on the due date."). However, the Co-Publishing Agreement here contains no such language. Wall Street's claim is therefore governed by New York's statutory limitations period for breach of contract claims, and not by the language in paragraph 8(b).

When not otherwise overridden by a valid contractual provision, the statute of limitations for a breach of contract claim in New York is six years. See New York Civil Practice Law and Rules § 213; T & N PLC v. Fred S. James & Co., 29 F.3d 57, 58 (2d Cir.1994). The limitations period begins to run upon breach of the agreement, independent of whether the plaintiff was aware of the breach. T & N PLC, 29 F.3d at 59–60; Clarendon National Insurance Co. v. Culley, No. 11 Civ. 2629, 2012 WL 1453975, at *3 (S.D.N.Y. April 25, 2012). The contract between the parties in this case was entered into in June 2009, and BuVision's failure to submit an accounting to Wall Street at the first semi-annual date, September 30, 2009, commenced the running of the statutory limitations period. (Pl. Memo. at 3; Co-Publishing Agreement at 4). Because Wall Street filed its complaint in February 2013, its claims are well within the limitations period.

C.   Wall Street's Breach of Contract Claim

Paragraph 6 of the Co-Publishing Agreement states that BuVision "shall pay to the Co-Publisher any and all royalties that are payable" in connection with the Songs and in accordance with a specific rate schedule[FN3 omitted] that is attached and incorporated into the provision. (Pl. Memo. at 3; Co-Publishing Agreement at 4). Paragraph 8(a) outlines BuVision's obligation to render semi-annual accountings as follows:

> On or before September 30 and March 31 of each year, Company shall render to you statements showing the amount of royalties payable hereunder for the preceding semiannual period ending June 30 and December 31, respectively, accompanied by payment of any royalties shown to be due in such statements.

(Pl. Memo. at 3; Co-Publishing Agreement at 4).

It is undisputed that the Co-Publishing Agreement was a valid contract and that Wall Street's performance was completed with the conveyance of the fifty percent interest in the Songs to BuVision. (Compl. ¶ 12; Ans. ¶ 12). Paragraphs 6 and 8(a) of the CoPublishing Agreement placed on the defendant the corresponding obligation to render royalty statements and pay Wall Street all applicable royalties. (Co-Publishing Agreement at 4). Finally, BuVision's failure to perform these obligations has resulted in damages to the plaintiff. . . . [¶]

* * * *

Conclusion

For the reasons set forth above, I recommend that Wall Street be granted summary judgment on liability only and that a trial be scheduled on damages. . . .

c. Determining Royalties for New Uses

A good illustration of the issues that arise in interpreting contractual provisions when technological innovation creates new methods of deriving revenue from existing works is the issue that arose between record labels and recording artists over whether digital downloads of full or partial recordings (e.g., iTunes downloads or ringtone downloads) qualified as a "sale" or a "license" under agreements that predated the invention of those uses of recordings. Because many standard recording agreements provided for a much lower royalty to artists for sales (e.g. 8–20% of retail sales price) than for licenses (typically 50%), artists received much less revenue when such transactions were treated as sales by record labels. Below, you will see two different courts wrestling with similar contractual language and reaching different results. Of course, modern recording agreements can expressly address how these types of uses will be treated, but the question still remains: how should royalties for new uses be treated under contracts that could not have expressly contemplated those uses?

The Allman Brothers Band in 1972
(Capricorn Records promotional photo)

ALLMAN V. SONY BMG MUSIC ENTERTAINMENT
2008 WL 2477465 (S.D.N.Y. June 18, 2008)

MEMORANDUM DECISION AND ORDER

GEORGE B. DANIELS, DISTRICT JUDGE.

This breach of contract action is brought on behalf of a purported class of recording artists who claim that defendant, Sony BMG Music Entertainment, has failed to pay them the full royalty amount owing under their recording agreements. Defendant moved, pursuant to Fed.R.Civ.P. 12(b)(6), to dismiss the amended complaint. The motion is granted.

[¶¶] ... Plaintiffs allege that they are entitled to royalties in the amount of fifty percent of the net licensing proceeds defendant obtains from sale of sound recordings by its licensees, music download services and ringtone providers, who distribute the recordings to purchasers via digital transmission. Plaintiffs' claim of entitlement is premised on the contractual language, which they identify as the "licensing provision," that states: "[i]n respect of any Master Recording[1] leased by [defendant] to others for their distribution of Phonograph Records in the United States, [defendant] will pay you fifty percent (50%) of [defendant's] net receipts from its Licensee."[2] (Am.Compl.¶¶ 36, 48). By its express terms, this provision pertains to the payment of fifty percent of net receipts when "any Master Recordings is leased . . ." Plaintiffs have not pled any allegations that the master recordings were leased. There is, therefore, no basis from which it can reasonably be inferred that payment pursuant to the master recording lease provision is applicable.

In calculating royalties, defendant utilizes the royalty provisions applicable to "Sales of Phonograph Records . . . consisting entirely of Master Recordings recorded under this agreement and sold by [defendant] or its Licensees Through Normal Retail Channels . . ." "Phonograph Records" is contractually defined as "all forms of reproductions, now or hereafter known, manufactured or distributed primarily for home use . . ." Plaintiffs acknowledge that digital music files, the form in which the subject recordings were distributed, fall within the definition of "phonograph records." Thus, the plain language of this royalty provision demonstrates its applicability to sales of sound recordings, by defendant's licensees through normal retail channels, including recordings that are distributed to consumers via transmission of digital music files. Plaintiffs do not argue otherwise.

Plaintiffs, however, stress that technological advances have rendered the agreed-upon royalty formula more advantageous to defendant. Advances in future technologies were clearly provided for in the agreements.[3] Thus, the emergence of a new era of digital sound recordings does not afford plaintiffs the right, under the guise of contract interpretation, to rewrite the terms of the contracts in order to secure a more favorable, or what they consider to be more equitable, royalty

---

[1]   The recording agreements define the term "Master Recording" as "every recording of sound . . . which is used or useful in the recording, production and/or manufacture of Phonograph Records."

[2]   The reference to "Licensee" only appears in two of the three named plaintiffs' recording agreements. The comparable section in the Cheap Trick contract reads: "In respect of any Master Recording leased by [defendant] to others for their distribution of Phonograph Records in the United States, [defendant] will pay you 50% of [defendant's] net receipts therefrom . . ." *Id.* ¶ 42).

[3]   The parties' contracts specifically provide that they govern the distribution of plaintiffs' recordings via "all forms of reproduction, now or hereafter known." Such language "clearly anticipate[s] development of new technologies." *Silvester v. Time Warner, Inc.*, 763 N.Y.S.2d 912, 917 (N.Y.Sup.Ct.2003), *aff'd* 787 N.Y.S.2d 870 (N.Y.App.Div.2005); *see also, Reinhardt v. Wal-Mart Stores, Inc.*, ___ F.Supp.2d ___, 2008 WL1781232, at *5 (S.D.N.Y. Apr. 18, 2008) ("The phrase 'now or hereafter known,' when referring to forms of reproduction, reveals that future technologies are covered by the agreement." "[Plaintiffs] argu[ment] that the license refers only to 'all forms' that are 'manufactured or sold,' and digital downloads do not fall within its purview because they are transmitted and licensed to end users rather than manufactured * * * is without merit.").

formula. *See, Greenfield v. Philles Records, Inc.*, 750 N.Y.S.2d 565, 572 (N.Y.2002).

Accordingly, the defendant's motion to dismiss is granted.

Eminem performing at DJ hero party in 2009
Author: http://www.glenjamn.com/ (CC-ASA-2.0)

F.B.T. PRODUCTIONS, LLC v. AFTERMATH RECORDS
621 F.3d 958 (9th Cir. 2010)

OPINION

SILVERMAN, CIRCUIT JUDGE:

This dispute concerns the percentage of royalties due to Plaintiffs F.B.T. Productions, LLC, and Em2M, LLC, under their contracts with Defendant Aftermath in connection with the recordings of Marshal B. Mathers, III, professionally known as the rap artist Eminem.[FN1 omitted] Specifically, F.B.T. and Aftermath disagree on whether the contracts' "Records Sold" provision or "Masters Licensed" provision sets the royalty rate for sales of Eminem's records in the form of permanent downloads and mastertones. Before trial, F.B.T. moved for summary judgment that the Masters Licensed provision unambiguously applied to permanent downloads and mastertones. The district court denied the motion. At the close of evidence, F.B.T. did not move for judgment as a matter of law, and the jury returned a verdict in favor of Aftermath. On appeal, F.B.T. reasserts that the Masters Licensed provision unambiguously applies to permanent downloads and mastertones. We agree that the contracts are unambiguous and that the district court should have granted summary judgment to F.B.T. We therefore reverse the judgment and vacate the district court's order awarding Aftermath its attorneys' fees.

BACKGROUND

F.B.T. signed Eminem in 1995, gaining exclusive rights to his recordings. In 1998, F.B.T. signed an agreement transferring Eminem's exclusive recording services to Aftermath. The "Records Sold" provision of that agreement provides that F.B.T. is to receive between 12% and 20% of the adjusted retail price of all "full price records sold in the United States . . . through normal retail channels." The agreement further provides that "[n]otwithstanding the foregoing," F.B.T. is to receive 50% of Aftermath's net receipts "[o]n masters licensed by us . . . to others for their manufacture and sale of records or for any other uses." The parties refer to this provision as the "Masters Licensed" provision. The contract defines "master" as a "recording of sound, without or with visual images, which is used or useful in the recording, production or manufacture of records." The agreement does not contain a definition of the terms "licensed" or "normal retail channels."

In 2002, Aftermath's parent company, Defendant UMG Recordings, Inc., concluded an agreement with Apple Computer, Inc., that enabled UMG's sound recordings, including the Eminem masters, to be sold through Apple's iTunes store as permanent downloads. Permanent downloads are digital copies of recordings that, once downloaded over the Internet, remain on an end-user's computer or other device until deleted. The contract between UMG and Apple is but one example of the many agreements that Aftermath has concluded to sell sound recordings in digital formats since approximately 2001. Since 2003, Aftermath has also concluded contracts with major cellular telephone network carriers to sell sound recordings as mastertones, which are short clips of songs that can be purchased by users to signal incoming calls, popularly known as ringtones.

In 2003, F.B.T. and Aftermath entered into a new agreement that terminated the 1998 agreement. The 2003 agreement increased some royalty rates, but incorporated the wording of the Records Sold and Masters Licensed provisions from the 1998 agreement. In 2004, the parties amended the agreement to provide that "Sales of Albums by way of permanent download shall be treated as [U.S. Normal Retail Channel] Net Sales for the purposes of escalations." Escalations are increases in the royalty rate when total album sales surpass certain targets. The amendment further provides, "Except as specifically modified herein, the Agreement shall be unaffected and remain in full force and effect."

F.B.T. brought suit after a 2006 audit showed that Aftermath had been applying the Records Sold provision to calculate the royalties due to F.B.T. for sales of Eminem's recordings in the form of permanent downloads and mastertones. Before trial, F.B.T. moved for summary judgment that the

Masters Licensed provision unambiguously applied to those sales. Aftermath cross-moved for summary judgment. It argued, in part, that the 2004 amendment showed that the parties intended the Records Sold provision to apply to permanent downloads.

After provisionally reviewing the undisputed extrinsic evidence, the district court concluded that the agreements were reasonably susceptible to either party's interpretation and denied both motions for summary judgment. . . . The jury returned a verdict in favor of Aftermath, and the district court awarded Aftermath its attorneys' fees of over $2.4 million. F.B.T. timely appealed the district court's final judgment and award of attorneys' fees. We have jurisdiction pursuant to 28 U.S.C. § 1291 and we reverse.

DISCUSSION

* * * *

II. The District Court Erred in Determining that the Contracts Were Ambiguous.

Turning to the agreements in question, the Records Sold provision contains the royalty rate for "full price records sold in the United States . . . through normal retail channels." On summary judgment, Aftermath argued that the Records Sold provision applied because permanent downloads and mastertones are records, and because iTunes and other digital music providers are normal retail channels in the United States.

However, the agreements also provide that "notwithstanding" the Records Sold provision, F.B.T. is to receive a 50% royalty on "masters licensed by [Aftermath] . . . to others for their manufacture and sale of records or for any other uses." The parties' use of the word "notwithstanding" plainly indicates that even if a transaction arguably falls within the scope of the Records Sold provision, F.B.T. is to receive a 50% royalty if Aftermath licenses an Eminem master to a third party for "any" use. A contractual term is not ambiguous just because it is broad. Here, the Masters Licensed provision explicitly applies to (1) masters (2) that are licensed to third parties for the manufacture of records "or for any other uses," (3) "notwithstanding" the Record Sold provision. This provision is admittedly broad, but it is not unclear or ambiguous.

Accordingly, to determine whether the Masters Licensed provision applies, we must decide whether Aftermath licensed the Eminem masters to third parties. Aftermath argues that there was no evidence that it or F.B.T. used the term "licensed" in a technical sense. See Cal. Civ.Code § 1644 ("The words of a contract are to be understood in their ordinary and popular sense, rather than according to their strict legal meaning; unless used by the parties in a technical sense. . . ."). In the ordinary sense of the word, a license is simply "permission to act." WEBSTER'S THIRD NEW

International Dictionary of the English Language 1304 (2002). Aftermath did not dispute that it entered into agreements that permitted iTunes, cellular phone carriers, and other third parties to use its sound recordings to produce and sell permanent downloads and mastertones. Those agreements therefore qualify as licenses under Aftermath's own proposed construction of the term.

The conclusion that Aftermath licensed the Eminem masters to third parties also comports well with and finds additional support in federal copyright law. When one looks to the Copyright Act, the terms "license" and "sale" have well differentiated meanings, and the differences between the two play an important role in the overall structures and policies that govern artistic rights. For example, under the language of the Act and the Supreme Court's interpretations, a "sale" of a work may either be a transfer in title of an individual copy of a work, or a sale of all exclusive intellectual property rights in a work. *See* 17 U.S.C. § 109 (describing the "first sale" doctrine); *Quality King Distribs. v. L'anza Research Int'l*, 523 U.S. 135, 145, 118 S.Ct. 1125, 140 L.Ed.2d 254 (1998) (describing the transfer of an individual copy of a work as a sale); *see also* 3–10 Nimmer On Copyright § 10.02 (2009) (describing a transfer of all ownership in a copyright as a sale).

There is no dispute that Aftermath was at all relevant times the owner of the copyrights to the Eminem recordings at issue in this case, having obtained those rights through the recording contracts in exchange for specified royalty payments. Pursuant to its agreements with Apple and other third parties, however, Aftermath did not "sell" anything to the download distributors. The download distributors did not obtain title to the digital files. The ownership of those files remained with Aftermath, Aftermath reserved the right to regain possession of the files at any time, and Aftermath obtained recurring benefits in the form of payments based on the volume of downloads.

Much as Section 109 describes a "sale" under the "first sale" doctrine, various other sections of the Copyright Act illuminate the meaning of the term "license." For example, section 114(f), titled "Licenses for Certain Nonexempt Transmissions," describes the statutory authorization for a third party to exercise public performance rights that otherwise remain the exclusive rights of a copyright holder and defines this authorization as a "license." 17 U.S.C. § 114(f); *see also* 17 U.S.C. §§ 111(a), 114(d)(2). Section 115, titled "Scope of Exclusive Rights in Nondramatic Musical Works: Compulsory License for Making and Distributing Phonorecords," refers directly to the statutory authorization for artists to exercise the copyright owner's right to make and distribute phonorecord "covers" as a license, but again makes it clear that title remains with the copyright owner. 17 U.S.C. § 115.

Under our case law interpreting and applying the Copyright Act, too, it is well settled that where a copyright owner transfers a copy of copyrighted material, retains title, limits the uses to which the material may be put, and is compensated periodically based on the transferee's exploitation of the material, the transaction is a license. *See, e.g., Wall Data Inc. v. Los Angeles County Sheriff's Dep't,* 447 F.3d 769, 785 (9th Cir.2006); *MAI Sys. Corp. v. Peak Computer, Inc.,* 991 F.2d 511 (9th Cir.1993); *United States v. Wise,* 550 F.2d 1180, 1190–91 (9th Cir.1977); *Hampton v. Paramount Pictures Corp.,* 279 F.2d 100, 103 (9th Cir.1960).

It is easily gleaned from these sources of federal copyright law that a license is an authorization by the copyright owner to enable another party to engage in behavior that would otherwise be the exclusive right of the copyright owner, but without transferring title in those rights. This permission can be granted for the copyright itself, for the physical media containing the copyrighted work, or for both the copyright and the physical media.

When the facts of this case are viewed through the lens of federal copyright law, it is all the more clear that Aftermath's agreements with the third-party download vendors are "licenses" to use the Eminem master recordings for specific purposes authorized thereby—i.e., to create and distribute permanent downloads and mastertones—in exchange for periodic payments based on the volume of downloads, without any transfer in title of Aftermath's copyrights to the recordings. Thus, federal copyright law supports and reinforces our conclusion that Aftermath's agreements permitting third parties to use its sound recordings to produce and sell permanent downloads and mastertones are licenses.

Furthermore, the sound recordings that Aftermath provided to third parties qualify as masters. The contracts define a "master" as a "recording of sound ... which is used or useful in the recording, production or manufacture of records." Aftermath admitted that permanent downloads and mastertones are records. The sound recordings that Aftermath supplied to third parties were "used or useful" in the production of permanent downloads and mastertones, so those sound recordings were masters. Because Aftermath permitted third parties to use the Eminem masters to produce and sell records, in the form of permanent downloads and mastertones, F.B.T. is entitled to a 50% royalty under the plain terms of the agreements.

Aftermath argues that the 2004 amendment to the agreements clarified that the Records Sold provision sets the royalty for permanent downloads. However, the 2004 amendment states only that albums sold as permanent downloads are to be counted "for purposes of escalations" under the Records Sold provision, and that "[e]xcept as specifically modified herein, the Agreement shall be unaffected and remain in full force and effect." Read in context, the plain language of the amendment provides that sales of permanent downloads by third parties count towards escalations on the royalty owed when Aftermath itself sells records through normal retail channels. It does not state, and in no way implies, that the royalty rate for the sale of the permanent downloads by third parties is set by the Records Sold provision.

Nor did any of the evidence regarding industry custom or the parties' course of performance support Aftermath's interpretation that the Records Sold provision applies. Aftermath's expert explained that the Masters Licensed provision had in the past been applied "only to compilation records and incorporation into movies, TV shows, and commercials." It was, however, undisputed that permanent downloads and mastertones only came into existence from 2001 to 2003. Consequently, the fact that the Masters Licensed provision had never previously been applied to those forms of licensing is immaterial. There is no indication that the parties intended to confine the contract to the state of the industry in 1998. To the contrary, the contract contemplated advances in technology. It provided that Aftermath had the right to exploit the "masters in any and all forms of media now known and hereinafter developed." Aftermath's evidence of how the Masters Licensed provision had been applied in the past therefore did not cast doubt on its application to permanent downloads and mastertones.

Furthermore, Aftermath renewed its agreement with F.B.T. in 2003, by which time permanent downloads and mastertones were coming into existence. Aftermath argued that subsequent to renewal, F.B.T. had "never objected to Defendants' payment of royalties under the Records Sold provision until the auditor raised the issue in 2006." ... F.B.T. had no obligation to audit the statements any earlier than it did, and it immediately raised the issue with Aftermath after the audit. Accordingly, Aftermath cannot use F.B.T.'s lack of objection to payments made before 2006 to prove how it interpreted the agreements. *See Barnhart Aircraft v. Preston,* 212 Cal. 19, 297 P. 20, 22 (1931) (holding that a party's acts can be used to construe its interpretation of an agreement only where such acts were "direct, positive and deliberate and ... done in an attempted compliance with the terms of the contract or agreement"). The undisputed extrinsic evidence provisionally reviewed by the district court therefore did not support Aftermath's interpretation that the Records Sold provision applies.

In sum, the agreements unambiguously provide that "notwithstanding" the Records Sold provision, Aftermath owed F.B.T. a 50% royalty under the Masters Licensed provision for licensing the Eminem masters to third parties for any use. It was undisputed that Aftermath permitted third parties to use the Eminem masters to produce and sell permanent downloads and mastertones. Neither the 2004 amendment nor any of the parole evidence provisionally reviewed by the district court supported Aftermath's interpretation that the Records Sold provision applied. Because the agreements were unambiguous and were not reasonably susceptible to Aftermath's interpretation, the district court erred in denying F.B.T. summary judgment.

The judgment in favor of Aftermath is REVERSED, the district court's order granting Aftermath its attorneys' fees is VACATED, and the case is REMANDED for further proceedings consistent with this opinion.

———————————

d. Income Attributable to Entire Catalogs or Multiple Works

In recent years, there have been increased occurrences of record companies and/or publishers acquiring equity stakes in particular companies as part of their licensing arrangement with those companies. This can happen especially with new or developing licensees (such as new digital service companies) that choose to provide equity in exchange for a reduced license fee. Such practices have attracted the attention of certain industry interests, some of whom are advocating for the labels and publishers to adopt "equitable" sharing policies with the performers and songwriters. For example, Taylor Swift famously included a provision in her November, 2018 recording deal with Universal Music Group in which the record company agreed to share the proceeds of any sale of its Spotify equity with *all* of its artists—without recoupment of any advances.[19] Both Sony and Warner had previously sold their stakes in Spotify, and both publicly stated that they would share the proceeds with their artists (although the process was treated differently among the different labels).[20] In 2009, the Future of Music Coalition—an artists' advocacy group—proposed that new business models within the music industry embrace a host of general principles favoring equitable and transparent reporting to artists, including equitable sharing of revenues relating to creative works such as unattributable income from investment in new distribution models and monies received as a result of copyright infringement litigation or settlements.[21]

Similar controversies have arisen regarding allotment of proceeds among a label's stable of artists (or a publisher's stable of songwriters) that

———————————

[19] Melinda Newman, *With New Contract, Taylor Swift Secures Better Deal For All UMG Artists*, BILLBOARD (Nov. 19, 2018), *available at* https://www.billboard.com/articles/business/8485 682/taylor-swift-universal-umg-deal-spotify-equity-payouts.

[20] Rachel England, *Taylor Swift ensures UMG artists will profit from Spotify shares*, ENGADGET (Nov. 20, 2018), *available at* https://www.engadget.com/2018/11/20/taylor-swift-umg-artists-profit-spotify-shares/.

[21] Future of Music Coalition, *Principles for Musician Compensation in New Business Models* (April 2, 2009), *available at* http://futureofmusic.org/article/article/principles-artist-compensation-new-business-models-0.

result from litigation recoveries. Although rejected by the court, the arguments made by the plaintiffs in **Silvester v. Time Warner, Inc.**, 1 Misc.3d 250, 763 N.Y.S.2d 912 (N.Y. Sup. Ct. 2003), excerpted above regarding new media, are suggestive of the position taken by many artists regarding litigation proceeds. They claimed that "various members of the recording industry, by prosecuting claims against MP3.com and Napster, Inc., obtained settlements of approximately $15 to $20 million and warrants to purchase shares of MP3.com common stock and licensing fees of at least $6 million in exchange for releases" and sought " 'equitable' shares of defendants' recovered damages for copyright infringement in the federal courts, specifically one-half of the infringement damages or other proceeds obtained by defendants from MP3.com in the MP3.com litigation and an accounting of all payments already made to songwriters and others to recoup improper payments." The court also noted the plaintiffs' argument that the defendant record labels had " 'judicially admitted' that they will share the MP3.com proceeds with all artists whose sound recordings appeared on the MP3.com website, based on a statement during argument before the Second Circuit."[22] In rejecting the plaintiff's arguments, the court stated:

> Plaintiffs' claim for equitable apportionment pursuant to Section 501(b) of the Copyright Act does not state a cause of action and, if it did, would not be enforceable in this Court. The Copyright Law does not give rights to "beneficial owners" to equitable apportionment of damages recovered for infringement. It merely allows legal or beneficial owners to bring actions for copyright infringement. 17 U.S.C. § 501(b). . . .

> Plaintiffs' claim for equitable apportionment under New York law is also unsupported. The only such claim recognized by New York law arises out of apportionment of damages among tortfeasors, which is not the case here. Plaintiffs also claim that in the MP3.com litigation, they were promised 50% of the recovery because of a statement made by defendants in the Second Circuit, which they deem a judicial admission, entitling them to an equitable claim in this court. However, such a claim belongs in the forum where it was allegedly made and where its validity can be determined in an appropriate context. . . .

––––––––––––

––––––––––––

[22]   763 N.Y.S.2d at 915.

NOTES AND QUESTIONS

1.   What lessons do you take from the above cases involving disputes over applying contractual language to new distribution methods and uses? How might you explain the different outcomes in the Allman Brothers and Eminem cases—does it all come down to the language used in the agreement at issue, or are there other forces in play?

2.   Do you think there is merit to the argument in the *Allman* case that the language covering royalty calculations for sales of recordings was negotiated under circumstances that made the royalty split fair given the relative manufacturing and distribution efforts by record labels but that it is unfair to apply the same split to newer, relatively cost-free distribution models? How might you alter the standard provisions to allow adjustments to the royalty split for new distribution models to avoid a similar result in the future?

3.   If recording artists and composers wish to participate in settlement proceeds from infringement litigation or equity interests that labels and publishers take in entities that license their works, what language would you recommend inserting into a standard recording or publishing contract to allow for such a sharing arrangement?

4.   Look back at the description of the Big Machine/Warner/Clear Channel deals regarding payment of performance royalties to recording artists from Chapter 4. What potential disputes can you anticipate regarding what the artists' share should be for payments attributable to terrestrial broadcasts of sound recordings? What language might you include in future agreements on behalf of artists (or labels) to address novel business deals like the one struck between Big Machine and Clear Channel?

CHAPTER XI

MUSIC INDUSTRY CONTRACTS PART 2:
YOU REALLY GOT A HOLD ON ME[1]

■ ■ ■

CONSIDER AS YOU READ . . .

- Just as statutory language is incapable of fully contemplating future technological and business innovations, so, too, is contractual language incapable of fully anticipating every eventuality. How do you think parties to music industry agreements can best ensure that the contract terms will remain equitable over a long period of time, particularly when these contracts create continuing rights and obligations well beyond the expiration of the personal service obligations?

- The music industry has been in a state of rapid change since the digital revolution upended traditional roles of parties in the industry. How do you think contracts should/will evolve to address the new marketplace?

A. OBLIGATIONS TO PROMOTE/ EXPLOIT THE WORKS

From the point of view of the songwriter or recording artist, one of the main obligations of their publisher or label is to "exploit" the works created under the agreement to the fullest extent permitted by the contract, thereby maximizing revenues from the agreement. Indeed, a primary driver in selecting a particular record label or a publisher to sign with is their ability to successfully promote the creative work and achieve successful placement in a variety of areas of commerce. However, publishers and labels seek to retain control over their ability to determine the level of effort and resources they commit to various works; they do not want to be contractually compelled to put good money after bad if a work is not likely to return their investment.

---

[1] Smokey Robinson (1962); released by the Beatles on WITH THE BEATLES (1963).

When songwriters or recording artists are able to negotiate express obligations from a publisher or label to promote or exploit a work, those obligations are often tied to the grant of rights in the work or the materiality of any breach. For example, some authors are able to negotiate a reversion right in the work if the publisher or label does not meet specified promotion or exploitation requirements—e.g., if a certain promotional budget is not met or if a work is not commercially released by a certain date. Of course, given the ease of distribution in the digital age, current contractual provisions incorporating such a right would need to be quite specific about what actions are necessary to constitute a commercial release; the parties should consider whether or not simply offering a track for sale through iTunes without any promotion is sufficient to satisfy the composer's or recording artist's interests. Typically, any reversion right would be conditioned upon repayment by the author of unrecouped advances or costs relating to the work, sometimes with a premium, making it difficult for many authors to exercise the right even if the opportunity arises.

SAMPLE PROVISION FROM RECORDING AGREEMENT

Company shall have no obligation to release or to promote masters that it, in its sole discretion, deems not to be commercially satisfactory. Should Company fail to release any master recordings delivered by Artist during the term of this Agreement, all right, title, and interest, including copyright ownership, in such recordings shall revert to Artist upon the expiration of this Agreement.

SAMPLE PROVISION FROM SONGWRITING AGREEMENT

Writer shall perform the services required under this Agreement, solely and exclusively for Publisher. Publisher is however not obligated to commercially exploit any of the rights granted to Publisher hereunder and there is no warranty or obligation for Publisher to produce or distribute any Records.

The cases below illustrate how courts have dealt with the obligation to promote or exploit. In some instances, it is an expressly-negotiated and drafted provision in the agreement. In other instances, courts may imply an obligation not to interfere with the promotion or exploitation of a work covered by a publishing or recording agreement—but no such implied obligation will be recognized in contracts that expressly refuse to create an obligation to promote or exploit as long as other consideration is present.

LP of Virgin: The Mission
Rock Opera by Father John T. O'Reilly

CONTEMPORARY MISSION INC. V. FAMOUS MUSIC CORP.
557 F.2d 918 (2d Cir. 1977)

Before MANSFIELD, VAN GRAAFEILAND and MESKILL, CIRCUIT JUDGES.

Opinion

MESKILL, CIRCUIT JUDGE:

This is an appeal by Famous Music Corporation ("Famous") from a verdict rendered against it in favor of Contemporary Mission, Inc. ("Contemporary"), in the United States District Court for the Southern District of New York, after a jury trial before Judge Richard Owen. . . . The dispute between the parties relates to Famous' alleged breach of two contracts.

I.   The Facts.

Contemporary is a nonprofit charitable corporation organized under the laws of the State of Missouri with its principal place of business in Connecticut. It is composed of a small group of Roman Catholic priests who write, produce and publish musical compositions and recordings.[1] In 1972 the group owned all of the rights to a rock opera entitled VIRGIN, which was composed by Father John T. O'Reilly, a vice-president and member of the group. Contemporary first became involved with Famous in 1972 as a result of O'Reilly's efforts to market VIRGIN.

Famous is a Delaware corporation with its headquarters in the Gulf + Western Building in New York City. . . . and, until July 31, 1974, it was engaged in the business of producing musical recordings for distribution throughout the United States. Famous' president, Tony Martell, is

---

[1]   For a further description of the group see Robert Stigwood Group, Ltd. v. O'Reilly, 346 F.Supp. 376, 379 (D.Conn.1972), rev'd, 530 F.2d 1096 (2d Cir. 1976).

generally regarded in the recording industry as the individual primarily responsible for the successful distribution of the well-known rock operas TOMMY and JESUS CHRIST SUPERSTAR.

* * * *

The relationship between Famous and Contemporary was considerably more harmonious in 1972 than it is today. At that time, Martell thought he had found, in VIRGIN, another TOMMY or JESUS CHRIST SUPERSTAR, and he was anxious to acquire rights to it. O'Reilly, who was encouraged by Martell's expertise and enthusiasm, had high hopes for the success of his composition. On August 16, 1972, they executed the so-called "VIRGIN Recording Agreement" ("VIRGIN agreement") on behalf of their respective organizations.

The terms of the VIRGIN agreement were relatively simple. Famous agreed to pay a royalty to Contemporary in return for the master tape recording of VIRGIN and the exclusive right to manufacture and sell records made from the master. The agreement also created certain "Additional Obligations of Famous" which included, inter alia: the obligation to select and appoint, within the first year of the agreement, at least one person to personally oversee the nationwide promotion of the sale of records, to maintain contact with Contemporary and to submit weekly reports to Contemporary; the obligation to spend, within the first year of the agreement, no less than $50,000 on the promotion of records; and the obligation to release, within the first two years of the agreement, at least four separate single records from VIRGIN. The agreement also contained a non-assignability clause which is set out in the margin.[3]

On May 8, 1973, the parties entered into a distribution contract which dealt with musical compositions other than VIRGIN. This, the so-called "Crunch agreement," granted to Famous the exclusive right to distribute Contemporary's records in the United States. Famous agreed to institute a new record label named "Crunch," and a number of records were to be released under it annually. Contemporary agreed to deliver ten long-playing records and fifteen single records during the first year of the contract. Famous undertook to use its "reasonable efforts" to promote and distribute the records. Paragraph 15 of the Crunch agreement stated that a breach by either party would not be deemed material unless the non-breaching party first gave written notice to the defaulting party and the defaulting party failed to cure the breach within thirty days. The notice

---

3   Paragraph 29 of the VIRGIN agreement provides, in full, as follows:

This Agreement shall not be assignable by FAMOUS, except in the voluntary sale of FAMOUS' entire business in which the present work is used, or in connection with a merger between FAMOUS and another business organization, or to a majority-owned subsidiary or division of FAMOUS engaged in the same business as FAMOUS, all conditioned upon the execution and delivery to (Contemporary) of an agreement whereby the assignee agrees to be bound by the obligations of this Agreement. (emphasis added).

was to specify the nature of the alleged material breach. The contract prohibited assignment by Contemporary, but it contained no provision relating to Famous' right to assign.

Although neither VIRGIN nor its progeny was ever as successful as the parties had originally hoped, the business relationship continued on an amicable basis until July 31, 1974. On that date, Famous' record division was sold to ABC Records, Inc. (ABC). When O'Reilly complained to Martell that Famous was breaking its promises, he was told that he would have to look to ABC for performance. O'Reilly met with one of ABC's lawyers and was told that ABC was not going to have any relationship with Contemporary. On August 21, 1974, Contemporary sent a letter to Famous pursuant to paragraph 15 of the Crunch agreement notifying Famous that it had "materially breached Paragraph 12,[4] among others, of (the Crunch) Agreement in that (it had) attempted to make a contract or other agreement with ABC-Dunhill Record Corporation (ABC Records) creating an obligation or responsibility in behalf of or in the name of the Contemporary Mission." This lawsuit followed.

II. The Jury Verdict.

Contemporary brought this action against several defendants and asserted several causes of action. By the time the case was submitted to the jury the only remaining defendant was Famous and the only remaining claims were that (1) Famous had failed to adequately promote the VIRGIN and Crunch recordings prior to the sale to ABC, (2) Famous breached both the VIRGIN and Crunch agreements when it sold the record division to ABC. . . .

The district judge submitted the case to the jury in two parts: the first portion as to liability and the second concerning damages. The court's questions and the jury's answers as to liability and damages are set forth below:

Liability Questions

1.   Has plaintiff established by a fair preponderance of the credible evidence that Famous breached the Virgin agreement by failing to adequately promote Virgin in its various aspects as it had agreed?

Yes.

2.   If you find a failure to adequately promote, did that cause plaintiff any damage?

---

[4]   Paragraph 12 of the Crunch agreement provides, in full, as follows:

This agreement shall not be construed as one of partnership or joint venture, nor shall it constitute either party as the agent or legal representative of the other. Neither party shall have the right, power or authority to make any contract or other agreement, or to assume or create any obligation or responsibility, express or implied, in behalf of or in the name of the other party or to bind the other party in any manner for anything whatsoever.

Yes. . . .

4. Did plaintiff establish by a fair preponderance of the credible evidence that Famous failed to use "its reasonable efforts consistent with the exercise of sound business judgment" to promote the records marketed under the Crunch label?

No.

5. Did plaintiff establish by a fair preponderance of the credible evidence that there was a refusal by ABC to perform the Crunch contract and promote plaintiff's music after the assignment?

Yes.

6. If your answer is "yes" to either 4 or 5 above, did such a breach or breaches of the Crunch agreement cause plaintiff any damage?

Yes. . . .

* * * *

III. Discussion.

On this appeal, Famous attacks the verdict on several grounds. Their first contention is that the evidence was insufficient to support the jury's response to liability question number 1. Their second contention is that the jury's response to liability question number 4 precludes a recovery for non-performance of the Crunch agreement. . . . We find none of these arguments persuasive.

A. The VIRGIN Agreement.

Judge Owen charged the jury as a matter of law that Famous breached the VIRGIN agreement by assigning it to ABC without getting from ABC a written agreement to be bound by the terms of the VIRGIN agreement. A reading of paragraph 29 of the agreement[FN7 omitted] reveals that that charge was entirely correct, and Famous does not challenge it on this appeal. Famous vigorously contends, however, that the jury's conclusion, that it had failed to adequately promote VIRGIN prior to the sale to ABC, is at war with the undisputed facts and cannot be permitted to stand. O'Connor v. Pennsylvania R.R. Co., 308 F.2d 911, 915 & n.5 (2d Cir. 1962). In particular they argue that they spent the required $50,000[8] and

---

[8]   Martell testified that he was certain that over $50,000 had been spent. Melvin Schlissel, Famous' Vice-President of Finance, testified that in early 1973 he prepared a report that indicated that approximately $50,000 had been spent on the promotion of VIRGIN as of the date of the report. . . . Although Famous' proof that it spent over $50,000 was uncontradicted, the proof itself was not particularly strong; indeed, it was rather imprecise and self-serving. The jury could quite properly have concluded that the proof was insufficient.

Famous contends that Contemporary waived the $50,000 spending requirement. In return for an advance of $7,500, Contemporary agreed that

appointed the required overseer for the project.[9] The flaw in this argument is that its focus is too narrow. The obligations to which it refers are but two of many created by the VIRGIN agreement. Under the doctrine of Wood v. Lucy, Lady Duff-Gordon, 222 N.Y. 88, 118 N.E. 214 (1917), Famous had an obligation to use its reasonable efforts to promote VIRGIN on a nationwide basis. That obligation could not be satisfied merely by technical compliance with the spending and appointment requirements of paragraph 14 of the agreement.

Even assuming that Famous complied fully with those requirements, there was evidence from which the jury could find that Famous failed to adequately promote VIRGIN. The question is a close one, particularly in light of Martell's obvious commitment to the success of VIRGIN and in light of the efforts that were in fact exerted and the lack of any serious dispute between the parties prior to the sale to ABC. However, there was evidence that Famous prematurely terminated the promotion of the first single record, "Got To Know," shortly after its release, and that Famous limited its promotion of the second record, "Kyrie," to a single city, rather than promoting it nationwide.[10] Moreover, there was evidence that, prior to the sale to ABC, Famous underwent a budget reduction and cut back its promotional staff. From this, the jury could infer that the promotional effort was reduced to a level that was less than adequate. On the whole, therefore, we are not persuaded that the jury's verdict should be disturbed.

Famous Music Corporation shall be relieved of its obligation to expend a minimum of $50,000.00 in the promotion of "Virgin" record sales if, as and when, in the sole option of Famous Music Corporation, such promotion shall cease to be effective and profitable.

This agreement did not operate as a present waiver of the spending requirement, as Famous contends. It granted Famous an option not to spend "if, as and when, in the sole option of Famous," the promotion became ineffective and unprofitable. Famous' argument is premised upon the notion that it had "absolute discretion concerning how much, if any, of the $50,000 to spend, and its opinion could not be challenged." This is not true. Under New York law there is implied in every contract a covenant of fair dealing and good faith. Kirke La Shelle Co. v. Paul Armstrong Co., 263 N.Y. 79, 87, 188 N.E. 163, 167 (1933); see, e. g., Van Valkenburgh, Nooger & Neville, Inc. v. Hayden Pub. Co., Inc., 30 N.Y.2d 34, 45, 330 N.Y.S.2d 329, 333, 281 N.E.2d 142, 144, cert. denied, 409 U.S. 875, 93 S.Ct. 125, 34 L.Ed.2d 128 (1972). Thus, Famous' determination of effectiveness or profitability of promotion would have to be made in good faith. There is no indication that such a good faith determination was in fact made.

[9]   It is clear that the personal overseer requirement was met. Martell himself was actively and extensively engaged in the promotional effort. In addition, Herb Gordon was clearly put in charge of the day-to-day supervision of the promotion. This adequately complied with the provisions of paragraph 14.

[10]   We recognize that the limited promotion of "Kyrie" was a result of "test marketing," i. e., the concentration of promotional efforts in one area before expanding the efforts to the rest of the country. However, because the promotion of "Kyrie" was thus limited, Famous only marketed three single records on a nationwide basis, and the contract required the nationwide promotion of four.

THIRD STORY MUSIC V. WAITS

41 Cal. App. 4th 798 (1995)

EPSTEIN, ACTING P. J.

This case involves a dispute between a company which owned the rights to the musical output of singer/songwriter Tom Waits from 1972 to 1983 and the party which purchased those rights. The issue is whether a promise to market music, or to refrain from doing so, at the election of the promisor is subject to the implied covenant of good faith and fair dealing where substantial consideration has been paid by the promisor. We conclude that the implied convenant does not apply.

Factual and Procedural Summary

According to the complaint, Waits agreed to render his services as a recording artist and songwriter exclusively to Third Story Productions (predecessor in interest to plaintiff and appellant Third Story Music, Inc.) from 1972 to 1983, pursuant to written agreements dated July 1, 1972, and July 1, 1977. Third Story Productions transferred its rights in Waits's music to Asylum Records (predecessor in interest to defendant/respondent Warner Communications, Inc.) on August 31, 1972, and to Elektra/Asylum Records (currently a division of Warner Communications, Inc.) pursuant to an agreement dated June 15, 1977.[FN1 omitted] Under these agreements, TSM was to produce master recordings featuring performances by Waits. Warner obtained from TSM the worldwide right to "manufacture, sell, distribute and advertise records or other reproductions (visual or nonvisual) embodying such recordings, to lease, license, convey or otherwise use or dispose of the recordings by any method now or hereafter known, in any field of use, to release records under any trademarks, trade names or labels, to perform the records or other reproductions publicly and to permit the public performance thereof by radio broadcast, television or any other method now or hereafter known, all upon such terms and conditions as we may approve, and to permit others to do any or all of the foregoing . . . ." This clause of the agreements also specifically stated that Warner "may at our election refrain from any or all of the foregoing."[2]

     * * * *

So far as can be ascertained from the record, the parties operated under these agreements without controversy until 1993. At that time, an affiliate of TSM known as Bizarre/Straight Records sought to compile and market an album of previously released Waits compositions, including four which were the subject of the TSM/Warner agreement: *On the Nickel, Jitterbug Boy, Invitation to the Blues,* and *Ruby's Arms.* Bizarre/Straight presented a licensing proposal to Warner through its agent Warner Special Products. During negotiations, Bizarre/Straight and TSM learned that

---

    [2]   Nearly identical language appears in the agreements between Waits and TSM.

Warner had no objection to the deal, but that it would not be made final unless Waits personally approved the licensing request. For reasons unknown, but which TSM claims have to do with Waits's desire to maximize profit on music created after his association with TSM, Waits refused consent. TSM brought suit for contract damages based on breach of the implied covenant of good faith and fair dealing, claiming that Warner "has created an impediment to [TSM] receiving material benefits under the [parties'] agreements and has wrongfully interjected that requirement [the requirement of Waits's approval] into an unknown number of potentially lucrative licensing arrangements, in so doing preventing at least the issuance of the four licenses described above, and other licenses, which TSM will ascertain through discovery."

Warner demurred to the complaint, alleging that the clause in the agreement permitting it to "at [its] election refrain" from doing anything to profitably exploit the music is controlling and precludes application of any implied covenant. The demurrer was sustained on those grounds. TSM contends on appeal, and argued below, that when a party to a contract is given this type of discretionary power, that power must be exercised in good faith, and that permitting the artist to decide whether a particular licensing arrangement was or was not acceptable did not represent a good faith exercise.

Discussion

I

When an agreement expressly gives to one party absolute discretion over whether or not to perform, when should the implied covenant of good faith and fair dealing be applied to limit its discretion? Both sides rely on different language in the recent Supreme Court decision in Carma Developers (Cal.), Inc. v. Marathon Development California, Inc. (1992) 2 Cal.4th 342[, 6 Cal.Rptr.2d 467, 826 P.2d 710] to answer that question. In Carma, the parties had entered into a lease agreement which stated that if the tenant procured a potential sublessee and asked the landlord for consent to sublease, the landlord had the right to terminate the lease, enter into negotiations with the prospective sublessee, and appropriate for itself all profits from the new arrangement. In the passage relied on by TSM, the court recognized that "[t]he covenant of good faith finds particular application in situations where one party is invested with a discretionary power affecting the rights of another." (2 Cal.4th at p. 372.) The court expressed the view that "[s]uch power must be exercised in good faith." (Ibid.)

At the same time, the Carma court upheld the right of the landlord to freely exercise its discretion to terminate the lease in order to claim for itself-and deprive the tenant of all profit from the expected sublease. In this regard, the court stated: "We are aware of no reported case in which a court has held the covenant of good faith may be read to prohibit a party from doing that which is expressly permitted by an agreement. On the contrary, as a general matter, implied terms should never be read to vary express terms. [Citations.] 'The general rule [regarding the covenant of good faith] is plainly subject to the exception that the parties may, by express provisions of the contract, grant the right to engage in the very acts and conduct which would otherwise have been forbidden by an implied covenant of good faith and fair dealing. . . . [¶] As to acts and conduct authorized by the express provisions of the contract, no covenant of good faith and fair dealing can be implied which forbids such acts and conduct. And if defendants were given the right to do what they did by the express provisions of the contract there can be no breach.' " (2 Cal.4th at p. 374, quoting VTR, Incorporated v. Goodyear Tire & Rubber Company (S.D.N.Y. 1969) 303 F.Supp. 773, 777–778.)

. . . . [¶] In situations such as the present one, where a discretionary power is expressly given by the contractual language, the quoted passages from Carma set up an apparent inconsistency between the principle that the covenant of good faith should be applied to restrict exercise of a discretionary power and the principle that an implied covenant must never vary the express terms of the parties' agreement. We attempt to reconcile the two.

II

. . . . [¶] In each of these cases, the courts were forced to resolve contradictory expressions of intent from the parties: the intent to give one party total discretion over its performance and the intent to have a mutually binding agreement. In that situation, imposing the duty of good faith creates a binding contract where, despite the clear intent of the parties, one would not otherwise exist. Faced with that choice, courts prefer to imply a covenant at odds with the express language of the contract rather than literally enforce a discretionary language clause and thereby render the agreement unenforceable. . . . [¶]

. . . . As we have seen, the implied covenant of good faith is also applied to contradict an express contractual grant of discretion when necessary to protect an agreement which otherwise would be rendered illusory and unenforceable. Does a different result ensue where the contract is unambiguous, otherwise supported by adequate consideration, and the implied covenant is not needed to effectuate the parties' expressed desire for a binding agreement? We believe it does, and the cases cited by the court in Carma illustrate this point.

* * * * . . . The conclusion to be drawn is that courts are not at liberty to imply a covenant directly at odds with a contract's express grant of discretionary power except in those relatively rare instances when reading the provision literally would, contrary to the parties' clear intention, result

in an unenforceable, illusory agreement. In all other situations where the contract is unambiguous, the express language is to govern, and "[n]o obligation can be implied ... which would result in the obliteration of a right expressly given under a written contract." (Gerdlund v. Electronic Dispensers International, supra, 190 Cal.App.3d at pp. 277–278.)

III

We turn to the question of whether it is necessary in this case to imply a covenant of good faith to protect the enforceability of the contract, or otherwise to effectuate the clear and obvious intent of the parties.

The TSM/Warner agreement states that Warner may market the Waits recordings, or "at [its] election" refrain from all marketing efforts. Read literally, as the trial court did and respondent would have us do, this is a textbook example of an illusory promise. At the same time, there can be no question that the parties intended to enter into an enforceable contract with binding promises on both sides. Were this the only consideration given by Warner, a promise to use good faith would necessarily be implied under the authorities discussed.

The illusory promise was not, however, the only consideration given by the licensee. Under paragraph 33 of the 1977 agreement and paragraph 34 of the 1972 agreement, Warner promised to pay TSM a guaranteed minimum amount no matter what efforts were undertaken. It follows that, whether or not an implied covenant is read into the agreement, the agreement would be supported by consideration and would be binding.[5]

As we see it, Warner bargained for and obtained all rights to Waits's 1972 to 1983 musical output, and paid legally adequate consideration. That it chose not to grant a license in a particular instance cannot be the basis for complaint on the part of TSM as long as Warner made the agreed minimum payments and paid royalties when it did exploit the work. "The courts cannot make better agreements for parties than they themselves have been satisfied to enter into or rewrite contracts because they operate harshly or inequitably. It is not enough to say that without the proposed implied covenant, the contract would be improvident or unwise or would operate unjustly. Parties have the right to make such agreements. The law refuses to read into contracts anything by way of implication except upon grounds of obvious necessity." (Walnut Creek Pipe Distributors, Inc. v. Gates Rubber Co. (1964) 228 Cal.App.2d 810, 815 [39 Cal.Rptr. 767].) TSM

---

[5]   The guaranteed payments involved do not appear to be large in relation to what might be earned from the music of a successful recording artist. But unless the consideration given was so one-sided as to create an issue of unconscionability, the courts are not in a position to decide whether legal consideration agreed to by the parties is or is not fair. The $8,800 annual payments due under the 1972 agreement and the $50,000 minimum payment, plus $100,000 to $150,000 for each LP produced by TSM, due under the 1978 agreement amounted to more than the peppercorn of consideration the law requires.

was free to accept or reject the bargain offered and cannot look to the courts to amend the terms that prove unsatisfactory.

* * * *

The judgment is affirmed.

NOTES AND QUESTIONS

1.   In *Mellencamp v. Riva Music Ltd.*, 698 F.Supp. 1154 (S.D.N.Y. 1988), the court expressly recognized that, under New York law, "every contract includes an implied covenant of good faith and fair dealing which precludes a party from engaging in conduct that will deprive the other contracting party of his benefits under their agreement" in the context of a lawsuit filed by singer/songwriter John Cougar Mellencamp regarding exploitation of his songs. Noting Mellencamp's entitlement to royalties from exploitation of the works covered by the contract, the court stated: "When the essence of a contract is the assignment or grant of an exclusive license in exchange for a share of the assignee's profits in exploiting the license, these principles imply an obligation on the part of the assignee to make reasonable efforts to exploit the license." *Id.* at 1157. However, the court specifically refused to find a more general fiduciary duty, noting that the obligation is "one founded in contract rather than on trust principles." *Id.*

2.   Although courts will in some circumstances imply a duty to promote/exploit as a component of the duty of good faith and fair dealing, there is no guarantee that such a duty will be found in individual cases. The sample provisions above illustrate how publishing and recording agreements might be crafted to avoid any such obligation. Do you think that they accomplish their goal in light of the cases above? How might you craft opposing provisions that create an affirmative obligation to exploit/promote? What issues do you contemplate arising in connection with any such affirmative language?

3.   A famous dispute over allegations regarding a label's failure to promote an album arose in 1964 between **Johnny Cash and Columbia Records**. Johnny Cash had collaborated with songwriter Peter La Farge to record *Bitter Tears*, a collection of storytelling folk ballads chronicling injustices against Native Americans—something totally unlike his prior hits for label Columbia Records. The album was criticized as un-American and widely censored. In response to the outcry, Columbia Records pulled its advertising for the album. The lead single, which had been banned by many country radio stations, was "The Ballad of Ira Hayes"; it told the story of the Native American Marine who was immortalized as one of six men raising the American flag at Iwo Jima but later died a destitute alcoholic. When Columbia refused to promote it, Cash bought a thousand copies of the single from Columbia and sent one to every radio station in the United States, personally imploring disc jockeys with whom he had developed relationships over the years to play the song. He also

wrote an open letter to the music industry that he published in a paid, full-page ad in *Billboard Magazine*, asking "Where are your guts?" (pictured below). The song reached the Billboard Top 10 in December 1964, and *Bitter Tears* ultimately peaked at No. 2 on the Album chart.

It is an astounding experience, the power that touches everyone who walks around the gigantic statue of the N.W. II flag-raising based on that classic picture from Iwo Jima. There are 5 Marines and one Navy corpsman depicted in that bronze giant at Arlington national cemetery.

I "chilled" like that recently, then went to Columbia records and recorded "The Ballad of Ira Hayes."

D.J.'s—station managers—owners, etc., where are your <u>guts</u>?

(I know many of you "Top 40," "Top 50" or what-have-you. So . . . a few of you can disregard this "protest" and that is what it is.)

I think that you do have "<u>guts</u>" . . . that you believe in something deep down.

I'm not afraid to sing the hard, bitter lines that the son of Oliver La Farge wrote.

(And pardon the dialect—mine is one of 500 or more in this land.)

Still . . . actual sales on Ballad of Ira Hayes are more than double the "Big Country Hit" sales average.

Classify me, categorize me—STIFLE me, but it won't work.

I am fighting no particular cause. If I did, it would soon make me a sluggard. For as time changes, I change.

This song is not of an unsung hero. The name Ira Hayes has been used and abused in every bar across the nation.

These lyrics, I realize, take us back to the truth—as written by his cousin, Peter La Farge (son of the late Oliver La Farge . . . author, and hard worker in the department of Indian Affairs, Washington, D. C., until 2 years ago.)

You're right! Teenage girls and Beatle record buyers don't want to hear this sad story of Ira Hayes—but who cries more easily, and who always go to sad movies to cry??? Teenage girls.

Some of you "Top Forty" D.J.'s went all out for this at first. Thanks anyway. Maybe the program director or station manager will reconsider.

This ad (go ahead and call it that) costs like hell. Would you, or those pulling the strings for you, go to the mike with a new approach? That is, listen again to the record?

Yes, I cut records to try for "sales." Another word we could use is "success."

Regardless of the trade charts—the categorizing, classifying and restrictions of air play, this is not a country song, not as it is being sold. It is a fine reason though for the <u>gutless</u> to give it thumbs down.

"Ballad of Ira Hayes" <u>is</u> strong medicine. So is Rochester—Harlem—Birmingham and VietNam.

In closing—at the Newport Folk Festival this month I visited with many, many "folk" singers—Peter, Paul & Mary, Theodore Bikel, Joan Baez, Bob Dylan (to drop a few names) and Pete Seeger.

I was given 20 minutes on their Saturday nite show (thanks to Mr. John Hammond, pioneer for Columbia by way of A/R).

The Ballad of Ira Hayes stole my part of the show. And we all know that the audience (of near 20,000) were not "country" or hillbillies. They were an intelligent cross-section of American youth—and middle age.

I've blown my horn now, just this once, then no more. Since I've said these things now, I find myself not caring if the record is programmed or not. I won't ask you to cram it down their throats.

But as an American who is almost a half-breed Cherokee-Mohawk (and who knows what else?)—I had to fight back when I realized that so many stations are afraid of "Ira Hayes."

Just one question: WHY???

4.   What should the baseline requirement for sufficient promotion or exploitation be in any recording or publishing agreement? Should it be left to individual negotiations, or should courts or state statutes articulate a minimum standard?

B. CONTROL OVER CONTENT

It is safe to say that parties on both sides of recording and songwriting agreements would like to retain as much control as they can over the content of and manner in which works produced under those agreements may be used. Even when the record label or publisher is granted all rights in the works, however, authors may still be granted specifically defined approval, or in some cases consultation, rights over aspects of the works. For example, composers may seek preapproval rights over licenses for new arrangements of their compositions; both composers and recording artists may seek preapproval or veto rights regarding licenses for synchronization of their works in certain types of audiovisual works, such as advertisements or films with potentially objectionable content. From a practical perspective, exploiting the works in a publisher or label's catalog becomes more complex and difficult when authors retain approval rights over uses of those works (see Chapter 9 for examples of disputes over licensing of musical works for advertising and political purposes).

SAMPLE RECORDING CONTRACT PROVISION
RE ARTIST APPROVAL RIGHTS

Company shall obtain verbal approval (not to be unreasonably withheld) from Artist in connection with all third-party licenses necessary for the exploitation of any of the Masters hereunder. Notwithstanding the foregoing, Artist has sole approval rights with respect to the third party licensing of any of the Masters to the extent such licensing implicates the following topics and/or subjects: political campaigns, affiliations and/or political issues, including but not limited to, gun control, climate change, and abortion; drugs, alcohol, and tobacco products; animal rights and the glorification of cruelty to animals; entertainment products with adult only ratings.

Recording artists may also seek to have approval over the selection and sequence of recordings on an album, artwork for an album cover, and specific types of distribution methods. As discussed above in connection with the "commercially satisfactory" requirement for delivery of masters under a recording agreement, record labels retain some level of control over the content of albums by virtue of the fact that they have the contractual right to refuse delivery of masters that they deem not commercially viable.

Even when recording artists are given broad control over the content of their albums, the agreement may give the label control over which recordings will be released as singles and require delivery of a specified number of recordings that the label accepts as appropriate for single release. The next case, involving a dispute between rapper Dr. Dre and his former label, Death Row Records, provides an illustration of a broad contractual grant of control to an artist regarding the manner in which the label could exploit the works produced under the recording agreement. Note that the artist's control was not given in his original deal with the label and was instead granted as a part of a renegotiation, after the successful release of the recordings. Note, too, as you read this excerpt, how the concept of control overlaps with applying contractual language to new uses and distribution methods.

Dr. Dre at Coachella 2012
Photo by Jason Persse (CC-ASA-2.0)

YOUNG V. WIDEAWAKE DEATH ROW ENTERTAINMENT LLC
2011 WL 12565250 (C.D. Cal. April 19, 2011)

ORDER GRANTING IN PART AND DENYING IN PART CROSSMOTIONS FOR PARTIAL SUMMARY JUDGMENT

CHRISTINA A. SNYDER, DISTRICT JUDGE.

I.   INTRODUCTION

On February 11, 2010, plaintiff Andre Young, professionally known as the rap artist Dr. Dre, filed the instant action against defendants Wideawake Death Row Entertainment, LLC; Wideawake Entertainment Group, Inc. . . . . [T]he only surviving claims are for breach of contract and imposition of a constructive trust.

On January 5, 2011, plaintiff filed a motion for partial summary judgment on the first claim for relief for breach of contract. On March 15, 2011, defendants filed a motion for summary judgment, or, in the alternative, partial summary judgment. . . . After carefully considering the arguments set forth by both parties, the Court finds and concludes as follows.

II. FACTUAL BACKGROUND

Plaintiff alleges that he is an "internationally renowned and immensely popular composer, producer, recording artist and performer, with an excellent reputation among the public and the critical community for his music." Compl. ¶ 1. In 1991, plaintiff cofounded the rap music record label Death Row Records ("Death Row") with Marion "Suge" Knight ("Knight"). Defendants' Statement of Genuine Issues of Material Fact ("DSGIMF") ¶ 1. From 1991 until 1996, plaintiff co-owned Death Row with Knight and was a producer, performer, and writer on the record label. Id. On December 15, 1992, plaintiff released the album "The Chronic." Id. ¶ 2.

On March 14, 1996, plaintiff entered into a written agreement surrendering his ownership interest in Death Row and resigning as an officer, employee and director of the company (the "1996 Agreement"). Plaintiff's Statement of Genuine Issues of Material Fact ("PSGIMF") ¶ 3. Paragraph 3 of the 1996 Agreement provides, in relevant parts:

(a) Nothing contained in this Agreement shall affect any artist's royalties, mechanical royalties or producer's royalties due or to become due by Death Row to Young on or after January 1, 1996.

(b) Subject to paragraph 3(a) hereof, Young hereby irrevocably assigns, transfers, conveys and quitclaims to Death Row all vested or contingent right, title and interest of every kind and description, including all copyrights, in and to the master recordings embodied in sound recordings heretofore released by Death Row, including but not limited to the sound recording entitled "The Chronic". . . .

(c) . . . unless the parties hereto otherwise agree in writing, the foregoing master recordings shall only be distributed in the manners heretofore distributed.

(d) Subject to paragraph 3(a) hereof, Young hereby irrevocably consents to the inclusion of any or all of the foregoing master recordings in one Death Row "Greatest Hits" or "Best of" album.

Declaration of Stephen D. Rothschild (Rothschild Decl.), Exh. 1 (1996 Agreement) at 2–3. . . .

Plaintiff's recordings were not available on the internet for digital download prior to the execution of the 1996 Agreement.[2] DSGIMF ¶ 4. In March 2000, Death Row concluded an agreement with third party internet vendor Musicmaker.com ("Musicmaker"), making plaintiff's recordings, including "The Chronic," available for digital download over the internet. Declaration of Michael D. Holtz ("Holtz Decl."), Exhs. E and F.

On January 15, 2009, defendants acquired Death Row's assets from Death Row's bankruptcy estate. PSGIMF ¶ 5. Defendants' purchase of Death Row's assets included the rights to plaintiff's recordings subject to the terms of the 1996 Agreement. Id.

Plaintiff claims that since acquiring Death Row's assets in bankruptcy, defendants have distributed digital copies of "The Chronic," and individual songs from the album, through internet retailers such as iTunes and Amazon.com. Plaintiff's Statement of Undisputed Material Facts ("PSUMF") ¶ 6. Furthermore, Death Row has distributed the following albums that include plaintiff's recordings along with recordings by other artists: (1) "Death Row Greatest Hits;" (2) "The Very Best of Death Row;" (3) "Death Row Records—15 Years on Death Row;" (4) "Dr. Dre Chronicles Deluxe—Death Row Classics;" (5) "Dr. Dre Chronicles—Death Row Classics;" (6) "Death Row Records—The Singles Collection;" and (7) "Ultimate Death Row Box Set" (collectively, "the post-1996 albums"). Id. ¶ 7.

The gravamen of the dispute is whether defendants breached the 1996 Agreement by making available for digital download plaintiff's album "The Chronic," among other works, and releasing multiple "Best of or Greatest Hit" albums, without his authorization.

* * * *

IV. DISCUSSION

A. Breach of Contract

The parties' cross-motions raise three fundamental issues: (1) whether defendants breached paragraph 3(c) of the 1996 Agreement by distributing digital downloads of "The Chronic," allowing internet retailers to sell plaintiff's recordings as singles, and including plaintiff's recordings on the post-1996 albums; (2) whether defendants breached paragraph 3(d) of the 1996 Agreement by distributing plaintiff's recordings on the post-1996 albums; and (3) whether defendants have any colorable affirmative defenses. Because these issues require the Court to construe the 1996 Agreement, the Court begins with an overview of the principles of contract interpretation under California law.

---

[2]   Digital or "permanent" downloads are "are digital copies of recordings that, once downloaded over the Internet, remain on an end-user's computer or other device until deleted." F.B.T. Prods., LLC v. Aftermath Records, 621 F.3d 958, 962 (9th Cir.2010).

Under California law, "[t]he language of a contract is to govern its interpretation, if the language is clear and explicit, and does not involve an absurdity." Cal. Civ.Code § 1638. The trial court's goal is to give effect to the parties' mutual intent at the time of contracting. . . . If the contract is reduced to a writing, the court should attempt to determine the parties' intent from the writing alone, if possible. Id.

Where contract terms are disputed, however, the trial court must provisionally consider extrinsic evidence which is relevant to show whether the contractual language is reasonably susceptible to the competing interpretations advanced by the parties. . . . "If in light of the extrinsic evidence the court decides the language is 'reasonably susceptible' to the interpretation urged, the extrinsic evidence is then admitted to aid in . . . interpreting the contract." Winet v. Price, 4 Cal.App.4th 1159, 1165, 6 Cal.Rptr.2d 554 (1992); see also Aftermath Records, 621 F.3d at 963. . . .

1.   Paragraph 3(c)

Plaintiff argues that defendants breached paragraph 3(c) of the 1996 Agreement by making "The Chronic" available for digital download on the internet, allowing internet retailers to sell as singles his recordings that were not sold as singles prior to the execution of the 1996 Agreement, and distributing his recordings on the post-1996 albums. Pl.'s Mot. at 7–10; Pl.'s Reply at 2.

Paragraph 3(c) provides that "unless the parties hereto otherwise agree in writing, the foregoing master recordings shall only be distributed in the manners heretofore distributed." Rothschild Decl., Exh. 1 at 2. Plaintiff argues that this provision unambiguously prohibits defendants from distributing his recordings in any other way than they were distributed prior to the execution of the 1996 Agreement. Pl.'s Mot. at 9–10. In support of his argument, plaintiff asserts that "distribution" is how record companies disseminate recorded music to consumers, and case law supports the conclusion that digital downloads are a manner of distribution. . . . Moreover, plaintiff asserts that legal commentators have recognized that the usage of "distribution" in the music industry includes digital downloading as a form of distribution. Id. at 9 (citing secondary sources).

Disputing plaintiff's interpretation, defendants argue that paragraph 3(c) is intended to address the "manner" in which the recordings are distributed—meaning that the songs on "The Chronic" should not be remixed, mixed in a different order than how they appeared on the original album, or mixed together with other recordings.[FN3 omitted] Deft.'s Opp'n at 12. Defendants further maintain that they have not breached paragraph 3(c) by distributing the post-1996 albums because the only songs by plaintiff included on those albums are songs that Death Row distributed as singles prior to the execution of the 1996 Agreement.[FN4 omitted] Deft.'s Opp'n at 9.

As an initial matter, the Court finds that the language in paragraph 3(c) providing, "the foregoing master recordings shall only be distributed in the manners heretofore distributed," precludes defendants from distributing plaintiff's recordings in any way other than how they were made available prior to the execution of the 1996 Agreement. Thus, the plain language of paragraph 3(c) prohibits defendants from exploiting plaintiff's works through new distribution channels—such as the internet—and bars defendants from altering plaintiff's recordings or distributing them in different configurations—including as singles or on new albums. The terms "manners" and "distribution" are admittedly broad, but they do not appear to be unclear or ambiguous. See Aftermath Records, 621 F.3d at 964 ("A contractual term is not ambiguous just because it is broad.").

Nevertheless, because the terms of the 1996 Agreement are in dispute, the Court must provisionally consider the extrinsic evidence to determine whether paragraph 3(c) is "reasonably susceptible to the competing interpretation advanced by [defendants] ." Pac. Gas & Elec. Co., 69 Cal.2d at 39, 69 Cal.Rptr. 561, 442 P.2d 641. Defendants offer no compelling evidence why the phrase "manners heretofore distributed" should be limited to remixing plaintiff's songs, putting the songs in a different order, or mixing them together with other recordings. Although these actions may breach the 1996 Agreement, there is no evidence supporting defendants' interpretation they are the only actions that constitute a breach. Indeed, unlike many other recording contracts, paragraph 3(c) appears to expressly confine Death Row's ability to exploit plaintiff's recordings to the manners in which they had been previously released, and the state of the industry as it existed in 1996. See Cohen v. Paramount Pictures Corp., 845 F.2d 851, 853–54 (9th Cir.1988) (holding that a contract granting rights to "[t]he exhibition of [a] motion picture . . . by means of television " did not encompass the right to distribute the film in videocassette form where the contract contained a broad restriction reserving the licensor "all rights and uses in and to said musical composition, except those herein granted.") (emphasis in original); see also Boosey & Hawkins Music Publishers, Ltd. v. Walt Disney Co., 145 F.3d 481, 487 (2d Cir.1998) ("new-use analysis should rely on neutral principles of contract interpretations. . . . If the contract is more reasonably read to convey one meaning, the party benefitted by that reading should be able to rely on it; the party seeking exception or deviation from the meaning reasonably conveyed by the words of the contract should bear the burden of negotiating for language that would express the limitation or deviation.").

The conclusion that paragraph 3(c) broadly restricts defendants' ability to distribute plaintiff's recordings on the internet and in different configurations comports with what appears to be the parties' purpose in including the provision in the 1996 Agreement. . . . At the same time the parties were negotiating the 1996 Agreement, plaintiff was orchestrating an exclusive agreement to form his own record label, "The Aftermath," under Interscope Records. Paragraph 3(c) was intended as a restriction on Death Row's right to exploit plaintiff's work so he would be able to negotiate higher royalty rates for any new manner of distribution of his recordings. See Rothschild Opp'n Decl., Exh.1 (Paterno Depo.) at 215:3–24; Holtz Decl., Exh. A (Paterno Depo.) at 103:2–104:9. In addition, because plaintiff was relinquishing his creative control in Death Row and striking out on his own, he sought to retain some measure of security in how Death Row presented his art to the public after his departure. Id.[5]

* * * *

Moreover, plaintiff's subsequent conduct does not demonstrate that he acquiesced in the digital distribution of his recordings on the internet. When plaintiff's recordings were first made available for digital downloading, plaintiff's counsel wrote cease and desist letters to third parties and to Death Row demanding that internet retailers immediately remove downloads containing plaintiff's recordings. See Rothschild Decl., Exhs. 15 and 17; Holtz Decl., Exhs. G, H, and I. For example, plaintiff's counsel wrote to Musicmaker that "Death Row Records has no right to distribute individual tracks containing Mr. Young's performance, whether by digital download or traditional compact disc distribution." Rothschild Decl., Exh 15 at 1. In a more detailed letter sent to Musicmaker on April 5, 2000, plaintiff's counsel objected to the distribution of plaintiff's performances "unless they are distributed as part of, and in the same configuration, of albums previously released by Death Row Records." Rothschild Decl., Exh. 17 at 1. Similarly, in a letter to Death Row dated March 26, 2000, plaintiff's counsel wrote, "Death Row Records only has the right to distribute Mr. Young's tracks as part of the albums on which they originally appeared. Death Row Records has no right to distribute individual tracks in any other configuration." Holtz Decl., Exh. H at 1.

Defendants argue that because plaintiff's protestations focused on the online distribution of his recordings as single tracks, he acquiesced to Death Row's internet distribution in all other respects. The Court disagrees. It does not follow that because plaintiff primarily challenged

---

[5]   Peter Paterno, plaintiff's lawyer who was involved in the negotiation of the 1996 Agreement, testified that the reasons plaintiff wanted to restrict future rights was so that he would be in a position to negotiate when those rights became available and because "the primary purveyor of digital music . . . iTunes will not let you sell albums as a single package, so . . . you wanted the ability to control how your art got presented to the public." Rothschild Opp'n Decl., Exh.1 (Paterno Depo.) at 215:3–24. Paterno further testified that "all that . . . Death Row could do with [plaintiff's recordings] is continue to distribute them in the way they had been distributing them until then. There was no new methods, no new coupling, no new licenses, nothing." Hotlz Decl., Exh A. at 104:4–9.

Death Row's distribution on one ground, he necessarily acceded to the distribution on all other grounds. Rather, viewed its entirety, plaintiff's subsequent conduct cannot be interpreted as permitting Death Row to distribute his recordings via digital download.

. . . . As discussed above, paragraph 3(c) unambiguously limits Death Row's right to distribute plaintiff's recordings in configurations different from the manners in which they were released prior to the execution of the 1996 Agreement. Death Row's release of certain songs from "The Chronic" as singles prior to 1996 only permits defendants to continue distributing those songs as singles. Distributing a song as a single is not the same as distributing it on a compilation. Therefore, paragraph 3(c) unambiguously prohibits Death Row from distributing compilation albums containing plaintiff's recordings without plaintiff's written approval.

[¶] . . . In sum, the Court concludes that paragraph 3(c) unambiguously prohibits defendants from distributing plaintiff's recordings in any fashion other than how they were made available prior to the execution of the 1996 Agreement without plaintiff's written consent. This includes making "The Chronic" available for digital download on the internet, allowing online retailers to sell as singles plaintiff's recordings that were not sold individually prior to 1996, and distributing plaintiff's recordings on compilation albums.[FN8 omitted] The undisputed extrinsic evidence does not support defendants' interpretation that the scope of paragraph 3(c) is limited to remixing plaintiff's songs, putting the songs in a different order, or mixing them together with other recordings.

* * * *

V. CONCLUSION

In accordance with the foregoing, the Court hereby GRANTS in part and DENIES in part plaintiff's and defendants' cross-motions for partial summary judgment.

IT IS SO ORDERED.

NOTES AND QUESTIONS

1.   As you might imagine, the more successful an author is before entering into a particular agreement, the more control he or she is likely to be able to exercise over the final product released under the agreement. Agreements run the gamut from total control for high-profile artists to total control for the companies acquiring the works produced under an agreement. What do you see as the pros and cons in granting total creative control to one party? Can control be easily shared—i.e., can contractual language adequately articulate how the parties are to reach agreement about creative issues if control is shared?

2.   As the Dr. Dre case illustrates, control can also involve not only approvals over the final works released to the public, but also over the manner in which those works may be used. What advice would you give to a potential copyright licensee for use of a work in an arguably controversial context to ensure that no approvals other than the copyright license are needed for the use? Do you think contracts between a label and recording artist or publisher and composer should be allowed to encumber uses of a work by a copyright licensee?

C. PERMISSIONS AND LIMITATIONS ON USE OF NAME AND LIKENESS

As was discussed in Chapter 9, an issue for many composers and performing artists is how their names, likenesses, and recorded voices, as well as works publicly associated with their identities, may be used in exploiting the works they create and related works. Most publishing and recording agreements include a general grant of permission to the publisher/label to use the author's name and likeness in connection with promotion and exploitation of the works delivered under the agreement. Some contracts have even broader language that purports to grant rights to use the author's name and likeness generally, rather than solely for promotion/exploitation purposes, and others include reservations by the authors of the right to approve or veto specific types of uses that they might find offensive.

SAMPLE PROVISION FROM RECORDING AGREEMENT

Company and its designees shall have the right throughout the universe in perpetuity to use and to permit others to use Artist's name, photographs and other likenesses of Artist, and biographical material concerning Artist in connection with the exploitation of any or all of the Works, and for trade or otherwise in connection with this Agreement. Artist shall be deemed to have approved any such likenesses, biographical material, and/or other identification if Artist fails to submit to Company specific objections thereto within ten (10) business days after Company has notified Artist of their availability for Artist's inspection.

SAMPLE PROVISION FROM SONGWRITING AGREEMENT

Publisher shall have the right, and may grant to others the right, to reproduce, print, publish, or disseminate, in any medium, Writer's name, portrait, picture and likeness and biographical material concerning Writer in connection with uses of the Compositions (including, but not limited to, print uses of the Compositions) and for the purpose of indicating Writer's association with Publisher. During the Term of this Agreement Writer shall not authorize any party other than Publisher to use Writer's name and likeness in connection with musical compositions that are subject to this Agreement. Writer agrees, during the Term of this Agreement and at Publisher's reasonable request, to furnish to Publisher biographies and likenesses. If Publisher desires to use any likeness not supplied by Writer or biographical material different from that supplied by Writer, Writer shall have the right to approve same in writing, which approval Writer shall not unreasonably withhold.

The cases and materials discussed in Chapter 9 give an overview of how the right of publicity and Lanham Act might provide non-contractual protection to composers and recording artists who complain about uses of their name, voice, or likeness in ways that could confuse the public or damage the composers/artists, but keep in mind that those legal claims are premised upon unauthorized uses. Where a contract expressly grants permission for certain uses or provides a general approval for all uses, composers and recording artists will have no recourse under those legal theories. However, when a publisher or label fails to seek required contractual approvals or exceeds them, a breach of contract may be found. The case below gives an example of how the right of publicity, Lanham Act, and contractual provisions in a recording artist's agreements with different record companies can interact in a given dispute.

Slip-N-Slide Records, Inc. v. TVT Records, LLC

2005 WL 8155006 (S.D. Fla. Sept. 30, 2005)[2]

REPORT AND RECOMMENDATION

Stephen T. Brown, U.S. Magistrate Judge

This cause is before the Court on the Plaintiff's Emergency Motion for Preliminary Injunction, filed July 8, 2005, and on Counterclaimant's Emergency Motion for Preliminary Injunction, filed July 18, 2005. . . .

Procedural Facts

On March 28, 2005, Plaintiff Slip-N-Slide Records, Inc. ("S-N-S"), a record producer and distributor filed a three count complaint in the Circuit Court for Miami-Dade County, Florida . . . in connection with the release and distribution of a record album entitled "Welcome to the 305." That action was subsequently removed to this Court. On April 29, 2005, Defendant/Counterclaimant TeeVee Toons, Inc., d/b/a TVT Records ("TVT") filed a counterclaim against S-N-S, . . . alleging Federal Trademark Infringement in Violation of 15 U.S.C. § 1125(a) (Count I), and False Designation of Origin and False Advertising in Violation of 15 U.S.C. § 1125(a) (Count II).

FACTS

"Welcome to the 305" and "M.I.A.M.I."

On September 1, 2001, Armando Perez, a recording artist professionally known as "Pitbull," ("Pitbull") entered into a recording contract with producer Julian Boothe ("Boothe"), President of Rudebwoy ("the Boothe contract"). That contract gave Boothe exclusive copyright ownership as to the master recordings made under the agreement, which were to be deemed "works made for hire." Ex. 3, ¶ 7. The contract also provided that Boothe could use Pitbull's name, likeness, photographs and biographical information in connection with publicizing the Boothe Masters. ¶ 7b.

In 2001, pursuant to the Boothe contract, Pitbull made recordings (the "Boothe Masters"), at least portions of which were later used in the recording of "Welcome to the 305," ("305"). . . .

In October 2003, Pitbull, through his agent The Diaz Brothers Music Group, Inc. ("DBMG") entered into an agreement with TVT ("the TVT contract," dated October 23, 2003), which provided that Pitbull would furnish exclusive recording services to TVT. The TVT contract further provided as follows:

5. (a)   You warrant and represent that you have the right to enter this agreement and Exhibit "A" annexed hereto and made a

---

    [2]   Footnotes omitted.

part hereof, and to grant the rights provided for hereunder and fully perform hereunder. . . . You and Artist hereby assign to us in perpetuity and will deliver to us hereunder all demonstration recordings, all masters and recordings embodying Artist's performances recorded prior to the date hereof and not heretofore commercially released. . . .

* * *

(c) All other terms and conditions where not inconsistent with the terms hereof will be set forth in our standard exclusive "long form" recording agreement attached hereto as Exhibit "A", it being agreed that in the event of any inconsistency, this agreement will take precedence over said "long-form" agreement . . . .

Ex. 13, ¶¶ 5(a), (c).

Jacqueline Sussman, Vice President of Business and Legal Affairs for TVT, testified that the "TVT Exclusive Recording Artist" agreement which is attached to Exhibit 13 is the "long form" agreement which became "Exhibit A," to the TVT contract, and which provides, inter alia:

* * *

5.04 TVT shall have the perpetual right, which right shall be exclusive during the Term, without any liability to any Person, to use and to authorize other Persons to use the names (including any professional names or sobriquets), approved likenesses (including pictures, portraits and caricatures), and approved biographical material of or relating to you and Artist, . . ., for purposes of advertising and promotion in connection with the making and exploitation of Records hereunder and in TVT's general goodwill advertising. . . .

* * *

10.04 During the Term, subject to the foregoing provisions of this paragraph 10, Artist's recording services will be rendered exclusively to TVT. . . .

* * *

10.08 . . . . Subject to the foregoing provisions of this paragraph 10, neither you, Artist, nor any person deriving any rights from you or Artist, shall use or authorize or permit any Person other than TVT to use Artist's name (including any professional name or sobriquet), likeness (including picture, portrait or caricature) or biography in connection with the manufacture and/or exploitation of Master Recordings or Records (including Audio-Visual Devices). (emphasis added).

Ex. 13. Exhibit B, the Artist Inducement Agreement, was also signed by Pitbull.

Pursuant to this agreement, on August 24, 2004, TVT released Pitbull's debut album, entitled "M.I.A.M.I." It contains twelve tracks with Pitbull and other featured artists, and although Pitbull wrote all of the songs, other writers are also credited. The cover of the album contains a photograph of Pitbull, wearing a black shirt and a green fatigue colored cap with "305" on the front. TVT's art director created also created a logo for the cover, which was the name "Pitbull" in a stylized format (essentially Old English font with a stylized "P") (See Ex. 34) ("TVT's Pitbull logo"). TVT's Pitbull logo was used in connection with its promotion and advertising of M.I.A.M.I. and Pitbull's recordings as a TVT artist (Ex. 15), with TVT investing close to four million dollars in the project. Sales of the M.I.A.M.I. album achieved "gold" status. [¶] . . . .

The Allegedly Infringing Conduct

Sometime after there had been substantial sales of M.I.A.M.I, S-N-S began advertising and marketing for the release of 305, which contains some of the Boothe Masters. That album, which has not yet been released, also includes instrumental tracks, vocal tracks from other artists, and "skits," or short conversational recordings. Pitbull performs to some extent on every musical track, although he does not appear on the skits.

S-N-S placed an advertisement for 305 which describes it as containing "Never Heard Previously Unreleased Material" from Pitbull and includes the titles of some of the tracks. . . .

The cover art created for 305 (Ex. 7) includes a photograph of Pitbull, again in the same clothes but a third pose. It also contains a Pitbull logo which is similar but not identical to TVT's Pitbull logo, in that all letters, including the "P" are in Old English font (as opposed to the stylized "P"). Mr. Boothe testified that the graphic designer suggested this design after stating that "people are familiar" with the TVT Pitbull logo. There is no indication on the cover as to the date when Pitbull recorded his songs, or that the songs are based on prior unreleased recordings.

Cover art for *Welcome to the 305*   Cover art for *M.I.A.M.I.*

One-sheet ad for *Welcome to the 305* (Exhibit B to Counterclaim)

S-N-S also issued a promotional "one sheet" for 305 (Ex. 17), which contains the same photograph as contained in the ad, and the Pitbull logo that is contained on the album cover and states, inter alia:

> Pitbull's current album "M.I.A.M.I." is one of the top selling albums in the country. This Pitbull special edition called "Welcome to the 305" is finally becoming available for the first time. This rare collection of songs was recorded when Pitbull first started in the rap game. The biggest producers in the Hip Hop game helped in reproducing this album. . . .

> Pitbull has made a name for himself with hard work, catchy songs, and street creditability [sic]. The full-length album is something

has [sic] fans have been waiting for and it's perfect timing when he's on top of his career.

The young 23 Cuban-American has dominated the charts with hit songs collaborating with Lil Jon, Ying Yang Twins[,] Daddy Yankee, Nina Sky, and many others. Now with this collection of songs that has never been released before, fans will get a chance to catch him in rare form.

Ex. 17. The one-sheet also refers to M.I.A.M.I. by stating: "Top Selling Independent artist of 2004 with his current album still selling strongly weekly" and "Album sales for Pitbull's Debut album 'M.I.A.M.I.['] surpass 300,000 copies as Pitbull prepares Video for next bilingual single 'Toma,' the follow-up to his breakthrough hit 'Culo'." Ex. 17.

The Cease and Desist Letter

Ms. Sussman, after seeing the advertisement and one-sheet for 305 sometime prior to March, 2005, and noting that the TVT contract did not contain a schedule of "previously unreleased masters," contacted Angela Martinez, Esq., President and Director of Pitbull Productions, who told her that 305 contained old songs Pitbull had recorded for Boothe. On March 2, 2005 Ms. Sussman wrote a letter to the attorneys for Pitbull Productions and DBMG demanding that 305 not be released, that they refrain from using Pitbull's name, likeness and biography in connection with 305, and further demanding an assignment of the previous unreleased masters. (Ex. 43).

. . . . [¶] On March 28, 2005, Ms. Sussman, on behalf of TVT, sent out Cease and Desist letters (the "Letter" or "Letters"), possibly one hundred in number, to numerous distributors, including Alternative Distribution Alliance, Inc., ("ADA"), the intended distributor of 305, with whom S-N-S had a non-terminable contract, stating inter alia:

. . . . The album known as "Welcome to the 305," currently being advertised for release by Slip-N-Slide Records, has been compiled and is being promoted without TVT's authorization and is in violation of TVT's rights.

You are hereby notified that:

1. The sale, placement, distribution, marketing, advertisement and/or promotion of the "Welcome to the 305" album violates TVT's rights and constitutes, without limitation, violation of the Lanham Act.

2. TVT will enforce all of its rights and will seek redress for any violation of those rights, to the fullest extent of the law.

Ex. 2. . . .

On April 28, 2005, TVT filed a trademark application for the TVT Pitbull logo for use in "musical sound recordings and musical video recordings by the recording artist with the same name." Ex. 9.

Effect of the Letters

Ted Lucas, President of S-N-S, testified that he had received 103,000 pre-orders, totaling over $800,000 copies of 305 before the Letters were received by the distributors. According to Mr. Lucas, he was originally going to release 305 in April, 2005 and agreed to change it to May at the request of TVT, but was unable to release it in May because virtually every distributor who received the Letters refused to sell it. . . . [¶¶]

* * * *

DISCUSSION

In order to be entitled to injunctive relief, the moving party must show: (1) a substantial likelihood of success on the merits; (2) a substantial threat of irreparable injury if the injunction is not granted; (3) that the threatened injury to the moving party outweighs the harm an injunction may cause the non-moving party; and (4) that the injunction would not disserve the public interest. See e.g. American Red Cross v. Palm Beach Blood Bank, Inc., 143 F.3d 1407, 1410 (11th Cir. 1998). A preliminary injunction is an extraordinary remedy that should only be granted when the movant has made a clear showing of its burden of proof. Café 207 v. St. Johns County, 989 F.2d 1136, 1137 (11th Cir. 1993).

* * * *

II. COUNTERCLAIM

A. Count I—Trademark Infringement

TVT maintains that the Counter-defendants have violated its trademark rights with respect to the TVT Pitbull logo. To establish a claim for trademark infringement, TVT must establish that the Counter-defendants "used the mark in commerce without its consent and 'that the unauthorized use was likely to deceive, cause confusion, or result in mistake.'" Nitro Leisure Products, L.L.C. v. Acushnet Co., 341 F.3d 1356, 1359 (11th Cir. 2003) (quoting McDonald's Corp. v. Robertson, 147 F.3d 1301, 1306 (11th Cir. 1998)).

Counter-defendants respond that TVT does not have any underlying trademark rights to the name "Pitbull," in that the trade name "PITBULL" is owned by Pitbull Productions. See also TVT contract ¶ 10.01.2. Additionally, the TVT contract only grants to TVT a limited right to use Pitbull's trade name, and only in connection with the promotion and sale of recordings "Delivered" under the contract or recorded by Pitbull "during the Term" of the contract. ¶ 5.01. See also M& J Enterprises v. Outler, 717 So. 2d 620 (Fla. 3d DCA 1998) (citing the rule that "the name of an artist,

[or] musician . . . is not regarded as a trade name, and, as such, salable or assignable") (citing 74 Am.Jur.2d Trademarks and Tradenames § 22 (1974)). The Counter-defendants likewise had contractual rights to use the Pitbull name in connection with the advertising and promotion of the Boothe Masters under the Boothe contract.

. . . . [¶¶] As to the issue of whether TVT has any protectible rights in the stylized Pitbull logo it created for "M.I.A.M.I." and registered for trademark protection, TVT must show that the defendant's use of the mark (the name "Pitbull" in Old English font with a stylized "P") is likely to deceive or cause confusion. Nitro Leisure Products, 341 F.3d at 1359. . . . The only evidence regarding the public's awareness of TVT's Pitbull mark was Boothe's testimony that his logo designer stated that people were "familiar" with the TVT Pitbull logo. There was no evidence, however, that the music industry or buying public associates the TVT Pitbull logo with TVT, as opposed to any other music label or producer, or with Pitbull himself.

Accordingly, the Court finds that TVT has failed to show a reasonable likelihood of success on its claim for trademark infringement.

B. Count II—False Advertising/False designation of Origin

Similarly, in order to prove a claim for false designation of origin, TVT must establish that the Counter-defendants adopted a mark confusingly similar to TVT's mark such that there was a likelihood of confusion as to the origin of the goods. Ross Bicycles, Inc. v. Cycles USA, Inc., 765 F.2d 1502, 1503 (11th Cir. 1985); Conagra, Inc. v. Singleton, 743 F.2d 1508, 1512 (11th Cir. 1984). . . . TVT argues that advertising for 305 was misleading on several fronts, including by making a claim that the recordings were "new," as opposed to previously recorded unreleased masters. Even assuming that this representation would be false or misleading, the Court first finds no evidence that the Counter-defendants advertised 305 as a "new" album or a "follow-up" album to MIAMI, or anything other than previously unreleased recordings. . . .

Nor do the photographs of Pitbull which are displayed on the 305 cover and included in the advertisement and the one sheet infringe on any of TVT's rights or constitute false advertising in that (1) it is uncontested that TVT has no rights in the photographs themselves; (2) there is no evidence that the public associates those photographs specifically with the M.I.A.M.I. album or with TVT, and (3) there is no evidence that Pitbull's "look" or "style" has changed in such a manner that it can be related to any particular "period" in his career. This third factor distinguishes this case from the case of Rich v. RCA Corp., 390 F. Supp. 530 (S.D.N.Y. 1975), which concerned a new recording with a "current" likeness of Charlie Rich on the front and back of the jacket, but which contained songs recorded by Rich ten to fourteen years earlier. In that case, the court noted that "[i]t appears from the affidavits and exhibits that Rich's singing style and appearance has undergone considerable change over the last ten years." Ms. Sussman testified that she is not aware of any change in appearance between the time the Boothe Masters were recorded and the release of M.I.A.M.I., and Mr. Boothe testified that Pitbull's look has not changed from that time to the present. There is also no competent evidence that Pitbull's singing style has changed. To the extent that TVT complains that the CD cover notes do not state the dates of Pitbull's recordings, Counter-defendants have proffered that they will place on the jacket a sticker which states that the CD contains previously unreleased masters.

Finally, even if TVT had proven that the public would be "confused" into thinking that this was a "Pitbull album" when it actually is not, that it was a "new" Pitbull album when it was not, or that it was a TVT album when it was not, there is no evidence that this will work to the detriment of TVT (i.e., that TVT will be irreparably harmed). The only evidence that the album will "disparage" Pitbull or his image (and therefore TVT's interests) is one posting to a message board suggesting that 305 is "not as good" as M.I.A.M.I. and is not a "party album," in that writer's opinion. The Court finds this showing to be woefully inadequate.

Accordingly, the Court finds that TVT has failed to establish a likelihood of success on the merits of its Counterclaim.

RECOMMENDATION

Accordingly, it is respectfully recommended

as follows:

1.   That Plaintiff's Emergency Motion for Preliminary Injunction be GRANTED, and that Defendant TVT be enjoined from interfering in any way with the distribution and/or release of "Welcome to the 305"; provided, however, that Plaintiff shall place on all copies of the CD a label which states "Contains Previously Unreleased Material."

2.   That Counterclaimant's Emergency Motion for Preliminary Injunction be DENIED. . . .

DONE AND ORDERED this 28th day of September, 2005 at Miami, Florida.

NOTES AND QUESTIONS

1.   Do the sample provisions provided at the start of this section regarding permission to use name and likeness raise any issues for you, assuming you were acting as counsel for either of the parties to the contract? If so, what? How might you seek to revise those provisions to address those issues?

2.   Recall the discussion in Chapter 9 regarding the distinction between assessing likelihood of consumer confusion under the Lanham Act and unauthorized commercial use under state right of publicity protections. Do you think that the analysis in the *Slip-n-Slide Records* case adequately addressed those issues? Can you think of ways to revise the contractual language between the parties in the *Slip-n-Slide Records* case to avoid the assertion of claims like those raised in the litigation in that case?

3.   Note that the Report and Recommendation excerpted above in the *Slip-n-Slide Records* case was a decision at the preliminary injunction stage of the case. After over a year of discovery in the case, the court denied cross-motions for summary judgment, concluding that there were compelling arguments on both sides and that the issues thus should be decided by a jury. With respect to the Lanham Act and false advertising claims by TVT, the court noted:

> [T]he parties have presented colorable arguments concerning whether the TVT Pitbull logo is sufficiently stylized and distinct enough to be susceptible to trademark protection. When the record is examined with an eye toward drawing reasonable inferences in favor of TVT's position, the Court can see, at least for now, that TVT may be able to convince a reasonable jury that its logo merited trademark protection. If, on the other hand, one looks at this record from the movant's perspective and draws inferences in favor of SNS, one can see how a reasonable jury could agree with Magistrate Judge Brown. That inference, however, cannot be drawn at the summary judgment stage. Therefore, the factual question as to whether TVT had protectible legal rights in the logo must be left for the trier of fact. . . .
>
> [¶] Pitbull testified it would be detrimental to his career if his fans confused the 305 Album as the follow-up studio album to his M.I.A.M.I. album. Whether TVT, the party in this case, would also have been injured, and to what extent, are arguably unresolved questions. Whether previously unreleased recordings are properly termed "new," and if not, whether such representations had a material effect on the purchasing decisions of consumers, are additional questions for the jury to resolve. Accordingly, the cross motions for summary judgment on the false designation of origin and false advertising must be denied.

Slip-N-Slide Records, Inc. v. TVT Records, LLC, No. 05-21113-CIV-TORRES, 2007 WL 473273, at *7–11 (S.D. Fla. Feb. 8, 2007). The jury ultimately ruled against TVT and in favor of Slip-N-Slide, rejecting TVT's claims based on use of the Pitbull logo and awarding Slip-N-Slide more than $2 million in compensatory damages for tortious interference stemming from the cease and desist letters sent by TVT and more than $6 million in punitive damages (which were later reduced by the court). See *Slip-N-Slide Records, Inc. v. TVT Records, LLC*, No. 05-21113-CIV, 2007 WL 3232274, at *37 (S.D. Fla. Oct. 31, 2007).

D. NATURE OF THE PARTIES' LEGAL RELATIONSHIP

Publishing and recording agreements often include a number of different ways of articulating the nature of the parties' relationship—independent contractors, work-for-hire, *not* employee/employer—but courts will often look beyond the language of the agreement to the actual facts and circumstances of the relationship to determine whether the contract is the sole source of rights and obligations between the parties. The law is fairly settled that—typically—no fiduciary duty or trust relationship arises out of songwriting or recording agreements without specific provisions in the agreement that create such obligations. Of course, the duty to account for revenues when royalties are provided for in an agreement provides a trust-like obligation to properly collect and distribute revenues covered by the agreement, but that obligation is limited and does not extend generally to the parties' relationship. Below, we provide cases that analyze both the general rule and its exceptions.[3]

John Mellencamp in
Germany, June 2011
Photo by Andrea Sartorati
(CC-BY-2.0)

MELLENCAMP V. RIVA MUSIC LTD.

698 F.Supp. 1154 (S.D.N.Y. 1988)

OPINION AND ORDER

CONBOY, DISTRICT JUDGE:

Plaintiff John J. Mellencamp, professionally known as John Cougar Mellencamp, is a songwriter, performer, and recording artist who has enjoyed enormous success in recent years. Defendants (collectively "the

---

[3] Note that the *Mellencamp* and *Silvester* cases were both also excerpted above with respect to other aspects of the parties' contractual disputes.

Riva companies") are affiliated corporations owned and/or controlled by William A. Gaff. On May 12, 1977, Mellencamp entered into a written publishing agreement with defendant G.H. Music, Ltd. Pursuant to the 1977 agreement, Mellencamp assigned to G.H. Music the worldwide copyrights in and to the compositions to be authored by him during the term of the agreement. The 1977 agreement was modified by a written agreement, dated February 28, 1979, and by letter agreement, dated February 21, 1980. On June 15, 1981, John Cougar, Inc. entered into a written publishing agreement with defendant Riva Music, Ltd. whereby John Cougar, Inc. assigned Mellencamp's songwriting and composing services and copyrights to Riva. On June 1, 1983, Mellencamp entered into a third publishing agreement with defendant Riva Music, Inc. Finally, by written agreement dated July 26, 1985, among Riva Music, Inc., Riva Music, Ltd., G.H. Music, Ltd, Mellencamp, and John Cougar Inc., each of the prior publishing agreements was amended in certain respects. In exchange for the assignment of the copyrights, Mellencamp received a percentage of the royalties earned from the exploitation of his music.

By virtue of the publishing agreements, according to the complaint, the Riva companies became fiduciaries for Mellencamp's interests. In his first and second claims, Mellencamp alleges that defendants breached their fiduciary duties by failing to actively promote his songs and to use their best efforts to obtain all the monies rightfully due him from third parties. In his third claim, Mellencamp contends that the Riva companies breached the various publishing agreements controlling their relationship by consistently underreporting royalties due him and by failing to timely render royalty statements and payments. In his fourth and final claim, Mellencamp contends that he entered into a binding agreement with the Riva companies pursuant to which the defendants agreed to release him from all obligations under the publishing contracts and to return all the rights to and in his musical compositions in exchange for $3 million dollars. This agreement was reached, according to plaintiff, at a luncheon meeting in a New York City restaurant among Sigmund Balaban, Mellencamp's accountant and advisor, William Gaff, and Milton Marks, Gaff's attorney. Both sides agree that the sale of the Riva companies' rights in Mellencamp's compositions was discussed, at least in general terms, at this meeting. The parties are in sharp dispute, however, over the legal consequences of their discussions.

Defendants now move pursuant to Rule 12(b)(6) to dismiss the complaint on the ground that it fails to state any valid claim for relief. Specifically, defendants contend 1) that the first two claims fail as a matter of law because no fiduciary duties are owed by a publisher to an author under a publishing agreement . . . .

ANALYSIS

I. Fiduciary Duties

Under New York law, the existence of fiduciary obligations in a particular relationship cannot be determined by recourse to fixed formulas or precedents:

> Broadly stated, a fiduciary relationship is one founded upon trust or confidence reposed by one person in the integrity and fidelity of another. It is said that the relationship exists in all cases in which influence has been reposed and betrayed. The rule embraces both technical fiduciary relations and those informal relations which exist whenever one man trusts in, and relies upon, another (see *Mobil Oil Corp. v. Rubenfeld,* 72 Misc.2d 392, 399–400, 339 N.Y.S.2d 623, affd. 77 Misc.2d 962, 357 N.Y.S.2d 589, revs. on other grounds 48 A.D.2d 428, 370 N.Y.S.2d 943). Such a relationship might be found to exist, in appropriate circumstances between close friends (see *Cody v. Gallow,* 28 Misc.2d 373, 214 N.Y.S.2d 127) or even where confidence is based upon prior business dealings (see *Levine v. Chussid,* 31 Misc.2d 412, 221 N.Y.S.2d 311).

Penato v. George, 52 A.D.2d 939, 942, 383 N.Y.S.2d 900, 904–05 (2d Dep't 1976). Notwithstanding this broad rule, defendants, relying on *Van Valkenburgh, Nooger & Neville, Inc. v. Hayden Publishing Co.,* 30 N.Y.2d 34, 330 N.Y.S.2d 329, 281 N.E.2d 142 (1972), *cert. denied,* 409 U.S. 875, 93 S.Ct. 125, 34 L.Ed.2d 128 (1972), argue that the relationship between an author and a publisher can never be a fiduciary relationship. *Van Valkenburgh* does not support this proposition.

There, a publisher and an author entered into a written agreement which provided, *inter alia,* that the publisher was obligated to use its best efforts to promote the author's books. *Id.,* 30 N.Y.2d at 43, 330 N.Y.S.2d at 331, 281 N.E.2d at 144. The agreement also provided that the author would receive a 15% royalty on all books sold. *Id.* The trial court found that the publisher did not use its best efforts to promote the books, the publisher occupied a fiduciary relationship to the author, and the publisher failed to act in good faith in that relationship. *Id.* at 44, 330 N.Y.S.2d at 332, 281 N.E.2d at 144. On appeal, the Appellate Division determined that no fiduciary relationship existed between the parties. *Id.* Instead, the court concluded, the relationship between the parties was one of ordinary contract. *Id.* The court also concluded that the publisher did not breach its duty of good faith but found that the publisher did breach its contractual obligation to use its best efforts to promote the author's books. *Id.* The New York Court of Appeals affirmed, concluding that "it *could* be found, as a matter of law, *on the record,* that there was no fiduciary relationship." *Id.* at 46, 330 N.Y.S.2d at 334, 281 N.E.2d at 145 (emphasis added). *See also*

Lane v. Mercury Record Corp., 21 A.D.2d 602, 252 N.Y.S.2d 1011 (1st Dep't 1964) (a royalty or percentage arrangement would not in and of itself establish a fiduciary relationship), *aff'd*, 18 N.Y.2d 889, 276 N.Y.S.2d 626, 223 N.E.2d 35 (1966). The Court did not hold that fiduciary obligations could never arise in a relationship based at least in part on publishing agreements.

The complaint as drafted, however, goes further than this, suggesting that fiduciary obligations attach to the publisher-author relationship as a matter of law and, consequently, that the Riva companies' alleged failure to meet their express or implied contract obligations amounts to a breach of trust. In addition, there is language in several older state cases, as well as in federal cases interpreting New York state law, that arguably supports the view that a publisher-author contract creates a "technical fiduciary relation." If these cases can be so interpreted, they are directly at odds with the greater weight of authority which teaches that the conventional publisher-author arrangement is not a per se fiduciary relationship. . . .

Under New York law, every contract includes an implied covenant of good faith and fair dealing which precludes a party from engaging in conduct that will deprive the other contracting party of his benefits under their agreement. *Filner v. Shapiro*, 633 F.2d 139, 143 (2d Cir.1980). A contract is also deemed to include any promise which a reasonable person in the position of the promisee would be justified in believing was included. *Rowe v. Great Atlantic & Pacific Tea Co., Inc.*, 46 N.Y.2d 62, 69, 412 N.Y.S.2d 827, 831, 385 N.E.2d 566, 570 (1978). When the essence of a contract is the assignment or grant of an exclusive license in exchange for a share of the assignee's profits in exploiting the license, these principles imply an obligation on the part of the assignee to make reasonable efforts to exploit the license. *Havel v. Kelsey-Hayes*, 83 A.D.2d 380, 382, 445 N.Y.S.2d 333, 335 (4th Dep't 1981). *See also Zilg v. Prentice-Hall, Inc.*, 717 F.2d 671 (2d Cir.1983) (promise of publisher to publish book which it has obtained exclusive rights to implies good faith effort to promote the book). The critical point here is that a publisher's obligation to promote an author's work is one founded in contract rather than on trust principles.

While it is true that several of the cases cited by plaintiff discuss certain "trust elements that are part of the relationship between a writer and a publisher," *Nolan v. Sam Fox Publishing Company, Inc.*, 499 F.2d 1394, 1400 (2d Cir.1974), it is apparent that the courts were in fact discussing a publisher's implied-in-law contract obligations or were relying on trust principles in situations where the publisher tolerated or participated in tortious conduct against the author. [¶¶] . . . .

To the extent the cases discussed above intended to posit a per se rule that a publisher with exclusive rights in a work is a fiduciary for the author's interests, they must be rejected as inconsistent with *Van*

Valkenburgh. The better view, and the one consistent with *Van Valkenburgh,* is that the "trust elements" in a publisher-author relationship come into play when the publisher tolerates infringing conduct, *Manning, Cortner,* or participates in it, *Nelson v. Mills.* Ordinarily, however, the express and implied obligations assumed by a publisher in an exclusive licensing contract are not, as a matter of law, fiduciary duties. *See Sobol v. E.P. Dutton, Inc.,* 112 F.R.D. 99, 104 (S.D.N.Y.1986) (Weinfeld, J.); *Ekern v. Sew/Fit Company, Inc.,* 622 F.Supp. 367, 373 (N.D.Ill.1985) (citing *Van Valkenburgh*). *Cf. Beneficial Commercial Corp. v. Murray Glick Datsun,* 601 F.Supp. 770, 772 (S.D.N.Y.1985) (absent assumption of control or responsibility and corresponding repose of trust, arm's length business transaction does not give rise to fiduciary relationship). Accordingly, since plaintiff's first two claims are predicated solely upon the professional relationship between the parties and do not plead any specific conduct or circumstances upon which trust elements are implicated, they are dismissed. In the unlikely event that plaintiff can repair his pleadings in this regard, he is given leave to replead within twenty days of the date of this order.

The next case excerpt is from *Silvester v. Time Warner, Inc.,* a case that raised numerous legal theories and was first introduced above with respect to the **scope of a contractual grant of rights**. Here, we provide the court's discussion and analysis in that same opinion regarding the plaintiffs' claims that the defendant recording companies breached a fiduciary duty and the covenant of good faith and fair dealing in connection with the digital release of their works and online piracy that occurred through P2P networks.

"The Main Ingredient" in San Diego, CA, September 2008
Photo by Phil Konstantin (released to public domain)

SILVESTER V. TIME WARNER, INC.
1 Misc.3d 250, 763 N.Y.S.2d 912 (N.Y. Sup. Ct. 2003)

HELEN E. FREEDMAN, J.

* * * *

Parties

Plaintiffs are individual recording artists who, as long ago as the 1950's, signed recording contracts with defendant companies or their predecessors, which granted master recording and licensing rights to defendants or their assignors. Plaintiff Tony Silvester d/b/a the Main Ingredient, is a citizen of New York who has recording contracts with RCA Records, as predecessor to defendant BMG Entertainment, Inc., dated 1969, 1972, 1980 and 1981, and one or more record contracts with Polydor Records, as predecessor to defendant Universal Music Group, Inc., dated 1989. Silvester and the other plaintiffs were primarily members of the named groups, and still hold rights to perform under those names. . . .

Defendants Time Warner Inc, Universal Music Group, Inc. ("UMG"), Sony Music Entertainment, Inc. ("Sony"), and BMG Entertainment, Inc ("BMG") are successors in interest to companies with which plaintiffs have recording contracts. . . .

* * * *

[P]laintiffs claim that defendants negligently and recklessly exposed class members to the risk of music piracy by releasing sound recordings in digital audio files on CDs, and that defendants breached both implied covenants of good faith and fair dealing and a fiduciary obligation to protect plaintiffs' beneficial interests or property rights in their sound recordings.

* * * *

[¶]. . . Discussion

Motion to dismiss [¶] . . . Breach of Fiduciary Obligation

Plaintiffs' complaint states a claim that defendants breached a fiduciary obligation owed to defendants. However, under New York law, an artist's assignment of rights to a record company in exchange for royalties is contractual and does not create a fiduciary relationship or duty. Unless parties can show a separate duty other than to perform under the contract, no fiduciary relationship between them is established. *Sony Music Entertainment, Inc. v. Robison*, 2002 WL 272406 (S.D.N.Y.2002), *Savage Records v. Jones*, 247 A.D.2d 274, 667 N.Y.S.2d 906 (1st Dept.1998), *Rodgers v. Roulette Records, Inc.*, 677 F.Supp. 731 (S.D.N.Y.1988), *Mellencamp v. Riva Music, Ltd.*, 698 F.Supp. 1154 (S.D.N.Y.1988), *Carter v. Goodman Group Music Publishers*, 848 F.Supp. 438 (S.D.N.Y.1994). See also, *Evans v. Jelly's Jams LLC.* Index No. 601308/01 (Sup.Ct.N.Y.Co.2002) ("a contract for the collection and payment of royalties on music, does not, by itself, give rise to a fiduciary relationship."). Moreover, actions for monetary damages from breach of fiduciary duty are governed by the three year statute of limitations set forth in CPLR 214(4). . . . Plaintiffs' claims that creation and distribution of their works through digital media resulted in a breach of fiduciary duty accrued in the early 1980's when digital audio files on CD's were first released and sold. The argument that there was a continuing breach is unavailing because the underlying alleged breach occurred when the production of digital audio files permitted piracy to occur in the first instance. See *Woodlaurel, Inc. v. Wittman*, 199 A.D.2d 497, 606 N.Y.S.2d 39 (2d Dept.1993) (holding that the statute of limitations runs when a party making the demand first becomes entitled to make it whether or not the party is aware that it may have a cause of action). Plaintiffs' further claim that the damages did not accrue until the late 1990's, when third parties downloaded the digital files and transmitted them over computer networks, does not state a claim against defendants. In fact, once the downloading occurred, defendants aggressively pursued claims against these third parties, in the Napster and MP3.com litigations, the results of which will accrue to the benefit of plaintiffs.

Breach of Covenant of Good Faith and Fair Dealing

The claims for breach of good faith and fair dealing do not state an independent cause of action. Every contract contains an implied covenant of good faith and fair dealing. However, such covenant does not impose any obligation upon a party to the contract beyond what the explicit terms of the contract provide. *Poley v. Sony Music Ent., Inc.*, 163 Misc.2d 127, 619 N.Y.S.2d 923 (Sup.Ct.N.Y.Co.1994). Where, as here, no party has acted in a way to prevent the performance of or the rights under the contract, the claim must fail. *Maxon Int'l, Inc. v. International Harvester*, 82 A.D.2d 1006, 442 N.Y.S.2d 588 (3d Dept.1981) *aff'd*, 56 N.Y.2d 879, 453 N.Y.S.2d

428, 438 N.E.2d 1143 (1982) (where defendant did what the contract expressly permitted, there is no evidence of bad faith). Here, here is no claim that defendants intentionally interfered with plaintiffs' rights to obtain royalties under their contracts. *PVM Oil Futures, Inc. v. Banque Paribas,* 161 A.D.2d 220, 554 N.Y.S.2d 606 (1st Dept.1990). In fact, the pursuit of claims in the copyright litigations indirectly furthered plaintiffs' interests under the contracts, inasmuch as in the federal actions, defendants sought to eliminate piracy to protect recording sales, the source of plaintiffs' royalties.

    * * * *

Based on the foregoing, the claims set forth, are hereby dismissed and the clerk is directed to ENTER Judgment for defendants.

The Beatles at Kennedy Airport, 2/7/64,
from United States Library of Congress Prints
and Photographs division, ID cph.3c11094

APPLE CORPS LIMITED V. CAPITOL RECORDS, INC.

13 Misc. 3d 1211(A), 2006 WL 2726809 (N.Y. Sup. Ct. 2006) (unpublished disposition)

KARLA MOSKOWITZ, J.

Plaintiffs, the individual members of the Beatles (or their representatives) and their recording label, Apple Corps Limited and Apple Records, Inc. ("Apple"), claim that defendants Capitol Records, Inc. and EMI Records Limited (collectively, "EMI/Capitol") owe them royalties. Plaintiffs charge EMI/Capitol with breaching the parties' contracts, abusing plaintiffs' trust, and engaging in fraudulent schemes in order to pilfer millions of dollars of royalties due and owing to plaintiffs and to obtain collateral benefits at plaintiffs' expense.

EMI/Capitol moves, pursuant to CPLR 3211(a)(1) and (a)(7) and CPLR 3016(b), to (1) dismiss the first cause of action (breach of fiduciary duty); (2) dismiss the third cause of action (fraud); (3) to strike the prayer for what it describes as "partial rescission;" and (4) to strike the demand for punitive damages in the complaint dated December 15, 2005 ("Complaint"). . . . For the reasons set forth herein, the court denies the motion.

BACKGROUND

The decision of the Appellate Division, First Department in *Apple Records, Inc. v. Capitol Records, Inc.* (137 A.D.2d 50 [1st Dept 1988] ["*Apple I* "]) sets forth the relevant facts pertaining to the parties' relationship through 1987. Therefore, I will not repeat these facts except where necessary. Plaintiffs sued EMI/Capitol in 1979 based on a variety of legal theories, including EMI/Capitol's alleged fraud, violation of fiduciary duties and breach of contract. In *Apple I,* the lower court, *inter alia,* granted EMI/Capitol's motion to dismiss with respect to the fraud cause of action (based on the conclusion that there was no fraud separate and distinct from the alleged claim sounding in contract), but denied the motion with respect to the breach of fiduciary duty cause of action (based on the conclusion that the pleading sufficiently alleged a fiduciary relationship). On appeal, the First Department held that plaintiffs' fraud claim did not repeat its contract claim. In reaching its conclusion the Appellate Division, First Department considered the allegations involving "defendants' improper disposition of Beatles' recordings and their fraudulent concealment and misrepresentation of those transactions through the rendering of false statements and accountings." (*Apple I,* 137 A.D.2d at 56).

Specifically, the Appellate Division, First Department considered the following allegations:

That defendants claimed they had "scrapped" as destroyed or damaged over $19,000,000 Beatles' recordings when in fact they secretly sold them and retained the proceeds;

That defendants distributed an excessive number of promotional copies of the Beatles recordings so that Capital Records could gain a promotional advantage for its other artists thereby diluting the market for the sale of the Beatles recordings

(*Id.* at 56–57)

In upholding the claim for breach of fiduciary duty, the Appellate Division, First Department found:

The business dealings between Capitol Records and the Beatles date back to 1962, when the still unacclaimed Beatles entrusted their musical talents to defendant Capitol Records. It is alleged that this relationship proved so profitable to defendant that at one point the Beatles constituted 25 to 30% of its business. Even after the Beatles attained their remarkable degree of popularity and success, they still continued to rely on Capitol Records for the manufacture and distributing of their recordings. *It can be said that from such a long enduring relation was born a special relationship of trust and confidence, one which existed independent of the contractual duties, and one which plaintiffs argue was betrayed by fraud in secretly selling records claimed as scrapped and in diluting the market and exploiting the Beatles' popularity with excessive distribution of promotional copies to benefit other aspects of defendants' business. Plaintiffs' allegations, then, are sufficient to support their claim that an injury separate and distinct from the breach of contract has been committed and is actionable as a tort.*

(Emphasis added; *Id.* at 57–58).

The Appellate Court also found further support for the fraud claim in plaintiffs' allegations that the defendants were bailees of the Beatles' recordings and breached their fiduciary duties as such:

Plaintiffs argue that pursuant to certain provisions of the contract they retained ownership rights to the Beatles' recordings until same were paid for by Capitol Records. During this interim period, Capitol Records was entrusted with the care and custody of these recordings. These claims in conjunction with plaintiffs' allegations of defendants' misappropriation of Beatles' recordings for their own benefit and in total disregard of plaintiffs' ownership rights, are sufficient to state a valid cause of action for fraud based on violations of duties distinct from defendants' contractual obligations.

(*Id.* at 58).

The parties entered into a global settlement agreement and new royalty agreements in November 1989, in the aftermath of *Apple I* and other related litigation. The 1989 Agreements and other agreements of the parties through 1995 (the "Royalty Agreements") are the subject of this current lawsuit.

In this action, plaintiffs complain of wrongful conduct by EMI/Capitol similar to that in *Apple I*. Specifically, plaintiffs complain that defendants:

designated various items as "scrap" but then really resold those items;

classified distribution of certain recordings as "promotional" and therefore non-royalty bearing, but then really sold the material;

entered into licenses with third-parties without plaintiffs' required consent;

failed to disclose money received from third-party exploitation, such as deals with record clubs like Columbia House and AEI Music Networks, a company that compiles and distributes tape programs to companies for various uses, such as airlines for in-flight music;

under-reported the number of units sold;

utilized incorrect royalty calculations.

Plaintiffs assert three causes of action against EMI/Capitol in the Complaint: fraud (first cause of action), breach of contract (second cause of action) and breach of fiduciary duty (third cause of action). Plaintiffs contend that EMI/Capitol concealed the true extent of sales of Beatles recordings and paraphernalia to avoid paying millions of dollars in royalties due under the relevant agreements. Plaintiffs allege that EMI/Capitol's allegedly deceitful behavior came to light after plaintiff conducted an audit examination of EMI/Capitol's books and records for the period 1994 to 1999. . . .

DISCUSSION

EMI/Capitol moves to dismiss the fraud and breach of fiduciary causes of action in the Complaint as well as a portion of the prayer for relief and the demand for punitive damages. Plaintiffs oppose the motion.

Breach of Fiduciary Duty Claim

EMI/Capitol contends that the court must dismiss the third cause of action for breach of fiduciary duty because a fiduciary relationship requires trust and/or confidence and here, despite the relationship of trust and confidence the parties may have had 25 years ago, distrust and contention has permeated the parties' post-*Apple I* relationship.

Plaintiffs argue that EMI/Capitol's nearly half-century exclusive right to exploit commercially the Beatles' recordings on a worldwide basis gives rise to a fiduciary relationship. Plaintiffs further allege that EMI/Capitol has become so integrated in the Beatles' careers, plaintiffs' Beatles-related business interests and the solo recordings of the individual Beatles' members, that plaintiffs and EMI/Capitol do not share a conventional business relationship. Rather, plaintiffs allege that there exists an intimacy between the parties that far exceeds mere commercial or contractual relationships. Plaintiffs further rely on the First Department's *Apple I* decision that the parties' relationship is one of "trust and confidence":

"from such a long enduring relation[ship] [between Capitol/EMI and The Beatles] was born a special relationship of trust and confidence, one which existed independent of the contractual duties, and one which plaintiffs argue was betrayed by fraud in secretly selling records claimed as scrapped and in diluting the market and exploiting the Beatles' popularity with excessive distribution of promotional copies to benefit other aspects of defendants' business."

(*Apple I,* 137 A.D.2d at 57).

Because of the allegations plaintiffs make here and the *Apple I* decision, I cannot hold, as a matter of law, that the parties no longer have a fiduciary relationship. Rather, plaintiff has pled a viable, continuing fiduciary relationship. Whether or not the level of contentiousness and distrust was so great as to destroy the fiduciary relationship the parties had is an issue that must await development of the factual record. Further, while ordinarily record companies owe no fiduciary duties to recording artists, the law recognizes circumstances where the parties' relationship elevates an arms length transaction to a fiduciary relationship. (*See e.g. Licette Music Corp. v. A.A. Records, Inc., supra*). Plaintiff has made such allegations here and, accordingly, the court denies defendants' request for dismissal of the cause of action for breach of fiduciary duty.

* * * *

Appropriateness of Remedy Sought by Plaintiffs

Plaintiffs request an order "terminating the rights" of EMI/Capitol "under the Royalty Agreements and directing that all rights to the Beatles Group and Solo Masters thereunder be transferred to the plaintiffs." (Complaint, ¶ 138). EMI/Capitol characterizes this as an impermissible demand for "partial rescission." EMI/Capitol seeks to strike this demand for relief arguing that there is no such thing as partial rescission of a contract (citing *Merryman v. Gottlieb* 99 A.D.2d 893, 894 [3d Dept 1984]). However, plaintiffs, in the Complaint, do not seek partial rescission, but rather seek to exercise their right to terminate the parties' agreements based on EMI/Capitol's alleged breach of contract, breach of fiduciary duties and fraud. Therefore, the court denies the request to strike this relief.

* * * *

CONCLUSION

Accordingly, it is ORDERED that defendants' motion to dismiss the Complaint is denied, and defendants are directed to serve their answers to the Complaint within 20 days after the date of service of a copy of this order with notice of entry.

NOTES AND QUESTIONS

1.   Fiduciary relationships often involve situations in which one party has superior knowledge or control over the other party. Do you think that the relationships between performers and labels or songwriters and publishers necessarily fit that description? If so, why? If not, what specific facts would be important in evaluating whether the relationship is fiduciary in nature? If you represented a record label or music publisher and wanted to avoid incurring the obligations of a fiduciary vis-à-vis your recording artists or songwriters, what language might you insert into your recording agreements to protect against the result in the Beatles case?

2.   Should the question of whether there is a fiduciary duty be analyzed differently in cases that are more substantively like a joint venture (e.g., Madonna's and Jay-Z's 360 deals with Live Nation) than in cases where a publisher or label is undertaking only to exploit a copyrighted work in exchange for royalty payments to a composer or artist?

3.   How do you reconcile the Beatles case with other cases finding no fiduciary duty? Do you think the case was rightly decided? Is longevity of the relationship enough, or do the fortunes of the two parties need to be intertwined in some significant way for the "Beatles exception" to apply?

E. CHOICE OF GOVERNING LAW

We leave this one for last, as choice of law is often viewed as a "boilerplate" provision that appears near the end of an agreement. However, a choice of law provision can have powerful repercussions for the parties' rights and obligations to one another in the event of a dispute and thus deserves attention. As the discussion of the variety of state law approaches to the right of publicity made clear in the prior chapter, the same dispute could have widely varying outcomes depending upon what state's law applies, both in terms of liability and in terms of available remedies. Of course, it is impossible to anticipate every type of dispute that might arise and research every state law governing such a possible dispute to determine which state's law, all things considered, would be best for one's client. One would typically expect to see a contract adopt the law of the place of domicile of one of the parties, or the law of the place where the contract is to be performed, or the law of the place where the contract is entered into, as the choice of governing law in a contract. If some other jurisdiction is identified as the choice of governing law, one would want to better understand why that jurisdiction's law is selected before agreeing to it as the law that will govern the parties' relationship.

We do not provide cases here regarding choice of law provisions, as the validity of the choice of law provisions within music industry contracts is rarely challenged. We only highlight the issue so that you take note of the contractual governing law provision in the cases and in any contracts that you might have cause to review and consider how it might affect the outcome of any litigation over potential disputes about the interpretation of the contract.

SAMPLE PROVISION RE GOVERNING LAW

This Agreement shall be governed by and construed under the laws of the State of New York and venued in a state or federal court situated in New York and the parties hereto consent to the jurisdiction of said courts.

NOTES AND QUESTIONS

This chapter introduced common provisions and issues in music industry contracts between music publishers and songwriters and between record labels and recording artists. It really is just the tip of the iceberg in terms of the breadth and depth of contractual relationships in the music industry, and the changing nature of the industry itself has led to innovative approaches to what were for decades "standard" provisions in music industry contracts. There is room for invention of new ways of crafting relationships in the industry—and thus an opportunity for lawyers, businesspeople, and artists to think outside the box and influence the direction that industry contracts will move in the future.

CHAPTER XII

MISCELLANEOUS MUSIC LAW ISSUES: *HERE, THERE, AND EVERYWHERE*[1]

■ ■ ■

This chapter provides a snapshot of additional legal and policy issues that have arisen from time to time in the music industry. The materials provided for each topic are intended to inspire discussion and to underscore the breadth of legal issues that lawyers in the music industry must consider in representing their clients.

First, we return to the central role that copyright law plays within the music industry by addressing the **termination right** granted to authors of works created under the 1976 Copyright Act. Termination rights allow authors to reclaim their interest in a copyright from a label or publisher after a specified period and subject to certain conditions. These provisions have the potential to play an important role in relationships—and bargaining power—between composers/musicians and publishers/labels.

Second, we highlight the role of **agents and managers** in the music industry and state laws governing their conduct that have particular relevance to musical performers. The role of agents and managers has evolved considerably in recent years, and entities serving in each role have moved beyond the traditional structure from past decades. Focusing on exactly "who" can be a manager or agent, and exactly "what" they are permitted to oversee, is a dynamic topic in the modern music industry.

Third, we touch on **consolidation** within the music industry. Like many industries, various aspects of the music industry have experienced increased concentration in some of the larger market actors. We will focus first on consolidation in the radio broadcasting industry following the Telecommunications Act of 1996, and then on the general trend toward broad vertical and horizontal consolidation within the entertainment and media industries in recent years and its particular impact on participants within the music business.

Finally, we introduce how the law has dealt with **payola**—the practice of paying for radio airplay of recordings. This practice has witnessed a complex history, including less savory practices in the earlier periods of the

---

1   John Lennon & Paul McCartney (1966); released by the Beatles on REVOLVER (1966).

industry, and periodically is given new attention by enforcement authorities.

A. TERMINATION RIGHTS IN SOUND RECORDINGS AND WORK FOR HIRE DOCTRINE

The discussion in Chapter 10 of duration of copyright grants in compositions and sound recordings briefly mentioned the 1976 Copyright Act's inclusion of a termination right for grants of rights in works by the author. The policy underlying adoption of the termination right is based upon the notion that copyright interests are not permanent in nature and that there is often unequal bargaining power at the outset of a contract conveying copyright interests to a label or publisher. In addition, there is significant uncertainty regarding the ultimate commercial value of a song or recording at the time the work is created, and many recording and publishing agreements grant copyright interests to label and publishers before specific works are actually in existence, covering all works created during a specified time period. Allowing for termination of the grant at some point (decades) in the future enables a "reset" on the commercial terms surrounding a song or recording. An author may reclaim control of the work during the statutory termination period, which allows him or her to capitalize on that ownership either directly or through a new deal with another third-party for the remainder of the copyright term. Alternatively, the statutory termination period can serve as an opportunity for authors to renegotiate the commercial terms of their original grants of copyright interests in their works even if those grants are not ultimately terminated.

The statute created a somewhat complex process for exercising the termination right in the event an author wished to reclaim copyrights granted to a label or publisher as part of an earlier contract. The Act excluded certain types of works from eligibility for termination, including "works made for hire" (defined as including collective works and compositions specially commissioned from the author and referred to in the industry as "work-for-hire"). How the law and the courts define those categories has become critical because authors are unable to terminate their rights in such works.

When the earliest time window for exercising termination rights—2013—began to approach, there was speculation in the music industry regarding its impact on publishers' and record labels' existing catalogs of copyrighted works.[2] Some argued that the work-for-hire exception would apply to compositions and sound recordings, as many publishing and recording contracts included language that characterized the works

---

[2] *See, e.g.,* Randy S. Frisch & Matthew J. Fortnow, *Termination of Copyrights in Sound Recordings: Is There a Leak in the Record Company Vaults?*, 17 COLUM.-VLA J.L. & ARTS 211, 211–229 (1993).

produced under the agreements as works-for-hire. As the termination right began to accrue for the first group of works, several high-profile songwriters and performing artists served notices of termination on the music publishers or record labels from their original songwriting or recording agreements.[3] In some instances, publishers and labels rejected termination notices on the grounds that (among other things) the work-for-hire exception applied. Lawsuits were predictably filed—but the majority were settled without reaching any holdings on the work-for-hire issue.

SAMPLE WORK-FOR-HIRE CONTRACTUAL LANGUAGE

Artist and all other persons rendering services in connection with the Works shall be deemed to be Company's employees for hire and the Works shall be considered a "work made for hire" pursuant to the copyright laws of the United States. If, for any reason, it is determined that any portion of the Works are not considered a work made for hire, then Artist shall be deemed to have hereby irrevocably assigned and otherwise transferred to Company an irrevocable royalty-free license for all right, title and interest in and to such Works and any part thereof including, without limitation, all rights of every kind and nature throughout the universe, for the life of copyright, including all extensions and renewals thereof.

Courts generally look to the actual relationships of the parties, rather than the language of their contracts, to determine whether an employer-employee relationship existed under the Copyright Act's work made for hire definition. In other words, simply calling something a "work made for hire" does not necessarily make it so. As these disputes have played out, most music industry termination notices have been ultimately addressed through private negotiations. These settlements are generally confidential, highly fact-specific, and of no weight in terms of legal precedent. Because there are few dispositive court decisions on this point, there remains a great deal of uncertainty about whether individual composers or recording artists have an enforceable termination right.

Below, we provide provisions of the Copyright Act relevant to the termination right and some pertinent case excerpts, including one from the governing Supreme Court case interpreting part of the work-for-hire language of the Copyright Act (albeit in the context of a sculptor's creation

---

[3]   For example, it was widely reported that Billy Joel, Bruce Springsteen, and the Eagles, among others, began serving notices of termination with respect to their 1978 works almost as soon as the statute permitted. *See, e.g.,* Ted Johnson, *Legal Landmark: Artists Start to Reclaim Rights to Their Music,* Variety (Apr. 16, 2013), http://www.variety.com/2013/biz/features/artists-reclaim-rights-to-music-1200334132.

of a work for an organization to use in a pageant rather than in the context of a recording or publishing relationship.) As you read these materials, think about what you learned in Chapter 10 regarding common publisher/songwriter and label/recording artist relationships and how the termination right might impact those relationships.

CONSIDER AS YOU READ . . .

- How is the termination right likely to apply to relationships between songwriters and publishers or recording artists and record labels?

- How does the work made for hire definition in the statute likely apply to a typical recording or publishing deal from before the advent of 360 deals? What factors should weigh heavily in the determination?

- As works created pursuant to recording contracts with "360" provisions begin to approach the 35-year termination notification period, how do you think the work-for-hire analysis might be different than in more traditional label/artist relationships?

- Is an album a collective work or compilation that might be exempt from the termination provisions of Section 203? What are the arguments on both sides?

- In the current digital era, the viability of the "album" format is waning. More and more artists and labels are opting for more frequent releases of fewer tracks (or even a single track), electing to provide increased consumer touchpoints instead of a crafted album. What impact do you think this trend might have on the work made for hire debate?

1. COPYRIGHT ACT PROVISIONS

§ 101. DEFINITIONS

Except as otherwise provided in this title, as used in this title, the following terms and their variant forms mean the following:

. . . .

A "collective work" is a work, such as a periodical issue, anthology, or encyclopedia, in which a number of contributions, constituting separate and independent works in themselves, are assembled into a collective whole.

A "compilation" is a work formed by the collection and assembling of preexisting materials or of data that are selected, coordinated, or arranged in such a way that the resulting work as a whole constitutes an original work of authorship. The term "compilation" includes collective works.

. . . .

A "work made for hire" is—

(1) a work prepared by an employee within the scope of his or her employment; or

(2) a work specially ordered or commissioned for use as a contribution to a collective work, as a part of a motion picture or other audiovisual work, as a translation, as a supplementary work, as a compilation, as an instructional text, as a test, as answer material for a test, or as an atlas, if the parties expressly agree in a written instrument signed by them that the work shall be considered a work made for hire. For the purpose of the foregoing sentence, a "supplementary work" is a work prepared for publication as a secondary adjunct to a work by another author for the purpose of introducing, concluding, illustrating, explaining, revising, commenting upon, or assisting in the use of the other work, such as forewords, afterwords, pictorial illustrations, maps, charts, tables, editorial notes, musical arrangements, answer material for tests, bibliographies, appendixes, and indexes, and an "instructional text" is a literary, pictorial, or graphic work prepared for publication and with the purpose of use in systematic instructional activities.

§ 203. TERMINATION OF TRANSFERS AND
LICENSES GRANTED BY THE AUTHOR

(a) Conditions for Termination.—In the case of any work other than a work made for hire, the exclusive or nonexclusive grant of a transfer or license of copyright or of any right under a copyright, executed by the author on or after January 1, 1978, otherwise than by will, is subject to termination under the following conditions:

(1) In the case of a grant executed by one author, termination of the grant may be effected by that author or, if the author is dead, by the person or persons who, under clause (2) of this subsection, own and are entitled to exercise a total of more than one-half of that author's termination interest. In the case of a grant executed by two or more authors of a joint work, termination of the grant may be effected by a majority of the authors who executed it; if any of such authors is dead, the termination interest of any such author may be exercised as a unit by the person or persons who, under clause (2) of this subsection, own and are entitled to exercise a total of more than one-half of that author's interest. . . .

(3) Termination of the grant may be effected at any time during a period of five years beginning at the end of thirty-five years from the date of execution of the grant; or, if the grant covers the right of publication of the work, the period begins at the end of thirty-five years from the date of publication of the work under the grant or at the end of forty years from the date of execution of the grant, whichever term ends earlier.

(4) The termination shall be effected by serving an advance notice in writing, signed by the number and proportion of owners of termination interests required under clauses (1) and (2) of this subsection, or by their duly authorized agents, upon the grantee or the grantee's successor in title.

(A) The notice shall state the effective date of the termination, which shall fall within the five-year period specified by clause (3) of this subsection, and the notice shall be served not less than two or more than ten years before that date. A copy of the notice shall be recorded in the Copyright Office before the effective date of termination, as a condition to its taking effect.

(B) The notice shall comply, in form, content, and manner of service, with requirements that the Register of Copyrights shall prescribe by regulation.

(5) Termination of the grant may be effected notwithstanding any agreement to the contrary, including an agreement to make a will or to make any future grant. . . .

(b) Effect of Termination.—Upon the effective date of termination, all rights under this title that were covered by the terminated grants revert to the author, authors, and other persons owning termination interests under clauses (1) and (2) of subsection (a), including those owners who did not join in signing the notice of termination under clause (4) of subsection (a), but with the following limitations:

(1) A derivative work prepared under authority of the grant before its termination may continue to be utilized under the terms of the grant after its termination, but this privilege does not extend to the preparation after the termination of other derivative works based upon the copyrighted work covered by the terminated grant.

(2) The future rights that will revert upon termination of the grant become vested on the date the notice of termination has been served as provided by clause (4) of subsection (a). The rights vest in the author, authors, and other persons named in, and in the proportionate shares provided by, clauses (1) and (2) of subsection (a).

(3) Subject to the provisions of clause (4) of this subsection, a further grant, or agreement to make a further grant, of any right covered by a terminated grant is valid only if it is signed by the same number and proportion of the owners, in whom the right has vested under clause (2) of this subsection, as are required to terminate the grant under clauses (1) and (2) of subsection (a). Such further grant or agreement is effective with respect to all of the persons in whom the right it covers has vested under clause (2) of this subsection, including those who did not join in signing it. If any person dies after rights under a terminated grant have vested in him or her, that person's legal representatives, legatees, or heirs at law represent him or her for purposes of this clause.

(4) A further grant, or agreement to make a further grant, of any right covered by a terminated grant is valid only if it is made after the effective date of the termination. As an exception,

however, an agreement for such a further grant may be made
between the persons provided by clause (3) of this subsection and
the original grantee or such grantee's successor in title, after the
notice of termination has been served as provided by clause (4)
of subsection (a).

(5) Termination of a grant under this section affects only those
rights covered by the grants that arise under this title, and in no
way affects rights arising under any other Federal, State, or
foreign laws.

(6) Unless and until termination is effected under this section,
the grant, if it does not provide otherwise, continues in effect for
the term of copyright provided by this title.

As noted above, there is uncertainty about how broadly or narrowly
the termination right established by the 1976 Copyright Act might be
interpreted in the context of works created under "typical" songwriting or
recording agreements. In the litigation over termination rights to date, few
courts have had the opportunity to evaluate the scope of the work-for-hire
exception or the question of whether record albums qualify as "collective
works" or "compilations" within the meaning of the Copyright Act. Labels
and publishers consistently assert the work-for-hire exception in response
to lawsuits regarding the termination right, but of the cases that have been
litigated more fully to date, most involve ownership/authorship questions[4]
or standing to assert the right.[5] In one of the most recent cases, the
Southern District of New York denied a motion to dismiss a purported class
action brought by recording artists against Sony Music Group, alleging
that Sony Music Group was infringing copyrights that had reverted to the
artists after notices of termination had been filed and the termination
dates had passed.[6] The motion to dismiss in *Johansen v. Sony Music
Entertainment, Inc.* focused on the adequacy of the termination notices
themselves, but in refusing to recognize the legitimacy of the termination
notices, Sony asserted that "'the Works are works made for hire,' and thus
not subject to termination."[7] As of the date of this writing, the case
remained pending, so there may well be a developing body of law that will
directly address these issues.

---

[4] *E.g., Everly v. Everly*, 352 F. Supp. 3d 834 (M.D. Tenn. 2018); *Scorpio Music (Black
Scorpio) S.A. v. Willis*, 2013 WL 6865559 (S.D. Cal. Dec. 26, 2013).

[5] *E.g., Ray Charles Foundation v. Robinson*, 795 F.3d 1109 (9th Cir. 2015).

[6] *Johansen v. Sony Music Entertaiment Inc.*, No. 19 CIV. 1094 (ER), 2020 WL 1529442, at
*1 (S.D.N.Y. Mar. 31, 2020).

[7] *Id.* at *1.

Below, you will first find excerpts from a Supreme Court case that sets out the key factors in evaluating whether an employer-employee or independent contractor relationship exists between two parties, which is essential to the first means of satisfying the work-for-hire definition. Then, we provide a case excerpt from one of the few opinions to at least preliminarily address the work-for-hire issue in the context of an attempt to terminate a grant of copyright in a sound recording, which briefly addresses whether a record album might qualify as a collective work or compilation within the "work made for hire" definition.

COMMUNITY FOR CREATIVE NON-VIOLENCE V. REID
490 U.S. 730 (1989)

JUSTICE MARSHALL delivered the opinion of the Court.[8]

In this case, an artist and the organization that hired him to produce a sculpture contest the ownership of the copyright in that work. To resolve this dispute, we must construe the "work made for hire" provisions of the Copyright Act of 1976 (Act or 1976 Act), 17 U.S.C. §§ 101 and 201(b), and in particular, the provision in § 101, which defines as a "work made for hire" a "work prepared by an employee within the scope of his or her employment" (hereinafter § 101(1)).

I.

Petitioners are the Community for Creative Non-Violence (CCNV), a nonprofit unincorporated association dedicated to eliminating homelessness in America, and Mitch Snyder, a member and trustee of CCNV. In the fall of 1985, CCNV decided to participate in the annual Christmastime Pageant of Peace in Washington, D.C., by sponsoring a display to dramatize the plight of the homeless. As the District Court recounted:

"Snyder and fellow CCNV members conceived the idea for the nature of the display: a sculpture of a modern Nativity scene in which, in lieu of the traditional Holy Family, the two adult figures and the infant would appear as contemporary homeless people huddled on a streetside steam grate. The family was to be black (most of the homeless in Washington

---

8   Footnotes are omitted from this excerpt.

being black); the figures were to be life-sized, and the steam grate would be positioned atop a platform 'pedestal,' or base, within which special-effects equipment would be enclosed to emit simulated 'steam' through the grid to swirl about the figures. They also settled upon a title for the work—'Third World America'—and a legend for the pedestal: 'and still there is no room at the inn.' " 652 F.Supp. 1453, 1454 (DC 1987).

Snyder made inquiries to locate an artist to produce the sculpture. He was referred to respondent James Earl Reid, a Baltimore, Maryland, sculptor. In the course of two telephone calls, Reid agreed to sculpt the three human figures. CCNV agreed to make the steam grate and pedestal for the statue. Reid proposed that the work be cast in bronze, at a total cost of approximately $100,000 and taking six to eight months to complete. Snyder rejected that proposal because CCNV did not have sufficient funds, and because the statue had to be completed by December 12 to be included in the pageant. Reid then suggested, and Snyder agreed, that the sculpture would be made of a material known as "Design Cast 62," a synthetic substance that could meet CCNV's monetary and time constraints, could be tinted to resemble bronze, and could withstand the elements. The parties agreed that the project would cost no more than $15,000, not including Reid's services, which he offered to donate. The parties did not sign a written agreement. Neither party mentioned copyright. . . .

Throughout November and the first two weeks of December 1985, Reid worked exclusively on the statue, assisted at various times by a dozen different people who were paid with funds provided in installments by CCNV. On a number of occasions, CCNV members visited Reid to check on his progress and to coordinate CCNV's construction of the base. . . . Reid and CCNV members did not discuss copyright ownership on any of these visits.

On December 24, 1985, 12 days after the agreed-upon date, Reid delivered the completed statue to Washington. There it was joined to the steam grate and pedestal prepared by CCNV and placed on display near the site of the pageant. Snyder paid Reid the final installment of the $15,000. The statue remained on display for a month. . . . Several weeks later, Snyder began making plans to take the statue on a tour of several cities to raise money for the homeless. Reid objected, contending that the Design Cast 62 material was not strong enough to withstand the ambitious itinerary. He urged CCNV to cast the statue in bronze at a cost of $35,000, or to create a master mold at a cost of $5,000. Snyder declined to spend more of CCNV's money on the project.

In March 1986, Snyder asked Reid to return the sculpture. Reid refused. He then filed a certificate of copyright registration for "Third World America" in his name and announced plans to take the sculpture on a more modest tour than the one CCNV had proposed. Snyder, acting in his capacity as CCNV's trustee, immediately filed a competing certificate of copyright registration.

Snyder and CCNV then commenced this action against Reid and his photographer, Ronald Purtee, seeking return of the sculpture and a determination of copyright ownership. The District Court granted a preliminary injunction, ordering the sculpture's return. After a 2-day bench trial, the District Court declared that "Third World America" was a "work made for hire" under § 101 of the Copyright Act and that Snyder, as trustee for CCNV, was the exclusive owner of the copyright in the sculpture. 652 F.Supp., at 1457. The court reasoned that Reid had been an "employee" of CCNV within the meaning of § 101(1) because CCNV was the motivating force in the statue's production. . . .

The Court of Appeals for the District of Columbia Circuit reversed and remanded, holding that Reid owned the copyright because "Third World America" was not a work for hire. 270 U.S.App.D.C. 26, 35, 846 F.2d 1485, 1494 (1988). . . .

II.

* * * *

. . . . Classifying a work as "made for hire" determines not only the initial ownership of its copyright, but also the copyright's duration, § 302(c), and the owners' renewal rights, § 304(a), termination rights, § 203(a), and right to import certain goods bearing the copyright, § 601(b)(1). . . . The contours of the work for hire doctrine therefore carry profound significance for freelance creators—including artists, writers, photographers, designers, composers, and computer programmers—and for the publishing, advertising, music, and other industries which commission their works.

* * * *

The dispositive inquiry in this case therefore is whether "Third World America" is "a work prepared by an employee within the scope of his or her employment" under § 101(1). The Act does not define these terms.

* * * *

In the past, when Congress has used the term "employee" without defining it, we have concluded that Congress intended to describe the conventional master-servant relationship as understood by common-law agency doctrine. . . . Nothing in the text of the work for hire provisions indicates that Congress used the words "employee" and "employment" to describe anything other than " 'the conventional relation of employer and employee.' " *Kelley, supra,* 419 U.S., at 323, 95 S.Ct., at 476, quoting *Robinson, supra,* 237 U.S., at 94, 35 S.Ct., at 494; cf. *NLRB v. Hearst Publications, Inc.,* 322 U.S. 111, 124–132, 64 S.Ct. 851, 857–861, 88 L.Ed.

1170 (1944) (rejecting agency law conception of employee for purposes of the National Labor Relations Act where structure and context of statute indicated broader definition). On the contrary, Congress' intent to incorporate the agency law definition is suggested by § 101(1)'s use of the term, "scope of employment," a widely used term of art in agency law. See Restatement (Second) of Agency § 228 (1958) (hereinafter Restatement).

In past cases of statutory interpretation, when we have concluded that Congress intended terms such as "employee," "employer," and "scope of employment" to be understood in light of agency law, we have relied on the general common law of agency, rather than on the law of any particular State, to give meaning to these terms. . . . This practice reflects the fact that "federal statutes are generally intended to have uniform nationwide application." *Mississippi Band of Choctaw Indians v. Holyfield,* 490 U.S. 30, 43, 109 S.Ct. 1597, 1605, 104 L.Ed.2d 29 (1989). Establishment of a federal rule of agency, rather than reliance on state agency law, is particularly appropriate here given the Act's express objective of creating national, uniform copyright law by broadly pre-empting state statutory and common-law copyright regulation. See 17 U.S.C. § 301(a). We thus agree with the Court of Appeals that the term "employee" should be understood in light of the general common law of agency.

* * * *

We turn, finally, to an application of § 101 to Reid's production of "Third World America." In determining whether a hired party is an employee under the general common law of agency, we consider the hiring party's right to control the manner and means by which the product is accomplished. Among the other factors relevant to this inquiry are the skill required; the source of the instrumentalities and tools; the location of the work; the duration of the relationship between the parties; whether the hiring party has the right to assign additional projects to the hired party; the extent of the hired party's discretion over when and how long to work; the method of payment; the hired party's role in hiring and paying assistants; whether the work is part of the regular business of the hiring party; whether the hiring party is in business; the provision of employee benefits; and the tax treatment of the hired party. See Restatement § 220(2) (setting forth a nonexhaustive list of factors relevant to determining whether a hired party is an employee). No one of these factors is determinative. See *Ward,* 362 U.S., at 400, 80 S.Ct., at 792; *Hilton Int'l Co. v. NLRB,* 690 F.2d 318, 321 (CA2 1982).

Examining the circumstances of this case in light of these factors, we agree with the Court of Appeals that Reid was not an employee of CCNV but an independent contractor. 270 U.S.App.D.C., at 35, n. 11, 846 F.2d, at 1494, n. 11. True, CCNV members directed enough of Reid's work to ensure that he produced a sculpture that met their specifications. 652 F.Supp., at

1456. But the extent of control the hiring party exercises over the details of the product is not dispositive. Indeed, all the other circumstances weigh heavily against finding an employment relationship. Reid is a sculptor, a skilled occupation. Reid supplied his own tools. He worked in his own studio in Baltimore, making daily supervision of his activities from Washington practicably impossible. Reid was retained for less than two months, a relatively short period of time. During and after this time, CCNV had no right to assign additional projects to Reid. Apart from the deadline for completing the sculpture, Reid had absolute freedom to decide when and how long to work. CCNV paid Reid $15,000, a sum dependent on "completion of a specific job, a method by which independent contractors are often compensated." *Holt v. Winpisinger*, 258 U.S.App.D.C. 343, 351, 811 F.2d 1532, 1540 (1987). Reid had total discretion in hiring and paying assistants. "Creating sculptures was hardly 'regular business' for CCNV." 270 U.S.App.D.C., at 35, n. 11, 846 F.2d, at 1494, n. 11. Indeed, CCNV is not a business at all. Finally, CCNV did not pay payroll or Social Security taxes, provide any employee benefits, or contribute to unemployment insurance or workers' compensation funds.

Because Reid was an independent contractor, whether "Third World America" is a work for hire depends on whether it satisfies the terms of § 101(2). This petitioners concede it cannot do. Thus, CCNV is not the author of "Third World America" by virtue of the work for hire provisions of the Act. However, as the Court of Appeals made clear, CCNV nevertheless may be a joint author of the sculpture if, on remand, the District Court determines that CCNV and Reid prepared the work "with the intention that their contributions be merged into inseparable or interdependent parts of a unitary whole." 17 U.S.C. § 101. In that case, CCNV and Reid would be co-owners of the copyright in the work. See § 201(a).

For the aforestated reasons, we affirm the judgment of the Court of Appeals for the District of Columbia Circuit.

It is so ordered.

John Waite at sound check before
Surf & Song Festival, January 2011
Photo by Matthew Straubmuller
(CC-BY-2.0)

WAITE V. UMG RECORDINGS, INC.
No. 19-CV-1091 (LAK), 2020 WL 1530794, at *1–3 (S.D.N.Y. Mar. 31, 2020)

MEMORANDUM OPINION

LEWIS A. KAPLAN, DISTRICT JUDGE.

Aspiring singers, musicians, authors and other artists—sometimes young and inexperienced and often not well known—tend to have little bargaining power in negotiating financial arrangements with recording companies, publishers, and others who promote and commercialize the artists' work. They often grant copyright in that work as part of the bargain they strike for promotion and commercialization. Accordingly, when an artistic work turns out to be a "hit," the lion's share of the economic returns often goes to those who commercialized the works rather than to the artist who created them. Section 203 of the Copyright Act of 1976 established a limited opportunity for artists to terminate the copyright ownership that they had granted to commercializers decades earlier in order to address this issue. The idea was that termination of these rights would more fairly balance the allocation of the benefits derived from the artists' creativity.

Termination is effectuated by serving the grantee with written notice.[1] This notice lists, among other information, the effective date of termination.[2] Once the effective date of termination has passed, the grantee becomes the owner of the copyright and therefore holds exclusive right to reproduce and distribute the sound recordings.[3]

---

[1]   17 U.S.C. § 203(a)(4).

[2]   Id. § 203(a)(4)(A).

[3]   Id. § 106.

This is a purported class action by recording artists[4] whose albums were released by predecessors in interest of defendant UMG Recordings, Inc. ("UMG") pursuant to agreements the artists signed in the 1970s and 1980s that granted copyright in their works to UMG's predecessor recording companies. These grants allowed those companies (and now UMG) to market, distribute, and sell the artists' sound recordings.

Each member of the class allegedly has terminated that grant as to the sound recordings comprising certain albums.[5] UMG disputes the validity of those terminations.[6]

Plaintiffs argue that UMG is infringing the artists' copyrights by continuing to market and sell the recordings for which the effective date of termination has passed. . . . The matter is before the Court on UMG's motion to dismiss the first amended complaint ("FAC").

Discussion

I. *Legal Standards*

. . . .

B. *Section 203 of the Copyright Act of 1976*

Recording artists often transfer copyright ownership in their works to record labels and music publishers. Recognizing that publishers often hold more bargaining power than authors and the "impossibility of determining a work's value until it has been exploited," Congress created a termination right to provide authors with an opportunity to enjoy a greater share of their work's economic success.[11] Authors of works created on or after January 1, 1978 may terminate transfers of a license or copyright in those works thirty-five years from the date of the grant's execution or, if the grant covers publication rights, the earlier of thirty-five years after the work's publication or forty years after the execution of the grant.[12] The termination right for the first eligible works therefore did not vest until January 1, 2013.

---

[4]   In one instance, the plaintiff is an alleged successor in interest to the artist. FAC [DI 45] ¶ 12.

[5]   Id. ¶¶ 31–32, 37, 43–44, 53–54, 69–70, 76–77. Plaintiffs seek to validate the termination notices for the following albums: Ignition, No Brakes, and Mask of Smiles (Waite); Honky Tonk Masquerade, Down the Drag, Live Shots, and Musta Notta Gotta Lotta (Ely); Surprise (Harris); Kasim (Sulton); Dawn of the Dickies (Phillips/Sobol/Caballero, "The Dickies"). Id. ¶¶ 32, 37, 44, 54, 77.

Ely's termination notice lists an additional album, Hi-Res, see FAC Ex. C at 3, which is not referenced in the FAC. The Court therefore assumes that Ely does not seek to enforce the termination notice as to that album.

[6]   Id. ¶ 4.

[11]   H.R. Rep. No. 94-1476, 124 (Sept. 3, 1976).

[12]   17 U.S.C. § 203(a)(3).

Termination under Section 203 is available for all works "executed by the author," other than those "made for hire."[13] Termination is not automatic. The earlier grant will remain in effect absent a termination notice.[14] These notices must include the effective date of termination, which may fall on any date in the five-year period after the work becomes terminable, and other requirements set forth by regulation.[15] The notice must be recorded with the Copyright Office and served upon the grantee prior to the effective date of termination.[16] Upon the effective date of termination, the grant is terminated and the copyright reverts to the author.[17]

For instance, if an author executed a grant transferring the copyright in Work A in January 1980, the grant for Work A may be terminated on a date between January 2015 (thirty-five years from the date of execution) and January 2020. If the author selected January 1, 2018 as the effective date of termination, assuming the termination notice comports with all applicable requirements, the grantee can continue to distribute Work A until December 31, 2017. On January 1, 2018, copyright ownership reverts to the author. At that point, any continued exploitation of that work by the grantee is an infringement on the author's copyright.

II. *Plaintiffs' Claims Cannot be Dismissed Based on Section 203's "Works Made for Hire" Exception*

Under Section 101 of the Copyright Act, a work made for hire is either a work "prepared by an employee within the scope of his or her employment" or certain types of "specially ordered or commissioned" work, so long as the parties agree in writing that the work will be considered a work made for hire.[18] The statute enumerates nine categories of works that can qualify as commissioned works: a contribution to a collective work, a part of a motion picture or other audio visual work, a translation, a supplementary work, a compilation, an instructional text, a test, answer material for a test, and an atlas.[19]

The legal author (creator of the work) and owner of a "work made for hire" is the employer or person who specially ordered it, rather than the artist.[20] Section 203 excludes these works from the termination right precisely for this reason: "The hired [or commissioned] party, although the 'author' in the colloquial sense . . . never owned the copyrights to assign. It

---

[13] Id. § 203(a).

[14] Id. § 203(a)(3).

[15] Id. § 203(a)(4).

[16] Id. § 203(a)(4)(A)–(B). The grantee must be served with the termination notice within two and ten years before the effective date of termination.

[17] Id. § 203(b).

[18] Id. § 101.

[19] Id.

[20] Id. § 201(b); Cmty. for Creative Non-Violence v. Reid, 490 U.S. 730, 737, 109 S.Ct. 2166, 104 L.Ed.2d 811 (1989) (distinguishing between copyright authors and owners).

stands to reason, then, that there are no rights the assignment of which [the artist or] his or her heirs may now terminate."[21]

Though plaintiffs' agreements with UMG's predecessors contained "works made for hire" language—which stated that the recording company, rather than the artist, was the legal author and owner of the works[22]—neither party argues, at this stage, that plaintiffs' works were specially commissioned. Nor do the parties contend that there was an employee-employer relationship between the artists and recording companies. As will be explained in more detail in the following section, defendant, for purposes of the motion to dismiss, argues only that the "works made for hire" language is relevant to the question of when the statute of limitations began to run on plaintiffs' claims.[23] The Court therefore need not resolve, for purposes of this motion, whether the agreements conferred "for hire" status on the works.

III. Plaintiffs' Claims: Copyright Infringement and Declaratory Relief

[¶]. . . . Defendant argues that a dispute over authorship and ownership is at the core of plaintiffs' claims.[35] This argument is premised on plaintiffs' allegations that they are the owners—or will be the owners following the effective dates of termination—of the copyrights to sound recordings that make up certain albums. However, as explained above, plaintiffs could not become the owners of the works if the works were "made for hire." Defendant contends that plaintiffs were put on notice of an authorship and ownership dispute—thereby triggering the three-year statute of limitations period—in the 1970s and 1980s when they signed agreements containing "works made for hire" provisions, as this language

---

[21] Marvel Characters, Inc. v. Kirby, 726 F.3d 119, 137 (2d Cir. 2013).

[22] See Declaration of Rollin A. Ransom [hereinafter "Ransom Decl."] [DI 51] Exs. A, B, C, D, E, G, H, I, J, K.

[23] Defendant suggests only in a footnote that sound recordings comprising an album constitute either a "compilation" or "contributions to a collective work," two of the nine enumerated categories of works that can be made "for hire." Defendant's Reply in Support of its Motion to Dismiss [DI 59] at 2 n.1. However, UMG makes no other arguments on this point and instead focuses on the consequences of a "works made for hire" agreement in light of the statute of limitations for Copyright Act claims. See id. 1–2 (stating that the "merits of a work for hire claim" is "beyond the scope of UMG's motion"); Defendant's Memorandum in Support of its Motion to Dismiss [hereinafter "Def's. Mem."] [DI 50] at 8 ("Resolution of the dispute [as to whether sound recordings on an album may be a 'work made for hire'] is irrelevant to the [statute of limitations] argument.").

The Court notes also that, in any event, defendant's limited cited authority is unpersuasive. In support of the position that sound recordings on an album could be "contributions to a collective work," defendant includes two sentences uttered during a congressional hearing. Defendant then cites to Bryant v. Media Right Productions, 603 F.3d 135, 140 (2d Cir. 2010), for the proposition that albums are "compilations." While Bryant concluded that "a[n] album falls within the Act's expansive definition of compilation," this classification was considered for purposes of statutory damages under a provision that, by its very terms, is limited to "the purposes of [that] subsection." Id. 140–141; 17 U.S.C. § 504(c)(1). The Circuit's conclusion in Bryant is thus not dispositive in the "works for hire" context.

[35] Defendant argues that this is true for all claims, regardless of whether the effective date of termination has or has not passed. See Def's. Mem. at 6–15.

was an "express assertion of sole authorship or ownership" and reflected a "repudiation" of any authorship or ownership claim by plaintiffs.[36] On this ground, defendant argues that plaintiffs' claims are now time barred, and that this is true whether or not the works qualify as "made for hire" within the meaning of the Act. The salient fact, UMG contends, is that plaintiffs knew when they executed their contracts that another party was declaring itself to be the legal author and owner.

In support of its argument, defendant analogizes plaintiffs' claims to those brought in *Aday v. Sony Music Entertainment*.[37] There, recording artist Meat Loaf entered into an agreement with a production company. The 1977 agreement included a work made for hire clause, stating "[s]olely for the purposes of any applicable copyright law, all persons rendering services in connection with the recording of master recordings shall be deemed 'employees for hire' of [the record company.]"[38] Almost thirty years later, Meat Loaf sought a declaration stating that he was "not, and never was, an 'employee for hire.' "[39] In other words, Meat Loaf argued that he always had been the sole owner of his copyright. The Court held that the three-year statute of limitations began to run in 1977 when Meat Loaf was put on notice "about any of the problems with the 'work for hire provision' " and his ownership claim was now barred.[40]

The issue here is a close one. Defendant correctly points out that authorship is relevant to plaintiffs' claims. The FAC acknowledges this. For example, the FAC alleges that, for claims based on effective dates of termination which have passed, the artists are "currently the owner of the United States copyright" in the sound recordings[41] and that the artists with future effective termination dates "authored" the recordings.[42] Further, plaintiffs seek a declaratory judgment that "[s]ound recordings cannot be considered 'a work made for hire' " within the meaning of Section 101.[43]

Yet relevance is not enough. An ownership claim is masked as an infringement claim, for purposes of statute of limitations accrual, when plaintiffs' cause of action is "rooted in [a] contested assertion of ownership in the copyright[.]"[44] In the archetypal case, "the lawsuit is between two parties who claim ownership of the copyrights . . . and one party's claim of

---

[36] Id. at 8–15 (citing Consumer Health Info. Corp. v. Amylin Pharm., Inc., 819 F.3d 992, 997 (7th Cir. 2016); Cooper v. NCS Pearson, Inc., 733 F.3d 1013, 1016 (10th Cir. 2013), Kwan, 634 F.3d at 228, Aday v. Sony Music Entertainment, No. 96-cv-0991 (MGC), 1997 WL 598410, at *5 (S.D.N.Y. Sept. 25, 1997)).

[37] 1997 WL 598410.

[38] Id. at *2.

[39] Id. at *4.

[40] Id. at *4–*5.

[41] See, e.g., FAC ¶ 40.

[42] See e.g., id. ¶¶ 68, 75.

[43] Id. ¶ 82(A).

[44] See Simmons v. Stanberry, 810 F.3d 114, 116 (2d Cir. 2016).

infringement is entirely a function of whether the other party is the sole owner of the disputed copyrights."[45] Here, while authorship is certainly pertinent, plaintiffs' infringement claim is a function of defendant's failure to comply with plaintiffs' termination notices. This distinction reveals why defendant's reliance on *Aday* is misplaced. Though plaintiffs indirectly challenge the validity of their "works made of hire" provisions by virtue of their infringement claim, unlike Meat Loaf in *Aday*, the gravamen of plaintiffs' claim is defendant's refusal to recognize their termination rights. Termination rights are, by their very nature, about the "nature, extent, or scope of copying" a particular work. Indeed, it is impossible for there to be a legally cognizable infringement claim until a termination right vests, a valid and timely termination notice is sent, is ignored, and the copyright's grantee continues to distribute the work.

b.   *Section 203*

Congress's explicit rationale for enacting Section 203 and the text of Section 203(a)(3) suggests that a "repudiation" of authorship or ownership did not trigger the running of the statute of limitations on plaintiffs' claims.

Section 203(a)(3) prescribes the time period in which an author may terminate his or her grant. At the earliest, the termination right may be exercised thirty-five years after copyright ownership was transferred.[46] That the statute of limitations would begin to run against an artist the day the contract is signed would be incongruent with a termination right that does not vest for at least thirty-five years from that date.

The explicit purpose of Section 203 reinforces the conclusion that plaintiffs' copyright claims could not have accrued upon the signing of their contracts. Congress enacted the termination provision to safeguard "authors against unremunerative transfers."[47] These authors needed statutory protection "because of the unequal bargaining position of authors, resulting in part from the impossibility of determining a work's value until it has been exploited."[48] To restrict the termination right based on the artist's failure to bring a claim within three years of signing a recording agreement—a time during which the artist and recording company may still have disparate levels of bargaining power—would thwart Congress's intent and eviscerate the right itself.[49]

---

[45]   Flo & Eddie, Inc. v. Sirius XM Radio Inc., 80 F. Supp. 3d 535, 542–43 (S.D.N.Y. 2015).

[46]   17 U.S.C. § 203(a)(3).

[47]   H.R. Rep. No. 94-1476, 124 (Sept. 3, 1976).

[48]   Id.

[49]   See Marvel Characters, Inc. v. Simon, 310 F.3d 280, 292 (2d Cir. 2002) (noting that the Copyright Act termination provisions "necessarily contemplate[ ] the likelihood that long-dormant copyright ownership issues will be awakened and litigated once the original . . . copyright term expires."). Marvel involved Section 304(c) of the Copyright Act, "a close but not exact counterpart of Section 203." H.R. Rep. No. 94-1476, 140 (Sept. 3, 1976).

Defendant's argument is weakened further by the music industry's practice of frequently inserting "work made for hire" language into recording contracts.[50] Its position requires that many artists, often early in their careers, would confront a choice when presented with a "works made for hire" provision. They could refuse to sign the contract and jeopardize their chance for the record company to record or distribute the artist's music. Or the artist could sign the contract and then bring a claim within three years to dispute the effect of the "work made for hire" provision in order to protect the copyright. Either outcome would be inconsistent with Section 203. The first would exemplify the unequal bargaining power Section 203 sought to correct. The second would render Section 203 meaningless, as its very purpose is to provide a mechanism by which artists can reclaim their copyright after the work has had time to become more valuable. Defendant's argument simply does withstand scrutiny in light of the unequivocal purpose of the termination provision.

2.   *Whether Plaintiffs' Copyright Infringement Claims are Time Barred*

For the foregoing reasons, the Court concludes that the statute of limitations for plaintiffs' infringement claim accrued after the effective date of termination passed. Plaintiffs brought these claims within the three-year statutory period and are not time-barred.[51]

NOTES AND QUESTIONS

1.   Applying the factors laid out in the *Reid* case, above, how do you think the "typical" recording or publishing agreement would be interpreted—are labels/publishers likely to be able to prove an employer/employee relationship? Why or why not? What about the alternative definition of work-for-hire in Section 203—what arguments might be made that a composition or sound recording was specially commissioned for one of the nine categories listed in the statute (in this context, the most relevant categories in the statute to consider are collective works, compilations, motion pictures or other audiovisual works)? Note that this second definition involving specially commissioned works requires that the parties agree in writing that the work is "for hire." As noted above, many songwriting and recording contracts contain standard language to that effect.

2.   In *Reid*, the Supreme Court noted that CCNV might be deemed a "joint author" with Reid if the evidence showed that the parties intended "that their contributions be merged into inseparable or interdependent parts of a unitary whole." How likely do you think it is that a record label and performing artist

---

[50]   1 Nimmer on Copyright § 5.03 (2019) (noting that since sound recordings earned copyright protection in 1972, "virtually all contracts" between artists and recording companies include "work made for hire" provisions).

[51]   The earliest effective date of termination alleged is May 22, 2017. FAC ¶ 32. The FAC was filed two years later, on June 5, 2019.

might be considered joint authors of the sound recordings or albums produced pursuant to a recording agreement? What evidence might support such an outcome?

3.   Although the *Waite* case did not address the merits of the work-for-hire exception under Section 203, in footnote 23, it briefly addressed and rejected the labels' arguments that the "specially commissioned works" piece of the work-for-hire definition governed because record albums were "collective works" or "compilations" within the meaning of the Copyright Act. In noting that it found those arguments unpersuasive, the court dismissed the applicability of *Bryant v. Media Right Prods., Inc.*, 603 F.3d 135 (2d Cir. 2010), a case that had found record albums to meet the statutory definition of "compilations" in the context of determining whether statutory damages should be calculated on a per-song basis or on a per-album basis. In so holding, the *Bryant* court reasoned:

> The Conference Report that accompanied the Act and explains many of its provisions, states that a "compilation" "results from a process of selecting, bringing together, organizing, and arranging previously existing material of all kinds, regardless of whether . . . the individual items in the material have been or ever could have been subject to copyright." H.R.Rep. No. 1476, 94th Cong., 2d Sess. 162, reprinted in 1976 U.S.C.C.A.N. 5659 (emphasis added).

> An album falls within the Act's expansive definition of compilation. An album is a collection of preexisting materials—songs—that are selected and arranged by the author in a way that results in an original work of authorship—the album.

Id. at 140–41. As you can see from the excerpt above, *Bryant* did not interpret the work-for-hire definition in the Copyright Act, but it did expressly rule that albums meet the statute's definition of "compilation." Do you think that record albums should be considered to be compilations for purposes of the work made for hire definition of the Copyright Act? Why or why not? Could the court's reasoning in *Bryant* lead to a result in which a recording artist could terminate and recover the copyright in the master recordings of individual songs but the record label would retain copyright ownership of the albums it released?

4.   If a recording agreement specifically requires the recording artist to deliver an "album" made up of a certain number of individual songs, should that be sufficient evidence that the album is a "specially commissioned work" within the meaning of the work-for-hire definition in Section 101? Why or why not? What do you think of the argument that neither compositions nor sound recordings are included in the nine types of works listed in the "specially commissioned work" prong of the work made for hire definition, and thus that publishers and labels cannot succeed in establishing a work made for hire under that prong?

5.   The *Waite* court placed particular emphasis on the purposes of Section 203 in reaching its conclusion that inclusion of a "work-for-hire" provision in the

parties' recording agreements did not immediately trigger the statute of limitations for disputing ownership of the copyrights to recordings produced under the agreements. Do you agree with the court's conclusion that recording artists could wait to challenge the "work-for-hire" provisions in their recording agreements until 35 years later, when the termination right accrued? Why or why not?

6.   The termination provisions of the 1976 Copyright Act, with their effective dates beginning to come into play at the height of the digital disruption of the recording industry, presented another potential blow to the industry if labels were to lose the rights to back catalogs of recordings or if forced to renegotiate with artists for higher royalties. Of course, the termination right has existed since the 1976 Act was enacted, and thus the notices of termination that the labels began receiving were not a complete surprise—and as time goes by, copyright ownership of more and more songs and recordings will be subject to potential termination and reversion to the authors of those works. Given that few of these termination notices to date have led to either transfer of ownership to the authors or dispositive rulings as to the application of the termination right to the copyright transfer and work-for-hire provisions in music industry contracts, what do you make of the impact of the termination provisions of the Act? Do they have their intended consequence if they give artists some room to negotiate for better contract terms, even if termination is rarely accomplished? What risk is there to publishers and labels, on the one hand, or to songwriters and recording artists, on the other hand, in having these issues resolved by the courts?

7.   Several cases have addressed the question of whether Section 203 preempts state laws that might permit termination of nonexclusive licenses earlier than the 35-year term in the Copyright Act. The Seventh and Eleventh Circuits have found that the Section 203 termination provision of the Copyright Act serves only as a ceiling—the longest period of time that a grant of rights, whether exclusive or non-exclusive, may extend before the author is given a right to terminate. According to these cases, state law or contractual provisions may permit earlier termination than the 35-year period provided for in federal copyright law.[9] By contrast, the Ninth Circuit has found that Section 203 is preemptive in nature and that state laws permitting termination at will for nonexclusive licenses are not enforceable: "Under Section 203 of the Copyright Act, licensing agreements are not terminable at will from the moment of creation; instead, they are terminable at the will of the author only during a five year period beginning at the end of thirty-five years from the date of execution of the license unless they explicitly specify an earlier termination date." *Rano v. Sipa Press, Inc.*, 987 F.2d 580, 585 (9th Cir. 1993), *as amended* (Mar. 24, 1993). Later, the Ninth Circuit clarified that the *Rano* holding only

---

[9]   *See, e.g., Walthal v. Rusk*, 172 F.3d 481 (7th Cir. 1999) (finding that agreement granting nonexclusive right to manufacture and sell copies of the Butthole Surfers' musical performances in return for a 50 percent share of the net profits with no specified term was terminable at will under Illinois state law and did not conflict with Section 203, which only provided a "ceiling" on license duration); *Korman v. HBC Florida, Inc.*, 182 F.3d 1291 (11th Cir. 1999).

applied to contracts of an indefinite duration, finding that when "the contract at issue is of a definite duration, neither Section 203, nor any other provision of the Copyright Act, governs" termination, but, instead, state law prevails.[10] The *Rano* decision has been criticized by scholars and seems inconsistent with the legislative history of Section 203, as both the House and Senate Reports stated that Section 203 was not intended to extend shorter contractual license periods or to limit application of state laws that would allow earlier termination.[11] Still, currently, the circuit courts seem to be split as to the impact of Section 203 on state laws that might permit earlier termination. What do you think the better rule is with respect to enforcement of state laws permitting earlier termination than Section 203? Why?

B. STATE LICENSING REQUIREMENTS FOR ARTIST REPRESENTATIVES

As in other branches of the entertainment industry, artists in the music industry are often represented by agents, managers, and lawyers who play a variety of roles for them, such as negotiating agreements, arranging for performances, and taking care of finances. Broadly speaking, an agent's role is to find work for the artist; a manager's role is to provide career guidance and manage the day-to-day schedule of the artist; and a lawyer's role is to negotiate and draft necessary legal documents for the artist. An agent represents multiple artists and is usually compensated on a commission basis, typically between 5–10% of the artist's earnings for work procured by the agent. A manager often represents only a small number of clients (if not just one) and may be either paid a salary or a commission—and if paid by commission, a manager typically will take 15–20% of the artist's earnings. An artist's lawyer will typically have multiple clients and may either bill by the hour for work performed for the artist or take a percentage (typically not more than 5%) of the artist's compensation arising from the agreements she documents or from the artist's total earnings.

However, the boundaries between these roles are often not clearly defined. For example, managers for performing artists will sometimes take a leading role in scheduling "gigs" for their clients. Lawyers representing musicians and songwriters are sometimes asked to perform services that cross boundaries into the territory of what is traditionally the role of an agent or manager, providing career advice and initiating negotiations with third parties for the artist's services. These blurred boundaries are problematic when state laws require licensing for particular activities,

---

[10]   *Scholastic Entm't, Inc. v. Fox Entm't Grp., Inc.*, 336 F.3d 982, 988 (9th Cir. 2003).

[11]   *See* H.R.Rep. No. 94–1476, at 128; S.Rep. No. 94–473, at 111, U.S.Code Cong.& Admin.News 1976, at 5743.

such as providing legal advice. As you will see in the materials that follow, many states have licensing requirements for artists' representatives who "procure employment" for the artist, regardless of whether the agreement between the artist and representative characterizes the representative as an agent or manager or lawyer.

The materials below address the licensing requirements for talent agents in California and New York, both of which have particularly important implications for participants in the music industry. First, we give you the relevant text of some of the main statutory and regulatory provisions governing licensing of talent agencies. Second, we provide excerpts from several of the most relevant cases that have interpreted and applied those provisions. Finally, we provide some questions to consider in connection with state regulation of those who perform the functions of agents in the music industry.

CONSIDER AS YOU READ . . .

- How might the statutory provisions below that govern talent agents in California and New York apply in the music industry?

- How might a performing artist's manager avoid being subject to licensing under the talent agent statutes?

- What are the risks of serving as an unlicensed talent agent in California and New York?

- What are the risks to artists of using the services of an unlicensed talent agent?

- Should exceptions to these licensing provisions apply to particular types of services that are performed by artist representatives in the music industry?

1. CALIFORNIA LABOR CODE—TALENT AGENCIES: §§ 1700 ET SEQ.

[SEC. 1700] "Person" defined

As used in this chapter, "person" means any individual, company, society, firm, partnership, association, corporation, limited liability company, manager, or their agents or employees.

[SEC. 1700.2] Definitions

(a) As used in this chapter, "fee" means any of the following:

(1) Any money or other valuable consideration paid or promised to be paid for services rendered or to be rendered by any person conducting the business of a talent agency under this chapter.

(2) Any money received by any person in excess of that which has been paid out by him or her for transportation, transfer of baggage, or board and lodging for any applicant for employment.

(3) The difference between the amount of money received by any person who furnished employees, performers, or entertainers for circus, vaudeville, theatrical, or other entertainments, exhibitions, or performances, and the amount paid by him or her to the employee, performer, or entertainer.

(b) As used in this chapter, "registration fee" means any charge made, or attempted to be made, to an artist for any of the following purposes:

(1) Registering or listing an applicant for employment in the entertainment industry.

(2) Letter writing.

(3) Photographs, film strips, video tapes, or other reproductions of the applicant.

(4) Costumes for the applicant.

(5) Any activity of a like nature.

[SEC. 1700.4] "Talent agency" and "artists" defined

(a) "Talent agency" means a person or corporation who engages in the occupation of procuring, offering, promising, or attempting to procure employment or engagements for an artist or artists, except that the activities of procuring, offering, or promising to procure recording contracts for an artist or artists shall not of itself subject a person or corporation to regulation and licensing under this chapter.

Talent agencies may, in addition, counsel or direct artists in the development of their professional careers.

(b) "Artists" means actors and actresses rendering services on the legitimate stage and in the production of motion pictures, radio artists, musical artists, musical organizations, directors of legitimate stage, motion picture and radio productions, musical directors, writers, cinematographers, composers, lyricists, arrangers, models, and other artists and persons rendering professional services in motion picture, theatrical, radio, television and other entertainment enterprises.

[SEC. 1700.5] Necessity and posting of license

No person shall engage in or carry on the occupation of a talent agency without first procuring a license therefor from the Labor Commissioner. The license shall be posted in a conspicuous place in the office of the licensee. The license number shall be referred to in any advertisement for the purpose of the solicitation of talent for the talent agency.

Licenses issued for talent agencies prior to the effective date of this chapter shall not be invalidated thereby, but renewals of those licenses shall be obtained in the manner prescribed by this chapter.

[SEC. 1700.20] Restriction of license's protection to person and place for which issued; Consent prerequisite to transfer

No license shall protect any other than the person to whom it is issued nor any places other than those designated in the license. No license shall be transferred or assigned to any person unless written consent is obtained from the Labor Commissioner.

[SEC. 1700.21] Revocation or suspension of license; grounds

The Labor Commissioner may revoke or suspend any license when it is shown that any of the following occur:

(a) The licensee or his or her agent has violated or failed to comply with any of the provisions of this chapter.

(b) The licensee has ceased to be of good moral character.

(c) The conditions under which the license was issued have changed or no longer exist.

(d) The licensee has made any material misrepresentation or false statement in his or her application for a license.

[SEC. 1700.23] Forms of contracts for services of talent agency; Approval; Prerequisites

Every talent agency shall submit to the Labor Commissioner a form or forms of contract to be utilized by such talent agency in entering into written contracts with artists for the employment of the services of such talent agency by such artists, and secure the approval of the Labor Commissioner thereof. Such approval shall not be withheld as to any proposed form of contract unless such proposed form of contract is unfair, unjust and oppressive to the artist. Each such form of contract, except under the conditions specified in Section 1700.45, shall contain an agreement by the talent agency to refer any controversy between the artist and the talent agency relating to the terms of the contract to the Labor Commissioner for adjustment. There shall be printed on the face of the contract in prominent type the following: "This talent agency is licensed by the Labor Commissioner of the State of California."

[SEC. 1700.25] Trust fund accounts; Disbursement of funds; Recordkeeping requirements

(a) A licensee who receives any payment of funds on behalf of an artist shall immediately deposit that amount in a trust fund account maintained by him or her in a bank or other recognized depository. The funds, less the licensee's commission, shall be disbursed to the artist within 30 days after receipt. However, notwithstanding the preceding sentence, the licensee may retain the funds beyond 30 days of receipt in either of the following circumstances:

    (1) To the extent necessary to offset an obligation of the artist to the talent agency that is then due and owing.

    (2) When the funds are the subject of a controversy pending before the Labor Commissioner under Section 1700.44 concerning a fee alleged to be owed by the artist to the licensee.

(b) A separate record shall be maintained of all funds received on behalf of an artist and the record shall further indicate the disposition of the funds. . . .

(e) If the Labor Commissioner finds, in proceedings under Section 1700.44, that the licensee's failure to disburse funds to an artist within the time required by subdivision (a) was a willful violation, the Labor Commissioner may, in addition to other relief under Section 1700.44, order the following:

    (1) Award reasonable attorney's fees to the prevailing artist.

(2) Award interest to the prevailing artist on the funds wrongfully withheld at the rate of 10 percent per annum during the period of the violation. . . .

[SEC. 1700.32] Prohibition against false or misleading information; Advertisements

No talent agency shall publish or cause to be published any false, fraudulent, or misleading information, representation, notice, or advertisement. All advertisements of a talent agency by means of cards, circulars, or signs, and in newspapers and other publications, and all letterheads, receipts, and blanks shall be printed and contain the licensed name and address of the talent agency and the words "talent agency." No talent agency shall give any false information or make any false promises or representations concerning an engagement or employment to any applicant who applies for an engagement or employment.

[SEC. 1700.33] Sending artist to unsafe place; Duty of reasonable inquiry

No talent agency shall send or cause to be sent, any artist to any place where the health, safety, or welfare of the artist could be adversely affected, the character of which place the talent agency could have ascertained upon reasonable inquiry.

[SEC. 1700.34] Prohibition against sending minor to place where intoxicating liquor sold or consumed

No talent agency shall send any minor to any saloon or place where intoxicating liquors are sold to be consumed on the premises.

[SEC. 1700.35] Prohibition against permitting persons of bad character at place of business

No talent agency shall knowingly permit any persons of bad character, prostitutes, gamblers, intoxicated persons, or procurers to frequent, or be employed in, the place of business of the talent agency.

[SEC. 1700.36] Prohibition against accepting application or placing minor in unlawful employment

No talent agency shall accept any application for employment made by or on behalf of any minor, as defined by subdivision (c) of Section 1286, or shall place or assist in placing any such minor in any employment whatever in violation of Part 4 (commencing with Section 1171).

[SEC. 1700.37] Contract between minor and talent agency; Absence of right to disaffirm approved contract; Approval by Labor Commissioner; Proceeding for judicial approval

A minor cannot disaffirm a contract, otherwise valid, entered into during minority, either during the actual minority of the minor entering into such contract or at any time thereafter, with a duly licensed talent agency as defined in Section 1700.4 to secure him engagements to render artistic or creative services in motion pictures, television, the production of phonograph records, the legitimate or living stage, or otherwise in the entertainment field including, but without being limited to, services as an actor, actress, dancer, musician, comedian, singer, or other performer or entertainer, or as a writer, director, producer, production executive, choreographer, composer, conductor or designer, the blank form of which has been approved by the Labor Commissioner pursuant to Section 1700.23, where such contract has been approved by the superior court of the county where such minor resides or is employed.

Such approval may be given by the superior court on the petition of either party to the contract after such reasonable notice to the other party thereto as may be fixed by said court, with opportunity to such party to appear and be heard.

[SEC. 1700.39] Division of fees

No talent agency shall divide fees with an employer, an agent or other employee of an employer.

[SEC. 1700.40] Registration fees; Referral to entity in which agency has financial interest; Acceptance of referral fee

(a) No talent agency shall collect a registration fee. In the event that a talent agency shall collect from an artist a fee or expenses for obtaining employment for the artist, and the artist shall fail to procure the employment, or the artist shall fail to be paid for the employment, the talent agency shall, upon demand therefor, repay to the artist the fee and expenses so collected. Unless repayment thereof is made within 48 hours after demand therefor, the talent agency shall pay to the artist an additional sum equal to the amount of the fee.

(b) No talent agency may refer an artist to any person, firm, or corporation in which the talent agency has a direct or indirect financial interest for other services to be rendered to the artist, including, but not limited to, photography, audition tapes, demonstration reels or similar materials, business management, personal management, coaching, dramatic school, casting or talent brochures, agency-client directories, or other printing.

(c) No talent agency may accept any referral fee or similar compensation from any person, association, or corporation providing services of any type expressly set forth in subdivision (b) to an artist under contract with the talent agency.

[SEC. 1700.47] Equal opportunity

It shall be unlawful for any licensee to refuse to represent any artist on account of that artist's race, color, creed, sex, national origin, religion, or handicap.

Ed. Note: In 2018, a new Article 4 was added to the California Talent Agencies statute requiring that talent agencies provide their clients with specified education and training materials, including materials on sexual harassment, nutrition, and eating disorders. See Cal. Labor Code ¶ 1700.50–.54.

2. NEW YORK ARTS & CULTURAL AFFAIRS LAW: §§ 37.01 ET SEQ.

[SEC. 37.01] Definitions

As used in sections 37.03 and 37.05 of this article:

1. "Person" means any individual, company, society, association, corporation, manager, contractor, subcontractor, partnership, bureau, agency, service, office or the agent or employee of the foregoing.

2. "Fee" means anything of value, including any money or other valuable consideration charged, collected, received, paid or promised for any service, or act rendered or to be rendered by an employment agency, including but not limited to money received by such agency or its emigrant agent which is more than the amount paid by it for transportation, transfer of baggage, or board and lodging on behalf of any applicant for employment.

3.   "Theatrical employment agency" means any person (as defined in subdivision one hereof) who procures or attempts to procure employment or engagements for an artist, but such term does not include the business of managing entertainments, exhibitions or performances, or the artists or attractions constituting the same, where such business only incidentally involves the seeking of employment therefor.

4.   "Theatrical engagement" means any engagement or employment of an artist in employment described in subdivision three of this section.

5.   "Artist" shall mean actors and actresses rendering services on the legitimate stage and in the production of motion pictures, radio artists, musical artists, musical organizations, directors of legitimate stage, motion picture and radio productions, musical directors, writers, cinematographers, composers, lyricists, arrangers, models, and other artists and persons rendering professional services in motion picture, theatrical, radio, television and other entertainment enterprises.

[SEC. 37.03] Theatrical employment; contracts

Contracts between a theatrical employment agency and an artist shall include the gross commission or fees to be paid by the artist to the theatrical employment agency consistent with section one hundred eighty-five of the general business law. Such contracts shall contain no other conditions and provisions except such as are equitable between the parties thereto and do not constitute an unreasonable restriction of business. In addition, such contracts in blank shall be first approved by the commissioner of labor, except that in the city of New York, such contracts in blank shall be first approved by the commissioner of consumer affairs of such city, pursuant to section one hundred eighty-nine of the general business law, and his or her determination shall be reviewable by certiorari. Each such contract shall also include the name, address, phone number and license number of the theatrical employment agency in addition to the name of the artist, the type of services covered by the contract, and all terms and conditions associated with the payment of such commission or fees. The theatrical employment agency shall keep on file a copy of each contract entered into with an artist and provide a copy of each contract to the artist. Separately from the contract, the agency shall provide to the artist, at the time of each audition or interview for specific employment, information as to the name and address of the person to whom the artist is to apply for such employment, the service to be performed, the anticipated rate of compensation, where such compensation is known prior to the audition or interview, and any other material terms and conditions of such employment that are known by the agency prior to the audition or interview. Such information may be provided by electronic communication.

[SEC. 37.05] Theatrical employment; financial investigations and security

A theatrical employment agent shall investigate whether or not any employer (person, firm or corporation) who is offering employment to an applicant for employment, has defaulted in the payment of salaries, fees or other compensation to any performer or group of performers or has left stranded any performing companies or individuals or groups, during the five years preceding the date of the application. An agent shall not procure or undertake to procure employment or engagements on the part of any performer or groups of performers for an employer who has failed to pay salaries, fees or other compensation, or who has left stranded any performer or groups of performers or any performing companies or individuals during the five years preceding the date of the application, unless such employer (person, firm or corporation) shall provide sufficient security for the direct benefit of the performer or performers and in an amount ample to pay the performer or performers their full compensation for the specified employment or engagement designated in the employment or engagement contract. The provisions of this section shall not apply to employment or engagements in modeling.

[SEC. 37.07] Performing artists; ads for availability of employment

1. It shall be unlawful for any person, firm, corporation, association, or agent or employee thereof, holding itself out to the public by any designation indicating a connection with show business including, but not limited to, talent agent, talent scout, personal manager, artist manager, impresario, casting director, public relations advisor or consultant, promotion advisor or consultant, to

(a) Make, publish, disseminate, circulate or place before the public or cause directly or indirectly to be made, published, disseminated, circulated or placed before the public in this state an advertisement, solicitation, announcement, notice or statement which represents that such person, firm, corporation or association has employment available or is able to secure any employment in the field of show business, including, but not limited to, theatre, motion pictures, radio, television, phonograph records, commercials, opera, concerts, dance, modeling or any other entertainments, exhibitions or performances when an advance fee of any nature is a condition to such employment; or

(b) Accept from a member of the public any fee, retainer, salary, advance payment or other compensation of any nature in return for services or otherwise, other than (i) repayment for advances or expenses actually incurred for or on behalf of such member of the public, or (ii) agreed commissions, royalties or similar compensation based upon payments received by or on behalf of such member of the public as a result of his employment in the field of show business.

2.   Whenever there shall be a violation of this section, an application may be made by the attorney general in the name of the people of the state of New York to a court or justice having jurisdiction to issue an injunction, and upon notice to the defendant of not less than five days, to enjoin and restrain the continuance of such violations; and if it shall appear to the satisfaction of the court or justice that the defendant has, in fact, violated this section, an injunction may be issued by such court or justice, enjoining and restraining any further violation, without requiring proof that any person has, in fact, been injured or damaged thereby. In any such proceeding, the court may make allowances to the attorney general as provided in paragraph six of subdivision (a) of section eighty-three hundred three of the civil practice law and rules, and direct restitution. In connection with any such proposed application, the attorney general is authorized to take proof and make a determination of the relevant facts and to issue subpoenas in accordance with the civil practice law and rules.

Below is an excerpt from an often-cited California Supreme court case interpreting the California talent agency statute. Although it arose in the context of the relationship between an actor and her representative, it provides some useful context for the purposes underlying state law regulation of talent agencies and the way that the California statute has been enforced. Excerpts from cases involving musical artists in both New York and California follow to highlight the application of the statutes to artist representatives in the music industry.

MARATHON ENTERTAINMENT, INC. V. BLASI
42 Cal. 4th 974 (2008)

Opinion

WERDEGAR, J.

In Hollywood, talent—the actors, directors, and writers, the Jimmy Stewarts, Frank Capras, and Billy Wilders who enrich our daily cultural lives—is represented by two groups of people: agents and managers. Agents procure roles; they put artists on the screen, on the stage, behind the camera; indeed, by law, only they may do so. Managers coordinate everything else; they counsel and advise, take care of business arrangements, and chart the course of an artist's career.

This division largely exists only in theory. The reality is not nearly so neat. The line dividing the functions of agents, who must be licensed, and of managers, who need not be, is often blurred and sometimes crossed. Agents sometimes counsel and advise; managers sometimes procure work. Indeed, the occasional procurement of employment opportunities may be standard operating procedure for many managers and an understood goal when not-yet-established talents, lacking access to the few licensed agents in Hollywood, hire managers to promote their careers.[FN1 omitted]

We must decide what legal consequences befall a manager who steps across the line and solicits or procures employment without a talent agency license. We hold that (1) contrary to the arguments of personal manager Marathon Entertainment, Inc. (Marathon), the strictures of the Talent Agencies Act (Lab.Code, § 1700 et seq.) (Act) apply to managers as well as agents; (2) contrary to the arguments of actress Rosa Blasi (Blasi), while the Labor Commissioner has the authority to void manager-talent contracts *ab initio* for unlawful procurement, she also has discretion to apply the doctrine of severability to partially enforce these contracts; and (3) in this case, a genuine dispute of material fact exists over whether severability might apply to allow partial enforcement of the parties' contract. Accordingly, we affirm the Court of Appeal.

FACTUAL AND PROCEDURAL BACKGROUND

In 1998, Marathon and Blasi entered into an oral contract for Marathon to serve as Blasi's personal manager. Marathon was to counsel Blasi and promote her career; in exchange, Blasi was to pay Marathon 15 percent of her earnings from entertainment employment obtained during the course of the contract. During the ensuing three years, Blasi's professional appearances included a role in a film, Noriega: God's Favorite (Industry Entertainment 2000), and a lead role as Dr. Luisa Delgado on the television series *Strong Medicine*.

According to Marathon, Blasi reneged on her agreement to pay Marathon its 15 percent commission from her *Strong Medicine* employment contract. In the summer of 2001, she unilaterally reduced payments to 10 percent. Later that year, she ceased payment altogether and terminated her Marathon contract, stating that her licensed talent agent, John Kelly, who had served as her agent throughout the term of the management contract with Marathon, was going to become her new personal manager.

Marathon sued Blasi for breach of oral contract, quantum meruit, false promise, and unfair business practices, seeking to recover unpaid *Strong Medicine* commissions. Marathon alleged that it had provided Blasi with lawful personal manager services by providing the downpayment on her home, paying the salary of her business manager, providing her with professional and personal advice, and paying her travel expenses.

After obtaining a stay of the action, Blasi filed a petition with the Labor Commissioner alleging that Marathon had violated the Act by soliciting and procuring employment for Blasi without a talent agency license.[2] The Labor Commissioner agreed. The Commissioner found Marathon had procured various engagements for Blasi, including a role in the television series *Strong Medicine*. Concluding that one or more acts of solicitation and procurement by Marathon violated the Act, the Commissioner voided the parties' contract *ab initio* and barred Marathon from recovery.

Marathon appealed the Labor Commissioner's ruling to the superior court for a trial de novo. (See § 1700.44, subd. (a); *Buchwald v. Katz* (1972) 8 Cal.3d 493, 500–501, 105 Cal.Rptr. 368, 503 P.2d 1376.) . . .

Blasi moved for summary judgment on the theory that Marathon's licensing violation had invalidated the entire personal management contract. Blasi submitted excerpts from the Labor Commissioner hearing transcript as evidence that Marathon had violated the Act by soliciting or procuring employment for her without a talent agency license. Blasi did not specifically argue or produce evidence that Marathon had illegally procured the *Strong Medicine* employment contract.

The trial court granted Blasi's motion for summary judgment and invalidated Marathon's personal management contract as an illegal contract for unlicensed talent agency services in violation of the Act, denied Marathon's motion for summary adjudication of the Act's constitutionality, and entered judgment for Blasi.

The Court of Appeal reversed in part. It agreed with the trial court that the Act applied to personal managers. However, it concluded that under the law of severability of contracts (Civ.Code, § 1599), because the parties' agreement had the lawful purpose of providing personal

---

[2]   The Labor Commissioner has original and exclusive jurisdiction over issues arising under the Act. (*Styne v. Stevens* (2001) 26 Cal.4th 42, 54–56, 109 Cal.Rptr.2d 14, 26 P.3d 343; Lab.Code, § 1700.44, subd. (a).) All further undesignated statutory references are to the Labor Code.

management services that are unregulated by the Act, and because Blasi had not established that her *Strong Medicine* employment contract was procured illegally, the possibility existed that Blasi's obligation to pay Marathon a commission on that contract could be severed from any unlawful parts of the parties' management agreement. In reaching this conclusion, the Court of Appeal distinguished prior cases that had voided management contracts in their entirety (*Yoo v. Robi* (2005) 126 Cal.App.4th 1089, 24 Cal.Rptr.3d 740; *Waisbren v. Peppercorn Productions, Inc.* (1995) 41 Cal.App.4th 246, 48 Cal.Rptr.2d 437) and in some cases expressly refused to sever the contracts (*Yoo,* at pp. 1104–1105, 24 Cal.Rptr.3d 740).

We granted review to address the applicability of the Act to personal managers and the availability of severance under the Act.

DISCUSSION

I. *Background*

A. *Agents and Managers*

In Hollywood, talent agents act as intermediaries between the buyers and sellers of talent. (*Regulation of Attorneys, supra,* 80 Cal. L.Rev. at p. 479.) While formally artists are agents' clients, in practice a talent agent's livelihood depends on cultivating valuable connections on both sides of the artistic labor market. (Birdthistle, *A Contested Ascendancy: Problems with Personal Managers Acting as Producers* (2000) 20 Loyola L.A. Ent. L.J. 493, 502–503 (hereafter *Contested Ascendancy*); *Regulation of Attorneys,* at p. 479.) Generally speaking, an agent's focus is on the deal: on negotiating numerous short-term, project-specific engagements between buyers and sellers. (*Conflicts in the New Hollywood, supra,* 76 So.Cal. L.Rev. at p. 981.)

Agents are effectively subject to regulation by the various guilds that cover most of the talent available in the industry: most notably, the Screen Actors Guild, American Federation of Television and Radio Artists, Directors Guild of America, Writers Guild of America, and American Federation of Musicians. (*Regulation of Attorneys, supra,* 80 Cal. L.Rev. at p. 487.) Artists may informally agree to use only agents who have been "franchised" by their respective guilds; in turn, as a condition of franchising, the guilds may require agents to agree to a code of conduct and restrictions on terms included in agent-talent contracts. (*Conflicts in the New Hollywood, supra,* 76 So.Cal. L.Rev. at pp. 989–990; *Contested Ascendancy, supra,* 20 Loyola L.A. Ent. L.J. at p. 520.) Most significantly, those restrictions typically include a cap on the commission charged (generally 10 percent), a cap on contract duration, and a bar on producing one's client's work and obtaining a producer's fee. (Screen Actors Guild, Codified Agency Regs., rule 16(g); American Federation of Television and Radio Artists, Regs. Governing Agents, rule 12–C; *Matthau v. Superior Court* (2007) 151 Cal.App.4th 593, 596–597, 60 Cal.Rptr.3d 93; *Conflicts in the New Hollywood,* at pp. 989–990; *Contested Ascendancy,* at pp. 520–521.) These restrictions create incentives to establish a high volume clientele, offer more limited services, and focus on those lower risk artists with established track records who can more readily be marketed to talent buyers. (*Conflicts in the New Hollywood,* at p. 981; *Contested Ascendancy,* at p. 503.)

Personal managers, in contrast, are not franchised by the guilds. (*Conflicts in the New Hollywood, supra,* 76 So.Cal. L.Rev. at p. 991; *Contested Ascendancy, supra,* 20 Loyola L.A. Ent. L.J. at p. 522.) They typically accept a higher risk clientele and offer a much broader range of services, focusing on advising and counseling each artist with an eye to making the artist as marketable and attractive to talent buyers as possible, as well as managing the artist's personal and professional life in a way that allows the artist to focus on creative productivity. (*Waisbren v. Peppercorn Productions, Inc., supra,* 41 Cal.App.4th at pp. 252–253, 48 Cal.Rptr.2d 437; Cal. Entertainment Com., Rep. (Dec. 2, 1985) p. 9 (hereafter Entertainment Commission Report); *Regulation of Attorneys, supra,* 80 Cal. L.Rev. at pp. 482–483.) "Personal managers primarily advise, counsel, direct, and coordinate the development of the artist's career. They advise in both business and personal matters, frequently lend money to young artists, and serve as spokespersons for the artists." (*Park v. Deftones* (1999) 71 Cal.App.4th 1465, 1469–1470, 84 Cal.Rptr.2d 616.) Given this greater degree of involvement and risk, managers typically have a smaller client base and charge higher commissions than agents (as they may, in the absence of guild price caps); managers may also produce their clients' work and thus receive compensation in that fashion. (*Conflicts in the New Hollywood,* at p. 992; *Talent Agencies Act, supra,* 28 Pepperdine L.Rev. at p. 383; *Contested Ascendancy,* at pp. 508, 526–527; *Regulation of Attorneys,* at p. 483.)

B.   *The Talent Agencies Act*

Aside from guild regulation, the representation of artists is principally governed by the Act. (§§ 1700–1700.47.) The Act's roots extend back to 1913, when the Legislature passed the Private Employment Agencies Law and imposed the first licensing requirements for employment agents. (*Buchwald v. Superior Court* (1967) 254 Cal.App.2d 347, 357, 62 Cal.Rptr. 364; *Talent Agencies Act, supra,* 28 Pepperdine L.Rev. at p. 387; *Regulation of Attorneys, supra,* 80 Cal. L.Rev. at p. 493.) From an early time, the Legislature was concerned that those representing aspiring artists might take advantage of them, whether by concealing conflicts of interest when agents split fees with the venues where they booked their clients, or by sending clients to houses of ill-repute under the guise of providing "employment opportunities." (See Stats.1913, ch. 282, § 14, pp. 519–520 [prohibiting agents from fee-splitting, sending artists to "house[s] of ill fame" or saloons, or allowing "persons of bad character" to frequent their establishments]; *Talent Agencies Act,* at pp. 386–387; *Regulation of Attorneys,* at p. 493.) Exploitation of artists by representatives has remained the Act's central concern through subsequent incarnations to the present day. (See *Styne v. Stevens, supra,* 26 Cal.4th at p. 50, 109 Cal.Rptr.2d 14, 26 P.3d 343.)

In 1978, the Legislature considered establishing a separate licensing scheme for personal managers. (See Assem. Bill No. 2535 (1977–1978 Reg. Sess.) as amended May 1, 1978, § 41; Assem. Com. on Labor, Employment & Consumer Affairs, Analysis of Assem. Bill No. 2535 (1977–1978 Reg. Sess.) as amended May 1, 1978, pp. 1–4; Entertainment Com. Rep., *supra,* at p. 8.) Unable to reach agreement, the Legislature eventually abandoned separate licensing of personal managers and settled for minor changes in the statutory regime, shifting regulation of musician booking agents to the Labor Commissioner and renaming the Artists' Managers Act the Talent Agencies Act. (Stats.1978, ch. 1382, pp. 4575–4583.)

[¶] . . . . In its present incarnation, the Act requires anyone who solicits or procures artistic employment or engagements for artists[3] to obtain a talent agency license. (§§ 1700.4, 1700.5.) In turn, the Act establishes detailed requirements for how licensed talent agencies conduct their business. . . . (§§ 1700.23–1700.47.) No separate analogous licensing or regulatory scheme extends to personal managers. (*Waisbren v. Peppercorn Productions, Inc., supra,* 41 Cal.App.4th at p. 252, 48 Cal.Rptr.2d 437.)

With this background in mind, we turn to two questions not previously addressed by this court: whether the Act in fact applies to personal managers, as the Courts of Appeal and Labor Commissioner have long assumed, and if so, how.

II. *The Scope of the Talent Agencies Act: Application to Managers*

Marathon contends that personal managers are categorically exempt from regulation under the Act. We disagree; as we shall explain, the text of the Act and persuasive interpretations of it by the Courts of Appeal and the Labor Commissioner demonstrate otherwise.

We begin with the language of the Act. . . . Section 1700.5 provides in relevant part: "No *person* shall engage in or carry on the occupation of a *talent agency* without first procuring a license therefor from the Labor Commissioner." (Italics added.) In turn, "person" is expressly defined to include "any individual, company, society, firm, partnership, association, corporation, limited liability company, *manager,* or their agents or

---

[3]   " 'Artists' means actors and actresses rendering services on the legitimate stage and in the production of motion pictures, radio artists, musical artists, musical organizations, directors of legitimate stage, motion picture and radio productions, musical directors, writers, cinematographers, composers, lyricists, arrangers, models, and other artists and persons rendering professional services in motion picture, theatrical, radio, television and other entertainment enterprises." (§ 1700.4, subd. (b).)

employees" (§ 1700, italics added), and " '[t]alent agency' means a person or corporation who engages in the occupation of procuring, offering, promising, or attempting to procure employment or engagements for an artist or artists" other than recording contracts (§ 1700.4, subd. (a)).

The Act establishes its scope through a functional, not a titular, definition. It regulates *conduct,* not labels; it is the act of procuring (or soliciting), not the title of one's business, that qualifies one as a talent agency and subjects one to the Act's licensure and related requirements. (§ 1700.4, subd. (a).) Any person who procures employment—any individual, any corporation, any manager—is a talent agency subject to regulation. (§§ 1700, 1700.4, subd. (a).) Consequently, as the Courts of Appeal have unanimously held, a personal manager who solicits or procures employment for his artist-client is subject to and must abide by the Act. (*Park v. Deftones, supra,* 71 Cal.App.4th at pp. 1470–1471, 84 Cal.Rptr.2d 616; *Waisbren v. Peppercorn Productions, Inc., supra,* 41 Cal.App.4th at p. 253, 48 Cal.Rptr.2d 437 . . . .)[4] The Labor Commissioner, whose interpretations of the Act we may look to for guidance, . . . has similarly uniformly applied the Act to personal managers. . . .[FN 5 omitted]

As to the further question whether even a single act of procurement suffices to bring a manager under the Act, we note that the Act references the "occupation" of procuring employment and serving as a talent agency. (§§ 1700.4, subd. (a), 1700.5.) Considering this in isolation, one might interpret the statute as applying only to those who regularly, and not merely occasionally, procure employment. (See *Wachs v. Curry* (1993) 13 Cal.App.4th 616, 628, 16 Cal.Rptr.2d 496 [Act applies only when "the agent's employment procurement function constitutes a significant part of the agent's business as a whole"].) However, as we have previously acknowledged in dicta, "[t]he weight of authority is that even the incidental or occasional provision of such services requires licensure." (*Styne v. Stevens, supra,* 26 Cal.4th at p. 51, 109 Cal.Rptr.2d 14, 26 P.3d 343, citing *Park v. Deftones, supra,* 71 Cal.App.4th 1465, 84 Cal.Rptr.2d 616, and *Waisbren v. Peppercorn Productions, Inc., supra,* 41 Cal.App.4th 246, 48 Cal.Rptr.2d 437.)[FN6 omitted] In agreement with these decisions, the Labor Commissioner has uniformly interpreted the Act as extending to incidental procurement. (See, e.g., *Gittelman v. Karolat* (Cal.Lab.Com., July 19, 2004)

---

4   The Legislature clearly agreed with this understanding of the Act. In 1978, it considered but ultimately rejected a special exemption that would have specifically authorized personal managers to procure employment for artists already represented by licensed talent agencies. (See Assem. Bill No. 2535 (1977–1978 Reg. Sess.) as amended May 10, 1978 [deleting proposal to enact new § 1708, which would have codified special exemption].) In 1986, it made permanent section 1700.44, subdivision (d), which creates a safe harbor for an unlicensed person or entity to "act in conjunction with, and at the request of, a licensed talent agency in the negotiation of an employment contract." Both the originally contemplated exemption and the ultimately adopted safe harbor provision would have been largely superfluous if unlicensed entities were already free to procure employment, so long as they did not label themselves as talent agencies. (See *Waisbren v. Peppercorn Productions, Inc., supra,* 41 Cal.App.4th at p. 259, 48 Cal.Rptr.2d 437.)

TAC No. 24–02, p. 14; *Kilcher v. Vainshtein* (Cal.Lab.Com., May 30, 2001) TAC No. 02–99, pp. 20–21; *Damon v. Emler* (Cal.Lab.Com., Jan. 12, 1982) TAC No. 36–79, p. 4.) The Labor Commissioner's views are entitled to substantial weight if not clearly erroneous (*Styne v. Stevens,* at p. 53, 109 Cal.Rptr.2d 14, 26 P.3d 343); accordingly, we likewise conclude the Act extends to individual incidents of procurement.

[¶¶] . . . . Marathon correctly notes that in 1978, after much deliberation, the Legislature decided not to add separate licensing and regulation of personal managers to the legislation. (See Assem. Bill No. 2535 (1977–1978 Reg. Sess.) as amended May 10, 1978, pp. 16–18 [deleting new licensure provisions].) The consequence of this conscious omission is not, as Marathon contends, that personal managers are therefore exempt from regulation. Rather, they remain exempt from regulation insofar as they do those things that personal managers do, but they are regulated under the Act to the extent they stray into doing the things that make one a talent agency under the Act.[8]

III. *Sanctions for Solicitation and Procurement Under the Act*

A. *Marathon's Procurement*

We note we are not called on to decide, and do not decide, what precisely constitutes "procurement" under the Act. The Act contains no definition, and the Labor Commissioner has struggled over time to better delineate which actions involve mere general assistance to an artist's career and which stray across the line to illicit procurement. Here, however, the Labor Commissioner concluded Marathon had engaged in various instances of procurement, the trial court concluded there was no material dispute that Marathon had done so, and Marathon has not further challenged that conclusion. We thus take it as a given that Marathon has engaged in one or more acts of procurement and that (as the parties also agree) Marathon has no talent agency license to do so.

We also take as a given, at least at this stage, that Marathon's unlicensed procurement did not include the procurement specifically of Blasi's *Strong Medicine* role. . . .

Finally, although Marathon argued below that it fell within section 1700.44, subdivision (d)'s "safe harbor" for procurement done in conjunction with a licensed talent agency, it has not preserved that

---

8   The Entertainment Commission articulated precisely this rationale in concluding there was no need to separately license personal managers: "It is not a person who is being licensed [under] the [Act;] rather, it is the activity of procuring employment. Whoever performs that activity is legally defined as a talent agent and [must be] licensed, as such. Therefore, the licensing of a personal manager—or anyone else who undertakes to procure employment for an artist—with the [Act] already in place would be a needless duplication of licensure activity." (Entertainment Com. Rep., supra, at pp. 20–21.)

argument here. Accordingly, we assume for present purposes that the safe harbor provision does not apply.

B.   *The Applicability of the Doctrine of Severability to Manager-talent Contracts*

We turn to the key question in Blasi's appeal: What is the artist's remedy for a violation of the Act? In particular, when a manager has engaged in unlawful procurement, is the manager always barred from any recovery of outstanding fees from the artist or may the court or Labor Commissioner apply the doctrine of severability (Civ.Code, § 1599) to allow partial recovery of fees owed for legally provided services?

Again, we begin with the language of the Act. On this question, it offers no assistance. The Act is silent—completely silent—on the subject of the proper remedy for illegal procurement.

On the other hand, the text of Civil Code section 1599 is clear. Adopted in 1872, it codifies the common law doctrine of severability of contracts: "Where a contract has several distinct objects, of which one at least is lawful, and one at least is unlawful, in whole or in part, the contract is void as to the latter and valid as to the rest." (*Ibid.*) By its terms, it applies even—indeed, only—when the parties have contracted, in part, for something illegal. Notwithstanding any such illegality, it preserves and enforces any lawful portion of a parties' contract that feasibly may be severed.[FN9 omitted]

Under ordinary rules of interpretation, we must read Civil Code section 1599 and the Act so as to, to the extent possible, give effect to both. . . . The two are not in conflict. The Act defines conduct, and hence contractual arrangements, that are illegal: An unlicensed talent agency may not contract with talent to provide procurement services. (Lab.Code, §§ 1700.4, subd. (a), 1700.5.) The Act provides no remedy for its violation, but neither does it repudiate the generally applicable and long-standing rule of severability. Hence, that rule applies absent other persuasive evidence that the Legislature intended to reject the rule in disputes under the Act.

The conclusion that the rule applies is consistent with those of the Labor Commissioner's decisions that recognize severability principles may apply to disputes under the Act. In *Almendarez v. Unico Talent Management, Inc.* (Cal.Lab.Com., Aug. 26, 1999) TAC No. 55–97, a radio personality sought a determination that his personal manager had acted as an unlicensed talent agency. The Labor Commissioner concluded the manager had engaged in unlawful procurement—indeed, that procuring employment was the manager's primary role (*id.* at pp. 2, 14)—but stopped short of voiding all agreements between the parties in their entirety. Citing and applying Civil Code section 1599, the Labor Commissioner concluded that a 1997 agreement between the parties had both a lawful purpose (repayment of personal expenses the manager had fronted for Almendarez) and an unlawful purpose (payment of commissions for unlawful procurement services) and should be partially enforced. (*Almendarez*, at pp. 18–21.) On numerous other occasions, the Labor Commissioner has severed contracts and allowed managers to retain or seek commissions based on severability principles without expressly citing Civil Code section 1599.[FN10 omitted]

Until two years ago, Court of Appeal decisions under the Act had neither accepted nor repudiated the general applicability of the severability doctrine.[FN11 omitted] In 2005, in *Yoo v. Robi, supra,* 126 Cal.App.4th 1089, 24 Cal.Rptr.3d 740, however, the Court of Appeal considered whether to apply Civil Code section 1599 to allow a personal manager to seek commissions for lawfully provided services. It noted, correctly, that severance is not mandatory and its application in an individual case must be informed by equitable considerations. (*Yoo,* at p. 1105, 24 Cal.Rptr.3d 740.) Civil Code section 1599 grants courts the power, not the duty, to sever contracts in order to avoid an inequitable windfall or preserve a contractual relationship where doing so would not condone illegality. (*Armendariz v. Foundation Health Psychcare Services, Inc.* (2000) 24 Cal.4th 83, 123–124, 99 Cal.Rptr.2d 745, 6 P.3d 669.) The *Yoo* Court of Appeal concluded the windfall for the artist, Robi, was not so great as to warrant severance.

[¶¶] . . . . More generally, the conclusion that severance is available is consistent with a wide range of cases that have applied the doctrine to partially enforce contracts involving unlicensed services. . . .

Blasi contends that even if severability may generally apply to disputes under the Act, we should announce a rule categorically precluding its use to recover for artist advice and counseling services. She relies on three sources in support of this rule: the legislative history, case law interpreting the Act, and decisions of the Labor Commissioner. None persuades us that the Legislature intended to foreclose the application of severability, as codified in Civil Code sections 1598 and 1599, to manager-talent contracts that involve illegal procurement, either generally or with regard to recovery specifically for personal manager services.

[¶¶] . . . . We recognize, however, that in more recent decisions, the Labor Commissioner has expressly adopted the position Blasi advocates: severance is never available to permit partial recovery of commissions for managerial services that required no talent agency license. (*Smith v. Harris* (Cal.Lab.Com., Aug. 27, 2007) TAC No. 53–05, pp. 16–17; *Cham v. Spencer/Cowings Entertainment, LLC* (Cal.Lab.Com., July 30, 2007) TAC No. 19–05, pp. 17–18.) The weight accorded agency adjudicatory rulings such as these varies according to the validity of their reasoning and their overall persuasive force. (*Yamaha Corp. of America v. State Bd. of*

Equalization, supra, 19 Cal.4th at pp. 12–15, 78 Cal.Rptr.2d 1, 960 P.2d 1031.) Here, the Labor Commissioner's views rest in part on a reading of the legislative history as suggesting such a rule, in part on a reading of past Court of Appeal decisions as announcing such a rule, and perhaps in part on a policy judgment that voiding contracts in their entirety is necessary to enforce the Act effectively. With due respect, the Labor Commissioner's assessment of the legislative history and case law is mistaken; as we have explained, neither requires the rule she proposes. And any view that it would be better policy if the Act stripped the Labor Commissioner (and the superior courts in subsequent trials de novo) of the power to apply equitable doctrines such as severance would be squarely at odds with the Act's text, which contains no such limitation. Neither we nor the Labor Commissioner are authorized to engraft onto the Act such a limitation neither express nor implicit in its terms. We are thus unpersuaded and decline to follow the Labor Commissioner's interpretation.

In sum, the Legislature has not seen fit to specify the remedy for violations of the Act. Ordinary rules of interpretation suggest Civil Code section 1599 applies fully to disputes under the Act; nothing in the Act's text, its history, or the decisions interpreting it justifies the opposite conclusion. We conclude the full voiding of the parties' contract is available, but not mandatory; likewise, severance is available, but not mandatory.

C. *Application of the Severability Doctrine*

Finally, we turn to application of the severability doctrine to the facts of this case, insofar as those facts are established by the summary judgment record. Given the procedural posture, our inquiry is narrow: On this record, has Blasi established as a matter of law that there is no basis for severance?

In deciding whether severance is available, we have explained "[t]he overarching inquiry is whether ' "the interests of justice . . . would be furthered" ' by severance." (*Armendariz v. Foundation Health Psychcare Services, Inc., supra,* 24 Cal.4th at p. 124, 99 Cal.Rptr.2d 745, 6 P.3d 669.) "Courts are to look to the various purposes of the contract. If the central purpose of the contract is tainted with illegality, then the contract as a whole cannot be enforced. If the illegality is collateral to the main purpose of the contract, and the illegal provision can be extirpated from the contract by means of severance or restriction, then such severance and restriction are appropriate." (*Ibid.;* accord, *Little v. Auto Stiegler, Inc.* (2003) 29 Cal.4th 1064, 1074, 130 Cal.Rptr.2d 892, 63 P.3d 979.)

Blasi does not contend that particular evidence in the record unique to this contract establishes severance cannot apply. Instead, she offers two arguments applicable to this contract and to manager-talent contracts in general.

First, Blasi points to the nature of the compensation. In the Marathon-Blasi contract, as with most such contracts, there is no match between services and compensation. That is, a personal manager provides an undifferentiated range of services; in exchange, he receives an undifferentiated right to a certain percentage of the client's income stream.

This compensation scheme is essentially analogous to a contingency fee arrangement, in which an attorney provides an undifferentiated set of services and is compensated not for each service but as a percentage of the ultimate recovery her efforts yield for her client. . . . While an undifferentiated compensation scheme may in some instances preclude severance (see Civ.Code, § 1608; *Hyon v. Selten* (2007) 152 Cal.App.4th 463, 471, 60 Cal.Rptr.3d 896), *Birbrower* demonstrates that it does not represent a categorical obstacle to application of the doctrine.[FN15 omitted] Accordingly, we may not affirm summary judgment on this basis.

Second, Blasi argues that once a personal manager solicits or procures employment, all his services—advice, counseling, and the like—become those of an unlicensed talent agency and are thus uncompensable. We are not persuaded. In this regard, the conduct-driven definitions of the Act cut both ways. A personal manager who spends 99 percent of his time engaged in counseling a client and organizing the client's affairs is not insulated from the Act's strictures if he spends 1 percent of his time procuring or soliciting; conversely, however, the 1 percent of the time he spends soliciting and procuring does not thereby render illegal the 99 percent of the time spent in conduct that requires no license and that may involve a level of personal service and attention far beyond what a talent agency might have time to provide. Courts are empowered under the severability doctrine to consider the central purposes of a contract; if they determine in a given instance that the parties intended for the representative to function as an unlicensed talent agency or that the representative engaged in substantial procurement activities that are inseparable from managerial services, they may void the entire contract. For the personal manager who truly acts as a personal manager, however, an isolated instance of procurement does not automatically bar recovery for services that could lawfully be provided without a license. (See *Lindenstadt v. Staff Builders, Inc., supra,* 55 Cal.App.4th at p. 894, 64 Cal.Rptr.2d 484.)

Inevitably, no verbal formulation can precisely capture the full contours of the range of cases in which severability properly should be applied, or rejected. The doctrine is equitable and fact specific, and its application is appropriately directed to the sound discretion of the Labor Commissioner and trial courts in the first instance. As the Legislature has not seen fit to preclude categorically this case-by-case consideration of the doctrine in disputes under the Act, we may not do so either. [¶¶] . . . .

DISPOSITION

For the foregoing reasons, we affirm the Court of Appeal's judgment and remand this case for further proceedings consistent with this opinion.

We Concur: KENNARD, ACTING C.J., BAXTER, CHIN, MORENO, CORRIGAN, JJ., and MCADAMS, J.

PINE V. LAINE

321 N.Y.S.2d 303 (Sup. Ct. App. Div. 1971)

Before STEVENS, P.J., and CAPOZZOLI, NUNEZ, KUPFERMAN and STEUER, JJ.

Opinion

PER CURIAM

Order of the Supreme Court, New York County, entered on September 30, 1970, denying defendant's motion for summary judgment, unanimously reversed, on the law, the motion granted, and the complaint dismissed. The clerk is directed to enter judgment in favor of defendant dismissing the complaint, with costs. Appellant shall recover of respondent $50 costs and disbursements of this appeal.

Plaintiff sues for $35,000 for work, labor and services performed in arranging a recording contract between the defendant and ABC Records. The court at Special Term determined that there was an issue of fact "as to whether the plaintiff was acting as an employment agency or as the personal manager of the defendant when he performed the alleged services for the defendant.

* * * *

Inasmuch as the plaintiff was not licensed as an employment agency pursuant to article 11 of the General Business Law, unless he comes within the exception of subdivision 7 of section 171 as a personal manager where the seeking of employment is only incidental to the business of managing, he may not recover. (See Mandel v. Liebman, 303 N. Y. 88.)

It is clear that the defendant had a manager, and that the only service performed by the plaintiff, although he sought to become the manager of the defendant, was this one procurement of a recording contract.

Under the circumstances, plaintiff cannot come within the exception.

Deftones singer Chino Moreno
performing at Maquinária Festival,
São Paulo, Brazil (Nov. 2009)
Photo by Luiz Alberto Fiebig Jr.
(CC-BY-2.0)

PARK V. DEFTONES

71 Cal. App. 4th 1465 (Cal. Ct. App. 1999)

NOTT, ACTING P. J.

Dave Park appeals from the summary judgment entered against him in his action for breach of contract and intentional interference with contractual relations. His action arises from the termination of his personal manager contract by the Deftones, a music act whose members are Camillo Wong Moreno, Stephen Carpenter, Abe Cunningham, and Chi Ling Cheng (referred to collectively as the Deftones), without paying him commissions which he asserts are due him. In addition, Park alleges that after he secured a recording contract for the Deftones with Maverick Records (Maverick), the record company and one of its agents, Guy Oseary, purposefully interfered with Park's contractual relationship with the Deftones. The trial court granted summary judgment on the ground that the management contract between the Deftones and Park was void, Park having violated the Talent Agencies Act (the Act) by securing performance engagements for the Deftones without being licensed as a talent agency. (Lab. Code, § 1700 et seq.)[1] We affirm on that ground.

Procedural and Factual Background

Park filed this action in October 1996, alleging breach of certain management agreements against the Deftones and the individual band members and intentional interference with contractual relations against Maverick and Oseary. He attached to his complaint his written agreements

---

[1]   All statutory references are to the Labor Code, unless otherwise indicated.

with the Deftones entered into in February 1992, February 1993, and January 1994. In February 1997, the Deftones filed a petition before the Labor Commissioner, seeking to void the management agreements. Park unsuccessfully sought dismissal of the petition as untimely filed. The Labor Commissioner determined that Park had violated the Act by obtaining performance engagements for the Deftones on 84 occasions without a license. He issued an order stating that the personal management agreements entered into in 1992, 1993, and 1994 were "null, void and unenforceable." Park demanded a trial de novo in the administrative proceeding.

Maverick and Oseary filed a motion for summary judgment on the grounds that the undisputed facts showed that (1) Park and the Deftones entered into a written contract for management services dated January 18, 1994, (2) between September 1991 and September 1994, Park procured numerous performances for the Deftones, and (3) Park was not a licensed talent agency during that period. Maverick and Oseary relied in part upon the transcript of the Labor Commission proceeding to establish the facts. The Deftones filed a similar motion.

Park opposed the motions. He objected to use of the Labor Commission hearing transcript, but admitted that he had obtained more than 80 engagements for the Deftones. He asserted that the Deftones' petition before the Labor Commission was untimely filed and that his services did not require a talent agency license because they were rendered without a commission and were undertaken in order to obtain a recording agreement. The trial court entered summary judgment in favor of all defendants.

Discussion

* * * *

II. *Incidental procurement of employment*

The Act provides that "No person shall engage in or carry on the occupation of a talent agency without first procuring a license therefor from the Labor Commissioner." (§ 1700.5.) A talent agency is "a person or corporation who engages in the occupation of procuring, offering, promising, or attempting to procure employment or engagements for an artist or artists, except that the activities of procuring, offering, or promising to procure recording contracts for an artist or artists shall not of itself subject a person or corporation to regulation and licensing under this chapter. . . ." (§ 1700.4, subd. (a).)

Unlike talent agents, personal managers are not covered by the Act. Personal managers primarily advise, counsel, direct, and coordinate the development of the artist's career. They advise in both business and personal matters, frequently lend money to young artists, and serve as spokespersons for the artists. (See *Waisbren v. Peppercorn Productions, Inc.* (1995) 41 Cal.App.4th 246, 252–253 [48 Cal.Rptr.2d 437] (*Waisbren*).)

Park argues that as a personal manager his goal in procuring engagements for the Deftones was to obtain a recording agreement. He contends that his actions were therefore exempt from regulation. That position was rejected in *Waisbren, supra,* 41 Cal.App.4th at page 259. In *Waisbren,* a promoter brought an action for breach of contract against a company engaged in designing and creating puppets. The defendant moved for summary judgment on the ground the parties' agreement for the plaintiff's services was void because he had performed the duties of a talent agent without obtaining a license. The plaintiff asserted that a license was unnecessary because his procurement activities were minimal and incidental. He had also assisted in project development, managed certain business affairs, supervised client relations and publicity, performed casting duties, coordinated production, and handled office functions. In return, he was to receive 15 percent of the company's profits. *Waisbren* holds that even incidental activity in procuring employment for an artist is subject to regulation under the Act.

The reasoning of *Waisbren* is convincing. It relies upon the remedial purpose of the Act and the statutory goal of protecting artists from long recognized abuses. The decision is also based upon the Labor Commissioner's long-held position that a license is required for incidental procurement activities. The court in *Waisbren* found the Labor Commissioner's position to be supported by legislative history and, in particular, by the recommendations contained in the Report of the California Entertainment Commission, which were adopted by the Legislature in amending the Act in 1986.

Wachs v. Curry (1993) 13 Cal.App.4th 616 [16 Cal.Rptr.2d 496], relied upon by Park, does not further his cause. In *Wachs,* the personal manager plaintiffs brought a declaratory relief action challenging the constitutionality of the Act on its face. They took the position that the Act's exemption for procurement activities involving recording contracts violated the equal protection clause and that the Act's use of the term "procure" was so vague as to violate due process. *Wachs* rejected both of those positions. It also interpreted the Act, which applies to persons engaged in the occupation of procuring employment for artists, as applying only where a person's procurement activities constitute a significant part of his business. (*Id.* at pp. 627–628.) The court did not define "significant part." The court acknowledged that ". . . the only question before us is whether the word 'procure' in the context of the Act is so lacking in objective content that it provides no standard at all by which to measure an agent's conduct" (*id.* at p. 628, italics omitted). We agree with *Waisbren* that the interpretation stated in *Wachs* is dictum and that even incidental procurement is regulated.

III. *Absence of a commission*

Park also contends that his procuring employment for the Deftones is not regulated by the Act because he was not compensated for that work. We disagree.

Park's 1993 and 1994 agreements with the Deftones expressly provided that Park was to receive a 20 percent commission on all income earned from employment that Park secured. Although Park stated in declaration testimony that he received no commission for procuring engagements for the Deftones, the contracts appear to provide for compensation.[3] In addition, Park would receive compensation for his services ultimately from commissions for obtaining a recording contract for the Deftones. Thus, it is not clear that Park should be treated as one who was not compensated for his services.

Park's position, moreover, is not supported by the language of the Act. The Act regulates those who engage in the occupation of procuring engagements for artists. (§ 1700.4, subd. (a).) The Act does not expressly include or exempt procurement where no compensation is made. . . . One may engage in an occupation which includes procuring engagements without receiving direct compensation for that activity.

As explained in *Waisbren*, the purpose of the Act is remedial, and its aim goes beyond regulating the amount of fees which can be charged for booking acts. For example, an agent must have his form of contract approved by the Labor Commissioner, maintain his client's funds in a trust fund account, record and retain certain information about his client, and refrain from giving false information to an artist concerning potential employment. (See §§ 1700.23, 1700.25, 1700.26, 1700.32, and 1700.41.) Because the Act is remedial, it should be liberally construed to promote its general object. (See *Buchwald v. Superior Court* (1967) 254 Cal.App.2d 347, 354 [62 Cal.Rptr. 364].) The abuses at which these requirements are aimed apply equally where the personal manager procures work for the artist without a commission, but rather for the deferred benefits from obtaining a recording contract.

. . . . [¶] We conclude that the Act requires a license to engage in procurement activities even if no commission is received for the service.

NOTES AND QUESTIONS

1.   States other than California and New York also have their own versions of licensing requirements for talent agencies. As noted above, lawyers representing recording artists and composers are also often asked to play roles

---

[3]   The agreements acknowledge that Park is not a licensed talent agent and is under no obligation to procure employment for the Deftones.

that overlap significantly with the defined role of agents under state law. Under what circumstances should a lawyer be required to also acquire a talent agent license from California? New York? In general? Is it relevant that lawyers are held to professional and fiduciary obligations that are more extensive than, but different from, those imposed on talent agents?

2.   What are the key differences that you note between New York and California law regarding regulation of talent agents that might be significant for those who work with recording artists? What policies might justify the requirements and approaches of each state? Which state's approach to regulating talent agents do you think is the better approach? Why?

3.   Although the California Supreme Court's decision in *Marathon Entertainment* did not address relationships within the music industry, it is one of the most significant and relatively recent rulings interpreting the scope of talent agency licensing statutes. Do you agree with its holding that the California Talent Agencies Act regulates personal managers when their actions cross the line into acting like a talent agent? What do you think about the possibility of severance of conduct that falls outside of the licensing requirements of the statute, and thus the ability of managers to recover commissions for work that does not require licensing even if those managers engaged in some unlicensed conduct that violated the statute? Does the likelihood that managers might lose all of their revenue from representing a client serve as a reasonable deterrent against unlicensed activity?

4.   In 2011, Texas repealed its talent agency law because the legislature found that the state's antifraud laws sufficiently protected artists from reprehensible representatives. Some have argued that the talent agency laws, specifically in New York and California, are used by rising artists to separate from their early representatives in order to get a high-powered agent once they obtain a measure of success—in other words, rather than serving to protect powerless artists against unscrupulous agents, these statutes may also be used by successful artists as a means of severing their relationships (and the corresponding obligation to pay the fee) with managers who helped them to procure employment that led to their success. As was alluded to in the *Marathon Entertainment* case, managers may end up procuring employment for their clients even though they are unlicensed because agents are incentivized to only represent established artists and therefore will not sign artists with no reputations. Artists will therefore have no representation and no way to find employment and create a reputation unless their manager assists them. Are California and New York's laws serving their underlying purposes when they are used by successful artists to sever relationships with representatives who helped them to achieve their success? If so, how? If not, how might you suggest amending them to serve those purposes? How might they (or how should they) attempt to distinguish between managers and agents when the line between the two varies so much in both individual circumstances and across different branches of the entertainment industry?

5.   Under New York's law, an unlicensed talent agent can be enjoined from further activity and future commissions, in addition to voiding any contracts, and under California's law, an unlicensed agent not only could be enjoined from future commissions but could be ordered to disgorge previous commissions. Given what the previous note said about artists utilizing the talent agency laws to cut out their early managers in favor of high-powered agents once their careers are established, are these remedies fair? Can you think of alternative remedies or enforcement mechanisms that would address any perceived unfairness? Would a separate licensing system for managers be helpful? Why or why not?

6   Consider Live Nation's relationships with the artists that it manages—particularly those like Madonna, U2, Shakira, and Jay-Z with whom it entered into 360-like deals—and how statutes like those in California and New York excerpted above might be argued to apply. Live Nation owns concert venues throughout the country, promotes concerts, and sells tickets to concerts through its ownership of Ticketmaster. It also manages artists and invests in their careers, serving a recording company-like function for some of its artists. Can the California or New York talent agent statutes apply to what Live Nation does for its artists? Should all of its various arms/subsidiaries be considered, or just the artist management division? How are the policies underlying these statutes implicated in situations like this?

C. RADIO DEREGULATION, CONSOLIDATION, AND ITS EFFECT ON THE MUSIC INDUSTRY

As noted in the introductory chapters to this textbook, the music industry has seen a period of massive consolidation in recent decades, both horizontal and vertical. As of the writing of this text, only three major publishers and three major recording companies remain, and some of those companies are part of even larger entertainment conglomerates. It is possible for a singer-songwriter to be under contract with a label and publisher owned by the same company, to have all of his or her merchandising and touring licensed to related companies, and to have works falling under the contract be licensed to film, cable, and television entities also owned by the same company. Other entities control large segments of the music industry, such as iHeartMedia (formerly Clear Channel), which at one point owned radio stations, outdoor advertising companies, and concert venues in every major market and which remains the largest radio station owner in the U.S, earning 22 percent of music radio revenue in 2019.[12] Live Nation Entertainment currently owns or controls more than 140 concert venues in North America and the major online ticket seller, Ticketmaster, while also serving as a management company for a number of major recording artists.

In some ways, such consolidation has the potential for providing easier access and more efficient licensing for those artists and composers who are fortunate enough to have a deal with one of these large companies. It may also increase overall value by enabling companies to leverage one aspect of an artist's career onto another aspect. In other ways, such consolidation makes entry into the market more difficult for newcomers and discourages the development of local "sounds" and genres, given the market's current preference for nationwide playlists on radio and bookings in venues. It may also have the effect of hampering market opportunities for certain artists or songwriters when dealing with venues or companies outsides of their "family" of providers.

A countervailing force in the past few decades of consolidation in the industry has been the rise of the Internet as a distribution and promotion mechanism for artists and, albeit to a lesser degree, songwriters. Challenges to new merger proposals on antitrust grounds are often countered by arguments that the "relevant market" to consider (for

---

[12] In 2020, iHeartRadio owned more than 850 radio stations—twice the number of its nearest competitor. Although it owns about 5.5% of U.S. radio stations, its 2019 share of music station revenue was almost 22%. *See* iHeartMedia Inc., Annual Report (Form 10-K) (Feb. 27, 2020); Broad. Station Totals as of Dec. 31, 2019, 2020 WL 132482, at *1 (OHMSV Jan. 3, 2020); Massarsky Consulting 2020. More generally, stations with revenue of $5 million and up made up only 4.5% of total stations but earned 39% of revenue. Massarsky Consulting 2020. iHeartMedia spun off its concert promotion subsidiary in 2005 (which is now Live Nation Entertainment). In 2019, iHeart underwent a Chapter 11 reorganization, which slimmed down both its debt and the diversity of its holdings to better focus on positioning itself as a multi-platform audio company.

purposes of evaluating competition) should include online avenues for consumers to access music and for competing entities to distribute them.

Below is a cross-section of materials to introduce you to some of these issues and to highlight the considerations present in the tension between the broadcast industry, content creators, consumers/listeners, and the government in a highly regulated sector of the music industry. First, we provide key language from the Telecommunications Act of 1996. This statute expanded the ability of a single entity to own multiple radio stations, television stations, and newspaper publishers in the same market and nationwide, and it was a driving force behind consolidation in the radio industry. Next, we provide summaries of and excerpts from the ongoing reviews by the Federal Communications Commission ("FCC") of the regulations implemented pursuant to the Telecommunications Act of 1996 and related litigation in order to give you a sense of the issues and arguments relating to radio ownership that continue to percolate in the industry. Finally, we include a case study to highlight the issues that arise more generally in the context of consolidation within the music industry, drawn from the 2012 merger of two of the then "Big Four" record labels that left the industry with three major labels.

CONSIDER AS YOU READ . . .

- What are the pros and cons of consolidation in the current music marketplace from the perspective of artists, labels, broadcasters, and consumers?

- What role do you see broadcast radio playing in the music industry moving forward?

- Should the FCC be concerned about music when it considers the impact of its regulations on competition, diversity, and localism? Should program diversity be important in the FCC's consideration of how many radio stations in a given market may be owned by a single company? Why or why not?

- What are the strongest arguments for permitting vertical and horizontal consolidation within the music industry that are illustrated by the EMI/UMG merger debate? What are the strongest arguments against such consolidation? Should further consolidation be permitted by antitrust authorities, and if so, under what conditions?

TELECOMMUNICATIONS ACT OF 1996,
PUB. L. NO. 104-104, § 202

An Act to promote competition and reduce regulation in order to secure lower prices and higher quality services for American telecommunications consumers and encourage the rapid deployment of new telecommunications technologies. . . .

SEC. 202. BROADCAST OWNERSHIP.

(a) NATIONAL RADIO STATION OWNERSHIP RULE CHANGES REQUIRED.—The Commission shall modify section 73.3555 of its regulations (47 C.F.R. 73.3555) by eliminating any provisions limiting the number of AM or FM broadcast stations which may be owned or controlled by one entity nationally.

(b) LOCAL RADIO DIVERSITY.—

(1) APPLICABLE CAPS.—The Commission shall revise section 73.3555(a) of its regulations (47 C.F.R. 73.3555) to provide that—

(A) in a radio market with 45 or more commercial radio stations, a party may own, operate, or control up to 8 commercial radio stations, not more than 5 of which are in the same service (AM or FM);

(B) in a radio market with between 30 and 44 (inclusive) commercial radio stations, a party may own, operate, or control up to 7 commercial radio stations, not more than 4 of which are in the same service (AM or FM);

(C) in a radio market with between 15 and 29 (inclusive) commercial radio stations, a party may own, operate, or control up to 6 commercial radio stations, not more than 4 of which are in the same service (AM or FM); and

(D) in a radio market with 14 or fewer commercial radio stations, a party may own, operate, or control up to 5 commercial radio stations, not more than 3 of which are in the same service (AM or FM), except that a party may not own, operate, or control more than 50 percent of the stations in such market.

(2) EXCEPTION.—Notwithstanding any limitation authorized by this subsection, the Commission may permit a person or entity to own, operate, or control, or have a cognizable interest in, radio broadcast stations if the Commission determines that such ownership, operation, control, or interest will result in an increase in the number of radio broadcast stations in operation.

In *Prometheus Radio Project v. F.C.C.*, 373 F.3d 372 (3d Cir. 2004), the Third Circuit provided a helpful description of the background for government limitations on media ownership leading up to the deregulatory movement in the 1980's and the Telecommunications Act of 1996:

> In 1934 Congress authorized the Commission to grant licenses for private parties' exclusive use of broadcast frequencies. Recognizing that the finite radio frequency spectrum inherently limits the number of broadcast stations that can operate without interfering with one another, Congress required that broadcast licensees serve the public interest, convenience, and necessity. Communications Act of 1934, 47 U.S.C. § 309(a); see also id. §§ 307(a), 310(d), 312.

> "In setting its licensing policies, the Commission has long acted on the theory that diversification of mass media ownership serves the public interest by promoting diversity of program and service viewpoints, as well as by preventing undue concentration of economic power." FCC v. Nat'l Citizens Comm. for Broad., 436 U.S. 775, 780, 98 S.Ct. 2096, 56 L.Ed.2d 697 (1978) ("NCCB"). The Commission's early regulations reflected its presumption that a single entity holding more than one broadcast license in the same community contravened public interest. . . . At the same time, the Commission prohibited common ownership of stations within the same broadcast service (AM radio, FM radio, and television) in the same community. . . . Regulations limiting an entity to the common ownership of seven AM radio stations, seven FM radio stations, and seven television stations survived judicial scrutiny in 1956. See United States v. Storer Broad. Co., 351 U.S. 192, 76 S.Ct. 763, 100 L.Ed. 1081 (1956). In the 1970s the Commission adopted its first cross-ownership bans, which prohibited, on a prospective basis, the common ownership of television and radio stations serving the same market, as well as combinations of radio or broadcast stations with a daily newspaper in the same community.

Although Congress had initially placed strict limits on national radio station ownership, it began relaxing those restrictions during the Reagan era in the 1980s. Prior to the 1996 Act, federal regulations precluded any radio station owner from owning more than 40 radio stations nationwide. As illustrated in the chart below, radio station ownership became greatly consolidated in the years after national ownership limits were removed upon enactment of the Telecommunications Act of 1996:

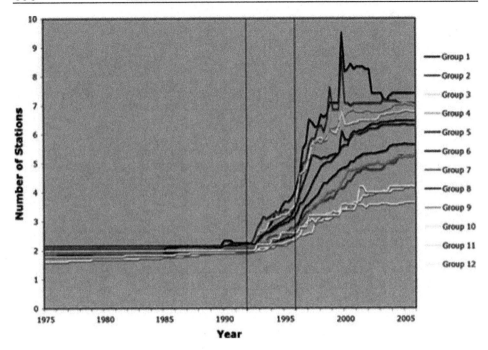

**Number of Stations Owned in a Market by the Largest Owner
in a Market, 1975–2005, Average by Market Group**
from the Future of Music Coalition False Premises, False Promises Report (2006),
available at https://futureofmusic.org/false-premises-false-promises-executive-summary

Following the 1996 Act's elimination of national limits on ownership and loosening of restrictions on ownership of multiple radio stations within individual markets, there have been numerous regulatory proceedings and associated litigation over those proceedings relating to proposed changes in existing ownership limitations based upon the evolving marketplace. The FCC was tasked by Congress with regularly reviewing the existing regulations on broadcast ownership, which it now does every four years (the "quadrennial reviews"). Below, we summarize some of those proceedings, which raise questions about the appropriate nature and scope of government regulation of radio. As you will see, much of the debate has been framed in the context of the FCC's overriding purpose of serving the public interest in its oversight of radio broadcasters. This admonition to act in the public interest has been described by the FCC as follows:

> [T]he "public interest" standard is not limited to purely economic outcomes. It necessarily encompasses the "broad aims of the Communications Act," which include, among other things, a deeply rooted preference for preserving and enhancing competition in relevant markets, accelerating private-sector deployment of advanced services, ensuring a diversity of information sources and services to the public, and generally

managing spectrum in the public interest. . . . The leading examples may come from broadcast transactions, where the Commission has long applied the congressional admonition to promote localism in programming, and especially news programming, available to communities.[13]

Although the public interest analysis is more concerned with access to information and to diverse viewpoints than to music, consolidation in ownership of radio stations has arguably led to more homogenous music programming throughout the nation and less local diversity in playlists across and within the various genres of music radio. For example, one 2006 report from the Future of Music Coalition indicated that just fifteen music formats made up three quarters of the airplay on commercial radio, with playlists for commonly owned stations in the same format overlapping up to 97% and up to an 80% overlap in songs played even across different formats. The same study found that "niche musical formats like Classical, Jazz, Americana, Bluegrass, New Rock, and Folk, where they existed, were provided almost exclusively by smaller station groups."[14] As you read the summaries below, consider how the questions and arguments addressed might apply to diversity in music programming as well as diversity of viewpoints.

1. SUMMARY OF FCC RULEMAKING PROCESS PURSUANT TO 1996 TELECOMMUNICATIONS ACT THROUGH 2016 REVIEW PROCEEDINGS

The FCC's regulatory review process relating to broadcast ownership limitations has been long and complex. The numerical limits on local radio station ownership set out in the 1996 Telecommunications Act have been a recurring part of that review process over the years, but the FCC has continued to find these tiered, numerical limitations based on market size to serve the public interest and thus they have remained unchanged as of 2020. The elimination of national ownership limits has not been the subject of review by the FCC, and the main focus of the FCC's regulatory review of broadcast ownership rules has been on ownership of local television stations and media cross-ownership limitations.

Because they are most relevant to the music industry, below we summarize FCC determinations relating to **local radio station ownership** since 2002 and related litigation.

---

[13] Jon Sallet, FCC General Counsel, *FCC Transaction Review: Competition and the Public Interest* (August 12, 2014—12:39 pm) at https://www.fcc.gov/news-events/blog/2014/08/12/fcc-transaction-review-competition-and-public-interest#fn3.

[14] Peter DiCola, Research Director, Future of Music Coalition, *False Premises, False Promises: A Quantitative History of Ownership Consolidation in the Radio Industry* 6–7 (Dec. 13, 2006), at http://futureofmusic.org/article/research/false-premises-false-promises.

2002 Review: Changes to Local Market Calculations

In its 2002 Biennial Review, although it recommended no changes in the numerical limits to local radio station ownership, the FCC adopted a final rule in 2003 that added noncommercial stations to the calculation of radio stations within a market, which had the effect of potentially allowing ownership of more stations in a local market where the total number of commercial and noncommercial stations placed the market into a different "tier" for ownership limits.[15] The FCC's 2003 Report and Order adopting the final rule stated in relevant part:

162.   The Commission concludes that the numerical limits in the local radio ownership rule are "necessary in the public interest" to protect competition in local radio markets. The Commission concludes, however, that the rule in its current form does not promote the public interest as it relates to competition because (1) its current contour-overlap methodology for defining radio markets and counting stations in the market is flawed as a means to protect competition in local radio markets, and (2) the current rule improperly ignores competition from noncommercial radio stations in local radio markets. To address those concerns, the Commission modifies the rule to replace the contour-overlap market definition with an Arbitron Metro market and to count noncommercial stations in the radio market. . . . Although the Commission primarily relies on competition to justify the rule, the Commission recognizes that localism and diversity are fostered when there are multiple, independently owned radio stations competing in the same market; its competition-based rule, therefore, will also promote those public interest objectives. . . .

200.   The Commission concludes that the ownership tiers in the current rule represent a reasonable means for promoting the public interest as it relates to competition. In radio markets, barriers to entry are high because virtually all available radio spectrum has been licensed. Radio broadcasting is thus a closed entry market, i.e., new entry generally can occur only through the acquisition of spectrum inputs from existing radio broadcasters. The closed entry nature of radio suggests that the extent of capacity that is available for new entry plays a significant role in determining whether market power can develop in radio broadcasting. Numerical limits on radio station ownership help to keep the available capacity from becoming "locked-up" in the

---

[15]   Final Rule, *Broadcast Ownership Rules, Cross-Ownership of Broadcast Stations and Newspapers, Multiple Ownership of Radio Broadcast Stations in Local Markets, and Definition of Radio Markets*, 68 FR 46286-01 (Aug. 5, 2003).

hands of one or a few owners, and thus help prevent the formation of market power in local radio markets.

201.   Although competition theory does not provide a hard-and-fast rule on the number of equally sized competitors that are necessary to ensure that the full benefits of competition are realized, both economic theory and empirical studies suggest that a market that has five or more relatively equally sized firms can achieve a level of market performance comparable to a fragmented, structurally competitive market. The current tiers ensure that, in markets with between 27 and 51 radio stations, there will be approximately five or six radio station firms of roughly equal size. An analysis of the top 100 Metro markets indicates that many of them fall within this range.

202.   The Commission finds that the concentration levels permitted by the current rule represent a reasonable and necessary balance for radio broadcasting that comports with general competition theory, and we decline to relax the rule to permit greater consolidation in local radio markets. . . .

203.   For markets with more than 51 radio stations, the number of radio station firms ensured by the rule increases as the size of the market increases. Because of this, some parties argue that we should raise the numerical limits to permit common ownership of more than eight radio stations in larger markets. The Commission rejects that argument. There is no evidence in the record that indicates that the efficiencies of consolidating radio stations increase appreciably for combinations involving more than eight radio stations. . . . By capping the numerical limit at eight stations, we seek to guard against consolidation of the strongest stations in a market in the hands of too few owners and to ensure a market structure that fosters opportunities for new entry into radio broadcasting.

204.   The Commission also declines to make the numerical limits more restrictive. In the smallest radio markets, the current rule provides that one entity may own up to half of the commercial radio stations in a market. Although this would be considered highly concentrated from a competitive point of view, greater levels of concentration may be needed to ensure the potential for viability of radio stations in smaller markets. Given these concerns, we find it reasonable to allow greater levels of concentration in smaller radio markets, but to require more independent radio station owners as the size of the market increases and viability concerns become less acute. . . .

206.   Although the Commission reaffirms the ownership tiers in the local radio ownership rule, we conclude that it is not necessary in the public interest to exclude noncommercial radio stations in determining the size of the radio market. Although noncommercial stations do not compete in the radio advertising market, they compete with other radio stations in the radio listening and program production markets. Indeed, noncommercial stations can receive a significant listening share in their respective markets. Their presence in the market therefore exerts competitive pressure on all other radio stations in the market seeking to attract the attention of the same body of potential listeners. . . .

207.   Rejection of Repeal and Other Modifications. The Commission rejects arguments that we should repeal the local radio ownership rule. We see nothing in the record that persuades us that the acquisition of market power in radio broadcasting serves the public interest. Competition breeds innovation in programming and creates incentives to continually improve program quality. Because competition—and the benefits that flow from it—is lessened when the market is dominated by one or a few players, the Commission seeks through its rules to prevent that type of market structure from developing. . . .

209.   The Commission does not dispute that a certain level of consolidation of radio stations can improve the ability of a group owner to make investments that benefit the public. Our responsibility under the statute, however, is to determine the level at which the harms of consolidation outweigh its benefits, and to establish rules to prevent that situation from developing. . . .

213.   Aside from the positive effect on localism that ensues from a competitive radio market, we see little to indicate that the local radio ownership rule significantly advances our interest in localism. . . . Although some parties suggest that localism has suffered as a result of consolidation, the source of the alleged harm appears to be the overall national size of the radio station group owner rather than the number of radio stations commonly owned in a local market. National radio ownership limits are outside the scope of this proceeding. . . .

216.   Programming Diversity. In theory, program diversity promotes the public interest by affording consumers access to a greater array of programming choices. The difficulty is in finding a way to measure program diversity in a coherent and consistent manner so that we can determine how it is affected by

concentration. The record indicates that different measures of format diversity produce strikingly different results. Overall, the results suggest that consolidation in the radio industry neither helped nor hindered playlist diversity between radio stations.

217.   The studies on program diversity also do not draw a sufficiently reliable causal link between ownership concentration and the purported increase in format diversity. After a careful review of the economic literature, however, the Commission cannot confidently adopt the view that we should encourage more consolidation in order to achieve greater format diversity.

218.   In light of this record, the Commission cannot conclude that radio ownership concentration has any effect on format diversity, either harmful or beneficial. Accordingly, we do not rely on it to justify the local radio ownership rule.[16]

The above Report and Order was challenged on numerous grounds by multiple parties in *Prometheus Radio Project v. F.C.C.* ("*Prometheus I*"), and in 2004 the Third Circuit found, inter alia, that Order lacked "a reasoned analysis for retaining" the numerical limits structure of the local radio ownership rule, remanding for additional justification by the Commission.[17] However, the court affirmed the Order's addition of noncommercial stations in calculating the number of radio stations in a given market and the decision to change the methodology used for defining local markets, and the regulation governing numerical limits on local radio station ownership was amended accordingly.[18] The Third Circuit retained jurisdiction over the regulatory review process.

2006 Review: Expanded Justification for Retaining Local Radio Numerical Limits

The FCC took up the remand of the 2002 Review's conclusions as to the numerical limits on local radio station ownership as part of the 2006 Review. The 2006 Review was released in February of 2008, reaffirming the Commission's conclusions that existing numerical limitations on local radio station ownership should be maintained.[19] However, the Commission adjusted and expanded its justification for maintaining the existing, tiered numerical limits:

---

[16]   *Id.*

[17]   *Prometheus Radio Project v. F.C.C.*, 373 F.3d 372, 432 (3d Cir. 2004), *as amended* (June 3, 2016).

[18]   47 C.F.R. § 73.3555(a)(1).

[19]   Report and Order and Order on Reconsideration, *In the Matter of 2006 Quadrennial Regulatory Review—Review of the Commissions Broad. Ownership Rules & Other Rules Adopted Pursuant to Section 202 of the Telecommunications Act of 1996 2002 Biennial Regulatory Review; Review of the Commissions Broad. Ownership Rules & Other Rules Adopted Pursuant to Section 202 of the Telecommunications Act of 1996*, 23 F.C.C.R. 2010, 2072–78 (Feb. 4, 2008).

118.   The evidence in the record indicates that retaining the numerical limits at the current level is necessary to protect against excessive market concentration. Prior to 1992, our radio ownership rules prohibited most radio mergers. In 1992, we relaxed our local radio ownership rules in recognition of the fact that our rules prevented some firms from achieving the economies of scale that they needed to survive financially. Congress further relaxed the local radio ownership limits in the 1996 Telecommunications Act. Congress's 1996 radio ownership rules revisions have had a substantial effect on the market structure of radio broadcasting, resulting in further consolidation of radio station ownership at both the national and the local level. By maintaining the current numerical limits, we seek to guard against additional consolidation of the strongest stations in a market in the hands of too few owners and to ensure a market structure that fosters opportunities for new entry into radio broadcasting. The number of commercial radio station owners declined by 39 percent between 1996 and 2007, with most of the decline occurring during the first few years after the 1996 Act. Although the average number of commercial owners across all Arbitron radio markets currently is 9.4, the largest commercial firm in each Arbitron Metro market has, on average, 46 percent of the market's total radio advertising revenue, and the largest two firms have 74 percent of the revenue. . . . The top four commercial firms also dominate audience share. And evidence in the record indicates that the increase in concentration in commercial radio markets has resulted in appreciable, albeit small, increases in advertising rates. All of this data in the record supports the conclusion that the current numerical limits are not unduly restrictive and that additional consolidation would not serve the Commission's competitive goals. . . .

120.   In addition, further tightening of the local radio ownership rule would disrupt the marketplace by necessitating widespread divestitures. . . . Requiring widespread divestitures would undermine settled expectations in a market where broadcasters needed regulatory relief to achieve the economies of scale necessary to compete just 10 years ago. Many broadcasters incurred significant financial risks by acquiring the additional stations permitted under this rule and are creating business development plans for the future based on these current economies of scale. Decreasing the limit would thus be a significant shock to the market. . . . We should not cause such a disruption absent persuasive evidence that further tightening of the local radio ownership rule would serve the public interest more effectively than the current rule. . . .

124. *Localism.* Our localism goal stems from our mandate to ensure that licensed broadcast facilities serve and are responsive to the needs and interests of the communities to which they are licensed. By preserving a healthy, competitive local radio market, the local radio ownership rule helps promote our interest in localism. Aside from the positive effect on localism that ensues from a competitive radio market, however, the Commission has never found that the local radio ownership rule significantly advances our interest in localism.

125. Although some parties suggest that localism has suffered as a result of consolidation, others forcefully argue that consolidation has benefited localism by giving group owners more resources to provide local news and public interest programming and to undertake initiatives responsive to the local needs and interests of the communities that they serve. For example, some critics of consolidation cite to a Future of Music Coalition Study, which contends that consolidation permitted under our rule reduces opportunities to air music from local artists. In addition, these commenters refute studies showing that large radio groups air a greater number of local programs. . . . In contrast, NAB argues that the record establishes that station groups are rolling out more news and talk stations and are otherwise providing substantial service to their local listeners; thus, NAB concludes that common ownership provides affirmative benefits to the public by increasing listening choices and enhancing local service.

126. Based on our examination of the record, the evidence does not show that consolidation in local markets has harmed localism. . . . We also note that the parties who criticize the effect of consolidation on localism often focus on the overall *national* size of the radio station group owner rather than the number of radio stations commonly owned in a local market. For example, several commenters criticize the practice of airing national music playlists by large national radio station groups. As we noted in the *2002 Biennial Review Order,* however, this criticism seems to focus more on Congress's decision to eliminate the national radio ownership cap, which we are not reviewing in this proceeding. In any event, these concerns do not address whether consolidation of radio stations in a *local* market harms localism.

127. *Diversity.* Although media other than radio play an important role in the dissemination of local news and public affairs information, the Commission previously has concluded that its competition-based limits on local radio ownership promote diversity by ensuring a sufficient number of independent radio voices and by preserving a market structure that facilitates and

encourages new entry into the local media market. The Commission has declined to rely on format diversity to justify the local radio ownership rule. . . .

129. Based on our examination of the record, we cannot conclude that the local radio ownership rule is necessary to protect format diversity. Nevertheless, we find that retaining the current, competition-based numerical limits on local radio ownership will promote diversity indirectly for the same reasons that the Commission pointed to in the *2002 Biennial Review Order*. Thus, it is proper for us to retain the status quo, as the ownership tiers serve the public interest in light of competition.[20]

The FCC's 2008 Report and Order was subsequently challenged by numerous interested parties in *Prometheus Radio Project v. F.C.C.*, 652 F.3d 431 (3d Cir. 2011) ("*Prometheus II*"). In *Prometheus II*, the Third Circuit vacated parts of the FCC's order in the 2006 Review, but found that the Commission's decision to retain existing numerical limits for local radio ownership was based on reasoned analysis and supported by the evidence before the FCC.

2010 and 2014 Reviews: Arguments Regarding Competition from New Audio Platforms

The Third Circuit's ruling in *Prometheus II* came in the early stages of the 2010 Quadrennial Review, with the FCC publishing its Notice of Proposed Rulemaking in December of 2011.[21] In its 2011 Notice, the FCC proposed retaining its existing local radio ownership rules but abandoning the existing radio/television cross-ownership restrictions based on the belief "that the local radio and television ownership rules adequately protect our localism and diversity goals." In seeking comment on its proposed retention of the local radio ownership rules, the FCC noted the competing arguments of broadcasters and public interest groups:

67. *Market.* Broadcasters generally assert that they are facing increased competition from new audio platforms and that this increased competition has led, at least in part, to a reduction in advertising revenues, which could threaten the continued viability of the broadcast radio industry. Broadcasters contend that Internet-based audio platforms such as Pandora and Apple's iTunes have "transitioned—in just a few years—from new market entrants to full-fledged competitors of terrestrial radio broadcasters." Broadcasters assert that none of the new competitors to free, over-the-air radio broadcasting are constrained by government-imposed limits on the number of outlets that can be owned, and therefore, limiting ownership of

---

[20] *Id.* (footnotes omitted).
[21] 26 F.C.C.R. 17489, 2011 WL 6540519 (F.C.C.) (Dec. 22, 2011).

broadcast stations places broadcasters at a disadvantage. For this reason, according to broadcasters, we should modify our local radio ownership rule to permit increased common ownership in local markets.

68. We tentatively conclude that broadcast radio stations compete in the radio listening market and that it is not appropriate, at this time, to expand the relevant market to include nonbroadcast sources of audio programming. We note that the current record suggests that the audio marketplace has changed since the last media ownership review in terms of the number of choices consumers have to access audio programming, the number of audio programming providers, and audio programming choices. For instance, satellite radio subscribership has grown significantly, and millions of listeners now access audio content via the Internet. However, satellite radio still only serves a small portion of all radio listeners and millions of listeners do not have broadband Internet access. Moreover, these audio programming alternatives are national platforms that are not likely to respond to conditions in local markets. Therefore, we propose that our local radio ownership rule continue to focus on promoting competition among broadcast radio stations in local radio listening markets. We seek comment on these tentative conclusions.[22]

The public comment period for the 2010 Quadrennial Review was further extended in April, 2014 in a long report and recommended rulemaking issued by the FCC in which the Commission formally initiated its 2014 Quadrennial Review and incorporated the existing record from the 2010 Review, essentially merging the two review periods. The FCC summed up its ongoing action as follows:

2. The existing record demonstrates not only the dynamic changes that are taking place in the media marketplace but also the continued and vital importance of traditional media outlets to local communities. The proliferation of broadband Internet connections and other technological advances have changed the ways in which many consumers access entertainment, news, and information programming. Yet traditional media outlets are still essential to achieving the Commission's goals of competition, localism, and viewpoint diversity. . . .

4. While broadband Internet has impacted the lives of many consumers in myriad ways, including access to media content, millions of Americans continue to lack access to broadband at speeds necessary to take advantage of online content available via streaming or download. For these Americans—disproportionately

---

[22] *Id.* at 17513-14, 17515-16 (footnotes omitted).

those in rural areas, in low-income groups, on Tribal lands, and in
U.S. Territories—traditional media still may be their only source
of entertainment and local news and information content.

5.   It is clear that the impact of new technologies on the media
marketplace is already significant. If broadband penetration
continues to rise, which is a policy priority of the Commission, it
may have major implications for a future review of our broadcast
ownership rules. At this time, however, we believe that the
broadcast ownership rules proposed herein remain necessary to
protect and promote the Commission's policy goals in local
markets.[23]

On November 1, 2016, the FCC published its final rule in the 2010 and
2014 Quadrennial Regulatory Reviews, 81 FR 76220-01, which essentially
retained the existing limitations on local radio broadcast ownership with
only minor modifications—and then it issued a revised final rule a year
later after granting motions for reconsideration.

After the FCC issued its November 20, 2017 Order on Reconsideration
and Notice of Proposed Rulemaking,[24] further proceedings were
commenced in the *Prometheus* litigation, with various parties challenging
the FCC's order and proposed rule. In September, 2019, the Third Circuit
ruled on the parties' challenges to the November 2017 Order on
Reconsideration and proposed rulemaking, essentially upholding all of the
FCC's determinations except for its consideration of the impact of its
rulings on diversity in broadcast media ownership, which it found
inadequate. However, because of that finding, the Third Circuit vacated
and remanded the entirety of the Commission's 2017 Order on
Reconsideration.[25]

The National Association of Broadcasters filed a petition for certiorari
in April of 2020, seeking review by the U.S. Supreme Court of the Third
Circuit's September ruling . The NAB's petition noted:

When Congress enacted Section 202(h), the FCC's ownership
rules were already relics from a time when traditional television
and radio broadcasts and print newspapers were virtually the
only means by which Americans received news, as well as the
dominant forms of video and audio entertainment. By 1996,

---

[23]   *In the Matter of 2014 Quadrennial Regulatory Review—Review of the Commission's
Broadcast Ownership Rules and Other Rules Adopted Pursuant to Section 202 of the
Telecommunications Act of 1996*, 29 F.C.C.R. 4371, 60 Communications Reg. (P&F) 1, 2014 WL
1466887 (April 15, 2014).

[24]   *See F.C.C. Order on Reconsideration* (MB Docket Nos. 14-50, 09-182, 07-294, 04-256, and
17-289), 83 Fed. Reg. 733; FCC 17-156 (adopted on November 16, 2017, and released on November
20, 2017).

[25]   *Prometheus Radio Project v. F.C.C.*, No. 17-1107, 2019 WL 4593318, at *15 (3d Cir. Sept.
23, 2019).

technological changes had sparked an "explosion of video distribution technologies and subscription based programming sources" that gave consumers new media options and challenged the dominance of newspapers and "free over-the-air broadcasting." H.R. Rep. No. 104-204, at 55 (1995). Yet a quarter century later, FCC rules fashioned when the Internet and outlets such as satellite television and radio were in their infancy—or did not even exist—continue to govern the media marketplace.

Despite Congress's mandate, those long-outdated rules are still in force because the same divided panel of the Third Circuit has purported to retain jurisdiction over all FCC ownership reviews and—time and again—prevented the FCC from implementing the reforms Section 202(h) requires. *See* Pet. App. 46a (Scirica, J., dissenting). In the *Reconsideration Order* under review, the FCC made necessary adjustments to its ownership rules by repealing certain provisions and modifying others that the FCC concluded no longer served the public interest in light of "dramatic changes in the marketplace." Pet. App. 67a (alteration omitted). The Third Circuit, however, vacated the *Reconsideration Order* in its entirety, thus reinstating *all* the prior rules. *Id.* at 41a. [¶¶] . . . .

Unless rectified by this Court, the Third Circuit's misguided interpretation and unworkable evidentiary standards will continue to distort every future quadrennial review of the FCC's ownership rules. In the meantime, the Third Circuit panel's ossification of the FCC's rules has had a concrete and negative impact on America's broadcast and newspaper industries—represented by petitioners here—by hampering their ability to compete with existing and emerging media sources (including multichannel video providers, social media networks, and online video and audio platforms) that are not governed by comparable restrictions. In sum, this petition presents a question of indisputable national importance on which there is no possibility of a circuit split.[26]

Regardless of whether and how the Supreme Court might address the NAB's petition, the debate over continued limits on broadcast media ownership continues in the context of the 2018 Quadrennial Review.

Commencement of 2018 Quadrennial Review

The FCC announced its initiation of the 2018 Quadrennial Review in December of 2018. In its Notice of Initial Rulemaking, it provided some initial background information, summing up arguments made by various

---

[26] *National Association of Broadcasters v. Prometheus Radio Project*, No. 19-1241 (April 17, 2020, U.S. Supreme Court), 2020 WL 1957376 (footnotes omitted). As of the date of this writing, the petition was still pending.

parties for changes in the local radio ownership rules and posing a variety of questions on which it invited public comment:

2.   As the Commission has observed, the media marketplace has seen dramatic changes since the Commission began conducting its periodic media ownership reviews in the late 1990s—an evolution that continues to this day. Most notably, the growth of broadband Internet and other technologies has given consumers access to more content on more platforms than ever before. For instance, an overwhelming majority of Americans now have access to broadband Internet service, and they are increasingly using it to access online audio and video programming for entertainment and news content. . . . [T]he largest audio and video streaming services count their users in the tens of millions. . . .

3.   In the face of these trends, however, broadcast television and radio stations remain important fixtures in local communities. Despite new technologies competing for viewers' attention, . . . more than 90 percent of Americans still listen to the radio each week. Total broadcast industry revenues have appeared fairly stable in recent years. . . .

5.   Today, as required by Congress, we start a new proceeding to take a fresh look at our rules in light of the media landscape of 2018 and beyond. . . .

13.   In anticipation of this 2018 review, NAB submitted a letter to the Chief of the Media Bureau recommending that the Commission relax its radio ownership limits in light of today's audio marketplace in which, it argues, radio stations compete for both listeners and advertisers with a host of other services, including streaming services, satellite radio, podcasts, Facebook, and YouTube. NAB suggests allowing an entity in the top 75 Nielsen Audio Metro markets to own or control up to eight commercial FM stations and unlimited AM stations in any of those markets. NAB also proposes that entities in those markets should be permitted to own up to two additional FM stations if they participated in the Commission's incubator program. Finally, NAB proposes eliminating all limits on FM and AM ownership in all other markets. Below we describe NAB's arguments and the counterarguments made in response thereto, and we invite interested parties to comment and to put forth other ideas and proposals. . . . [¶¶]

17. In the *2010/2014 Quadrennial Review Order*, the Commission concluded that the broadcast radio listening market remains the relevant product market for purposes of the Local Radio Ownership Rule. Accordingly, the Commission declined to

expand its definition of the market to include non-broadcast audio sources, such as satellite radio and online audio services. The Commission reached its determination by assessing whether alternate sources of audio programming provide a meaningful substitute for local broadcast radio stations. The Commission's analysis centered on the fact that broadcast radio stations provide "free, over-the-air programming tailored to the needs of the stations' local markets." In contrast, satellite radio is a subscription service, online audio requires an Internet connection, and neither typically provides programming responsive to local needs and interests.

18.   In its recent letter proposing a relaxed radio rule, NAB argues that current ownership limits constrain the ability of radio broadcasters to compete on a level playing field in the digital audio world of 2018, particularly in smaller markets. NAB suggests that the dominance of broadcast radio has faded alongside streaming services such as Pandora and Spotify, satellite radio, podcasts, Facebook, and YouTube. NAB posits that the tailoring of needs and interests "now occurs on the basis of specific listeners, not just on the basis of local radio markets." It suggests that the pertinent fact for consumers is not where providers of audio services like Sirius XM, Spotify, and Pandora are headquartered but where their services are accessible, which is in the same spaces where consumers can listen to AM/FM radio (e.g., their cars, homes, and offices). NAB claims that allowing radio station owners to achieve economies of scale and scope would enable them to improve the quality of their informational and entertainment programming. It argues that "the Commission cannot continue to ignore multiple major sources of competition for both listeners and advertisers in the audio marketplace." . . .

20.   The Commission received several comments in response to its request for information regarding the status of competition in the marketplace for the delivery of audio programming. . . . For example, NAB provides information and statistical data purporting to show how fragmented the listening market has become. A coalition of radio broadcasters agrees with NAB that new marketplace entrants have disrupted the traditional radio market and claims that, despite data showing that 93 percent of Americans still listen to AM and FM radio weekly, the amount of their radio listening has shrunk as they divide their time among other audio providers, which, it notes, are not subject to the same regulatory burdens as radio licensees. . . . On the other hand, coalitions representing musicians, recording artists, and representatives of the music industry argue in that proceeding

that AM/FM radio continues to dominate the audio marketplace and that history shows that consolidation in the radio industry harms small broadcasters and leads to the homogenization of programming. REC Networks claims that unlike free, over-the-air radio, online audio services are unavailable to many Americans due to cost or lack of broadband coverage.

21. We seek comment on these different perspectives of the state of the audio marketplace and on whether and how they should affect our understanding of the market for purposes of the Local Radio Ownership Rule. . . .

22. *Market Definition.* We seek comment on whether we should continue to consider only local broadcast radio stations for purposes of the Local Radio Ownership Rule or whether we should revise our market definition to include other audio sources. Do local radio stations face direct competition today from satellite radio and online audio services? To what extent has radio's ability to attract listeners and advertisers been affected by satellite radio and online audio? . . . Do consumers view non-broadcast audio services as meaningful substitutes for local radio stations? Do non-broadcast audio services provide programming that responds to the needs and interests of local markets? Does radio's free, over-the-air availability make it unique or non-substitutable in the audio marketplace? . . . . If we were to revise our market definition, what non-broadcast sources should we include, and how should we count them or otherwise factor them into our rule for purposes of determining market size tiers and numerical limits? . . . How would an expanded definition better serve our policy goals, if at all? . . . .

24. . . . We seek comment on whether the Commission should retain its approach of using market size tiers, and if so, also on whether the current demarcations should remain in place. We also seek comment on whether there is any reason to discontinue including noncommercial radio stations in market counts. How well has the rule's tiered structure served the rule's purposes, and does it promote the policy goals of competition, localism, and viewpoint diversity in today's radio marketplace? NAB's proposal would divide radio markets into only two tiers—the top 75 Nielsen Audio Metro markets and all other markets (i.e., Nielsen Audio Metro markets outside of the top 75 and all undefined markets). What would be the advantages and disadvantages of creating a different number of tiers, including moving from a four-tiered to a two-tiered approach? If we were to collapse four tiers into two, should we draw the line where NAB proposes? We invite

commenters to offer alternative proposals for a tiered approach or for a different type of approach altogether. . . .

27. We seek comment on whether it is necessary as a result of competition to maintain the numerical limits for any or all of the market size tiers. Do the current limits adequately prevent a radio broadcaster from amassing excessive local market power? Conversely, do they permit sufficient growth to enable radio broadcasters to obtain the additional assets they may need to improve the quality of their service? Commenters should provide concrete, actual examples of markets where the current limits are either too restrictive or too lenient, explain how those examples typify other markets in that tier, and specify the benefits to those markets that would be gained by revising the limits.[27]

The public comment period for the 2018 Quadrennial Review closed in 2019 and dozens of comments from a broad spectrum of interested parties were submitted, with some arguing that regulation of broadcast ownership should be relaxed or eliminated and others arguing that it should be tightened. As of this writing, the FCC had not yet issued an Order associated with that review period, but some in the industry have speculated that the current body of FCC Commissioners may be more sympathetic to the arguments about changes to the broadcast marketplace in the digital era than in the past review periods, and thus may recommend further loosening of local radio ownership restrictions.[28]

In spite of reports of declining listeners, broadcast radio still plays an important role within the music industry. Artists and labels still want to have their recordings played on the radio. Songwriters and publishers still earn considerable income from performance royalties paid to PROs through blanket licenses purchased by broadcasters. Most radio broadcasters are for-profit entities that are necessarily concerned with profitability. They have a commercial interest in increasing market share and reducing overhead by owning multiple local stations, and they view heightened government regulations and court-imposed limitations as harmful to the overall business interests of broadcasters. On the other hand, the government has an interest promoting a diversity of viewpoints and local access through the broadcast licenses that it issues to only a limited number of stations in each broadcast area. This "public interest" mandate is one of the responsibilities that has been attached to the privilege of being granted exclusive control over one of only a limited number of pieces of the

---

[27] Notice of Proposed Rulemaking, *In the Matter of 2018 Quadrennial Regulatory Review F Review of the Commission's Broad. Ownership Rules & Other Rules Adopted Pursuant to Section 202 of the Telecommunications Act of 1996*, 33 F.C.C.R. 12111 (Dec. 13, 2018) (footnotes omitted).

[28] See, e.g., Marissa Moss, *One More Scoop of Vanilla: A New Proposal Looks To Loosen Radio Ownership Rules*, NPR Music News (June 7, 2019), at https://www.npr.org/2019/06/07/7303 23196/one-more-scoop-of-vanilla-a-new-proposal-looks-to-loosen-radio-ownership-rules.

broadcast spectrum. The regulations that the FCC enacts and enforces must serve citizens in both rural and urban settings across the nation and distinguish radio broadcasters from other types of content providers.

The interests of musicians and songwriters are less of a focus in these debates, but are nonetheless significant and are not monolithic. Successful songwriters and musicians benefit from nationwide playlists in their particular format. Additionally, local artists may have styles and fan bases grown on local histories, reputations, and ties to the communities in ways that would enhance local listener numbers and help smaller stations to compete in local markets. However, consolidation of radio ownership makes it harder for new artists without a major label deal to get radio airplay when nationwide playlists are the norm and there are fewer and fewer music directors making those decisions.

The arguments about consolidation and competition in the radio marketplace—and who the main competitors of broadcast radio are and will be in the coming years—are being echoed in the broader context of widespread horizontal and vertical integration and consolidation across the entertainment and media industries. Of particular concern for purposes of this text are the effects of consolidation on the various participants in the music industry, with a special focus on songwriters and musical performers who are trying to break into the business. As you will see in the case study in the next section, consolidation in the music industry has an impact on emerging musical artists in other contexts beyond broadcast radio.

NOTES AND QUESTIONS

1.   How would you answer the questions posed by the FCC in its 2018 request for public comment relating to local radio ownership rules? In particular, do you think that non-broadcast sources of audio programming should be considered as the FCC evaluates whether the interests of competition, localism, and diversity of content are served by a particular regulatory approach? How do you think today's alternatives to broadcast radio affect broadcast owners' programming and/or business decisions and their impact on local markets? Should these non-broadcast sources impact determinations of market size or be considered in setting local ownership limits? Can you think of other ways to require broadcasters to support localism and diversity in their programming that do not impact ownership? What do you think is the best regulatory approach?

2.   Do you agree with the FCC's reasoning in deciding to maintain existing numerical limits for local radio station ownership summarized in the 2002, 2006, and 2010/2014 Reviews? Why or why not? If, as the FCC suggested in these prior reports, program diversity has decreased as a result of consolidation following the elimination of national ownership limits (rather

consolidation in local markets), do you think that new national radio station ownership limits should be considered? Why or why not?

3.   Given the changes in the radio industry over the past two decades, what do you think the impact, if any, would be on radio ownership if expanded performance rights were to be granted to sound recordings? Would it likely have an impact on the localism and diversity concerns discussed in the Quadrennial Review process? How?

4.   Do you think that consolidation in the radio industry should concern songwriters and musicians in light of the array of promotional opportunities available outside of traditional broadcast radio?

5.   Is terrestrial radio relevant to your own enjoyment of music in today's market? Where do you find new music? Regardless of the importance of broadcast radio to your own consumption of music, what do you think of the FCC's stated concerns about the limited availability of satellite and Internet platforms in some parts of the country or to citizens without the financial resources to access them? Do these concerns support more or less (or different) regulation of local radio ownership?

2.   THE EMI/UNIVERSAL MERGER: A CASE STUDY

This section briefly addresses the broader issue of consolidation within the entertainment industry as a whole over the past twenty years. This consolidation impacts sectors across the sprawling industry, as demonstrated by the following:

- There remain only three "major" record labels (Universal Music Group, Sony Music Entertainment, and Warner Music Group), down from six "major" labels in the 1990s.

- There are only a handful of major music publishers, the top three of which are affiliated with the three major labels.

- Across the entertainment industry in general, there has been consolidation of film, music, print publishing, and television companies within a small number of corporate conglomerates, some of which overlap with the companies mentioned above.

As you read the materials that follow, consider the impact of this larger trend toward consolidation from the perspective of various participants in the industry. In particular, does such consolidation help or hurt consumers and their choices? Does it help or hurt artists? How does it impact emerging distribution technologies for music? Do you think the government should exercise its antitrust authority in this area, similar to how it has regulated PROs? Why or why not?

In 2012, the proposed merger between Universal Music Group and EMI, two of the then "Big Four" music labels in the United States, was addressed in both Senate Hearings before the Antitrust Subcommittee and in a Federal Trade Commission (FTC) review. Ultimately, the merger was approved.[29] Below, we provide excerpts from statements by interested parties in some of those proceedings relating to the proposed merger to illustrate the nature of the debate over the impact of further consolidation in the music industry. As you read the statements below, note the arguments made in support of approval of the merger and those made in opposition and consider what your own views are as to the FTC's rationale for closing its investigation of the proposed merger between record label giants Universal and EMI.

a. Statement of Senator Patrick Leahy, United States Senate, Antitrust Subcommittee Hearing re Proposed Universal Music Group/EMI Merger, June 21, 2012

Today, the Antitrust Subcommittee will examine the proposed merger of Universal Music Group and EMI and, importantly, discuss broader trends in the distribution of music online. Senator Kohl is continuing his efforts to highlight competition issues that will affect American consumers. This discussion comes at a time of growth and change in the world of music distribution. Users can access music in more ways and at a broader range of price points than ever before. . . . New technologies are promoting consumer choice and giving artists better ways to connect with fans.

Even as our ways of accessing music continue to grow, all platforms for delivering music still rely on one thing—quality content. As in all markets, it is important to protect competition to ensure that new music services can emerge and that existing distribution outlets can fairly negotiate reasonable prices. Our antitrust laws establish a review process by federal authorities to analyze competition issues in proposed mergers, and I have confidence that the Federal Trade Commission will consider the issues presented by the Universal Music Group acquisition of EMI fairly and thoroughly in its review of this transaction.

---

[29] At around the same time, EMI sold its music publishing operations to a consortium led by Sony/ATV Music Publishing. EMI's publishing catalog included songs by Queen, Carole King, The Police, Kanye West, Alicia Keys, Drake, and Pharrell Williams, as well as the Motown catalog. In November of 2018, Sony/ATV Music acquired 60% of the interest of EMI's music publishing catalog held by the consortium, giving Sony a 25% share of music publishing revenues in 2019, compared to Universal Music Publishing Group's 21% share and Warner Chappell Music's 11.6% share. See Music & Copyright Blog, https://musicandcopyright.wordpress.com/tag/market-share/ (May 20, 2020).

Today's discussion with some of the leading participants in the music industry ties in with the Committee's ongoing focus on developments in music distribution and online innovation. . . . As the landscape for music distribution continues to evolve, we must ensure that our system encourages quality content by compensating songwriters and recording artists, while also ensuring the different platforms can compete and thrive. . . .

b. Written Submission of Universal Music Group, Before the Senate Committee on the Judiciary Subcommittee on Antitrust, Competition Policy and Consumer Rights (Lucian Grainge, Chairman & CEO), June 21, 2012[30]

Mr. Chairman, Ranking Member Lee, and Members of the Subcommittee, thank you for the opportunity to appear here today. My name is Lucian Grainge, and I am the Chairman and CEO of Universal Music Group. We at Universal are pleased to assist the Subcommittee by testifying about our pending acquisition of EMI's recording music business. We appreciate the opportunity to share our vision for combining EMI's rich heritage with Universal's track record of investing in the future of music. Our coming together will benefit consumers, artists, and all those committed to a diverse and healthy music business.

Over the course of my 33 years in this business, I signed many talented songwriters and artists. I have worked with great bands that never became household names, as well as stars such as U2, Elton John, ABBA, Eurythmics, Paul Anka, Rihanna, Mika, Duffy, and Amy Winehouse. I still consider myself a talent scout today, but now my talent search has expanded to include writers, producers, sound engineers, creative executives, startups, entrepreneurs, and digital platforms.

The music business has changed dramatically, as the Judiciary Committee is well aware. You have studied and assessed the challenges presented by the Internet, and I appreciate the many actions that you have taken to bolster and support businesses that depend on the protection of intellectual property. Many of the basic principles of law that have been acknowledged and protected by the Judiciary Committee have enabled us to invest in innovative artists that connect with audiences around the globe. . . .

Universal Is Committed To Innovation And Embracing Wide Distribution

The future success of the music industry is going to depend on the distribution of music through as many platforms as possible. Universal is committed to investing and innovating to meet the competitive challenges

---

[30] Footnotes are omitted from this excerpt.

of the digital age—which means providing consumers what they want, when they want it, and how they want it.

The challenges to the music industry are significant. Extensive piracy has curtailed sales, resulting in lost profits and significant pricing pressure. Over the past decade, the recording industry in the United States has been almost cut in half—from about $13 billion in 2002 to $6.5 billion last year. This lost revenue has caused a great many people to lose their jobs and has limited the resources available to enable aspiring artists to pursue their dreams.

We have responded to these challenges by embracing distribution via the broad range of emerging technologies. Universal has a strong record of embracing ground-breaking innovations to market artists and recorded works through multiple channels. . . . In order to sell music and support our artists, Universal must get the music to the consumer, whenever and however consumers are looking for it. Universal has learned that we need as many lines going to as many shores as possible.

With our commitment to embracing digital platforms and new opportunities, our revenues leveled off between 2010 and 2011. That is not the same as growth—but after a decade of significant decline, it's a start. Universal is committed to working with our technology partners and innovators so that we can succeed in this fiercely competitive and dynamic market, empower our artists, and provide consumers with high quality, diverse, creative music.

Universal's Resources, Expertise, And Innovation Will Reinvigorate EMI

EMI has a storied history—it has brought the world some of the greatest artists in history—from the Beatles to Frank Sinatra. It is built on the foundations of the creative hubs at Capitol Records and its associated studios here in the US and, of course, the EMI UK labels and the incredible Abbey Road studios. Yet, the past decade has been undeniably difficult for EMI. EMI is currently owned by Citigroup, which acquired EMI following a default by EMI's previous owner, a private equity group. During this time, its owners have significantly reduced EMI's ability to invest in the search for new artists and innovative sounds. The team at EMI have done a masterful job under trying circumstances—and with the right financial support, long term commitment, and stability, they can contribute mightily to the global music scene.

With Universal's infusion of resources and commitment to investing in artistic development, there will be a healthy future for the company. We are absolutely committed to investing in EMI as a distinct business that can help us develop even more music and more choice for consumers and fans everywhere. EMI's labels will be reinvigorated and artists will have more choices, which will lead to more competition in this dynamic market. . . .

The Music Industry Is An Increasingly Competitive, Dynamic Market

Universal and EMI are both committed to music—committed to our artists and committed to the exploration and development of new sounds.

To Succeed In Today's Marketplace, Universal And EMI Must Embrace And Nurture The Broad Range Of Continuously Developing Platforms Consumers Demand

[¶¶] . . . . The range of digital services is increasingly complex. No two services are exactly the same, which is a good thing, because these services expand the range of choices for artists and consumers.

In order to compete in a world where music is readily, if illegally, available for free, we know that our future is contingent on the vitality of legitimate digital music services. . . . [¶]

It is in Universal's interest to engage with the broad range of new distribution channels available to consumers. We need robust, vibrant, and successful legitimate music services in order to compete with pirate sites that carry substitutes of our artists' works. We want a large number of innovative digital music services to flourish. We are not a tech company, but our viability is contingent on the success of legitimate online and mobile music services and digital models.

I have seen this industry transition from eight-track tape to instantaneous download onto smart phones. I know that I cannot predict which platforms consumers will demand, but I can predict that consumers will continue to demand their music on new and evolving platforms and, as our track record demonstrates, Universal's catalog and repertoire will be on those services.

[¶¶] . . . . The Universal/EMI Deal Will Expand The Options Available To Artists

Universal is committed to expanding the options available to artists and growing the music industry.

Artists And Musicians' Unions Support The Universal/EMI Deal

As recognized by the unions that represent America's recording artists, professional musicians, and other entertainment and media industry professionals, Universal is committed to its artists and respects industry collective bargaining agreements. These unions agree that Universal will be able to reinvigorate EMI and position it for the future.

SAG-AFTRA's Kim Roberts Hedgpeth expressly stated that Universal has "best weathered" the "daunting and unprecedented challenges" of the past decade "by maintaining its commitment to the art and the music industry, and by investing in new artists and innovative musical genres." She also concluded that, "[f]rom a labor perspective, UMG's compliance with and respect for its collective bargaining agreements and relationships has been unique among recording companies. As such, sustaining the EMI legacy under UMG's oversight appears to be a benefit to SAG-AFTRA's recording artist members."

American Federation of Musicians' Ray Hair has also recognized our commitment to artists and to ensuring that they receive their due compensation through our industry-leading compliance with collective bargaining agreements. We also value AFM's observation that recording musicians will benefit from Universal's oversight of EMI's legacy and its future. Universal looks forward to providing the same levels of respect to EMI's artists to further support their musical success.

Artists Have Choices

We are not just competing against the other major labels, Sony and Warner, who are already vigorous competitors. We compete with the significant "Indie" market, which, according to A2IM, the Indie trade association, represents over 30% of the market in the US. [Ed. Note: in 2020, A2IM reportedly represented over 35% of the US market.][31] Indeed, the global rights agency Merlin, which represents independent music rights, refers to itself as the "the virtual fifth major." And we compete with DIY (do-it-yourself) artists, who can record, promote, and sell their own music.

Smaller labels have agreed that the Universal/EMI deal will not limit their success. Scott Borchetta, chief executive of Big Machine Records, has said that consolidation does not matter as much in the digital age. "When the major labels controlled the distribution channels, it was a different deal, but now the barrier to entry is literally turning on your computer," he said. "If I continue to make great records by great artists, nobody can stop us." Mike Chadwick, an experienced UK Indie label and distribution expert, has said that the Universal/EMI deal is "great" for the Indie market:

> Is it good for us? It's great for us: there are loads of middle-level artists who are perfect for us. If we sell 10,000 records, I'm happy—we don't have to sell a million records to make a profit. Artists who are unhappy gravitate towards companies like us. These huge amalgamations or mergers are really good for the indies.

---

[31] See Linked In page for American Association of Independent Musicians (A2IM), at https://www.linkedin.com/company/a2im-american-association-of-independent-music-/about/.

The Indie labels are strong competitors in the age of digital distribution. Furthermore, technological advances mean that neither a "major" label deal nor an "Indie" label deal are essential for an artist. As David Pogue, the New York Times technology columnist, wrote in the May 9, 2012 New York Times, "In the online world, you can take your music straight to the public. No more gatekeepers, record executives or rejection letters. If you're any good, you'll soon win your fame and fortune—or at least sky-high view counts."

Mr. Pogue was referring to DIY (do it yourself) products that offer artists key services—services that had traditionally been offered only by record labels. This is a dynamic, competitive market where artists can choose their own path to success.

Universal's Plan Going Forward

We are in a world of the unknown in an unpredictable, dynamic industry. With such revolutionary distribution channels developing all the time, the music industry is constantly changing and ever more competitive. Everything we thought we knew about the music business is changing— but that can be said about music itself. And that is why I love it. Universal/EMI will continue to promote artists, invest in the future of the industry, and explore new business models in as many sales outlets as possible—digital, streaming/subscription, ad-based, DVDs/CDs—and whatever other outlets I hope are currently being developed.

Through our acquisition of EMI, Universal will enhance the creative investment in the company and further broaden the support for digital services. This will provide more opportunities for artists and more music and choice for consumers than ever before.

c. Statement of Roger C. Faxon, Chief Executive, EMI Group, Before the U.S. Senate Judiciary Committee Subcommittee on Antitrust, Competition, and Consumer Rights, Hearing on The Universal Music Group/EMI Merger and the Future of Online Music, June 21, 2012[32]

Thank you, Mr. Chairman, Ranking Member Lee, members of the Subcommittee. I am Roger Faxon, and as the Chairman has said, I am chief executive of the EMI Group, and I am pleased to join you today to discuss the Universal Music Group's proposed acquisition of our recorded music division.

To appreciate the competitive implications of this transaction, I think it is important to place it in the context of the market for recorded music as it is today, and not as it may have been in the past. Without a doubt, the

---

[32]   https://www.govinfo.gov/content/pkg/CHRG-112shrg76045/pdf/CHRG-112shrg76045.pdf.

music landscape has changed beyond all recognition from where it was even 10 years ago.

In that time, overall industry revenues have more than halved, even as digital revenues have soared. The forces that have produced this decline have substantially shifted the impact of record company consolidation, on both consumers and the wider music business. I would like to take you through why I believe that to be so.

As digital exploded, the CD fell through the floor. Specialist retailers, which were the backbone of our industry, all but became extinct. For the vast majority of the thinning ranks of retailers that remain, music is not at the center of their offering. But they are central to record companies and the careers of their artists. So, inevitably, it is they, not the labels, that are in control. It is the retailers who decide which albums they stock and what commercial terms they will take.

Retail concentration is even more pronounced on digital platforms. Between the iTunes and Amazon services, you have two players accounting for 90 percent of the download business and over 80 percent of all digital revenues. In this environment, pricing again does not sit with the gift of the record companies, regardless of size or market position.

Digital distribution has created a music meritocracy. There is no limit to the amount of music that can be stocked. That means any band, budding or established, can have their music distributed on digital platforms. Major record companies, if they ever were, are no longer the gatekeepers.

In this meritocracy, good music rises to the top. The skill is in finding that music and helping to connect it with an audience, and that skill is not confined to one company or group of companies.

The Internet has also democratized music promotion. The explosion in media has taken promotional power away from the editors and radio program directors and put it firmly in the hands of music fans through Facebook, Twitter, YouTube, and a myriad of other sites and services—all essential to an artist's ultimate success. These fans do not care about market position of an artist's record company. They care about the music and whether it is any good. And radio stations are focused on playing only the music that their extensive callout research tells them will connect with the highest possible audience, irrespective of its source. Again, it is the music that matters, not the source.

Technology has significantly reduced the cost of entry for new music companies. As a result, the market is more crowded and competitive than it has been in my experience. So record companies cannot control consumer pricing, do not control access to consumers, cannot exert control over promotional platforms or music discovery tools that fans use, and they have to compete with the vastly increased number of alternative paths to market for artists. If there ever were antitrust issues implicated with label consolidation, it seems to me they are not present today.

As a result of all this change, the focus of the music industry has returned to where it should be—on helping artists develop the most compelling music and working with them to ignite passion for it in their fans. And I think we are doing a very good job of that.

But we also have to assure that the creators of that music are properly rewarded for their contribution. And there we are not doing as well as we should. The ambiguity and unenforceability of our intellectual property laws is failing our creators. Individual rights holders are no longer able to protect their music, ISPs are not held responsible for their actions, and safe harbor provisions designed to encourage innovation are instead being used as a shield by bad actors seeking to build their own business without compensating the creators whose music underpins those new businesses.

Technological and musical innovation are not mutually exclusive. Content created by great artists and songwriters can drive consumers toward new ventures, and exciting new platforms and products can open up a wider market for the works of creators. But our institutions have allowed the balance to shift too far in favor of big technology. The impact on our creative community has been devastating and will only worsen if the scales continue to tip unchecked.

Music touches us in a way that nothing else can. For me it has been an absolute privilege to be able to represent some of the greatest artists this world has ever seen. Yet without a solid framework of intellectual property rights to underpin that creativity, we do not just threaten labels or jobs, but America's ability to nurture the next Jay-Z, the next Beach Boys, the next Norah Jones. That will not be the fault of any merger or acquisition. It will be the fault of our own unwillingness to stand up to protect one of the greatest cultural strengths this country has to offer. Thank you.

d.   Testimony of Gigi B. Sohn, President, Public Knowledge, on Behalf of Public Knowledge and Consumer Federation of America, Before the U.S. Senate Judiciary Committee Subcommittee on Antitrust, Competition, and Consumer Rights, Hearing on The Universal Music Group/EMI Merger and the Future of Online Music, June 21, 2012[33]

The proposed merger of the major record labels UMG and EMI Music comes at an important time for music fans and the music industry. Innovative companies using digital technologies have found new ways to give musicians and consumers more choices for how and where to create

---

[33] Footnotes are omitted from this excerpt.

and experience recorded music. Digital music distribution in particular has benefitted consumers by enabling them to access music more conveniently and more directly from the artists. . . . Digital platforms also dramatically decrease distribution costs, which in a competitive market results in cost savings for the consumer. However, nothing is immune to market power and a merger of this magnitude can easily stifle the consumer benefits of digital distribution.

These technologies hold great promise for recording artists and consumers, but nascent entrants in the market dependent on licenses from incumbent labels are vulnerable to anticompetitive behavior by the major labels. For example, the company Deezer, digital music streaming service similar to Spotify, has enjoyed success in 81 countries around the world, but does not offer its service in the U.S. Deezer has also partnered with numerous other companies, including social networks like Facebook and Twitter, mobile telephone services like T-Mobile, stereo system manufacturers like Sonos and Logitech, and car manufacturers like Nissan and Parrot. These partnerships create new services that increase music fans' opportunities to enjoy music conveniently and at a reasonable price. But when asked why none of these innovative new services have reached the U.S. market, Deezer representatives point to the cost of licensing the music from the major labels.

The major labels can thwart or seize control of innovation with anticompetitive behavior against new market entrants that cannot operate without sound recording licenses from the major labels. The merger between UMG and EMI would create a new super-major label that controls 41% of the recorded music market, and could use that market share to stifle the development of new digital platforms while raising prices to the detriment of both musicians and their fans. To prevent this result, antitrust authorities must block this merger to protect the future of innovation, competition, and pricing in the music business.

Digital technology's ability to let artists reach fans directly has been a powerful, consumer-friendly, competition-friendly force in the music industry. However, it is not immune from the abuse of market power by entrenched physical space incumbents. Incumbent major record labels have the incentive to stifle new digital distribution platforms because those platforms begin to level the playing field among major labels, independent labels, and unsigned artists. Digital platforms are more likely to license unknown or niche music because, unlike their physical space predecessors, they are not constrained by time limits (like radio) or space limits (like physical stores). As a result, the major record labels lose one of their main selling points to musicians—namely, that they have the connections and influence that a musician absolutely needs to get his or her music out in the marketplace. Thus, the dominant incumbent labels are particularly incentivized to stifle digital platforms that will decrease their influence as compared to smaller competitors or unsigned acts. [¶] . . . .

EMI Music Has Historically Been Willing to Take Risks and Innovate

As the fourth largest label in the marketplace, EMI must continuously explore opportunities to grow market share by attracting customers and recruiting new talent. Unlike its larger competitors, EMI cannot be complacent and focus on merely preserving its market share but rather must be a scrappy contender willing to try the unorthodox. With regard to digital music services, EMI Music has consistently been the first major label willing to take risks and innovate. As a result, consumers have reaped the benefit of music that can play on more devices and services than ever before at price points they demand and artists have benefited from having a label more willing to meet their needs in exchange for their talent. For example:

- In 2000, EMI became the first major label to license its catalog to the online subscription streaming service Streamwaves, and in 2001 EMI became the first label to license to a digital music service, PressPlay, without demanding an equity interest in the service. . . .

- In 2007, EMI became the first of the major labels to offer digital downloads through the iTunes music store without digital locks on the files. . . .

- In 2009, EMI was the first major label, with the band Depeche Mode, to offer an iTunes Pass, a digital music product similar to a deluxe CD package with additional limited edition material included. . . .

- EMI has launched OpenEMI, a partnership with The Echo Nest, which allows application developers to access parts of the EMI Music catalog to develop new ways to distribute music. . . .

New Digital Distribution Services Benefit Consumers

EMI's leadership in the industry has helped promote the growth of digital music services, which has benefited both musicians and audiences by offering new opportunities for artists to create, promote, distribute, and monetize their works. Digital technology lets consumers choose when and where they want to enjoy music, and enables consumers to purchase music at the click of a button. Innovative new digital services also decrease the cost of manufacturing and distribution, which in a competitive marketplace would be passed on to consumers as cost savings. [¶] . . . .

When record labels and other copyright owners are willing to explore new digital distribution technologies, new services that benefit both consumers and artists enter the marketplace. . . . [¶¶]

A Combined UMG/EMI Would Have the Power to Prevent or Control new Digital   Music Services to the Detriment of Consumers

Digital music services often depend upon the cooperation or collaboration of the record labels that own the relevant sound recording copyrights or the publishers that control the musical compositions. As audience demand currently turns to a streaming, cloud-based model, new distribution services will have trouble launching without a major label willing to be the first to grant licenses, and ultimately may never succeed if a single major label can withhold 41% of the recorded music market even after other labels have started working with the service. Even in today's marketplace, a major label can wield sufficient power to demand that potential new digital music services pay the label hefty advances and a high percentage of future revenue, or give the record label an equity stake in the new company. A combined Universal/EMI entity would only be able to exert even more control over new music services. [¶¶] . . . .

If both the UMG/EMI record label merger and Sony/EMI publisher merger are approved, UMG and Sony's combined sound recording and composition catalogs would give them enormous leverage over a nascent digital music service. In essence, the two majors' whims would control the emergence of new distribution options for the entire industry. Digital services that do not require performance rights or non-statutory mechanical rights in music publishing would still come up against Universal, as the dominant player in recorded music, while services requiring performance rights licenses or non-statutory mechanical rights licenses would need to deal with both Universal and Sony, on each company's own terms, in order to launch a viable service. Access to the content of the majors remains indispensable to building new distribution models. It is not feasible to succeed on the basis of unsigned artists alone. The concentration of control of albums in the hands of a dominant player in a highly concentrated market poses a severe threat to competition and dynamic innovation in this space. As the majors gain greater leverage, alternatives and artists lose out. [¶¶] . . . .

The Merger Fails Under Traditional Antitrust Analysis

The antitrust laws are intended to protect innovation and competition, and to prevent firms from using their market power to arbitrarily raise prices for consumers. Traditional antitrust analysis shows that the UMG-EMI merger contains significant competitive harms, particularly in light of the merger's potential effects on the development of new digital music distribution models. The merger must therefore be scrutinized closely and its harms must be remedied in order to preserve a competitive, productive music distribution market.

The post-merger market share of the combined UMG/EMI entity would give it the power to distort the development of digital music distribution models or even determine the fate of new digital music services. UMG and EMI's combined market share of 41% would likely give it the power to veto emerging distribution models, and would certainly empower the combined entity to lead other record labels in doing so. With a post-merger three-firm market share of 90%, and with one or two companies following the lead of the dominant firm—here, UMG/EMI—the market would be vulnerable to anticompetitive harm resulting from conscious parallelism. [¶¶] . . . .

Based on 2010 year-end figures, the four major record labels account for almost 90% of recorded music sales in the U.S. UMG is the largest company, with a share of 30.8% followed by its nearest competitor, Sony (at 28.0%), then Warner Music Group (WMG) (20.0%), and EMI (10.2%). This leaves only an 11.0% market share for independent labels. . . . This situation raises serious concerns that the top three labels will coordinate or engage in conscious parallelism that reinforces the lead of the dominant firm.

Other aspects of this merger only increase concerns under antitrust analysis. The top four to six firms in the market have remained remarkably stable for the past 25 years, despite an unprecedented technological upheaval. This kind of stability raises concerns that the dominant companies have entrenched themselves and that barriers to market entry prevent new companies from competing with the incumbent labels. . . . [¶¶]

Conclusion

Competition among production and distribution intermediaries in the music industry ultimately gives more choice to musicians and leads to better market offerings for consumers. Competition increases the diversity of choices for consumers, empowering consumers to choose the services that best fit their needs at the best price. If one or two major labels obtain enough influence to stifle the development of new digital music services, those services never will be able to gain traction in the marketplace, and potential competitors will fail, not on their merits, but based on the service's inability to strike a deal with an inordinately powerful supplier. As a result, both musicians and audiences will suffer for lack of innovative competitors in the online music service marketplace. . . .

e. Statement of Irving Azoff, Executive Chairman and Chairman of the Board, Live Nation Entertainment, Inc., and Chairman and Chief Executive Officer, Front Line Management Group, Before the U.S. Senate Judiciary Committee Subcommittee on Antitrust, Competition, and Consumer Rights, Hearing on The Universal Music Group/EMI Merger and the Future of Online Music, June 21, 2012

Thank you, Mr. Chairman, and thanks to the Committee for having me here today. . . . For more than 43 years in the music business, I have focused on one thing: serving artists. The music industry I joined was a vibrant, emerging, and entrepreneurial business whose format of choice was vinyl. Throughout all the choices—vinyl, 8-track, cassette, and compact disc—one thing remained constant: the power of the record label. The emergence of the Internet has changed that.

I work with acts big and small, some that are household names and some who should be but just have not yet gotten there yet. Let me be very clear. None of them have to sign to a major label anymore. Majors cannot sign every act, and the door is open for many others to do so.

In fact, independent labels are capturing more and more market share every year. Bon Iver won the Grammy for Best New Artist this year. Esperanza Spaulding won last year. And Mr. Mills' XL has brought us the biggest selling artist of 2011 in Adele.

Approximately 40 percent of our artists are not even on labels. I have no doubt that labels add value, but you just do not have to have one in a world where artists can deliver an album direct to fans themselves. It is a little like hiring an interior decorator to redo your house. The experience and results can be great, but some acts enjoy and prefer to do it on their own and put their own imprint on things. With services like iTunes, CD Baby, Top Spin, 9 Reverb Nation, Pro Tools, Facebook, Spotify—you name it—artists can do everything themselves on their own very professionally.

It used to be that bands could not make a professional album without the backing of a label. Labels used to be THE gatekeepers to fans. But today those barriers have been blown away. The new gatekeepers are the fans. Facebook and other social media make fans the essential promotional power. If a fan "likes" a song and tells a friend or two or 10,000, an artist is on their way. The power today rests with consumers, not record labels. So while the Internet has brought challenges for many, it has also given bands opportunities, access, and control previously unknown to any generation of artists.

The reason a combined UMG/EMI is a good thing rests in the much bigger picture. Our industry has been turned on its head in the last decade.

With all the great developments the Internet has brought us, the economics are still daunting.

Most musicians make a living today from touring, not record sales as they once did. And it makes sense, since consumers are not buying $15 CDs anymore, they are paying for a single track download from Amazon or iTunes or listening to ad-supported services that result in mere fractions of a penny-per-play being paid to the artist; or worse, still, they just go to a torrent site and get it for free. Late to embrace the Internet, labels are playing catch-up. But any way you slice it, recorded music sales are still the core of a label's business model.

Those who speculate about the demise of competition simply do not live in the hyper-competitive music world that I see every day. Competition is fierce between the major labels and fierce between the majors and indies. Competition is fierce as mobile services vie against one another and against Apple.

As for the brouhaha around this deal, Mr. Bronfman has been talking about combining Warner and EMI for the better part of a decade. The entire industry expected it to happen, Wall Street expected it to happen, journalists expected it to happen. Warner had a chance to outbid Universal in this process but chose not to. Now they regret their decision and are spending millions to fight this deal. Well, I do not think the Government should step in to give them another bite at the apple. That is not how our free economy works.

The fact is it would have been great if EMI could have made a go of it on its own. But the recession, piracy, and the facts surrounding Terra Firma and Citi combined to make that a pipe dream. The aura of uncertainty made EMI a risky place for an artist to sign. This business is about relationships and confidence that the team you sign with will be right beside you through the entire journey.

Uncertainty made it hard for EMI to compete. With Universal taking over and their commitment to resurrecting Capitol Records, there will actually be another record company for artists to explore if they want to. As I see it, it is not one less company—it is one more choice.

Bottom line, the people concerned that a combined UMG/EMI would have too much power really just do not get what has happened to the business over the last decade. Labels do not control 10 artists. Those days are gone. And no label in the world can control the supremacy of the modern music fan. The power shift has already taken place, and no one should worry for a minute that it rests with the labels any longer.

f. Statement of Martin Mills, Founder, Beggars Group, London, U.K., Before the U.S. Senate Judiciary Committee Subcommittee on Antitrust, Competition, and Consumer Rights, Hearing on The Universal Music Group/EMI Merger and the Future of Online Music, June 21, 2012

I am honored to be here. Thank you. Please forgive me if I use some strong words today, but having read the statements of those on the monopolists' bench, I believe they are needed. I speak not just for myself but also for thousands of independent labels and artists worldwide.

Seven letters: C-O-N-T-R-O-L. It spells "control." That is what this is about.

Do not believe them when they say the music market is now a Garden of Eden in which any young artist can become famous overnight without a label. That is simply not true. Ask them who these fortunate artists are.

Mr. Azoff says that 40 percent of his artists manage without a label. When I Google his company, I find the Eagles, Christine Aguilera, Kings of Leon, John Mayer, Van Halen, Jennifer Hudson, Miley Cyrus, Kenny Chesney, Kid Rock, Avril Lavigne, Aerosmith, and Jimmy Buffett—all on the front page. I do not recall any of them becoming successful without a record label. Do you? And all of them, I believe, released their last albums in association with a major. Whereas established stars may plow their own furrow these days, often with the benefit of services from a major label, any new artist needs a label just as much as Steven Tyler did. Even our artist Adele needed Sony's strength in the U.S.A.

Do not believe them when they say market share is not market power. Market power is why they are doing this—the power to dominate digital services and impose their demands upon them, the power to leverage a disproportionately onerous deal, the power to squeeze out the competition, the power to impose what Universal wants on the consumer. You will see how they do that in the written evidence. It is all true.

Do not believe them when they say the independents represent a countervailing competitive force, the thousands of tiny, fragmented indies. Do not believe the 30-percent of the market figure for indies in this context. Two-thirds of that has digital rights controlled by the majors.

Do not think that the resulting Universal/EMI 40-percent market share figure is as simple as it looks. Universal/EMI's share of hit Billboard's Top 100 for the last year was nearly 70 percent when you include controlled shares and negative rights to block its repertoire. Indeed, looking at just last week's Billboard's charts, eight of the top ten singles will be post-EMI controlled by Universal. That is 80 percent.

When you hear Universal downplay its market share today, you should ask yourselves what market share do they insist on in their commercial negotiations, for splitting anti-piracy proceeds, for advances for music services. Very different. This is about Universal leveraging new acts who are already successful acts and obtaining 13 more than their fair share of the oxygen of exposure. Even today, contrary to what Mr. Faxon says, major labels have 92 percent of radio play.

Most great music, the music that changes tastes and lives, starts outside the mainstream, and that means on independent labels. Elvis Presley, Muddy Waters, R.E.M., Adele—they all did that. In fact, the economics of the majors these days means that signing artists without mass market potential makes no sense for them. If this transaction goes through, the next great artist may never be found.

With the kind of increased market dominance that Universal seeks here, it will completely control the shape of all new digital services. No one will be able to deny them. Look at their ability to raise prices of iTunes' new music. . . . [¶] Modern society sees unlawful monopolies as being bad, with good and with obvious reason. Some are worse than others. If airlines merge or soft drinks companies, is the effect on consumer choice that bad? Isn't one seat or one soft drink pretty much the same as another? But that is certainly not the case with music. Music matters to people. It affects. It changes lives. It is human. It is personal. You cannot substitute a Katy Perry for a Lady Gaga for an Adele.

Yet in the world Universal seeks, great music will suffer, and we will be headed for a lowest common denominator music market with consumers having less choice and probably paying more.

Universal is a great company. Do not get me wrong. It has got great people. But there is big and there is too big. Give them the position of increased power and greater dominance that they seek, and they will exploit it. And specifically for a new company to start and grow in this environment, as mine did, will quite simply be impossible.

Please forgive my passion today, but not only do I absolutely believe what I say, I know it to be true.

g. Statement of FTC Bureau of Competition Director Richard A. Feinstein *In the Matter of* Vivendi, S.A. and EMI Recorded Music, September 21, 2012

UNITED STATES OF AMERICA
FEDERAL TRADE COMMISSION
WASHINGTON, D.C. 20580

Office of the Director
Bureau of Competition

Today, the Commission voted to close its investigation of the proposed acquisition by Vivendi, S.A. parent company of Universal Music Group ("Universal"), of EMI Recorded Music ("EMI"). After a thorough investigation into the likely competitive effects of the merger, Commission staff did not find sufficient evidence that the acquisition would substantially lessen competition in the market for the commercial distribution of recorded music in violation of Section 7 of the Clayton Act.

Universal is the largest recorded music company in the world. EMI is the fourth largest. Together with Sony Music and Warner Music Group, Universal and EMI are among the four "Majors" in the recorded music industry. . . . Although independent recorded music companies, including a large number of independent record labels and distributors, compete in the market for commercial distribution of recorded music, the majority of independent record labels rely on the Majors to provide distribution services.

Based on its review of company documents, discussions with industry participants, and empirical analysis, Commission staff did not find sufficient evidence of head-to-head competition to conclude that the combination of Universal and EMI would substantially lessen competition. In the recorded music business, the products are highly differentiated, and companies compete for distribution in multiple ways, including: (1) the sale of new titles in large retailers; (2) the sale of catalog titles; and (3) the opportunity to promote artists and records. Commission staff therefore considered the level of direct competition between Universal and EMI across all of these different channels. Universal is very strong in popular new releases, but EMI—the smallest of the Majors—has a portfolio much more heavily weighted toward older titles. Further, while all of the Majors participate to different degrees in a variety of catalog discount programs, the competition between Universal and EMI in this area is relatively insignificant. . . .

Commission staff also assessed the impact of the acquisition on the development of interactive music streaming services. Staff focused on whether Universal would have enhanced bargaining leverage after the acquisition, allowing it to extract from streaming services superior financial terms, or advantaged positioning for its content. Commission staff sought to determine whether the transaction would lead to higher costs to interactive streaming consumers or a more limited selection of recorded music. Commission staff found considerable evidence that each leading interactive streaming service must carry the music of each Major to be competitive. Because each Major currently controls recorded music necessary for these streaming services, the music is more complementary than substitutable in this context, leading to limited direct competition between Universal and EMI. In the end, insufficient evidence existed showing that Universal and EMI offer products that could be viewed by streaming services as direct substitutes.

Commission staff also did not find sufficient evidence to support the concern that Universal's acquisition of EMI would significantly increase the potential for coordination among recorded music companies. Market conditions have changed since previous antitrust enforcement actions, such as in the unique situation of *Three Tenors*. The evidence showed that recorded music products are differentiated, with each record label offering a wide portfolio of titles, the success of which, in many instances, is uncertain and not strongly correlated with the success or failure of other titles. The net price for each title often is not particularly transparent because of the complexity of negotiated arrangements between record labels, distributors, retailers, and other rightsholders. Further, many factors impact sales of a particular title, and the transaction does not change competitors' ability to monitor each other or respond to competitive activity. In addition, the absence of evidence that EMI's competitive behavior has been disruptive to the status quo in recent years undermined the argument that it had functioned as a maverick.

We worked closely with the European Commission throughout the investigation, but reached different conclusions because of different evidence unique to each jurisdiction. For example, concentration levels in a number of EU Member States were significantly higher than the combined market share of Universal and EMI in the United States. In addition, the markets in Europe have a different, larger, and more diverse set of customers, and it appears that the market dynamics relating to digital streaming services differ significantly from those found in the United States. Although the Commission did not conclude that a remedy was needed to protect competition in the United States, we note that the remedy obtained by the European Commission to address the different market conditions in Europe will reduce concentration in the market in the United States as well.

NOTES AND QUESTIONS

1.   Considering the disparate views reflected in the above materials regarding the EMI/Universal merger and your own experiences with the available variety of music platforms and promotional opportunities for artists, should the merger have been permitted? Is there a risk that new technologies/platforms will be repressed if too much control over content is in the hands of too few entities? Are there concerns on either side of the debate that you did not see raised in the statements provided above? Will there be stronger arguments against the next proposed merger (i.e., when the day comes that we move from three big recording companies to just two, if that has not yet happened by the time that you read this), or do the options available to artists and consumers outweigh concerns about consolidation among record labels?

2.   Although the FTC did not take any action with respect to the EMI/Universal merger, the European Union approved the merger in 2012 with certain conditions imposed, including that Universal would divest itself of one-third of its operations to other music industry companies. To comply with this condition, in 2013, Universal sold a number of its and EMI's labels to Warner Music Group, including Chrysalis Records, EMI Classics, Virgin Classics, Sanctuary Records, Mute Records, and a number of EMI's regional European labels. (Universal retained ownership of the Beatles' library, however, moving it to a newly-formed subsidiary called Calderstone Productions.) As is reflected in the chart below, as compared to its 2012 pre-merger U.S. market share of 23.9%, in 2019, UMG's market share was 28.8%, reflecting an almost 5% increase. Sony Music Entertainment and Warner Music Group showed more modest shifts, with Sony's share decreasing from 22.5% in 2012 to 20.19% in 2019 and Warner Music Group's share increasing from 14.8% to 15.86%. In the same time period, the combined U.S. market share for independent labels increased from 32.6% to 35.13%.[34]

---

[34]   See   https://www.statista.com/statistics/317632/market-share-record-companies-label-ownership-usa/. Note that the missing 6.2% of the U.S. market share total from 2012 was likely attributable to EMI's then-share of the U.S. market.

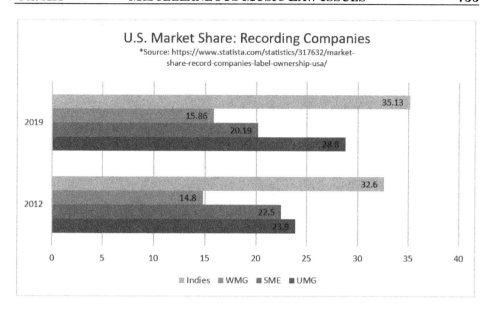

Although these numbers only give a superficial picture of the relative positions of the Big Three given the complexities of the marketplace for recorded music and the distribution interrelationships between major and independent labels, what, if anything, might you glean from the changes in the U.S. market share for record companies since the UMG/EMI merger? Do you think that any of the arguments for or against the merger have been proven right or wrong, or have the rapid changes in the music marketplace in the period since the merger muddied the waters?

3.   Each of the Majors has a host of brand labels within its umbrella. In 2020, Universal's web page identified the following labels within its catalog:

UMG's Labels and Brands, from https://www.universalmusic.com/labels/
(July 2, 2020)

Sony Music Entertainment is reported to have the following record labels within its catalog in 2020:

Sony Music Entertainment Labels 2020
See https://www.sonymusic.com/labels/

Warner Music Group lists the following labels in its catalog in 2020:

WMG's Labels, from https://www.wmg.com/services (July 20, 2020)

Partially in response to the growing consolidation and market share of the major record labels, in 2018 the indie label community formed their own digital agency called Merlin. Merlin does not own its label members, but rather acts as a global licensing body which enables indie labels to level the playing field by pooling their negotiation power when negotiating with large digital service providers, using a collective bargaining approach. Merlin's website states that Merlin "adds value to the global digital marketplace by ensuring that independents have a vehicle to enhance their ability to compete in the ever-changing world of digital music as well as to protect the value of their rights." As of 2020, Merlin's membership represented 15% of the global market share, having grown to include over 800 members[35] representing tens of thousands of labels in over 60 countries worldwide. In many instance, the combined market share of all Merlin labels allows it to rival—or even surpass—the market share of the largest major label.

4.   Is collective action by independents, such as that by Merlin's members, a panacea for any negative impact that you might see in consolidation of the major record labels? Why or why not?

5.   Why do you think artists might care which "brand" within a Major or which of many independent labels is associated with their recordings? Does it matter to you as a consumer? Do you think that maintaining the various brand labels under the Major's umbrellas has an impact on the diversity of acts that the Majors might sign or the nature of the contractual relationships that the companies enter into with artists?

---

[35]   Merlin's members include Altafonte Distribution, Amuse, Armada Music, AVL Group (including CD Baby and FUGA), AWAL, Because Music, Beggars Group, Better Noise Music, Cinq Music Group, Curb Records, Dim Mak, Domino, Entertainment One, Epitaph Records, FaroLatino, Freeme Digital, Foundation Media, IDJDigital, !K7, Kontor New Media, KVZ Music, Mad Decent, Mom + Pop, mtheory, Mushroom Music, Ninja Tune, ONErpm, [PIAS], Pony Canyon, Secretly Group, Symphonic Distribution and Sub Pop, Ultra Records and Warp Records.

D. PAYOLA INVESTIGATIONS AND ALLEGATIONS IN THE MUSIC INDUSTRY[36]

Dating as far back as the Tin Pan Alley days of music publishing, there have been cycles of allegations within the music industry of improper payments for promotion of compositions or, most recently, sound recordings. For example, Variety first coined the term "payola" in the 1930s, using it to refer to the practice of music publishers paying prominent musicians to publicly perform their latest songs; many performers earned a weekly stipend from publishers to do so, and some reportedly earned more from these stipends than they did from performance fees.[37] Congressional investigations in the 1950s and 1960s of payments by record labels to radio disc jockeys in exchange for radio airplay of their recordings called public attention to the practice:

> The House committee called famed deejays such as Dick Clark, of American Bandstand notoriety, and Alan Freed, often credited with coining the term "rock 'n' roll," to testify about their participation in the payola scandal. Dick Clark's appearance before the committee revealed that payola practices intertwined with every part of the music and broadcast industries, from recording and distributing companies to talent agencies. In fact, Clark supposedly had connections with "six small music publishing houses, seven small recording companies, two distributing companies, one record pressing company, two production companies and one talent agency." While Clark was thereafter merely required to divulge his financial interests in music enterprises, Freed eventually pled guilty to charges of commercial bribery, thereby effectively ending his career.[38]

---

[36] For good general discussions of and background on this issue, see RUSSELL SANJEK, PENNIES FROM HEAVEN: THE AMERICAN POPULAR MUSIC BUSINESS IN THE TWENTIETH CENTURY 373–76, 441–58, 602–07 (Da Capo Press 1996); Kristen Lee Repyneck, Note, *The Ghost of Alan Freed: An Analysis of the Merit and Purpose of Anti-Payola Laws in Today's Music Industry*, 51 VILL. L. REV. 695–697, 698–707 (2006).

[37] *See* DAVID SUISMAN, SELLING SOUNDS: THE COMMERCIAL REVOLUTION IN AMERICAN MUSIC 83–84 (Harvard Univ. Press 2009); RUSSELL SANJEK, PENNIES FROM HEAVEN: THE AMERICAN POPULAR MUSIC BUSINESS IN THE TWENTIETH CENTURY 199–204 (Da Capo Press 1996).

[38] Kristen Lee Repyneck, Note, *The Ghost of Alan Freed: An Analysis of the Merit and Purpose of Anti-Payola Laws in Today's Music Industry*, 51 VILL. L. REV. 695–97 (2006).

Trading card photo of Alan Freed
(Topps Gum Cards 1957)

In response to these investigations, in 1960, Congress passed amendments to the Communications Act of 1934 that made it a criminal offense to fail to include an announcement disclosing when consideration was paid to broadcast material.[39] These requirements are outlined in the first section below. Note that they do not outright prohibit accepting payments for airplay; they prohibit *undisclosed* payments for broadcasting particular promoted content.

Notwithstanding the federal prohibition of accepting payment for playing material on broadcast radio without disclosure of the "sponsorship," the practice continued to occur at some level. In part, this was because radio airplay of new recordings was viewed as essential to successful sales of records. As noted in our earlier discussions of the promotion/substitution theme, in the latter half of the 20th century record sales were the main source of income for the recording industry, and broadcast radio was an important marketing tool to help drive those sales by increasing public awareness of recordings.

To help navigate the requirements of the federal statute, a system of "independent promotion" developed, in which third-party promoters established exclusive relationships with program directors or station managers. Such promoters were "independent" of the record label, but worked to help highlight and market particular releases to the program managers at radio stations. The promoter would then invoice record labels whenever a record released by the label was added to the playlist of a station with which the promoter was affiliated.

In the early through mid-2000s, payola moved back into the spotlight with high-profile investigations by the New York Attorney General's office,

---

[39] The FCC promulgated regulations in furtherance of that statutory prohibition in 47 C.F.R. § 73.1212.

leading to settlements with record labels and radio networks. Below, we first provide the text of the relevant statutory provisions governing payola. Then, the 2006 New York investigations and settlements are summarized, followed by the Rules of Engagement that were agreed to by labels and broadcast radio in 2007.

CONSIDER AS YOU READ . . .

- What are the harms that the federal payola statute seeks to prevent?

- Do the policies underlying disclosure requirements for pay-for-play on the radio still apply in today's audio distribution marketplace? Why or why not?

- Should new entrants to the audio distribution marketplace that provide radio-like services via satellite or the Internet be subject to similar pay-for-play disclosure requirements? What justifications might exist for treating broadcast radio differently?

1.   RELEVANT FEDERAL STATUTES

47 U.S.C. § 317(a)(1). ANNOUNCEMENT OF PAYMENT FOR BROADCAST

All matter broadcast by any radio station for which any money, service or other valuable consideration is directly or indirectly paid, or promised to or charged or accepted by, the station so broadcasting, from any person, shall, at the time the same is so broadcast, be announced as paid for or furnished, as the case may be, by such person: *Provided*, That "service or other consideration" shall not include any service or property furnished without charge or at a nominal charge for use on, or in connection with, a broadcast unless it is so furnished in consideration for an identification in a broadcast of any person, product, service, trademark, or brand name beyond an identification which is reasonably related to the use of such service or property on the broadcast.

47 U.S.C. § 508. DISCLOSURE OF PAYMENTS TO INDIVIDUALS CONNECTED WITH BROADCASTS

(a) Payments to station employees

Subject to subsection (d) of this section, any employee of a radio station who accepts or agrees to accept from any person (other than such station), or any person (other than such station) who pays or agrees to pay such employee, any money, service or other valuable consideration for the broadcast of any matter over such station shall, in advance of such broadcast, disclose the fact of such acceptance or agreement to such station.

(b) Production or preparation of programs

Subject to subsection (d) of this section, any person who, in connection with the production or preparation of any program or program matter which is intended for broadcasting over any radio station, accepts or agrees to accept, or pays or agrees to pay, any money, service or other valuable consideration for the inclusion of any matter as a part of such program or program matter, shall, in advance of such broadcast, disclose the fact of such acceptance or payment or agreement to the payee's employer, or to the person for whom such program or program matter is being produced, or to the licensee of such station over which such program is broadcast.

(c) Supplying of program or program matter

Subject to subsection (d) of this section, any person who supplies to any other person any program or program matter which is intended for broadcasting over any radio station shall, in advance of such broadcast, disclose to such other person any information of which he has knowledge, or which has been disclosed to him, as to any money, service or other valuable consideration which any person has paid or accepted, or has agreed to pay or accept, for the inclusion of any matter as a part of such program or program matter.

(d) Waiver of announcements under section 317(d)

The provisions of this section requiring the disclosure of information shall not apply in any case where, because of a waiver made by the Commission under section 317(d) of this title, an announcement is not required to be made under section 317 of this title.

(e) Announcement under section 317 as sufficient disclosure

The inclusion in the program of the announcement required by section 317 of this title shall constitute the disclosure required by this section.

(f) "Service or other valuable consideration" defined

The term "service or other valuable consideration" as used in this section shall not include any service or property furnished without charge or at a nominal charge for use on, or in connection with, a broadcast, or for use on a program which is intended for broadcasting over any radio station, unless it is so furnished in consideration for an identification in such broadcast or in such program of any person, product, service, trademark, or brand name beyond an identification which is reasonably related to the use of such service or property in such broadcast or such program.

(g) Penalties

Any person who violates any provision of this section shall, for each such violation, be fined not more than $10,000 or imprisoned not more than one year, or both.

2. PAYOLA INVESTIGATIONS IN NEW YORK AND SUBSEQUENT SETTLEMENTS[40]

As noted above, the 1960 statutes intended to curb payola practices were not entirely effective in minimizing the influencing of radio playlists; they just altered the manner in which the practice worked. In subsequent years, a system developed whereby independent promoters would establish exclusive relationships with radio stations and commit to pay "promotional expenses" to radio stations, as well as offering hotel stays and other perks (some legal, some not) to radio station employees. Then, every time a new release from a record label's artist was added to a station playlist, record companies would make a payment to the independent promoter who had established a relationship with the radio station.[41] Unlike the early days of

---

[40] For an in-depth look at payola in the context of record label/radio station relationships, see FREDRIC DANNEN, HIT MEN: POWER BROKERS AND FAST MONEY INSIDE THE MUSIC BUSINESS (Vintage 1996); Devin Kosar, *Payola—Can Pay-for-Play Be Practically Enforced?*, 23:1 J. CIV. RIGHTS AND ECON. DEVEL., art. 6 (2008).

[41] In 2001, journalist Eric Boehlert published a series of articles (winning him a journalism award in 2002) that detailed how independent promoter, record label, and radio station relationships worked at the time and that are a good resource for understanding the system as it then existed. *See, e.g.*, Eric Boehlert, *Fighting Pay-for-Play: Sources in the Music Industry Call for a Federal Clampdown on the New Payola*, SALON.COM (April 3, 2001), *archived at* https://web.archive.org/web/20090215060509/http://dir.salon.com/ent/music/feature/2001/04/03/payola2/index.html; Eric Boehlert, *Pay for Play: Why Does Radio Suck?*, SALON.COM (March 14, 2001), *archived at* https://web.archive.org/web/20090301015407/http://dir.salon.com/ent/feature/2001/03/14/payola/index.html.

record promotion that spawned the 1960 statute, which involved station-by-station promotion in a diversely-held marketplace, by the turn of the millennium, radio consolidation had placed control over radio playlists in almost two-thirds of the market into the hands of just a few people—the program directors for nation-wide radio conglomerates. Thus, as playlists became more standardized nation-wide, it became harder and harder for labels to "break" a new recording into broadcast radio and promoters became more and more important, with fees increasing accordingly.

The dollars alleged to be involved in this process were huge: roughly speaking, labels would rely on about 1,000 of the largest stations in the largest markets to play their artists' recordings and stimulate sales; each station would add only about three new songs per week to its playlist; and independent promoters would get paid about $1,000 (or more) for each new song added. In other words, independent promoters were being paid about $3 million each week by labels for their work in getting the labels' records on the air. None of this may have violated the 1960 statute, however, if the "promotional" payments by independent promoters to radio stations were not directly tied to the addition of a specific record to a station's playlist.

In July of 2005, the Attorney General for the State of New York, Eliot Spitzer, announced the settlement with Sony Music after a year-long investigation of pay-for-play practices in the recording industry, which were claimed to violate both state and federal law. The settlement described a variety of improper inducements that Sony BMG employed to increase airplay of their releases, including bribes to radio programmers (such as expensive vacation packages and gifts), fictitious contest giveaways for audiences, payments directly to radio stations to cover operational expenses, and various "spin programs" operated under the guise of advertising. The investigation revealed that Sony BMG employees took steps to conceal some of the payments and that executives at various levels of the company were aware of the practices. As part of the settlement, Sony BMG acknowledged the improper conduct and enacted a series of company-wide reforms. The company also agreed to a $10 million payment for programs aimed at funding music education and appreciation.

Settlements with other major labels, including Warner, Universal, and EMI, followed this announcement in succeeding months. Attorney General Spitzer's investigation also extended to radio corporations, and CBS was the first radio corporation to settle with his office in October of 2006.[42] CBS agreed to implement more stringent policies in dealings with record labels and to pay $2 million to New York charities. The investigation continued into other radio broadcasters, including Clear Channel Communications, Entercom Communications, and Citadel Broadcasting, with the FCC also stepping in to request information from the companies about their

---

[42]   *See* Jeff Leeds, *CBS Radio Tightens Policies in Settlement Over Payola*, NEW YORK TIMES (Oct. 20, 2006), *available at* http://www.nytimes.com/2006/10/20/business/media/20payola.html.

practices. Later that year, a civil lawsuit filed by the AG's Office against Entercom was settled in exchange for payment of almost $5 million dollars to New York charities and a commitment to enhanced protocols to prevent payola practices from continuing.

AG Spitzer referred the investigation to the FCC, which ultimately entered into a series of consent decrees beginning in 2007 with different entities in the radio broadcast industry that involved "voluntary" payments to the U.S. Treasury and committed the entities to implementation of internal protocols to deter future pay-for-play practices.[43]

Also in 2007, as a part of the FCC settlement, the major radio broadcasters negotiated a set of Rules of Engagement with the independent music community, setting out standards to prevent future incidences of pay-for-play activity that might violate state or federal law. Those Rules of Engagement are set out below.

3. RULES OF ENGAGEMENT NEGOTIATED BETWEEN MAJOR RADIO BROADCASTERS AND INDEPENDENT MUSIC COMMUNITY IN 2007[44]

The following Rules of Engagement were voluntarily adopted by The American Association of Independent Music (A2IM), representing independent record labels, and major radio broadcasters Entercom, CBS Radio, Citadel, and Clear Channel. They attempt to reduce pay-or-play practices in the industry, as well as securing more airtime for independent music to be played on nation-wide radio networks.

Rules of Engagement

1. Radio should establish, and appropriately publicize, clear and non-discriminatory procedures for music submissions and access to radio station music programmers (to the extent any such access is provided).

2. Radio should not be allowed to sell or barter access to its music programmers.

3. Radio should not form relationships with any music companies, independent promotion companies, or other parties which provide for exclusive access to radio station music programmers, nor should Radio restrict access to its music programmers to those who contribute promotional consideration.

---

[43] *See, e.g.*, Federal Communications Commission, *Payola and Sponsorship Identification*, http://www.fcc.gov/eb/broadcast/sponsid.html (listing consent decrees against Clear Channel Communications Inc., CBS Radio Inc., Citadel Broadcasting Corp., Entercom Communications Corp, and Univision Radio Inc., relating to payola investigations).

[44] *Originally available at http://www.a2im.org/UploadedFiles/Payolaeducationguide.pdf;* print copy available from authors.

4.   Radio should not exclude independent promotion companies, as a class, from gaining access to music programmers except for independent promotion companies which are compensated based upon playlist additions or increased spins.

5.   Radio shall not ask for or expect, either directly or indirectly, any quid pro quo to play music, including but not limited to: (a) Any promotional considerations including cash and prizes (b) Local concert appearances (c) Exclusive relationships with recording artists.

6.   Radio (individual stations or their parent companies) shall not act in a coercive manner, make or imply threats to withhold or reduce airplay or make or imply promises to commence or increase airplay, in connection with the solicitation of any promotional consideration, or any promotional consideration promised or given to competitor stations, including concert appearances and artist "exclusives."

7.   Disclosure: All cash and non-cash consideration (above a reasonable threshold) made by labels, artists, or their agents shall be confirmed in writing and shall be subject to internal tracking controls, with the information gathered as a result of these controls available to the FCC upon its request.

8.   Contest prize recipients to the extent permitted by applicable law must be identified publicly, and confirmed as not employees of the radio station or members of their immediate families or households.

March 6, 2007.

NOTES AND QUESTIONS

1.   The FCC has described the purpose of the federal payola regulations as existing to prevent consumers from being misled as to the source of the material they are hearing over the radio airwaves. In 2009, the Future of Music Coalition published a study that attempted to evaluate whether the FCC and NY Attorney General investigations and settlements effectively curtailed pay-for-play practices in the U.S. *See* http://futureofmusic.org/article/research/same-old-song. The report concluded that there had been no measurable change in station playlists over the period from 2005–2008, but asserted that the terms of the settlements, consent decrees, and Rules of Engagement were too vague in both their underlying policies and their language to measure their effectiveness. As a result, the FMC recommended three policies for the FCC to implement to assist it in enforcing prohibitions against pay-for-play practices: improved data collection, focusing on localism, and expanding the number of

voices on the public airwaves. How well do you think the Rules of Engagement addressed the alleged payola practices that were investigated by the NY AG's Office and the FCC?

2.   What do you think about the pay-for-play practices that were addressed in the above investigations? Are the underlying concerns about misleading consumers relevant in today's marketplace? Are consumers relying as much today on disc jockeys and radio program managers to curate their music for them, or has the Internet streaming era made these concerns irrelevant? Do you think there might be some corollaries in the Internet era for potential pay-for-play conduct that should be monitored and curtailed by state and federal agencies if they are found to exist—e.g., paying for streaming service algorithms to favor recordings by certain artists? Why or why not?

3.   Recently, some have suggested the potential for reexamining the anti-payola regulations in the context of new and alternative technologies for public consumption of music. In January of 2020, the FCC Commissioner sought information from the major record labels regarding their current policies for complying with the payola regulations and expressly commented on the potential inequities of regulating payola in the context of broadcast radio but not in the context of other music distribution platforms. The Commissioner's letter noted:

> Despite competing for the same listeners, the U.S. radio industry finds itself subject to payola restrictions when alternative technologies, such as streaming, Internet radio, podcasts and other commercial audio distribution platforms, do not. This asymmetric treatment has an impact on the radio industry's financial well-being, perhaps even affecting its long-term sustainability. Moreover, as the lines between these different technologies are becoming more blurred each day, the compliance difficulties facing dynamic radio companies that deliver content via multiple distribution methods and those that interact with them increase as well.[45]

In their responses to the Commissioner, the labels did not express any opinions about the equities in treating broadcast radio differently from other audio distribution technologies.[46] What do you think? Is it fair that broadcast radio is the only strictly regulated form of music distribution given the wide array of alternative distribution technologies available to consumers? If you think that other distribution platforms should be held to similar obligations, should those distribution technologies be regulated as much as broadcast radio, or should the regulations on broadcast radio be dialed back to match the obligations of other technologies? If disclosure should be required for online services, should written disclosure be sufficient for online music services that have a visual display available to their users, or should an audio disclosure be required? Or should the payola rules be abandoned for all distribution channels? Do the

---

[45]   https://docs.fcc.gov/public/attachments/DOC-361998A1.pdf.

[46]   All three responses were posted on Twitter by the Commissioner at https://twitter.com/ mikeofcc/status/1252662055674482695.

rationales underlying the disclosure rules still apply to today's music consumers? What possible reforms to the current regulations would you recommend?

INDEX

References are to Pages